UNDERSTANDING BUSINESS AND PERSONAL LAW

EIGHTH EDITION

GORDON W. BROWN, J.D.
Member of the Massachusetts Bar
Professor of Business Law
North Shore Community College
Beverly, Massachusetts

PAUL SUKYS, J.D.
Member of the Ohio Bar
Professor of Law
North Central Technical College
Mansfield, Ohio

LOIS ANDERSON
Utah State Specialist
Business Education/Technology
Salt Lake City, Utah

GREGG DIVISION
McGRAW-HILL BOOK COMPANY

New York   Atlanta   Dallas   St. Louis   San Francisco   Auckland
Bogotá   Guatemala   Hamburg   Lisbon
London   Madrid   Mexico   Milan   Montreal   New Delhi
Panama   Paris   San Juan   São Paulo   Singapore
Sydney   Tokyo   Toronto

ABOUT THE AUTHORS

Gordon W. Brown is a professor with over 20 years' experience teaching business law, real estate law, and legal terminology at North Shore Community College in Beverly, Massachusetts, where he has served as Business Division chairman. He is coauthor of *Business Law With UCC Applications*, and contributes articles to Business Education World. In addition, he is a speaker at workshops and conferences on methods of law instruction. Mr. Brown is a practicing attorney and a member of the Massachusetts Bar.

Paul A. Sukys is professor of law and legal studies at North Central Technical College in Mansfield, Ohio. He is also an adjunct professor at Cuyahoga Community College in Cleveland and a freelance writer. He received his law degree from Cleveland State University. Mr. Sukys is a member of the Ohio Bar.

Lois H. Anderson is Utah State Specialist for Business Education/Technology. She has served as curriculum specialist for Utah Schools, and has been named "Teacher of the Year." Past president of the Utah Vocational Association, and recipient of the Delta Pi Epsilon "Leadership Award," she has recently been nominated for the National Business Education Association's "Distinguished Administrative Service Award."

Sponsoring Editor: Michael Buchman
Editing Supervisor: Nicola von Schreiber
Design and Art Supervisor/cover and Interior Design:
    Annette Mastrolia-Tynan
Production Supervisor: Albert Rihner
Photo Editor: Rosemarie Rossi
Cover Photographer: © H. Mark Weidman

Library of Congress Cataloging-in-Publication Data

Brown, Gordon W., 1928–
    Understanding business and personal law.

    Includes index.
    1. Business law—United States.   I. Sukys, Paul.
II. Anderson, Lois,   III. Title.
KF889.6.B68   1988   346.73'07   87-2636
ISBN 0-07-008433-5   347.3067

Understanding Business and Personal Law, Eighth Edition

Copyright © 1988, 1984, 1979, 1973, 1967, 1963, 1957 by McGraw-Hill, Inc. All rights reserved. Copyright 1949 by McGraw-Hill, Inc. All rights reserved. Printed in the United States of America. Except as permitted under the United States Copyright Act of 1976, no part of this publication may be reproduced or distributed in any form or by any means, or stored in a data base or retrieval system, without the prior written permission of the publisher.

Previously published under the title *Understanding Business and Consumer Law*, Sixth Edition.

1 2 3 4 5 6 7 8 9 0 VNHVNH 8 9 4 3 2 1 0 9 8 7

ISBN 0-07-008433-5

CREDIT LIST

Page 46: National Coalition to Prevent Shoplifting; page 84: Richard Hackett; page 91: Sears Roebuck and Co.; page 126: Will Faller; page 147: Richard Hackett; page 160: Michael Weisbrot; page 182: Will Faller; page 201: General Electric; page 205: Will Faller; page 213: Reprinted from the Consumers Resource Handbook, published by the United States Office of Consumer Affairs; page 227: General Motors Corp.; page 230: Ford Motor Co.; page 255: Emery Worldwide; page 270: Will Faller; page 274: Courtesy of Buckeye Educational Systems, Doug Wolf photographer; page 287: Will Faller; page 302: Associated Press; page 316: Social Security Administration; pages 330 and 347: Giuseppe Cavalieri; pages 406 and 447: Will Faller; page 470: Jules Allen; page 480: Kidder Peabody & Co.; page 503: Jules Allen; page 517: Copyright © 1986 Chicago Mercantile Exchange; page 524: Reprinted with permission from American Appraisal Associates, Inc.; page 534: Will Faller; page 544: Reprinted with permission of the Society for the Right to Die, 250 West 57th St., New York, NY, 10107; page 554: Will Faller; page 566: Courthouses of the Commonwealth, photograph by George Peet and Gabrielle Keller, copyright © 1984.

CONTENTS

■ PREFACE

Few subjects are as dramatic and challenging as the law. Because laws grow from human conflict, lawsuits are often emotional, complex, and costly. Despite these costs, more and more business and personal disputes are being settled in court everyday. Ours is a "litigious society." We train more lawyers than engineers. Liability insurance rates have skyrocketed, partly as a result of large court awards for damages. A professional might be sued for malpractice. A business might be sued for negligence, breach of contract, or product liability. Neighbors sue neighbors over disagreements that reasonable adults should be able to settle themselves.

Knowing more about the law can help you avoid legal conflicts in your professional and personal lives. If you cannot resolve a dispute, a background in the law will help you preserve your rights. *Understanding Business and Personal Law,* Eighth Edition, is not designed, however, as merely a practical guide. Our aim, rather, is to help you to (1) get an overview of the substance of the law, (2) understand the general procedures of law, and (3) gain insight into the spirit of the law.

Along the way you will study some fascinating cases and recognize some persistent problems. You will learn many principles and rules and be able to apply these principles to both simple and complex legal cases. You will learn the vocabulary of a new "language." In the end, you will have mastered a challenging body of knowledge and be capable of using this knowledge in your daily life.

**STUDY
MATERIALS**

As the core of the course, the textbook structures your study of business and personal law. There is a presentation of the subject, followed by questions, exercises, and cases to help you master the subject. The Performance Guide is a paperback with review and enrichment activities. Puzzles, exercises, study questions, and cases reinforce the material covered in class. Legal documents, forms, and readings expand your experience by allowing you to apply the principles you have mastered.

In addition, your teacher may use a set of tests to evaluate your progress. Do not be intimidated by these tests. Studying the text regularly for class discussion and reviewing your notes weekly will prepare you for a test every two or three chapters. You will also have an opportunity to consolidate your knowledge by reviewing for both mid-term and final examinations. (In a one-semester course, a mid-term exam may be omitted.)

Your teacher may also supplement tests and class discussions with extra cases. You may also have the chance to conduct a "mock trial" based on material in your text.

Other sources of material for studying business and personal law include newspaper articles, movies, and television programs related to your class studies. For your teacher's convenience, we have collected a number of cases from *The People's Court* television series available on videotape. Study guides for each case are found at the back of the Performance Guide.

USING THE TEXTBOOK

Before you begin the course, review the table of contents of this textbook. You will notice the book is divided into 39 chapters, which are grouped into 8 units. The first unit explores the foundations of U.S. law. The second unit is a comprehensive presentation of contract law. Together, the 13 chapters in Units 1 and 2 will give you an overview of public and private law while touching topics of interest, including individual rights, classes of crimes, minors and the law, shoplifting, drug abuse, white collar crime, computer crime, the process of a lawsuit, how to make a contract, and how to enforce your contractual rights. The remainder of the book is organized around the "life-cycle" concept, enabling you to study law as you may encounter it in life. We explore laws related to consumer issues (Unit 3); employment (Unit 4); marriage, housing, and insurance (Unit 5); borrowing and credit (Unit 6); starting a business (Unit 7); and pensions and wills (Unit 8). Throughout the text we focus on both business and personal aspects of the law.

The Drama of the Law

Each chapter begins with a brief "play" in which characters encounter a number of legal issues (questions of law). Your task is to identify legal issues in these plays and to read each chapter with the purpose of applying the law. Legal Issues questions at the end of each play will guide your work. Notes in the margin refer you to appropriate sections of text to help you answer each question. We hope you will enjoy following the lives of the cast of characters through each unit.

The Spirit of the Law

Following the Legal Issues questions, each chapter discusses "The Spirit of the Law." These brief sections present general principles and social issues and link the ideas of different chapters. To help put the law in perspective, reread The Spirit of the Law when you complete a chapter.

In-Text Case Examples

Every chapter has several examples of cases to highlight legal principles. As you read these examples, restate the facts in your own words; then apply the principles you have just read about. Reading cases actively will help you remember material.

Boldfaced Vocabulary

Legal thinking requires you to learn a new vocabulary. Words with special legal meanings appear in boldprint. Make notes as you read, or return to these terms when completing the Language of the Law exercises at the end of each chapter.

Tables, Cartoons, and Illustrations

We have selected a variety of visual displays to emphasize key points. Study the illustrations and tables and relate them to your reading. Our captions often ask questions to challenge your thinking.

Suggestions for Reducing Legal Risks

The text discussion of each chapter ends with Suggestions for Reducing Legal Risks. You may use these suggestions as practical pointers and as a study tool. Identify the topic in the chapter that relates to each point and state a reason for the advice. In this way you will review your reading with a purpose.

Chapter Exercises

Each chapter has four sets of activities.

1. Language of the Law reviews vocabulary.
2. Questions for Review reinforces main ideas.
3. Cases in Point are closely focused cases to solve.
4. Cases to Judge are more complex situations taken from actual lawsuits.

Answering case problems is crucial to your study of business and personal law. Developing this skill enables you to recognize the rights of all parties and to identify the major principles of law that will control the court's decision.

Unit Cases

Each unit presents two types of case activities, a Case to Discuss and a Case to Brief. Both provide some of the actual language used in a judge's decision. This material will be challenging, but you will also enjoy the flavor of the language and the insight into legal reasoning.

Trial Procedures

The major steps in a lawsuit are presented in the Trial Procedures activities at the end of each unit. In these activities you will take the role of a trial participant and create legal documents crucial to the success of a case.

Appendix: A Day in Court— Conducting a Mock Trial

If time permits, your teacher may involve the class in a mock trial, which is an enactment of a lawsuit. The appendix to this text provides the background and the rules of evidence.

MEETING THE CHAL-LENGE

Studying the law holds many delights. The drama of human conflict lives in every case. The potential for justice rests in every decision. A subject as complex as the law, however, requires discipline and hard work. We hope this book provides you with a framework for careful and rewarding study, as well as the satisfaction of mastering challenging, vital, and useful subject matter.

ACKNOWL-EDGMENTS

We gratefully acknowledge the contribution of the reviewers of this text: Ted Dinges, Longview Community College, Lee Summit, Missouri; Eileen Frumkin, Chairperson, Business Education, Albertus Magnus HS, Bardonia, New York; Karen Atherton, Philomath HS, Philomath, Oregon; Ray Rogina, Business Education, St. Charles High School, St. Charles, Illinois; Martha Domiguez, Business Law Supervisor, Ysleta Independent School District, El Paso, Texas; Robert Dellinger, Business Department Head, Northrup HS, Fort Wayne, Indiana; Bernard Flashberg, Cranford High School, Cranford, New Jersey; Dr. Jack Lee, Ridgewood Sr. High School, Ridgewood, New Jersey; Philip Green, Patchogue HS, Patchogue, New York.

We also thank the many teachers who responded to our questionnaire for their suggestions for improving the previous edition.

We wish to give special thanks to Jane A. Brown for her work on the Performance Guide and introductory plays, for her proofreading of the text manuscript, and for her many suggestions which helped to improve this law program.

Gordon W. Brown
Paul Sukys
Lois Anderson

KNOWING MORE ABOUT THE LAW

UNIT
1

Chapter 1

THE NATURE AND SOURCES OF LAW

In this unit you will meet Mike DeFazio, his sister, Sue, their friends, Steve and Pam, and their cousin, Tony. Two other characters, Wayne and Rick, appear to be heading into conflict with the law. Each chapter begins with a dramatic scene, followed by a series of questions that draw your attention to legal issues raised in the chapter. These questions are guidelines to direct your reading of the text. Try to answer the questions after you have completed your reading assignment.

Scene: The front steps of an apartment building. Mike is talking to his friend Steve.

Steve: Can you imagine that? I got a speeding ticket yesterday for doing 65 miles an hour on the freeway! Everybody goes that fast!

Mike: You can say that again. When I go 55 miles an hour, everybody passes me. We ought to get that law changed. What is it anyway, a state or a federal law?

Steve: They have it all over the country, so it must be a federal law. I still can't believe that it happened to me. I ran right into a speed trap. They stopped about ten cars in a row.

Mike: We ought to write to our senator and try to get it changed. It's ridiculous. I'm going to vote next year when I'm 18. I think I'll write to the senator and tell him that he'll have to change that law if he wants my vote.

Steve: I don't think that you can vote when you're 18 anymore. I heard that you have to wait until you're 21. Remember when they raised the drinking age? That affected the voting age, too.

Mike: I didn't know that.

Steve: When they stopped me for speeding, they made me open the trunk of my car. They said they were looking for illegal drugs and things like that.

Mike: Did you let them search the trunk?

Steve: What else could I do? They caught me speeding with the radar.

Mike: I don't think that they can search the trunk of your car like that. (*At that moment, Sue steps out of the apartment onto the steps.*)

Sue: Hi, guys!

Steve and Mike: Hi, Sue!

Steve: I hear you're going to school to be an auto mechanic.

Sue: I thought I was, but the community college won't let me into the auto mechanic program. They said that it's only for boys. They said I could be a hairdresser, or a secretary, or a nurse, but not an auto mechanic.

Steve: What a bummer! That's discrimination. You should fight that. We have the equal rights amendment in this country, you know. That's something else you can write to the senator about, Mike.

(*Just then, a young girl delivers the newspaper to the apartment building steps where the three are sitting.*)

Mike (*picking up the paper*): Look at this! That guy who killed the 78-year-old lady is getting off easy. It says here that they're only charging him with assault and battery.

Sue: Are you sure? That was a terrible crime. That guy broke into her house and hit her over the head with a pipe, and she was in a coma for over a year.

Mike: It says here that he can't be charged with homicide because she lived too long after he struck her. Do you believe that?

Steve: I believe just about anything these days. It's getting late. I've got to go home. See you tomorrow.

Sue: Bye, Steve.

Mike: Drive slow, hear?

LEGAL ISSUES

1. Is the 55-mile-per-hour speed limit a state or federal law?
2. At what age may a person vote in a federal election?
3. Is there a law in this country that prohibits an unreasonable search?
4. May state colleges discriminate on the basis of sex?
5. Is there an equal rights amendment to the U.S. Constitution?
6. What law prevents people from being charged with homicide when the victim lives for a certain length of time following the assault?

THE SPIRIT OF THE LAW

We hold these truths to be self-evident, that all men are created equal, that they are endowed by their Creator with certain unalienable Rights, that among these are Life, Liberty, and the pursuit of Happiness.—That to secure these rights, Governments are instituted among Men, deriving their just powers from the consent of the governed,—That whenever any Form of Government becomes destructive of these ends, it is the Right of the People to alter or to abolish it, and to institute new Government, laying its foundation on such principles and organizing its powers in such form, as to them shall seem most likely to effect their Safety and Happiness. . .

In Congress, July 4, 1776
The unanimous Declaration of the
thirteen united States of America

The term *law* means different things to different people. For some, it means following legal principles that developed in the past—those that have withstood the test of time. For others, it means following rules of logic in the development of legal principles. For still others, it means developing legal principles by seeking divine sources for determining what is right and wrong. The Declaration of Independence, part of which is quoted above, falls within this latter school of legal thought. There is no doubt, in any event, that custom, history, logic, and ideals have had an important influence on the development of law.

If you lived alone on an island and no other person ever came to your island, you might be free from human-made laws. You might stretch your imagination a little more and give yourself a smart sports car to drive on your island. Imagine also that you have a long, straight concrete highway running the length of your island. You could drive just as fast as you wished. You could drive on the right side of the road, on the left side, or down the middle. It would not make any difference. Let one other person come to your island paradise, however, with another automobile, and some rules are going to be necessary—or else someone is going to get hurt. This is but one example of why some rules of conduct are necessary if you are going to live in harmony and safety with other people.

Law, then, can be said to consist of the rules of conduct that govern people in their dealings with one another. The function of law is to maintain peace, order, and harmony among people in society. It does this by spelling out what is considered right and what is considered wrong and by defining the legal rights and duties of people. It also provides a means of enforcing legal rights and duties through law enforcement agencies, the courts, and special regulatory agencies.

THE EFFECT OF THE LAW

The law touches our lives from before we are born until after we die.

EXAMPLE 1 Bruce Applegate was killed in a boating accident while vacationing at a lakeside resort. His wife, Angela, and their three-year-old son, Thomas, were injured in the same mishap but survived. At the time of the accident, Angela was expecting their second child. A daughter was born two months later. Applegate's will left part of his estate to his wife, Angela, and the balance in trust for "all of his children who survived him." The child who was born after the death of her father inherited from her father's estate.

In the above example, the law gave rights to Applegate's daughter before she was born. It also controlled the distribution of Applegate's estate after he died.

Think of the things you may do today. You might ride on a bus, drive a car, buy something in a store or restaurant, or work for someone part time. In each of these situations, the law plays an important role. When you buy something in a store or restaurant or pay to ride on a bus, you are governed by the laws of contracts. When you drive a car, you are governed by motor vehicle laws. When you work for someone, you are governed by the laws of contract, agency, and employment. These are only a few illustrations of how the law affects your daily life. Even after you die, the laws of wills and inheritance, among other laws, have an effect on you (indirectly) and on the people you leave behind.

It is clear, then, that you cannot escape legal dealings with others and that you need to know something about law. The ordinary business person and the average citizen can hope to learn only the basic rules. A knowledge of these basic rules, however, will help you over many rough spots when you are on your own.

THE DEVELOP- MENT OF LAW

According to some experts, the earliest laws governing people probably were created when cave dwellers first began to hunt together. These primitive people found that they could protect themselves better and find more game by working in groups. Some rules governing the hunt had to be worked out. As primitive people began to live in larger and still larger tribal groups, it became necessary to develop laws that would permit them to work, hunt, play, and get along together for their mutual benefit. They quickly learned that a person cannot be an "outlaw" and still be accepted in a social system. Each person must learn to conform to the rules that govern all the people.

The first laws were tribal laws. As time went on, larger units of government developed. Laws were expanded to regulate these larger units.

Roman, or Civil, Law

One of the great contributions of the Roman Empire was a system of laws known as the **Roman,** or **civil, law.** Rome conquered almost all the known civilized world of its day. To administer this great empire, the Romans organized a complex set of laws. Through the influence of Emperor Justinian and other emperors who followed him, a complete code of laws was drawn up. An attempt was made in this code to write down all the laws and regulations of every kind that were to govern the Romans and their subjects. Almost all the laws of Europe have been built around the **Roman Code.** Colonists who settled in the New World brought the code of laws of the particular European nation from which they came. Thus all the Latin American countries follow the Roman Code. In this country the laws of the state of Louisiana are based on it because Louisiana was settled by the French, and France had developed its legal system after the pattern set by the Roman Code.

English Common Law

Laws in the United States, with the exception of the state laws of Louisiana, are almost all based on English common law.

England in medieval days was governed by the **feudal system**—a system in which the feudal lord had supreme power within his domain. The feudal lord owned all the land surrounding his castle. This land was worked by serfs, who had few, if any, rights. Because the lords settled arguments over rights with their neighboring lords by fighting, little law was needed.

As common men began to rise from serfdom to the status of tenant farmers, however, they began to acquire some rights. (Women at this time in history still had very few rights.) The rights of one tenant might come into conflict with the rights of another. The earliest disputes were probably settled by the feudal lord. He would hear the arguments of each tenant and then make his decision. There

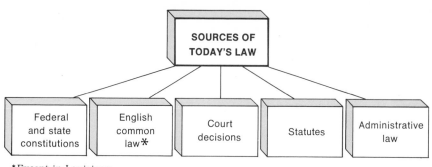

*Except in Louisiana

American law develops from five main sources.

was no formal body of law to guide him. He followed his own reason and best judgment. Later, civil officers having judicial powers (**magistrates**) were appointed to hear and settle disputes; but still there was no law to guide them. Quite logically, a magistrate might say to himself, "Now, I decided a case much like this one 6 months ago. How did I decide that one?" To refresh his memory, he began to write down his decisions so that he could refer to them. As communication with neighboring magistrates became better, he might exchange notes and ideas with them. Agreement on certain principles of law slowly began to emerge.

At the same time the central government of the king, which at first was very weak, was becoming stronger, and the king began to establish courts. The king's courts made decisions and kept records. But the king also had no written laws. By the time the central government of the king had become strong enough to pass a code of laws, the laws regulating the rights of the common man were already well established by the day-to-day rulings of the early courts. This body of law is called the law of precedent, or the **common law.**

Parliament, the English legislature, did not disturb these common-law precedents but merely picked up where they left off. The new laws that were passed by Parliament, called **statutes,** changed the common law as needed to meet new situations or to fill needs that were not present in earlier days.

A more detailed study of the common law would illustrate how some customs became law. Many of the early court rulings that became law were based on custom. One of the sources of these customs was the law of the church, known as **ecclesiastical law.** Another source was the customs of merchants and traders. These customs formed the basis of what is known as the **law merchant.** It was logical for a judge who had no written law to look at the customs of merchants and traders to find the answer to an argument between two business people. Once the judge gave a decision on the point in dispute, the decision became a part of the way of doing things, or the common law.

When the early settlers founded this country, they brought with them from England these common-law principles. The English common law formed the basis of the law in force in the colonies, and it is still the basis of some of our law today.

SOURCES OF UNITED STATES LAW

Constitutional Law

Today's law in the United States, in general, comes from (1) federal and state constitutions, (2) common law, (3) appellate court decisions, (4) federal, state, and local statutes, and (5) administrative regulations.

Every law in the United States, regardless of its source, must be **constitutional**—that is, allowed by both the U.S. Constitution and the constitution of the state where it is enforced.

The U.S. Constitution The Constitution of the United States is the broad, basic foundation for our laws in this country. It sets forth the fundamental rights of citizens, defines the limits within which the federal and the state governments may pass laws, and describes the functions of the various branches and divisions of our national government. It consists of 7 short articles and 26 amendments.

The first three articles of the Constitution set forth the structure and the powers of the three branches of the federal government. Article I gives legislative powers to Congress; Article II gives executive powers to the presidency; Article III gives judicial power to the Supreme Court and to courts established by Congress.

Article IV of the Constitution requires each state to accept the laws of all other states, that is, give "full faith and credit" to them.

Article V tells how the Constitution may be amended; this may be done in either of two ways: (1) by a two-thirds vote of each house of Congress, or (2) by a convention called by Congress upon application of the legislatures of two-thirds of the states. In either case, to be effective, any amendment must be ratified by the legislatures of three-fourths of the states.

EXAMPLE 2 In 1972, Congress proposed an amendment to the U.S. Constitution calling for equal rights for men and women. It read: "Equality of rights under the law shall not be denied or abridged by the United States or by any State on account of sex." The proposed amendment did not become law because it was not ratified by the legislatures of three-fourths of the states within the required time period.

Legal Issue No. 5

Article VI states that the U.S. Constitution and the laws of the United States and treaties shall be the supreme law of the land.

Article VII provided for ratification of the Constitution, which took place in 1787.

The first ten amendments, passed in 1791, are called the **Bill of Rights.** These amendments granted individuals many rights in an effort to curb potential abuses by the government. The First Amendment gives to all Americans the freedom of religion, the freedom of speech, the freedom of the press, and the freedom of assembly. Recognizing the need for a well regulated militia, the Second Amendment gives the right to the people to keep and bear arms. The Third Amendment prevents soldiers from being housed in private homes without the owners' consent. The Fourth Amendment prevents unreasonable searches and seizures by requiring that search warrants be obtained before peo-

Legal Issue No. 3

ple or places may be searched. In addition, the place searched must be particularly described, and there must be probable cause to obtain a search warrant. The Fifth Amendment protects against **double jeopardy** (being tried twice for the same offense) and **self-incrimination** (being a witness against oneself). It also protects against being deprived of ''life, liberty, or property, without due process of law'' (the due process clause). The Sixth Amendment guarantees to anyone charged with a crime the right to a speedy and public jury trial. In addition, people accused of crimes are given the right to be confronted with the witnesses against them and to have the assistance of counsel for their defense.

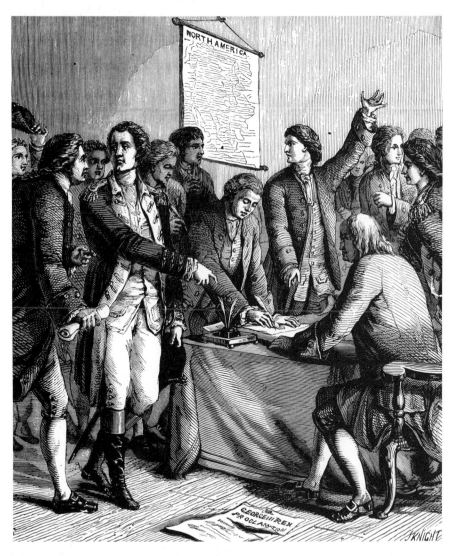

The founders of our nation reacted to abuses of power by the English king by making individual rights a cornerstone of American government.

The right to a jury trial in noncriminal cases is preserved by the Seventh Amendment, and the Eighth Amendment prevents excessive bail, excessive fines, or cruel and unusual punishment. The Ninth Amendment gives to the people all rights not otherwise in the Constitution, and the Tenth Amendment states that all powers not given to the federal government are reserved to the states or to the people.

In addition to the Bill of Rights, two other amendments bear discussion here. The Fourteenth Amendment provides that no state shall "deprive any person of life, liberty, or property, without due process of law; nor deny to any person within its jurisdiction the equal protection of the laws" (the equal protection clause). A major principle of justice, then, requires equal treatment of all people under the law. This amendment requires state governments to give to their citizens the same rights that the federal government must give under the Fifth Amendment.

EXAMPLE 3 Joe Hogan was denied admission to the Mississippi University for Women's School of Nursing solely because of his sex. Located in Alabama, the university is supported by the state. The U.S. Supreme Court held, in 1982, that the single-sex admissions policy of the state school violated the equal protection clause of the Fourteenth Amendment. The court said that the policy perpetuated the stereotyped view of nursing as an exclusively woman's job. Hogan was admitted to the school of nursing.

Legal Issue No. 4

The Twenty-Sixth Amendment, the most recent, was enacted in 1971. It gives 18-year-olds the right to vote. Section 1 of the amendment reads: "The right of citizens of the United States, who are 18 years of age or older, to vote shall not be denied or abridged by the United States or by any state on account of age."

Legal Issue No. 2

If any state law violates the federal Constitution, a state or federal court can declare that law unconstitutional—that is, make it no longer valid. The Supreme Court of the United States is the ultimate authority regarding the constitutionality of laws at all levels of government.

State Constitutions The states each have their own constitutions. Although similar, they are not identical to the federal Constitution. Sometimes, they are more protective, narrower, and more restrictive than the federal Constitution.

EXAMPLE 4 The Massachusetts legislature wanted to have a graduated income tax like the federal income tax. This tax requires people with larger incomes to pay a higher tax rate than people with smaller incomes. The legislature could not assess such a tax, however, because the Massachusetts Constitution requires all people to be taxed at an equal percentage rate.

Existing Common Law

Many states still follow parts of the common law exactly as it was practiced in England.

EXAMPLE 5 Under common law, no one may be convicted of homicide (murder or manslaughter) unless the victim died within a year and a day after the striking of the blow. The common law places an outer limit on the time that can elapse between the injury and death. It is presumed that the injury did not cause the death if the interval exceeded a year and a day. This early English law that dates back to the year 1278 is followed in the United States today, except in the states of New York, New Jersey, Ohio, Massachusetts, Oregon, Pennsylvania, and California.

Legal Issue No. 6

Appellate courts and legislatures have the power to change the common law. Thus much of the original common law has changed since this country was founded.

Appellate Court Decisions

People involved in lawsuits may appeal to a higher court if they believe an error of law was made by the lower court. This right of appeal comes from the due process clause of the U.S. Constitution. Courts that hear cases initially are called **lower courts, trial courts,** or **courts of original jurisdiction. Jurisdiction** is the power granted to a court to try an individual or disagreement and to make a judgment. Courts that hear cases on appeal are known as **appellate courts** or **courts of appellate jurisdiction.** Many states have intermediate appellate courts to which cases must be appealed before going to the highest appellate court.

Decisions made by the highest appellate court of any state become the law of that state and must be followed by other courts in that state thereafter. This is known as the law of **precedent.** It is also called the doctrine of **stare decisis** (ˌster-ē-di-ˈsī-səs), which means ''to stand by the decision.''

Cases decided by appellate courts are put in writing so that lawyers, judges, and other interested parties will know about them. Once written down, the cases are published in books called **reporters.** A case is identified by a **citation,** which consists of the names of the parties followed by the volume number, the name of the reporter, and the beginning page number of the case.

EXAMPLE 6 In *State v. Zerban,* 617 S.W.2d 458 (Missouri), John Paul Ladefian was allegedly assaulted by Jeffrey Zerban on August 26, 1978. Ladefian died on January 18, 1980, and Zerban was charged with his murder. The Missouri Court of Appeals dropped the murder charge, holding that Missouri still follows the common law *year-and-a-day* rule. The court said that Zerban could not be charged with murder because the death of Ladefian did not occur within a year and a day from the date of the attack.

The criminal action in Example 6 was brought by the state of Missouri (the plaintiff or prosecution) against Jeffrey Zerban (the defendant). The case is reported in volume 617 of the Southwestern Reporter, second series, on page 458. The common law year-and-a-day rule remains in effect in Missouri.

Each state in the United States has its own appellate court. Each court makes its own decisions. They are often different from the decisions of the appellate courts of other states.

EXAMPLE 7 In *State v. Young,* 372 A.2d 1117 (New Jersey), Roosevelt Young fired five shots at Samuel Story on September 17, 1972, upon finding him in his estranged wife's home. Story died on November 17, 1973, and Young was convicted of his murder. Young appealed the conviction, arguing that the common law year-and-a-day rule was part of New Jersey law. In upholding the conviction, the Appellate Division of the Superior Court said: "The common law 'year-and-a-day rule' does not conform to present-day medical realities, principles of equity or public policy. We reject it as an anachronism and declare that it is no longer part of the common law of this State." Young appealed further to the Supreme Court of New Jersey, that state's highest court. In that decision (*State v. Young*, 390 A.2d 556) the majority of justices agreed that the year-and-a-day rule should no longer be followed. The court reversed Young's conviction, however, saying that the change in the law will apply only to future cases, not to this one. Young's conviction was reduced to assault with intent to kill.

This is an example of an appellate court decision being the source of a state law. As a result of this court decision the common law year-and-a-day rule is no longer in effect in New Jersey.

Subsequent Case Citations Are Analyzed Attorneys preparing for trial research related cases in order to strengthen their arguments. As the *Young* case demonstrates, attorneys must know the validity of each case in question. Some

While every individual has rights under the law, the law must be applied equally, regardless of the power or influence of an individual. (*Drawing by Joseph Farris. Copyright © 1986, The New Yorker Magazine, Inc.*)

"It really wasn't my fault, Your Honor. I was led to believe I was above the law."

cases are followed in later court decisions; others are discussed and disregarded; still others are overruled by a higher level court or the same court that made the decision initially. To determine if a case is cited in a later case, attorneys use a set of books called *Shepard's Citations,* published by Shepard's/McGraw-Hill, Inc. Each book is called a "citator" and together they show every instance in which a case has been referred to by any state or federal court decision as reported in the National Reporter System, the U. S. Supreme Court reports, and other selected legal publications.

Using this method of legal research is commonly referred to by lawyers as **Shepardizing** a case. After locating the list of citations, a legal researcher reads the cases indicated. In these cases there would be found the citation to the case being researched and the court's reasoning. Because much law is based on previous decisions, Shepardizing is an essential step in preparing a case for argument in court.

The citation in the first line of Example 7 shows that a criminal action was brought by the state of New Jersey against Roosevelt Young. The case is reported in volume 372 of the *Atlantic Reporter,* second series, on page 1117.

Statutory Law

Statutes are laws specifically passed by a governing body created for that purpose. Thus, laws passed by the English Parliament, the U.S. Congress, the state legislatures, local city councils, or town meetings can all be called **statutory law.**

These laws consist of additions to or modifications of the original common law to meet modern situations. Also, modern living raises many problems that were never thought of during the common-law period; therefore much new legislation is necessary. These new laws, passed by legislatures, are found in state and federal statutes, city **ordinances,** and town **bylaws.** (The terms *ordinance* and *bylaw* tell us at which level of government a law was passed.)

State Statutes   In the United States there are 50 different state legislatures, each enacting statutes that are often quite different from those in other states. The law in one state is not necessarily the law in another state.

EXAMPLE 8   In 1969, the California legislature changed the common-law year-and-a-day rule by enacting the following statute: "To make the killing either murder or manslaughter, it is requisite that the party die within three years and a day after the stroke received or the cause of death administered" (Penal Code section 995). The statute reset the time limit within which people can be held responsible for homicide in California to 3 years and 1 day.

It is a basic principle of constitutional law that statutes must not be vague. They must give people of ordinary intelligence a reasonable opportunity to know what is prohibited, so that they may act accordingly. The U.S. Supreme Court has said, "Vague laws trap the innocent by not providing fair warning." Appellate courts can strike down statutes that are vague. When this is done, the statutes are said to be "void for vagueness" and cannot be enforced by any court.

This is a part of a page taken from *Shepard's Atlantic Reporter Citations*. In Example 7 on page 9, the case of *State of New Jersey v. Young*, 372 A.2d 1117 is mentioned. To find other cases where State v. Young is cited, open *Shepard's Atlantic Reporter Citations* at volume 372 (shown at the top of the page) and find page 1117 (in bold type near the bottom of the page). Notice that the following cases cite *State v. Young*:

(148 NJS 405) Parentheses indicate this is a "parallel cite" because it is where the case was originally reported in the New Jersey reporter before it was appealed.)

r 390 A2d 556 (The small "r" means that the case was reversed on appeal.)

s 384 A2d 519 (The small "s" means that it is the same case as the one above it.)

384 A2d[7] 1172 (The raised number refers to a paragraph in the case that is cited.)

421 NE2d 600 (an Indiana case)

366 NE2d 749 (a Massachusetts case)

409 NE2d 773 (a Massachusetts case)

617 SW2d 459 (a Missouri case)

60 A3 1323 (American Law Reports 3d—a legal encyclopedia)

115

EXAMPLE 9 A Texas statute made it a criminal offense to ''sell, serve, or deliver beer to a person showing *evidence of intoxication.''* In a 1985 case, the Texas Court of Appeals held the statute to be unconstitutionally vague. The court said that the words ''evidence of intoxication'' are not precise enough to define the crime. It gave the example that bloodshot eyes may be evidence of intoxication; yet people can have bloodshot eyes for other reasons too.

Federal Statutes Federal statutes regulate matters that concern the nation as a whole, and they are based on the powers given to the federal government by our Constitution. In some instances both federal and state statutes may govern a situation. For example, kidnapping, taxation, and narcotics control may be regulated by both federal and state statutes.

TITLE 18, SECTION 3056 OF THE CODE OF THE LAWS OF THE UNITED STATES OF AMERICA (18 USCS 3056)

(a) Under the direction of the Secretary of the Treasury, the United States Secret Service is authorized to protect the following persons:

(1) The President, the Vice President (or other officer next in the order of succession to the Office of President), the President-elect, and the Vice President-elect.

(2) The immediate families of those individuals listed in paragraph (1).

(3) Former Presidents and their spouses for their lifetimes, except that protection of a spouse shall terminate in the event of remarriage.

(4) Children of a former President who are under 16 years of age.

(5) Visiting heads of foreign states or foreign governments.

(6) Other distinguished foreign visitors to the United States and official representatives of the United States performing special missions abroad when the President directs that such protection be provided.

(7) Major Presidential and Vice Presidential candidates and, within 120 days of the general Presidential election, the spouses of such candidates. As used in this paragraph, the term ''major Presidential and Vice Presidential candidates'' means those individuals identified as such by the Secretary of the Treasury after consultation with an advisory committee consisting of the Speaker of the House of Representatives, the minority leader of the House of Representatives, the majority and minority leaders of the Senate, and one additional member selected by the other members of the committee.

The protection authorized in paragraphs (2) through (7) may be declined.

This federal statute, enacted by Congress in 1984, tells whom the U.S. Secret Service may protect. Why do you think Congress found it necessary to enact this law?

Legal Issue No. 1

EXAMPLE 10 Although automobile speed limits are set by each state, Congress passed a federal statute in 1975 that reduced the speed limit on U.S. highways to 55 miles per hour. The federal law prohibits a state from receiving money for federally aided highway projects if it has (1) a maximum speed limit on any public highway within its jurisdiction in excess of 55 miles per hour, or, with exceptions, (2) a speed limit on any portion of a public highway within its jurisdiction which is not uniformly applicable to all types of motor vehicles using it. States will lose money if they fail to follow this law.

Administrative Regulations

Federal, state, and local legislatures sometimes find it desirable to regulate certain kinds of activities in the public interest. Legislators, however, often do not have expert knowledge of a particular field. They also do not have the time to give their complete attention to any one kind of activity. For these and other

TABLE 1-1
EXAMPLES OF FEDERAL ADMINISTRATIVE AGENCIES

Agency	What Is Regulated
Department of Transportation (DOT)	Highway safety
Department of Energy (DOE)	Research, production, and marketing of energy sources
Interstate Commerce Commission (ICC)	Truck, railroad, and pipeline transportation between states
Internal Revenue Service (IRS)	Federal income taxes
Federal Aviation Administration (FAA)	Aircraft and airport safety
Federal Maritime Commission (FMC)	Shipping on all navigable waterways
Nuclear Regulatory Commission (NRC)	Supervision of atomic energy plants and procedures
Federal Power Commission (FPC)	Electrical industry
Securities and Exchange Commission (SEC)	Sale of stocks and bonds
Federal Reserve System (FRS)	Banking and credit
National Labor Relations Board (NLRB)	Union-management relations
Occupational Safety and Health Administration (OSHA)	Employment safety
Equal Employment Opportunity Commission (EEOC)	Job discrimination
Environmental Protection Agency (EPA)	Pollution
Federal Trade Commission (FTC)	Business-consumer relations
Food and Drug Administration (FDA)	Food, drugs, and cosmetics

TABLE 1-2
ADMINISTRATIVE PROCEEDINGS VERSUS COURT PROCEEDINGS

Administrative Proceedings	Court Proceedings
1. The proceeding does not judge criminal wrongdoing or award damages to injured parties.	1. Criminal and/or civil complaints may be filed against the accused.
2. Some due process rights are not granted to the accused (for example, the right against self-incrimination).*	2. Due process rights are guaranteed by the U.S. Constitution.
3. There is no trial by jury.	3. There is a trial by jury, in most cases, when requested.
4. An examiner or officer, who is usually an expert in the field being regulated, conducts the hearings.	4. A judge conducts the trial.
5. A lawyer may advise the accused but does not necessarily participate in the hearing as a matter of right.	5. A lawyer represents the accused and participates in the trial as a matter of right.†
6. The agency may make findings of fact, reach decisions, and take action even before the hearing is held.	6. The decision and action by the court usually follow the trial and the determination of the guilt or innocence of the accused.
7. Administrative remedies must be exhausted before a court will hear a case.	7. Lower court decisions may be appealed immediately to a higher court.
8. Penalties take the form of sanctions—the seizure of property, loss of license, cease and desist orders (orders to stop or prevent a prohibited act or acts), or fines. No jail sentences are imposed.	8. A wide range of criminal and/or civil penalties may be imposed, including jail sentences, fines, injunctions, and other penalties.

*Practice varies depending on the administrative agency conducting the hearing.
†The right to participate in the trial is not an absolute one. The lawyer may be barred from the trial if he or she is found guilty of contempt of court.

reasons, legislatures often give the power to regulate a particular kind of activity to an administrative agency. An administrative agency, often called a **regulatory agency,** is a department of government formed to administer particular legislation. Such agencies are separate from the executive, legislative, and judicial branches of government.

Administrative agencies tend to have an unusually wide range of powers. They often have the power to act in the following ways: (1) as legislators by making their own rules, (2) as police officers by enforcing their rules, (3) as prosecutors by investigating violations of their rules, and (4) as judges by deciding on the guilt or innocence of those who violate their rules. The rules and procedures established by regulatory agencies are called **administrative law.**

The courts have ruled such agencies to be constitutional. Even though they perform all three functions of government, there are checks and balances on their power. The legislature that created an agency always has the power to end that agency's existence or to change its powers, and any final decision by an agency can always be reviewed by a court. The number of administrative agencies in all levels of government has increased tremendously in recent years. These have a direct effect on daily American life.

Administrative Agency Proceedings   Acting as a judge, an administrative agency conducts hearings that differ in several ways from the proceedings in a regular court. Table 1-2 (page 15) summarizes the important differences between administrative hearings and regular court hearings.

Although administrative regulations often have the force of law, the violators of such regulations do not enjoy the same basic rights as those accused of violating statutory laws. In recognition of this fact, there has been an attempt in recent years to obtain the same rights for accused violators of administrative regulations as those that are given to persons accused of breaking criminal and civil laws. It seems likely, however, that the courts and elected government officials will continue to recognize the necessary role that administrative agencies play in regulating complex areas of our business life and the nation's economy.

Summary

1. The law is a body of rules that governs people's dealings with each other. In general, today's law has five main sources: common law, appellate court decisions, statutory law, administrative law, and constitutional law. Federal and state constitutions represent the ground rules that other laws must follow. The highest court in each state may rule that a state law violates its own constitution. The Supreme Court of the United States may rule on the constitutionality of any state or federal law.
2. The Bill of Rights of the U.S. Constitution guarantees many individual rights that protect people from abuses of power by government.
3. Courts depend on precedent when deciding cases. Therefore lawyers preparing for court, research the cases cited in related decisions. A common source of this information is *Shepard's Citations.*
4. Lawmakers often establish administrative agencies to create and enforce rules about special activities. These agencies can become expert in their areas and regulate efficiently. Administrative agencies have broad powers, but their rulings can be appealed, and the legislatures that created them may change their powers.

Language of the Law

Define or explain each of the following words or phrases:

law
Roman law, civil law,
  or Roman Code
feudal system
magistrates
common law
statutes
ecclesiastical law
law merchant

constitutional
Bill of Rights
double jeopardy
self-incrimination
lower courts
trial courts
courts of original
  jurisdiction

jurisdiction
appellate courts
courts of appellate
  jurisdiction
precedent
stare decisis
reporters
citation

Shepardizing
statutes
statutory law
ordinances
bylaws
regulatory agency
administrative law

Questions for Review

1. Why does society need laws? Describe some of the ways the law affects your everyday life.
2. What might have been some of the earliest laws governing people?
3. Why are the laws of Louisiana based on the Roman Code?
4. Briefly describe how the common law developed.
5. Name five sources of United States law.
6. What is the purpose of the first three articles of the U.S. Constitution?
7. How may the U.S. Constitution be amended?
8. What freedoms are given to all Americans by the First Amendment?
9. Why is the Fifth Amendment important to Americans?
10. What is the purpose of the twenty-sixth Amendment to the U.S. Constitution?
11. What court is the ultimate authority regarding the constitutionality of laws at all levels of government?
12. Give an example of a rule of law that developed in early England and is still followed in this country by some states, but not by others.
13. Read the following: *City of Kansas City v. Taylor*, 689 S.W.2d 645. What is it called? What is the meaning of each of its parts?
14. Explain the rule of law that is referred to by the following quote: "Vague laws trap the innocent by not providing fair warning."
15. Give some examples of administrative agencies.

Cases in Point

In each of the following cases, give your decision and state a legal principle that applies to the case:

1. Richard Lovina was arrested for stealing 1 pound of hamburger from a supermarket. This was the third time that he had been arrested for shoplifting. At Lovina's trial, the prosecuting attorney suggested to the judge that Lovina's hand be cut off as punishment for the crime. How would you decide?
2. Angela Ganon was given a ticket for driving 70 miles per hour in a 55-mile-per-hour

zone. In addition, she was cited for not wearing a seat belt, which violated a state law. One day earlier, the highest court of that state had held that the seat belt law was unconstitutional under its state constitution. If you were the trial judge, how would you decide Ganon's case?

3. A week after reaching the age of 18, Irving Adler went to the town clerk's office in his home town to register to vote. He was told by an assistant there that he could not vote until he reached the age of 21. Was the assistant correct? Why or why not?

4. While serving as a juror in a criminal case, Caleb Rakov argued that the defendant must be guilty because she didn't take the stand to testify. Do you agree with Rakov? Explain.

5. Alex Barsky refused to register for the draft when he learned that his cousin Lena did not have to register. Barsky claimed that men and women must be treated equally under the equal rights amendment to the United States Constitution. Do you agree? Explain.

6. Ann Chun's will became the subject of a court hearing in New Hampshire, where she lived at the time of her death. Her will had been drawn years earlier by an attorney who followed the law of California, where she lived at the time. Can the New Hampshire court refuse to recognize the will if the Cali-

fornia law differs from the New Hampshire law with regard to making wills?

7. Urszula Sydlo's apartment was searched by the police while she was at work. Sydlo had been in this country for only a short time and was not sure of her legal rights in this situation. Explain Sydlo's legal rights.

8. Lucy Demps was charged by her employer with stealing. After Demps was found not guilty of larceny by a jury, her employer brought new charges against her for the same offense, this time calling it embezzlement. How would you decide? Why?

9. A bank robber in the state of Missouri shot and wounded Lillian Shultz, who was an innocent customer standing in the bank lobby. Shultz died from the wounds 13 months later. The robber was charged with her murder. How will the court decide? Explain.

10. Carroll Corporation, a manufacturing company, was inspected by an official of the Occupational Safety and Health Administration (OSHA). The official found many safety violations and gave the company a specific number of days to correct them. The company refused to make the corrections. In court, Carroll Corporation's attorneys argued that OSHA was unconstitutional because it performed all three functions of government. How would you decide?

Cases to Judge

1. A dispute arose between the state of South Carolina and the Sloan Construction Company over the ownership of a riverbed. There were no state statutes or appellate court decisions in South Carolina on that particular subject. What law will the court follow in making its decision? *State Ex Rel. McLeod v. Sloan Const. Co., 328 S.E.2d 84 (South Carolina)*

2. A 4-year-old child who was in the care of foster parents was bitten by a dog while left unattended. Suit was brought against the foster parents for leaving the child unattended. Under common law, parents could not be sued by their children. Does an appellate court have the power to change the common law? Explain. *Mayberry v. Pryor, 352 N.W.2d 322 (Michigan)*

3. A parent allegedly insulted his daughter's teacher in the presence of several students. The parent was charged with violating the following Kentucky state statute: "No person shall upbraid, insult or abuse any teacher of the public schools in the presence of the school or in the presence of a pupil of the school." The parent argued that the statute is unconstitutionally vague. Do you agree? Why? *Com v. Ashcraft*, 691 S.W.2d 229 (Kentucky)

4. On December 15, Stevenson attempted to rob the registrar's office of Aquinas College in the state of Michigan. A young man tried to intervene and was shot twice in the abdomen. He died from the gunshot wounds on December 19, the following year, 1 year and 4 days after being shot. Stevenson was charged with first-degree felony murder. How should the court decide? Explain. *People v. Stevenson*, 300 N.W.2d 449 (Michigan)

5. Stephen Taylor was fined $500 and given a 180-day suspended jail sentence for pasturing his horse too close to his neighbor's house. Although the horse was pastured only on Taylor's land, his neighbor's house was 47 feet 6 inches from the property line. A city ordinance prohibited the "keeping, maintaining, and pasturing of livestock, including horses and swine, within 200 feet of the nearest portion of a residence other than that of the keeper." Is this an example of common law or of statutory law? What issues might Taylor raise in the appeal of his conviction? *City of Kansas City v. Taylor*, 689 S.W.2d 645 (Missouri)

Chapter 2

CRIMINAL LAW

Scene: Sue and Mike are still sitting on the front steps of the apartment building. Their cousin, Tony, comes along.

Sue and Mike: Hi, Tony.

Tony: What's up?

Mike (*showing Tony the newspaper*): Did you see this? That guy who killed the old lady is getting off easy. They're not charging him with murder because she lived more than a year and a day after he hit her.

Tony: What happened? How'd he kill her?

Sue: The lady had her window partly open one afternoon, and he opened it further and climbed in, trying to steal something. She heard a noise and caught him sneaking through the house. She started screaming, and he hit her over the head with a pipe or something. The guy climbed back out the window, but a cop was walking by, heard the screams, and arrested him.

Tony: Serves him right. Anybody who does that to an old woman must be crazy! Did they get him for robbery?

Mike: The paper said that all he got charged with was assault and battery.

Sue: He should be sent up for life, but he'll probably claim he was crazy and get off free.

Mike: Yeah, that's what all those crooks do nowadays. They tell the judge they were crazy when they did the crime, and the judge lets them go.

Tony: Speaking of being crazy, I was with those friends of mine last week, you know, Wayne and Rick. . . .

Sue: I told you to stay away from them. They're troublemakers.

Tony: Well, they talked me into doing something real bad. We skipped school and spent the morning planning a way to steal a Walkman from Cohen's store. We decided that Rick and I would keep Mr. Cohen occupied—you know, by pretending to buy something—while Wayne went to the other side of the store and put the Walkman under his jacket.

Sue: That's robbery! You're as bad as the guy who killed the old lady!

Tony: Wait a minute. Don't get excited! I backed out at the last minute. After we had agreed on our plan, we walked to Cohen's store and I chickened out and went home.

Mike: I'm glad you didn't commit a crime.

Sue: What did those idiots do? They'll spend the rest of their lives in jail.

Tony: They went into the store, and Mr. Cohen must have been in the back room. Instead of taking a Walkman, they took off with some VCRs worth over $1,000. The barber next door saw the whole thing and called the cops.

Sue: Did they get caught?

Tony: They came to my house and told me what happened, and I hid them out from the cops. The cruiser drove up and down the street for a couple of hours looking for them. We kept really quiet.

Sue: I told you they were bad news. You had better get some new friends, or get measured for a striped suit.

Tony: At least I didn't commit a crime.

LEGAL ISSUES

1. Is there a ''breaking'' when someone raises a partially opened window farther and climbs through?
2. What is the significance today of breaking into and entering another's house in the daytime?
3. Does a criminal who successfully uses the insanity defense automatically go free?
4. When someone climbs through the window of another's house and steals property, is it called robbery?
5. Is it robbery to shoplift from a store?
6. Is it a criminal offense to plan a crime with others?
7. Is it a crime to hide someone from the police with the knowledge that the person has committed a felony?

THE SPIRIT OF THE LAW

When people commit crimes, they harm not only the individual victim but all of society as well. There are certain acts which are not allowable in our society. These acts threaten the peace, safety, and well-being of the whole community. For this reason, a **crime** is considered an offense against the public at large. Also for this reason, the state or federal government, representing the public at large, is the **plaintiff** or **prosecution,** that is, the one who brings the criminal action. A person accused by a court of a crime or other legal wrongdoing is called a **defendant.**

A crime consists of the performance of an act which is punishable by a fine, imprisonment, or both. No act can be considered criminal unless it is prohibited by the law of the place where it is committed and unless the law provides for the punishment of offenders.

CLASSIFI-CATION OF CRIMES
Treason

Crimes are classified into three basic categories: treason, felonies, and misdemeanors.

Under the common law of England, **treason** was divided into "high treason" (acts against the king) and "petit treason" (acts against one's master or lord). Such a division, however, was never followed in this country. Under our Constitution, "Treason against the United States shall consist only in levying war against them, or in adhering to their enemies, giving them aid and comfort."

A crime similar to treason is espionage. **Espionage** is the gathering, transmitting, or losing of information related to the national defense with reason to believe that it will be used to injure this country or to aid a foreign government. It is prohibited by a federal statute with penalties as high as life imprisonment and death.

Felonies

A **felony** is defined in most states as a crime punishable by death or imprisonment in a state prison. It is a major crime. To determine whether or not a crime is a felony, we look at the statute to see what the punishment is for the commission of that particular crime. Murder, manslaughter, burglary, grand larceny, robbery, and arson are examples of felonies. A few states define a felony as a crime subject to "punishment by hard labor," "an infamous crime," or a crime subject to "infamous punishment." The federal Comprehensive Crime Control Act of 1984 defines a felony as "any offense punishable by death or imprisonment for a term exceeding one year."

Persons Who Commit Felonies A person who actually commits a felony—who pulls the trigger or strikes the blow—is called a **principal in the first degree.** Someone who does not actually commit the act but who is present, assisting another in the commission of a felony, is called a **principal in the second degree.** For example, a person who serves as a lookout for others who are committing a crime is considered present in the eyes of the law and is a principal in the second degree. In most states a principal in the second degree is given the same punishment as that given to a principal in the first degree.

A person who gets someone else to commit a felony but is not present when the felony is committed is an **accessory before the fact.** Such an accessory is generally responsible for things that the principal does. Thus, even if the accessory tells the principal not to use a gun in a robbery, the accessory is responsible if the principal uses a gun and shoots someone. In general, an accessory before the fact is subject to the same punishment as a principal. An **accessory after the fact** is one who gives aid and assistance to another with the knowledge that that person has committed a felony. The punishment for being an accessory after the fact varies from state to state. The Massachusetts statute, for example, provides that an accessory after the fact shall be punished by imprisonment in the state prison for not more than 7 years or in jail for not more than 2½ years or by a fine of not more than $1,000.

In most states a close relative, such as a husband, wife, parent, grandparent, child, grandchild, brother, or sister, cannot be *convicted* (found guilty) of being an accessory after the fact. The theory underlying this rule is that such persons will naturally protect and aid their loved ones when they are in trouble.

Legal Issue No. 7

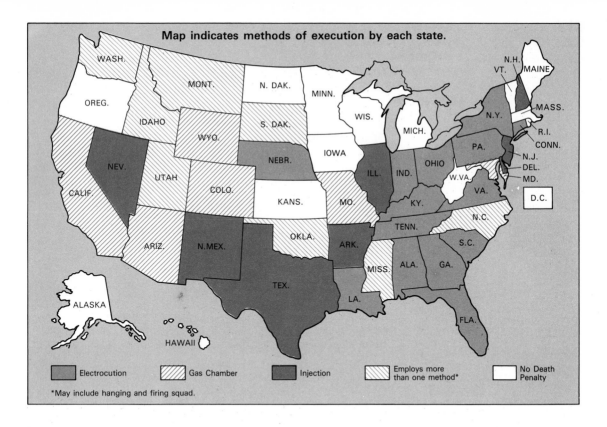

Map indicates methods of execution by each state.

Electrocution | Gas Chamber | Injection | Employs more than one method* | No Death Penalty

*May include hanging and firing squad.

The Death Penalty The U.S. Supreme Court in 1972 held that the death penalty was cruel and unusual treatment and was, therefore, unconstitutional. The Court said that the death penalty would be constitutional, however, if there were enough guidelines to ensure that people were treated fairly and if juries and judges were not allowed to give out the death sentence whenever they wished. Without proper guidelines, blacks, the poor, and the uneducated were more likely than anyone else to receive the death sentence.

After the 1972 Supreme Court decision, many states changed their death penalty laws. In 1976 the Supreme Court approved newly revised death penalty laws in Florida, Georgia, Texas, and Utah. Other states soon followed and passed death penalty laws within the Supreme Court's guidelines. In general the new death penalty laws provide for trials to go through three phases. In the first phase, the jury determines the guilt or innocence of the person charged with the crime. If the person is found guilty, the second phase, called a **presentence hearing,** takes place. In a presentence hearing, the judge or jury listens to lawyers' arguments and examines other evidence to help determine the punishment to be given. The state's laws must clearly set forth factors to be considered before deciding on the punishment. The third phase is an appeal to the state's highest court.

In 1982, the U.S. Supreme Court ruled that the death penalty was unconstitutional for juveniles. The law as it applies to juveniles is discussed further in Chapter 3.

Traffic violations are crimes because they endanger the public at large. People who are charged with crimes have the right to appear in court to defend themselves.

Misdemeanors

All crimes which are not treason or felonies are **misdemeanors.** They require a lighter penalty such as a fine or imprisonment in a county or local jail. Some examples of misdemeanors are petty larceny, driving an automobile without a license, assault and battery (without a dangerous weapon), lying about one's age to purchase alcoholic beverages, and leaving the scene of an automobile accident.

INCOMPLETE OFFENSES

Sometimes crimes are begun but not completed. Either the criminal act was planned and not carried out, or it was attempted and not completed. In either case, under the law a crime has actually occurred.

Conspiracy

Conspiracy is the crime that takes place when two or more people get together and agree to commit a crime. The crime that is agreed upon does not have to be committed for someone to be convicted of conspiracy. In most states, the very act of getting together with other people and agreeing to accomplish something unlawful is itself a crime. By statute in some states, conspiracy must also include an overt act by one of the parties toward the commission of the crime.

Legal Issue No. 6

Attempts to Commit Crimes

An attempt to commit a crime, even if it fails, is a crime itself. An **attempt** (such as attempted robbery or attempted murder) may be defined as an act done with the intent to commit a crime that falls short of its commission (or completion).

Mere preparation to commit a crime is not enough for a person to be found guilty of an attempt. There must be some noticeable act toward the commission of the crime itself.

EXAMPLE 1 A man whose business was in financial trouble placed a candle in a dishpan containing turpentine. He trailed oil-soaked wood shavings leading from the pan to other combustible material in his shop. He left the shop and asked an employee to light the candle. The employee refused. Later that evening the man started toward his shop with the intent of lighting the candle but changed his mind and went home. He was charged with attempted arson. The court found him not guilty, saying that there was no present intent to set the fire. Mere preparation alone is not enough for someone to be convicted of attempted arson.

In Example 1, if the man actually lit the candle and the candle had failed to function properly, he could have been found guilty of attempted arson. If he had planned the arson with his partner, he could be found guilty of conspiracy in most states.

PARTICULAR CRIMES

Each crime must have an exact definition. These exact definitions come from either the common law or the statutory law of each state. This is necessary so that everyone will know, without any doubt, what is against the law. Some of the more common crimes and their definitions are explained in the paragraphs that follow.

Assault and Battery

Battery is the unlawful touching of another person. An accidental bumping of another person on a crowded subway or bus would not be battery, since the crime requires criminal intent or reckless behavior. Although battery most commonly involves the forceful use of a person's hand, a knife, or a gun, other examples of battery are giving poison or drugs to another without the other's knowledge, exposing a helpless baby to severe weather conditions, spitting in someone's face, or siccing a dog on someone. An unwelcome kiss can be battery, too.

An **assault** is an attempt to commit battery. The pointing or shooting of a gun at someone is the assault; the bullet striking the person is the battery. There can be and often is an assault without a battery, but a battery necessarily includes an assault. Some states no longer follow the common-law distinctions between assault and battery. Ohio, for example, has eliminated the term ''battery'' from its criminal code and substituted ''assault'' by itself.

Simple assault and battery is generally a misdemeanor. **Aggravated assault,** however, is a felony in most states. Examples of aggravated assault are assault with the intent to murder, assault and battery with a dangerous weapon, assault with the intent to commit robbery, and assault with the intent to commit rape.

Burglary

Burglary is defined under common law as the breaking (opening) and entering of a dwelling house at night with the intent to commit a felony. This definition is still used today; but, as you can see, it does not cover every situation. For this reason, each state has passed laws covering other kinds of breaking and entering incidents. Such incidents include breaking and entering in the daytime, breaking and entering a place that is not a dwelling house, and breaking and entering a place with the intent to commit a misdemeanor. If any part of the definition of burglary cannot be proved, the defendant cannot be found guilty.

Legal Issues Nos. 2 and 4

EXAMPLE 2 A number of years ago, while walking along a sidewalk after dark, a man noticed a house with a partly opened window. He raised the window farther, climbed inside, and stole some expensive shoes. He was charged with committing the crime of burglary. However, the court held that he was not guilty because there was no breaking. The window was already open. He simply opened it farther. Most state laws today say that a breaking has occurred when someone raises a partly opened window.

Larceny and Embezzlement

Larceny is the legal name for stealing. It is the wrongful taking and carrying away of the **personal property** (things other than real estate) of another with the intent to steal. In many states the crime is divided into **petty larceny,** which is a misdemeanor, and **grand larceny,** which is a felony, depending on the value of the stolen property. Shoplifting is a form of larceny.

Embezzlement is similar to larceny in that it too is a form of theft. **Embezzlement** is the wrongful taking away of another's property by a person who has been entrusted with or given rightful control over that property by the owner.

EXAMPLE 3 Virginia Waddell worked as a cashier in a supermarket. A customer bought some groceries and paid Waddell the money. Waddell put the money directly into her pocket instead of placing it in the cash register drawer. She intended to steal the money. This was embezzlement because she was entrusted with the money (she had it rightfully) before she stole it. If Waddell had placed the money in the cash register drawer when she first received it and then had taken it out and put it in her pocket, her crime would have been larceny rather than embezzlement. This is because there would have been a wrongful (rather than a rightful) taking before she placed it in her pocket.

Robbery

Robbery is the wrongful taking and carrying away of the personal property of another from the other's person, against the victim's will, by the use of force, violence, or the threat of bodily harm. The principal difference between larceny and robbery is that in robbery there is a taking ''from the person''—that is, from the body or from close to the body of the victim, by the use of force or threats—whereas in larceny this is not so.

EXAMPLE 4 Suppose, in Example 3, that someone came into the store while Waddell was working as a cashier, pointed a gun at her, and demanded the money from the cash register drawer. This would be armed robbery because it would be taking the money from Waddell's personal custody, and it would be done against her will. Pointing the gun at her would be an instance of force and violence.

The penalty for robbery is greater than that for larceny. In one state, for example, the punishment for robbery (whether armed or unarmed) is ''imprisonment in the state prison for life or for any term of years.'' In contrast, the punishment for grand larceny is ''imprisonment in the state prison for not more than five years or by a fine of not more than $600 and imprisonment in jail for not more than two years.'' The punishment for petty larceny is ''imprisonment in jail for not more than one year or by a fine of not more than $300.''

Arson

The common-law definition of **arson** is the willful and malicious burning of the dwelling house of another. (**Malicious** means "with evil intent.") The law originally was aimed at protecting people rather than property, and therefore it required that the building be a dwelling house. Even though most states have kept the common-law definition of arson and still follow it, they have added statutes to cover other forms of arson, such as the burning of a building other than a dwelling house. The scorching or blackening of a part of a building is not enough to be considered an act of arson. Some portion of the building must actually have been on fire so that the wood or any other building material is charred.

Homicide

Homicide is the killing of a human being by another human being. **Justifiable homicide** occurs when a convicted criminal is legally executed or when a soldier is killed in battle. **Excusable homicide** occurs when someone kills another person in self-defense. Neither justifiable nor excusable homicide is a crime as such. All other homicides are serious felonies. They consist of two types of crimes—murder and manslaughter.

Murder **Murder** is the unlawful killing of a human being by another with malice aforethought. **Malice aforethought** means having an evil intent before the killing takes place. In many states the crime is divided into first-degree murder and second-degree murder.

■ The definition of **first-degree murder** differs somewhat from state to state, but generally it is murder committed in any one of the following three circumstances: (1) killing someone after **premeditation** (thinking about it and planning it in advance); (2) killing someone in a cruel way, such as with torture; or (3) killing someone while committing a major crime such as rape, robbery, or kidnapping. If none of these three conditions apply, the crime is **second-degree murder.**

Manslaughter **Manslaughter** is the unlawful killing of one human being by another without malice aforethought. The major difference between murder and manslaughter is that malice (evil intent) is found in murder, but it is not found in manslaughter. Manslaughter is of two types—voluntary manslaughter and involuntary manslaughter.

Voluntary manslaughter occurs when one person intends, at the time the act is committed, to kill another but does so suddenly and as the result of great personal distress. The wrongdoer must have become very upset before the killing.

EXAMPLE 5 Harry Hegarty asked Kim Clark to marry him. She accepted, and they were both very happy. The next evening, when Hegarty went to visit Clark, he found her kissing another man. He became enraged and struck her with an iron pipe that was lying nearby. She died from the blow. Hegarty was

---

■ This symbol indicates that there may be a state statute that varies from the law discussed here. Whenever you see this symbol find out, if possible, what the statute in your state says about this point or principle of law.

charged with voluntary manslaughter. Hegarty had intended to hit Clark, but he did so without malice, in the heat of emotional upset.

Involuntary manslaughter occurs when one person, while committing an unlawful or reckless act, kills another. There is no intent to kill.

EXAMPLE 6 Claudine Makimbo was driving her car at a speed of 65 miles per hour in an area where the speed limit was 35 miles per hour. A child ran out in front of the speeding car and was killed. Makimbo had no intent to kill anyone. She was charged with involuntary manslaughter because she killed the child while violating the law. In some states, this is called reckless or vehicular homicide.

WHITE-COLLAR CRIMES

White-collar crimes are crimes that are fraud-related and are carried out in a nonviolent way. Some of them are larceny by false pretenses, forgery, bribery, extortion, and computer theft.

Larceny by False Pretenses

Larceny by false pretenses is the taking of someone else's money or property by the intentional use of false statements. The false statements must be calculated to mislead and must induce the victim to rely on them.

EXAMPLE 7 Dennis Joyce told Lin Hau that her husband had been placed under arrest and was being held by the police. He told her that he could have her husband released on bail if she would give him something of value to pawn. She gave him a valuable diamond ring. It turned out to be a fraud: Hau's husband had not been arrested. Joyce had committed larceny by false pretenses.

Forgery

Forgery is the false making or changing of a writing with the intent to defraud. The signing of another person's name without authority to a check or other document is a forgery.

EXAMPLE 8 In an attempt to defraud a client, an attorney made up a bogus court order on which he reproduced the signatures of a judge and a court clerk by the use of a photocopy machine. The court held this to be a forgery of the two signatures.

Signing one's own name, pretending to be someone else of the same name, is a forgery. Similarly, the creation of a fictitious identity and the signing of the name of the fictitious person with a fraudulent purpose is considered forgery.

In order for there to be a crime in these circumstances, there must be an intent to defraud, and the item forged must have some legal effect. Thus, it would not be forgery to write someone else's signature on a will that was never witnessed, because an unwitnessed will has no legal effect.

Uttering a forged instrument is also a crime. **Uttering** means to offer a forged instrument to another person, knowing that it is forged and intending to defraud. Similarly, issuing counterfeit currency is a federal crime and a crime in many states as well.

Bribery and Extortion

It is illegal to pay or give anything of value to public officials in order to influence their official activity. This is known as **bribery** and is defined as the giving or receiving of a reward to influence any official act. It is a crime at any level of government, whether federal, state, or local.

The penalty for bribery at the federal level is a fine of not more than $20,000 or three times the monetary equivalent of the "thing of value," whichever is greater, or imprisonment for not more that 15 years, or both. In addition, the offender may be disqualified from holding a federal office.

Extortion, under the common law, is the taking of money or a thing of value unjustly by a public official. Some states have extended the crime to include the taking of property by people other than public officials. In extortion, the victim consents to the surrender of the money or property, but the consent has to be brought on by using force or putting the victim in fear.

EXAMPLE 9 Joseph Peluso, a member of the city council, told Miguel Rosa that he would have to pay him $2,000 if he wanted to keep the rubbish collection contract in that city for another year. In fear of losing the contract, Rosa paid Peluso the money. Later, when the crime was discovered, Peluso was convicted of extortion.

Computer Crime

There is a growing concern about computer crime. This relatively new area of criminal law ranges from the theft of computer programs and the wrongful use of computer time to the illegal access of information belonging to others.

EXAMPLE 10 In a Texas case, Hancock, who was employed to write computer programs for his company, attempted to sell 59 programs (valued at $2.5 million) to another company. His plan was discovered, and he was convicted of theft. The court held that computer programs come within the definition of property as it is used in statutes defining theft.

Some states have enacted special computer crime statutes. Generally, they cover such things as the unauthorized access to computer programs and the destruction of computer programs and equipment. Louisiana's statute makes it a crime for users of software to violate the license printed on a software box. Some people oppose this latter type of legislation, claiming that it protects only the seller and not the buyer of the software.

The Los Angeles–based National Center for Computer Crime Data publishes a monthly newsletter called *Conscience in Computing*. The publication's goal is to build a mainstream computer ethic about what is right and what is wrong when people use computers.

DEFENSES TO CRIMES

All crimes have exact definitions and can be broken down into precise elements. Thus, a defense that is used quite often in criminal cases is the failure of the prosecution to prove a necessary element of the crime. To illustrate, the man who raised the partly opened window and climbed inside and stole the shoes, in Example 2, was able to establish that the prosecution had failed to prove a breaking. This is a necessary element of the crime of burglary.

Some other defenses that are used in criminal cases are self-defense, entrapment, and insanity.

Self-Defense

Self-defense is an excuse for the use of force in resisting attack. Except in one's own home (under modern statutes), the person claiming self-defense must retreat, if possible, before resorting to excessive force. When self-defense is used as a defense to homicide, it must be shown that the only possible way to escape death or bodily injury was to kill the assailant.

Entrapment

If a police officer induces someone who is not a law violator to commit a crime, **entrapment** may be used as a defense. The person using the defense must show that the crime would not have been committed had it not been for the inducement of the officer.

Insanity

The oldest legal test of insanity, called the McNaughten Rule, was developed in England in 1843. McNaughten killed the British Prime Minister's secretary, in an attempt to kill the Prime Minister himself. He simply shot the first person wearing a top hat to leave the Prime Minister's house. McNaughten was found to be not guilty by reason of insanity.

Under the McNaughten Rule, "it must be clearly proved that, at the time of the committing of the act, the party accused was labouring under such a defect of reason, from disease of the mind, as not to know the nature and quality of the act he was doing; or, if he did know it, that he did not know he was doing what was wrong." This test is still used in about two-fifths of the states. In addition, it is the basis for the definition of insanity in the federal Comprehensive Crime Control Act of 1984.

A more modern insanity test was developed in 1962 by the American Law Institute (ALI). Under the ALI test, a person is not responsible if "as a result of mental disease or defect he lacks substantial capacity either to appreciate the criminality [wrongness] of his conduct or to conform his conduct to the requirements of law." About three-fifths of the states follow the ALI test.

Legal Issue No. 3

People found not guilty by reason of insanity do not automatically go free. Often they are committed to institutions and must undergo periodic psychological examinations. Sometimes they actually spend more time in psychiatric hospitals than they would have spent in prison if they had been convicted of the crime.

CRIMINAL ARREST

An **arrest** occurs when a person is deprived of his or her freedom. A person under arrest has the right, under the U.S. Constitution, not to answer questions if he or she chooses not to do so.

An officer may arrest a person at any time if the officer has a warrant for that person's arrest. An **arrest warrant** is an order issued by a court saying that a person is charged with a crime and is to be arrested. An officer may arrest a person without a warrant if the officer has good reason to believe that the person has committed or is presently committing a felony. In addition, an officer may, without a warrant, arrest someone who has committed a misdemeanor if the misdemeanor involves a breach of the peace and is done in the officer's pres-

What is the purpose of a frisk? Is a warrant needed for this kind of search?

ence. Various state statutes also allow officers to make arrests for specific misdemeanors done in their presence, even if there is no breach of the peace.

Search and Seizure

A police officer may search a person, a motor vehicle, a house, or other building at any time if permission is given or if the officer has a search warrant. A **search warrant** is a court order allowing an officer to conduct the search. The search must be limited to the area mentioned in the warrant. The one whose person or property is being searched has a right to see the search warrant or to have it read out loud. The officer keeps the warrant, however, since it must be returned to the court.

If an officer has reason to believe that a person is carrying a hidden weapon, the officer may conduct a limited search called a **frisk.** This is done by patting the outer clothing of a person. If the frisk reveals something that feels like a weapon, the officer may search for and remove that object. The officer must return any lawful object that is found. When the search is over, the person must be either released or arrested. Persons who have been arrested may be searched without a warrant.

When someone is arrested in a house or building, the police may conduct a limited search of the area in which the arrest took place without a search warrant. They must have a warrant, however, to search the entire building. A limited search of a car may be made without a warrant if someone is arrested in the car. A more complete search of the car may be made if there is good reason to believe that the car contains something illegal that the police may take as evidence. In addition, the police have the right to **impound** (take possession of) a car until a search warrant is obtained from the court.

EXAMPLE 11 In a 1976 case, a car was impounded by the police in a South Dakota community for a number of parking violations. While making a routine list of the car's contents, the police found a bag of marijuana. They charged the owner with possession of the substance. The Supreme Court of the United States held that the search without a warrant was constitutional in this case because the police of this community had followed a standard procedure of writing down the contents of every car they impounded.

Police may seize suspicious items, such as illegal drugs or weapons, that are in plain view without obtaining a warrant. This is known as the **plain-view exception** to the requirement of obtaining a search warrant. The U.S. Supreme Court has said that "information obtained from observing an object in plain sight may be the basis for probable cause or reasonable suspicion of illegal activity."

In 1981, the Supreme Court said that police can search the entire passenger area of a car without a search warrant once the occupants are placed under arrest. A year later, the Court held that police officers who have legitimately stopped an automobile and who have probable cause to believe that **contraband** (illegal goods or substances) is concealed somewhere within, may conduct a warrantless search of the vehicle, including compartments and containers within the vehicle whose contents are not in plain view.

EXAMPLE 12 Acting on information from a reliable informant, police officers stopped an automobile driven by a person whose description matched the description given by the informant. They had been told that the automobile contained drugs. The police opened the trunk, without a warrant, and discovered a bag of heroin inside. In holding the warrantless search legal, the U.S. Supreme Court said, "If probable cause justifies the search of a lawfully stopped vehicle, it justifies the search of every part of the vehicle."

In 1985 the Supreme Court said that the Constitution permits school officials to search students without a search warrant. The officials must have reasonable grounds to believe that the search will turn up evidence that the student has violated either the law or rules of the school. Also, the search must be done in a reasonable manner.

Police roadblocks are becoming increasingly popular to detect illegal activity. In 1979 the Supreme Court ruled that a single car could not be pulled over without cause but said that roadblocks where everybody is stopped for a license check are legal. It is uncertain, however, whether that decision allows roadblocks solely for the purpose of detecting drunken drivers. Since that time, police roadblocks, following specific guidelines, have been allowed by the courts in New York, Massachusetts, and Kansas to detect drunken drivers. The Massachusetts court said, "For a roadblock to be permissible, the selection of motor vehicles to be stopped must not be arbitrary, safety must be assured, motorists' inconvenience must be minimized, and assurances must be given that the procedure is being conducted pursuant to a plan devised by law enforcement supervisory personnel." In contrast, the courts of Illinois and Oklahoma have held roadblocks to be unconstitutional in their states.

Rights of the Arrested

When people are arrested they must be informed of their constitutional rights, as affirmed in the case of *Miranda v. Arizona*. Under the *Miranda* warnings, people have the right to know the crimes with which they are charged and the names of the police officers making the arrest. They have the right to use the telephone soon after they are brought to the police station to call their families, a friend, or a lawyer, or to arrange for bail. **Bail** is money or other property that is left with the court to assure the court that the person will return to stand trial. People who are arrested also have the right to remain silent. If they decide to answer questions, they have the right to talk to an attorney beforehand. They can also have an attorney present during the questioning. People who cannot afford an attorney have the right to have the court appoint one to represent them free of charge. In addition to the Miranda warnings, the accused also have a constitutional right to a fair trial and to the presumption of innocence until proven guilty of a crime by a court of law. Many other rights of the accused are spelled out in the Bill of Rights. The aim of the Bill of Rights and of our entire judicial system is to protect the rights of all people accused of crimes and to presume people innocent until proven guilty.

Suggestions for Reducing Legal Risks

If you are arrested:

1. Do not under any circumstances resist arrest or run from the police.
2. You do not have to answer any questions or to say anything.
3. Anything you say may be used against you in court.
4. You do not have to sign anything.
5. You have a right to have an attorney represent you, whether or not you can afford one.

Language of the Law

Define or explain each of the following words or phrases:

crime	presentence hearing	malicious	forgery
plaintiff	misdemeanor	homicide	uttering
prosecution	conspiracy	justifiable homicide	bribery
defendant	attempt	excusable homicide	extortion
treason	battery	murder	self-defense
espionage	assault	malice aforethought	entrapment
felony	aggravated assault	first-degree murder	arrest
principal in the first degree	burglary	premeditation	arrest warrant
	larceny	second-degree murder	search warrant
principal in the second degree	personal property	manslaughter	frisk
	petty larceny	voluntary manslaughter	impound
accessory before the fact	grand larceny	involuntary manslaughter	plain-view exception
	embezzlement	white-collar crimes	contraband
accessory after the fact	robbery	larceny by false pretenses	bail
	arson		

Questions for Review

1. Compare a felony with a misdemeanor.
2. How does a principal in the first degree differ from a principal in the second degree? What is the difference in their punishment?
3. What is the name given to someone who gets another person to commit a felony but is not present when the felony is committed?
4. Why does the law in most states say that a close relative cannot be convicted of being an accessory after the fact?
5. Generally, the new death penalty laws provide for trials to go through three phases. What are these phases?
6. What must be proved for a person to be found guilty of common-law burglary?
7. What is the difference between robbery and larceny? larceny and embezzlement?
8. Explain the difference between battery and assault.
9. Homicide is divided into murder and manslaughter. How do these two crimes differ?
10. Define an attempt to commit a crime.
11. What are the rights of a person arrested for an alleged crime?
12. When may police conduct a warrantless search of an automobile?
13. What did the U.S. Supreme Court set forth in the plain-view exception to the requirement of obtaining a search warrant?
14. When and in what way may school officials search students without a search warrant?

Cases in Point

For each of the following cases, give your decision and state a legal principle that applies to the case:

1. Flora Wright paid Ernest Todd $200 to beat up her brother Albert. Later, Wright claimed that she was not guilty of a crime because Todd, not she, had done the wrongful act. Is she correct?
2. Sol Feder, Ann Feeney, and René Faucett got together one evening. They agreed to break into a house in a wealthy section of town in order to steal whatever they could find. The wrongful act was never carried out. Was a crime committed? If so, what crime?
3. José Urena committed armed robbery and was wanted by the police. His sister, Maria, who knew he had committed the crime, allowed him to stay at her house. She was later charged with being an accessory after the fact to the crime. Is she guilty or innocent? Why?
4. Rosemary Morrison smashed a window and entered a television store at 2 a.m. She was caught attempting to carry out a $500 color television set and was charged with committing common-law burglary. Is she guilty or innocent? Why?
5. Lena Gorin gave her state representative $1,500 in exchange for his promise to award her company a state contract. Was a crime committed? Explain.
6. Oscar Brumer accidentally bumped into Elvira Neely on a crowded subway. Neely claimed that Brumer had committed the crime of assault and battery. Is she correct? Why or why not?
7. Joseph E. Moore, who had a history of passing bad checks, went to court and legally changed his name to Daniel E. Moore. Later, he bought groceries with a $20 check which he signed Joseph E. Moore. The check was returned by the bank with the notation ''No account.'' Was this a forgery? Explain.

8. A thief picked Angelo Renza's pocket and stole his wallet containing several hundred dollars. The episode was witnessed by Sandra Sims, who notified a police officer. Renza did not know that it had happened until the thief was apprehended. Did the thief commit robbery? Explain.

9. While walking along the school corridor, Kathy Holt saw John Link place a handgun under a bookbag on the top shelf of his locker. Kathy told the assistant principal, who searched the locker and found the gun. Link claimed that the search of his locker was illegal without a search warrant. Do you agree? Explain.

10. Being upset over the loss of a sale, and seeing no one in the reception area, Kent Gibbs started to walk off with a portable computer as he left the Acme Supply Company. To his surprise, the computer was attached to the desk by a strong cord. Gibbs was able to move the computer only as far as the length of the cord before being discovered by a receptionist. Can Gibbs be convicted of larceny? Explain.

Cases to Judge

1. Davenport's brother had broken into a house through a basement window. His brother then came out through the patio door and went back home and told Davenport about it. Davenport had not previously known about the crime. Then both of them went to the house and stole a number of items. Davenport was charged as a principal in the first degree of breaking and entering a dwelling house with intent to commit larceny. Is he guilty? Why or why not? *People v. Davenport*, 332 N.W.2d 443 (Michigan)

2. While exiting a trolley in Philadelphia, Jackson kicked the person in front of him in the rear. He then followed the person and punched him in the eye, knocking his glasses to the ground. Jackson was joined by several trolley-riding colleagues who punched and kicked the victim for a few seconds and attempted to snatch a chain from his neck. One member of the group picked up the victim's glasses, and the entire group returned to the trolley. Jackson was apprehended and charged with robbery. How would you decide? Give reasons for your answer. *Com. v. Jackson*, 463 A.2d 1036 (Pennsylvania)

3. Oxendine was charged with arson after setting fire to his aunt's house. His aunt testified that after hearing her son exclaim, "Fire!" she went into the bedroom and saw fire and smoke coming out of it. By the time the fire truck arrived, the aunt and four neighbors had doused the blaze. A police officer testified, "The curtains were burned, and there were dark or burned patches over the wall; the wallpaper was burned, and there was a heavy odor of kerosene. Smoke was throughout the house." In his defense, Oxendine argued that the state had not proved that the building had been charred. Do you agree with Oxendine? Explain. *State v. Oxendine*, 286 S.E.2d 546 (North Carolina)

4. Michael Price lived in Texas, and James, his brother, lived in California. With his brother's cooperation, Michael had procured a driver's license that bore Michael's own picture but James' name. At James' request, Michael used the altered license to open a Texas bank account. Michael represented himself to be James Price and, as identification, showed the license. Michael signed the signature card using James' name. He then sent a book of checks to James in California, the checks being imprinted with James' name but with Michael's Texas address. James drew 11 checks on the Texas account totalling $28,500. There was not enough

money in the account to cover any of the checks. Is James guilty of forgery? Why or why not? *United States v. Price,* 655 F.2d 958 (9th Circuit)

5. A police officer observed a parked pickup truck in the parking lot of an all-night grocery store at 4:45 a.m. Both doors of the truck were open, and no one was visibly near the vehicle. A rash of car break-ins had occurred at that parking lot a week or two earlier. The officer, being suspicious, walked toward the driver's side of the truck. He noticed legs sticking out of the driver's side entrance to the vehicle. As he approached the truck, Miller got out. The officer asked him what was going on, while at the same time looking into the open vehicle in search of possible weapons. The glove compartment was open, and the officer observed a clear plastic baggie containing a green substance that he believed to be marijuana. At that moment, Miller instructed another person in the truck to shut the glove compartment, which was done. The officer opened the compartment and found that the plastic bag contained marijuana. Was this an illegal search? Why or why not? *Miller v. State,* 686 S.W.2d 725 (Texas)

Chapter 3

PROBLEMS IN SOCIETY

Scene: Steve's car is stopped in front of the apartment building where Mike lives. Steve and Mike are leaning against the car, talking.

Steve: You know those kids Wayne and Rick? They got caught shoplifting last week in a store downtown.

Mike: I knew they'd get caught sooner or later. My cousin, Tony, almost got mixed up with them.

Steve: A store detective caught them inside the store. They both had a brand new Sony Walkman underneath their jackets.

Mike: How stupid can you get.

Steve: They're arguing that they can't be charged with shoplifting because they didn't walk out of the store with the goods. They claim that they were on their way to the checkout counter.

Mike: With the goods under their jackets?

Steve: They're a couple of real jerks. You should have seen them in school last year when they got caught with drugs. A teacher smelled pot in the men's room just after they had walked out, so the principal searched their lockers.

Mike: Oh yeah?

Steve: They made a big deal of it, saying the school couldn't search their lockers without a search warrant.

Mike: They may have been right, you know?

Steve: When they were questioned at the police station, they claimed that they had the right to remain silent and to have a lawyer just like adults do. The police told them that kids don't have those rights.
(At that moment, Sue walks out of the apartment building.)

Steve and Mike: Hi, Sue!

Sue: Hi, guys! Uncle Gino just called Mom. He's all upset. He had a few too many drinks last night at his friend's house, and the police stopped his car on the way home. They had him take a breathalizer test, and it came out .11 percent, which is over the amount the law allows.

Mike: What a shame. Gino's such a nice guy.

Sue: He's a wonderful person. He'll do anything for you.

Steve: He could have got out of that. They couldn't do anything if he refused to take the test.

Mike: Are you sure? *(seeing Tony walking toward them)* Here comes

Tony. Let's ask him about his friends, Wayne and Rick.

Sue, Steve, and Mike: Hi, Tony!

Tony: What's up?

Mike: We heard that your two nit-wit friends finally got busted.

Tony: Where'd you hear that?

Sue: Word gets around fast in this neighborhood. I told you to stay away from those two. They're weird!

Tony: I saw them today and they're pretty sure that they'll get off easy the way they did last time, when they got caught with pot in their school lockers.

Sue: Didn't they go before a juvenile court that time?

Tony: Yeah, and the judge gave them a warning and told them to shape up and keep away from drugs.

Steve: How old are they now?

Tony: They're both 17. I hope they don't get the same judge they had before.

LEGAL ISSUES

1. Is the concealment of goods on one's person in a store evidence of intent to steal?
2. Are minors entitled to the same due-process rights as adults?
3. What happens to a person who refuses to submit to a breathalizer test?
4. May a 17-year-old person charged with a crime be tried in a juvenile court?

THE SPIRIT OF THE LAW

In today's fast-moving and complicated society, some problems seem to stand out more than others. On the international level, terrorism and highjacking head the list. On the national level, child abuse and the disappearance of children have become major concerns. Alcohol and drug abuse continue to plague society and are the cause of many other social problems, including criminal activity. With goods so easily accessible on store shelves, shoplifting has become a costly activity that has increased prices for all consumers and lessened profits for business people. Juvenile delinquency and vandalism are continuing problems as well.

TERRORISM AND HIGH-JACKING

People all over the world are becoming increasingly concerned about terrorism. It is a violent crime that injures and kills innocent people of all ages and walks of life. The following definition of **international terrorism** comes from the U.S. Code (50 USCS 1801):

"International terrorism" means activities that—
(1) involve violent acts or acts dangerous to human life that are a violation of the criminal laws of the United States or of any State, or that would be a criminal violation if committed within the jurisdiction of the United States or any State;

(2) appear to be intended—
    (A) to intimidate or coerce a civilian population;
    (B) to influence the policy of a government by intimidation or coercion; or
    (C) to affect the conduct of a government by assassination or kidnapping; and
(3) occur totally outside the United States or transcend national boundaries in terms of the means by which they are accomplished, the persons they appear intended to coerce or intimidate, or the locale in which their perpetrators operate or seek asylum.

The highjacking of airplanes is a crime that sometimes occurs in the United States and in other parts of the world. Under the Federal Aviation Act, the penalty for aircraft piracy is imprisonment for not less than 20 years. If the death of another results from the piracy, the punishment is death or imprisonment for life. In 1984, Congress increased the penalty for carrying weapons or explosives aboard aircraft to $25,000 or imprisonment for not more than 5 years, or both.

ALCOHOL ABUSE

Alcohol, the major chemical found in beer, wine, whiskey, and other distilled beverages, is the most commonly abused drug in the United States, despite the strict laws controlling its sale.

Drunk driving is a particularly serious problem. Recently it was estimated that in an average week nearly 500 Americans died in alcohol-related automobile accidents. Many states toughened the punishment for drunken driving. (See Table 3-1.) In Florida, for example, a first conviction would bring a minimum fine of $250 plus 50 hours of required community service and a 6-month loss of license. For a second offense, the minimum penalties would jump to $500 and 10 days in jail.

Innocent civilians are often the victims of terrorist activities. Can a U.S. federal law be effective against terrorism?

TABLE 3-1
LICENSE REVOCATION AND SUSPENSION FOR DRUNK DRIVING*

State	Drinking Age	Refusal to Submit to Breath Test	Driving While Intoxicated
Alabama	21	Suspension	*Suspension (1)* Revocation (2)
Alaska	21	Either suspension or revocation	Revocation
Arizona	21	Suspension	Suspension (1, 2) Revocation (3)
Arkansas	21	Revocation	Suspension (1) Revocation (2)
California	21	Revocation	Suspension (1, 2) Revocation (3)
Colorado	18/21	Revocation	Suspension (1) Revocation (2)
Connecticut	21	Either suspension or revocation	Suspension
Delaware	21	Revocation	Revocation
Florida	21	Suspension	Revocation
Georgia	21	Suspension	Suspension (1, 2) Revocation (3)
Hawaii	18	Revocation	Suspension (1, 2) Revocation (3)
Idaho	19	Suspension	Suspension
Illinois	21	*Suspension*	*Revocation*
Indiana	21	Suspension	*Suspension (1)* Suspension (2)
Iowa	19	Revocation	Revocation
Kansas	18/21	Suspension	Suspension (1) Revocation (2)
Kentucky	21	Revocation	Revocation
Louisiana	18	Suspension	Suspension (1) Revocation (2)
Maine	21	Suspension	Suspension
Maryland	21	Suspension	*Either suspension or revocation*
Massachusetts	21	Suspension	Revocation
Michigan	21	Suspension	*Suspension*
Minnesota	19	Revocation	Revocation
Mississippi	21	Suspension	Suspension
Missouri	21	Revocation	Suspension (1) Revocation (2)
Montana	19	Suspension	Suspension (1, 2) Revocation (3)

TABLE 3-1 (Continued)

State	Drinking Age	Refusal to Submit to Breath Test	Driving While Intoxicated
Nebraska	21	Revocation	Revocation
Nevada	21	Suspension	*Suspension (1)* Suspension (2) Revocation (3)
New Hampshire	21	Revocation	Revocation
New Jersey	21	Revocation	Revocation
New Mexico	21	Revocation	Revocation
New York	21	Revocation	Revocation
North Carolina	21	Revocation	Revocation
North Dakota	21	Revocation	Suspension
Ohio	19/21	Suspension	Either suspension or revocation
Oklahoma	21	Revocation	Revocation
Oregon	21	Suspension	Suspension (1, 2) Revocation (3)
Pennsylvania	21	Suspension (1) Revocation (2)	Suspension (1) Revocation (2)
Rhode Island	21	Suspension	Suspension
South Carolina	21	Suspension	Suspension
South Dakota	19/21	Revocation	*Revocation (1)* Suspension (2)
Tennessee	21	Suspension	Revocation
Texas	21	Suspension	Suspension
Utah	21	Revocation	Revocation
Vermont	18	Suspension (1) Revocation (2)	Suspension (1) Revocation (2)
Virginia	19/21	Suspension	Suspension (1, 2) Revocation (3)
Washington	21	Revocation	Suspension (1, 2) Revocation (3)
West Virginia	19	Suspension	Revocation
Wisconsin	19	Revocation	Suspension (1) Revocation (2)
Wyoming	19	Suspension	Suspension (1, 2) Revocation (3)

*Laws subject to change. Check latest state regulations. Words in italics indicate that the penalty is optional with the court. Words in regular roman type indicate penalty is mandatory. Numbers in parentheses indicate the number of convictions necessary before the court may impose a particular penalty. Under "drinking age," where two ages are given, purchasing beverages relatively low in alcohol, such as beer, is permitted at the younger age.

Note that the courts may also impose jail sentences and/or fines in addition to license revocation and suspension for drunk-driving convictions in some states.

Sources: American Insurance Association and Federal Highway Administration National Transportation Safety Board

Because so many young people commonly drink alcoholic beverages, it is easy for them to forget that such drinking on their part is illegal. They also tend to forget that drinking can lead to even more serious problems. People who are drunk can all too easily commit crimes that they would never commit while sober.

In an effort to protect young people, state laws throughout the country strictly control the sale of alcoholic beverages to them. In 1984, Congress provided an incentive for the states to raise the drinking age to 21. It passed a law requiring the withholding of federal highway trust fund money to any state "in which the purchase or public possession in such State of any alcoholic beverage by a person who is less than twenty-one years of age is lawful." Since that time, many states have increased the drinking age to 21.

A merchant or bartender convicted of selling an alcoholic beverage to a minor may be jailed or fined and may lose the license required to sell such beverages. The minor also may be prosecuted for making the illegal purchase or for misrepresenting his or her age when making the purchase.

EXAMPLE 1   Jane Evans, 17 years old, went with some older friends to a tavern in upstate New York. She had borrowed a driver's license from a 22-year-old friend to use as identification in case she was asked her age. But the bartender never asked for proof of age and served her hard liquor. A plain-clothes agent for the state liquor-control board witnessed the purchase, asked Evans for identification, and noted that her physical description did not match the one on the license. Under questioning, Evans admitted her true age. The bartender was arrested, convicted of selling liquor to a minor, and fined $500. The owner of the tavern lost his liquor license. Evans was charged with juvenile delinquency for using the false identification and was placed on probation by a juvenile court judge.

Recent court decisions have held that bartenders who sell drinks to intoxicated customers are liable for injuries caused by the customers' drunk driving. Similarly, an Indiana court held a barroom customer liable for buying "one more drink" for another customer who was intoxicated. The intoxicated customer struck and killed a jogger while driving home. Going even further, courts in New Jersey and Iowa have extended the same liability to social hosts (people having parties). When hosts serve alcohol to intoxicated guests, they become liable for injuries to others caused by the drunken guests. Under the laws of many states, social hosts are criminally responsible for having alcoholic beverages available for guests who are minors.

DRUG ABUSE

The increase in alcohol abuse in society has been accompanied by a significant increase in other kinds of drug abuse. **Drugs** are chemical substances that have an effect on the body or mind. **Drug abuse** is the use of such substances in a way that can harm the body or mind. As with alcohol, drug abuse can lead to even more serious crimes. For example, some drugs, such as heroin, can cause **addiction**—the people taking them become physically and mentally dependent

TABLE 3-2
NARCOTICS AND DANGEROUS DRUGS PENALTIES IN SELECTED JURISDICTIONS

	Federal	Louisiana	Minnesota
MARIJUANA			
Possession	1 year–$5,000	6 months–$500	Small amount, $100 Large amount, 3 years $3,000
Subsequent Offense	2 years–$10,000	5 years–$2,000 Third offense, 20 years	--
Sale	Under 50 kilograms, 5 years–$50,000 50 kilograms and over, 15 years–$125,000	10 years at hard labor–$15,000	5 years–$15,000
Subsequent Offense	Under 50 kilograms, 10 years–$10,000 50 kilograms and over, 30 years–$250,000		1–10 years–$30,000
NARCOTIC DRUGS (Cocaine and Heroin)			
Possession	1 year–$5,000	4–10 years at hard labor–$5,000	5 years–$5,000
Subsequent Offense	2 years–$10,000	--	--
Sale	Over 100 grams of heroin or 1 kilogram of cocaine, 20 years–$250,000	Life (mandatory) at hard labor–$15,000	15 years–$25,000
Subsequent Offense	Over 100 grams of heroin or 1 kilogram of cocaine, 40 years–$500,000	--	1–30 years–$50,000

Each state establishes penalties for possession and sale of prohibited drugs, and these penalties vary. Penalties include imprisonment and/or fines. In Minnesota, possession of a small amount of marijuana is punishable by a fine of $100, while in Louisiana an offender may be jailed for up to 6 months and fined $500. Possession or sale of heroin and cocaine carry serious penalties in all states.

Source: *Shepard's Lawyer's Reference Manual*, McGraw-Hill, Inc., New York, 1985 Supplement, pp. 230, 234, and 236.

on them. To obtain such drugs, which can only be bought illegally and are therefore usually very expensive, addicts may become habitual thieves.

In 1970, in an attempt to curb drug abuse, Congress passed the Federal Controlled Substances Act. This act categorizes drugs on the basis of medical use, potential for abuse, and potential for addiction. The law prohibits the unauthorized possession of controlled substances for an individual's own use. It also prohibits drug trafficking. **Drug trafficking** is the unauthorized manufacture or distribution of any controlled substance or the possession of such a substance with the intention of manufacturing or distributing it illegally. This makes it illegal not only to sell drugs but also to give them away to friends.

The federal law has been used as a model for state laws and has now been adopted by most states. However, the Federal Controlled Substances Act does not establish fixed penalties for drug violations. Each state adopting the law sets its own penalties. Thus sentences often vary widely for identical crimes committed in different states. In spite of this variation, some generalizations can be made. All states consider the sale of drugs to be a much more serious offense than mere possession or use. Also, harsher penalties are set for the abuse of such "hard" drugs as heroin and LSD than for so-called "soft" drugs such as amphetamines and barbiturates.

Possession of marijuana is a criminal offense with rather harsh penalties in most states. For example, the penalty for possession of any amount of marijuana in Alabama can be up to 1 year in jail and/or a fine of up to $1,000. Eleven states* have decriminalized possession of small amounts of marijuana. **Decriminalization** does not mean that marijuana is legal. It means that possession of a small amount may result in a fine (usually about $100) but no jail term. The trend toward decriminalization of small amounts of the drug, which occurred in the late 1970s, has not continued in the 1980s. This may be due to the increasing number of reports that indicate that there are harmful effects from smoking marijuana. There are still severe penalties for trafficking in the drug in almost every state. The debate over whether or not to decriminalize marijuana is likely to continue for years. Meanwhile, young people must make the choice between staying within the law as it exists in their state or being prepared to face the legal consequences.

In addition, young people must be aware that even if they personally have nothing to do with drugs, they can be prosecuted for associating with those who do. For example, if drugs are found by the police during the search of a car, everyone in the car may be charged with possession.

EXAMPLE 2 A state highway police officer chasing a speeding car in Ohio saw one of the two occupants of the rear seat throw a packet out the window. The packet was picked up and was found to contain marijuana. Both the driver and the front-seat passenger claimed that they should not be prosecuted because only the two rear-seat passengers had the marijuana. But the court disagreed, ruling that there were reasonable grounds to believe that each occupant of the car was in possession of the marijuana. The court said that the police were within their rights when they arrested everyone in the car.

*Alaska, California, Colorado, Maine, Minnesota, Mississippi, Nebraska, New York, North Carolina, Ohio, Oregon.

MOTOR VEHICLE VIOLATIONS

Being issued a license to drive a motor vehicle is considered a privilege, not a right. It is a privilege that can be suspended temporarily or revoked permanently if the driver abuses it. Therefore, as new drivers, young people should know and strictly obey the motor vehicle laws in their own states. In most states young people with driver's licenses who break these laws do not have the protection of being classified as juveniles. They may be tried in traffic court and can be fined or have their licenses suspended or revoked, as would be the case if they were adults.

Legal Issue No. 3

One of the most serious motor vehicle violations is driving while under the influence of drugs or alcohol. Tests called **sobriety tests** have been devised to permit police to check a motorist's condition by analyzing the alcohol content of the motorist's blood or by having the motorist take a breathalizer test. The results of such tests indicate whether driving ability has been impaired. A blood alcohol reading of 0.10 percent or more is considered evidence of intoxication in most states. Some states impose stricter limits (e.g., 0.08 percent blood alcohol defines intoxication in Utah). A motorist may legally refuse to take such a test, but he or she may lose the right to drive for doing so. Many states require suspension or revocation of the driver's license of anyone who refuses a sobriety test. In addition, drunk driving is punishable by large fines and severe penalties, especially if any damage has been done by the drunken driver.

Another problem for the driver who violates the motor vehicle laws is the payment for damages. Because young drivers as a group have so many more accidents than the general population, their insurance rates are higher. With each accident that a young driver has, that driver's rates are increased. Finally, the insurance company may refuse altogether to issue a policy. Since insurance is required by law in many states, this would be another way of taking away a young person's driving privileges.

SHOP-LIFTING

Shoplifting is the act of stealing goods from a store. It is a form of larceny and can be either petty larceny or grand larceny, depending on the value of the goods stolen. Shoplifting has become almost a form of sport for some young people who like to pit their wits against those of the guards that many stores now hire. These young people do not consider this to be stealing, because they think that the storekeepers make so much money that they will never miss what is taken.

Shoplifting, however, is a serious crime. Shoplifting costs Americans billions of dollars each year. This includes the costs of security and prevention as well as the value of the merchandise stolen. It is estimated that one out of three small businesses goes into bankruptcy directly as a result of shoplifting and employee thefts. Shoplifting losses and the cost of extra security increase retail prices an average of 2 to 3 percent. Thus the shoplifters are actually hurting themselves, their families, and all other consumers as well.

Legal Issue No. 1

Shoplifting can be very hard to prove, because the person can claim that he or she intended to pay for the item but either forgot or had not yet had a chance to do so. Many states have laws that regard the concealment of an article offered for sale on one's person as **prima facie evidence** (pronounced ˈprī·mə-fā·shə) of an intent to steal. This means that the evidence is legally sufficient to estab-

The FBI, which collects crime statistics, reports about 800,000 shoplifting incidents annually. Many more incidents are unreported. Who pays for the cost of these crimes?

lish a fact or a case unless disproved. Under these laws, the storekeeper would not have to prove that the suspect intended to steal. Rather, the suspect who concealed merchandise would have to prove that he or she did not intend to steal.

These special shoplifting laws also give storekeepers the right to detain someone in a reasonable manner if reasonable grounds exist to think that the accused is a shoplifter. However, many storekeepers wait until the suspect has actually carried the goods out of the store before making an accusation. This is to avoid any possibility of being sued by the suspect for false arrest or imprisonment. As we will discuss in Chapter 4, this is the act of unlawfully restraining someone or restricting his or her freedom of movement.

EXAMPLE 3 Jeff Burns had a bet with a friend that he could get a soccer ball out of the local sporting goods store without being caught. Burns asked to try on some ski pants and was able to get the soccer ball into the dressing room with him while the owner was busy elsewhere. There he let the air out of the ball and put it under his shirt. He put on his jacket, thanked the storekeeper for letting him try on the ski pants, and started to leave. The owner, who had been less busy than Burns thought, challenged Burns. Burns was unable to claim that he was not intending to steal the ball, since he had concealed it on his person. The juvenile court judge placed Burns on probation and ordered him to give two Saturdays' worth of work to the storekeeper.

▌VANDALISM

In many communities today vandalism is a serious problem. **Vandalism** (also called **malicious mischief**) is defined as the willful or malicious causing of damage to property. If the value of what is damaged is not very great, the charge is a misdemeanor. Vandalism may also be considered a felony, however, especially if the damage is extensive and if breaking and entering are involved.

Because the cost of repairing the damage resulting from vandalism is so high, young vandals are often required either to pay the cost or to provide the work needed to restore the damaged property. In recent years some states have passed **parental liability laws.** These laws require the parents of vandals to pay for the damage done by their children. However, the amount of the parents' liability is limited, ranging from $300 in some states to $2,000 in others.

To be guilty of malicious mischief or vandalism, a young person does not have to be the person who actually does the damage. Anyone who keeps watch for passersby while others commit the act is considered guilty, too.

EXAMPLE 4 Helen Jenkins was out walking with a group of friends one night. They had been drinking some wine. They passed the home of a teacher who had that day sent one of them to the principal for disciplining. The house was obviously empty, and they decided that this would be a good time to "get even" with the teacher. They entered the house through an unlocked window, leaving Jenkins outside with a whistle in case anyone came. Once inside, they broke eggs and smeared the tops of tables with them. Then they slashed pillows and shook the feathers, many of which stuck to the egg-covered tables. Ultimately, they were identified by a neighbor and arrested. Jenkins claimed that she was not guilty, since she had been outside. However, the court ruled that she was as guilty as the others. The young people were required to do yard work and other chores for the teacher, and their parents were required to pay for the damages.

CHILD ABUSE

Children are protected by the state from neglect, ill treatment, and abuse. State laws provide for the removal of mistreated children to places where they will be treated properly. The laws also provide for the punishment of people who abuse children. Although parents have the natural right to the control and custody of their children, this right can be taken away from them if children are mistreated.

Under the Connecticut statute, an abused child is defined as any person under 16 years of age who

(a) has had physical injury or injuries inflicted upon him other than by accidental means, or (b) has injuries which are at variance with the history given of them, or (c) is in a condition which is the result of maltreatment such as, but not limited to, malnutrition, sexual molestation, deprivation of necessities, emotional maltreatment or cruel punishment.

Under New Mexico law,

Abuse of a child consists of a person knowingly, intentionally or negligently, and without justifiable cause, causing or permitting a child to be: (1) placed in a situation that may endanger the child's life or health; or (2) tortured, cruelly confined or cruelly punished.

The laws of many states require teachers, doctors, and nurses to report suspected cases of child abuse. In addition, some states grant immunity from prosecution to people who report child abuse incidents.

CRIMES BY YOUNG PEOPLE

At common law, children under the age of 7 were incapable of committing a crime. It was presumed that children under that age were incapable of having the intent to commit a crime. This presumption of innocence was **conclusive**—that is, it could not be overruled by any other evidence. At the same time, there was a **rebuttable presumption** that children between the ages of 7 and 14 were incapable of having the intent to commit a crime. This means that evidence could be introduced in court to show that a particular child was capable of having the intent necessary to commit a crime. If the evidence showed that the child between the ages of 7 and 14 did have a criminal intent, he or she would be tried for committing the crime and punished if found guilty. Children 14 and older were presumed to be capable of committing a crime. With some exceptions, these common-law principles have been preserved today and are found in the statutes of many states.

Juvenile Delinquents

Legal Issue No. 4

In addition to the law stated above, every state in the United States has passed laws defining juvenile delinquency. A **juvenile delinquent** is generally defined as a minor, under a certain age (17 in many states), who has committed an act that would be a crime if done by an adult. These minors are tried in juvenile court instead of criminal court so that their cases can be dealt with in a different way. The goal of the juvenile court system is **rehabilitation**—to steer the individual offender in the right direction rather than to impose harsh penalties. As explained in Chapter 5, the proceedings against juvenile delinquents are held in private and are not criminal in nature—that is, the juvenile does not usually acquire a criminal record.

■ In some states, minors over a certain age (usually 14) under certain circumstances are tried as adults in the criminal court instead of the juvenile court. This occurs when the minor has been in serious trouble previously or has committed an offense that caused serious bodily harm. In deciding whether or not to **transfer** or take the case out of the juvenile court, the following factors are considered: (1) the seriousness of the offense; (2) the child's family, school, and social history; (3) the child's court and juvenile delinquency record; (4) the protection of the public; (5) the nature of past treatment efforts; and (6) the likelihood of rehabilitation.

EXAMPLE 5 Sam Martin, 16, was caught committing armed robbery of a gas station. Because of the seriousness of the offense and because he had been before the juvenile court several times previously, the case was removed from the juvenile court and tried in the adult criminal court. Martin was convicted of a felony and acquired a lifelong criminal record.

The Rights of Minors to Due Process of Law

Legal Issue No. 2

The term **due process of law** refers to those fundamental rights and principles of justice that limit the government's power to deprive people of their lives, liberty, or property. In the case of people who have been accused of wrongdoing, *due process* refers to certain procedures that have been established by law to give them the chance to prove their innocence.

Before 1967 the courts did not recognize minors as being entitled to the same due-process rights as adults. In that year, however, the U.S. Supreme Court ruled that persons who go before juvenile courts must be given the same consti-

If a minor had no criminal intent in the process of committing an offense, may he or she be punished for the act? How is "intent" determined?

tutional rights as people who go before other types of courts. The court said that juveniles have the right to remain silent when arrested. They have the right to know the specific charges made against them and the right to be represented by a lawyer. They may confront and cross-examine the people who bring charges against them. The high court's decision was an important one, because it stated in very decisive language that full protection of the Constitution must be extended to everyone, regardless of age.

Disposition of Juvenile Cases

To try to list the exact punishment that would be given to juvenile delinquents for specific offenses would be impossible. Not only are there variations in state laws, but there are also variations in the interpretation that different judges give to these laws. In addition, the juvenile court system is set up so that the case of each young lawbreaker can be considered individually. Often there are special circumstances that the judge takes into consideration.

As a first step, therefore, the judge usually holds a **detention hearing.** The purpose of such a hearing is to find out whether there are good reasons for keeping the accused in custody and whether or not there are special circumstances affecting the case. An investigation into the minor's background and home life is undertaken by the court's probation department or by a child welfare agency. If the investigation shows that there are special circumstances, or that the matter is not serious enough to pursue further, or that the youth was wrongly accused, the judge might dismiss the charges at this point.

If the charges are not dismissed, the judge then conducts an **adjudicatory hearing.** This is the actual hearing of the case by the court. It is quite informal. The judge may question the youth and his or her parents, listen to witnesses, and seek advice from the probation officer. Some courts decide what action to take at this point. Other courts hold a third hearing, called a **dispositional hearing,** to decide how to dispose of the case.

After one of these two types of hearings has taken place, the judge decides the outcome of the case. The matter is generally settled in one of three ways:

1. The judge may allow the offender to return home, while placing him or her on probation for a period of time, under the supervision of a probation officer. The judge may set certain conditions of behavior for the offender and have the probation officer check on the offender's compliance. Failure to meet these requirements may result in more severe punishment.
2. The judge may place the offender in an agency or foster home. The natural parents will then be required to pay what they can toward the offender's support.
3. The judge may commit the offender to a training school or reformatory. This is usually a last resort, when both probation and foster care have already been tried and have failed, or when they seem unlikely to work.

Besides these alternatives, the judge can also order the juvenile delinquent to pay for the damages, with money or work or both. The parents of the offender may also be ordered to reimburse (pay back) the victim in some cases. This is true for a variety of offenses, including shoplifting as well as vandalism.

The sentence for youthful offenders is also set with rehabilitation in mind. It is generally limited to probation under court supervision, confinement for not more than 3 years in some kind of reformative institution, or some other course of action designed to help, rather than punish, the youthful offender.

Language of the Law

Define or explain each of the following words or phrases:

international terror- ism	decriminalization	parental liability laws	transfer
drugs	sobriety tests	conclusive	due process of law
drug abuse	shoplifting	rebuttable presump- tion	detention hearing
addiction	prima facie evidence	juvenile delinquent	adjudicatory hearing
drug trafficking	vandalism	rehabilitation	dispositional hearing
	malicious mischief		

Questions for Review

1. Describe international terrorism.
2. What is the penalty for carrying weapons or explosives aboard aircraft?
3. How did Congress persuade the states to raise the drinking age to 21?
4. What can happen to a merchant or bartender who sells an alcoholic beverage illegally to a minor? What can happen to the minor?
5. Are the penalties for drug offenses the same in all states? Explain.
6. A blood alcohol reading of what percent or more is considered evidence of intoxication in most states?
7. Describe the rights given to storekeepers under some special shoplifting laws.
8. When is vandalism a felony? a misdemeanor?
9. When may the right to control and custody of children be taken away from parents?
10. Explain why a 5-year-old child who steals a toy from a store cannot be charged with theft.
11. What is the idea behind trying juvenile delinquents in juvenile court instead of criminal court?
12. What are the rights that a young person has if accused of a crime?
13. Why is it impossible to list the exact punishments that would be given for specific offenses by juvenile delinquents?

Cases in Point

For each of the following cases, give your decision and state a legal principle that applies to the case:

1. Jeanette Kepler lived in Alaska, where she sometimes smoked marijuana in her home. She went to Iowa on a visit and took 3 ounces of marijuana with her. When arrested there for the possession of marijuana, Kepler claimed the arrest was invalid because it was legal to use marijuana in her home state. Do you agree?
2. Clarence Bilandic was 17 but looked older. He tried to obtain liquor at a barroom. The bartender asked his age, and Bilandic said he was 21. When the bartender requested written proof of age, Bilandic said he had none with him. The bartender served him the liquor. Could the bartender be prosecuted?
3. Edna Carlucci was arrested on a drunk-driving charge. A police officer asked her to submit to a breathalyzer test to determine whether she had been driving while intoxicated. Did she have the legal right to refuse?
4. Hank Lefcourt, who was 19 and had no previous offense, was out with some younger friends on Halloween. They had a can of paint, which they splattered on five parked cars before they were caught by a police patrol. Lefcourt argued that he was too young to be charged with a crime. Do you agree?
5. Sally Smith had been shopping and had a bag with her. She went into a stationery store, looking for a birthday present for a friend. She wandered up and down the aisles, trying to get an idea of what to buy, but couldn't find anything. As she started to leave the store, the owner stopped her and demanded to see what was in her bag. What were Smith's rights in this matter?
6. Georgette Johnson, 16, was picked up in her car for speeding and given a ticket. Since this was her third traffic offense, the judge in the traffic court suspended her license for one year. Was it legal for the judge to do this?
7. Joseph Cameron was caught carrying an explosive aboard a major airline plane at the

Miami airport. He argued that since there had been no explosion, he had not committed a crime. Do you agree? What punishment, if any, can he receive?

8. Henry Garbowski, a bartender, served alcohol to Joe DeLuca, who was 18 years old. When cited by the police, Garbowski argued that the drinking age is the same as the voting age, that is, 18. Is he correct? Explain.

9. Gail, a young teenager, confided to her friend Denise that she had been abused by her stepfather. Denise suggested that she tell the school nurse. Was this good advice? What do the laws provide to take care of situations like this?

10. A 9-year-old boy was caught snatching a purse from an elderly woman. Is the boy too young to have criminal intent and be charged with a crime?

Cases to Judge

1. A boy who was 14 years 11 months old shot and killed his mother. He was tried as an adult, found guilty of first-degree murder, and given a mandatory sentence of life imprisonment. On appeal, the boy's lawyer argued (a) that the trial should have been held in the juvenile court, and (b) that a child of his age did not have the capacity to commit murder. Do you agree? Why or why not? *Com. v. Sourbeer,* 422 A.2d 116 (Pennsylvania)

2. An employee of a self-service liquor store watched Lee pick up two $16.47 bottles of cognac. Lee concealed one of the bottles in his pants and held the other in his hand. When approached by the employee, Lee returned both bottles to the shelf and fled the store. He was chased by the employee, who flagged down a police cruiser, and was arrested for shoplifting. Is he guilty of the crime? Explain. *Lee v. State,* 474 A.2d 537 (Maryland)

3. Dorothy Lucero, a widow with two children, lived with a man. He beat her and, on one occasion, broke her jaw. After she gave birth to his child, he started beating her 5-year-old son. Lucero was charged with violating the child abuse law of New Mexico because she did not get help to stop the man from beating her son. Lucero claims that she was afraid to seek help for fear of injury to her. Should she be convicted of child abuse? Explain. *State v. Lucero,* 647 P.2d 406 (New Mexico)

4. A highway patrolman found a car parked about 20 feet from the right side of a highway at 11:30 p.m. The engine was not running, none of the lights were on, and the keys were in the ignition but in the off position. Mark Adams was in the driver's seat of the car, unconscious and intoxicated, with a blood alcohol reading of 0.152 percent. He was arrested for violating the following statute: "It is unlawful for any person who is under the influence of intoxicating liquor, to a degree which renders him incapable of safely driving a motor vehicle, to drive or have actual physical control of any vehicle within this state." Should he be found guilty? Why or why not? *Adams v. State,* 697 P.2d 622 (Wyoming)

5. A police officer stopped a van when he saw the driver acting suspiciously and overheard him telling his companions: "Let's get going. Here comes a cop." The van smelled of marijuana smoke. Inside, the police officer found 13 pounds of marijuana, an ounce of cocaine, and 252 LSD tablets. He also found $4,010 in cash inside the van and $500 in the driver's pocket. Among other things, the driver was charged with unlawful possession of LSD and cocaine with the intent to sell. The driver argued that there was no evidence proving he intended to sell the drugs. Do you think he was correct? Explain. *Commonwealth v. Miller,* 349 N.E.2d 362 (Massachusetts)

Chapter 4

THE LAW OF TORTS

Scene: Steve stops his car in front of Mike's apartment and backs into a parking space. He rings the bell of the apartment.

Sue (*opening the door*): Hi, Steve. Come in.

Steve: How're you doing, Sue? (*walking into the apartment*) I heard that the community college is going to let you into the auto mechanic program after all.

Sue: Yes. Isn't that good news? I start next week.

Steve: You'll be the first girl that ever took that program, won't you?

Sue: I wish they wouldn't make such a big deal about it. Someone from the college came and took my picture last week. They want to use it to advertise their program, and I don't want my picture in their ads.

Steve (*hearing loud music*): Where's that music coming from?

Sue: The apartment next door. It's not too bad now. You should hear it at 5 o'clock in the morning. These walls are paper-thin, and the noise wakes up everyone in our family. We asked them politely to turn it down, but they don't pay any attention to us.

Steve: There must be something you can do.

Sue: What did you say? The music's so loud I can't hear you!

Steve (*shouting*): Is Mike around?

Sue: Yes. He's in the den with Pam. Go ahead in.
(*Steve walks into the den where Mike and Pam are sitting.*)

Mike and Pam: Hi, Steve!

Steve: Hi! How was your vacation, Pam?

Pam: Wonderful! I was just telling Mike about it. We were at my parents' cottage up on the lake, and it was great! In between soaking up rays, we played miniature golf and went roller skating—and you should have seen me para-sailing!

Steve: Para-sailing? What's that?

Pam: Well, you go out to a flat-bottomed boat where they strap you into a harness. Then you get attached to a parachute brought by a speed boat that goes real fast and pulls you way up into the air for a long ride. The trip ends when you float down by parachute to the same point you started from.

Steve: You'd never get me to do that!

Pam: I went three times! It was great until some people complained that the parachute was going through the air over their land. They stopped the whole operation. I was really disappointed.

Mike: Can they stop you from using the air over somebody else's land?
(*Just then the screech of brakes is heard above the music, and there is the sound of crashing metal and broken glass.*)

Pam: Oh-oh, that sounds like it's out front.

Steve (*getting up*): My car's out there!
(*They all go to the front door.*)

Mike: Somebody smashed into your car, Steve.

Pam: It looks like those nitwits, Wayne and Rick!
(*Steve looks speechlessly at his car as Wayne and Rick approach them.*)

Wayne: Sorry about that. It wasn't my fault—a squirrel ran out in front of me. I couldn't hit the squirrel!

LEGAL ISSUES

1. What legal wrong, if any, occurs when someone uses another's picture in an advertisement without permission?
2. Does a legal wrong take place when one neighbor disturbs another with loud music?
3. May the public use the airspace over private property without permission of the property owner?
4. What is the legal wrong that causes most automobile accidents?

THE SPIRIT OF THE LAW

One of the primary purposes of the law is to protect you from the wrongful acts of other people. This protection is given, first, by preventing or discouraging other people from doing wrongful acts that might injure you and, second, by giving you a remedy for an injury resulting from a wrongful act of another person. The remedy usually given is the right to recover what you have lost or to receive payment for your loss.

THE LAW OF TORTS

Under law, all people are entitled to certain rights. These rights include, among others, (1) the right to be free from bodily harm, (2) the right to enjoy a good reputation, and (3) the right to have one's property free from damage or trespass by others. In addition, the law imposes a duty upon all people to respect the rights given to others. The assorted group of rights and duties is known as the law of torts.

A tort, from a word meaning "wrong" in French, is a wrong against an individual. A tort is different from a crime, which is a wrong against the public at large. **Tort** may be defined as one person's interference with another's rights, either by an intentional act or through negligence. Tort lawsuits are brought against wrongdoers by injured persons themselves to recover damages for a loss or an injury. Criminal actions, on the other hand, are brought by the state in order to punish wrongdoers. In some situations a wrong is both a tort and a crime.

EXAMPLE 1 Stephen Shalit, in violation of the Motor Vehicle Code, was driving his car at 70 miles per hour on the city streets. While speeding, he ran into Rachel Crossett's car and seriously damaged it. Shalit will find himself involved in two court actions—one brought by the state or the city for violating the Motor Vehicle Code and another brought by Crossett for damages done to her automobile. Shalit's speeding is a crime, whereas the damage he did to Crossett's automobile is a tort.

In Example 1, the law gives Crossett the right to recover money from Shalit for the damage done to her car. In addition, the law may punish Shalit if he is found guilty of the crime of violating the Motor Vehicle Code.

Minors are held responsible for their own torts. Parents, in most instances, are not responsible for the torts of their children other than the willful acts of minors, and then only up to a limited sum of money.

INTENTIONAL TORTS

Torts are classified as being intentional or unintentional. We will discuss the more common intentional torts here and present negligence (the most common unintentional tort) later in the chapter.

Assault and Battery

Assault and battery usually occur together and form the common tort of assault and battery. Assault and battery is an example of a tort which is also a crime. It is a tort because the person injured can sue for recovery of damages. It is a crime because the state can bring criminal charges against the offending party in the interest of the public. As discussed in Chapter 2, assault is an attempt to commit a battery; battery is the unlawful touching of another person.

EXAMPLE 2 John Allen picked up a stick and threatened Joe Ryle with it, but did not strike him. This is an assault, which is a separate tort by itself. If Allen were actually to hit Ryle with the stick, this would be a battery. The two acts together are assault and battery.

If, in Example 2, Allen had had no stick and no stick had been nearby and he had said to Ryle, ''If you weren't my friend, I'd go find a stick and hit you,'' Allen would have committed neither assault nor battery. Why not? To commit an assault, Allen must also have the ''apparent present ability'' to commit the battery. By conditioning his statement, he has indicated he really will not commit the battery.

Trespass

A **trespass** is a wrongful injury to or interference with the property of another. The term **property** refers to everything we own, including movable items such as automobiles, pencils, or books, and nonmovable items such as land and buildings. Today the tort of trespass is most commonly used with reference to land and buildings, which are called **real property.**

EXAMPLE 3 Nichols and some friends went fishing in Englehardt's private lake without his permission. Entering on Englehardt's property and fishing in the lake without proper authority to do so is a trespass. Englehardt, therefore, may bring a suit for damages against Nichols and the others.

Legal Issue No. 3

Real Property Under common law, ownership of real property extended from the center of the earth to the highest point in the sky. A person owned not only a portion of the earth's crust but also the ground under it and the airspace over it. It was a trespass to go on, under, or over another's land without permission. Today, however, property owners no longer own the airspace to the highest point in the sky. Under the laws of most states, they generally own the airspace up to as high as they can effectively use it. It is a trespass to enter another person's airspace without permission.

Nuisance

The tort of **nuisance** may be defined as anything that interferes with the enjoyment of life or property. Such things as loud noises late at night, noxious odors, and smoke or fumes coming from a nearby house are examples of nuisance. A **public nuisance** is one that affects a large group of people, such as all the residents of a neighborhood or community. A **private nuisance,** on the other hand, is one that affects one person only.

Legal Issue No. 2

EXAMPLE 4 Planes landing and taking off at a city airport made loud noises and emitted smoke and fumes over a particular neighborhood. The residents brought suit against the airport for nuisance. The court ordered the airport to change the takeoff and landing patterns of the planes so that they would not disturb that neighborhood. The airport could also be sued for trespass if the planes flew too close to the tops of houses as they took off and landed.

Interference With Contractual Relations

It is a wrongful act to interfere with other people's contracts. Called **interference with contractual relations,** this tort comes about in either of two ways: (1) intentionally causing one person not to contract with another person or (2) intentionally causing one person to breach a contract with another person.

EXAMPLE 5 David Ackerman was under contract to work for Ellen Bodek for 3 years. Celia Colby, who knew that Ackerman's contract with Bodek had more than 2 years to run, offered Ackerman $25,000 if he would breach the contract with Bodek and go to work for her. Ackerman did so. Bodek would be able to sue Colby in tort for interference with contractual relations. She would also be able to sue Ackerman for breaching the employment contract. This type of contract is discussed further in Chapter 22.

Deceit

A false statement or other deceitful practice done with the intent to injure another person is **deceit.** This tort is often referred to as **fraud** and has five elements which the plaintiff must prove in order to recover damages. People

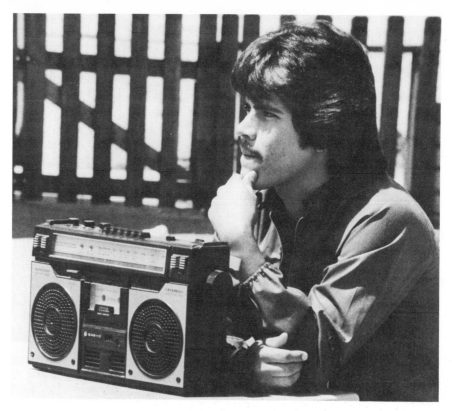

People's tastes in music differ. What constitutes a public nuisance?

who are induced by fraud to enter into contracts have the choice of either suing for money damages or rescinding (getting out of) the contract on the ground of fraud. The elements of fraud are discussed in further detail in Chapter 9.

Conversion

Conversion is the unauthorized taking of the personal property of someone else for the use of the person taking it. This includes such actions as stealing property or using borrowed property in an unauthorized way. It also includes the misdelivery of goods by a transportation company.

False Arrest

The unlawful physical restraint of a person's liberty, whether in prison or otherwise, is **false arrest.** This tort is also called **false imprisonment.** Police officers must have probable cause (supported by circumstances) or a warrant to arrest someone; they are susceptible to suit for false arrest if they make an arrest without meeting these requirements. Shop owners and store detectives must also use good judgment in detaining suspected shoplifters. Because of the large amount of shoplifting that occurs in our society, most states have laws allowing stores to detain suspected shoplifters. The store must have reasonable grounds to suspect the shoplifting and must detain the suspected person in a reasonable manner; otherwise, it may be sued for false arrest.

EXAMPLE 6 An innocent customer in a store was suspected of shoplifting. She was locked in a stock room closet by a store detective for 3 hours. In court she was able to prove her innocence. She also proved that the store detective did not have reasonable grounds to suspect her of shoplifting. The court awarded her a large sum of money as compensation for her humiliation and emotional suffering.

Malicious Prosecution

Malicious prosecution is the bringing of a legal action with malice and without probable cause. It is legally wrong, and thus a tort to bring false and malicious criminal or civil charges against others. A successful suit for malicious prosecution requires all of the following conditions:

1. The defendant (the person against whom suit is brought) must have brought either criminal or civil charges against the plaintiff at an earlier time.
2. The plaintiff (the person bringing the suit) must have won that earlier case.
3. The plaintiff must prove that the earlier case was brought by the defendant with malice and without probable cause.

When all of these occur, the plaintiff may be able to recover money damages from the defendant for having to stand trial without good reason.

EXAMPLE 7 Robert Hilton disliked his next-door neighbor, Eugene Kessner. Hilton brought criminal charges against Kessner, falsely claiming that Kessner had broken into his house and stolen a valuable painting while Hilton was away on vacation. Kessner was tried for burglary and found not guilty. He then sued Hilton in tort for malicious prosecution. Kessner won the case because he was able to prove that the burglary charges against him were trumped up by Hilton and motivated by hatred and ill will.

Defamation

Defamation is the wrongful act of injuring another's reputation by the use of false statements. Defamation is divided into two classes—libel and slander. **Libel** is an untruthful written or printed statement that injures another person's reputation or reflects upon that person's character. **Slander** is similar to libel except that the untrue statement is made orally (by word of mouth) to a third person. Radio and television statements are generally held to be the subject of libel rather than slander.

You can usually sue someone for libel as long as the written statement is damaging to your reputation, is untruthful, and is communicated to at least one other person. You cannot, however, always sue someone for slander. You can sue someone for slander only if the oral words do one of the following:

1. Accuse you of committing a crime, such as assault, rape, murder, and so on.
2. Accuse you of having a communicable disease, such as leprosy or venereal disease.
3. Injure you in your business, trade, or profession.
4. Actually cause some special damage which can be proved, such as loss of money.

EXAMPLE 8   Amy Gant said to Paula Schuessler, "You're drunk. You're a liar and a no-good so-and-so." Sue Lewis overheard the conversation. Even if the accusations were false, Schuessler probably could not sue Gant for slander because the words do not fall into any of the four classes mentioned above. If the message had been in writing, however, and had been shown to Lewis by Gant, Schuessler might recover damages from Gant for libel.

People are allowed to speak and write the truth without being sued for defamation as long as it is done without ill will or spite. In addition, statements made by senators and representatives on the floor of the House and Senate and statements made in a court of law are **privileged.** This means that such statements are not subject to defamation lawsuits. Privileged speech protects the open discussion of legislative and judicial matters.

Persons who are in the public view, such as public officials, entertainers, and other public figures, are subject to a greater amount of criticism than are persons who are not well known. Therefore, under the constitutional guarantees of free speech and a free press, such people cannot win a suit for libel and slander unless they can prove actual malice. Actual malice means that the statement was made either with knowledge that it was false or with reckless disregard as to whether or not is was false.

Invasion of Privacy

Invasion of privacy is interference with the right to be let alone. The right of privacy includes the right to be free from unwarranted publicity and interference in private matters. In most states, but not all, the invasion of this legal right is a tort. Some states, such as New York, have established this right by statute. The state of California, on the other hand, has established the right of privacy by adding it to the state constitution.

Legal Issue No. 1

The Federal Privacy Act of 1974 provides safeguards for individuals against the invasion of privacy by agencies of the federal government. With some exceptions, the act requires federal agencies to allow individuals to determine what personal records will be kept by any agency. It also permits individuals to know what records concerning them are being kept. Individuals have a right to receive copies of such records and to correct errors in them. Agencies must get an individual's permission to use records for purposes other than those for which the records were gathered.

The following is part of the New York State right of privacy law. An **equitable action** seeks an injunction (a court order from a judge). **Exemplary damages** act as a punishment to deter other wrongdoers.

Any person whose name, portrait or picture is used within the state for advertising purposes or for the purposes of trade without the written consent first obtained as above provided may maintain an equitable action in the supreme court of this state against the person, firm or corporation so using his name, portrait or picture, to prevent and restrain the use thereof; and may also sue and recover damages for any injuries sustained by reason of such use and if the defendant shall have knowingly used such person's name, portrait or picture in such manner as is forbidden or declared to be unlawful by section fifty of this article, the jury, in its discretion, may award exemplary damages.

Emotional Suffering

A tort called **emotional suffering** has come into existence in recent years. Under earlier law, people who suffered emotionally from the wrongful acts of others could not recover damages without an accompanying bodily injury. Today, in many states, people who intentionally or recklessly cause emotional suffering to others will be responsible even without an accompanying bodily injury. The conduct complained of must be extreme and outrageous and must cause severe emotional distress.

EXAMPLE 9 Agis was employed by the Ground Round Restaurant as a waitress. The manager of the restaurant called a meeting of all waitresses and told them that there was some stealing going on and that the identity of the person responsible was not known. He said that until the person responsible was discovered, he would begin firing all the present waitresses in alphabetical order, starting with the letter "A." He then fired Agis. She became greatly upset, began to cry, sustained emotional distress and mental anguish, and suffered the loss of wages. The court allowed her to recover damages for her emotional suffering.

▮NEGLIGENCE

Legal Issue No. 4

Negligence is an accidental or unintentional tort. It is the tort which occurs most often in society. It may be present, for example, when there is an automobile accident, when a doctor commits **malpractice** (improper professional practice), or when someone trips on a broken floorboard. **Negligence** is the failure to exercise the degree of care that a reasonably prudent person would have exercised under the same circumstances and conditions. In order to recover damages for negligence, the plaintiff must prove all of the following:

1. The defendant owed the plaintiff a duty of care.
2. The defendant failed to use the degree of care required under the circumstances.
3. The failure of the defendant to use care caused the plaintiff to suffer damages or injuries.

Degree of Care

Under common law, the degree of care that one person owed to another depended on the relationship of the parties. People who were invited onto another's property to do business, for example, were owed a higher degree of care than people who were invited as social guests. Also, negligence was categorized into three degrees—slight negligence, ordinary negligence, and gross (very great) negligence.

EXAMPLE 10 Cathy Dooley was riding as a passenger in Paul Beaulieu's car. She was injured when Beaulieu exceeded the speed limit on a wet, slippery road and his car skidded into a tree. Dooley would not be able to win a lawsuit for her injuries against Beaulieu or his insurance company in many of those states which still follow the common-law rule. The reason is that she was a guest of Beaulieu's, and a court would consider his act to be ordinary negligence rather than gross negligence.

How can negligence cause an automobile accident?

Many states have done away with the different degrees of negligence and maintain that we owe a duty to use ordinary or reasonable care toward all people who are rightfully on our property. In the case of a trespasser, on the other hand, we usually can be negligent without being liable to the trespasser for his or her injuries. Property owners must, however, refrain from **willful, wanton, and reckless conduct** toward trespassers. Such conduct includes the intentional commission of an act which a reasonable person knows would cause injury to another.

EXAMPLE 11 A 14-year-old boy, while riding his bicycle, noticed a chain dangling from a slow-moving truck. He took hold of the chain and was pulled along by the vehicle. The truck driver saw the boy in the mirror, laughed, increased his speed to 35 miles per hour, and swerved onto the shoulder of the road. The boy was thrown over the handlebars of the bicycle and was severely injured. The court held the truck driver's action to be willful, wanton, and reckless conduct. The boy won the lawsuit against the owner of the truck, even though technically he would be considered a trespasser.

There are some occasions when the law imposes no duty upon us to act. For example the law usually does not impose a duty on persons to assist others who are in trouble. However, when we do act (even if not required to do so by law) we must avoid being negligent.

EXAMPLE 12 A passenger on a train was so drunk that he was incapable of standing. When the train arrived at the passenger's station, the conductor helped him off the train, walked with him halfway up a flight of stairs, left him in a standing position, and returned to the train. The passenger fell down the stairs and landed on his head. When he sued the railroad for his injuries, the court found in his favor. The ruling said that the railroad was under no obligation to assist the passenger after he left the train, but because it did so, it was bound to use reasonable care.

Attractive Nuisance Doctrine

The law recognizes that young children may be attracted to areas where they do not belong. Although they are trespassers, they are given protection from dangerous things, such as swimming pools, that are on people's property. Under a rule of law called the **attractive nuisance doctrine,** property owners must use reasonable care toward children who are attracted to their property by something that is dangerous.

Strict Liability

Under a doctrine known as **strict liability,** or **absolute liability,** people may be liable for injuries to others whether or not they have done something wrong. This rule of law applies when people keep dangerous things such as wild animals on their property. It also applies to people who use explosives or dangerous chemicals in their business.

EXAMPLE 13 In building an extension to an interstate highway, the Enrique Rueda-Puerto Construction Company used every safety precaution available in blasting through several miles of solid granite. In spite of the precautions that were taken, windows were broken and other damage was done to several houses in the nearby community. The company is legally required to pay for the damages under the doctrine of absolute liability.

In recent years, the doctrine of strict, or absolute, liability has also been applied in **products liability** cases. These are cases in which people are injured from defects in products they buy in the marketplace. The company that manufactures a product is liable, regardless of fault, for injuries to users of the product if there was a defect in the product which caused the injury.

Defenses to Negligence

People who are sued for negligence sometimes defend themselves by proving that the act they committed was not a negligent act at all, or that the act did not cause the injuries, or that there were no injuries actually suffered. Other commonly used defenses are contributory negligence, comparative negligence, and assumption of the risk.

Contributory Negligence **Contributory negligence** is negligence on the part of the plaintiff who assisted in causing the injuries. Under the doctrine of contributory negligence, if a plaintiff sues a defendant for negligence but the defendant can prove that the plaintiff was also negligent (no matter how slight), the plaintiff can recover nothing. Many states no longer follow this doctrine because of its unfairness to plaintiffs who were only slightly negligent. These states have adopted the doctrine of comparative negligence in its place.

Comparative Negligence Under the doctrine of **comparative negligence,** the negligence of each party is compared and the amount of the plaintiff's recovery is reduced by the percent of his or her negligence.

EXAMPLE 14 Jason Cohen sued Mark Goodhue for damages suffered in an automobile accident. The jury found that the damages suffered by Cohen amounted to $100,000. In addition, the jury found that Cohen was 10 percent negligent and that Goodhue was 90 percent negligent in causing the accident. Cohen recovered $90,000 from Goodhue instead of $100,000, which he would have recovered had he not been negligent at all. In the same case, had the jury found that each party was 50 percent negligent, Cohen would have recovered only $50,000. If the jury had found that Cohen was 51 percent negligent and that Goodhue was 49 percent negligent, Cohen would have recovered nothing.

Assumption of the Risk In a suit for negligence, if the defendant can show that the plaintiff knew of the risk involved and took the chance of being injured, he or she may claim **assumption of the risk** as a defense. This defense has sometimes been used by baseball clubs when they have been sued by spectators injured when baseballs were hit into the stands.

REMEDIES FOR TORTS

If a wrongdoer has injured you by committing a tort, your injury usually can be measured in terms of money damages.

EXAMPLE 15 When Stephen Shalit damaged Rachel Crossett's car by his negligent driving, Crossett's damages were the difference between the fair market value of the car before the accident and the fair market value of the car after the accident. When Shalit pays that amount to Crossett, Crossett's money loss will be restored.

In some cases, however, money will not repay the injured party for the damages.

EXAMPLE 16 Josephine Jones had a beautiful locust tree on her lawn. Al Chambers, who lived next door, did not like the tree because it shaded his house. Chambers threatened to go onto Jones's property and cut down the tree. If Chambers did this, money damages would not properly restore Jones to her original position because a similar locust tree cannot be grown in a normal lifetime.

If Chambers's threat seemed serious, Jones could go to court and ask the judge to order Chambers not to trespass on her property and not to remove the tree.

A court order issued by a judge ordering a person to do or not to do a certain act is called an **injunction.** The remedy of injunction, however, is available only in special circumstances where money damages will not adequately repay the injured party for the wrong done.

If Chambers violated the judge's order and cut down the tree, he would be guilty of contempt of court. **Contempt of court** is a deliberate violation of the order of a judge or a refusal to perform as ordered by a judge. Contempt of court is a crime, and Chambers could be sent to jail for his wrongdoing. Table 13-1 on page 175 explains the different types of damages.

Language of the Law

Define or explain each of the following words or phrases:

tort
trespass
property
real property
nuisance
public nuisance
private nuisance
interference with
  contractual relations
deceit

fraud
conversion
false arrest
false imprisonment
malicious prosecution
defamation
libel
slander
privileged
invasion of privacy

equitable action
exemplary damages
emotional suffering
malpractice
negligence
willful, wanton, and
  reckless conduct
attractive nuisance
  doctrine

strict liability, abso-
  lute liability
products liability
contributory negligence
comparative negligence
assumption of the risk
injunction
contempt of court

Questions for Review

1. Give an example of a tort that is also a crime.
2. To what extent do property owners own the airspace above their land under today's law?
3. What is the difference between a public and a private nuisance?
4. In what two ways may someone illegally interfere with other people's contracts?
5. Persons who are induced by fraud to enter into contracts have two choices. What are they?
6. Give an example of conversion.
7. For a successful suit for malicious prosecution, what conditions must occur?
8. On what occasions can someone be sued for slander?
9. What must a public official prove in order to win a lawsuit for libel?
10. What kind of conduct is required for someone to be sued for emotional suffering?
11. Name the tort which occurs most often today.
12. List the three things that the plaintiff must prove to recover damages from the defendant for negligence.
13. What duty does a property owner owe to a trespasser?
14. What is required of property owners under the attractive nuisance doctrine?
15. When does the doctrine of strict liability apply?
16. When may people avail themselves of the remedy of an injunction?

Cases in Point

In each of the following cases, give your decision and state a legal principle that applies to the case:

1. Without permission, Anne Trigg took her next-door neighbor's lawn mower from the garage and mowed her own lawn. Did she commit a tort? Explain.
2. At 2 a.m. every morning when she arrives home from work, Ruth Ward plays her stereo with the volume high. She refuses to turn it down when asked to do so by the

neighbor in the apartment next door. What tort, if any, has Ward committed? What can the neighbor do to obtain relief?

3. A photographer took a picture of Juanita Lao without her permission when she was sunbathing beside a swimming pool in New York. Later, Juanita discovered that the picture was used in an advertisement for the bikini bathing suit she was wearing. What tort, if any, was committed by the photographer?

4. Tom Hada lived two houses away from Lou Lombardi. Their houses were separated by a narrow lot of land with a house on it owned by Mrs. McDuffie. One afternoon, Hada and Lombardi were playing catch with a baseball. Each was standing on his own property, throwing the ball to the other through the air across McDuffie's land. She threatened to sue them for trespass. Does she have a good case? Explain.

5. As she was about to leave a department store without buying anything, Donna Grant was stopped by a store detective, accused of shoplifting, taken into a back room, and detained for an hour before being released. Later, the detective learned that he had stopped the wrong person. What tort, if any, did the store detective commit?

6. Roberto Medero kept a dangerous snake in a glass container in his college dormitory room. He was very careful about keeping it from getting loose and harming anyone. One day, when he was in class, two students broke into his locked room and let the snake loose. Peggy Gardner was injured by the snake. Is Medero legally responsible for Gardner's injuries? Explain.

7. In a certain community an elderly woman was beaten and robbed by an unknown person. Emily Simpson told several people that Max Newmark was guilty of the crime. This was a false statement. Has Simpson committed a tort for which Newmark can recover damages?

8. Natalie Duval purchased a car from Michael O'Hara. She bought the car because O'Hara told her that he had just had the engine rebuilt a month earlier. Later, the car broke down and Duval learned that O'Hara had lied. The engine had not been rebuilt. What tort, if any, did O'Hara commit?

9. Shirlee Zucaro pointed a toy gun at Alphonso Johnson and told him to hand over his money. Johnson, who had no money, suffered a heart attack. What tort, if any, has Zucaro committed? If Johnson sues Zucaro and wins, what will he recover in damages?

10. James Lee, while leaving a shopping center, accidentally backed his car into a parked car owned by Barbara Faustino. The radiator, the front of the engine, and part of one fender of Faustino's car were smashed in. It was an old car, but the body shop and garage gave a repair estimate for $1,200. What tort did Lee commit? How much money will Faustino be able to recover in court?

Cases to Judge

1. A bar in Provincetown, Massachusetts, called Fo'cs'le, Inc., had a house rule that children were not allowed on the premises after 6 p.m. Mr. and Mrs. Ziemba refused to leave with their 3-year-old son when told to do so by a barmaid. The barmaid called the police, who came and told them to leave. When the Ziembas refused, they were arrested by the police. In court they were found not guilty of criminal trespass. The Ziembas sued both the barmaid and Fo'cs'le, Inc. for false imprisonment, malicious prosecution, and emotional suffering. How would you decide? Explain. *Ziemba v. Fo'cs'le, Inc.*, 475 N.E.2d 1223 (Massachusetts)

2. Two amateur hockey teams played each other in a hockey game. After the game ended, a fight broke out between Kadella and a member of the opposing team. The fight soon became general, with players leaving the benches to join the melee. During the fight, Kadella struck Overall, knocking him unconscious and fracturing the bones around his right eye. Overall brought suit against Kadella for assault and battery. Kadella claimed that Overall could not sue him for an injury incurred while Overall was voluntarily participating in a hockey game. Do you agree with Kadella? Give a reason for your answer. *Overall v. Kadella*, 361 N.W.2d 352 (Michigan)

3. Franklin Pork, Inc. constructed a pig feeding and breeding facility next to Jack and Ruth Cline's farm. According to the Clines, there was a "nauseating type of smell" that varied in intensity "from a slight hog smell to just absolutely horrid." The odor from the facility was so rank that they had to keep their doors and windows closed. They could not entertain friends or relatives. During one week in July, 12,976 flies were exterminated on their premises. The following week, 14,900 flies were exterminated. What type of tort action might the Clines bring in this situation, and what remedy should they seek? Explain. *Cline v. Franklin Pork, Inc.*, 361 N.W.2d 566 (Nebraska)

4. Hamilton was injured when he fell while chasing three ducks that had strayed onto his property. He claimed that the ducks were permitted by their owner, Green, to run loose onto his property in violation of a statute that read: "Hereafter, it shall be unlawful for any animal of the species of horse, ass, mule, cattle, sheep, goat, swine, or geese to run at large in the state of Illinois." Hamilton also claimed that the act of allowing ducks to stray onto his premises was a negligent act and was the proximate cause of his injuries. Can Hamilton recover money damages from Green for his injuries? Explain. *Hamilton v. Green*, 358 N.E.2d 1250 (Illinois)

5. Johnson's mother was a patient in a state hospital. Another patient with the same name died. The hospital erroneously informed Johnson that her mother was dead. In fact, she was alive and well in another wing of the hospital. Johnson engaged an undertaker, notified relatives and friends, and arranged for a funeral. On the day of the wake, when she viewed the body for the first time, Johnson realized that the deceased was not her mother. She became hysterical and had to be helped from the funeral chapel. Later, the hospital admitted that it had pulled the wrong patient record. May Johnson recover from the state for the funeral expenses and for her emotional suffering? Explain. *Johnson v. State*, 334 N.E.2d 590 (New York)

Chapter 5

THE COURT SYSTEM

Scene: Mike, Pam, Steve, and Sue are sitting on the front steps of the apartment building where Mike and Sue live.

Sue: Mom said that Uncle Gino's all upset again. He's got to go to court on that drunk driving charge, and he's afraid he'll lose his license. This is the first time he's ever been in any trouble.

Mike: All because he had one drink too many. What a shame. He hardly ever drinks much. He just stayed too long at his friend's house and had one too many. He's my favorite uncle.

Sue: Mine too. He's going to help me when I start studying auto mechanics at the community college. He knows a lot about cars.

Pam: Do you think he'll have to go to jail?

Steve: I doubt it. But they stopped him on the interstate, so his trial will probably be in the federal court.

Sue: You have to go to court soon, don't you, Steve?

Steve: Yeah, for that speeding ticket I got. Instead of paying the fine, I decided to fight it. I'm going directly to the court of appeals and explain to the judge that all the cars go 65 miles an hour now, the same as I did. I don't

think they should enforce the 55-mile speed limit. Nobody goes that slow any more.

Pam: I wish you luck!

Mike: Here comes Tony. I haven't seen him for a week.
(Tony approaches and stops at the front steps.)

Everyone: Hi, Tony!

Tony: What's up?

Pam: Where've you been? We haven't seen you for a week!

Mike: I saw those jerks, Wayne and Rick, yesterday. They said that their shoplifting trial is coming up next month in the small claims court. They said that they haven't seen you lately either.

Sue: A shoplifting trial in the small claims court?

Mike: They said that it's being held there because the things they stole were small. You know, each one got caught with a Sony Walkman underneath his jacket.

Sue: They're bad news. They stole more than that. That's all they got caught stealing.

Steve: I still haven't collected for the damage Wayne did to my car. The jerk smashed up my car to avoid hitting a squirrel. Can you imagine that? I'll probably have to sue him. I'll take him to the Supreme Court of the United States if I have to.

Tony: I'm glad that I stopped hanging around with them. They almost got me into a lot of trouble. They'll end up in jail.

Sue: We're all glad you did too, Tony. But we knew you were too smart to stay with them for long.

Tony: Thanks.

LEGAL ISSUES

1. Is a person charged with drunk driving on an interstate highway tried in a federal, state, or local court?
2. Can a person who gets a speeding ticket have the case heard the first time in a court of appeals?
3. Are criminal trials for shoplifting held in small claims courts if the item stolen is worth a small amount of money?
4. Can a plaintiff take an automobile accident case all the way to the U.S. Supreme Court?

THE SPIRIT OF THE LAW

The establishment of courts and court procedures is one of the great achievements of the human race. By providing peaceful means for settling disputes between parties, courts make an important contribution to the preservation of law and order.

If someone cannot get a satisfactory settlement of a claim by a voluntary agreement, it is possible to bring an action to court and to ask the court to decide. Some courts may hear both criminal and civil cases. In addition, courts have been established for special needs ranging from administrative cases to small civil claims. Furthermore, if an individual disagrees with a court's decision, it may be possible to appeal the case to a higher court. Someone might well ask, "In what court should I bring my action? There seem to be so many of them."

STATE AND FEDERAL COURTS

First of all, there are two court systems to consider: those of a state and those of the federal government. Each has exclusive jurisdiction over specific types of controversies. **Jurisdiction** is the power and authority given to a court or a judge to hear a case and to make a judgment. When a court has exclusive jurisdiction over certain cases, the court has the sole right to try these specific cases. In other types of cases, however, a person may have the choice of bringing an action in one or the other of these two court systems.

Remember: In either case, the functions of the court are the same. These functions are (1) to find the facts of the case and (2) to apply the proper law to the facts.

State Courts

■ Each state has its own court system. Therefore, in order to learn about the exact organization of all the courts in your own state, you must usually ask a local attorney or judge. The general pattern, however, is the same in all states. You can think of your state court system as a pyramid. Many small local courts form the base of the pyramid. Decisions of these local courts may be appealed to area, or county, courts, usually called courts of general jurisdiction. Courts of general jurisdiction, in turn, may have their decisions appealed to appellate, or appeal, courts. At the top of the pyramid is always one court of highest appeal, which makes final decisions on state cases.

Local Courts

Local courts are called courts of limited jurisdiction. This means that they have jurisdiction only in minor matters, petty crimes, and civil actions involving small amounts of money.

Justice of the Peace Courts **Justice of the peace courts,** or magistrate's courts, as they are sometimes called, were the only local courts in the early days of our country. They were established to furnish a way to try small claims cases and to punish petty crimes in each local community. They continue to serve that function today in many communities. The justice of the peace, or magistrate, hears both criminal and civil cases without a jury, both to determine the facts

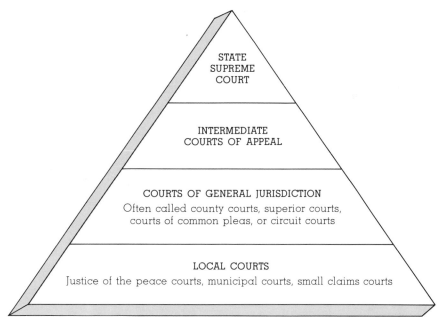

The state court system is like a pyramid with the right of appeal going from bottom to top.

and to apply the law. In most states the defendant may appeal the justice's decision to the county court.

Legal Issue No. 1 *Municipal Courts* In larger communities, justice of the peace courts have been replaced by **municipal courts.** These courts serve the same function as justice of the peace courts, but in the larger cities these functions may be divided among several specialized courts. These specialized courts may be, for example, traffic courts, police courts, juvenile offenses courts, family courts, and small claims courts.

Legal Issue No. 3 *Small Claims Courts* Many cities have courts for special cases, such as **small claims courts.** These courts may hear civil, but not criminal, cases involving claims up to amounts ranging from $500 to $5,000, depending on the state law. Small claims courts are valuable because the parties (the plaintiff and the defendant) may act as their own attorneys. Trials in these courts are conducted very informally. Such courts provide a relatively inexpensive means of obtaining justice in minor civil cases.

Courts of General Jurisdiction In most states each county has at least one **court of general jurisdiction.** These courts are called by various names, such as county court, superior court, court of common pleas, circuit court, and, in a few states, supreme court.

Usually, any case may be started in the court of general jurisdiction, but minor cases are commonly begun in the more informal local courts. An appeal to the court of general jurisdiction is made if one of the parties feels that he or she has not obtained justice in the local court. All cases involving major crimes and large amounts of money must be started in the court of general jurisdiction.

In these courts of general jurisdiction the most important matters are tried. These courts have the duty to determine the facts, usually with the aid of a jury, and to apply the appropriate law to these facts.

Legal Issue No. 2 *Intermediate Courts* The function of **intermediate courts** is to hear appeals from the courts of general jurisdiction rather than to hear cases for the first time. Appeals may be taken to an intermediate court by the parties if they believe that they did not have a fair trial in the lower court or that the judge in the court of original jurisdiction did not properly interpret the law. Intermediate courts hear appeals only on questions of law, not on questions of fact. The facts, which are determined in the trial court—that is, the court of general jurisdiction—usually cannot be redetermined in an intermediate court. It is only when there is evidence that the jury has been prejudiced and has decided contrary to the evidence presented in the trial that the intermediate court will review the facts.

EXAMPLE 1 Slocum sued Archbold for injuries suffered in a two-car crash. The case was tried in a local county court, and the court supported the defendant. If Slocum's lawyer finds grounds for an appeal founded upon errors in the county court's interpretation of the law, she would then appeal to a higher court and ask for another trial.

Intermediate courts are usually called **appellate courts,** district courts of appeal, or some similar term. Over half of the states have intermediate courts. In those that do not, appeals are taken directly from the trial court to the highest court of the state.

Highest Courts of Appeal In forty states the highest court is called the **state supreme court.** In the others it is called court of appeals, court of errors, or some similar name.

It is the function of these high courts to make a final decision on matters of law that are appealed from the lower courts. Here, again, they do not retry a case and redetermine the facts; they only decide whether an error was made in the lower courts in the determination of the law involved. In many states, the highest court selects the cases it wishes to hear.

Federal Courts

The federal courts have exclusive jurisdiction over (1) all actions in which the United States or a state is a party, except those actions between a state and its own citizens; (2) all cases arising under the Constitution or involving a violation of a federal law; (3) all admiralty (pertaining to the sea), patent-right, copyright, and bankruptcy cases; and (4) cases involving citizens of different states where the amount of money involved exceeds $10,000. Even in these cases, however,

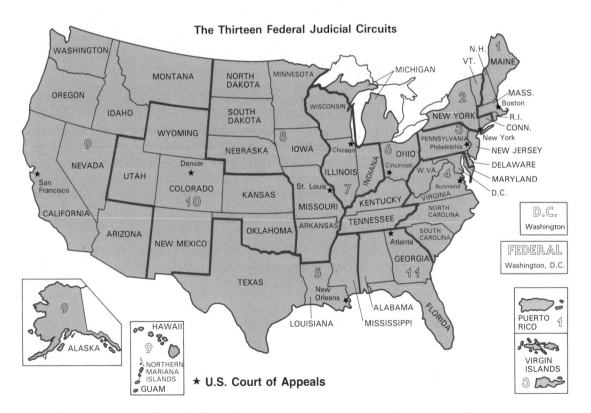

The Thirteen Federal Judicial Circuits

★ **U.S. Court of Appeals**

The U.S. federal court system is divided into 13 "circuits," including the D.C. and federal circuits. Each circuit has several district courts. ★ Indicates the location of the court of appeals in each circuit.

states cannot be sued by citizens of other states unless they agree to be sued. Under the Eleventh Amendment to the U.S. Constitution, an unconsenting state is immune from suits brought in federal court by citizens of other states.

Federal District Courts At the bottom of the pyramid in the federal system are the **federal district courts.** The United States and its territories are divided into judicial districts, and many of the districts are subdivided still further. District courts are the courts of original jurisdiction in the federal system. Most federal cases are first tried in district courts.

EXAMPLE 2 A local FBI office was broken into and robbed of a large sum of money. The thief was arrested by the state police and turned over to the authorities for trial in the federal district court. This was proper since the offense was committed against a federal agency.

Courts of Appeals The entire United States is divided into 13 judicial circuits. In each circuit there is a **U.S. Court of Appeals.** These courts hear appeals from the federal district courts. The U.S. Court of Appeals from the District of Columbia Circuit hears appeals from federal administrative agencies and from the district court in Washington, D.C. The U.S. Court of Appeals for the Federal Circuit hears appeals in patent and custom cases. Most appeals are given final judgment in the U.S. Courts of Appeals because the Supreme Court of the United States hears only a selected number of appeal cases.

The U.S. Supreme Court **The U.S. Supreme Court** is the highest court in the land. It has both original and appellate jurisdiction. It has *original jurisdiction* (power to hear a case first) in all cases affecting ambassadors, other public ministers, and consuls and those in which a state is a party. Its *appellate jurisdiction* (power to hear cases on appeal) is the Court's main function, however.

Legal Issue No. 4

The Court decides, by a vote of four of its nine justices, which cases it will hear. The justices attempt to select only those cases that will have an impact on American society, such as the constitutionality of important legislation.

EXAMPLE 3 On a busy street corner, Cora Swartz was delivering a political speech criticizing the current mayor and the police force of the city. Several police officers arrested Swartz for blocking the pedestrian traffic flow on the sidewalks—a violation of a city ordinance. A city judge fined Swartz $10 for the violation. She then appealed her case to a higher court, claiming that the city ordinance interfered with her right of free speech.

Although the fine was small, this case involves constitutional rights and might be appealed through the courts, even up to the U.S. Supreme Court.

Special Courts

Courts have been established by the federal and state governments to handle certain specialized cases. Among the more common of these special courts are courts of claims (established by the federal and state governments) and surrogate, or probate, courts (established by the states). There are also juvenile courts (established by state and local governments).

TO COURTROOM ←

WHAT'S DISCOURAGING IS BEING CHEATED OUT OF YOUR LIFE'S SAVINGS AND HAVING TO GET IT BACK IN SMALL CLAIMS COURT.

© 1986 by NEA, Inc.

What is the purpose of small claims court? Where could you appeal a small claims court judgment? (*Copyright © 1986, Newspaper Enterprise Association, Inc.*)

Courts of Claims Neither the federal government nor a state government may be sued by individuals, except with the permission of the government. However, the federal government and most state governments have set up special courts, called **courts of claims,** to which cases may be brought by individuals who have claims against these governments.

Family Courts In most states, each county has a special court known as a **family, probate,** or **surrogate court** to supervise the administration of the estates of deceased persons. The work of these courts—the distribution of property according to the laws governing wills and inheritance—is explained further in Chapter 39. These courts also handle divorce and child custody (see Chapter 28) cases and other family matters.

Juvenile Courts **Juvenile courts** are courts that have special jurisdiction over delinquents and neglected children up to an age set by state statute. Such courts exist in every state in the United States. They exist at the state level of government and also at the local level.

In some states the juvenile court is a separate court, not connected with any other court. In other states special sessions to handle juvenile cases are held in the district court or the probate court. Procedures in these courts differ somewhat from those of other types of courts. The sessions are often held privately in the judge's chambers or in some other room not as formal as a courtroom. It has also been generally held that persons who appear before juvenile courts have no right to a trial by jury or to be released on bail. These rules are based on the theory that such a hearing is not criminal but rather civil in nature. In addition, the U.S. Supreme Court has held that there must be proof beyond a reasonable doubt to charge a child with an act that would be a crime if it had been committed by an adult.

Criminal Courts

An adult offender* is tried in a criminal court at the local, state, or federal level. Many of our federal and state courts have jurisdiction over both civil and criminal cases. In both criminal and civil trials the courts perform the same basic

*As discussed in Chapter 3, some states, by a device called *transfer,* allow a juvenile offender above a certain age to be tried as an adult in criminal court if the minor has been accused of committing a serious felony.

functions—that is, they (1) determine the facts and then (2) apply the law to those facts. This is often the task of a **jury,** a body of persons selected to determine the truth in questions of fact. In cases tried without juries the judge performs these functions. Obviously, the honesty and judgment of the trial jury are very important.

Serving on a jury is a duty of great importance. Every citizen has an obligation to serve when called and to attempt to serve without bias. If unqualified, dishonest, or prejudiced persons are allowed to sit on juries, serious injustice may result. A wrong or misguided judgment can result in financial loss and personal harm for innocent people.

EXAMPLE 4   Vera Jenson, the defendant in a case, tried to bribe a juror to insist on a verdict in Jenson's favor or to "hang"* the jury. The juror reported Jenson's offer to the court. Jenson could be charged by the judge with contempt of court and could also be tried by a jury separately for this offense.

Criminal and civil actions begin differently. In civil cases, the injured party begins the suit by filing a complaint. In a criminal case, the action is usually started by a district attorney. It is the duty of the district attorney to make investigations to determine whether crimes have been committed and whether certain individuals should be tried. The district attorney often has the assistance of a grand jury.

A **grand jury** is a jury of inquiry. It is a group of citizens called together by a court official to determine whether there is enough evidence to justify accusing certain persons of certain crimes. There is a clear difference between a grand jury and a petit jury. A grand jury conducts a preliminary hearing in secret to determine whether someone must stand trial. In this way an innocent party may be spared undue publicity. A **petit jury** decides on the guilt or innocence of the person tried, and this trial is a matter of public record. A trial jury is called a petit jury because it usually has a smaller number of jury members than a grand jury.

Unlike a petit jury, a grand jury carries on its own investigations, usually under the leadership of the district attorney. The jury calls witnesses, makes investigations, and considers all evidence. The members of a grand jury do not make final determinations of fact, however; they only indicate their suspicions. If the members of a grand jury believe, after hearing the evidence and listening to the testimony of witnesses, that a crime has been committed by the named individual or individuals, they issue what is known as an **indictment.** This is a written accusation issued by a grand jury, charging the individual or individuals named in it with a certain crime. An indictment does not mean that the named person is guilty of the crime. It only means that the grand jury believes that a crime has been committed and that there is a possibility that the person named in the indictment is guilty of the crime.

The next step in the process is for the district attorney to bring an action in court, charging the indicted party with the commission of the crime. The person's guilt or innocence is then established by a trial in court. This trial of a criminal action in court is similar to that of a civil action. A jury is called; the

*A juror "hangs" the jury by refusing to agree with the decision of the others, thereby preventing the jury from giving a verdict. (In most cases a verdict must be a unanimous decision).

attorneys present evidence, question witnesses, and sum up their arguments for the jury. Then the jury determines the facts, decides on guilt or innocence, and the judge pronounces sentence.

Remember: In the trial of a criminal case, the guilt or innocence of the accused is the most important matter to be determined. The accused is innocent until proven guilty.

Language of the Law

Define or explain each of the following words or phrases:

jurisdiction	court of general	U.S. Court of	surrogate court
local courts	jurisdiction	Appeals	juvenile court
justice of the peace	intermediate courts	U.S. Supreme Court	jury
courts	appellate courts	courts of claims	grand jury
municipal courts	state supreme court	family court	petit jury
small claims courts	federal district courts	probate court	indictment

Questions for Review

1. What two separate systems of courts do we have in this country?
2. What are the two main functions of each court system?
3. Ordinarily, the intermediate courts hear appeals only on matters of law. What is meant by this statement?
4. Under what conditions might an intermediate court be willing to review the facts of a case?
5. What different names are given to the highest court of appeals in the various states?
6. What is the principal function of these highest courts of the states?
7. The U.S. Supreme Court has original jurisdiction over what types of cases? It has appellate jurisdiction over what types of cases?
8. Why are special courts necessary? Name some special courts.

Cases in Point

In each of the following cases, give your decision and state a legal principle that applies to the case:

1. Annie Carney was arrested for shoplifting a camera valued at $45. Will her trial be in a small claims court? Explain.
2. Ben Freedman was indicted for armed robbery, a felony. Will his trial be in a local court? Why or why not?
3. Edith Gold appealed to the U.S. Supreme Court after losing her case in her own state's highest court. Must the U.S. Supreme Court hear the case? Explain.
4. Angela Harding, who is 12 years old but looks 16, was charged with a misdemeanor. In what court will her case be heard?
5. Peter Kafka was charged with murder. Because of the seriousness of the crime, may he have a grand jury decide on whether he

is guilty or innocent? Explain.

6. Jana Listner was seriously injured on a state highway and threatened to sue the state for $50,000 damages. May Listner bring a suit against the state? If so, in which court must her claim be tried?

7. Andrea Adams alleges that she suffered injuries as a result of an assault on her person by Harry Jackson. She seeks to recover the sum of $5,000 as damages. To save time and money, she wants to have the case tried before the court of appeals in her state. May she do so? Why?

8. Fred Kawabata was arrested for a traffic violation. He was fined $100 by the local justice of the peace. Kawabata maintained that this was excessive and unfair. He said he would appeal the case to the federal courts where he could get a fair trial. May he do so? Why?

9. Josephine Barnes, who lives in Pennsylvania, owes $15,000 to Rita Carson, who lives in Ohio. Is Carson entitled to bring an action against Barnes for this amount in Pennsylvania? In a federal court? Why?

10. The Missouri River, forming a boundary line between Missouri and Kansas, changed its course and cut a new channel east of its old bed. Kansas claims the land between the old and new river beds. Will this controversy be tried first by the U.S. Supreme Court? Why?

Cases to Judge

1. Watson was charged with murder. Testimony about a telephone conversation was presented by the victim's friend to the grand jury. Similar evidence was given to the petit jury but later held to be inadmissible by the court of appeals. The question arose whether or not the grand jury was responsible for determining the guilt or innocence of the accused. What is your opinion? *People v. Watson*, 486 N.Y.S.2d 592 (New York)

2. Jurgens brought suit in a small claims court against her former employer, Ram Leather Care, for $500. Ram Leather Care responded with a counterclaim against Jurgens for $15,500. By state statute, the small claims court can hear civil actions that do not exceed $5,000. Can the court decide the case? Explain. *Jurgens v. Ram Leather Care*, 687 S.W.2d 955 (Missouri)

3. Townsend was arrested by federal officers for using abusive language during a demonstration that took place on the steps of the Pentagon. Later, the charges were dismissed, and Townsend brought suit against the officers in a federal court. What must be the amount of money damages suffered by the plaintiff for the suit to be brought before the federal court? *Townsend v. Carmel*, 494 F. Supp. 30 (Washington, D.C.)

4. Arthur, a citizen of Ohio, was injured in an automobile accident while driving in Florida. He brought suit against the state of Florida in a federal court, claiming that the state was negligent in the construction and maintenance of the road where the accident occurred. The state of Florida claims that an individual cannot bring suit against a state in a federal court. Do you agree? Explain. *Arthur v. Fla. Dept. of Transp.*, 587 F. Supp. 974 (Florida)

5. When the Greenleafs were divorced, they entered into a separation agreement in which Mr. Greenleaf agreed to place $18,570.41 in trust for the benefit of their children. The agreement was never carried out. When Mrs. Greenleaf died, one of the children (now an adult) brought suit in the probate court against her father for breach of contract. Does the probate court have jurisdiction over breach of contract actions? Explain. *Glick v. Greenleaf*, 403 N.E.2d 947 (Massachusetts)

Lambert v. State
694 P.2d 791 (Alaska)

David R. Lambert was charged with driving while intoxicated in violation of an Alaskan statute that read: "A person commits the crime of driving while intoxicated if the person operates or drives a motor vehicle . . . while under the influence of intoxicating liquor."

Trooper Jeff Slamin stopped Lambert because Lambert's vehicle was weaving within its own lane and had crossed the divider and fog lines. When he stopped Lambert, Lambert smelled of alcohol and refused to perform sobriety tests. At trooper headquarters Lambert was videotaped. The videotape showed that Lambert's speech was slurred and his gait unsteady.

THE TRIAL

Lambert testified that for 2 weeks prior to his arrest he had been sick with flu; he had been taking Contac, Nyquil, and Terpin hydrate. On the evening of his arrest, he had stopped at the Chatanika Lodge, where he had drunk some coffee and some unidentified prescription cough medicine furnished him by the lodge's owner. When asked at trial how he was measuring the cough syrup, Lambert said that when he "got to the top of his bottom teeth, he would stop swallowing."

Lambert's expert witness, Mark Gilberts, a pharmacist, testified that Nyquil was 25% alcohol, which makes it 50 proof. Terpin hydrate is 41% alcohol, or 82 proof, and also contains codeine. Gilberts stated that the Nyquil bottle includes a warning not to drive while taking it.

At the close of trial, the jury was instructed, in relevant part, as follows:

You are further instructed that a person is *under the influence of intoxicating liquor* and/or a controlled substance when he has *consumed alcohol* and/or a controlled substance to such an extent as to impair his ability to operate a motor vehicle. *Under the influence of intoxicating liquor* and/or a controlled substance means that the defendant *consumed some alcohol* and/or ingested a controlled substance, whether mild or potent, in such a quantity, whether great or small, that it adversely affected and appreciably impaired his actions. . . .

The jury sent Judge Crutchfield the following note during its deliberations: "Judge, is the alcohol in Nyquil considered an intoxicating liquor?"

The judge responded: "Jurors, the alcohol in Nyquil is the same as alcohol found in beer or liquor."

The jury found Lambert guilty of driving under the influence of intoxicating liquor.

THE ARGUMENTS ON APPEAL

Lambert's theory of defense rested on the contention that he was driving under the influence of medicinal alcohol rather than recreational alcohol and that medicinal alcohol does not fall within the definition of "intoxicating liquor." He contends that the phrase "intoxicating liquor" is so vague that its use in the statute deprives him of due process of law. He also objects to the instruction given after the jury had commenced deliberations and returned with the question whether Nyquil was an intoxicating liquor. Lambert contends that the phrase "intoxicating liquor" is not defined anywhere in the Alaska statutes.

QUESTIONS FOR DISCUSSION

1. How should the court treat a word or phrase that is not defined in a state statute?
2. What is the definition of "intoxicating liquor"?
3. Are the cough medicines Nyquil and Terpin hydrate intoxicating liquors?
4. Is the phrase "intoxicating liquor" unconstitutionally vague?
5. Based on your reading of the chapters in Unit 1, what law or laws might apply to this case?
6. If you were an appellate court judge hearing this case, for whom would you decide? Why?

READING AND BRIEFING CASES

A well-recognized method of studying law is the reading and briefing of appellate court decisions. A case brief consists of a short summary and analysis of a case that was decided by an appellate court. The purpose of briefing a case is twofold: (1) to obtain a better understanding of the court's decision and the principles of law involved in the case, and (2) to have an efficient method of recalling a case for the purposes of discussion and examination.

HOW TO WRITE A CASE BRIEF

A case brief consists of five parts:

1. *Heading* Write the names of the parties and the citation of the case.
2. *Statement of Facts* Write a short description of the activities that caused this lawsuit to come about. This should be a very short story about the things that happened to the people involved in the case.
3. *Legal Issue* Determine one question of law that must be decided by the court of appeals. Most cases have more than one of these; just select the most important one. Write the legal issue in one sentence in the form of a question. It should be obvious to anyone reading your question that it arises from the statement of facts you wrote above.
4. *Court's Decision* Write the answer to the question (legal issue) you wrote above. (Note: If the question calls for a yes or no answer, just write "yes" or "no.")
5. *Reason for the Court's Decision* Copy from the decision the main reason the court decided as it did. Do not write citations in your brief.

SAMPLE CASE

Here is the report of a case that was decided by the Appellate Division of the Superior Court of New Jersey. Following this case is a sample brief for you to use as a guide when you are asked to write a case brief.

Schomp v. Wilkens by Leen
501 A.2d 1036 (New Jersey)

(**Note:** David Wilkens, a minor, was represented in this action by his guardian, Philip Leen.)

This case involves the novel question of the interplay between the legislatively expressed intent to regulate bicyclists in accordance with motor vehicles statutes and the deeply rooted principle of our jurisprudence that in assessing negligence children ordinarily are to be measured against a standard of care which would be exercised by one of similar age, judgment, and experience.

Here plaintiffs, Gregory Schomp and his father, John, challenge a trial court judgment entered upon a jury verdict of no cause for action in connection with the complaint they instituted against David Wilkens. The complaint alleged that Gregory was injured in a bicycle collision as a result of the negligence of David Wilkens who was riding the other bicycle involved in the accident. Answers were filed and the case proceeded to trial where the following facts were established.

On June 16, 1981, Gregory Schomp, who was then 17½ years old, was riding his bicycle near his home in Watchung. Proceeding down Washington Drive, he made a right turn onto Scott Drive which is in a recently developed residential area. There were no cars travelling on the street or parked between the corner of Washington Drive and the scene of the accident. Gregory was riding about two feet from the curb and looking straight ahead. He estimated his speed to be approximately 10 m.p.h. As he rode down a slight decline, gently applying his brakes to maintain a constant speed, he was struck by the bicycle ridden by David Wilkens who was exiting his driveway on Scott Drive. As a result of the collision Gregory was injured. The Wilkens' driveway declines sharply to the street. There is sufficient foliage surrounding the Wilkens' driveway to prevent a clear view of it on approach from Washington Drive. Gregory testified that he neither saw David approach nor heard any kind of warning. David presented no evidence at trial. The trial judge instructed the jury, over the Schomps' objection, that the standard of care for a minor is that exercised by a person of similar age, judgment and experience. He declined to charge the jury, as requested by the Schomps, on the effects of violation of the motor vehicle statutes relevant to the situation. The jury returned a verdict of no cause for action and this appeal ensued in which the Schomps claim that a reversal is warranted because the trial judge erroneously instructed the jury as to the applicable standard of care, improperly declined to charge violations of the motor vehicle statutes as evidence of negligence and because the verdict was against the weight of the evidence.

We begin with the Schomps' claim that the trial judge erred when he described the standard of care applicable to this case: ". . . the law tells us that the degree of care required of a child is such as is usually exercised by a person of similar age, judgment and experience." We view this instruction as entirely proper. In this respect, we conceive the Schomps' reliance on *Goss v. Allen* [a New Jersey case decided in 1976] to be misplaced. In that case, the plaintiff was injured in a skiing accident with a 17 year old skier. Faced with the question of the standard of care applicable to the minor skier . . . the Supreme Court held that while "certain activities engaged in by minors [for example, hunting, driving, operating a boat] are so potentially hazardous as to require that the minor be held to an adult standard of care . . . " skiing, as a recreational activity engaged in by persons of all ages, is governed in each individual case by the standard applicable to the age of the person so engaged. The Schomps here contend that bicycle riding is a "hazardous" activity as described in *Goss* and urge that because of the hazard the standard which ordinarily would have applied to David as a minor should have been replaced by an adult standard. We reject this argument. Bicycling is an ordinary recreational activity engaged in by persons at every stage of life from babyhood to old age. As is true with other relatively innocuous activities it is, of course, possible to ride a bicycle in a dangerous manner. Generally however bicycling is viewed as a safe method of exercise and recreation. . . .

Nor are we persuaded to the contrary by the Schomps' argument that in analyzing this issue it is critical to consider the provisions of [a New Jersey statute] which require bicyclists to obey the motor vehicle statutes. Clearly . . . the motor vehicle statutes are relevant to a charge of negligence made against a bicyclist. But this is a far cry from concluding, as the Schomps urge, that the applicability of these statutes in itself evidences a strong legislative expression as to the dangerousness of bicycling which translates into the "hazardousness" described in *Goss*. . . . [Here the court cited two cases, one in Arkansas and one in Michigan. Each case involved a minor bicyclist in an accident.]

In each of these cases the appropriate standard of care was held to be that of a child of similar age, experience and judgment under similar circumstances. It should be noted that both cases were cited with approval in *Goss* and there is no contrary authority in any jurisdiction. Rather the great weight of authority supports the application of the child's standard of care to a minor bicyclist. The only cases which have applied an adult standard of care to children have involved activities which clearly pose substantial risk of injury to others. One of the cases cited by plaintiffs, for example, deals with a 12 year old who seriously injured another 12 year old with a pistol. . . . Similarly, an adult standard is applicable to a minor who causes injury to another while playing golf because a golf ball, like a power-driven vehicle, is [dangerous]. . . .

In sum, we are satisfied that the trial judge properly charged the jury that David Wilkens' conduct was to be evaluated by the standard applicable to a person of "similar age, judgment and experience."

(**Note:** The court decided that a new trial *was* necessary, however, because the trial judge did not instruct the jury that violation of a motor vehicle statute is evidence of negligence. A New Jersey statute makes bicyclists subject to the same duties as motorists.)

SAMPLE BRIEF

Schomp v. Wilkens by Leen
501 A.2d 1036 (New Jersey)

1. *Statement of Facts:* Gregory Schomp, 17½, was riding his bicycle on Washington Drive, near his home. He made a right turn onto Scott Drive. He was riding about 2 feet from the curb, looking straight ahead, at a speed of approximately 10 miles per hour. As he rode down a slight decline, he was struck and injured by a bicycle ridden by David Wilkens, who was exiting his driveway on Scott Drive. The Wilkens' driveway declines sharply to the street. Foliage at the entrance of the driveway prevents a clear view of it from Washington Drive. Gregory testified that he neither saw David approach nor heard any kind of warning.

2. *Legal Issue:* Is the degree of care required of a teenage bicyclist the same as is usually exercised by a person of similar age, judgment, and experience?
3. *Court's Decision:* Yes.
4. *Reason for the Court's Decision:* Bicycling is an ordinary recreational activity engaged in by persons at every stage of life. It is not a hazardous activity that would warrant an adult standard of care in all situations. Although the motor vehicle statutes are relevant to a charge of negligence made against a bicyclist, this does not mean that bicycling is especially hazardous. The required standard of care of a teenage bicyclist is that of a person of a similar age, experience, and judgment under similar circumstances.

CASE TO BRIEF

After reading *How to Write a Case Brief* on page 78, and examining the sample brief above, write a brief of the following case:

Matter of Julio R.
492 N.Y.S.2d 912 (New York)

Is the detention of a truant teenager for the purpose of returning the youth to school a "lawful duty" of a New York City policeman? This is the question presented by this juvenile delinquency proceeding. Julio R. (respondent) is charged with acts which if committed by a person over the age of 16 years would constitute assault in the second degree. Second degree assault occurs when: "With intent to prevent a peace officer, police officer or a fireman . . . from performing a lawful duty, a person causes physical injury to such peace officer, police officer or fireman." (Penal Law 120.05(3))

The facts proved beyond a reasonable doubt are as follows: On February 13, 1985 respondent arrived at Susan Wagner High School at 8:45 a.m. Although he was fifteen minutes late, he avoided the "late pass" procedure by saying he was going in to see his guidance counselor. Ten minutes later he was seen outside the school, walking away from the school, by a school safety officer, who alerted New York City Police Officer Timothy Farrell. Officer Farrell, who was in uniform and who knew respondent by name, got in his police car and located respondent near the football field in the company of a group of youths. Officer Farrell told everyone to return to school, and all the other young people obeyed the instruction. Respondent, however, became obscene and refused to return. After an exchange of words the officer told respondent to get in the police car. When respondent refused, Officer Farrell got out of the car and attempted to handcuff respondent. It was Officer Farrell's intent to put respondent in the car and drive him back to the school, in accordance with Patrol Guide 180–18. Respondent then shoved the officer, punched him in the mouth and bit him on the hand. Back-up officers arrived and subdued respondent.

At the time of the hearing, four months after the incident, Officer Farrell's hand still displayed a large discoloration, approximately one inch long, resulting from the bite, and several smaller discolorations on his knuckles. He was treated at Staten Island Hospital emergency room where the wound was cleansed. He also received a tetanus shot, and antibiotics for one month were prescribed. He missed five days of work as a result of his injuries.

In pursuing respondent, Officer Farrell was carrying out his normal assigned duties, which include patrol of the perimeter of Susan Wagner High School to look for truants and bring them back to school. In preparation for this assignment, Officer Farrell, a patrolman assigned to the 122 Precinct, was given one week of special training specifically relating to truants, over and above the regular police training. His assignment is part of the New York City Police Department's "Truancy Patrol Program," which was initiated in January, 1981.

Respondent does not contend that Officer Farrell's pursuit was the result of whim or caprice; rather, it is the lawfulness of the assignment which respondent challenges. School attendance is compulsory for youngsters in New York City under seventeen. . . . Enforcement power is specifically conferred on certain school officials: "A supervisor of attendance, attendance teacher or attendance officer, as the case may be, may arrest without warrant any minor who is unlawfully absent from attendance upon instruction." (Education Law 3213(2)(a))

[Respondent argues that since attendance officers are responsible for arresting truants, police officers are excluded from this duty.] The Presentment Agency [The Commissioner of Social Services], on the other hand, contends that the Education Law must be read together with section 435(a) of the New York City Charter which confers upon the police the power and duty, ". . . to preserve the public peace, prevent crime, detect and arrest offenders, . . . protect the rights of persons and property, guard the public health, . . . enforce and prevent the violation of all laws and ordinances in force in the city, . . . "

We conclude that the deployment of police to pick up truants is a legitimate exercise of police power and hold that Officer Farrell was performing a lawful duty when he was injured by respondent. . . .

. . . The compulsory education law is fundamentally a child protective statute, intended to insure to every child the schooling he needs to function in the adult world. The problem of truancy in New York City, however, has reached crisis proportions, going beyond the interests of the individual child to have an economic and social impact on the life of the entire city. Statistics compiled in 1983 revealed that more than one-third of New York City high school students were chronically absent from school without excuse. That most of these undereducated young people are unemployable upon leaving school is self-evident. The correlation between school failure and juvenile crime is also widely recognized and crime prevention appears to have been the primary purpose for the institution of the Truancy Patrol Program.

The conduct of the police in exercising crime prevention functions must be subject to close judicial scrutiny because of the inherent potential for abuse. . . . The duty performed by Officer Farrell as a member of the truancy patrol withstands such scrutiny. Certainly the function performed is properly an executive one, so that the separation of powers is in no way compromised. Neither does the procedure condone or invite free-wheeling police intervention in the lives of juveniles. . . . Officer Farrell's conduct in the present case was a straightforward . . . response to a well-defined and statutorily outlawed activity, truancy. . . .

Here the charge is not resisting arrest, and the presentment agency need not show a valid criminal arrest; it is sufficient that the presentment agency has proved that Officer Farrell was engaged in the performance of a lawful duty, to wit, the noncriminal detention of respondent for truancy.

The presentment agency having carried its burden of proof at the fact-finding hearing, the matter is set down for disposition on September 17, 1985. The Probation Department and Family Court Clinic are to prepare reports to submit to the court on that date. Respondent's parole is continued to that date.

TRIAL PROCEDURES

PARTICIPANTS IN A TRIAL

The procedure for taking a case to court is governed by rules established by federal and state laws and courts. In civil cases, the rules are called *rules of civil procedure*. In criminal cases, they are known as *rules of criminal procedure*. In the Trial Procedures section that ends each unit, you will be introduced to these rules and become familiar with legal documents. Although rules vary from state to state, they are generally similar to federal trial rules. Their aim is to provide a structure for finding the truth and applying the laws to the facts. Of the many people involved in a trial, the principal participants are described below.

THE PARTICIPANTS

Plaintiff: The injured person who brings a lawsuit or legal action. In a criminal case, the victim is a witness for the state. The state or the United States takes legal action against criminal suspects.

Plaintiff's Attorney: The lawyer who is the advocate for the plaintiff. In a criminal trial, the *prosecutor* or *district attorney* represents the community.

Clerk of the Court: The person who receives and files all papers relating to the trial, sets up the trial calendar, and tends to all other clerical matters for the court. In some states, the clerk also has the power to hear minor offenses and to mediate disputes.

Process Server: A sheriff, marshal, other court official, constable, or attorney—sometimes the plaintiff—who gives notice to the parties and witnesses in a lawsuit by handing them official documents.

Defendant: The party being sued in court. In a criminal case, the person being tried for the commission of a crime.

Defendant's Attorney: The lawyer who is the advocate for the defendant.

Judge (sometimes referred to as the *court*): The person who presides over all court actions.

Court Reporter: The person who keeps a written record of the trial.

Jury: A group of citizens selected from a pool of community members to determine the guilt or innocence of an accused in a criminal case or the responsibility of a defendant for damages in a civil case.

Witnesses: The individuals called into court to testify with regard to the facts of the case.

Sheriff: An officer who enforces the court's orders.

Bailiff: A sheriff's deputy. A court officer who keeps order in the courtroom and helps the sheriff enforce the court's orders.

PRETRIAL PROCEDURES

As you can see, the cast of characters in a trial is large. Similarly, the cost of this legal drama can be enormous. With many people seeking civil justice in court, the courts are overburdened. As a result, procedures have been created to help establish the facts of a case. Many cases can be settled without the time and expense of an actual trial.

The figure on page 83 shows the main steps that come before the plaintiff and defendant face each other in a civil trial. This process will be discussed in greater detail at the end of the other units of this text.

THE CASE OF GRAZIO V. WILLIAMSON

In the skit in Chapter 4, Wayne smashed into Steve's car which was parked in front of the DeFazio apartment building. Wayne claimed that a squirrel ran out in front of him and that he swerved to avoid hitting the squirrel. Rick was a passenger in Wayne's car. No one was injured in the accident. Considerable damage was done to both cars. Wayne's insurance policy covered bodily injury liability, but it did not cover property damage. (See the chart on page 235).

Steve pointed out to Wayne that Wayne was responsible for the damage to Steve's car. In

Pretrial Civil Procedures

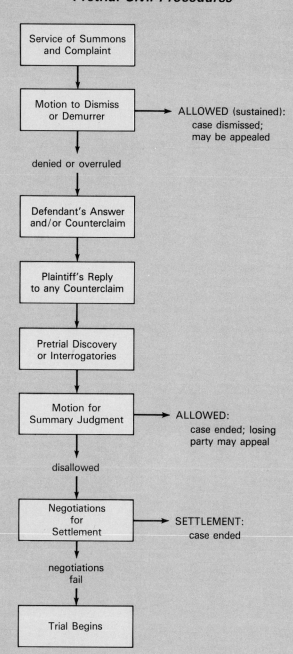

Service of Summons and Complaint

↓

Motion to Dismiss or Demurrer → ALLOWED (sustained): case dismissed; may be appealed

↓ denied or overruled

Defendant's Answer and/or Counterclaim

↓

Plaintiff's Reply to any Counterclaim

↓

Pretrial Discovery or Interrogatories

↓

Motion for Summary Judgment → ALLOWED: case ended; losing party may appeal

↓ disallowed

Negotiations for Settlement → SETTLEMENT: case ended

↓ negotiations fail

Trial Begins

response, however, Wayne argued that he was not at fault. He refused to pay for the damages to Steve's car. Steve's lawyer, Susan L. Powers, has written a letter to Wayne in an attempt to keep the case out of court but has received no reply. Attorney Powers has decided to bring suit against Wayne in the local district court. Her first step will be to write a complaint against Williamson and file it with the court. (The case of Grazio v. Williamson continues at the end of the next unit on page 181.)

QUESTIONS FOR REVIEW

1. In Grazio v. Williamson, who will be the plaintiff? the defendant?
2. What are the duties of the clerk of the court?
3. Describe the function of the process server.
4. What two names describe the person who presides over the court?
5. What is the duty of the court reporter?
6. From what area are members of the jury selected?
7. What do jurors decide?
8. How does a petit jury differ from a grand jury?
9. How does a sheriff differ from a bailiff?
10. How did Powers try to settle the case without bringing a legal action?

ENTERING INTO CONTRACTS

UNIT 2

Chapter 6

HOW CONTRACTS ARISE

In this unit you will meet the Williams family. Mrs. Williams is a widow raising three teenagers: Doug, 19; Denise, 17; and Lorna, 16. You will also hear about Marvin Maxwell, a friend of Mrs. Williams, who introduces a number of thorny legal issues.

Scene: The living room of the Williams home. Lorna Williams is talking with her younger sister, Denise.

Lorna (*glancing through the Sears anniversary sale advertisement that arrived with the daily newspaper*): Here's something that Mom would like for her birthday—a microwave oven.

Denise: That's a good idea. Mom has been talking about getting one of those for a long time. How much is it?

Lorna: $149.99.

Denise: We could get Doug to go in with us and each chip in $50.

Lorna: If I know Doug, he'll borrow the money from one of us. He's always broke—and he works all the time, too!
(*The telephone rings.*)

Denise: I'll get it. (*answering the telephone*) Hello. Yes, just a moment please. (*calling into the other room*) Mom! It's for you!

Mrs. Williams (*calling from the kitchen*): I'll take it in here!

Lorna: Is Doug awake yet?

Denise: I haven't seen him all morning. He went to a party last night and got home pretty late.
(*Doug enters the living room.*)

Doug: Hi.

Lorna: It's about time you woke up! Did anything exciting happen last night at the party?

Doug: Not much. Except that I made a deal to buy a car. I met a guy at the party who is selling his wheels for $490. It's in good shape. Not a dent in it, and it runs like a dream. I told him I'd buy it if I could borrow the money from my sisters, and we shook hands on it. He agreed to hold it for me for one week at that price.

Lorna: What did I tell you, Denise? Old moneybags himself.

Denise: Doug, before you start spending our money on yourself, did you get a present for Mom yet? It's her birthday tomorrow, you know.

Doug: That's right. I forgot about it.

Denise: We thought she might like the microwave oven that Sears has on sale this week. It's selling for $149.99. We can each chip in $50 toward it.

Doug: That's a good idea. She'd like that. I'm kind of short right now, but I'll pay you back in a couple of weeks.
(*Mrs. Williams walks into the room.*)

Mrs. Williams: That was Marvin on the phone. He's in my night class at the community college. He invited me out to dinner tomorrow night.

Lorna: You accepted, I hope!

Mrs. Williams: Yes. I hesitated at first because I didn't want to leave you kids alone, but after all, it is my birthday, so I accepted.

Doug, Lorna, and Denise: Good!
(*The next day, Lorna is at the small appliance department of Sears.*)

Lorna: I'd like one of those microwave ovens that's on sale for $149.99.

Salesperson: Oh, I'm sorry. There was a mistake in the ad. The correct price is $199.99.

Lorna: Are you sure? But the ad said $149.99!
(*It is 10:00 p.m. the following evening in the Williams's living room.*)

Mrs. Williams: Thank you for the beautiful microwave oven. It's something I've wanted for a long time. You must have paid a lot for it.

Doug: You can say that again!

Mrs. Williams: Who called you tonight, Doug?

Doug: That guy who promised to sell me his car. He called to tell me that he sold it to someone else.

Lorna: That's too bad. I'm sorry that guy Marvin never showed up, Mom. He could have at least called you if he couldn't make it.

Denise: You should sue Marvin for breach of contract.

Doug: Better still, I'll get my friend's brother to beat him up. He'll do anything for money.

Mrs. Williams: Douglas, I thought that I brought you up better than that!

LEGAL ISSUES

1. Does a conditional acceptance create a contract?
2. Is a promise to hold an offer open legally binding?
3. Does an offer to enter into a social engagement create a legal obligation?
4. Is a newspaper advertisement an offer to sell at that price?
5. Is a contract to do an illegal act valid?

THE SPIRIT OF THE LAW

In order to conduct business and daily affairs, people must rely on each other's promises. The laws governing contracts evolved to uphold and enforce promises that people make in reliance on promises or acts of others. A contract gives reasonable assurances to all parties that agreements will be fulfilled. The law provides remedies for those who suffer losses due to another's failure to keep a contractual promise. In fact, a **contract** may be defined as "any agreement enforceable at law."

CONTRACT REQUIRE-MENTS

Many people think of contracts as long and hard-to-read documents. While some contracts do fit this description, it is not an accurate picture of contracts in general. You have already made hundreds of contracts. You enter into a contract every time you buy something at a store, go to a movie, or mow someone's lawn for money. Every time you work for someone, your oral agreement to perform the work and your employer's oral promise to pay you constitute a contract. Similarly, a contract is created when you travel by bus, get a haircut, go to the doctor, or have the car repaired. Contracts are very much a part of your daily life.

Legal Issue No. 3

Some types of agreements are not enforceable at law. For example, you may agree to go to a movie with someone; you may accept a dinner invitation from a friend; someone may promise to call you next Friday night at 8:00 p.m. Such agreements are social engagements. They are not contracts and are not enforceable at law because they lack *consideration* (the exchange of things of value), an essential element of a contract that is explained in Chapter 7.

Legal Issue No. 5

The requirements of a contract are (1) that it be an agreement, (2) that it contain consideration, (3) that it be between two or more parties who have the capacity to contract, (4) that it be made by mutual consent, (5) that it be made for a legal purpose, and sometimes, but not always, (6) that it be in written form or evidenced by a writing. All of these requirements will be discussed in detail in subsequent chapters of this unit.

CONTRACT CHARAC-TERISTICS

Contracts are classified in the following four ways: (1) valid, void, voidable, or unenforceable; (2) express, implied in fact, or implied in law; (3) bilateral or unilateral; and (4) oral, written, or written and under seal. Any one contract would be classifiable in all four ways.

Valid, Void, Voidable, or Unenforceable

The word **valid** means "legally good." Thus, a valid contract is one which is legally binding and fully enforceable by the court. A **void contract,** on the other hand, amounts to nothing and has no legal effect whatever. A contract to do something illegal would be void.

A **voidable contract** is different from a void contract. It is one which is not void in itself but which may be avoided (canceled) by one of the parties if that party chooses. For example, a contract between a minor and an adult may be avoided by the minor but not by the adult. It is sometimes said that a voidable contract is one that is valid unless voided.

A contract which is **unenforceable** is one which is not void but which, because of some rule of law, cannot be enforced in court. An example of an unenforceable contract is an oral (spoken) contract to sell land. A contract for the sale of land must be evidenced by a writing to be enforceable.

Express, Implied in Fact, or Implied in Law

An **express contract** is stated in words and may be either oral or written. For example, someone may say to you, "I'll sell you my camera for $50," and you may say, "I'll buy it." This conversation would result in a valid, binding contract which is fully enforceable by a court.

A **contract implied in fact** (often called an implied contract) is one that comes about from the actions of the parties rather than from the words that the parties use. Very often people enter into contracts without exchanging a word.

EXAMPLE 1 You drop your fare into the coin box as you board a bus. Neither you nor the bus driver speaks. It is mutually understood by your acts that the driver of the bus is to allow you to ride to your desired destination.

Contracts implied in law, also called **quasi contracts,** are not true contracts at all. The law says there is a contract even though no contract has been made; it requires one party who has been unjustly enriched to pay money to the other party in order to be fair and equitable.

EXAMPLE 2 Delia J. King, who was 80 years old, promised Herman L. Heil that she would leave him something in her will if he would care for her. Heil and his wife cooked, cleaned, and cared for her for 11 years. King left nothing to Heil in her will. The oral promise was unenforceable in court because it was one of the kinds of contracts that have to be in writing. The court, however, allowed Heil to recover from King's estate, in quasi contract, an amount of money equal to the fair value of the services rendered to her. (A deceased person's *estate* consists of the things that person owned at death.)

Bilateral, Unilateral

The word *bilateral* means "two-sided." A **bilateral contract** contains two promises—one by each person. One person promises to do something in exchange for the other person's promise to do something. If someone says to you,

A public offer of reward creates a unilateral contract if accepted.

"I'll sell you my camera for $50," and you say, "I'll buy it," a bilateral contract comes into existence. Both persons have made promises—one has promised to sell, the other to buy. Most contracts come about in this way.

The word *unilateral* means "one-sided." A **unilateral contract** contains one promise only. One person promises to do something if and when the other person performs some act. If someone says to you, "I'll sell you my camera for $50 if you give me cash before noon tomorrow," only one person is making a promise—the one promising to sell. That person will not be required to keep the promise unless you hand over $50 in cash before noon the following day. If you deliver the money within that time, a unilateral contract will take place. A reward offer is one of the most common instances of this kind of contract. The acceptance of a reward offer must precisely comply with the offer.

Oral, Written, or Written and Under Seal

An oral contract is one that is created by word of mouth. It comes into existence when two or more people speak to each other. One person usually offers to do something, and the other person accepts and agrees to do something else in return. Most of the contracts that we make during our lives are of this type.

Sometimes, however, it is desirable to put contracts in writing. A contract is put into writing to allow the parties to know the exact terms of the contract and also to provide proof that the agreement was made. A law known as the Statute of Frauds requires that certain contracts must be evidenced by a writing to be enforceable. This topic is discussed further in Chapter 11.

In addition to being in writing, some contracts are also placed **under seal.** A **seal** is an impression made on a document. Under common law the seal was regarded as proof that the parties had exchanged something of value (consideration) in order to bind themselves to their agreement. Today, however, many states have done away with the common-law seal, saying that it is old-fashioned and no longer needed.

REACHING THE AGREEMENT

An agreement is reached by the acceptance of an offer. An **offer** is a proposal by one party, called the **offeror,** stating the terms under which he or she will contract. **Acceptance** is the unqualified assent of the other party, called the **offeree,** to the proposal stated. The offer and acceptance may be made orally in person or by telephone, by an exchange of letters or telegrams, by a formally drawn written agreement, or by a combination of these methods. The important thing is that the parties understand each other.

EXAMPLE 3 Lisa Young placed the following advertisement in her high school newspaper: "For Sale, One Polaris Camera, $75." Dom Santiago read the ad. He telephoned Young and said, "I'll buy that Polaris camera if it's the model I'm looking for."

A contract may eventually result from these preliminary statements, but there is no agreement between the two parties as yet. Young, even though she put an ad in the newspaper, has not said she will sell, nor has Santiago definitely said he will buy. There is no mutual assent or agreement by both to a clearly stated proposal. Without such an agreement, there can be no contract.

Requirements of an Offer

An offer has three basic requirements. (1) It must be seriously intended. (2) It must be definite and certain. (3) Finally, it must be communicated to the offeree.

Serious Intent An offer must be made with the intention of entering into a legal obligation. An offer made in heat of anger or as a joke would not meet this requirement. For instance, a friend complaining about her unreliable car might say, "Give me five bucks, and it's yours." In such cases, words are used that sound as though an offer is being made when, actually, no offer is intended.

Very often, an invitation to negotiate is confused with an offer. Sellers normally have limited merchandise to sell. They could not possibly sell the advertised product to everyone who read the ad. Not only would they not have enough products to go around, they might be unable to obtain more of the same product to satisfy the demand. For this reason, most advertisements in newspapers, circulars, and catalogs are treated in the eyes of the law as invitations to negotiate rather than offers. They are also called invitations to deal, invitations to make an offer, or invitations to trade.

Legal Issue No. 4

EXAMPLE 4 A newspaper advertisement that appeared in the evening paper read, "Cabbage Patch Dolls, $35." Marcia Petras walked into the store about noon the next day and said, "I accept your offer on the Cabbage Patch Doll." The sales clerk apologized, saying that the dolls had sold out within an hour after the store had opened. No one, including the manufacturer, had anticipated the high demand for the dolls.

The advertisement was merely an invitation to the public to come in, see the dolls, and make an offer. When Marcia said, "I accept your offer," she was actually making an offer to buy a doll for $35, which the store could accept or reject.

Advertisements are sometimes held to be offers by the courts when they contain very particular promises, use such phrases as "first come, first served," or limit the number of items that will be sold. In such cases, under the terms of the ad, the number of people who can buy the product becomes limited, making the ad an offer rather than an invitation to negotiate.

Price tags, signs in store windows and on counters, and prices marked on merchandise, in addition to advertisements, are treated as invitations to negotiate rather than offers. This rule of law probably stems from the days when people negotiated for products in the marketplace more than they do in today's society. The price marked on the item is a starting point for the bargaining that may occur between the buyer and the seller before the final price is decided.

Definiteness and Certainty An offer must be definite and certain to be enforceable. In a case in which a landlord agreed to pay "a share" of the cost if the tenant had the plumbing fixed, the court would not enforce the contract because it was too indefinite. It was impossible to determine what the parties meant by the word *share*. Similarly, in a case in which a person agreed to buy equipment at "competitive prices," the court said the words were too indefinite for the contract to be enforceable.

Even the most responsible merchants make mistakes in advertising prices. A newspaper ad is not an offer, but an invitation for an offer. Sears is not legally required to sell the microwave at the incorrect price.

EXAMPLE 5   Joe Vasquez was offered a position as an account executive with the International Corporation. He was to receive $800 a month plus a "reasonable" commission on total sales. Do you think that this is a definite and certain offer?

It is not definite and certain because it would be difficult to determine exactly what a "reasonable commission" is. The court, however, could fix a commission based upon general practices in the trade.

Communication to the Offeree   Offers may be made in many ways—by telephone, by letter, by telegram, or by other methods. To be effective, an offer must be communicated to the offeree.

EXAMPLE 6   Jean Lefèvre found a wallet on Main Street in her hometown. An identification card and the address of the owner was in the wallet. Lefèvre returned the wallet to its rightful owner. The owner thanked her but did nothing more. Later in the evening, while reading the local newspaper, Lefèvre discovered that the owner had offered a reward for the return of the wallet. Can Lefèvre collect the reward?

No, she cannot legally collect the reward. The offer had not been communicated to her. She did not know of the reward at the time she returned the billfold, so it cannot be said that she accepted the offer. There can be no agreement if the offeree does not know of the offer, even if he or she has done the act requested in the offer.

Requirements of an Acceptance

As in the case of an offer, there are certain basic requirements for an acceptance. These are discussed here.

Unconditional Acceptance by the Offeree

The acceptance must be made by the offeree without attaching any conditions to the original offer.

EXAMPLE 7 Ray offers to sell his boat to Doreen for $400 cash. Doreen replies, "I accept if you will allow me to pay $50 a week for 8 weeks." Edward, who is with Doreen at the time, speaks up and says, "I'll accept your offer and pay the $400 cash right now." Is there a valid acceptance?

No, there is no valid acceptance. This situation illustrates two important requirements of a valid acceptance. An offer is completely within the control of the offeror. The offeror may offer any terms desired and may make the offer to any person selected. No one else may change the terms, and no one but the offeree to whom the offer is made may accept. Thus, Doreen is not making a valid acceptance because she is changing the terms. Edward is not making a valid acceptance because the offer was not made to him.

Communication of Acceptance

The time at which an acceptance takes effect is very important. It is then that a contract comes into being. There is no special problem of communication when the parties are dealing face to face. When one of the parties speaks, the other party hears him or her and the offer or the acceptance is communicated. When the parties live at a distance, however, and must write or send telegrams, special rules indicate when the acceptance takes place.

When the offeree uses the same method of communication that the offeror used, the contract comes into existence *when the acceptance is sent.* Let's assume that Ray and Doreen live in different cities. Ray has made an offer by letter to sell his boat to Doreen. Doreen decides to accept. There is no contract yet. She writes a letter, addresses it to Ray, and puts a stamp on it. Still no contract. She carries the letter across the street to a post-office mailbox, pulls down the slide, puts the letter in, but holds her finger on the letter. Still no contract. When she lifts her finger, however, and the letter slides down into the mailbox beyond her control, a contract is made.

In contrast, under the common law, if the offeree used a method of communication which was different from that used by the offeror, the contract came into existence when the acceptance was *received* by the offeror rather than when it was sent by the offeree. The modern trend, under the Uniform Commercial Code (UCC), is to have the acceptance take place when it is sent, as long as the method of communication used is reasonable under the circumstances. (The UCC is discussed on page 185.)

Silence alone is not an acceptance of an offer, but this rule does not govern most record club agreements. This is because club members *agree* to accept the monthly selection unless they notify the club. What obligations do record club members undertake? Does the person filing this form make an offer or an acceptance?

If the offeror states in the offer the method that the offeree must use to accept, it must be complied with. Ray could have stated the time and place of acceptance in his offer, indicating that a contract would not come into existence until he received the acceptance. In that case, there would be a contract only if Ray received the acceptance within the specified time limit.

Sometimes an offer specifies that it must be accepted by an action. When this is true, then the action must take place before there is an acceptance. A promise to do the action is not enough. Thus, if Larry McNulty promised to pay Floyd Little $25 if Little would climb to the top of the school flagpole, Little would have to climb to the top in order to accept the offer.

Silence alone is not an acceptance. Ray, in his letter to Doreen offering the sale of the boat, could have said, ''If I do not hear from you, I shall assume that you have accepted my offer.'' Doreen's silence after receiving the offer would not bind her to pay. Ray has no right to try to force an acceptance through Doreen's lack of action. A person cannot be forced to speak or to write in order to avoid a binding agreement. A person is under no obligation to reply to an offer.

A contract is **executory** when it has come into existence through a valid offer and acceptance but its terms have not yet been carried out. It becomes **executed** when the parties do whatever they have agreed to do.

EXAMPLE 8 Ray offers to sell his boat to Doreen for $400. Doreen replies, "I'll buy it." At this point the contract comes into existence and is in its executory stage. When Ray turns the boat over to Doreen and she pays him the $400, the contract will be executed.

Termination of Offer

An offer comes to an end in any of the following ways: (1) by revocation, (2) by rejection, (3) by counteroffer, (4) by conditional or qualified acceptance, (5) by expiration of time, (6) by death or insanity.

By Revocation A **revocation** is the taking back of an offer by the offeror. The offeror has a change of mind and decides to withdraw the offer before it has been accepted. Two important rules govern revocation: (1) With the exception of an option and a firm offer (see page 95), an offer can be revoked any time before it has been accepted, and (2) a revocation becomes effective when it is received by or communicated to the offeree.

By Rejection A **rejection,** or refusal, of an offer by the offeree brings the offer to an end. For example, if someone says to you, "I'll sell you my camera for $50," and you say, "I don't want it," the offer has come to an end. If you later say, "I've changed my mind, I'll take the camera for $50," you are now making an offer that the other party can either accept or reject.

By Counteroffer A **counteroffer,** or an offer in return, ends the first offer. If someone says to you, "I'll sell you my camera for $50," and you say, "I'll give you $35 for it," no contract comes into existence unless the original offeror accepts your new offer. Your counteroffer had the effect of ending the first offer. If you later say, "Okay, I'll give you $50 for the camera," you will be making a new offer, which the original offeror may accept or reject.

By Conditional or Qualified Acceptance A **conditional or qualified acceptance** occurs when the offeree accepts the offer but adds some additional term or some condition to it. A conditional or qualified acceptance brings an offer to an end and does not create a contract. For example, if a friend writes and says to you, "I'll sell you my lakeside lot for $6,000," and you write in reply, "I'll take it if you'll give me your boat trailer too," no contract would be created. You have added a condition to the offer. (Actually, adding a condition to an offer makes your reply a counteroffer.)

There is an exception to this rule under the UCC. If the contract is for the sale of goods (movable items), minor changes may be made by the offeree, and a contract will still be created. For example, if someone says to you, "I'll sell you my camera for $50," and you answer, "I'll buy it and pay you next week," a contract will be created. The added term, "I'll pay you next week," may be accepted or rejected by the offeror. This rule allowing minor changes to be made by the offeree applies only to goods, however, and does not apply to other

Legal Issue No. 1

kinds of contracts. Thus, if the same type of offer were for real estate, no contract would result, since the added terms would amount to a counteroffer.

By Expiration of Time It is sometimes said that the offeror is the master of the offer. This means that anything contained within the offer must be complied with by the offeree in order to create a contract. Thus, if the offeror puts a time for acceptance in the offer, it must be complied with. Assume that Ray has offered to sell Doreen his boat for $400. Ray tells Doreen that the offer will remain open until noon on the following day. To create a contract, Doreen must accept within that time. If she waits until later, she will be too late; the offer will have ended at noon.

If no time for acceptance is stated within the offer, it must be accepted within a reasonable time. Otherwise, no contract is created. What is a reasonable time depends on the circumstances. For example, a reasonable time to accept an offer for the sale of a truckload of ripe tomatoes would be different from a reasonable time to accept an offer for the sale of a house.

Legal Issue No. 2

By Expiration of an Option Contract When an offeree pays money or other consideration to an offeror to hold an offer open for an agreed period of time, an option comes into existence. An **option** is a binding promise to hold an offer open for a specified time period. It confers upon the holder of the option, the **optionee**, the exclusive right to accept the offer within the agreed time, subject to the terms of the option.

EXAMPLE 9 Darrell Luff offered to sell his car to Harriet O'Shea for $499. O'Shea wanted 2 weeks to decide whether or not to buy the car at that price. Luff agreed to give her an option on the car. In exchange for $25 given to him by O'Shea, Luff promised to hold the offer open until 5:00 p.m. 2 weeks from that date. O'Shea has the exclusive right until that date and time to accept the offer. Luff may keep the $25, in any event, as consideration for holding the offer open.

For a binding contract to be reached, the option must be exercised by the optionee. This requires an absolute, unconditional, unqualified acceptance exactly according to the terms of the option. In the above example, if O'Shea does not accept Luff's offer by 5:00 p.m. on that date, Luff may sell the car to someone else.

The UCC has a special provision for the situation where the one promising to hold the offer open is a merchant and the promise is made in writing. A merchant's written promise to hold open an offer for the sale of goods, known as a **firm offer** rather than an option, needs no consideration to be binding. Such an offer will be firm (irrevocable) during the time stated in the offer, or for a reasonable time if none is stated, but in no event longer than 3 months.

EXAMPLE 10 Suppose that rather than being a private party in Example 9, Luff owned Luff Auto Sales and gave O'Shea a written statement that he agreed to hold the offer open for 2 weeks for her to buy the car for $499. She would not have had to give him the $25 (unless Luff made it a part of the deal) to hold open the offer. It would have been binding on Luff Auto Sales without any consideration.

By Death or Insanity If the offeror dies or becomes insane before the offer is accepted, the offer comes to an end. It should be noted that although death ends an offer, it does not end a contract, except for personal services.

Suggestions for Reducing Legal Risks

When you make an offer:

1. If the offer is important, decide whether or not you need to get legal counsel before making the offer.
2. If you send a written communication, be sure that it is not subject to more than one possible interpretation.
3. To be safe, you should state, "This is an offer," or "This is not an offer, but rather an invitation [or request] for an offer."
4. It is wise to specify in the offer the time and manner in which the acceptance is to take place.
5. Be definite and clear about the exact terms of the offer and any conditions that may apply to the terms.
6. If it becomes necessary to withdraw an offer, remember that a revocation does not become effective until it is received by the offeree.

When you make an acceptance:

1. Be sure that you understand clearly all the terms, conditions, and the legal meaning of accepting the offer.
2. If the contract is very important, decide whether or not you should get legal advice before agreeing to it.
3. Keep a correctly dated carbon copy, duplicate, or some written record of the acceptance, and indicate the date and time when the acceptance was sent or otherwise communicated.
4. Set up a calendar showing the dates when all agreements, financial and otherwise, must be met according to the terms of the contract.

Language of the Law ▬▬▬▬▬▬▬▬▬▬▬▬▬▬▬

Define or explain each of the following words or phrases:

contract	contract implied in	acceptance	counteroffer
valid	law	offeree	conditional or quali-
void contract	quasi contract	executory	fied acceptance
voidable contract	bilateral contract	executed	option
unenforceable	unilateral contract	revocation	optionee
express contract	seal	rejection	firm offer
contract implied in	offer		
fact	offeror		

Questions for Review

1. Give an example of an agreement that is not enforceable at law.
2. List the six requirements of a contract.
3. What is the difference between a void and a voidable contract? Give an example of each.
4. How does a contract implied in fact differ from a contract implied in law?
5. Give an example of a bilateral contract and an example of a unilateral contract.
6. What are the requirements of a valid offer?
7. How does a revocation differ from a rejection?
8. When does a revocation become effective?
9. Give an example of a counteroffer and of a conditional acceptance.
10. If the offeree uses a method of communication different from that used by the offeror, when does the acceptance take place under the common law? What is the trend today?

Cases in Point

In each of the following cases, give your decision and state a legal principle that applies to the case:

1. Judy Nelson said to Wayne Carlson, "Meet me at the theater entrance tomorrow afternoon at two o'clock. I have two tickets to a musical comedy." Carlson agreed but failed to show up. Does Nelson have a legal claim against Carlson?
2. Bob Goodman orally agreed to buy a pocket calculator from Howard Hermann for $35. When Hermann delivered the calculator, Goodman refused to accept it, stating that he was not bound by his oral agreement. Was the agreement enforceable?
3. Home Furniture Company advertised its waterbeds in a local newspaper. By mistake, the newspaper advertised the beds for $49 instead of $249. Must Home Furniture Company sell the beds at the advertised price?
4. Maria Servideo offered to sell her farm to Mark Sawyer. Sawyer told his friend Linda Wells of the offer and mentioned that he did not plan to accept it. He suggested to Wells that she might accept it if she wished to do so. Wells wrote an acceptance, which Servideo received. Is there a contract?
5. A firm advertised that it was selling 2,000 items of equipment for $20 each. Victoria Perkins ordered the entire lot at the price stated, but delivery was refused. Has Perkins a claim against the company?
6. Victor Archer mailed an offer to Sally Miles, and Miles mailed a properly addressed and stamped letter of acceptance 10 minutes before she received a revocation of the offer. Was the revocation effective?
7. Helene Black's letter to David Donovan contained an offer stating, "This offer subject to receipt of acceptance by June 10." Donovan wrote and mailed his acceptance on June 8, but it did not reach Black until June 11. Was there a valid contract?
8. Barbara Nichols offered to sell John Fisk a piano for $200 and agreed orally to keep the offer open for 5 days. The same day, a neighbor told Fisk that she had bought the piano from Nichols. Has Fisk any claim against Nichols?
9. On June 2, Eve Bristol wrote to Marvin Burton offering to sell her automobile for $1,000 and stated that the offer was "good for 10 days." Burton received the letter on June 5 and wrote and mailed a letter of acceptance on June 11. Because Bristol received the letter of acceptance on June 14, she claimed that there was no contract. Is she right?

Cases to Judge

1. Lee Calan Imports, Inc., placed an advertisement in the *Chicago Sun-Times* for the sale of a Volvo station wagon for $1,795. By mistake, the newspaper advertised the car for $1,095. A customer visited the car lot, examined the Volvo, and stated that he wished to purchase it for $1,095. The company refused to sell it at that price. The customer contends that the advertisement was an offer which he accepted, creating a binding contract. Do you agree? Why or why not? *O'Keefe v. Lee Calan Imports, Inc.*, 262 N.E.2d 758 (Illinois)

2. Georgia Marble Company offered to buy certain property from Sarah Shiver. The offer provided that the closing would take place "within 60 days of acceptance but not later than July 30, 1981." Instead of accepting the offer, Shiver offered to sell the property to Benton on the same terms and conditions as those offered to her by Georgia Marble. Benton accepted Shiver's offer with the stipulation that the closing would take place "by August 25, 1981." Was there a contract between Benton and Shiver? Why or why not? *Benton v. Shiver*, 326 S.E.2d 756 (Georgia)

3. As part of a divorce settlement Reba Tarpley gave Bobby Tarpley a 13-month option to buy five parcels of real estate for $250,000. During the final month of the option period, Mrs. Tarpley asked Mr. Tarpley whether he intended to exercise the option. He answered in the affirmative. Later, in an argument, she said to him "the deal is off." Mr. Tarpley made no attempt to offer the money to her and gave her no formal notice that he was exercising the option. He argues that she breached the option agreement. Is he correct? Why or why not? *Pinney v. Tarpley*, 686 S.W.2d 574 (Tennessee)

4. Bishop and Hendrickson were law partners who practiced together for many years before forming a professional corporation. At some point during their association, they orally agreed that "in the event any of their children ever became lawyers and wanted to practice law with the firm, there would be a place for such child or children in the law firm." Hendrickson's daughter worked for the firm for approximately 1 year as a law clerk but not as a lawyer. For personal reasons, she left the firm. Bishop's daughter began working with the firm after she graduated from law school. She worked for approximately 1 month. When she inquired about getting paid, she was told she would not be hired by the firm. Did the conversation between Bishop and Hendrickson create an enforceable contract to employ Bishop's daughter? Explain. *Bishop v. Hendrickson*, 695 P.2d 1313 (Montana)

5. Stoddard had leased 208 acres of Riverdale Plantation for over 20 years on the basis of an oral contract that was renewed annually. When the owner of the plantation died, the executor of her estate required a written lease. The first written lease covered a term ending December 31, 1980. Another lease was executed which covered 1981. In the fall of 1981, Stoddard planted winter wheat, which was to mature in the spring of 1982. He had done the same thing in 1980 and had harvested the wheat in the spring of 1981. At the time of planting, Stoddard was unaware of the proposed sale of the property to Shannon. Shannon purchased the plantation in March 1982 and harvested the wheat planted by Stoddard. What legal theory might Stoddard use to recover the value of the wheat taken by Shannon? Explain. *Kistler v. Stoddard*, 688 S.W.2d 746 (Arkansas)

Chapter 7

CONSIDERATION

Scene: The kitchen of the Williams home. Denise is talking to Mrs. Williams.

Mrs. Williams (*taking a steaming dish out of the microwave oven*): I've decided not to take that new job that I was offered, even though it would pay $50 more a week.

Denise: But $50 a week is a lot of money.

Mrs. Williams: Yes, but there are 6 months remaining on my 1-year contract to work for Mr. Ellis, even though I don't like him very much.

Denise: Can't you get out of it?

Mrs. Williams: When I told Mr. Ellis about the new job offer, he said he'd pay me a $500 bonus at the end of the year if I'd stay on with him and finish out the year. I agreed to do it for the bonus.
(*Lorna enters the room.*)

Lorna: The mail's here, Mom.

Mrs. Williams: Probably just bills. Put it on the counter.

Lorna: Here's a letter for Doug from Aunt Martha. What do you suppose she's writing to him for—it's not his birthday.

Denise: Any mail for me?

Lorna: Here's a letter for you, Mom. It looks like it's from a charitable organization.

Mrs. Williams: You can open it.

Lorna (*opening and reading the letter*): They want you to sign a pledge card promising to pay $10 a month for a year.

Mrs. Williams: I've given to that charity before, but I've never been asked to sign a pledge card. I wonder what happens if someone signs a pledge card but doesn't pay?

Lorna: Here's another letter for you, Mom. It's from somebody named Marvin Maxwell. Isn't that the guy who stood you up last week?

Mrs. Williams (*surprised*): Marvin Maxwell? Let me have that letter! (*She takes the letter from Lorna's hand, tears open the envelope, and begins to read it.*)
(*Doug walks into the room.*)

Lorna: The mail came, Doug. You got a letter from Aunt Martha.

Doug: Really?

Denise: And Mom got a letter from that jerk Marvin, who stood her up last week.

Mrs. Williams: He writes a beautiful letter—so poetic. He asks my forgiveness for not picking me up that night. He was out of town on a business trip and couldn't get back. That's understandable.

Doug: He could have called you on the telephone.

Mrs. Williams: Oh, listen to this: "To make up for my indiscretion, I have a small gift for you—a diamond and sapphire ring. It's yours, the next time we meet."

Denise: I wouldn't trust that guy. He doesn't come through with his promises.

Doug: Keep the letter! You've got him this time! He put it in writing, and you can make him give you that diamond ring.

Lorna: Why did Aunt Martha write to you, Doug?

Doug: Mom must have told her about the A I got on my last test. She says, "I'm very proud of you. Because you received an A on your last business law test, I am going to send you $25 from my next dividend check."

Lorna: How lucky can you get!

Doug: And listen to this! "Furthermore, I will give you $25 for each A you receive in the future."

Denise: That's discrimination! I always get A's!

Mrs. Williams: Send her a thank-you note right away.

LEGAL ISSUES

1. When someone is already under a contractual duty to do something, is a promise to give additional money to do that same thing binding?
2. Is a pledge to a charitable organization binding?
3. Is a promise to make a gift binding on the promisor?
4. Is a promise to give a gift of money in exchange for a past performance binding?
5. Is a promise to give a gift of money in exchange for a future performance binding?

THE SPIRIT OF THE LAW

From very early times, the law has not enforced **gratuitous** (free) agreements. This is because agreements must be bargained for if they are to be binding on those who are parties to them. An agreement is **bargained for** when (1) a promise is made in exchange for another promise, or (2) a promise is made in exchange for an act, or (3) a promise is made in exchange for a forbearance to act. The idea here is that if in relying on another's promise someone gives up nothing, then he or she is not injured if the promise is not kept. The legal name for that which is given up is *consideration*.

CONSIDERA-TION

Consideration is the exchange of benefits and detriments by the parties to an agreement. A **benefit** is something that a party was not previously entitled to receive. A **detriment** is any of the following:

1. Giving up something (or promising to give up something) that one has a legal right to keep. An example of this is a promise to sell something.
2. Doing something (or promising to do something) that one has a legal right not to do. Promising to paint someone's house would be an example of this.
3. Refraining from doing something (or promising not to do something) that one has a legal right to do. This is called **forbearance.** Because one has a legal right to eat cake, promising not to eat cake as part of a diet for 6 months would be an example of forbearance.

EXAMPLE 1 Suppose that you agree to sell your tape deck to Carol Adams for $50. Adams agrees to buy it at that price. You have made a promise to sell. Adams has made a promise to buy. Each promise is consideration for the other.

Your benefit is the receipt of the $50. Your detriment is your promise to give up the tape deck. Adams' benefit is the receipt of the tape deck. Her detriment is her promise to give up the $50. This is the most common way that consideration occurs in contracts. It is found in the promises of the parties.

A common forbearance is a promise not to bring a lawsuit. This promise is adequate consideration to support a contract, so long as the promisor has legal grounds to prosecute. Unless there is consideration to support a promise, the courts will not enforce the promise, and the agreement cannot be called a contract.

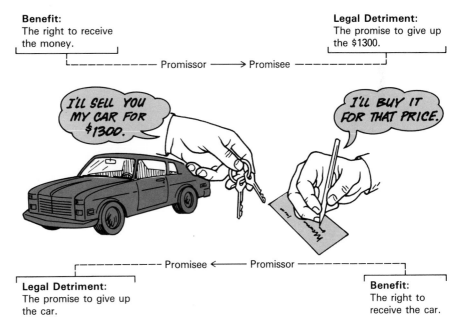

Benefit:
The right to receive the money.

Legal Detriment:
The promise to give up the $1300.

Promissor ⟶ Promisee

I'LL SELL YOU MY CAR FOR $1300.

I'LL BUY IT FOR THAT PRICE.

Promisee ⟵ Promissor

Legal Detriment:
The promise to give up the car.

Benefit:
The right to receive the car.

Consideration is an exchange of benefits and detriments by the parties to an agreement.

AGREEMENTS WITHOUT CONSIDERATION

Certain acts and promises do not provide consideration. These include promises to make a gift, to obey the law, or to fulfill another preexisting duty. In addition, past consideration and illusory promises are not consideration at all.

A Promise to Make a Gift

A gift is something given freely, for no consideration. Once given, a gift has the status of an executed contract, and the giver cannot force its return. However, the promise to make a gift is not enforceable and does not constitute a contract.

Legal Issue No. 3

EXAMPLE 2 Pete's favorite uncle, Steve, promises Pete a gift of $1,000 cash with no strings attached. His uncle tells him, "You are honorable. Your high school grades are excellent. You are also a great help to your parents at home. Next Tuesday I am going to give you $1,000 as a gift, because I like you. Is that acceptable to you?" Pete replies, "Yes!"

In this example there is no consideration for Steve's promise. This is because Pete gave nothing up (and promised nothing) and therefore suffered no detriment. Similarly, Steve received no benefit from the transaction. If Steve refuses to make the gift, Pete cannot sue him for breach of contract. If the gift were made, however, it would be Pete's property.

A Promise to Obey the Law

Since everyone is obligated to obey the law, a promise to do so is no detriment.

EXAMPLE 3 Suzanne Culman was arrested for smoking marijuana in a state in which the act is a criminal offense. Her wealthy Aunt Sylvia wrote to her, "If you will stop smoking marijuana for 1 year, I will give you $2,000." Culman did stop smoking marijuana for 1 year, but her aunt refused to give her the money.

Culman cannot enforce the agreement because it contained no valid consideration. Culman refrained from doing something that she had no legal right to do anyway; thus, she suffered no legal detriment.

Preexisting Duty

If a person is already under a legal duty to do something, a promise to do that same thing does not furnish consideration.

EXAMPLE 4 A city offered a reward to anyone who gave information that led to the conviction of the person who had been setting fires in the city. In addition, the city hired a night watchman to be on the lookout for anyone setting fires. The night watchman caught the person setting fires and sought the reward. The court held that he was not entitled to the reward because he was under a legal duty to do what he did and thus did not furnish consideration to the city for its promise to pay the reward.

Similarly, if someone is already under a contractual duty to do something, a promise to do that same thing does not furnish consideration.

EXAMPLE 5 Morgan entered into a contract to work for Davis for 1 year for $200 per week. After starting the job, Morgan was offered $250 per week by

Legal Issue No. 1

another company to do the same work. Morgan told Davis about the new offer, and Davis said to him, "Stay on with me and I'll give you a $1,200 bonus at the end of the year." Morgan finished the year, but Davis refused to give him the bonus as he had agreed. The court held that Morgan was not entitled to the bonus; he gave no consideration for it, since he was under a contractual duty to work for Davis for the entire year.

The parties can always end a contract by mutual consent. Thus, in the above example, Morgan and Davis could have terminated the old contract and formed a new one containing the new terms. In that case, Morgan could have enforced the promise for the $1,200 bonus.

Past Consideration

Legal Issue No. 4

The giving or exchange of benefits and detriments by the parties must take place when the contract is made. If consideration took place in the past or is given for something that has already been done, the courts will not regard the consideration as legal. The courts will not enforce any contract based on past consideration.

EXAMPLE 6 Suppose you had voluntarily helped out in your uncle's store for the past 2 years. Your uncle now promises to give you $500 for your work in the past. Months go by, but your uncle forgets about the promised award. You cannot enforce this promise. Your uncle's promise was the result of past performance on your part. No new consideration was given for his promise. In addition, you should note that your uncle has actually offered you a gift. A promise of a gift cannot be enforced by a court.

Illusory Promise

For a binding contract to be formed, both parties must be under a binding obligation to do something; otherwise, neither is bound to do anything. Some contracts are **illusory.** They appear at first glance to bind both parties, but upon further examination it is clear that they do not.

EXAMPLE 7 Isadore Karras agreed to sell, and Lorraine Patti agreed to buy at a stated price per bushel, all the potatoes that Patti might order within the next 2 months. Because Patti might not order any potatoes within the next 2 months, she is not bound to do anything. The contract is illusory. Karras will not be required to sell potatoes to Patti if he decides not to do so.

ADEQUACY OF CONSIDERA-TION

Generally, the court does not look into the adequacy of the consideration—that is, it does not look to see whether or not the value of the consideration was fair to both parties. It lets the parties make their own agreement, and it usually enforces that agreement.

EXAMPLE 8 Suppose that Lynne Turner sees a statuette marked $500 in an antique shop. She offers the proprietor $400 for the statuette, and the proprietor accepts. Later, Turner discovers that the figure is a cheap import worth not more than $10. She argues that there was no consideration for her promise.

Turner will have to pay the $400 that she agreed to pay. The court will not consider the inadequacy of the consideration. If, instead, the store proprietor had falsely represented to Turner that the statuette was a genuine antique and very valuable, the inadequacy of the consideration could be used along with other evidence to show fraud on the proprietor's part. The contract would then be set aside on the grounds of fraud.

An exception occurs when the inadequacy of the consideration is so great that it shocks the conscience of the court. However, the court's conscience is seldom shocked. A court may refuse to enforce a contract or any clause of it that it considers to be **unconscionable;** that is, where the consideration is ridiculously inadequate. This usually occurs in situations in which there is a vast difference in bargaining power. If a court as a matter of law finds a contract or any clause of a contract to have been unconscionable at the time it was made, (1) the court may refuse to enforce the contract, or (2) it may enforce the contract minus the unconscionable clause, or (3) it may so limit the application of any unconscionable clause so as to avoid any unconscionable result.

EXAMPLE 9 Mrs. O'Grady, an 85-year-old widow, lived alone in a small bungalow. A fast-talking door-to-door salesperson talked her into signing a contract to have vinyl siding put on her house for $40,000. A fair price for the job would have been about $4,000. Because of the difference in bargaining power of the parties and the exceptionally unfair price, it is unlikely that a court would enforce this contract.

When it is claimed or appears to the court that a contract may be unconscionable, the parties are given a reasonable opportunity to present evidence concerning the commercial setting, purpose, and effect of the contract in order to aid the court in making a decision. In examining the commercial setting, the court will look at the needs and practices of a particular trade or business to determine what is or is not accepted practice. What may seem unfair and unconscionable in one trade may be considered fair and reasonable in another.

SPECIAL APPLICA-TIONS OF CONSIDER-ATION
Partial Payment of a Debt

Each promise made as consideration for another promise must create a new obligation. If you promise to do something you are already legally bound to do, your promise does not create a new obligation and is not regarded as valid consideration.

EXAMPLE 10 Roger Bolton owes Guy Racine $300. Bolton admits that the money is owed and that payment is overdue. Racine is pressuring Bolton for payment and states, "If you will pay me $200, I will cancel the $300 debt." Bolton agrees and pays the $200, relying on Racine's promise. The following day Racine sues Bolton for the remaining $100.

■ Bolton will have to pay the $100. Racine's promise to forgive the balance is not binding on him because there was no consideration for it. Bolton paid the

■ This symbol indicates that there may be a state statute that varies from the law discussed here. Whenever you see this symbol, find out, if possible, what the statute in your state says about this point or principle of law.

$200, relying on Racine's promise. But Bolton already owed the $300; he was promising to do something that he was already legally bound to do. If Racine's release had been in writing and signed by Racine, it would have been binding in some states. Other states would require a seal in addition to the writing to make it binding.

EXAMPLE 11 Suppose, in Example 10, that the $300 owed by Bolton was not due for another month. Suppose also that Racine said to Bolton, "If you will pay me $200 today, I will cancel the $300 debt." Bolton agrees and pays the $200. Racine cannot sue for the balance because Bolton paid the debt before it was due. This provided consideration for Racine's promise to cancel the debt.

Settlement of Disputed Claims

Suppose that there is an honest difference of opinion as to how much is owed.

EXAMPLE 12 Clarence Judd claims that Terry Dees owes him $100 for typing services, but Dees maintains that she owes only $50. Judd thinks that the typing services were worth $100. Dees thinks that they were worth only $50. If Dees compromises on $75, each has given up something and the agreement is binding.

Parties often compromise on the amount owed, particularly in contracts for services. When you visit a doctor or take your car to a garage for repairs, unless a price is agreed on before the work is done, you are implying that you promise to pay the reasonable value of the services. The bill you receive for the services may be more than this. People sometimes handle this situation by sending a check for what they consider to be a reasonable amount. They write on the check the words "In full payment of the amount I owe you." If the amount has been agreed upon or is not in dispute, in most states the balance can be recovered even if the check is cashed. If the amount is in dispute or not agreed upon, however, the cashing of the check is treated as the acceptance of the smaller amount, and the balance cannot be recovered.

Extension of Time for Payment

EXAMPLE 13 Assume that Terry Dees owes an agreed amount of $100. Assume also that it is now due and payable but that Dees does not have the money. Clarence Judd promises to extend the time of payment 30 days if Dees will agree to pay at that time. Dees gives her promise, but the next day Judd sues her anyway.

Judd is not bound by his promise to extend the time of payment. Dees promised nothing new, and thus there is no consideration for the promised extension. ■ Some states have changed this rule by statute.

PROMISES ENFORCE-ABLE WITHOUT CONSIDER-ATION

Some promises are enforceable without consideration. In certain circumstances the courts find that a promise influences the behavior of other people. If such promises were not enforced, those relying on them may suffer damages. These special cases include pledges and subscriptions to charities, and promissory estoppel. In some states consideration is assumed in contracts in writing or under seal. Furthermore, the Uniform Commercial Code (UCC) does not require consideration for certain contracts to sell goods.

Pledges and Subscriptions

Legal Issue No. 2

■ Citizens and business firms are often asked to sign pledges to support community projects. Because these community projects are generally charitable and, therefore, work in the public interest, the courts usually try to find some way to enforce these pledges or subscriptions, even though, technically, they are promises to make a gift and are not based on formal consideration. Not all courts look at consideration for these pledges or subscriptions in the same way. Some courts hold that the promises of other persons who have subscribed to the same fund amount to consideration. Other courts hold that if the charitable institution had made commitments to spend the money as a result of relying on such subscriptions, the subscriptions are enforceable. Still other courts hold that there is an implied promise on the part of the institution to use the funds in the manner designated and that this promise amounts to consideration.

EXAMPLE 14 Arcadia College held a fund drive to raise $500,000 for the construction of an addition to its library. Gary Disanto, an alumnus of the college, signed a pledge card, promising to donate $1,000 per year for 3 years to the building fund. The construction was completed 1 year after he signed the pledge card. Under the laws of that state, the construction work that was completed in reliance on Disanto's pledge formed the consideration, making his pledge binding and enforceable.

Promissory Estoppel

Legal Issue No. 5

Under the doctrine of **promissory estoppel,** a promise may be enforceable without consideration. Certain conditions must be met, however, before a court will apply this principle: (1) The promise must be made in order to induce an action or a forbearance by another person, (2) the other person must have relied upon that promise and acted (or refrained from acting) in accordance with the promise, and (3) injustice can be avoided only by enforcing the promise. Under these circumstances, a court may hold that the promise must be fulfilled.

EXAMPLE 15 Hosuk Chai, knowing that his niece, Jill Chai, wishes to go to college, promises to give her $10,000. With the aid of student loans, and at a cost of more than $10,000, she goes to college and graduates. Hosuk then notifies his niece that he has changed his mind about the $10,000 gift. Hosuk's promise is binding, and Jill is entitled to the payment under the doctrine of promissory estoppel.

Significance of the Seal

At common law, a seal took the place of consideration. If the parties entered into an agreement, put the agreement in writing, and placed a seal on the paper, no further proof of consideration was necessary.

Historically, contracts under seal were used when most people could not read or write. In order to show that they agreed to contracts which they dictated to someone else, they would melt wax on the paper and press their own private seal into the wax.

Charitable institutions rely on pledges or promises of gifts. For instance, relying on pledges, a hospital may contract with a builder to construct a new facility. Is a promise to make a gift enforceable in this situation?

The original need for contracts formalized by a seal has long since passed. However, some states still use the seal and follow the common-law rule which held that the seal took the place of consideration. Other states take the position that a seal gives a contract the presumption of consideration unless the contrary can be proved. Still other states no longer recognize the seal.

■ In those states where the seal is still used, it is no longer necessary to melt wax and to press into it a signet ring or other private seal. It is enough if the person signing the contract attaches a special red paper wafer, or simply writes the word *Seal* after his or her signature, or even simply the letters *L.S.* The letters *L.S.* stand for **locus sigilli,** meaning "the place of the seal."

EXAMPLE 16 Roberto Fuentes requested payment from Ruth Hyde upon the following written statement: "I promise to pay Roberto Fuentes $700 on demand." This statement was signed "Ruth Hyde (Seal)."

In a state where the seal is recognized, Fuentes could enforce his claim for $700 whether or not he gave consideration to Hughes. In a state where a sealed instrument carries the presumption of consideration, however, Hyde would not have to pay the $700 if she could prove that no consideration was actually given by Fuentes.

In addition to this use, the seal is sometimes used to indicate genuineness or authority. Such seals are the seal of a corporation, the seal of a public official, or a seal attached by a **notary public** (an official who certifies that the person signing an instrument is the person he or she is supposed to be). These seals indicating genuineness or authority should not be confused with the private seals we have been discussing that are used to create a contract under seal.

The Uniform Commercial Code

Contracts for the sale of goods are governed by the UCC in all states. Since this particular law does not recognize the seal, it has a few special rules under which no consideration is required.

Firm Offer A merchant's written promise to hold open an offer for the sale of goods needs no consideration to be binding. As discussed in Chapter 6, this is known as a firm offer. Such an offer will be revokable during the time stated in the offer, or a reasonable time if none is stated, but in no event longer than 3 months.

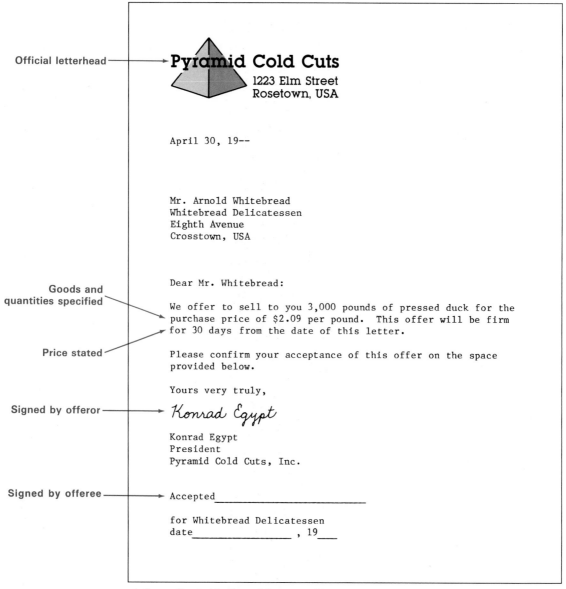

Official letterhead

Pyramid Cold Cuts
1223 Elm Street
Rosetown, USA

April 30, 19--

Mr. Arnold Whitebread
Whitebread Delicatessen
Eighth Avenue
Crosstown, USA

Dear Mr. Whitebread:

Goods and quantities specified

We offer to sell to you 3,000 pounds of pressed duck for the purchase price of $2.09 per pound. This offer will be firm for 30 days from the date of this letter.

Price stated

Please confirm your acceptance of this offer on the space provided below.

Yours very truly,

Signed by offeror

Konrad Egypt

Konrad Egypt
President
Pyramid Cold Cuts, Inc.

Signed by offeree

Accepted_____

for Whitebread Delicatessen
date_____ , 19___

A firm offer is binding without consideration. Mr. Whitebread has the right to buy 3,000 pounds of pressed duck for $2.09 per pound until May 30.

Modification of a Contract An agreement by the parties to modify (change) a contract for the sale of goods needs no consideration to be binding.

EXAMPLE 17 If the contract in Example 5 (page 102) were for goods rather than employment, the change in the contract would have been binding on Davis, even though Morgan gave no consideration for it.

Contracts in Writing

A few states have passed laws providing that contracts in writing need no consideration to be binding. Some states call this law the "written obligation act."

EXAMPLE 18 A Kansas statute (16-107) provides: "All contracts in writing, signed by the party bound thereby, or his authorized agent or attorney, shall import a consideration." In interpreting this law, the Kansas court has held that if a contract is written, the existence of consideration is presumed unless it is alleged and proved that there actually was none.

CONSIDERA-TION IN YOUR EVERYDAY LIFE

The following principles pertain to consideration in everyday situations:

1. To amount to consideration, the act done or promised must be legal and not involve any violation of the law.
2. If a person pays a debt in advance, it is something he or she is not legally bound to do, and this would amount to consideration for settling the debt for a lesser amount.
3. If a person has made a gift in the past, has performed services in the past as a gift, or has been paid for past services, he or she may not use these past performances as consideration for a new promise.
4. To constitute consideration, an act or a promise must be bargained for.

Suggestions for Reducing Legal Risks

1. Carefully analyze all your contractual obligations to decide whether or not the requirement of valid consideration is present.
2. Get legal advice on important agreements when you are in doubt about the nature or validity of the consideration.
3. If you are promised a gift, do not rely on getting it unless you promise something or do something that can be interpreted as a new obligation on your part.
4. ■ Obtain a statement in writing, signed by the promisor, and under seal in some states, in case (1) a promise to pay extra compensation is given, or (2) an agreement is reached on settling a disputed claim for less than the full amount.
5. ■ Obtain a written statement, signed by the creditor, and under seal in some states, in case (1) you agree to settle a past-due debt for less than the full amount, or (2) you are promised additional time in which to pay an existing debt and you do not provide additional consideration.

Language of the Law

Define or explain each of the following words or phrases:

gratuitous   benefit   gift   promissory estoppel
bargained for   detriment   illusory   locus sigilli
consideration   forbearance   unconscionable   notary public

Questions for Review

1. What are the most common forms of consideration?
2. Give an example of an agreement that is not enforceable because of a lack of consideration.
3. Why is the promise of a gift not enforceable? What is the legal status of a gift that has already been given? Can one be forced to return a gift?
4. Ordinarily, are the courts sufficiently interested in the value of the consideration to determine if it is equal in value to the promise? Under what circumstances may a court refuse to enforce a contract on the grounds of inadequacy of consideration?
5. Under what conditions may a debt be discharged by paying an amount less than the original debt?
6. How may one bind an agreement to extend the time payment of a debt? Explain.
7. On what grounds are pledges usually held to be enforceable promises?
8. Name three things that must occur before the doctrine of promissory estoppel can be used.
9. Describe the three positions that various states have taken regarding the legal effect of a seal.
10. Describe two special rules in the UCC under which no consideration is required.

Cases in Point

In each of the following cases, give your decision and state a legal principle that applies to the case:

1. John Corning promised to give his daughter a watch as a birthday present. Was this a legally enforceable promise?
2. Lisa Waring received a ticket for violating the speed limit. Her older brother who lived in another state learned of this and wrote, ''If you don't violate the speed limit for 1 year, I will give you $100.'' Waring did not violate the speed limit for 1 year. Is her brother's promise binding?
3. Hunter Johnston became annoyed at his neighbor, Joe Washington, and offered a hoodlum $1,000 to wreck Washington's car. The hoodlum wrecked the car, as agreed, but Johnston refused to pay. Can the hoodlum collect the $1,000 through legal proceedings?
4. Stephanie Strong claimed that Donna Perkins owed her $500, but Perkins claimed that the debt was only $300. Finally, Strong agreed to accept $400 in full settlement. After Perkins had paid the $400, Strong demanded the $100 balance. Was Strong legally entitled to the balance?

5. Lana Bertolli accepted $100 from James Arkin in full settlement of a past-due note of $150 and turned over a signed release (under seal) of the entire debt. Is the debt entirely canceled? Would your answer be different if there were no signed release under seal?

6. Horace Kushner, who had been injured by Vic Ling's automobile, agreed not to sue Ling if Ling would promise to pay $1,000. Ling promised. Was Kushner legally bound to the promise?

7. Tammy Carson's car ran out of gas. Ned Grover, driving by, saw Carson's problem and offered to tow her to the next filling station. Carson accepted the offer. After they reached the filling station, Carson said she would send Grover a check for $25 for his kindness. Is she legally bound to do so?

8. Lisa Lowe left her car at the Browning Garage for a motor tune-up and agreed to pay $75 for the job. Before the job was completed, Lowe said to the proprietor, "I'll pay you $10 extra if you do a good job." Is Lowe bound to her promise?

9. Mina Pratt promised her son $5,000 if he would enter and complete medical school. The son completed the course. Was he legally entitled to the $5,000?

10. Carmen Sanchez's debt to Bernie Martin was due on June 1, 1986. Martin signed a written promise on May 20, 1986, to give Sanchez an additional 2 months to pay the debt. Was this promise binding?

Cases to Judge

1. Thomas and Gary Edlin orally agreed in April to pay Brett Marshall $20 per acre to harvest their 450-acre crop the following October. Marshall agreed to do so with his combine. In October, however, the Edlins rented a combine and did their own harvesting. When sued for breach of contract, the Edlins argued that there was no consideration in the agreement. Do you agree? Why or why not? *Marshall v. Edlin*, 690 S.W.2d 477 (Missouri)

2. Siegel owed Codner $31,000. Although there was no dispute over the amount owed, Codner agreed in writing to accept $18,000 in full payment of $31,000. Is Codner's agreement binding? Why or why not? *Codner v. Siegel*, 271 S.E.2d 465 (Georgia)

3. Al Seier gave Freddie Peek a written promise to pay $10,000 in exchange for all the outstanding stock of a corporation. Seier failed to pay. He argued that the consideration given to him for the promise was inadequate because the stock was worthless. Will the court determine whether or not the consideration was adequate? Explain. *Seier v. Peek*, 456 So. 2d 1079 (Alabama)

4. Mary Gertrude Schloss was left $1 in her aunt's will. Schloss's sister, Suzanne McGinness was left a sizeable inheritance. Mary met with Suzanne and, although she had no legal grounds to do so, threatened to bring a court action to set aside the will. Suzanne agreed to share one-fourth of her inheritance in return for Mary's promise not to contest the will. Was there consideration in the agreement? Explain. *Schloss v. McGinness*, 474 N.E.2d 666 (Ohio)

5. Mack Trucks, Inc., left one of its trucks with Pitts Truck Air, Inc., to have an air-conditioning unit installed. The parties signed a contract requiring Pitts Truck Air to provide insurance coverage on the truck. The truck was stolen while in the possession of Pitts Truck Air, and Pitts Truck Air had failed to obtain insurance. Mack Trucks agreed not to bring suit against Pitts Truck Air for the loss of its truck in exchange for Pitts Truck Air's signing an agreement to pay for the value of the truck. Did this agreement contain consideration? Why or why not? *Pitts Truck Air, Inc. v. Mack Trucks, Inc.*, 328 S.E.2d 416 (Georgia)

Chapter 8

THE CAPACITY OF MINORS & OTHERS TO CONTRACT

Scene: Denise and her friend Kim are walking through a shopping mall.

Denise: My brother, Doug, got in trouble last weekend.

Kim: Really? What happened?

Denise: He filled out a card saying that he was 21 when he tried to buy a 6-pack of beer. He's only 19, you know.

Kim: That's no big deal—lying about your age to buy beer.

Denise: That's what you think! They reported him to the police, and he's got to go to court.

Kim: I didn't think it was that serious.

Denise: Neither did I until it happened to Doug, and the police told him that it's a crime.

Kim: Let's go into this store.
(*The girls enter a store; 20 minutes later they emerge with packages.*)

Kim: That sweater you bought is beautiful.

Denise: Thanks. I know that your mother will love the crystal set you bought her.

Kim: I hope so. It took all my savings, but I wanted to get her something nice for her birthday.

Denise: Speaking of birthdays, mine's next week. I'll be 18.

Kim: I'll be 18 next month . . . oops! (*Kim accidentally drops the package she is carrying, and the sound of broken glass echoes through the mall.*)

Denise: My gosh! Your mother's new crystal set!

Kim: It's ruined! (*Tears come to her eyes.*) It's completely smashed— my whole savings—I don't know what happened. It just fell out of my hand.

Denise: Calm down. Don't get upset. There must be something we can do. Maybe you can get your money back from the store.
(*In the Williams home, a week later, Mrs. Williams is talking with Lorna.*)

Mrs. Williams: Want to see what I got for Denise's birthday? I hope she likes it, because it can't be returned—all sales were final. (*She opens a small jewelry case and shows it to Lorna.*)

Lorna: Oh, a pearl necklace and bracelet! She'll love them! I don't know what to get her. I was going to get her a sweater, but she bought herself one last week. (*They hear the sound of the front door opening.*) That's probably her now.

Denise (*entering the room wearing the sweater she bought a week ago*): Hi.

Mrs. Williams: What have you been up to?

Denise: I've been shopping. Look what I bought—it's something I've always wanted. (*She holds open a small jewelry case identical to the one that Mrs. Williams showed to Lorna a moment ago.*)

Mrs. Williams: On the day before your birthday?

Lorna: Would you believe . . . Mom bought the same pearl necklace and bracelet for your birthday present.

Denise: You did? Oh, I'm sorry. I didn't know. . . .

Mrs. Williams: Why don't you return it right now and get your money back from the store.

Denise: I can't. The sales clerk told me that all sales were final, and there was a sign that said "no returns."

Mrs. Williams: Yes, but I think that that doesn't apply to minors. Your birthday isn't until tomorrow.

Lorna: Say, while you're doing it, why don't you take back that sweater you have on—you bought that when you were a minor—then I can get you a sweater for your birthday.

LEGAL ISSUES

1. Is it a criminal offense for a minor to lie about his or her age to buy alcohol?
2. Can minors get their money back even though the items that they purchased have been damaged or totally destroyed?
3. When does a person legally become an adult?
4. When and in what way may minors ratify their contracts?

THE SPIRIT OF THE LAW

As we read in Chapter 7, the exchange of benefits and detriments, known as consideration, binds people to their contracts. But do all people have the **capacity**—the legal ability to consent—to contract? Years ago, under English common law, **infants** (here meaning *minors*, persons under 21), insane persons, and intoxicated persons were given only limited capacity to contract. Married women were not allowed to enter into contracts because the law treated a husband and wife as one person and gave only the husband the right to contract for both of them.

Today's laws have done away with such discrimination and have given married women the same rights to enter into contracts as others have. The law has remained generally the same, however, with regard to protecting minors, insane persons, and intoxicated persons from mistakes they may make. For well over 700 years, the law has shielded such persons by giving them the right to get out of their contracts if they choose to do so. People who contract with minors, insane persons, or intoxicated persons do so at their own risk. (There are some exceptions to this rule. These are discussed later in this chapter.)

CONTRACTS OF MINORS

Legal Issue No. 3

■ The age at which minors reach legal maturity, usually called **majority** in legal language, is fixed by statute in each state. For hundreds of years the age of majority was fixed at 21 years. However, since 1972, when the voting age in the United States was lowered to 18 years, most states have lowered the age of majority to that age.

In most states, you become legally 18 years old at the beginning of the day before that birthday. This is because the day you were born is counted as the first day of your life. The law does not consider fractions of a day. Thus, on your eighteenth birthday, you are 18 years and 1 day old.

Voidable Contracts of Minors

Contracts of minors are voidable. This means that minors may disaffirm or **avoid** (not be bound by) their contracts if they choose. A long time ago, a famous judge made the statement, ''Infancy is a shield, not a sword.'' The law does not intend to give the minor the right to take advantage of other persons wrongfully. To protect the minor fully, however, the right to disaffirm is an almost absolute right. To **disaffirm** a contract means to show by a statement or by some act an intent not to live up to the contract. Thus there are times when a minor may legally take unfair advantage of an adult.

EXAMPLE 1   On his seventeenth birthday, Clinton Washington received $100 as a gift from his uncle. Washington was in a buying mood. The first thing he saw was a movie camera. It was a $250 camera on sale for 1 day only at $99.95. After he got it home, he realized that it was of no use unless he had film. Furthermore, he would also need a projector to enjoy his purchase. He found he could not buy these items because he had no more money.

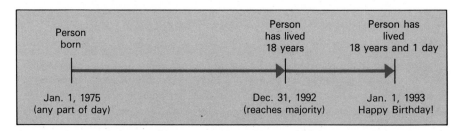

Teenagers become **18 years old at the beginning of the day** *before* **their eighteenth birthday, because the law does not count fractions of a day in calculating age.**

Washington, acting in haste, had made a poor investment. Because he was 17 years old, he could return the camera, disaffirm his contract, and ask for the return of his money. He would have to do this before reaching majority or within a reasonable time afterwards. The law gives young people a second chance when they have used poor judgment. Until they have reached a mature age, they may avoid their contracts. This is true even if the item is damaged or destroyed. In a few states, an amount can be deducted for damaged or soiled items that are returned by the minor.

Legal Issue No. 2

Returning Consideration ■

If minors still have whatever they received upon entering into a contract (the consideration), they must return it when they disaffirm the contract. This requirement can be complied with not only by an actual return of the consideration but also by a *tender* or offer to return it. If minors do not have the consideration, they may still disaffirm the contract, in most states, and get back the full amount they paid for the item.

Misrepresenting Age ■

If minors lie about their ages and say they are over the age of majority, it is a misrepresentation known as *fraud*. Fraud is a wrongful act, and minors are legally responsible for their own wrongful acts. Thus, in some states, when a minor lies about his or her age and then disaffirms a

Legal Issue No. 1

resulting contract, the other party can sue the minor for fraud. Other states follow the older law that does not allow minors to be sued for fraud when they disaffirm contracts, even though they may have lied about their ages. This is done on the theory that it would ''cut a tunnel under the shield of infancy'' if we allowed minors to be sued for fraud when they disaffirm contracts.

It is a criminal offense in most states to lie about one's age to buy alcohol.

```
.............., 19. .
    I, ....................., hereby represent to ....................,
a permittee of the Connecticut Department of Liquor Control, that I am over the age
of 21 years OR HAVE ATTAINED THE AGE OF TWENTY ON OR BEFORE SEPTEMBER 1, 1985,
having been born on ................. , 19..., at ....................
This statement is made to induce said permittee to sell or otherwise furnish
alcoholic beverages to the undersigned. I UNDERSTAND THAT TITLE 30 OF THE GENERAL
STATUTES PROHIBITS THE SALE OF ALCOHOLIC LIQUOR TO ANY PERSON WHO IS NOT TWENTY-ONE
YEARS OF AGE OR WHO HAS NOT ATTAINED THE AGE OF TWENTY ON OR BEFORE SEPTEMBER 1, 1985.
    I understand that I am subject to a fine of one hundred dollars for the first
offense and not more than two hundred fifty dollars for each subsequent offense for
willfully misrepresenting my age for the purposes set forth in this statement.
.................... (Name)
.................... (Address)
```

In Connecticut, people whose ages are in question must fill out a form like this before buying alcohol.

EXAMPLE 2 The New York Alcoholic Beverage Control Law provides for arrest, probation, and a fine of up to $100 for misrepresenting one's age to buy alcohol. This includes the giving of any written evidence of age which is false, fraudulent, or not the person's own.

Disaffirming the Whole Contract A minor may not affirm parts of a contract that are favorable and disaffirm the unfavorable parts. He or she must disaffirm all or none. A minor may, however, disaffirm one (or both) of two separate contracts.

EXAMPLE 3 José Orio contracted to purchase a fishing boat and an outboard motor for $650. Later, Orio decided that he would like to keep the outboard motor but not the fishing boat.

Orio cannot keep the motor and disaffirm the contract to buy the boat. If he had entered into two contracts—one to buy the boat for $550 and another to buy the motor for $100—he could disaffirm one and affirm the other.

Ratification of Minors' Contracts

After reaching adulthood (majority), persons may **ratify,** or approve, contracts made during childhood (minority) if they choose to do so. Ratification ends the privileges that the person enjoyed as a legal "child." Ratification can only be done upon reaching majority, and may be accomplished orally, or in writing, or by one's actions. Using the items purchased after reaching majority, selling the items after reaching majority, or keeping the items beyond a reasonable time after reaching majority all have the effect of ratifying a contract.

Legal Issue No. 4

EXAMPLE 4 Colleen Gregory, who was 17 years of age, bought a car. She made a down payment and promised to pay a certain amount each month for 18 months. After she reached 18, she continued to make payments for 2 months.

Gregory's act of making payments after reaching her majority was a ratification. She could no longer return the car and demand the return of her money. Even if she made no payments, she would be bound if she kept the car an unreasonable length of time after reaching majority without paying anything. "Reasonable time" has no exact definition. It varies with circumstances and is determined by a judge or jury. A reasonable time for a person to return a perishable item, for example, would be less than a reasonable time for returning an automobile or stereo set.

Minors' Contracts for Necessities

A minor is held responsible for the fair value of necessities. **Necessities,** sometimes called *necessaries,* include food, clothing, shelter, and medical care. Under common law, one's "station in life" has a bearing on determining whether or not an item is a necessity. A $125 pair of shoes, for example, might be considered a necessity for someone who is used to wearing designer clothing. In contrast, the same pair of shoes could well be considered a luxury and not a necessity for someone used to buying less expensive clothing. If a minor pays more than the fair value, he or she is entitled to the difference between the fair value and the price paid.

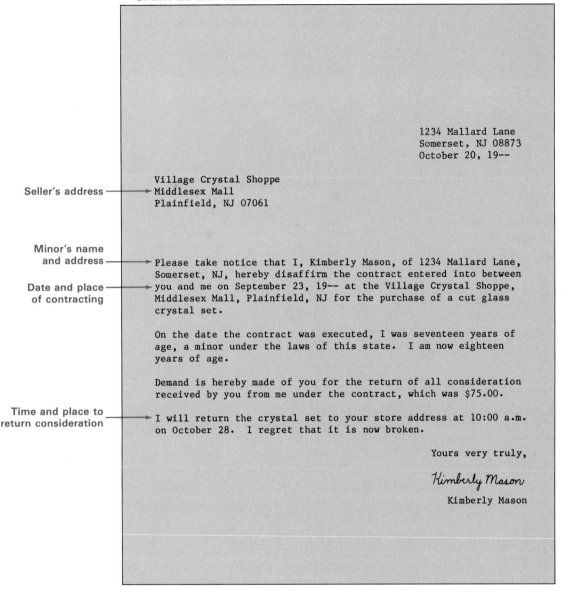

1234 Mallard Lane
Somerset, NJ 08873
October 20, 19--

Seller's address → Village Crystal Shoppe
Middlesex Mall
Plainfield, NJ 07061

Minor's name and address → Please take notice that I, Kimberly Mason, of 1234 Mallard Lane, Somerset, NJ, hereby disaffirm the contract entered into between

Date and place of contracting → you and me on September 23, 19-- at the Village Crystal Shoppe, Middlesex Mall, Plainfield, NJ for the purchase of a cut glass crystal set.

On the date the contract was executed, I was seventeen years of age, a minor under the laws of this state. I am now eighteen years of age.

Demand is hereby made of you for the return of all consideration received by you from me under the contract, which was $75.00.

Time and place to return consideration → I will return the crystal set to your store address at 10:00 a.m. on October 28. I regret that it is now broken.

Yours very truly,

Kimberly Mason

Kimberly Mason

Does the destruction of the consideration prevent a minor from disaffirming a contract?

EXAMPLE 5 Washington, in Example 1, might have spent his money more wisely. Suppose that, instead of a camera, he had bought a warm coat, a sweater, a cap, and a pair of overshoes. If these were things he actually needed, Washington would be bound to keep them and pay the fair value for them.

You will note, however, that Washington must actually need this clothing. In addition, it must be shown that he was not being adequately provided for by his parents or guardian. If he already had plenty of winter clothing or if his parents were willing and able to supply his needs, then the items would not be necessities and he could disaffirm his contract for them in the regular way.

Special Statutory Rules

■ Many states have made statutory changes in the capacity of minors to enter into contracts. For example, many states have given minors the capacity to enter into contracts for automobile insurance and life insurance. Some states give limited capacity to minors who are engaged in business in their own names to make contracts essential for the conduct of the business. Others treat minors who are married as adults. Still others consider the rental of an apartment by a minor as a necessity regardless of whether the minor needs it. These are but a few of the statutory changes—there are many, many more. Minors should consult the statutes of their own state to determine any special contractual capacities of their home state.

Note that the contracts of minors are only voidable, not void. When one of the parties to a contract is a minor, that person is the only one who can avoid the contract. If the minor chooses to enforce the contract, he or she may do so. Usually, such contracts are carried out by both parties, and it makes little difference that the contracts are voidable. It is only when the minor chooses to be released from his or her promise that the contract terminates.

The protection afforded minors also limits their rights. In effect, the law warns adults against contracting with minors, except for necessities. Consequently, minors may be asked to have their parents make major purchases for them or guarantee their contracts.

CONTRACTS OF MENTALLY ILL PERSONS

The same right given to minors to disaffirm contracts is also given to the mentally ill for the same reason. They are considered unable to make sound judgments. Before a guardian is appointed, a mentally ill person's contracts are voidable. Like a minor, he or she is responsible for the fair value of necessities. If a mentally ill person has been declared insane by a court action and a guardian is appointed to look after his or her affairs, the mentally ill person's contracts are void, not just voidable.

CONTRACTS OF INTOXI-CATED AND CERTAIN OTHER PERSONS

Persons who were intoxicated at the time they made contracts are sometimes able to disaffirm those contracts. Their contracts are treated in much the same way as contracts of minors and the mentally ill. Intoxication may be from alcohol or from drugs. To disaffirm a contract for this reason, a person must have been so intoxicated at the time of contracting that he or she did not understand the nature of the transaction. The judge or jury must decide that question. Intoxicated persons, like minors and people who are mentally ill, are responsible for the fair value of necessities.

Other classes of persons lack capacity to enter into certain types of contracts. In time of war, those foreign-born persons who are designated enemy aliens are denied certain legal capacity, and even in time of peace some states prevent aliens from entering into certain types of contracts by law. Convicts also have certain limitations put on their contracting powers in a few states.

Suggestions for Reducing Legal Risks

Minors:

1. Just before becoming of legal age, make an inventory of all your contractual obligations—those for purchases or sales, services, money payments, or important agreements of any kind. Decide just what you should do about each contractual obligation before you reach legal age. Decide whether you should affirm or disaffirm each agreement.
2. Follow the legal procedure for disaffirmance approved by the laws of your state. Before, or within a reasonable time after, reaching the age of majority, disaffirm those contracts you do not wish to be bound by.
3. If you decide to disaffirm a contract, be sure that you do not do anything after reaching majority that would ratify the contract.
4. If the obligation is important or extensive, obtain legal counsel regarding the manner of the disaffirmance so that you can be certain that the obligation has been discharged.

Adults:

1. Do not rely on a person's appearance when judging age or competency. Verify that the other party to a contract is of legal age, is not insane, and does not have other possible incompetencies.
2. When dealing with a minor, if the contract is for something other than the fair value of necessities, insist that one of the parents or a guardian sign the agreement.
3. Become familiar with the special statutes of your state, especially those that permit minors to enter into certain types of legal contracts before the age of majority.
4. If there is a question as to the possible interpretation of necessities for a minor in a particular station in life, ask for legal counsel before concluding a sales agreement with the minor. It is sometimes difficult to determine just what a necessity is for a particular person.

Language of the Law

Define or explain each of the following words or phrases:

capacity	majority	disaffirm	necessities
infant	avoid	ratify	

Questions for Review

1. Who is considered to be a minor?
2. Technically, when does a person become 18 years old?
3. May a minor avoid a contract even if he or she is unable to return the consideration or property received?

4. What risks do adults run if they contract with minors?
5. How can an adult reduce the risk involved when contracting with a minor?
6. Name several things for which a minor might contract and be held liable.
7. Name several items that a minor might buy for which he or she could *not* be held liable.
8. Why may minors avoid contracts, even though they have misrepresented their age?
9. Why does the law give special rights to minors?
10. What classes of persons, in addition to minors, have the same special rights?
11. List two special statutory rules that sometimes apply to contracts of minors.
12. May a minor affirm part and disaffirm part of the same contract? Explain.
13. Give an example of the ratification of a contract.
14. What is the legal difference between a contract made with a mentally ill person and one who has been declared insane by the court?
15. What is the possible legal effect of a contract made with an enemy alien? an alien in peacetime? an intoxicated person? a convict?

Cases in Point

In each of the following cases, give your decision and state a legal principle that applies to the case:

1. Tom Molinero, who was 17 years old, bought a car from Clyde Tait for $1,500. Three months later, while still a minor, Molinero was involved in an accident and damaged the car beyond repair. He sought the return of the $1,500 from Tait. Is he entitled to it?
2. Anna Long, who was 16 years old, bought an electronic typewriter for $485 from a department store. A 90-day manufacturer's limited warranty came with the typewriter. The typewriter stopped working 4 months later. A clerk at the store where she purchased the typewriter told Long that her only recourse would be to mail it to the factory and pay to have it repaired. Can you suggest another remedy that is available to Long?
3. On the day before his eighteenth birthday, David Loo bought a watch at a department store. A sign in front of the watches read, "Closeout Special! $165. All Sales Final. No Returns." The next day, David attempted to return the watch, arguing that he was a minor when he bought it. Is he entitled to the refund of his money?
4. Cesar Diaz, 17 years of age, bought a television set for $500 and told the dealer he was 19 years of age. Two months after the purchase, he returned the television set and demanded the return of his money. The merchant refused to comply with Diaz's demands. Can Diaz avoid the contract?
5. While on a fishing trip, Carol Larkin, a minor, broke her arm. She went to a doctor for treatment. Claiming infancy as a defense, she refused to pay the doctor. Was Larkin legally bound to pay?
6. Leah Carr, while a minor, bought a radio for $75. The day after her eighteenth birthday, she tried to return it, claiming that it did not satisfy her needs. Can Carr force the seller to accept the radio and return the purchase price to her?
7. Winston Perelmann, aged 17, owns and operates a radio repair shop. Claiming infancy as a defense, he seeks to avoid a contract made for the purchase of supplies necessary for his shop. Is this a good defense?
8. Two months before coming of age, Helen Smith bought a motorboat for $3,000, paying cash. Three years later, she sought to avoid the contract, claiming that she was a minor at the time of the purchase. Was she legally bound to the contract?

9. Tina Kepler was declared by the court to be insane, and a guardian was appointed to take care of her. Later, Kepler made an agreement to purchase certain clothes from a merchant. Was the agreement binding on Kepler?

10. Cheryl Garson sues Susan Harris for breach of contract. Harris proves she was intoxicated when the agreement was executed so that she did not understand the nature of the transaction. Is the contract enforceable?

Cases to Judge

1. Leo received serious job-related injuries to his left hand at 12:45 p.m. on August 3, 1977. The age of majority at that time in Rhode Island was 18. Under the worker's compensation law, people are entitled to triple damages if they are injured at a time when they are a minor. Leo was born on August 3, 1959, at 3:56 p.m. Is he entitled to triple damages? Explain. *Leo v. Maro Display, Inc.*, 412 A.2d 221 (Rhode Island)

2. Before reaching the age of 18, Brenda Sanchez sold some property to Norman and Mary Ann Sanchez for $3,000. Later, after reaching the age of 21, Brenda signed an official paper acknowledging that she had sold the property to Norman and Mary Ann. She then attempted to rescind the sale on the ground that she was a minor at the time. Can she do so? Explain. *Sanchez v. Sanchez*, 464 So. 2d 1009 (Louisiana)

3. Dalton placed vinyl siding on a house under a written contract with Walter and Kathy Bundy. He assumed that the house belonged to them, but learned later that it belonged to their 12-year-old daughter and that the Bundys were bankrupt. Dalton argues that their daughter, although a minor, would be unjustly enriched if she were not required to pay for the siding. He also argues that the siding is a necessity. Do you agree with Dalton? Why or why not? *Dalton v. Bundy*, 666 S.W.2d 443 (Missouri)

4. Youngblood, who was 17 years old, sold a wrecked Ford automobile to Blankensopp for $35 cash. Later, unknown to Blankensopp, Youngblood repossessed the vehicle and sold it to a second purchaser for $40. Youngblood was charged with the crime of unlawfully appropriating an automobile owned by another. Youngblood claims that he still owned the vehicle because of minority and could not be convicted of the crime. Do you agree with Youngblood? Explain. *Youngblood v. State*, 658 S.W.2d 598 (Texas)

5. Wallace, who was 16 years old, purchased a Datsun automobile from Whitley's Discount Auto Sales, Inc., for $3,080. He paid $1,200 cash and financed the remaining $1,880 with a car loan from Richmond County Bank. According to the credit application, Wallace was 18 years old. Eight and one-half months later, after paying $839.65 on the bank loan and being involved in two accidents, Wallace returned the car to Whitley's and demanded the return of the $3,080. Is he entitled to it? Explain. *Gillis v. Whitley's Discount Auto Sales, Inc.*, 319 S.E.2d 661 (North Carolina)

Chapter 9

DEFECTIVE AGREEMENTS

Scene: The kitchen of the Williams home.

Lorna: Did you get caught in the storm last night, Mom? You were late getting home.

Mrs. Williams: No. I went out with Marvin after class. He's so nice. It was a terribly stormy night—the wind was blowing, and there was a drenching rain, and Marvin was such a gentleman.

Doug: That jerk who stood you up?

Denise: How do you know he's a jerk? You've never met him.

Mrs. Williams (*holding her hand out*): Look at the beautiful ring he gave me. He said that the stones are real diamonds and sapphires.

Denise: It's beautiful!

Lorna: You shouldn't have taken that, Mom. You hardly know him!

Mrs. Williams: I didn't want to hurt his feelings. I said that I would just wear it until the end of classes and then return it to him. He's such a nice man.

Doug: I don't trust him. The stones are probably fake.

Mrs. Williams: He wants me to have an interest in a corporation that he owns. It's a company that searches the ocean for old shipwrecks. If it ever finds one, we'll be rich. I agreed to buy some stock in it.

Lorna: For how much?

Doug: I hope you didn't sign anything.

Mrs. Williams: I said that I would buy ten shares at $10 a share, and I signed this paper. (*She hands the paper to Doug.*)

Doug (*reading*): It says here that you agree to buy ten shares of stock a week for the next 5 years for $10 a share. Did you read what you signed, Mom?

Mrs. Williams: No. I didn't think it was necessary to read it. Marvin seemed like such a nice person.

Lorna: I think that your Marvin friend is a fraud.

Mrs. Williams: I signed another paper too, agreeing to buy a boat for you kids. You've wanted one for a long time, and he had one for sale. He said that it's worth $15,000 but that he'd sell it to me for $5,000. I think he gave me a good deal.

Denise: You bought a boat for us? When can we see it?

Doug: It's probably worthless.

Mrs. Williams: I haven't seen it yet. He said that it's tied to a mooring in the harbor.
(*The next day. Mrs. Williams arrives home from work.*)

Mrs. Williams (*calling in a loud voice*): Is anyone home?

Lorna: (*walking into the room*): Hi, Mom. How's everything?

Mrs. Williams: I'm not sure. I stopped at the jewelers on my lunch hour and had the ring that Marvin gave me appraised. The jeweler said that it's a cheap ring made of cut glass.

Lorna: You should sue that guy Marvin for fraud.

Mrs. Williams: Then I drove down to the harbor to look at Marvin's boat, and the harbormaster told me that it had sunk in the storm the other day. Can you imagine that? It was sitting on the bottom of the ocean when I signed that paper agreeing to buy it.

Lorna: That Marvin Maxwell is something else!

LEGAL ISSUES

1. Is it legally fraudulent for one making a gift of a ring to misrepresent the quality of gems in the ring to the person receiving the gift?
2. Are people bound to contracts that they sign without reading?
3. May a contract be rescinded when both parties are mistaken as to the existence of the subject matter of the contract?

THE SPIRIT OF THE LAW

We have seen in Chapter 8 that contracts of minors and insane or intoxicated people are voidable. Certain other types of contracts are voidable also. These include contracts that involve mutual mistake, fraud, duress, and undue influence. Such agreements, in many cases, may be avoided (canceled) by the injured party because there is a lack of real consent to the transaction.

EXAMPLE 1 Josephine Kyle agreed to sell and Marilyn Kavanagh agreed to buy four lots of land on Prospect Street in a particular city. Kavanagh refused to go through with the agreement when she discovered that the land she thought she was buying was on another Prospect Street in the same city. Kyle sued Kavanagh for breach of contract.

In this case there was both an offer and an acceptance; however, the agreement between the parties was not a real one because they did not have the same thing in mind. There was a defect in their mutual understanding. Kyle lost the case against Kavanagh.

First and foremost in any valid contract is the need that the parties understand each other. Only when there is understanding can a valid contract be created.

■MISTAKE

People sometimes enter into contracts in the mistaken belief that certain facts exist when they really do not, or that certain facts do not exist when they really do. When the parties discover the true facts, one or both of them may wish to avoid the contract.

Unilateral Mistake

A **unilateral mistake** is a mistake made by one of the parties only. With some exceptions, a person cannot get out of a contract because of a unilateral mistake.

> **EXAMPLE 2** Maureen Martori agreed to buy Diane Sutherland's desk for $75, mistakenly thinking it was made of mahogany and worth much more money. She later learned that it was made of pine and worth only $50. Martori made a unilateral mistake and will have to go through with the contract.

Legal Issue No. 2

Mistake as to the Nature of the Agreement A mistake as to the nature of an agreement cannot be used as an excuse to avoid a contract. Thus, people are bound by written agreements they sign without reading, even though they may be mistaken as to what the agreement says. By signing, they agree that the writing sets forth the terms of the agreement.

The same rule applies to people who cannot read English. The burden is on them to have the agreement read and explained to them by someone they can rely on. If they sign without doing this, they will still be bound to the terms of the writing they signed.

Mistake as to the Identity of a Party A mistake as to the identity of a party may cause a contract to be voidable.

> **EXAMPLE 3** Suppose you send an offer by letter to your friend Jill Gomez, who lives in a nearby town. The postmaster delivers your letter to another Jill Gomez, who happens to live in the same town. The wrong Jill Gomez likes your

Imagine that the seller of an appliance believed it was slightly used. If the seller later discovered the appliance was in fact new, could he or she get out of the sales contract? If the buyer discovered the appliance was really heavily used, could he or she get out of the contract? *(ZIGGY, by Tom Wilson. Copyright © 1986, Universal Press Syndicate. Reprinted with permission. All rights reserved.)*

offer and accepts it. The contract would be voidable because she is not the person you had in mind.

If, however, you are dealing face to face with a person who you think is Jill Gomez, but who really is not, your mistake as to her identity will not prevent the contract's being binding. You are making the offer to the person facing you. She is the person who may accept it. Mistaken identity of this kind will not be a ground for voiding the contract.

Mutual Mistake

When both parties are mistaken about some important fact—that is, there is a **mutual mistake**—the contract may be avoided by either party. This is also known as a **bilateral mistake.**

Mistake as to the Possibility of Performance If both parties entering into a contract believe that it can be performed when in fact it cannot, either party may get out of the contract because of the mutual mistake.

Legal Issue No. 3

EXAMPLE 4 Robert Houlihan agreed to sell his car to Cynthia Stamatopoulos for $1,400. Unknown to both of them, however, was the fact that the car had been totaled the night before and could not be repaired. Either party may avoid the contract on the ground of a mutual mistake as to the possibility of performance.

Mistake as to the Identity of the Subject Matter If both parties are mistaken about the identity of the subject matter when they enter into a contract, the contract may be avoided by either one of them. Example 1 illustrates this rule of law. Most lawsuits involving mistake result from a careless use of language by the parties.

Remember: Always state your offers and your acceptances in plain, clear, simple language. Be sure that the other party understands you.

▌FRAUD

Persons who are induced by fraud to enter into contracts have the choice, if they wish, of either getting out of the contract or suing in tort for money damages.

Fraud consists of (1) a misrepresentation of a material, existing fact, (2) known to be false by the party making it, (3) made with the intention that it be relied upon, (4) which is actually relied upon, and (5) which causes the party who was wronged to suffer damages. In order to bring suit for fraud, all five of the above conditions must be proved by the party bringing the suit.

Legal Issue No. 1

EXAMPLE 5 Let us suppose that Maureen Martori, in Example 2, asked Diane Sutherland, "What is this desk made of?" and Sutherland, knowing that it was made of pine, replied, "It's made of mahogany." If Martori relied on Sutherland's statement and bought the desk, she could either **rescind** (get out of) the contract or sue Sutherland for damages. Her damages would be the difference between the amount she paid for the desk and the cost of a desk made of mahogany.

A gem is represented as genuine when in fact it is fake. What must a purchaser prove to rescind a contract for fraud? If the false gem were given as a gift, could the donor be responsible for fraud?

Misrepresentation of Fact

The misrepresentation must be of a material, existing fact, not a promise of something to happen in the future and not someone's opinion. A **material fact** is one that is important—one that matters to one of the parties.

EXAMPLE 6   Suppose that instead of saying that the desk was made of mahogany, Sutherland said, ''That is the best desk on the market. It will be worth twice as much in 2 years.'' Martori would not have a cause of action against Sutherland for fraud if the statements turn out to be false.

The law allows a certain amount of ''sales talk'' (or ''puffing,'' as it is called) without considering it to be fraudulent. The statement, ''This is the best desk on the market,'' is an example of such sales talk. The statement, ''It will be worth twice as much in 2 years'' is not only the seller's opinion, it is also a promise of something to happen in the future, which is not an existing fact.

Misrepresentation Known to Be False

The misrepresentation must be known to be false by the person making it. This element may be satisfied by proving actual knowledge, or by showing that the statement was made recklessly, without regard to its truth or falsity or without an honest belief in its truthfulness. Without this element, we often have innocent misrepresentation, discussed below.

Misrepresentation Intended to Be Relied Upon

The misrepresentation must be made with the serious intent that it is to be relied upon.

EXAMPLE 7   Let us suppose that Maureen Martori, while visiting Diane Sutherland, asked, ''What is this desk made of?'' and that Sutherland, with no intention of selling the desk and knowing it was made of pine, replied, ''It's made of mahogany.'' If Martori went out and bought a similar desk elsewhere, thinking it was made of mahogany, she could not win a lawsuit against Sutherland for fraud. Sutherland did not intend that Martori rely on her statement.

Misrepresentation Actually Relied Upon

Sometimes persons will make misrepresentations to others who pay no attention to them. If one pays no attention to a misrepresentation, one cannot win a lawsuit for fraud. The misrepresentation must be reasonably relied upon by the other party at the time that it is made.

EXAMPLE 8 A used-car dealer, in attempting to sell a car to Charles Aho, said to him, "The brakes are in excellent condition. They are recently relined." Before buying the car, Aho tried it out and showed it to his mechanic friend, Ronald Silva. Silva removed the wheel and pointed out a worn brake lining to Aho. Aho bought the car anyway.

Aho could not later avoid the contract on the ground of fraud because he did not rely on the used-car dealer's false statement.

Resulting Damages

In order to recover for fraud, the person defrauded must suffer some loss. If someone makes a false statement to you and you rely on it and enter into a contract but suffer no loss, you cannot win a lawsuit for fraud.

INNOCENT MISREPRESENTATION

Sometimes a person will make an innocent statement of supposed fact that turns out to be false. The person making the statement honestly believes it to be true, but it really is not. If that person would be expected by others to have knowledge and makes a statement as of that knowledge, he or she will be held responsible for making the false statement. The court will give legal recourse to the injured party on the ground of **innocent misrepresentation.**

EXAMPLE 9 Let us suppose that Martori, in Example 2, asked Sutherland, "What is this desk made of?" and that Sutherland, honestly thinking so, replied, "It's made of mahogany." If Martori relied on Sutherland's statement and agreed to buy the desk, she would not have to go through with the agreement after finding out that the desk was made of pine.

Under the Uniform Commercial Code (UCC), Example 9 also illustrates a breach of express warranty, which would give Martori another ground for relief. An **express warranty** comes about whenever anyone sells goods and makes a statement of fact or promise about them to the buyer. The statement or promise must relate to the goods and be part of the basis of the bargain.

DURESS

An agreement must be entered into voluntarily by the parties; otherwise, it will not be enforced by the courts. Agreements made under duress are either void or voidable. **Duress** is the overcoming of a person's will by the use of force or by threat of force or bodily harm. When actual physical force is used to cause another to sign a contract, the contract is void.

EXAMPLE 10 One evening while driving his car on a country road, Victor Rebikov picked up a hitchhiker. The hitchhiker took over the car and forced Rebikov, at gunpoint, to endorse a bill of sale for the car. The car was found by police in a used-car lot some days later. The used-car dealer produced the bill of sale endorsed by Rebikov, claiming that the bill of sale gave him good title to the car. Rebikov would be entitled to the return of his car. Since the bill of sale was void, Rebikov would get the car back even if the dealer had sold it to an innocent buyer.

When a threat of physical force is used to cause another to sign a contract, the contract is voidable. Such a threat may be made against the contracting party or a member of his or her immediate family. The injured party may avoid the contract if he or she elects to do so.

Economic duress consists of threats of a business nature that cause another, without real consent, to enter into a contract.

EXAMPLE 11 The Elrod Company was under a contract to deliver some special parts to Bluebird Corporation by a certain date. Bluebird needed the parts by that date and could not get similar parts elsewhere. Elrod threatened to refrain from delivering the parts by the agreed date unless Bluebird signed a contract to buy additional products from them. Bluebird signed the contract. Bluebird would be able to avoid its contract with Elrod on the ground of economic duress.

Note, however, that a threat to exercise one's legal rights is not duress. For example, a party with grounds to sue may threaten to do so or demand satisfaction.

UNDUE INFLUENCE

Another factor that may cause a contract to be voidable is undue influence. **Undue influence** is unfair and improper persuasive pressure exerted by one person in a relationship of trust on another person. Usually, the undue influence is exerted by a strong person upon another who is weaker because of ill health, old age, or mental immaturity. The stronger person substitutes his or her will for the will of the weaker person. People who are in relationships of trust include attorney and client, doctor or nurse and patient, guardian and ward, trustee and beneficiary, principal and agent, husband and wife, parent and child, and clergy and parishioner.

EXAMPLE 12 Josephine Bernard, a childless widow in failing health, hired a nurse-companion. As Bernard's health worsened, she grew to rely on the nurse to an ever greater degree, even to the extent of entrusting private matters to her. Shortly before Bernard's death, the nurse induced her to sign a contract agreeing to deed over her house to the nurse for a fraction of its value.

This would probably be a case involving undue influence. On the other hand, if additional evidence tended to show that this was what Bernard wanted to do with her property, the court might hold otherwise.

Duress may or may not be present along with undue influence. Usually, we think of duress as involving a threat. Undue influence usually does not involve a threat but rather involves a persuasive pressure exerted by someone who is in a position of trust.

Suggestions for Reducing Legal Risks

If you are an offeror:

1. Do all in your power to avoid mistakes by making your offer as clear as you possibly can.
2. Be careful not to misrepresent innocently any material facts.
3. Never knowingly participate in a fraud by misrepresenting material facts with the intent to deceive the offeree.
4. Avoid any actions or words that might be seen as duress or undue influence in your business relationships.

If you are an offeree:

1. Check and recheck all possible material facts that are important.
2. Ask the offeror for further clarification of doubtful points.
3. If the contract is important, get legal advice.
4. Never rush into an important agreement.
5. If legal difficulties are possible, get a written statement signed by the offeror.

Language of the Law

Define or explain each of the following words or phrases:

unilateral mistake	fraud	innocent misrepre-	duress
mutual mistake	rescind	sentation	economic duress
bilateral mistake	material fact	express warranty	undue influence

Questions for Review

1. What are the four ways that someone may be led or forced into a defective agreement?
2. Name and describe the type of mistake for which a person cannot get out of a contract.
3. What kinds of mistakes will make a contract voidable or not enforceable by either party?
4. If you fail to read the fine print on a written contract, may you later avoid the contract when you are injured financially as a result of your failure to do so? Why?
5. What is the difference between dealing by mail and dealing face to face when there is a mistake as to the identity of a party?
6. How can you avoid making mistakes in your future contracts?
7. Give an example of innocent misrepresentation and an example of fraud.
8. What elements must be proved by the injured party to establish fraud?
9. What is meant by a false statement of a material, existing fact?
10. Give an example of a contract that might come into being as a result of duress.
11. Give an example of a contract that might come into being as a result of undue influence.

Cases in Point

In each of the following cases, give your decision and state a legal principle that applies to the case:

1. While out to sea, a fishing vessel took on a full load of fish. The captain radioed ashore to have an agent place insurance on the load of fish. As the agent was on the way to the insurance office, the ship sank. Insurance was placed on the load of fish without knowledge that the ship had sunk. Must the insurance company pay for the lost fish?

2. Ed Rodrigues was told by his ex-wife's boyfriend that he would be "taken care of" if he did not sign a particular paper. Rodrigues signed the paper against his will. It turned out to be an agreement to deed over his house to his ex-wife in exchange for her motorcycle. Is Rodrigues bound by the written agreement?

3. Marjorie Long decided to sell her car. She told Rupert Ames that it "is a bargain at $600." Ames bought the car. Later, he discovered that the motor was in bad condition, that the radiator leaked, and that there were other things wrong with the car. Does Ames have any legal claim against Long for fraud?

4. Olga Lark selected and purchased kitchen furniture that she thought was maple but later discovered was pine wood. Because of this mistake, Lark demanded that the merchant take back the furniture. Must the merchant comply with Lark's demands?

5. Akeo Shimazu hurriedly signed without reading a form that he assumed was a request for a sample copy of an expensive book. Later he found that he had actually signed an order for the book. When the book was delivered, Shimazu refused to accept it and claimed he was not bound to the agreement because of the mistake. Is Shimazu legally bound to his agreement?

6. Estelle Petkins put her summer cottage up for sale. Edith Ong, who was interested in buying it, asked Petkins, "Does the cottage have termites?" Petkins, who was not aware of any termites, replied, "No. It has no termites." Ong bought the cottage and discovered that it was infested with termites. Does she have any recourse against Petkins for fraud?

7. The basement of Rodney Wiseman's house flooded every time it rained. Nevertheless, when asked about water in the cellar by Phelps, a potential buyer, Wiseman lied, saying that the basement was dry. Before buying the property, however, Phelps had an expert in the field check the cellar for dryness. Can Phelps recover damages from Wiseman for fraud upon discovering the water problem?

8. May Dirk bought a tractor on the strength of a salesperson's statement that it would lessen the cost of planting and harvesting her wheat. At the end of the season, Dirk found her cost had increased rather than decreased and tried to recover the price paid for the tractor. Is Dirk within her rights?

9. Helena Crump was hired to take care of Lorna Boff, an elderly lady who was in poor health. Crump was a strong, persuasive person, and Boff was weak and ill. After caring for Boff for 3 weeks, Crump talked her into making a new will, leaving Crump the entire estate. Boff died a week later. On what legal grounds might the will be attacked? Why?

10. A sales clerk said to Gilbert Gold, "This is the best cassette recorder on the market." Gold bought the recorder and learned that there were better cassette recorders available in other stores. Did the sales clerk commit fraud? Explain.

Cases to Judge

1. Yost purchased two horses from Millhouse: a 2-year-old named Pandy for $425 and a yearling named Andy for $400. Millhouse gave Yost the registration papers for Pandy and told Yost that Andy was registered also, assuming this to be the case. He said that the registration papers would arrive later. It turned out that Andy was not registered. Yost would not have bought the horse had she known this fact and eventually sold it at a loss. Does Yost have legal grounds to win a lawsuit against Millhouse? Explain. *Yost v. Millhouse,* 375 N.W.2d 826 (Minnesota)

2. Glenn and Jean Rudell signed a contract with Comprehensive Accounting Corp. to buy an accounting franchise. The contract contained a clause providing for arbitration in the event of a dispute. (In *arbitration* a disagreement is presented to an unbiased person for judgement.) Later, a dispute arose. Comprehensive Accounting Corp. terminated the Rudells' franchise and sought arbitration. The Rudells refused to arbitrate, claiming that they did not know about the arbitration clause and had not agreed to it. How would you decide? Why? *Comprehensive Accounting Corp. v. Rudell,* 760 F.2d 138 (7th Circuit)

3. Benton signed some documents when she opened a cash management account with a stockbrokerage firm. She did not read the documents before signing them because she could not read the English language. The agent for the company did not know that she could not read English, and Benton did not ask him to read any documents to her. Is she bound to the terms of the document? Explain. *Merrill, Lynch, Pierce, Fenner & Smith v. Benton,* 467 So. 2d 311 (Florida)

4. Patricia Berger had apparently failed to report to the Internal Revenue Service substantial cash receipts from the operation of a beauty salon. Her husband threatened to turn her in to the IRS unless she signed a property settlement agreement with him. She signed an agreement giving him the custody of their children, their house, its furnishings, a truck, some cash, and other belongings. Can Patricia rescind the agreement? Why or why not? *Berger v. Berger,* 466 So. 2d 1149 (Florida)

5. A riot occurred at the Iowa State Penitentiary. Prison staff members were held as hostages by inmates. During negotiations to obtain the release of the hostages, the warden promised in writing that there would be no reprisals against certain inmates, including Everett Wagner. When the hostages were released and the prison returned to normal, Wagner received the punishment of 30 days in solitary confinement, 180 days of administrative segregation, and the loss of 1,283 days of good time earned. On what legal ground can the warden refuse to keep his promise to the inmates? Explain. *Wagner v. State,* 364 N.W.2d 246 (Iowa)

Chapter 10

LEGALITY OF A CONTRACT

Scene: The breakfast table of the Williams home. Members of the family arrive at different times to the kitchen and prepare their own breakfast as they arrive.

Denise: Did you see Marvin Maxwell in class last night, Mom?

Mrs. Williams: No, he didn't attend. I watched the door all evening, thinking that he might come in late, but he didn't arrive.

Doug: You should hire someone to beat him up after the things that he did to you!

Lorna: Would that be legal?

Mrs. Williams: Now don't talk like that, Doug. Marvin is really a very nice man. He probably thought there were real diamonds and sapphires in the ring that he gave me. It was such a nice gift—and he's a very handsome man . . .

Denise: They say that love is blind.

Mrs. Williams (*blushing*): Oh, stop that!

Lorna: He'll probably be in class next week, Mom. I'll bet he went on another business trip.

Doug: I'll bet you $5 that he won't be in class next week!

Lorna: I'll take you up on that, Doug! In fact, I'll double it! Let's make it $10. I say that Marvin Maxwell will be in class next week!

Mrs. Williams: Children, it's not right to gamble! It's illegal and it's wrong and Marvin is a very nice person!

Doug: You've got a deal, Lorna! Ten dollars says he won't be there!

Denise: Mom, won't you be late for work?

Mrs. Williams: Yes, I have to hurry. Mr. Ellis is not an easy person to work for, and I don't like to be late.

Doug: You should open your own business, Mom, as soon as the year is up on your contract with Mr. Ellis. You could do it!

Mrs. Williams: I'd love to, but I'm afraid I can't. The employment contract that I signed with Mr. Ellis has a clause in it prohibiting me from opening a competing business anywhere in the United States for the next 99 years. I'm afraid that that's another paper that I signed without reading.

Lorna: There must be something that you can do to get out of that.

Mrs. Williams: Well, I've got to go. Good-bye, children. Have a nice day.

Doug, Denise, Lorna: Good-bye, Mom!
(*Mrs. Williams leaves.*)

Lorna: Have you found a job yet, Doug?

Doug: I'm still looking, but I've been busy lately doing jobs on my own. Right now I'm doing some electrical work for Mrs. DeLuca. I'm rewiring her house.

Lorna: Don't you need a license to do that?

Doug: Yes, but she knows that I don't have a license. She's paying me very well, too. She agreed to give me $500 for the job.

LEGAL ISSUES

1. Is an agreement to beat up someone legal and valid?
2. Is a gambling agreement valid and enforceable?
3. Will a clause in an employment contract be upheld by the court if it prohibits similar employment anywhere in the United States for 99 years?
4. If an unlicensed person agrees to do work that requires a license, is the agreement valid?

THE SPIRIT OF THE LAW

As we learned in Chapter 9, contracts involving mutual mistake, fraud, duress, and undue influence are voidable. The injured party has the power to avoid the contract if he or she elects to do so; otherwise, the contract is valid. In contrast, illegal agreements are void. They have no legal effect whatsoever. With a few exceptions, the court will not aid either party to an illegal agreement. The law will let parties live with the consequences of their own acts.

ILLEGAL AGREEMENTS

An illegal agreement usually can be described in one or more of the following three ways:

1. The agreement requires the performance of an illegal act.
2. The agreement violates a statute.
3. The agreement is contrary to public policy.

Agreements Requiring an Illegal Act

EXAMPLE 1 Leonard Mason and Cora Tompkins agreed to rob a bank and split the proceeds. Mason was to stand guard, and Tompkins was to blow the safe. Tompkins, however, double-crossed Mason. Mason brought an action, asking the court to force Tompkins to split up the "loot," as they had agreed.

Of course, this is a simple case to solve. The courts are established to enforce the law. They will not help enforce an agreement which has as its object the performance of an illegal act.

Agreements That Violate Statutes

Common types of agreements that violate statutes are those involving usury, gambling agreements, agreements to violate licensing laws, and some Sunday agreements.

Usury ■ If you agree to pay a higher rate of interest than the law permits, your agreement is usurious. Most states specify the maximum rate of interest that may be charged for a loan of money. Charging more than the maximum legal rate is **usury.** A pressing need for money may make some people easy victims of loan sharks. Usury laws are designed to protect the public from this danger.

EXAMPLE 2 Linda Chavez wants to purchase a car just after she becomes 18 years of age. In order to make the down payment, Chavez borrows $600 from Robert Lightner. Chavez promises to pay Lightner $100 per month for 12 months, representing a payment of $1,200 for the use of $600—an absurdly high interest rate.

The law would not require Chavez to pay the full $1,200. She has promised to pay a higher rate of interest than the law permits. The bargain is illegal, and the courts would not enforce it.

The Truth in Lending Act, which will be discussed more fully in Chapter 16, is one step taken by the federal government to make the consumer aware of the cost of credit. The merchant or lender must now make clear to the buyer the annual percentage rate on each installment sale or loan. Before you sign any credit or loan agreement, be sure to take advantage of the protection provided by the Truth in Lending Act, and look for a statement of the true rate of interest.

Gambling Agreements ■ Another type of illegal agreement prohibited by statute is a gambling agreement. If you bet on the results of a basketball game or won an office pool, you could not collect in court because such agreements are
illegal.

Some types of gambling have been licensed in various states—for example, betting at race tracks in New York, Illinois, California, Massachusetts, and other states. This does not mean that all gambling is legal in these states. It is only the licensed types of gambling that are legal and then only when conducted strictly in accordance with the license. Lotteries, other than state-run lotteries, are considered illegal in many states. However, because legalized lotteries have become sources of additional money for governmental bodies, they have become popular in many states. A state-run lottery has been approved by the state legislature and is administered by an agency of the state government.

Sunday Agreements ■ In many states it is illegal to do certain types of work on Sunday. An agreement to perform the prohibited work on Sunday would be illegal. In recent years, many of these laws have been changed or repealed.

Three men pose as doctors and contract their services to a local hospital. If the hospital refuses to pay them, will a court enforce their contract?

Under common law contracts could be made on Sunday. The prohibitions came about many years ago through the passage of Sunday "blue laws" by state legislatures. Since the 1960s there has been a trend toward relaxing or doing away with Sunday laws altogether, either by state legislatures or by state courts. The courts of 18 states have held their Sunday laws to be unconstitutional either in whole or in part, saying that they are arbitrary and irrational or too protective of special interests.* In contrast, the courts of 13 states have upheld their Sunday laws, saying that they are constitutional.†

In states in which Sunday contracts are illegal, the following rules apply:

1. An agreement made on a Sunday is void.
2. If an offer is made on a day other than Sunday and accepted on a Sunday, the resulting agreement is void.
3. If an agreement is made on a Sunday but a date for a day other than a Sunday is placed on the paper, the agreement is void.
4. Sunday laws often apply to legal holidays.

Legal Issue No. 4

Agreements to Violate Licensing Laws To engage in certain trades or professions, a person is required by law to have a **license**—a legal document stating that the holder has permission from the proper authorities to carry on a certain business or profession. To engage in such a business or profession without a license is illegal.

EXAMPLE 3 Walter Jarvie went to work as a plumber but failed to get a license. He bought some new plumbing tools and contracted to install a new shower for Rachel Bloom. Jarvie installed the shower exactly as the contract required. He believed he had done a proper job. Bloom, however, refused to pay Jarvie.

---

*Alabama (1976), Arkansas (1982), Connecticut (1979), Georgia (1975), Illinois (1962), Kansas (1964), Kentucky (1966), Louisiana (1968), Minnesota (1968), Nebraska (1966), New York (1976), North Carolina (1972), Oklahoma (1972), Pennsylvania (1978), Utah (1971), Vermont (1982), Washington (1966), Wyoming (1964)

†Iowa (1971), Louisiana (1982), Maine (1976), Maryland (1974), Massachusetts (1977, 1983), Mississippi (1975), New Hampshire (1967), New Jersey (1978), North Dakota (1970, 1981), Rhode Island (1982), South Carolina (1970), Texas (1976), Virginia (1977)

■ Jarvie cannot collect for his work. The law requires that a person have a license in order to engage in the plumbing business. His contract was illegal, and the courts will not help him to collect.

Courts emphasize a difference between statutes for revenue and statutes for protection of the public health, safety, and welfare. If a statute requires licensing simply for the raising of revenue, its violation will not necessarily make a contract void. On the other hand, if a licensing law is designed to protect the public health, it is more likely that persons without licenses will be denied the enforcement of their contracts.

EXAMPLE 4 Kenneth Wheeler performed industrial engineering services for Bucksteel Company, an Oregon corporation. He was not a registered engineer. An Oregon statute provides that a person shall not "engage in the practice of engineering or land surveying without having a valid certificate or permit to so practice." Bucksteel refused to pay Wheeler for his services. The court held in favor of Bucksteel, saying: "The dangers of incompetent engineers to the public at large are obvious. The law provides for thorough regulation of the profession in order to maintain the necessary standards of competence and ethical behavior."

AGREEMENTS CONTRARY TO PUBLIC POLICY

Agreements in Unreasonable Restraint of Trade

An agreement that requires the performance of an act that is harmful to the public welfare is considered to be **contrary to public policy,** even though the act in itself may not be illegal. Such agreements are usually unenforceable.

Restraint of trade is the elimination of competition with the intent to control prices. Three types of contracts are generally considered to be in unreasonable restraint of trade: (1) outright contracts not to compete, (2) price fixing, and (3) agreements to defeat competitive bidding.

Outright Contracts Not to Compete Even though outright contracts not to compete are illegal, in some cases a reasonable restraint is allowed. In the sale of a business, for example, it is quite common for the seller to agree not to open a competing business for a period of time after the sale. This is done to protect the **goodwill** (the public approval and patronage) of the business. Such an agreement will be upheld by the court to the extent that it is reasonable both in time and geographic area. For instance, an agreement by the seller of a barbershop not to open another shop anywhere in the United States for the next 99 years would not be reasonable in either time or geographic area. It would be enforced only to the extent that the seller refrains from competing for a reasonable time. If the restraint is unreasonable considering the nature of the business sold, then the restraint is illegal and unenforceable.

Promises not to compete, called **restrictive covenants,** are sometimes found in employment contracts. Under these covenants, employees agree not to engage in similar employment for a period of time after they leave the company. Such covenants will be enforced only if reasonably limited in time and geographic area, and then only to the extent necessary to protect the employer from unfair competition. This issue is discussed further in Chapter 22.

Legal Issue No. 3

The Organization of Petroleum Exporting Countries successfully set crude oil prices in the 1970s. If American oil companies agreed to set the domestic price of gasoline, would their agreement be enforceable at law?

Price Fixing   The law views competition in the marketplace as an efficient way of determining prices. Producers compete to provide better products at attractive prices. Price fixing would discourage competition and raise prices for everyone. **Horizontal price fixing** occurs when competitors agree to sell a particular product or service at an agreed price. **Vertical price fixing** occurs when manufacturers dictate the price at which a product must be sold by retailers. Vertical price-fixing agreements are called *retail price maintenance agreements*. Being contrary to public policy, price-fixing agreements will not be enforced by courts. In fact, those who seek to fix prices may be stopped from doing so by state and federal government agencies.

Agreements to Defeat Competitive Bidding   In auction sales and in certain other types of contracts, particularly when the government contracts with private parties, competitive bidding is very important. If, before the bids are made, the bidders get together and agree not to bid more than a certain price, they are not bidding fairly. The bidders' agreements and their resulting contract are not enforceable.

EXAMPLE 5   Three new parks were to be built in a certain city. Only three contractors were available for bidding on the contracts to build the parks. Local law required the city government to open the contracts to competitive bidding and to accept the lowest bid submitted by a contractor on each construction job. Before the bidding began, however, the contractors met and fixed the bids so that each of them would be awarded one of the construction jobs. This agreement is not enforceable.

Agreements Interfering With Operation of the Courts

Any contract that tends to interfere with the administration of justice is illegal. Thus, an agreement to pay a nonexpert to testify at a trial is unenforceable. A nonexpert witness is one who testifies as to the facts of the case. Such witnesses are paid a regular fee by the courts to compensate them for their time. An agreement by one of the parties to pay a witness an additional amount might color the witness's testimony. Expert witnesses may also be called to court, but these are different from nonexpert witnesses. Expert witnesses are called to testify about technical matters. They may testify only on general principles, not on the facts of the case. These witnesses are paid by the party calling them.

Agreements Inducing Breach of Duty or Fraud

Many persons hold positions of trust. This means that they have a responsibility for the well-being of other people. Your representative in Congress, your state representative, and all other public officials come within this class. They owe a duty to work for the best interest of the public. Any contract that tries to influence these public officials to use their position for private gain is unenforceable. This rule also applies to private persons who are in positions of trust.

Another act contrary to public policy takes place when someone commits a tort, even though the act itself may not be a crime. A tort, or a civil wrong, is any violation of a person's rights. For example, a contract to defraud a third person or to injure that person in other ways would be a tort. The courts will not enforce such wrongful agreements.

Agreements Interfering With Marriage

The law encourages marriages and protects family relationships. A contract that would have the effect of discouraging or interfering with good family relationships may be illegal and, therefore, unenforceable in the courts.

EXAMPLE 6 If a father promises to give his daughter $1,000 if she never gets married, the contract would not be enforceable. The same would be true if the father promised $1,000 to a married daughter if she would leave her husband.

THE EFFECT OF ILLEGALITY

The general rule is that the court will not aid either party to an illegal contract. It will leave the parties where they placed themselves. Neither one can enforce the agreement or receive aid from the court.

An exception occurs, however, when the parties are not equally at fault. In such cases the court may aid people who are not at fault to get back anything they may have parted with.

There might be a case in which only part of the contract is illegal. If the legal part can be separated from the illegal part, the legal part can be enforced. In Example 3, for instance, the sale of the plumbing equipment and materials would be legal, and the seller could collect for the selling price of these things. It was the labor contract that was illegal because the plumber had no license; so this part would be uncollectible. If the legal part cannot be separated from the illegal part, however, the entire agreement will be void.

Suggestions for Reducing Legal Risks

1. When you are in doubt about the legality of the subject matter of an important agreement, see an attorney before entering into it.
2. Remember that almost all gambling and betting agreements are illegal in most states and that the courts will not enforce such agreements.
3. Become familiar enough with the statutes of your own state so that you will know which types of agreements are considered illegal in your state.

4. Where a license is required for you to perform services, obtain the license; otherwise, you may not be able to enforce a claim of payment for your services.
5. You run a grave risk of losing your reputation or possibly becoming a subject for blackmail if you enter into an agreement to commit a crime or enter into an agreement that is contrary to public policy. Don't take such a chance!

Language of the Law

Define or explain each of the following words or phrases:

usury	contrary to public policy	goodwill	horizontal price fixing
license	restraint of trade	restrictive covenants	vertical price fixing

Questions for Review

1. What is the legal effect, generally, of an illegal agreement?
2. Give an example of an agreement that requires an illegal act.
3. Name three types of agreements that would not be enforceable because they violate statutes.
4. What is the purpose of usury laws?
5. Name several types of gambling agreements that are not enforceable in your state. Name any types of gambling that are legal in your state.
6. What are some trades or professions that require a license in your state or community?

7. Name four types of agreements that are contrary to public policy. Why are these agreements considered to be contrary to public policy?
8. What is meant by unreasonable restraint of trade? When are agreements not to compete allowed?
9. Give an example of an agreement that may interfere with the operation of the courts. Why is such an agreement frowned upon?
10. What is meant by the breach of a private or a public duty? Give examples of agreements that would not be enforceable.
11. What do the courts generally do about agreements that are illegal?

Cases in Point

In each of the following cases, give your decision and state a legal principle that applies to the case:

1. John Harmeling met Ralph Campiola at a party one Saturday night and offered to sell him his camera. Campiola said he would think it over. The next day, Sunday, Campiola contacted Harmeling and said that he would buy the camera. Sunday contracts are illegal under the laws of that particular state. Is the contract valid?
2. Robert Armstrong agreed to sell Frank Karper an automobile for $2,000 and a submachine gun for $500. There is a law that prohibits the sale of submachine guns. If Armstrong fails to carry out his promises, what rights does Karper have?

3. Carla Carbone promised to pay Stacey Wilson $10,000 if Wilson would destroy some evidence needed in a criminal case against Carbone. Wilson destroyed the evidence. When Carbone refused to pay the $10,000, Wilson sued for the amount promised. Is Wilson entitled to the money?

4. To protect the public, a state statute requires real estate brokers to obtain a license. Burke, without getting a license, engages in buying and selling real estate for others. He sues one of his clients to collect a fee. Is he entitled to judgment?

5. Hazel Mahoney bet $5 in an office pool that was organized by a fellow worker, Harry Holt. Mahoney won the pool, but before she collected her winnings, Holt was laid off. If Holt does not pay the money to Mahoney, can she sue him for breach of contract?

6. Josie Hope sold Suzie Tanaka a camera repair shop located in Rochester, New York. In the contract Hope agreed never to engage in a similar business in New York State. Five years later, Hope opened a camera repair shop in New York City. Was Hope liable for breach of contract?

7. Olive Mower, a defendant, promised to pay $300 to Sonya Dorsey if she would testify falsely for Mower at her trial. Dorsey testified as agreed. Was she legally entitled to the $300?

8. Al Perkins promised his daughter $10,000 if she would never marry. Was she entitled to collect this amount from his estate when he died if she had not married?

Cases to Judge

1. Alberto-Culver Company had an opening in its data processing department for a senior programmer. West obtained the position through an employment agency. The agency was not licensed as required by Illinois law, and Alberto-Culver Co. refused to pay the agency fee. Must it do so? Why or why not? *T.E.C. & Assoc. v. Alberto-Culver Co.*, 476 N.E.2d 1212 (Illinois)

2. Anabas Export Ltd. sold and delivered to Alper Industries, Inc., stickers featuring a portrait of Michael Jackson. Alper Industries, whose place of business is in Mount Vernon, New York, planned to resell the stickers in the course of trade. Jackson's written permission to feature his portrait on the stickers was not obtained, in violation of the New York Right of Privacy Law (see page 59). Alper Industries refused to pay for the stickers, and Anabas brought suit. How would you decide? Why? *Anabas Export Ltd. v. Alper Industries Inc.*, 603 F. Supp. 1275 (New York)

3. A husband and wife entered into a contract. Under the contract, the wife agreed to sign a joint income tax return for the preceding year with the husband and to stay married to him. In return, the husband agreed to pay money periodically to the wife for her daughter's college tuition. Shortly thereafter, the wife obtained a divorce and sued the husband for failing to make some of the periodic payments required. The husband contends that a contract to remain married is against public policy and void. Do you agree? Explain. *Taylor v. Martin*, 466 So. 2d 977 (Alabama)

4. Noble and Odle signed a 1-year lease for an apartment. Before moving in, they decided not to take possession of the premises. When sued for damages, they argued that the lease was void because the landlady had not registered the premises as residential property with the city and had not obtained an occupancy permit. Both of these were required. Was the lease void? Why or why not? *Noble v. Alis*, 474 N.E.2d 109 (Indiana)

Chapter 11

FORM OF A CONTRACT

Scene: The Williams home. Mrs. Williams is talking on the telephone with her sister, Martha. Denise enters the room.

Mrs. Williams: Good-bye, Martha. I'll talk to you soon. Don't start making any wedding plans! (*She hangs up the phone.*) That sister of mine is unreal. Remember the time she tried to get me to marry that friend she introduced me to?

Denise: What a weirdo he was.

Mrs. Williams: Well, 2 weeks ago I showed her the ring that Marvin Maxwell gave me, and she thinks I'm going to marry him.

Denise: Are you kidding? Aunt Martha doesn't even know Marvin.

Mrs. Williams: I tried to tell her that I'm not interested in him, but she doesn't even listen. She just said to me that if I marry Marvin, she'll pay for the wedding and give us a free honeymoon trip to Bermuda.

Denise: I like Aunt Martha, but sometimes . . .
(*Doug enters the room.*)

Doug: I finished the electrical job for Mrs. DeLuca, but I just noticed the check that she gave me. It says $500 in figures, which is the correct amount, but on the line where it's written in words, it just says "Five Dollars." Do you think the bank will cash it?

Mrs. Williams: I'm sure they will. I've had an account there for years.

Denise: What are you going to do with all that money, Doug? Are you still planning to buy the car from that guy down the street?

Doug: No, I don't think so.

Mrs. Williams: But I thought that you agreed to buy it from him for $490.

Doug: I did, but I changed my mind. It was just an oral agreement, anyway. We didn't put it in writing, so there's no contract. What can he do? Take me to court?

Mrs. Williams: It's not honest to break your promise like that.
(*A loud noise can be heard coming from the front of the house.*)

Denise: That sounds like a truck stopping in front of our house. Were you expecting anything, Mom?

Mrs. Williams: That's probably the new couch that I ordered. It was supposed to arrive today. (*She goes to the door.*)
(*The couch is placed in the living*

room by the delivery men, and Mrs. Williams, Denise, and Doug take pleasure in the arrival of the new piece of furniture.)

Denise (*sitting on the new couch*): This is beautiful, Mom, and it is so comfortable!

Doug (*stretching out on the couch, pushing against his sister*): It sure is. I'm going to enjoy this!

Denise: Get off me! And keep your shoes off the new couch!

Mrs. Williams: Doug, you said that your agreement to buy the car was not a contract because it was oral. My agreement to buy this couch was oral too. The price was $800, and I haven't paid for it yet. Do you suppose that it's not a contract either?

Doug: Oh, come on Mom—that's different.

Mrs. Williams (*still thinking about Doug's promise to buy the car*): You should keep your word when you tell someone that you'll do something.

LEGAL ISSUES

1. Must contracts in consideration of marriage be in writing to be enforceable?
2. Which will prevail when there is a discrepancy in a check in the amount in words and the amount in figures?
3. Is an oral agreement to buy a car for $490 enforceable?
4. Is an oral agreement to buy a couch for $800 enforceable when the couch has been delivered and accepted by the buyers?

THE SPIRIT OF THE LAW

In Chapter 10 we saw that illegal agreements are void. They have no legal effect whatsoever. In contrast, some contracts are valid but unenforceable. Oral contracts of certain types fall into this category.

In early England, all contracts could be oral, and they were fully enforceable. During that time, however, persons brought to trial for breach of contract could not testify on their own behalf. If someone accused another of breach of contract, the accused could not go on the witness stand and tell his or her side of the story. Only persons who were not parties to the contract could be witnesses in the lawsuit. To protect their friends or their own interests, witnesses often committed **perjury;** that is, they made false statements under oath in court.

Because of such practices, the English Parliament passed a statute in 1677 requiring certain contracts to be evidenced by a writing in order to be enforceable. This statute became known as the **Statute of Frauds.** Most of the states in the United States have adopted the English Statute of Frauds. These laws and others like them require certain contracts to be evidenced by a writing. We commonly say such contracts must be ''in writing,'' although the written evidence need not be a formal contract itself.

Putting a contract in writing can help clarify an agreement for both parties and for the courts, if necessary. However, unless a contract is one of those required by statute to be in writing, it is fully enforceable if it is oral. The vast majority of contracts we enter into during our lives do not have to be in writing to be enforceable.

WHAT THE WRITING MUST CONTAIN

The writing and format necessary to satisfy a statute of frauds need not be formal. It is known as a **memorandum** and may consist of such things as a letter or several letters, a sales slip, an invoice, a telegram, or even words written on a check. Usually, it is sufficient if the writing identifies (1) the subject matter, (2) the parties, (3) the price and terms, (4) the quantity (instead of the price) in the case of goods, and (5) the respective intent of the parties to the contract. Furthermore, the writing must be signed by the party against whom it is to be used as evidence. This means that, if you were seeking to enforce your contract with Louise Tucker, it would have to be signed by her. If, however, Tucker were seeking to enforce the contract against you, the writing would have to be signed by you.

EXAMPLE 1 Joyce Hiro orally agreed to buy some land from Noyes Hanscome for $40,000. She gave Hanscome a check for $3,500 and wrote on the back of the check, "Deposit on property at 19 Sylvan St. Total price $40,000." Hanscome signed the back of the check and put it in his bank account. He later demanded $60,000 for the land. The court held that the oral contract was enforceable, since the words on the check satisfied the requirements of the Statute of Frauds. The words on the check identified the subject matter, the parties, the price and terms, and the intent of the parties to the contract.

Signed and unsigned writings relating to the same transaction and containing all the essential terms of a contract may be read together as the evidence of a binding contract.

Evaluating Contradictory Terms

Sometimes handwritten terms will be placed in a typewritten or printed contract. When the handwritten terms contradict the typewritten or printed terms, the handwritten terms will prevail. The court takes the position that the handwritten terms were placed in the writing after it was typed or printed and were, therefore, the final intent of the parties. Following this rule, handwriting prevails over typewriting or printing, and typewriting prevails over printing.

Legal Issue No. 2

When there is a discrepancy in an amount that is written in both words and figures, as in a check, the amount written in words will prevail over the amount written in figures.

Evaluating Ambiguous Clauses

Sometimes written contracts are ambiguous; that is, they can be understood in different ways. When this happens the court will lean in favor of the party who did not draft the contract and against the one who drafted it.

EXAMPLE 2 Katharine Black was involved in an automobile accident. Her insurance policy contained an ambiguous clause that could be interpreted in different ways. The insurance company refused to pay Black, interpreting the

LAST NATIONAL BANK

November 10, 19XX   56-292
                              213

Pay to the order of _Doug Williams_ $ *500.00*

Five and °°/100 ————————————— Dollars

Harriet DeLuca

⑆0213⑈0292⑈0240⑈0688⑈

Where there is a discrepancy in an amount which is written in both words and figures, the amount written in words will prevail over the amount written in figures.

clause against her. When Black took the case to court, the court interpreted the clause in her favor because the insurance company had drafted the ambiguous policy.

CONTRACTS THAT MUST BE IN WRITING

The principal classes of contracts that must be in writing are (1) contracts to pay the debts of others, (2) contracts by executors and administrators to pay debts of the deceased out of their own pocket, (3) contracts in consideration of marriage, (4) contracts to sell an interest in real property, (5) contracts for the sale of goods valued at $500 or more, and (6) contracts requiring more than a year to perform.

■ Some states have added other types of agreements to the principal classes. You might wish to consult the statutes of your own state to find out what additional classes of contracts must be in writing.

Contracts to Pay Debts of Others

An oral promise to pay the debts of someone else is not enforceable.

EXAMPLE 3 Roland Jackson's uncle took him into a clothing store and said, "If you will sell this young man a suit of clothes on credit, I will pay you if he doesn't." The merchant would be wise to get such a promise in writing.

If the promise were not in writing, Jackson's uncle could not be sued to enforce his promise. This is a promise to pay the debt of someone else, and the law would require written evidence to prove the promise in court.

If Jackson's uncle had said, "Give this young man a suit of clothes and charge it to me," no writing would be required. This would be the uncle's own debt from the beginning. It was never implied that Jackson would pay.

Contracts by Executors and Administrators

Promises by executors or administrators to pay claims against the estate out of their own pockets must be in writing to be enforceable. Executors and administrators perform the duty of settling estates of deceased persons. This is discussed in detail in Chapter 39.

Contracts Requiring More Than a Year to Perform

The law requires all contracts to be written if they cannot be performed within 1 year of the date of their making.

EXAMPLE 4 Suppose that on the first day of May you enter into an oral contract with Louise Tucker. The contract provides, among other things, that you are to work for 1 year and that you are to begin work on the first day of June.

This contract must be in writing. You cannot completely perform the contract in less than 13 months from the day you entered into your agreement. The written requirement applies only to contracts that cannot possibly be performed within a year of their making.

EXAMPLE 5 If, in the example described above, you had contracted to work for Louise Tucker for "as long as Tucker continues to be president of the Tucker Company," your agreement would not have to be in writing. The time involved would be uncertain.

<u>AGREEMENT</u>

This agreement made this 1st day of May, 19--, between Louise Tucker, 1506 Sylvan Glade, Austin, Texas, as Employer, and Edwardo Garcia, 416 S. Church St., Lockhart, Texas, as Employee.

1. The Employee agrees to give his undivided time and service in the employ of the Employer in such capacity as the Employer may direct, for the period of one year from and after the 1st day of June, 19--.

2. In consideration of the service so to be performed, the Employer agrees to pay to the Employee the sum of $20,800, payable in equal weekly installments at the end of each week, until the termination of this agreement.

3. This agreement shall terminate in the event the Employer's business ceases to operate for any reason.

In witness whereof, the parties have hereunto set their hands and seals the day and year first above written.

Louise Tucker

Edwardo Garcia

Must this agreement be in writing to be enforceable?

Tucker might continue to be president of the Tucker Company for many, many years; on the other hand, she might be president for only a few months longer. The contract, therefore, could be completed in less than a year. It is the possibility of performance within a year that is the deciding factor.

Contracts in Consideration of Marriage

Legal Issue No. 1

Contracts in consideration of marriage must be in writing to be enforceable. They are not common in our society. In early England, however, it was customary for a bride's father to provide a dowry (money or goods) to his future son-in-law. Often the dowry was delivered after the marriage. Frequently, disagreements arose as to the amount promised. To avoid bitter family disputes, the courts required that such contracts must be in writing.

EXAMPLE 6 William Maunsel orally promised to pay Albert Demille $10,000 in cash if Demille would marry Maunsel's daughter, Veronica. Demille did so. However, Maunsel would not be in any way obligated to pay Demille the $10,000, because the contract would have to be in writing to be enforceable.

When two persons, however, mutually agree to marry, they do not need to put their agreement in writing. Such agreements to marry do not, and never did, require a written contract. Under present-day laws, an agreement between two people to marry each other is generally not enforceable. Either party can break the agreement without being liable to the other.

In contrast, people today often enter into premarital agreements. These are explained in Chapter 24. A premarital agreement must be in writing to be enforceable.

Contracts to Sell Real Property

Contracts for the sale of real property—that is, land and the things that are permanently attached to it—must be in writing to be enforceable. One of the most important contracts you may ever enter into is the contract to buy or sell a house. It is often advisable to have a lawyer either write or look at such a contract before you sign it.

Equitable Estoppel There is an exception to the requirement that a contract for the sale of real property be evidenced by a writing to be enforceable. The exception is called **equitable estoppel** by some courts and **part performance** by others. The exception applies when a person relies on an owner's oral promise to sell real property and then either makes improvements on the property or changes his or her position in an important way.

EXAMPLE 7 Gladys Green orally agreed to sell a lot of land to Thomas and Patricia Hickey for $15,000. The Hickeys told Green that they intended to sell their present home and build a new house on the lot. They immediately advertised their house for sale and, within 10 days, found a buyer and signed a written contract to sell it. Green then decided to sell her lot to someone else for $16,000. The court held that the oral contract with the Hickeys was enforceable under the doctrine of equitable estoppel. The Hickeys had so changed their

When must a contract to buy a car be in writing?

position in reliance on the oral contract that Green was estopped from using the Statute of Frauds as a defense.

Contracts for the Sale of Goods of $500 or More

Goods consist of movable items, such as furniture, books, livestock, cultivated crops, clothing, automobiles, and all personal effects of any kind. A contract for the sale of goods (personal property) for the price of $500 or more is not enforceable unless there is some writing indicating that a contract of sale has been made between the parties.

EXAMPLE 8 Georgette Jaworski entered into an agreement with a friend for the purchase of the friend's car for $950. This agreement was not in writing. A short time later, Jaworski changed her mind and told her friend that she did not want to buy the car. Although seriously intended and made with mutual assent, the agreement was not enforceable because there was no written contract.

Legal Issue No. 3

Exceptions An oral contract for the sale of goods of $500 or more will be enforced when any of the following conditions are satisfied:

1. If such a contract is between two merchants, if a written confirmation is sent within a reasonable time, and if no objection to it is made within 10 days.
2. If such a contract involves goods that are to be specially manufactured and that cannot be resold easily.
3. If the buyer actually receives and accepts the goods or pays for them.
4. If the parties to the contract admit in court that they entered into an oral agreement.

Legal Issue No. 4

These conditions only apply to contracts for the sale of goods over $500 in value. Contracts for the sale of goods valued at under $500 do not have to be in writing to be enforceable.

Commonwealth of Massachusetts
District Courts of Massachusetts

ESSEX, ss

FIRST DISTRICT COURT OF ESSEX

65 Washington Street, Salem, MA

STEVEN GRAZIO, a minor, by
MATTHEW GRAZIO, his father
and next friend,   Plaintiff

v.

WAYNE WILLIAMSON,   Defendant

Civil Action No. _87-316_

SUMMONS
(Rule 4)

To defendant _Wayne Williamson_ of _709 Hale St., Beverly, MA_ :
                    (name)   (address)
    You are hereby summoned and required to serve upon _Susan L. Powers_ plaintiff('s
attorney), whose address is _28 Main St., Beverly, MA_ , a copy of your answer to
the complaint which is herewith served upon you, within 20 days after service of this summons, exclusive of the day of
service. You are also required to file your answer to the complaint in the office of the Clerk of this court either before
service upon plaintiff('s attorney), or within 5 days thereafter. If you fail to meet the above requirements, judgment by
default may be rendered against you for the relief demanded in the complaint. You need not appear personally in
court to answer the complaint.
    Unless otherwise provided by Rule 13(a), your answer must state as a counterclaim any claim which you may have
against the plaintiff which arises out of the transaction or occurrence that is the subject matter of the plaintiff's claim
or you will be barred from making such claim in any other action.

WITNESS _Samuel E. Zoll,_ , Presiding Justice, on _____ November 15, 19--
(SEAL)   (date)

James X. Flynn CLERK/MAGISTRATE

Note: (1) When more than one defendant is involved, the names of all defendants should appear in the action. If a separate summons is used for each defendant
           each should be addressed to the particular defendant.
      (2) The number assigned to the complaint by the Clerk at commencement of the action should be affixed to this summons before it is served.

RETURN OF SERVICE

On _____ I served a copy of the within summons, together with a copy of the
        (date of service)
complaint in this action, upon the within named defendant, in the following manner (see Rule 4 (d) (1-5)):

_____
(signature)

_____
(name and title)

_____
(address)

Note: (1) The person serving the process shall make proof of service thereof in writing to the court and to the party or his attorney, as the case may be, who has
           requested such service. Proof of service shall be made promptly and in any event within the same time during which the person served must respond to
the process. Rule 4 (f).
      (2) Please place date you make service on defendant in the box on the copy served on the defendant, on the original returned to the court, and on the copy
           returned to the person requesting service or his attorney.
      (3) If service is made at the last and usual place of abode, the officer shall forthwith mail first class a copy of the summons to such last and usual place of
           abode, and shall set forth in the return the date of mailing and the address to which the summons was sent. (G.L. c 223, sec 31).

This form prescribed by the Chief Justice of the District Courts

**A summons is a notice by the court to the defendant that a lawsuit has begun. In
the case of Grazio v. Williamson, this summons was handed to Wayne Williamson
by a sheriff. What must Williamson do in response to this summons?**

THE PAROL
EVIDENCE
RULE

When a contract is reduced to writing, it is important to make sure that the
writing contains everything that was agreed upon between the parties. This is
because of a long-established rule called the **parol evidence rule,** which says
that evidence of oral statements made before signing a written agreement is
usually not admissible in court. Such oral statements cannot change or contradict the terms of the written agreement. **Parol** means *word of mouth*. **Evidence,**
in this instance, refers to anything presented as proof at a court trial.

EXAMPLE 9 Sylvia Cohen needed reliable transportation to and from her new job. She went to several used-car lots and chose a particular car because the dealer said to her, "This car has a 90-day guarantee, but if it breaks down during the next year, we'll lend you a car for free while it's being repaired." She signed a written agreement to buy the car, but the writing did not contain the promise. Eight months later, when the car broke down, the dealer refused to lend Sylvia a car. The parol evidence rule would prevent Sylvia's telling of the dealer's statement in court.

There are exceptions to the parol evidence rule. Oral evidence may be introduced if its sole purpose is to clarify some point that is not clear in a written agreement. Terms may not be contradicted by oral evidence but may be explained or supplemented by it. In addition, oral evidence may be introduced in court to prove that someone has committed fraud in relation to a written contract.

CHANGING THE WRITING

Frequently, you will find yourself in a position in which you are asked to sign an order blank, sales slip, or other printed form. Such forms may contain small print on the front or reverse side. The words are often difficult to read, and the language may be hard to understand. Quite often the small print is not written in your favor. Be aware of the following guidelines whenever you are asked to sign your name:

1. Read the entire text of any document before you sign it.
2. If you don't understand something or don't agree to it, *cross it out before you sign*. Have the other party initial what you have crossed out.
3. If any promises are made to you, *write them in*. Don't be afraid to make changes on a printed form.
4. *Refuse to sign* if you do not agree with everything contained in the writing. You are sometimes in a better position with an oral agreement than with an agreement that is written but not in your favor.

Remember: A contract is an agreement between *two* parties, not just one. Any writing should be an expression of their mutual consent.

Suggestions for Reducing Legal Risks

1. Remember that certain types of contracts must be in writing to be enforceable. If you are in doubt about a particular contract, see a lawyer for legal advice.
2. Because the sale or purchase of real property is ordinarily an important contract, be sure to have a lawyer draw up the contract so that it will cover all necessary details and terms for your protection.
3. If at all possible, obtain some written evidence of your important agreements, even though the law does not require it. Written evidence will help you to prove your case if a problem arises in the future.
4. Standard preprinted contracts may be changed by the parties. Read all agreements and ask for changes before you sign.

Language of the Law

Define or explain each of the following words or phrases:

perjury   equitable estoppel   goods   parol
Statute of Frauds   part performance   parol evidence rule   evidence
memorandum

Questions for Review

1. Name the six types of contracts that must be evidenced by a writing.
2. When does the equitable estoppel exception apply to an oral contract to sell real property?
3. Describe the exceptions to the rule that contracts for the sale of goods of $500 or more must be in writing.
4. What five things must a writing identify to satisfy the Statute of Frauds?
5. When handwritten terms contradict typewritten or printed terms in a written agreement, which terms will prevail?
6. Which will prevail when there is a discrepancy in an amount written in both words and figures, as on a check?
7. When a written contract is ambiguous, in whose favor will the court lean in determining the contract's meaning?
8. What is the parol evidence rule?
9. Explain an exception to the parol evidence rule.
10. List some guidelines that should be followed when one is asked to sign a printed form.

Cases in Point

In each of the following cases, give your decision and state a legal principle that applies to the case:

1. On July 15, Karl Leib orally agreed to work for Elsie Levy until June 1 of the following year. Is the contract enforceable?
2. By telephone, Mary Portillo agreed to act for 2 years as manager of a store owned by Eva Kline at a salary of $20,000. Is this an enforceable contract?
3. Paul Cooper, meeting Sue Ames on the street, orally agreed to sell her his summer home for $15,000. Was this an enforceable contract?
4. Ruby Simpson orally agreed to sell and Pedro Pedilla orally agreed to buy a camera for $450. Simpson later argued that the agreement was not enforceable because it was not in writing. Is she correct?
5. In a telephone conversation Frank Larson promised Gena Little $10,000 if she would marry Larson's nephew. Little married the nephew, but Larson refused to pay the promised sum. Could Little have the promise enforced?
6. A. R. Norton orally agreed to sell her farm to E. J. Dillon for $20,000. She gave Dillon a written memorandum as follows: "On this date I hereby agree to sell my farm to E. J. Dillon for $20,000, A. R. Norton." Dillon later refused to carry out the agreement. May Norton recover from Dillon for breach of contract?
7. Carlos Beck made an oral agreement to buy a building lot from the Bitner Realty Company. At the same time, he wrote a memorandum of the agreement, which he signed and gave to the realty company, although the company did not sign. When Beck

failed to buy the property as agreed, the Bitner Realty Company brought an action for damages. Was the realty company entitled to judgment?

8. David Abrams agreed to buy printing equipment from Aaron Ackerman. A contract was drafted and typed to evidence the agreement, but before signing it, the parties added a handwritten clause in pen and ink. Later, it was discovered that the handwritten clause contradicted a typewritten clause in the agreement. Which clause will the court follow in determining the intent of the parties?

9. Hector Faria orally agreed to sell his house in Cleveland, Ohio, to Marie Ellis for $95,000. Ellis immediately sold her house in Nevada, gave up her job there, and moved her belongings to Cleveland. Faria refused to sell Ellis the house in Cleveland. Would a court help Ellis?

10. A used-car dealer told Irving Zack that if the car he purchased broke down in the next 6 months, the dealership would repair it free of charge. Later, Zack signed an agreement to buy the car, but the agreement contained only a 90-day guarantee. Will the 6-month oral guarantee be upheld in court?

Cases to Judge

1. As part of a business transaction, Buck H. Simpson orally promised to repurchase a particular parcel of real estate from Dr. Michell M. Young whenever Dr. Young decided to sell it. Simpson refused to repurchase the property when asked to do so by Young. Is Simpson's promise enforceable? Why or why not? *Young v. Simpson*, 607 F. Supp. 67 (Texas)

2. The city of Yonkers entered into a contract that required Otis Elevator Company to stay in Yonkers "for a reasonable period but not less than 60 years." The city of Yonkers argued that the contract could have been performed within a year and therefore did not need to be in writing. Do you agree with the city of Yonkers? Give a reason for your answer. *City of Yonkers v. Otis Elevator Co.*, 607 F. Supp. 1416 (New York)

3. Investors in a limited partnership entered into an agreement concerning the dissolution of the partnership and the division of its assets. A memorandum agreement was drawn up and dated but never signed. Later, the parties wrote letters to each other, referring to the memorandum agreement. Can the signed letters and the unsigned agreement all be used together as evidence to satisfy the Statute of Frauds? Explain. *Weiner & Co. v. Teitelbaum*, 483 N.Y.S.2d 313 (New York)

4. Attorney Sanford Kowal orally agreed to guarantee payment of certain medical bills due Dr. Richard Webster. This was in exchange for Webster's expert testimony in a civil suit in which Kowal was the attorney for Webster's former patient, Philip Soule. Soule's medical bills were to be paid out of any sums recovered in the event that Soule won the case. Kowal claims that the oral agreement is unenforceable. Do you agree? Why or why not? *Webster v. Kowal*, 476 N.E.2d 205 (Massachusetts)

5. When being interviewed for employment with A.T. Transport, Mr. and Mrs. Cowdrey asked questions about job security and made a special point of inquiring about the duration of the position. The representative of A.T. Transport promised Mr. Cowdrey a job saying, "as long as you do your job and A.T. Transport is in business, you'll never have a thing to worry about." Cowdrey was hired as a terminal manager and dispatcher. The parties did not enter into a written contract. Four and one-half years later, Cowdrey was discharged. Did the contract have to be evidenced by a writing to be enforceable? Explain. *Cowdrey v. A.T. Transport*, 367 N.W.2d 433 (Michigan)

Chapter 12

HOW CONTRACTS COME TO AN END

Scene: The Williams home. Doug and Lorna are sitting in the den.

Lorna: I hope you've got that $10 ready to hand over. Mom will be home from her evening class in a few minutes, and you'll find out that Marvin Maxwell was there. I'll win our bet for sure!

Doug: That's what you think! He'll never show his face again after the fraud he committed on Mom.

Lorna: Are you still going to buy that car from the guy down the street?

Doug: Well, I did agree to buy it from him, so I guess I'm going to have to go through with the deal. I'd like to get out of it, though. We had another deal going, too. He's a partner in that liquor store that's going out of business. He agreed to sell me 100 cases of beer at the wholesale price, and I was going to resell them for a profit.

Lorna: You're not 21. Can you buy beer?

Doug: Well, that's the problem. Before they raised the age to 21, I could legally buy beer. Now it's illegal.

Lorna: Do you think the deal will go through?

(Denise comes dashing into the room.)

Denise: You know that guy down the street? He just smashed up his car! He came around the corner too fast and couldn't make the turn and smashed into a telephone pole. I saw the whole thing! It was a miracle that he didn't get hurt!

Doug: Was it a red Mustang?

Denise: Yes, I think so.

Doug: That was the car I was going to buy from him.

Lorna: We were just talking about him before you came in.

(They hear the sound of a car pulling into the driveway.)

Lorna: That's probably Mom now. Get your money out, Doug—you're going to lose that bet.

(The door opens, and Mrs. Williams enters the room.)

Lorna (*eagerly*): Well? Was Marvin there?

Mrs. Williams (*tears come to her eyes*): He died! Marvin died! That handsome man . . .

Lorna: What happened?

Doug: Was he murdered?

Mrs. Williams: He was killed in an automobile accident. The woman who sits beside me in class told me. She knew him, too. It seems that he had agreed to paint her house for her, and she had given him half the money already for doing the work, and he hadn't started yet.

Doug: That sounds like him. There's no way they can make him paint the house now.

Mrs. Williams: I would have gone to his funeral if I'd known.

Lorna: Well, Doug, I guess I owe you the $10. You won the bet. He didn't show after all.

Doug: No. It wouldn't be fair to take your money. We had no idea that it would end this way.

Lorna: You're a nice brother.

Mrs. Williams: At least I have the ring to remember him by, even if it is made of glass.

LEGAL ISSUES

1. Does subsequent illegality make a contract void?
2. Does the destruction of the exact subject matter of a contract discharge the contract?
3. Is death of a party to a contract for personal services an excuse for nonperformance?
4. Can a contract be ended by agreement of the parties?

THE SPIRIT OF THE LAW

Contracts, like everything else, eventually end. When contracts end, they are said to be **discharged,** or **terminated.** The law specifies the ways that contracts end so that people will know when their rights and duties expire. Contracts may be discharged by (1) performance, (2) agreement, (3) impossibility of performance, or (4) operation of law. Each of these methods of termination is described in this chapter.

DISCHARGE BY PERFORMANCE

Most contracts are discharged by performance. Both parties do what they have agreed to do, and their obligations end.

Time for Performance

Occasionally the time for completing a contract is very important to one or both of the parties. If the time for performance is not mentioned in the contract, the court will say it must be completed within a reasonable time. A **reasonable time** may be defined as the time that is suitable to the objective in view. This time will vary with the circumstances of each individual case. For example, the reasonable time for the sale of a crate of ripe tomatoes would not be the same as the reasonable time for the sale of a house.

If the parties specify a time limit for the performance of the contract, the court will usually allow a longer time for its performance unless time is of the essence. **Time is of the essence** means that time is a vital or essential element of the contract.

EXAMPLE 1 Peter Miles agreed to paint Carol Wolloff's house and to begin on or before June 1. He showed up on June 3 to do the job. A court would probably excuse his tardiness because there was nothing to show that time was of the essence.

If the parties specify a time for performance in the contract and, in addition, state or imply that time is of the essence, the court will enforce the time period.

EXAMPLE 2 The Seasons Store agreed to buy 5,000 chocolate rabbits from Northern Confectionaries. Their contract specified delivery 3 weeks before Easter and stated that time was of the essence. The rabbits arrived 1 week before Easter, by which time Seasons had ordered and received substitute products from another supplier. Seasons refused the late delivery of rabbits. The court would probably uphold Seasons' refusal.

Satisfactory Performance

EXAMPLE 3 Marcia Morris, an artist, agreed to paint Joyce Merritt's portrait "to her satisfaction" for $250. When the painting was completed, all of Merritt's friends, relatives, and acquaintances thought that it was a perfect likeness of her. However, Merritt felt the nose was too long and did not like it.

Under the law of many states, if Merritt honestly did not like the portrait, she would not have to pay for it. Since Morris had agreed to paint it "to her satisfaction," Merritt could reject it if she were not satisfied. Merritt could not, of course, keep the painting in such a case.

Sometimes people will require in a contract that a job be done "in a satisfactory manner." On other occasions, the contract will say nothing about satisfaction. In both of these situations, when one party believes the job to be unsatisfactory and the other believes it to be satisfactory, the court uses the **reasonable-person test.** The court asks, "Would a reasonable person consider the job to be completed in a satisfactory manner?" The dispute will then be settled based on the answer to this very crucial question.

Substantial Performance

In order to discharge a contract by performance, both parties must fully perform their parts of the bargain. They must do everything they agreed to do. Someone who has not fully performed cannot, in most instances, win a lawsuit against the other for money owed or other damages. An exception to this rule is known as the doctrine of **substantial performance.** Under this doctrine, someone who has substantially performed (done everything except very minor and unimportant things) may win a lawsuit for the amount agreed upon under the contract, minus the cost of completing the job. This doctrine is often applied to construction contracts.

EXAMPLE 4 Suppose that Eugene Bell agreed to build a house for Ramon Ramirez. It was to be built according to certain plans and specifications on land owned by Ramirez. The specifications called for "Reading Pipe," but the person Bell hired to do the plumbing overlooked the word *Reading*. The pipe installed was just as good, but it was not Reading Pipe. When the house was finished, Ramirez refused to pay any of the contract price, claiming breach of contract.

Ramirez must pay. He may, however, deduct any damages suffered as a result of Bell's failure to use the correct pipe.

Tender of Performance

A **tender of performance** is an offer to do what you have agreed to do under a contract. If you agree to buy a car, for example, making tender would be offering to pay the money at the agreed time for performance. If you agree to sell a car, making tender would be offering to give the car to the buyer at the agreed time. It is important to make tender even if you know the other party is not going to perform his or her part of the contract. This is because it is necessary, in some states, to test the other party's willingness and ability to perform. If neither party has made tender, these courts hold that a breach of contract has not been established. Neither party is in a position to bring suit against the other.

Persons who must perform acts (such as selling goods or performing services) are excused from performing if they make proper tender and it is rejected. On the other hand, persons who must pay money are not excused from paying if their tender of payment is rejected. They are merely excused from paying further interest on their obligation.

EXAMPLE 5 Suppose that Keith Hanson owed Carla Miller $100, which was due on the first of July. Hanson did not tender payment until the first of August. Miller refused to take the money at that time and said, "You didn't pay the money when it was due. Now I'm going to sue you and make it cost you plenty."

Hanson still owes Miller $100. However, if Miller did sue, she could collect $100 plus interest on the $100 at the legal rate for the 1 month between the due date of tender and the actual tender of payment.

Tender of payment (an offer to pay the money) may be made, for the purchase of goods, by check or by any other manner normally used in business. However, the seller may demand **legal tender**—that is, U.S. currency. If the seller demands legal tender, he or she must give the buyer additional time to get it when the contract is for goods.

DISCHARGE BY AGREEMENT

Legal Issue No. 4

Contracts may be terminated by mutual agreement of the contracting parties.

EXAMPLE 6 Suppose that Lawrence Langham has contracted to sell his tractor to Jerry Bodoni for $1,200. Langham suddenly changes his mind. He decides not to sell the tractor. Langham visits Bodoni prepared to defend his decision but finds out that Bodoni has changed his mind also. Bodoni decides not to purchase the tractor. Each man agrees to call the agreement off. Langham and Bodoni shake hands amiably after agreeing to terminate the original agreement, and the contract no longer exists.

Whatever the parties agree to do in the first place, they may later mutually agree not to do. The agreement to terminate a contract may take any one of several forms.

Mutual Release

The agreement entered into by Langham and Bodoni terminating their agreement was a **mutual release.** Each released the other from his obligation. Each gave up something, so the agreement to terminate is binding. The release must be mutual, however; otherwise, there would be no consideration for the promised release.

Accord and Satisfaction

Another way in which an existing contract can be discharged is by substituting another contract for it. This is called an **accord and satisfaction.**

EXAMPLE 7   Suppose, in Example 6, that Bodoni still wants the tractor but does not have the money to make good on his agreement. He goes to Langham, explains the situation, and offers to give Langham his expensive camera and color television instead of the $1,200. If Langham agrees and accepts the camera and the television, Bodoni's promise to pay the $1,200 is discharged.

In the above example, Langham must actually accept the items. His promise to accept would not be binding. The promise to do so is the accord. The carrying out of the promise is the satisfaction.

DISCHARGE BY IMPOSSI-BILITY OF PERFOR-MANCE

If the performance of a contract is actually impossible and not merely difficult or costly, the court will generally excuse one of the parties for not performing. The principal situations in which the courts will allow a discharge for impossibility are (1) death or illness that prevents the performance of a personal service contract, (2) destruction of the exact subject matter or the means for performance, and (3) illegality—that is, when performance of a contract becomes illegal.

Death or Illness in a Personal Service Contract

The death or illness of a party to a contract is an excuse for nonperformance only if the contract requires the personal service of the person who has died or become ill. In Example 3, for instance, if Morris were to die before completing the portrait, the contract would be discharged. She was undoubtedly selected for her particular ability to do the work.

However, if the contract is such that the party who became ill or died had the right to hire someone else to perform the obligation, neither death nor illness will discharge the contract. In the case of death, the person appointed to settle the deceased's affairs would be obligated to hire someone else to carry out the contract.

Legal Issue No. 3

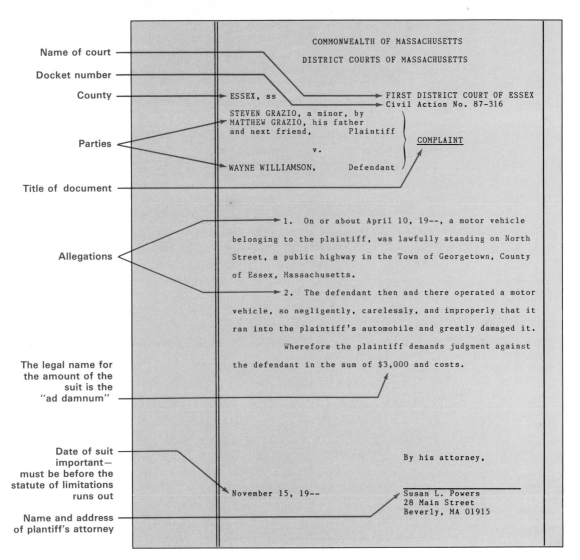

Name of court

Docket number

County

Parties

Title of document

Allegations

The legal name for the amount of the suit is the "ad damnum"

Date of suit important— must be before the statute of limitations runs out

Name and address of plantiff's attorney

COMMONWEALTH OF MASSACHUSETTS

DISTRICT COURTS OF MASSACHUSETTS

ESSEX, ss

FIRST DISTRICT COURT OF ESSEX
Civil Action No. 87-316

STEVEN GRAZIO, a minor, by
MATTHEW GRAZIO, his father
and next friend,   Plaintiff

COMPLAINT

v.

WAYNE WILLIAMSON,   Defendant

1. On or about April 10, 19--, a motor vehicle belonging to the plaintiff, was lawfully standing on North Street, a public highway in the Town of Georgetown, County of Essex, Massachusetts.

2. The defendant then and there operated a motor vehicle, so negligently, carelessly, and improperly that it ran into the plaintiff's automobile and greatly damaged it.

Wherefore the plaintiff demands judgment against the defendant in the sum of $3,000 and costs.

By his attorney,

November 15, 19--

Susan L. Powers
28 Main Street
Beverly, MA 01915

A summons is official notice to the defendant in a lawsuit that a complaint has been filed with the clerk of the court. What are the defendant's duties regarding this complaint?

Destruction of the Exact Subject Matter

When a particular item is chosen by the parties to be the subject matter of the contract and that item is destroyed after the contract is entered into but before it is carried out, the contract is discharged.

EXAMPLE 8   Edward Augulewicz went into Elena Grillo's secondhand furniture shop and picked out a couch for his apartment. It was agreed that the couch would be delivered the next day. That night, however, the couch was destroyed by fire. The contract would be discharged because of the destruction of the particular subject matter that had been identified to the contract.

Legal Issue No. 2

However, compare Example 8 with the following example:

EXAMPLE 9 Augulewicz went into the Big Value Furniture Mart and picked out a couch he liked from several samples. The salesperson told him that they had some of those couches in their warehouse and that one would be delivered to him the next day. That night a fire destroyed the Big Value Furniture Mart warehouse and all of its furniture. The store would still be obligated to obtain another couch for Augulewicz, because a particular couch had not been identified to the contract. A type of couch had been selected, but the exact one had not been chosen.

Sometimes the means for performance of a contract is destroyed so that the contract cannot be completed. For example, suppose a person contracts to reshingle the roof of a house. If the house is destroyed before the job is done, the contract is discharged because the job requires the existence of the house in order to be performed.

Illegality

Legal Issue No. 1

Another type of impossibility of performance arises when performance of the contract becomes illegal. You have seen that a contract whose performance would be illegal at the time it was entered into is void. The same general rules apply when performance becomes illegal after the contract is entered into.

EXAMPLE 10 Suppose that Holly Jones, who is 14 years of age, contracted to work for Frank Carlino for 3 months. At the time the agreement was made, such employment was perfectly legal. Shortly afterward, however, a new child labor law that prohibited the employment of anyone under 16 years of age took effect.

Jones and Carlino have no choice in the matter. The contract is terminated. Legal performance has now become impossible.

DISCHARGE BY OPERATION OF LAW
Wrongful Alteration

At times, the best interests of society demand that a contract be terminated. Under these circumstances, the law declares contracts discharged by **operation of law.**

Sometimes wrongful acts of one of the parties will discharge a contract by operation of law. One of these wrongful acts is altering (changing) a contract.

EXAMPLE 11 A written contract provided that Peter Merkle was to buy Bart Little's canoe for $95. Little secretly inserted a ''1'' in front of the ''95'' and then attempted to collect $195 from Merkle. Little outsmarted himself. The contract was discharged by his wrongful alteration. Not only may he not collect $195, but he also may not enforce the original contract.

The contract, however, is not discharged if Merkle chooses to enforce it. If Merkle still wants the canoe at $95, he can get it or can collect damages if Little will not deliver.

Statutes of Limitations

If you make a contract and your contract is breached by the other party, you ordinarily have a right to sue that party. Under some circumstances, however, this right to sue may be taken away from you. The law may specify the time within which a contract may be enforced.

■ In all states there are statutes that specify the length of time within which a legal action may be brought on a contract. These statutes are called **statutes of limitations.**

EXAMPLE 12 Suppose that Smart Shoppes, Inc., owed the Gould Corporation $1,000 for a shipment of dresses. Smart Shoppes did not pay, and for more than 10 years, Gould did not bring any action to collect. Gould probably can no longer collect. It has waited too long. You may not "sleep on your rights" and then expect the law to help you collect.

The statute of limitations for the failure to perform contracts for the sale of goods is 4 years in most states. This means that an action must be begun within 4 years after the contract is broken. The parties may reduce the period of limitations to not less than 1 year by the original agreement. They may not, however, extend the period to more than the limit set by their state.

The time begins to run at the very moment the failure to perform occurs, but a "time out" is called if the debtor is a minor or leaves the state. This also occurs when a creditor becomes mentally ill.

EXAMPLE 13 Suppose that Alice Briggs breached her contract and refused to pay Jill Hamilton the $100 she had borrowed from her. A month later Briggs went out of state and did not return until 10 years later. Prior to the time of Briggs's return, Hamilton was found to be insane and was committed to a state mental hospital. Even though she may remain in the mental institution for 10 additional years, Hamilton could still bring suit for the money due her as soon as she is released from the hospital and declared sane again.

The time of Briggs's absence from the state and the time of Hamilton's mental incapacity would not be counted in the statutory limitation period.

■ Under the law of some states, people who are in prison suffer **civil death;** that is, they lose the right to vote, to contract, and to bring and defend against civil lawsuits. In these states, the statute of limitations often stops running while a person is in prison. Also, if something is paid on account or if the debtor admits the existence of the debt after the time period has passed, the debt is renewed for another statutory period. In New York State and some other states, such a new promise must be in writing. There are many special statutes of limitations in every state. In order to protect yourself fully in important business relationships, you should refer to the most recent statutes in your state.

Bankruptcy

Sometimes people and businesses get hopelessly in debt—so hopelessly that they cannot meet the demands of their creditors. Their creditors become angry, and there is just no way for debtors to pay their bills. Under old English law, such debtors were placed in debtors' prisons. Most debtors had no hope of recovering. The drafters of the U.S. Constitution opposed the mistreatment of

If a contractor agreed to remodel a kitchen in a home, which subsequently burned, would the contract be binding on either party?

debtors and gave Congress the authority to pass laws to help people in this dilemma. Thus, since 1880, the U.S. Congress has passed various bankruptcy laws. The most recent is the Bankruptcy Reform Act of 1978, which was amended in 1984. Its aims are to give debtors who are overwhelmed with debt a fresh start and to provide a fair way of distributing a debtor's assets among all creditors. A bankruptcy order by a court will end a debtor's current contractual obligations.

The bankruptcy act is divided into eight odd-numbered chapters, the most important of which are Chapters 7, 9, 11, and 13. Chapter 7 provides for liquidation, or straight bankruptcy; Chapter 9 deals with cities and towns that must file bankruptcy; Chapter 11 is designed to allow businesses with financial problems to reorganize; and Chapter 13 allows for the adjustment of debts of individuals with regular income. Personal bankruptcies are filed under Chapter 7 or Chapter 13 of the bankruptcy act.

Chapter 7 (Liquidation)   In a Chapter 7 bankruptcy (sometimes called a *straight bankruptcy*), the debtor's belongings, with some exceptions, are **liquidated,** or turned into cash to pay creditors. The bankruptcy petition may be voluntary (brought by the debtor) or involuntary (brought by creditors). To file for voluntary bankruptcy, a debtor must be unable to pay debts as they become due. To file for involuntary bankruptcy, creditors must have **grounds for relief.**

These include the failure of the debtor to pay bills as they become due. If there are fewer than 12 creditors, anyone whose claim is $5,000 or more may file the petition. However, if a debtor has 12 or more creditors, at least 3 of them with claims of $5,000 or more must join the petition. The legal name for a bankruptcy judgment is an **order for relief.** Debtors who file under this chapter must wait at least 6 years before filing for bankruptcy again.

Chapter 11 (Reorganization)

Chapter 11 (Reorganization)   Chapter 11 of the bankruptcy act provides a method for businesses to reorganize their financial affairs and still remain in business. If allowed to continue in operation, companies may be able to overcome their difficulties, pay their creditors, and become profit-making organizations.

When a petition for reorganization is filed, either by the debtor or a creditor, the court appoints a committee of creditors to assist with the reorganization. The court may also appoint a trustee to operate the business or to protect creditors' interests. A reorganization plan is developed by the debtor, creditors, or trustee. The plan divides creditors into classes and sets forth ways in which their claims will be handled fairly. It may include giving creditors stock in the company in exchange for canceling the debts owed them. Once the plan is approved by a certain number of creditors and the court, it will go into operation. The business will be able to continue to operate without interference from its creditors.

Chapter 13 (Adjustment of Debts)   Sometimes debtors overextend their credit. They have regular income, but they cannot pay all of their bills. If given time, they may eventually be able to pay at least part of the amount they owe to each creditor. Chapter 13 of the bankruptcy act permits an individual debtor to develop a repayment plan and, upon completion of payments under the plan, to receive a discharge from most remaining debt. This avoids liquidation of the debtor's assets as in a Chapter 7 bankruptcy. The plan must provide either for partial payment of all creditors proportionately or full payment of all creditors over an extended period of time. During the period of the plan, which is usually 3 years, creditors are prevented from continuing their collection activities. The 6-year waiting period before the debtor is allowed to file for bankruptcy again does not apply, in most cases, to a Chapter 13 bankruptcy. In addition, debtors whose repayment plans under this chapter do not work out may file for liquidation under Chapter 7.

Exemptions   As part of the "fresh start" policy of the bankruptcy act, many assets are protected from liquidation. They may be kept by debtors even after bankruptcy with the hope that debtors will recover more easily from their misfortune if they are not completely wiped out of everything they own. Items that are exempt from liquidation include $7,500 equity in a personal residence and $1,200 in one car. **Equity** means the value of the residence less the mortgage. Also exempt are up to $200 of each item of ordinary household furnishings and personal apparel (not to exceed $4,000), $500 in jewelry, and $750 in professional books or tools of trade. In addition, there is a **pour-over provision,** which allows up to $3,750 of any unused portion of the real estate exemption plus $400 of any other unused exemption to be applied to other property and thus be exempt. Husbands and wives may file a joint petition in bankruptcy and receive double the amount of exemptions.

EXAMPLE 14 The Milroys found themselves in the position of being unable to pay their debts as they became due. After reviewing their financial situation, their lawyer advised them to file bankruptcy. Their residence, valued at $50,000, had a mortgage of $36,500. This gave them an equity of $13,500. Mr. Milroy's car, which he owned outright, had a market value of $1,400. Mrs. Milroy's car, on which $1,000 was still owed to the bank, was worth $2,700. This left an equity in the vehicle of $1,700. They had $1,600 in a joint bank account. Their double real estate exemption (2 × $7,500) amounts to $15,000. This means that the full $13,500 equity in their residence is exempt and there is a balance of $1,500 remaining. The first $1,200 of Mr. Milroy's car is exempt, leaving $200 not exempt. Similarly, the first $1,200 of Mrs. Milroy's car is exempt, leaving $500 not exempt. At this point the pour-over provision may be applied. The $200 and $500 may be subtracted from the $1,500 surplus, leaving a surplus balance of $800. This, added to each spouse's $400 exemption in any other property equals $1,600 ($800 + $400 + $400). Thus, the bank account balance of $1,600 is also exempt, along with their residence and their two cars.

For all practical purposes, an order for relief ends all the debtor's outstanding contractual obligations. Technically, these obligations still exist, but the remedy for enforcing them in court no longer exists. The bankruptcy act has modified the common law so that a person who becomes hopelessly in debt may be relieved of further obligation on contracts if the court grants that person relief. However, debts associated with fraud or wrongdoing are revived even after the debts have been discharged in bankruptcy.

Certain debts cannot be discharged under the bankruptcy act. Educational loans, for example, are not dischargeable during the first 5 years of the repayment period unless a judge finds that payment would impose an undue hardship on the debtor. Similarly, debts for taxes, alimony, support, and maintenance are not affected by a general discharge in bankruptcy.

Suggestions for Reducing Legal Risks

1. When you contract for services, decide clearly whether or not you expect to demand *personal* services. Remember, when time is an important factor, that impossibility of personal performance discharges the contract and this may create a hardship on you. There are advantages and disadvantages involved, so calculate your risks carefully. Many times it is an advantage not to require personal service when equally satisfactory service will be sufficient.

2. If you plan to enter into an important contract in which you might suffer a sizable loss in case of impossibility of performance due to the destruction of subject matter, discuss the potential risks with the other party. Come to an understanding about the sharing of risks and losses, and make that understanding a part of the original contract.

Language of the Law

Define or explain each of the following words or phrases:

discharged
terminated
reasonable time
time is of the
essence
reasonable-person
test

substantial perfor-
mance
tender of perfor-
mance
tender of payment
legal tender

mutual release
accord and satisfac-
tion
operation of law
statutes of limitations
civil death

liquidated
grounds for relief
order for relief
equity
pour-over provision

Questions for Review

1. If the time for performance is not mentioned in a contract, when must the contract be completed?
2. On what occasion will the court strictly enforce the time period that is stated in the contract?
3. What test does the court use when the person who does a job believes it is satisfactory and the client believes it is unsatisfactory?
4. Explain what is meant by the doctrine of substantial performance.
5. Give an example of tender of performance and tender of payment.
6. What must the seller do if a check is offered for the purchase of goods and the seller demands legal tender?
7. Explain how a contract for personal service might be discharged as a result of the destruction of the means for performance.
8. If one party changes a contract without the other party's consent, what can the other party do about this?
9. What are the statutes of limitations for different types of contracts in your state?
10. Under what conditions may the time be extended for an additional statutory period?
11. What are the aims of the Bankruptcy Reform Act of 1978?
12. Describe Chapter 7 of the bankruptcy act.
13. Describe Chapter 13 of the bankruptcy act.
14. What assets are exempt from liquidation under the bankruptcy act?

Cases in Point

In each of the following cases, give your decision and state a legal principle that applies to the case:

1. Marie Juliano agreed to paint George O'Shea's house for $1,500 and to begin on or before August 1. Juliano began the work on August 4. Did she breach the contract?
2. Earl Kirton agreed to put vinyl siding on Ben Finkel's house for $4,500. After completing almost the entire job and with only one row of clapboards remaining to be installed, he could not stand Finkel's watching his every move any longer. Kirton picked up his tools and left; Finkel argued that he didn't have to pay Kirton because Kirton did not complete the job. Is Finkel correct?
3. While browsing through a secondhand furniture store, Ruth Collins came upon an

antique table that she admired. She told the proprietor that she would buy it, and since she had no money with her, she agreed to pick it up and pay for it the next day. That night the antique shop and its contents burned to the ground. Is the contract to buy the table discharged?

4. Sam Norbert contracts to build a wooden garage for Charles Wills. Before work is begun, a local law is passed prohibiting the construction of wooden garages in the city. Is Wills liable to Norbert on the contract?

5. Jack Carson and Ruth Horton became engaged to marry, and Carson gave Horton a beautiful diamond ring. Later, they had an argument. Horton returned the ring and said, "I wouldn't marry you if you were the last man on earth." Carson replied, "That's okay with me." Has their contract been terminated? If so, on what basis?

6. Millicent White agreed to sell Claudine Burns all the peaches grown this year in her orchard. A severe frost ruined the peach crop, and White was unable to deliver any peaches. Was she liable to Burns for breach of contract?

7. Otto Mandel entered into a contract with the Hewlett Lumber Company for the purchase of 50,000 feet of yellow pine lumber. Mandel intended, as the lumber company knew, to use the wood in the manufacture of pinball games. After the contract was made, a law was passed making the manufacture and sale of these games anywhere in the state illegal. Did this new law relieve Mandel from liability on the contract?

8. A statute states that no action on a debt may be brought 4 years after the debt is due. Donna Simpson had owed Ralph Kerr $200 for 4 years, but 6 months later she gave Kerr $50 on the account. Simpson later refused to pay the balance, claiming that the statute of limitations bars recovery. Is this a valid defense?

9. Roger Goldberg took his television set to Catherine Jones for repairs. Jones agreed to repair it for $45. After a more careful inspection, Jones found that she could not repair the set without a sweep generator, an expensive electrical instrument that she did not have. Jones said that the contract was discharged because of impossibility of performance. Is her reasoning sound? If Jones does not repair the set, can Goldberg bring suit for breach of contract?

10. Lillian McNiff sold goods in the amount of $480 to Thurlow Rumpf on 30-day credit terms. Rumpf left the state a short time after and did not return until 5 years later. When McNiff learned of Rumpf's return, she immediately brought suit. The statute of limitations operating in her state provided that an action not begun within 4 years from the day that payment was due on a sale of goods was not permitted. Would McNiff win her suit? Explain.

Cases to Judge

1. Taylor took out several student loans to help pay for his college education. During the first year of the repayment period, when he owed $8,697, Taylor filed a petition for involuntary bankruptcy in the U.S. Bankruptcy Court. Must he repay the student loans? Explain. *Mass. Higher Educ. Assistance v. Taylor,* 459 N.E.2d 807 (Massachusetts)

2. Harris brought suit against Craig for medical malpractice. The time period for bringing such a suit under the statute of limitations had gone by, Harris, however, had been in prison during part of that time period. Is the time in prison included in the time period of the statute of limitations? *Harris v. Craig,* 697 P.2d 189 (Oregon)

3. Gary and Bill Stratton entered into a written contract with the Prudential Insurance Company of America under which they were to be paid $250 per acre to cut, pile, and burn all trees, brush, and other vegetation either standing or fallen on the land. Work was to commence "immediately" and be completed "no later than November 25, 1981." Due to rain and inclement weather, the Strattons' heavy equipment was unable to operate for a 3-week period. Does this cause the time of performance to be extended? Explain. *Prudential Ins. Co. of America v. Stratton,* 685 S.W.2d 818 (Arkansas)

4. At the age of 17, Donna Kowalski, who was married and the mother of one child, underwent a surgical operation. The operation resulted in the removal of her reproductive organs. Two days before her twentieth birthday, Kowalski brought suit against the surgeon and the hospital for malpractice. She claimed that the surgery was unnecessary and too radical. She also claimed that it was performed without her knowledge. Her suit was brought more than 2 years after the surgery took place. The statute of limitations in that state at the time was 2 years for medical malpractice. Is Kowalski barred by the statute of limitations from bringing suit? *Kowalski v. Liska,* 397 N.E.2d 39 (Illinois)

5. Erickson Construction built a concrete water slide for Congress-Kenilworth Corporation. The project, known as Thunder Mountain Rapids, opened to the public the day after the job was completed. Congress-Kenilworth refused to pay the amount due under the contract because there was extensive cracking of the concrete flumes within the water slide. The cracks did not affect the operation of the structure as a water slide. Erickson argued that under the doctrine of substantial performance it should be paid the amount of the contract less an amount to offset the defects. Congress-Kenilworth argued that it only owed Erickson the reasonable value for services rendered under a quasi-contract theory. For whom would you decide? Why? *W. E. Erickson Const. v. Congress-Kenilworth,* 477 N.E.2d 513 (Illinois)

Chapter 13

ASSIGNMENT, DELEGATION, AND BREACH OF CONTRACT

Scene: The Williams home. Denise, Lorna, and Doug are sitting in the den.

Denise: Let's do something special for Mom when she gets home from work tonight. This is her last day with Mr. Ellis, you know.

Lorna: That's a good idea! She's been waiting for this day for a long time.

Doug: I'll go out and buy a couple of pizzas.

Denise: Are you kidding? That's not special!

Lorna: Let's order some Chinese food. We haven't had that for a long time.

Denise: She loves Chinese food. We can buy it to bring home and surprise her when she gets here.

(Later, the family is sitting around the dining room table.)

Mrs. Williams: You children are so thoughtful to do this for me! What a pleasant surprise.

Lorna: Did Mr. Ellis give you the $500 bonus that he promised, Mom?

Mrs. Williams: No, I'm disappointed about that. He said that he couldn't afford to give it to me because business has fallen off.

Denise: He promised it to you, Mom! You can sue him for breach of contract!

Mrs. Williams: I just want to get away from him and go on to something more pleasant.

Doug: If you don't sue him, I will. I'll take him to small claims court.

Lorna: Let's talk about more pleasant things. Open your fortune cookie, Mom.

Mrs. Williams *(opening the cookie and reading the slip of paper inside)*: "The sun will shine on you today and brighten your life."

Denise: I knew that it would be something nice.

Mrs. Williams: I was talking with my friend at school last night—you know, the one who paid Marvin to paint her house.

Lorna: Did she ever get the money back that she paid Marvin?

Mrs. Williams: No, and she was furious. In fact, she was going to bring suit and have the court order his estate to paint the house.

Doug: Why didn't she?

Mrs. Williams: Well, an unusual thing happened. Some people from a painting company arrived last week and started to paint her house. It seems that before Marvin was killed in that accident, he transferred the job of painting the house to the painting company.

Lorna: Really? I didn't know you could do that.

Denise: Did you get your mail, Mom? It's on the counter.

Mrs. Williams: Thank you. (*She takes the mail and opens a letter.*) This is from an insurance company. (*There is a pause while she reads.*) I don't believe it! Marvin Maxwell named me the beneficiary of his life insurance policy! Can you imagine that? I hardly knew him!

Doug: Marvin did that?

Denise: And you called him a jerk.

Mrs. Williams: Wait a minute. It says here that they are not going to pay me—for some legal reason.

Doug: They can't do that!

Lorna: Can you sue the insurance company?

Mrs. Williams: I don't know. . . . (*looking through her other mail*) This looks like a letter from Marvin's corporation that I bought stock in— you know, the one that searches the ocean for old shipwrecks.

Doug: That was a ripoff if there ever was one.

Mrs. Williams: It's a notice to stockholders that they have found an old pirate ship off the New England coast! Marvin's company has struck it rich!

Doug: I don't believe it.

Denise: Do you mean that we're rich?

Lorna: I always liked that guy Marvin.

LEGAL ISSUES

1. Can someone who is not a party to a contract bring suit for breach of that contract?
2. Will a court order a person (or the estate of a deceased person) to paint a house when the person has breached a contract to do so?
3. Can duties, such as painting a house, be transferred to others without the approval of the original party?
4. Can the beneficiary of a life insurance policy bring suit against the insurance company to enforce the rights under the policy?

THE SPIRIT OF THE LAW

We saw in Chapter 7 that when people enter into contracts, they receive rights (benefits) and incur duties (detriments). In most cases, people keep the rights and carry out the duties themselves. Occasionally, however, people transfer their rights or their duties (or both) to someone else. With some exceptions, the law allows this to be done, if the parties have not agreed otherwise. There are also times when a party does not carry out the terms of a contract at all. When this happens and the other party to the contract suffers a loss, the law provides a **remedy,** that is, a legal means of correcting the wrong.

TRANSFER OF RIGHTS

The transfer of a right under a contract is called an **assignment.** The party who transfers the right is called the **assignor.** The party who receives the right is called the **assignee.**

EXAMPLE 1 Anthony Cuomo entered a contract with Cathy Michaud to paint her house for $1,800. Cuomo was pleased to get the contract because he owed $1,800 to his landlord, David Brown. Before painting the house, Cuomo assigned the right to receive the money to Brown. When it came time to pay for the paint job, Michaud would pay the $1,800 to Brown rather than to Cuomo.

How Rights May Be Assigned

No consideration is necessary for an assignment to be valid. In most cases, the law does not specify the form in which a right may be assigned by one party to another, but usually the assignment should be in writing. An oral assignment might be legal, but it would be hard to prove.

Perhaps the most important reason for a written statement is this: The party who owes the money or other duty of performance is entitled to notice of the assignment. If that party is not notified, he or she may pay the debt to the assignor and end the obligation. If that party is notified or shown the written assignment, then he or she is legally bound to pay the assignee only; payment to the assignor will not discharge the debt.

EXAMPLE 2 Suppose that in Example 1 Cuomo assigned his right to the $1,800 to his landlord, Brown. If Michaud were informed, then she would *have* to pay Brown, not Cuomo, to discharge the contract. If the assignment were in writing, Michaud's new duty and Brown's new right would be easily proven.

What Rights May Be Assigned

Most rights are assignable unless such an assignment would materially change the obligations of the other party to the contract. In Example 1, when Cuomo assigned the right to receive the $1,800 to Brown, Michaud's obligation (which was to pay out money) did not change. The assignment was valid. However, consider the following example:

EXAMPLE 3 In Example 1, Michaud has the right to have her house painted. If she were to assign that right to some other homeowner, Cuomo's obligation would be materially changed. He would be required to paint a house other than the one he had planned to paint. Such an assignment would be void. Rights to receive personal services are usually not assignable.

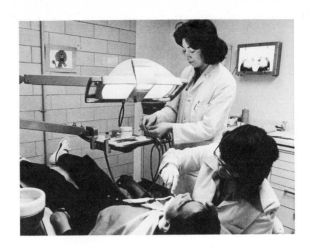

May personal services be unilaterally assigned or delegated?

An assignor can only assign the rights he or she has and nothing more. An assignee takes those rights subject to other people's defenses.

EXAMPLE 4 Suppose, in Example 1, that when Cuomo assigned the right to receive the $1,800 to Brown, Cuomo then did a very poor job of painting the house. Michaud could raise the defense of a poor paint job if she were sued by the assignee, who wanted to collect $1,800.

TRANSFER OF DUTIES

Duties may at times be transferred to someone else. This transfer of a duty is called a **delegation.** A delegation should not be confused with an assignment. An assignment is a transfer or rights, whereas a delegation is a transfer of duties.

EXAMPLE 5 Suppose, in Example 1, that Cuomo was in business for himself as a very busy painting contractor. Instead of promising Michaud that he would paint the house himself, he might simply promise her that the job would be done. He would then hire other people to do the actual labor.

Legal Issue No. 3

If the person having the work done and the person doing the work both understand the situation, it is perfectly all right for a contractor to delegate the duty of doing the work to someone else. This is really a form of subcontracting and occurs many times in business contracts. It is quite common, for example, in building contracts.

When Duties May Not Be Delegated

Duties may not be delegated when (1) a party agrees to perform the service personally, (2) the contract calls for the exercise of personal skill and judgment, or (3) the contract itself prohibits delegation.

EXAMPLE 6 Suppose, in Example 1, that Cuomo had told Michaud that he would personally paint the house for her. He could not then delegate the job to someone else. Duties that require personal skill and judgment, such as the

This format may be used to assign one person's rights in a contract to another person.

duties of teachers, writers, artists, or entertainers, cannot be delegated to others. Such persons are selected to perform their services because of the particular skill they have.

The offeror and the offeree may include in their contract an agreement that the contract may not be assigned or delegated. In this case, both parties are restrained.

EXAMPLE 7 Herbert Ryan contracted to build a garage for Roberta Mc-Govern. The contract said that Ryan would do the work himself and that he would not assign or delegate the contract to any outside third party. Although a contract of this type could, ordinarily, be assigned or delegated to another competent builder, the words of this contract would invalidate any attempt to do so in this case.

NOVATION

One party to a contract does not need permission of the other party to assign his or her rights or to delegate his or her duties to a third person. If he or she does receive permission to do so, however, and the other party agrees to deal with the assignee, the resulting contract is called a novation. A **novation** is an agreement whereby an original party to a contract is replaced by a new party. To be effective, the substitution of parties must be agreed to by all of the parties involved in the transaction.

EXAMPLE 8 Suppose that Cuomo delegated the job of painting the house and assigned the right to receive the money to Matthew Corkin. Suppose also that Corkin agreed to do the job and that Michaud agreed to release Cuomo from all obligations and deal solely with Corkin. The substitution of parties would be a novation.

THIRD-PARTY BENEFI-CIARIES

Legal Issue No. 1

Usually, only the parties to a contract have standing to bring suit when one of them breaches the contract.

EXAMPLE 9 Baxter Link agreed to put vinyl siding on Alice Squire's house, and Squire paid for the job in advance. Link breached the contract, however, and failed to do the job. Squire's next-door neighbor, Stanley Cooper, threatened to sue Link for breach of contract.

Squire has standing to sue Link because they were in **privity of contract,** that is, they contracted with each other. The transaction, however, is of no concern to Cooper. He might argue that he received some benefit under the contract by having a nice-looking house next door, but this would be only an incidental benefit. Cooper has no standing to bring suit for the breach.

Sometimes, a third person, called a **third-party beneficiary,** may enforce a contract when it is made specifically for that person's benefit.

EXAMPLE 10 George John bought a $50,000 life insurance policy, naming his wife Veronica as beneficiary. When John died, the insurance company refused to pay his widow, claiming that John had not disclosed to them that he had cancer. Veronica John claimed that her husband did not know that he had the illness when he took out the policy.

Legal Issue No. 4

Since Veronica John was an intended beneficiary of the life insurance contract, she has standing to bring suit against the insurance company. Although she was not a party to the original contract, she is entitled to enforce the rights under it.

BREACH OF CONTRACT

A **breach of contract** occurs when one of the parties does not do what he or she agreed to do. When parties refuse to fulfill their obligations, either by failing to carry them out or by carrying them out in an incomplete or unsatisfactory manner, they are said to have breached the contract.

Anticipatory Breach

When parties to a contract notify the other party of their intention not to go through with the contract before the time for performance, they are said to have made an **anticipatory breach.** They have, in other words, breached (violated) the agreement before they were required to act. Under the common law, the injured party would have to wait to bring suit until the time for performance had arrived and passed. However, modern decisions in many states permit the injured party to bring an action for damages immediately without waiting for the actual time for performance to arrive.

EXAMPLE 11 Suppose that you made a contract with a carpenter to build a playroom in the basement of your house. The carpenter was to begin work on June 20, but on May 9 she called you and said that she would not do the job as agreed. You have the right to bring an action for damages against the carpenter for an anticipatory breach.

The principle of anticipatory breach does not apply to promises to pay money at some future date. Someone who refuses to pay money owed on a future date cannot be sued until after the payment is due.

REMEDIES OF THE INJURED PARTY

When a contract is breached, the injured party has a choice of remedies (legal means of correcting a wrong). The injured party may (1) accept the breach; (2) sue for money damages; or, on some occasions, (3) ask the court to order the other party to do what he or she agreed to do.

Acceptance of Breach

When one party breaches a contract, it is an excuse for the other party not to perform. The other party may, if desired, simply accept the breach and consider the contract discharged. This may often be the best choice, especially if no damages have been suffered. Even if a lawsuit is won for breach of contract, if no damages are suffered, the winner of the suit will receive only **nominal damages.** Such damages are a very small sum of money, such as 1 cent or $1 to recognize that there has been a breach of contract but no real loss suffered.

Money Damages

If the injured party has suffered a loss, he or she may sue the offending party for money damages that resulted from the breach. In such a case, the injured party must make tender—that is, must offer to do what he or she agreed to do under the contract.

Actual and Incidental Damages In actions for breach of contract, the injured party is permitted to recover the **actual damages** caused by the other's failure of performance. The measure of damages for a buyer's breach of contract for the sale of land is the difference between the contract price of the land and its market value at the time of the breach. When a seller breaches a contract for the sale of goods, the measure of damages is the difference between the market price at the time of the breach and the contract price plus incidental damages. **Incidental damages** are any reasonable expenses resulting from a breach that have been incurred by the buyer.

EXAMPLE 12 Yukio Tanaka made a contract with a bookstore for the purchase of an encyclopedia set offered at a price of $500. The store failed to deliver the set of books according to the agreement. After investigation, Tanaka learned that the same set of books would cost $600 at any other bookstore. Tanaka is entitled, therefore, to sue for his actual damage, which is the difference between $500 and $600, or $100, plus any expenses incurred in getting the books at the other bookstore (incidental damages).

Liquidated Damages   Damages agreed upon by the parties when they first enter into a contract are called **liquidated damages.** The parties may include in their contract a statement of agreed damages, in case either one breaches the

```
                    COMMONWEALTH OF MASSACHUSETTS

                    DISTRICT COURTS OF MASSACHUSETTS

        ESSEX, ss                    FIRST DISTRICT COURT OF ESSEX
                                     Civil Action No. 87-316

        STEVEN GRAZIO, a minor, by        \
        MATTHEW GRAZIO, his father         \
        and next friend,     Plaintiff     \
                                            >    DEFENDANT'S ANSWER
                       v.                   /
                                           /
        WAYNE WILLIAMSON,    Defendant    /

                1.  The defendant has no knowledge or information

        sufficient to form a belief regarding the truth of the

        allegation of paragraph 1 of the complaint.

                2.  The defendant denies the allegations of

        paragraph 2 of the complaint.

                3.  Further answering, the defendant says that at

        the time of the alleged accident, the plaintiff's motor

        vehicle was parked next to a fire hydrant.  This violated

        the law and caused or contributed to the causing of the

        damages complained of.




                                     By his attorney,


        November 15, 19--            _____
                                     George Rodriguez
                                     792 Washington Street
                                     Peabody, MA 01960
```

A person who is served a summons must file a formal "answer" to the complaint in writing or forfeit the case. This document answers the complaint on page 157.

contract. They agree beforehand that these will be the damages to be sought in the event of a suit. If the contract is for the sale of goods, the law requires that liquidated damages be reasonable.

EXAMPLE 13 The Young Supply Company ordered a machine for its new plant, which was being built in Sacramento. The machine was a vital link in the production of a new product. The Young Company had inserted in its contract with the seller the following terms: "The Young Company will be paid $500 each day beyond the date agreed upon for delivery of said machine." Considering the profits that might be lost through delay in delivery, the liquidated damages provision would, no doubt, be considered reasonable and proper.

The different types of damages are explained in Table 13-1.

Specific Performance

Sometimes the remedy of money damages is not enough to repay an injured party for a breach of contract. On some occasions, the injured party may sue for **specific performance.** To obtain specific performance, the injured party asks the court to order the other party to do specifically what he or she agreed to do. This remedy can only be used, however, when money damages are not sufficient to give relief.

EXAMPLE 14 Doreen Russell contracted to sell Betsy Keller a valuable book, the only one of its kind in existence. Russell then breached the contract and refused to sell. Money damages would not be adequate in this case because the book could not be purchased elsewhere. The court would order Russell to turn the book over to Keller for the agreed price.

Legal Issue No. 2

As the case illustrated, specific performance can be granted when the subject matter of the contract is rare or unique. It will not be ordered in the case of contracts involving common and available goods or easily obtained services.

The uniqueness of the subject matter is especially important in real estate contracts. The law considers each parcel (separate piece) of real estate to be unlike any other parcel of real estate, if for no other reason than that the locations are different. For this reason, it is usually possible to sue for specific performance of an agreement to buy or sell real estate.

MINIMIZING OF DAMAGES

An injured party must take all available steps to minimize the damages that might result from the other party's failure of performance. At all times, the injured party will be obliged to protect the other party from any unnecessary losses. This principle is known as **mitigation of damages.**

EXAMPLE 15 Peter Lister contracted to deliver 1,000 baskets of tomatoes from his farm to a cannery. When he tried to deliver the tomatoes, however, the canner would not accept them. Lister would be obligated to try to sell the tomatoes to another buyer. Then he would be allowed to demand payment from the cannery for the difference between what he got for the produce and what the cannery had agreed to pay.

TABLE 13-1
DIFFERENT TYPES OF DAMAGES

Type of Damages	Definition or Description
Actual damages	An amount of money awarded for damages directly attributable to another party's breach of contract or tort; for example, physicians' fees when one party wrongly injures another, and financial losses resulting from failure to deliver goods already contracted for.
Compensatory damages	An award of an amount of money that compensates a complainant for the injuries suffered and nothing more.
Consequential damages	Damages, loss, or injury (such as loss of profits) that does not flow directly and immediately from the act of the party but only from some of the consequences or results of such act.
Incidental damages	Reasonable expenses that indirectly result from a breach of contract. They include such expenses incurred in stopping delivery of goods, transporting goods, and caring for goods that have been rightfully rejected by a buyer.
Liquidated damages	An amount of anticipated damages, agreed to by both parties and contained in a contract, to be the basis of any award in the event of a breach of the contract.
Nominal damages	Damages awarded by a court when a successful plaintiff has proven a legal injury but no actual resulting damage; 6 cents by common law, usually $1 today.
Punitive damages	Damages in excess of losses suffered by the plaintiff awarded to the plaintiff as a measure of punishment for the defendant's wrongful acts. Also called *exemplary damages*, because they set an example of punishment awaiting other wrongdoers.
Speculative damages	Damages not founded on fact but on the expectations that a party may have hoped for from a contract that has been breached; not allowed in any claim for money damages.

Suggestions for Reducing Legal Risks

1. To be safe, you should put a notice of assignment in writing and be sure that the third party receives a copy.

2. Since you may be held liable when you delegate a duty and the third party fails to perform, you should keep in touch with the third party and check on his or her performance.
3. In case of a breach of contract, explore the possibility of arriving at an acceptable settlement out of court before starting court action.

Language of the Law

Define or explain each of the following words or phrases:

remedy	delegation	breach of contract	incidental damages
assignment	novation	anticipatory breach	liquidated damages
assignor	privity of contract	nominal damages	specific performance
assignee	third-party beneficiary	actual damages	mitigation of damages

Questions for Review

1. Why is it desirable to have the notice of assignment in writing?
2. When may a right not be assignable?
3. An assignee takes rights subject to other people's defenses. Give an example of this.
4. Give two examples of duties that may not be delegated.
5. Give an example of a novation.
6. When may a third person enforce a contract between two other people?
7. When does a breach of contract occur?
8. Give an example of an anticipatory breach. What do modern decisions in many states permit the injured party to do if an anticipatory breach occurs?
9. What can an injured party do when a contract is breached?
10. How are actual damages determined if there is a breach in a contract for the sale of goods?
11. Give an example of an occasion when an injured party may be granted specific performance of a contract.
12. May an injured party make the damages as high as possible? Explain.

Cases in Point

In each of the following cases, give your decision and state a legal principle that applies to the case:

1. Mesmer Tanis entered into a contract to paint Gertrude Pearson's house for $1,200. Later, Tanis breached the contract and refused to do the job. Can Natalie Nichols, who lives across the street from Pearson, sue Tanis for breach of contract?
2. Dea Duk Sung bought a $100,000 life insurance policy naming Yung Shen Sung as the beneficiary. If the insurance company refuses to pay the proceeds of the policy to Yung Shen when Dea Duk dies, does Yung Shen have standing to sue?
3. Sergio Morales entered into a written contract to sell his car to Pedro Rodriguez for its fair market value of $3,000. The next day, Rodriguez notified Morales that he had changed his mind and would not buy the car. Morales sold the car to his brother-in-law as a favor for $100. Can Morales sue Rodriguez for $2,900?

4. Don Blair contracted to work as a mechanic for Henry Lee for 1 year. A month later, Lee assigned his right to receive Blair's services to Titus. Must Blair work for Titus?

5. The Turner Company sold goods to Pierre Moreau on credit. After waiting for several months after the account should have been paid, the Turner Company notified Moreau that it was assigning its rights to a collection agency. Is this legally permissible?

6. Carmen Vega contracted to sell a stove to Marie Ervine. Ervine later breached her contract and refused to accept delivery. May Vega sue Ervine for the full contract price?

7. Walt Melon engaged Sylvia Darr, a well-known artist, to do a painting. Before the picture was completed, Darr died. The executor of the estate engaged a former assistant in Darr's studio, an artist of outstanding ability, to finish the picture. Can Melon, knowing the facts, be required to accept and pay for the picture?

8. Janine Drake owed Duncan Coe $500. Coe assigned the right to receive the money to Abram Burke in payment of a debt. Coe then moved out of town. No one notified Drake of the assignment, however, so she mailed the $500 to Coe at his new address. Can Burke sue Drake for failing to honor the assignment?

9. Julia Spaulding, a concert violinist, contracted to purchase a rare old Italian violin from the Freeman Music Store for $15,000. The music store learned that the violin was worth much more and refused to deliver the violin to Spaulding upon tender of the money. The store then tried to get her to accept another violin. Spaulding refused. What could Spaulding do?

Cases to Judge

1. Williams agreed to buy a parcel of land from Cotten for $120,000 and paid a $20,000 deposit. Later, Williams breached the contract, refusing to buy the property. The court determined that the market value of the property was $120,000. In a suit against Williams for breach of contract, how much money will Cotten recover? *William v. Cotten*, 684 S.W.2d 837 (Arkansas)

2. Consolidated Rail Corporation owned a driveway easement (a right-of-way) to provide access from East 149th Street into the Penn Central Oak Point railroad yard in New York City. Without permission from the railroad, MASP Equipment Corp. stored construction equipment on the driveway, blocking its use. Consolidated Rail Corporation brought suit to stop MASP from blocking its driveway easement. The lower court ordered MASP to stop blocking the driveway. It also ordered the company to pay $1,000 per day, as liquidated damages, for each day that it blocked the driveway after a certain date. MASP appealed, arguing that liquidated damages did not apply to this case. How would you decide? *Consolidated Rail Corp. v. MASP Equipment*, 486 N.Y.S.2d 4 (New York)

3. Ward signed an agreement not to compete when he went to work for an insurance company. Ten years later, Ward was discharged by the insurance company in violation of the employment agreement. He then began selling insurance in violation of the agreement not to compete. Is Ward liable for breach of contract with the insurance company? Why or why not? *Ward v. American Mut. Liability Ins. Co.*, 443 N.E.2d 1342 (Massachusetts)

4. John Mohrlang agreed in writing to buy some land from Larry Draper for $14,875. The written agreement provided that Draper would pay the cost of relocating a gas line and paving the street. Later, Draper learned that the cost of relocating the gas line would be $10,050. He refused to sell the property to Mohrlang. Can Mohrlang force Draper to sell him the land? Explain. *Mohrlang v. Draper*, 365 N.W.2d 443 (Nebraska)

Presidio Enterprises v. Warner Bros. Distributing
784 F.2d 674 (5th Circuit)

In the late 1970s, "disaster" films such as *The Poseidon Adventure* and *The Towering Inferno* were box office hits. When the craze ended, however, Warner Bros. Distributing (Warner) found itself being sued for fraud. Presidio Enterprises (Presidio) claimed that it relied on Warner's promotional material in booking *The Swarm* in its theaters. When *The Swarm* turned into box office disaster, Presidio claimed that Warner's brochures and invitations to bid contained material misrepresentations. One brochure contained the following:

"THE SWARM" IS COMING!

Today, shooting started at Warner Bros. on your blockbuster for the summer of '78.

"THE SWARM" IS COMING!

From the man who brought you the stunning successes of "THE POSEIDON ADVENTURE" and "THE TOWERING INFERNO" now comes what we hope to be the greatest adventure-survival movie of all time.

"THE SWARM" IS COMING!

Starring Michael Caine, Katharine Ross, Richard Widmark, Olivia de Havilland, Ben Johnson, Lee Grant, Patty Duke Astin, Slim Pickens, Bradford Dillman, and Henry Fonda as Dr. Krim, this will be the most "want-to-see" movie of the year.

Warner also sent Presidio an invitation to bid for the rights to exhibit *The Swarm* that read in part:

Dear Exhibitor:

"SWARM" will be available in the Austin area on or about July 14, 1978, on an exclusive or non-exclusive basis for a maximum of two (2) runs.

Since the film is not yet complete, we will not be able to screen it at this time. This letter is being sent to you as a solicitation for a bid. If a bid is submitted by you and accepted by Warner Bros. such offer will be noncancellable.

In effect, Presidio was being invited to bid for the exhibition rights to the film sight unseen. This practice, known as "blind bidding," is relatively common in the film industry. Distributors want to be sure their films are solidly booked before they set in motion their expensive advertising campaigns (in this case, Warner spent over $4,000,000 advertising *The Swarm*), and exhibitors want to be sure they have promising films to show during periods of peak attendance.

In its bid letter Warner suggested a minimum "guarantee" of $35,000 for *The Swarm*. Presidio responded with bids of $35,000 and $30,000 as the guarantees for eight-week runs at two of its theatres; its remaining terms closely mirrored those suggested by Warner. Warner accepted Presidio's bids.

The Swarm opened as scheduled on July 14, 1978. It was not a big success. The film ran for only five weeks at one of Presidio's theatres, and four weeks at the other. Presidio calculated that, after subtracting the guarantees and operating expenses from box office revenues, it had sustained a loss of $56,056.69.

Presidio brought suit against Warner in federal district court, alleging common law fraud and negligent misrepresentation. Presidio also charged that Warner had violated the Texas Deceptive Trade Practices Act by engaging in "false, misleading, or deceptive acts or practices," by misrepresenting *The Swarm's* characteristics, benefits, and qualities, and by acting unconscionably.

THE TRIAL

At the trial, Charles Chick, president of Presidio, testified in part as follows:

Q. It is true, isn't it, that the distributors had been using superlatives to describe their movies ever since you've been in the industry?
A. It is generally true. They rarely tell you when they have got a bad picture, or use a negative term in talking about their pictures.

Q. And it's because of that through the years you people at Presidio have learned to more or less go on solid facts, and make up your own business judgments?

A. We always try to make up our own business judgments.

Q. At the time of "The Swarm," could you separate and recognize facts from exaggeration and superlatives, that kind of thing?

A. Yes, sir, I think so.

When questioned about the meaning of the term "blockbuster," Mr. Chick testified:

By "blockbuster," I guess they mean it's going to do good box office business, be an important box office picture.

A jury found Warner liable. The district court entered judgment in favor of Presidio with an award of $521,483.23. This included trebled damages, attorney's fees, interest, and costs.

THE ARGUMENTS ON APPEAL

On appeal, Warner argued that it had not made any misrepresentations of fact. The company claimed that its statements about the film were merely expressions of opinion or promises of something to happen in the future. Warner pointed out that expressions of opinion and promises are not statements of fact and, therefore, cannot be sued upon.

In addition, Warner claimed that the statements in the brochures and letters amounted to "puffery" or "puffing," which reasonable people do not take seriously. Warner asserted that professional film exhibitors could not have reasonably relied on such puffery.

QUESTIONS FOR DISCUSSION

1. Based on your reading of the chapters in Unit 2, what law or laws apply to this case?
2. In your opinion, is the statement "your blockbuster for the summer of '78" a statement of fact? Explain.
3. Do you think the statements in the brochures and letters were puffing and salestalk? Why or why not?
4. If you were an appellate court judge hearing this case, for whom would you decide?

CASE TO BRIEF

After reading *How to Write a Case Brief* on page 78, and examining the sample brief on page 80, write a brief of the following case:

Halbman v. Lemke
298 N.W.2d 562 (Wisconsin)

This matter was before the trial court upon stipulated facts. On or about July 13 . . . , James Halbman, Jr. (Halbman), a minor, entered into an agreement with Michael Lemke (Lemke) whereby Lemke agreed to sell Halbman a [used] Oldsmobile for the sum of $1,250. Lemke was the manager of L & M Standard Station in Greenfield, Wisconsin, and Halbman was an employee at L & M. At the time the agreement was made Halbman paid Lemke $1,000 cash and took possession of the car. Arrangements were made for Halbman to pay $25 per week until the balance was paid, at which time title would be transferred. About five weeks after the purchase agreement, and after Halbman had paid a total of $1,100 of the purchase price, a connecting rod on the vehicle's engine broke. Lemke, while denying any obligation, offered to assist Halbman in installing a used engine in the vehicle if Halbman, at his expense, could secure one. Halbman declined the offer and in September took the vehicle to a garage where it was repaired at a cost of $637.40. Halbman did not pay the repair bill.

In October of [the same year,] Lemke endorsed the vehicle's title over to Halbman, although the full purchase price had not been paid by Halbman, in an effort to avoid any liability for the operation, maintenance, or use of the vehicle. On October 15 . . . , Halbman returned the title to Lemke by letter which disaffirmed the purchase contract and demanded the return of all money theretofore paid by Halbman. Lemke did not return the money paid by Halbman.

The repair bill remained unpaid, and the vehicle remained in the garage where the repairs had been made. In the spring [of the next year] in satisfaction of a garageman's lien for the outstanding amount, the garage elected to remove the vehicle's engine and transmission and then towed the vehicle to the residence of James Halbman, Sr., the father of the plaintiff minor. Lemke was asked several times to remove the vehicle from the senior Halbman's home, but he declined to do so, claiming he was under no legal obligation to remove it. During the period when the vehicle was at the garage and then subsequently at the home of the plaintiff's father, it was subjected to vandalism, making it unsalvageable.

Halbman initiated this action seeking the return of the $1,100 he had paid toward the purchase of the vehicle, and Lemke counterclaimed for $150, the amount still owing on the contract. Based upon the uncontroverted facts, the trial court granted judgment in favor of Halbman, concluding that when a minor disaffirms a contract for the purchase of an item, he need only offer to return the property remaining in his hands without making restitution for any use or depreciation. . . .

The sole issue before us is whether a minor, having disaffirmed a contract for the purchase of an item which is not a necessity and having tendered the property back to the vendor, must make restitution to the vendor for damage to the property prior to the disaffirmance. Lemke argues that he should be entitled to recover for the damage to the vehicle up to the time of disaffirmance, which he claims equals the amount of the repair bill.

Neither party challenges the absolute right of a minor to disaffirm a contract for the purchase of items which are not necessities. That right, variously known as the doctrine of incapacity or the "infancy doctrine," is one of the oldest and most venerable of our common law traditions. Although the origins of the doctrine are somewhat obscure, it is generally recognized that its purpose is the protection of minors from foolishly squandering their wealth through improvident contracts with crafty adults who would take advantage of them in the marketplace. . . . Thus it is settled law in this state that a contract of a minor for items which are not necessities is void or voidable at the minor's option. . . .

Once there has been a disaffirmance, however, as in this case between a minor vendee and an adult vendor, unresolved problems arise regarding the rights and responsibilities of the parties relative to the disposition of the consideration exchanged on the contract. As a general rule a minor who disaffirms a contract is entitled to recover all consideration he has conferred incident to the transaction. . . . In return the minor is expected to restore as much of the consideration as, at the time of disaffirmance, remains in the minor's possession. . . . The minor's right to disaffirm is not contingent upon the return of the property, however, as disaffirmance is permitted even where such return cannot be made. . . .

The return of property remaining in the hands of the minor is not the issue presented here. In this case we have a situation where the property cannot be returned to the vendor in its entirety because it has been damaged and therefore diminished in value, and the vendor seeks to recover the depreciation. Although this court has been cognizant of this issue on previous occasions, we have not heretofore resolved it. . . .

[A] minor who disaffirms a purchase and recovers his purchase price should not also be permitted to profit by retaining the property purchased. The infancy doctrine is designed to protect the minor, sometimes at the expense of an innocent vendor, but it is not to be used to bilk merchants out of property as well as proceeds of the sale. Consequently, it is clear that, when the minor no longer possesses the property which was the subject matter of the contract, the rule requiring the return of property does not apply. The minor will not be required to give up what he does not have. . . .

Here Lemke seeks restitution of the value of the depreciation by virtue of the damage to the vehicle prior to disaffirmance. Such a recovery would require Halbman to return more than that remaining in his possession. It seeks compensatory value for that which he cannot return. Where there is misrepresentation by a minor or willful destruction of property, the vendor may be able to recover damages in tort. . . . But absent these factors, as in the present case, we believe that to require a disaffirming minor to make restitution for diminished value is, in effect, to bind the minor to a part of the obligation which by law he is privileged to avoid. . . .

[M]odifications of the rules governing the capacity of infants to contract are best left to the legislature. . . .

The decision of the court is affirmed.

TRIAL PROCEDURES

PLEADINGS

Pleadings are the papers that are filed with the court by the plaintiff and the defendant at the beginning of a lawsuit. They establish the issues by setting forth the plaintiff's *allegations* (claims or assertions) and the defendant's answer. Sometimes pleadings include a counterclaim made by the defendant against the plaintiff and the plaintiff's *reply*.

The first pleading filed is the plaintiff's *complaint* statement of the claim against the defendant. The complaint must contain sufficient facts so that the plaintiff will win the case if they are proved and there are no defenses to them. A *defense* is a reason that excuses an otherwise wrongful act. For instance, ''self-defense'' may excuse an assault charge.

A lawsuit begins when the complaint is filed with the court. The clerk of the court issues a *summons*, a notice to the defendant that a lawsuit has begun. A process server hands the summons and a copy of the complaint to the defendant (or leaves it at the defendant's residence). This procedure is known as *service of process*.

The defendant must answer the complaint within the time period allowed or lose the case by default. There are several ways to respond to the complaint. One is to file a *motion to dismiss,* which claims that the complaint does not allege sufficient facts to allow the plaintiff to win the case. In some states, a pleading called a *demurrer* is used for this purpose. If the motion to dismiss (or demurrer) is not allowed by the court, or if none is filed, the defendant must file an answer with the court. An *answer* admits or denies each allegation of the complaint and states any defenses.

THE CASE OF GRAZIO V. WILLIAMSON (continued from page 83)

Steve Grazio's lawyer had sent a letter to Wayne Williamson attempting to settle the automobile accident case out of court. Williamson did not answer. Steven decided to bring suit. Because he was a minor, the suit had to be brought by someone 18 years of age or older, in this case his father, Matthew Grazio.

Attorney Powers obtained a summons from the District Court and filled it in as shown on page 148. She also drafted the complaint shown on page 157 and filed it with the clerk of the court. The summons and a copy of the complaint were given to a deputy sheriff. The deputy sheriff delivered copies of the summons and complaint in person to Wayne Williamson, notifying him of the lawsuit. The deputy sheriff then returned the original complaint to the court with a notation that it had been served on the defendant.

Upon reading the summons, Williamson realized that he had 20 days to file a written answer with the court. Williamson retained Attorney George Rodriguez, who drew the defendant's answer (page 173), filed the original with the court, and sent a copy to Attorney Susan L. Powers.

LEGAL PRACTICUM

Martha Hawkens entered into an oral agreement to sell a vacant lot of land to William Parsons for $15,000. Parsons agreed to buy it for that price. Later, Parsons changed his mind and decided not to buy it. After much effort in locating another buyer, Hawkens sold the lot for $10,000 to someone else. Seven years later, Hawkens decided to sue Parsons for the damages she suffered as a result of the breach of contract. Parsons defended the suit by arguing that the action could not be brought because of the statute of frauds. He also argued that the statute of limitations had run out.

Assume that you work in the office of an attorney representing Martha Hawkens. Using the complaint on page 157 as a guide, write a complaint to begin a legal action against William Parsons. Then, assume that you work in the office of an attorney representing William Parsons. Write an answer using the defendant's answer on page 173 as a guide.

BEING A CONSUMER
UNIT 3

Chapter 14

CONTRACTS FOR THE SALE OF GOODS

In this unit you will follow the lives of the Chin family. Joe Chin, 17, and Dorothy Chin, 16, are high school students who live with their parents in the suburbs of a small city. Mr. and Mrs. Chin own a wholesale vegetable outlet.

Scene: The family room of the Chin residence. It is late afternoon.

Dorothy (*talking on the telephone to her friend, Debbie*):   . . . and the store manager promised to hold it for me. I didn't even say for sure that I'd buy it, but she could tell how much I liked it, and she said that she'd hold it for me for 2 weeks and I could decide later whether I wanted to buy it or not. It was the only one they had left. She offered it to me for $49.

Mrs. Chin (*in a loud voice*): Dorothy! Are you still on the telephone? Dad will be home soon and you haven't set the table!

Dorothy: I've got to go, Debbie. See you tomorrow.
(*One hour later, Mr. and Mrs. Chin, Joe, and Dorothy are sitting at the dining room table.*)

Mr. Chin: I made a good deal today. I contracted with a farmer out in Springdale to buy all the tomatoes and green beans that he raises this season—at a real good price.

Joe: Can you do that? We learned in our business law class in school that a contract has to be definite.

Mrs. Chin: You're right, Joe. I remember that from my evening course. It wouldn't be definite, because nobody knows how many tomatoes and beans the farmer will grow.

Mr. Chin: I suppose he could have a blight or something and not grow any at all.

Joe: I hope you got it in writing. If the price of goods is over a certain amount—I forget how much—the contract has to be in writing. I think tomatoes and beans are goods.

Dorothy: They're only good if you like them! Ha! Ha!

Joe: What a clown! Can't you be serious for a change?

Mr. Chin: I think they're called future goods when they're not grown yet. Anyway, they're our beans and tomatoes. We own them now!

Dorothy: Can't we talk about something more interesting?

Joe: Like what, for instance?

Dorothy: Well, like the sweater I looked at today at the mall. It was really nice, and it was the only one left, and they're going to hold it for me even if I decide not to buy it.

Joe: Clothes, that's all you think about—clothes and boys.

Mrs. Chin: I had a strange experience today. I went to the jeweler's to pick up the watch that I left there to be repaired, and they couldn't find it. It seems that they sold it to somebody by mistake.

Mr. Chin: They sold it? The watch I gave you?

Mrs. Chin: Yes, but they know the name of the customer. I told them how much that watch meant to me, and they're going to get it back.

Mr. Chin: I sure hope so. We sold a lot of green beans to get you that watch.

LEGAL ISSUES

1. Is an oral promise by a merchant to hold an offer open for the sale of goods binding?
2. Is a contract to buy all the products a farmer grows binding?
3. Must a contract for the sale of goods over a certain price be in writing to be enforceable?
4. Are tomatoes and beans considered to be goods?
5. Can title to future goods be transferred by a contract of sale?
6. Suppose that a person leaves an item, such as a watch, for repairs at a shop. If the shop owner sells the item to another individual, does the buyer really own the item?

THE SPIRIT OF THE LAW

The law of contracts that you have studied in the previous eight chapters is referred to as general contract law. It governs contracts for the sale of real estate, personal services, and many other types of transactions. Another law, called the **law of sales,** governs contracts for the sale of goods and is the subject of this chapter.

The law of sales began many years ago in England. It originated in the law merchant, which was the name given to the customs and practices of business-people, merchants, and mariners in early English times. In those days, merchants administered the law in their own courts. As time went on, the early law of sales combined with English common law and eventually was put into a code called the English Sale of Goods Act. In 1906, a code of law called the Uniform Sales Act was introduced in the United States. This law was similar to the English Sale of Goods Act and, over a period of years, was enacted by the legislatures of 35 states. As **interstate commerce** (trade between the states) developed, the need arose to modernize and make uniform many of our commercial laws. This led to the development of the Uniform Commercial Code (UCC), article 2 of which contains our present law of sales.

The UCC was written by the National Conference of Commissioners on Uniform State Laws. One purpose of this law is to combine the laws relating to commerce into a single uniform code. Under this law, many of the rules governing the various phases of a business transaction may be found in a single statute that is uniform throughout the land. The UCC is now the law in every state. Louisiana, a former French possession, has developed its legal system after the pattern set by the Roman Code. Its legislature has adopted part, but not all, of the UCC.

Another purpose of the UCC is to simplify, clarify, and modernize the law governing commercial transactions. A third purpose is to encourage the expansion of commercial practices through custom, usage, and agreement of the parties.

TRANS-ACTIONS INVOLVING GOODS

Legal Issue No. 4

The law of sales applies only to transactions involving goods. Whenever people buy or sell goods, whether or not they are merchants, Article 2 of the UCC governs the transaction. The term **goods** covers all things (including those that have been specially manufactured) that are movable at the time they are made part of a contract for sale. Goods also include the unborn young of animals, growing crops, and other identified things attached to real estate, such as timber, minerals, and the like—all of which may be removed. However, neither the money with which the price is to be paid nor investment securities, such as stocks and bonds, are considered goods.

To be valid subject matter of a contract for sale, goods must be tangible personal property. By **tangible** we mean something that occupies space—something that you can touch and put your hands on. Thus the law of sales does not apply to the sale of land (which is not movable), nor does it apply to employment contracts or contracts for services.

EXAMPLE 1 Kathleen Riley obtained a summer job in a local store on the same day that her parents bought a new house. To celebrate, they all went out to dinner. The day's activity involved three different contracts. Kathleen's employment contract (the store's oral promise to employ her, and her promise to work) and her parents' written contract to buy the house were both governed by the law of contracts discussed in Unit 2. The oral contract with the restaurant for the purchase of the food they ate at dinner was governed by the UCC.

CONTRACT FOR SALE VERSUS SALE

A **contract for sale** may be a contract for a present sale of goods or it may be a contract to sell goods at a future time. An actual **sale** takes place when the seller gives the buyer title to the goods for a price.

EXAMPLE 2 Gary Thompson contracted with the Clymer Hardware Store to buy a new power lawn mower. The hardware store agreed to order the mower and to deliver it to Thompson in a week. Thompson knew that Harriet Foster was interested in buying his used mower. That afternoon he pushed his used mower down the street to Foster's house and offered the mower to her for $20. She said, "I'll take it," and gave Thompson the money.

Thompson's contract with the hardware store is a contract for sale but not an actual sale because ownership of the mower will not be transferred to him until a week later. His transaction with Foster was both a contract for sale and a sale. It was a contract for sale when they agreed to buy and sell the mower; it was a sale when the mower was given to Foster for the price agreed upon.

SPECIAL RULES FOR SALES

The UCC has relaxed some of the strict rules of general contract law. These more flexible rules apply in all contracts for the sale of goods:

1. A contract for sale may be made in any manner including conduct by the parties. It may come about even though the exact moment of its making cannot be determined and some terms have been left open.
2. An offer may be accepted by any means and in any manner that is reasonable unless the offeror requests a particular method to be used for the acceptance.
3. An acceptance may have different or additional terms without being a rejection of the offer. The different or additional terms are treated as proposals for additions to the contract if the parties are not both merchants. If the parties are both merchants, the different or additional terms become part of the contract unless they make an important difference or the offeror objects.
4. A contract for sale may be made even though the price is not settled. Unless the parties later agree on a price, it will be a reasonable price at the time for delivery of the goods.
5. Output and requirement contracts are allowed even though they are not definite. For example, a shoe manufacturer might agree to sell to a buyer "all the shoes we manufacture." This would be an **output contract.** A trucking company might agree to buy from a gasoline distributor "all the gasoline we need to run our trucks." This would be a **requirement contract.**
6. No consideration is necessary to modify (change) a contract for the sale of goods. The modification may be oral unless the original agreement is in writing and states that it may only be modified in writing. In addition, any such statement in a form supplied by a merchant to a nonmerchant must be separately signed by the nonmerchant to be effective.

Legal Issue No. 2

Legal Issue No. 1

7. A merchant's written promise to hold an offer open for the sale of goods (called a firm offer) needs no consideration to be binding. Such an offer will not be revocable during the time stated in the offer, or for a reasonable time if none is stated; but in no event must the offer stand longer than 3 months.
8. The seal is not recognized. Therefore, a seal on a contract for sale has no effect.

FORMAL REQUIRE-MENTS OF A CONTRACT FOR SALE

Contracts for the sale of goods for a price of $500 or more are not enforceable unless there is some writing indicating that a contract for sale has been made between the parties. The writing need not be in any particular form, but must be signed by the person against whom enforcement is sought, that is, the defendant.

```
                    Contract for the sale of goods

_____ , of _____ ,
          (name of seller)                         (address)

                                    (name of buyer)
hereby sells, and _____ , of

_____ , hereby purchases for $_____ ,
          (address)

_____ , to be
          (quantity)                    (type of goods)

                                                           (date)
delivered by seller on or before _____ .

Dated _____        _____
                                            (Signature of seller)

                                   _____
                                            (Signature of buyer)
```

This form may be followed if you want to put a contract for the sales of goods in writing.

There are four situations, however, in which no writing is required even though the sales price is $500 or more:

If the contract is between two merchants and one of them sends a written confirmation of the transaction within a reasonable time and the other does not object within 10 days.
2. If the contract involves goods that are to be specially manufactured, that cannot be resold easily, and that the seller has either ordered or begun making.
3. If the buyer actually receives and accepts the goods or pays for them.
4. If the parties to the contract admit in court that they entered into an oral contract for the sale of goods.

Legal Issue No. 3

EVIDENCE OF OWNERSHIP OF GOODS

Let us assume that you received a wristwatch as a birthday present last year. You say that you own this watch. Exactly what do you mean when you make this claim? Did you ever stop to think about the nature of ownership and the rights that ownership gives? If you own the watch, you have the right to possess it, but you would have the right of possession even if you had just borrowed the watch. There is more to ownership than mere possession. As the owner of the watch, you have a right to do with it as you choose. You can give it away, you can sell it, and you can leave it to someone in your will. You can even destroy it. No one else has any right to the watch unless you give away that right. **Title,** technically, is the means by which you prove ownership; but in ordinary use, *title* has essentially the same meaning as *ownership*.

There are several types of evidence that are better than mere possession for proving title. The sales slip and the invoice that you receive when you purchase merchandise provide acceptable evidence of ownership.

Bill of Sale

When you buy goods that involve a considerable amount of money, it is always advisable to get a written statement that the seller is transferring ownership to you. Such a paper is called a **bill of sale.** A bill of sale, however, proves only that you once had title. It does not prove that you still own the goods.

EXAMPLE 3 Steven Forman bought a 12-gauge shotgun from Sylvia Boswell for $200 and received a bill of sale. Forman then sold the shotgun to Steve Bobick. The day after this sale, Forman wrongfully contracted to sell the same shotgun to Jim Johnson. In making the sale to Johnson, Forman presented the bill of sale from Boswell as proof of his ownership. The bill of sale meant nothing because Forman no longer had title.

Documents of Title

Some papers, called **documents of title,** serve as evidence that the person holding the paper has title. Perhaps the most common of these papers is the title certificate used in many states to show ownership of a car. A car owner receives a certificate of title from an agency of the state government. When the owner sells the car, he or she must sign the certificate of title and give it to the new owner. The new owner turns the certificate into the state agency and receives a new certificate showing that he or she has title to the car.

Documents of title have been used in business for many years. Some are called negotiable documents of title because they can be negotiated (transferred) from one person to another. Others are nonnegotiable and cannot be transferred. The bill of lading and the warehouse receipt are documents of title.

A **bill of lading** is a receipt for shipment of goods. It is given by a transportation company (known as a carrier) to a shipper when goods are accepted by the carrier for shipment. There are two kinds of bills of lading. One kind is a **straight bill of lading.** It is a receipt only, an acknowledgment by the carrier that the goods have been received. The other kind is an **order bill of lading.** In addition to acknowledging receipt of the goods, an order bill of lading provides that the goods will not be delivered to anyone unless the original bill of lading is presented to the carrier when the goods are called for. The goods may be called for by the shipper or by someone else to whom the shipper has transferred the bill of lading. The shipper may transfer a bill of lading to someone else by indorsing (signing) the back of the document. Thus possession of the order bill of lading is evidence of ownership of the goods.

EXAMPLE 4 Suppose that Danielle Becquerel, who lives in Pittsburgh, sells a freezer to Laura Echeverria, who lives in Detroit. Becquerel arranges to deliver the freezer by air freight and receives an order bill of lading from the airline. Becquerel then sends a letter to Echeverria informing her that the bill of lading will be mailed to her after her check for the purchase price is received. In this way Becquerel is assured of receiving the money due her.

The airline will not deliver the freezer to Echeverria until she produces the order bill of lading. (A bill of lading issued by an airline is called an **airbill.**) Echeverria cannot get the order bill of lading until she pays Becquerel for the freezer.

A **warehouse receipt** is similar to a bill of lading. It is given by a warehouse to a customer whose goods the warehouse is storing. Again, there are two kinds of warehouse receipts. A **nonnegotiable warehouse receipt** is like a straight bill of lading; it is only a receipt for the goods. A **negotiable warehouse receipt** is like an order bill of lading; the original copy must be presented to the warehouse before the goods will be delivered.

PASSAGE OF TITLE AND RISK OF LOSS

Sometimes it is necessary to determine who has title to goods—the seller or the buyer. In a bankruptcy case, for example, only goods to which the debtor has title can be taken by the court to satisfy creditors' claims. Some of the goods in the debtor's possession may be owned by someone else; other goods that have left the debtor's possession may still be owned by the debtor; still other goods that have not yet been delivered to the debtor may be owned by the debtor. Similarly, it is occasionally necessary to determine who must bear the **risk of loss** (responsibility for loss or damage) to goods. This is because goods may be stolen, damaged, or destroyed after a sales contract has been entered into but before the transaction is completed. Many years ago, the law provided that whoever had title to goods also bore the risk of their loss. Although this is sometimes still true, it is no longer always the case.

Title

Legal Issue No. 5

Title to goods cannot be transferred by a contract for sale until the goods have been identified. **Identified goods** are goods that presently exist and that have been selected or set aside to be the subject matter of a particular contract. Goods that are *not* both existing and selected are known as **future goods.** Crops that are not yet grown or items that have not yet been manufactured are examples of future goods. They may only be the subject matter of a contract for sale of goods at a later date.

Under a sales contract, the time at which title is transferred—unless the parties agree otherwise—depends on the method of delivery of the goods. If the contract requires the seller to send the goods to the buyer but does not require the seller to deliver them directly to the place of destination, title is transferred at the time and place that the shipment begins. This is called a **shipment contract.**

EXAMPLE 5 A machine is shipped to a customer f.o.b. St. Louis, the home city of the seller. The customer lives in Chicago. Title to the machine would be transferred to the customer as soon as the seller delivered it to the freight depot in St. Louis and it was accepted by the transportation company.

The abbreviation **f.o.b.** means "free on board." When a price is quoted for goods **f.o.b. shipping point,** the buyer must pay the freight charges from the shipping point to the destination. Thus *f.o.b. St. Louis* means that the seller will put the goods on freight cars or trucks at St. Louis, but that the buyer will pay all expenses from there. At the shipping point, the goods become the responsibility of the buyer. Title is transferred when the seller delivers the goods to the carrier (the transportation company) for shipment. The seller must take the goods to the carrier in the manner provided and bear the expense and risk of putting them into the possession of the carrier.

If the contract requires the seller to deliver the goods to the destination, title is transferred when the seller delivers the goods to the destination. Such goods are said to be shipped **f.o.b. destination,** and the contract is called a **destination contract.**

EXAMPLE 6 If the customer in Example 5 had not wished to accept the responsibility of ownership during the shipment of the machine, she could have said that the delivery would have to be made f.o.b. destination. The destination would be the city in which she lived. Since she lived in Chicago, the terms would have been f.o.b. Chicago. The seller, under such terms, would pay the freight charges from St. Louis to Chicago.

Goods sold under the terms *f.o.b. destination* remain the property of the seller until the merchandise reaches its destination. The seller must transport the goods to that place and there make delivery in the agreed way.

If delivery is to be made without moving the goods, title is transferred at the following times:

1. If the seller is to deliver a document of title, such as a bill of lading or a warehouse receipt, title is transferred when the document is delivered.
2. If no documents are to be delivered, title is transferred at the time and place of contracting.

EXAMPLE 7 Steven Marquez contracted to buy a CB radio from Maria Fossa, a private party. Marquez gave Fossa a $50 deposit at the time of contracting. He agreed to pick up the radio and pay the balance of the purchase price in 2 days. Title to the radio passed from Fossa to Marquez at the time of contracting because delivery was to be made without moving the goods.

Risk of Loss

When goods are to be shipped by carrier, the risk of loss passes to the buyer at the same time as the passage of title. In a shipment contract, the risk of loss passes to the buyer when the goods are delivered to the carrier. In a destination contract, the risk of loss passes to the buyer when the goods arrive at their destination.

When goods are not to be shipped by carrier, the passage of risk of loss depends on whether or not the seller is a merchant. If the seller is a private party (not a merchant), the risk of loss passes to the buyer when the seller makes **tender of delivery.** This occurs when the seller offers to turn the goods over to the buyer.

EXAMPLE 8 Maria Fossa, in Example 7, offered to turn the CB radio over to Steven Marquez at the agreed time. Marquez, however, refused to take it then, saying that he would pick it up in 2 weeks. Three days later, the radio was stolen from Fossa's house. Marquez must suffer the loss and pay the contract price to Fossa.

	BILL OF SALE
Price	In consideration of Two Hundred Dollars ($200) paid
Name and address of buyer	by Steven Forman, 7 Maple Ave., Youngstown, OH, the receipt
Receipt	of which is hereby acknowledged, I Sylvia Boswell, do
	hereby sell and convey to Steven Forman one Remington
Goods sold	12-gauge shotgun, No. 37119582.
	And I hereby covenant that I am the lawful owner of
Warranty	the goods and agree to warrant and defend their sale
The word "seal" provides consideration in some states	against any lawful claims and demands of all persons.
	Witness my hand and seal this 15th day of April, 19--.
Date	*Sylvia Boswell*
Signature of seller	Sylvia Boswell
Name and address of seller	11 Hemlock Drive Youngstown, OH

A bill of sales proves that title to goods was transferred. Is it proof of ownership? Does the holder of a bill of sale assume the risk of loss for the goods in question?

If the seller is a merchant, however, the risk of loss is transferred from the seller to the buyer when the buyer receives the goods. Thus, if Marquez had been in the same situation with a dealer instead of with a private party, Marquez would not have suffered the loss.

Instead of following these rules, the parties may agree, if they wish, to other times and places when the risk of loss shall pass.

Voidable Title

Sometimes people have **voidable title** to goods. This means that they can return the goods and get back the money they paid for them. Minors and people who obtain goods through fraud are examples of people with voidable title. Under the UCC, a purchaser with voidable title may transfer good title to someone else who buys them in good faith for something of value.

EXAMPLE 9 Andrea Lane, who was 16 years old, bought a car for $400. Six months later, she sold the car to her 19-year-old cousin, Jason, for $450. Even though Andrea had voidable title (because she was a minor), Jason was given good title because he was a good-faith purchaser for value.

Buying From a Merchant

Special rights are given to people who buy goods from a merchant who deals in goods of a particular kind. If someone entrusts goods with a merchant and the merchant sells them in the ordinary course of business, the buyer receives good title to the goods.

EXAMPLE 10 Janet Bergstrom left her watch at a jewelry store to be repaired. A salesperson at the jewelry store sold the watch to a customer in the ordinary course of business. The customer who bought the watch received good title to it and will be able to keep it. Bergstrom's claim is against the jewelry store for conversion. (Conversion, a tort, is discussed in Chapter 4.)

The purpose of this law is to assure people that they will receive good title to things that they buy from merchants. The law does not apply in the case of stolen goods, since only the rightful owner has title to stolen property.

AUCTION SALES

Auction sales are governed by the UCC. When the auctioneer at an auction asks, "What am I offered for this item?" he or she is inviting people to make a **bid.** When people in the audience make bids on the items, they are making offers. The acceptance occurs and the sale is made when the auctioneer brings down the gavel and cries "Sold!" Bids may be withdrawn at any time before the acceptance. When a new bid is made while the gavel is falling, the auctioneer has the choice of either reopening the bids or declaring the goods sold without considering the new bid.

In an auction sale **with reserve,** the auctioneer does not have to sell the goods for the highest bid. He or she may withdraw the goods at any time before a sale is completed. On the other hand, in an auction sale **without reserve,** the auctioneer must sell the goods to the highest bidder. He or she may not withdraw the goods after putting them up for bidding unless no bid is made. An auction sale is with reserve unless it is expressly stated that it is without reserve.

Owners of goods cannot bid on their own property being sold at an auction unless notice is given of this practice or unless it is a forced sale. A **forced sale** occurs when property is being sold against the will of the owner, as at a sheriff's sale. (A sheriff's sale is a sale of property carried out by a sheriff to satisfy a judgment of a court.)

BULK TRANSFERS

Businesses must follow special rules when they transfer their entire stock of merchandise and supplies in one transaction, which is called a **bulk transfer.** These rules have been made to protect creditors from loss. The rules that must be followed are found in the bulk transfer section of the UCC. Basically, they require the transferee of a bulk transfer to notify all of the transferor's creditors that the transfer will take place. The creditors then have the opportunity to take legal steps to get the money that is owed them before the transfer of the goods.

EXAMPLE 11 Alright Auto Parts, Inc. contracted to sell all of its inventory and supplies to Best Auto Supply Company. To satisfy the bulk transfer law, Alright and Best made a list of everything that was being sold. In addition, Best asked Alright for a list of Alright's creditors. Best then notified Alright's creditors of the sale 10 days before it was to take place. This procedure allowed Alright's creditors to take legal action, if they wished, against Alright for the money owed them (and have the sheriff take the goods) prior to the sale. If this hadn't been done, Alright's creditors would have been able to reach the goods sold to Best, even after Best took title to them.

REMEDIES FOR BREACH

The basic remedies that are available to the parties in the event of a breach of contract are discussed in Chapter 13. These remedies have been made more specific by the section of the UCC covering breach of a sales contract.

Seller's Remedies

Sometimes buyers refuse to accept goods after ordering them. They may also refuse to pay for the goods. In such situations, the seller may do the following:

1. Withhold delivery of any goods not yet delivered.
2. Stop delivery of any goods that are still in the possession of a carrier. This is known as **stoppage in transit.**
3. Resell any goods that have been rightfully withheld, and then sue the buyer for the difference between the agreed price and the resale price, plus expenses.
4. Sue the buyer for the difference between the agreed price and the market price, plus expenses. (The seller may do this *only* if the goods cannot be resold.)
5. Sue the buyer for the price of any goods that were accepted by the buyer.
6. Cancel the contract.

Buyer's Remedies

Sometimes the seller fails to make delivery of the goods after agreeing to do so. The seller may also send improper goods (goods other than those that were ordered, or goods that are damaged or defective). In these cases the buyer may do the following:

1. Cancel the contract.
2. Sue the seller for the return of any money that has been paid.
3. Sue the seller for the difference between the agreed price and the market price at the time the buyer learned of the breach, plus expenses.
4. Reject the goods (refuse to accept them) if they do not conform to the contract. The buyer is given a reasonable time to inspect the goods to see if they conform. The seller is entitled to be notified of the rejection of the goods and has a reasonable time in which to correct the error or defect.
5. **Cover** the sale—that is, buy similar goods from someone else and sue the seller for the difference between the agreed price and the cost of the purchase, plus expenses.
6. Give notice to the seller that the goods have been accepted (if that is the case) but that they do not conform to the contract. Then, if no adjustment is made, sue the seller either for breach of contract or for breach of warranty.
7. Revoke (take back) the acceptance. This is allowed if a defect is serious and could not be detected by the buyer or if the buyer was led to believe that the seller would fix the defect.

CONTRACTS FOR THINGS OTHER THAN GOODS

In general, contracts for things other than goods are governed by common law, as amended by statutes and judicial decisions in each state. For example, the law governing the sale of goods does not apply to the sale of real property (land and buildings), because real property is not considered to be a good.

EXAMPLE 12 Donald Kozak entered into a contract for the sale of his apartment building, which contained eight refrigerators, eight stoves, and eight portable air conditioners (not built in). He sold the entire property for $65,000. In the agreement he mentioned that the selling price of the land and building was $61,000 and that the other items (goods) were being sold for $4,000.

The common law of that state would govern the sale of the real property, and the UCC would govern the sale of the goods, because Kozak specifically mentioned that the goods were being sold separately. If this had simply been a contract for the sale of the apartment building as a whole (even though the goods were included), the UCC would not have applied.

Employment contracts and contracts for labor and services are two more types of contracts that are not governed by the UCC.

Suggestions for Reducing Legal Risks

1. If you are about to make a purchase, demand adequate proof of the seller's ownership of the goods before paying for them. Try to buy goods from a responsible seller who is known to be financially able to make good if called on as a result of a breach of contract.
2. If there is any doubt as to when title is to be transferred, try to obtain a written statement indicating exactly when the title is to be transferred.
3. If the seller breaches the contract, you (as the buyer) should consider carefully the various remedies available. Select the remedy that would be most advantageous to you.
4. If the buyer breaches the contract and refuses to accept the goods, you (as the seller) should also consider the available remedies. For example, if the market price of the goods has gone up, you will benefit by avoiding the sale and keeping the goods. If the market price has gone down, you will benefit by confirming the sale and bringing an action for the purchase price.
5. Because the law is so complicated and because different laws apply to different situations, it is best to talk to a lawyer before entering into a major agreement, such as the purchase of a house or a business. Very often a lawyer can anticipate problems and help you to avoid difficulties.

Language of the Law

Define or explain each of the following words or phrases:

law of sales	documents of title	risk of loss	tender of delivery
interstate commerce	bill of lading	identified goods	voidable title
goods	straight bill of lading	future goods	bid
tangible	order bill of lading	shipment contract	auction with reserve
contract for sale	airbill	f.o.b.	without reserve forced sale
sale	warehouse receipt	f.o.b. shipping point	bulk transfer
output contract	nonnegotiable ware-	f.o.b. destination	stoppage in transit
requirement contract	house receipt	destination contract	to cover a sale
title	negotiable warehouse		
bill of sale	receipt		

Questions for Review

1. List three purposes of the UCC.
2. What transactions are governed by article 2 of the UCC?
3. How may an offer be accepted under the UCC?
4. In what way may an acceptance differ from an offer without being a rejection?
5. How is the price determined if it is not settled or agreed upon?
6. What would be an example of an output contract? a requirement contract?
7. On what two occasions is consideration unnecessary?
8. When must there be some writing indicating that a contract for sale has been made?

What are the four exceptions to this requirement?
9. What is a negotiable document of title? What are two types of negotiable documents of title?
10. Why is it important to know the exact moment that title passes in a sale of goods?
11. What is the practice with respect to passing of title for an f.o.b. destination sale? an f.o.b. shipping point sale?
12. What remedies are available to the seller if the buyer refuses to pay for the goods and the goods are still in the possession of the seller?

Cases in Point

In each of the following cases, give your decision and state a legal principle that applies to the case:

1. Vera Norovich innocently purchased from Dora Lieb goods that had been stolen. Did Norovich get a legal title to these goods?
2. George Kane was planning to take a fishing trip. Before he left, he agreed to sell all the fish he might catch on the trip to Thomas Laird for $10. Was this a sale?
3. Chung's Restaurant sent an order to Lee Tu Chu's Oriental Supply House for 20 boxes of fortune cookies, terms 2/10, n/30 (a 2 percent discount may be taken if payment is made within 10 days; the net, or full, amount is due in 30 days). The supply house acknowledged the order but changed the terms to n/30. Is there a contract?
4. Vera Lovitt agreed to buy a car from José Morales, and Morales agreed to sell it to her. They had not, however, decided on the price. Is there a contract?
5. After going on a diet and losing 50 pounds, Diane Waller took some dresses to a dressmaker to be altered. Would the contract

with the dressmaker be governed by the UCC?
6. Erica Terza of Terza Appliances sold a new refrigerator to Ogden Kamen for a price of $620. The entire agreement was oral. Before the refrigerator was delivered, Kamen learned that another store was selling the same refrigerator for less money. He wanted to rescind (cancel) the agreement to buy Terza's refrigerator, on the ground that there was no written sales contract. May he do so? Why or why not?
7. Spencer Norton, of Topeka, Kansas, ordered electrical equipment from Janet Ming, of Warren, Ohio. The equipment was shipped (from Warren) f.o.b. Topeka. If the equipment were damaged en route, through no fault of the carrier, who would suffer the loss—Norton or Ming? Explain.
8. Clara Murray contracted to sell a stove to Bob Kent. Kent later breached his contract and refused to accept delivery. Murray brought an action for the contract price. Was this action proper? If not, what should Murray have done?

9. Sandy Jameson and Anna Dianopoulos, owners of a small beauty salon in San Jose, California, owed $5,000 for the installation of hair dryers and for a large assortment of beauty supplies. Both women decided that they would rather live in Portland, Oregon. They sold their entire business and moved to Portland. Do Jameson and Dianopoulos have any responsibilities under the bulk transfer section of the UCC? Explain.

10. Arthur Conklin contracted to sell a stereo of a specified make and model to Hannah Torme for $100. When Torme came in to pay for and pick up the stereo, she found that Conklin had sold it to someone else. Torme threatened to sue for breach of contract; but later in the day, she found that she could buy exactly the same stereo from the Appliance Store for $90. What should Torme do?

Cases to Judge

1. Arthur and Arline Chevalier made an offer on some town-owned land after reading the following advertisement: "The Town of Sanford will accept bids until 4 p.m. June 13th for the sale of the following property: [description of property]. All bids should be mailed to [name and address of town administrator]." The Chevaliers sent in the highest bid. When it was not accepted, they sued the town. The court, in its decision, followed the rules governing auction sales as found in the UCC. Must the town accept the highest bid? *Chevalier v. Town of Sanford*, 475 A.2d 1149 (Maine)

2. Jernigan put a for sale sign on his tractor in the front yard of his home. Rickman looked at the tractor and telephoned Jernigan, offering to purchase it for $2,250. Jernigan accepted. Rickman loaded the tractor onto his trailer and offered Jernigan a check. Jernigan refused to take the check, saying that he required cash. They agreed that since the tractor was already loaded, Rickman could take the tractor and return with the cash the next day. Rickman immediately sold the tractor to Memphis Ford Tractor, Inc. for $1,500. That company sold the tractor in the regular course of business for $2,300. Rickman did not pay Jernigan and was convicted of the crime of larceny by trick. Can Jernigan recover the money for the tractor from Memphis Ford Tractor, Inc.? Explain. *Jernigan v. Ham*, 691 S.W.2d 553 (Tennessee)

3. Roger and Sharon Russell, d/b/a (doing business as) Performance Marine, entered into an agreement to sell a 19-foot Kindsvater boat to Clouser for $8,500. Under the agreement, Clouser made an initial payment of $1,700, and the balance was to be paid when Clouser took possession of the boat. Also, under the agreement, the sellers were to retain possession of the boat in order to transfer an engine and drive train from another boat. Upon completion of these alterations, Clouser was to take delivery of the boat at the Russells' marina. No documents of title were to be delivered by the seller. While the boat was being tested by Russells' employees, it hit a seawall and was completely destroyed. At the time of the accident, who had title to the boat? Who had the risk of loss? Explain. *Russell v. Transamerica Ins. Co.*, 322 N.W.2d 178 (Michigan)

4. Estes purchased a late-model Chevrolet Caprice Sports Coupe from Howard, an automobile dealer in Mississippi. Later, it was discovered that the vehicle had been stolen from a Chevrolet dealership in Florida and, after a circuitous route, eventually had come to rest in Mississippi. The bill of sale to the vehicle had been forged. Estes contends that he has good title to the vehicle because he bought it from a dealer. Is Estes correct? Why or why not? *Allstate Ins. Co. v. Estes*, 345 So. 2d 265 (Mississippi)

Chapter 15

THE IMPORTANCE OF WARRANTIES

Scene: The Chin residence. Mr. and Mrs. Chin, Joe, and Dorothy are sitting around the dining room table celebrating Joe's eighteenth birthday.

Dorothy: How does it feel to be a man, man?

Joe: Not much different, I guess. (*looking at a small gift-wrapped box in front of him*) When do I get to open the presents?

Mrs. Chin: Not until after we have dessert! I've got your favorite ice cream to go with the cake.

Dorothy: Oh, come on, Mom! Let Joe open his presents first. I can't wait to have him open my present!

Joe: This must be yours, Sis. (*picking up the present in front of him*) It looks pretty small to me. (*He shakes the box.*)

Mr. Chin: Good things come in small packages, you know.

Dorothy: That's right, Dad!

Mrs. Chin: It's okay with me if you want to open the presents before we have dessert.

Joe: I'll open this first. (*He opens the small box and takes out a wrist-watch.*) Oh, it's beautiful! Thanks Sis! It's just what I need.

Dorothy: You're welcome. It should show the right time. I set it before I wrapped it.

Joe (*looking at the face of the watch*): It must have stopped. That's strange.

Mr. Chin (*leaving the table*): I'll be right back.

Joe (*attempting to reset the watch*): It doesn't seem to work. The second hand doesn't go at all. The stopwatch isn't working, either.

Dorothy: Really? My present doesn't work?

Joe: Don't worry about it. We can get it replaced. It says here "limited warranty."

Dorothy: What does that mean? I hope it's not too limited!

Mr. Chin (*returning with a large box*): Here you go, Joe!

Joe: Wow! (*looking at the box for a clue*) What is it?

Mr. Chin: You'll have to open it to find out.

Joe (*opening the box*): It looks like a . . . it is! It's a rowing machine! Just like the one we have at school! Thanks, Dad and Mom!

Mr. and Mrs. Chin: You're welcome, Joe.

Mr. Chin: I see it's not the same as the one they showed me as a model in the store, but if you like it, we'll keep it anyway.

Joe: It's wonderful! Thanks, everybody, for such nice presents.

Mrs. Chin (*putting a cake in front of Joe*): It's your day to cut the cake, Joe. Dorothy, you can put the ice cream on each plate.

Dorothy: Okay. It's a beautiful cake, Mom.

Joe: It's my favorite ice cream, too. (*Joe puts a spoonful of ice cream into his mouth.*)

Joe: Ow! (*He puts his hand to his mouth.*) I think I cut my mouth!

Mrs. Chin: Oh, Joe! Are you all right?

Joe (*removing something from his mouth*): There was a piece of glass in the ice cream. It cut me under my tongue.

Mrs. Chin: Oh, good heavens! Are you all right?

Mr. Chin: We better have a doctor look at your mouth, Joe. It's bleeding hard. Come on. I'll drive you to the hospital.

LEGAL ISSUES

1. Do buyers have any legal recourse when they purchase defective merchandise from a store?
2. What is the legal meaning of the term "limited warranty"?
3. What rights do buyers have when they select an item based on a model and receive something different in its place?
4. What legal recourse does a person have who is injured by impurities or foreign substances contained in food that was purchased from a store?

THE SPIRIT OF THE LAW

Warranties are important for everyone involved in the marketing process. Manufacturers, for example, give implied warranties to retailers, who, in turn, give the same warranties to consumers. In this way, all parties connected with the sale of a product are given protection. In addition, manufacturers often give express warranties directly to consumers as an incentive to buy their products. This helps retailers to sell more goods and takes some of the burden of standing behind products away from retailers. The law of warranties also helps to improve the quality of products found in the marketplace.

Have you ever bought something that did not work when you took it home? Have you ever purchased an item that turned out to be damaged or broken when you opened up the box? Have you ever paid for something that you wanted to use for a particular purpose, only to find that it would not do the job? Has a salesperson ever made a statement or a promise about a product that did not come true? Have you ever found an impurity or a foreign substance in food that you bought in a store or ate in a restaurant? The UCC provides you with protection in all of these types of situations under its law of warranties.

In ordinary usage, the term *guarantee* is often used in place of the term *warranty.* An **express warranty,** as the name implies, is a statement of fact expressed by the seller for the purpose of having the buyer make a purchase. An **implied warranty** is not stated in words but is implied by the acts of the parties, the nature of the sale, or the surrounding circumstances.

Under the UCC warranties come about only when there is a sale of goods. They do not arise in contracts for services. A sale, you will remember, is the passing of title from the seller to the buyer for a price.

EXPRESS WARRAN-TIES

An express warranty comes about in any of three ways: (1) by a statement of fact or promise made by the seller, (2) by a description of the goods, or (3) by the use of a sample or model.

Statement or Promise by Seller

Whenever anyone sells goods and makes a statement of fact or promise about them to the buyer, an express warranty is created. The statement must relate to the goods and become part of the basis of the bargain. It is not necessary for the creation of an express warranty that the seller use formal words such as *warranty* or *guarantee.*

The express warranty may be a statement of a present fact or a promise as to performance in the future. The following example illustrates the statement of a present fact.

EXAMPLE 1 In attempting to sell his used car, Winston Carter told Dorothy Naber that the car had a new engine. Naber bought the car and discovered that the engine was not new. The statement made by Carter created an express warranty. Naber may recover damages from Carter for the breach of warranty.

The example below illustrates a promise as to performance in the future.

EXAMPLE 2 Howard Turner purchased a car from Helen Sanderson. As part of the deal, Sanderson promised to obtain an inspection sticker for the vehicle. She refused to obtain the sticker, however, when she discovered that the vehicle would not pass inspection without major repairs. The failure of Sanderson to keep her promise was a breach of an express warranty.

Express warranties are often found in sales brochures, circulars, and advertisements.

EXAMPLE 3 The manufacturer of a liquid drain cleaner advertised the product as "safe" and capable of "fast action." A child was severely injured when she was accidentally splashed with the product. The court held that the advertisement was an express warranty that the product was safe, and the child recovered money damages against the company for breach of the express warranty.

An express warranty consists of the words used by the seller. It is important that you demand a warranty that is stated in clear, precise, and understandable terms if you want to minimize your risks. Suppose that the seller says, "This product is warranted," or "This product is guaranteed." These words alone are not enough to give you protection. You need to know exactly what the seller will do for you in the event a problem arises.

There is another precaution that is very important if you wish to avoid trouble later. Always try to get a warranty in writing. If, for example, you enter into a written contract to buy a television set, insist on a written warranty to support the contract of sale. Also insist that any oral promises that are made to you be written down on the sales slip. Warranties do not have to be in writing. But if they are not, oral statements are difficult to prove. Also, the parol evidence rule, which is discussed in Chapter 11, does not usually allow oral statements or promises to be introduced in court if there was a written contract.

The opinion of the seller is not a warranty. The law allows a certain amount of "puffing," or sales talk, as discussed in Chapter 9. A statement of the value of the goods or a statement that is merely the seller's opinion does not create a warranty.

Magnuson-Moss Warranty Act   A federal law known as the Magnuson-Moss Warranty Act gives further protection to consumers when written express warranties are made on items that cost more than $15. The law provides that written warranties must fully disclose in simple, readily understandable language the terms and conditions of the warranty.

EXAMPLE 4   Suppose, when you buy a television set, that the seller gives you a written guarantee which says, "This television set is guaranteed for 6 months from the date of delivery." Nothing more is said. A short time after the set is delivered, you ask the seller to send a repair person to make some needed minor adjustments. The seller refuses, saying that the guarantee covered only the replacement of parts that were manufactured defectively.

The seller, in the above example, violated the federal law because the warranty did not say exactly what was covered and what was not covered. In addition, the warranty did not say what the seller must do or what the buyer must do in the event that something went wrong with the set.

Under federal law there are two types of written warranties, a full warranty and a limited warranty. A **full warranty** is one in which a defective product will be fixed or replaced free within a reasonable time after a complaint has been made about it. The consumer does not have to do anything unreasonable, such as ship a heavy product back to the factory, to get service under the warranty. A full warranty is good for the period mentioned in the warranty. This is true regardless of who owns the item when it breaks down. If the product cannot be fixed, under a full warranty, consumers have the choice of either getting a new

GENERAL ELECTRIC COMPANY

(For Command Performance™ Series and Performance Plus™
Color Televisions)

What We Will Do

General Electric warrants this color television for normal home use within
the fifty states of the USA and the District of Columbia as follows:

- For one year from the original date of purchase General Electric
  will repair any manufacturing defects at no charge to you.

- For an additional twelve months, General Electric will furnish a
  free picture tube in exchange for a defective tube. Labor is not
  included during this period.

Parts supplied under this warranty may be new or rebuilt at General
Electric's option.

How To Obtain Warranty Service.

On sets with model numbers beginning with 19, 25 or 40, you will be
provided with service in your home or in the Service Shop, as required.
Owners in Alaska who live more than 15 miles from a franchised General
Electric Customer Care® Service Shop will be required, however, to
deliver and pick up their set at their own expense.

Where To Get Service:
To locate your nearest General Electric Customer Care® Service Shop.
- Contact your General Electric dealer.
- Check your yellow pages.
- Call The GE Answer Center™ 800.626.2000 consumer information
  service. Toll-free.

This warranty gives you specific legal rights, and you may also
have other rights which vary from state to state.

GENERAL ELECTRIC COMPANY
VIDEO PRODUCTS DIVISION
PORTSMOUTH, VIRGINIA 23705

G3

**A manufacturer offers a warranty to encourage sales. A warranty should make
clear the obligations of the maker and the purchaser. Why would General Electric
limit its warranty?**

Legal Issue No. 2

product or getting their money back. A warranty that provides less than this is
called a **limited warranty** under federal law, and it must be labeled as such.
When you see the words "limited warranty" on a product, it is a good idea to
read the warranty before you buy it to learn of its limitations.

Description of the Goods

Any description of the goods that is made part of the basis of the bargain creates
an express warranty. The seller warrants that the goods will be the same as the
description.

EXAMPLE 5 Suppose you order a stereo system after selecting it from a
catalog. The catalog described the system and showed a picture of it. When the
system arrives, you discover that it is not the same as the one pictured and
described in the catalog. A breach of an express warranty has occurred.

Sample or Model

Any sample or model that is made part of the basis of a bargain creates an
express warranty. The seller warrants that the goods will be the same as the
sample or model.

Legal Issue No. 3

EXAMPLE 6 Suppose you go to a store to purchase a stereo system. The salesperson shows you several different models. You look at them carefully and select the one you like best. You are then given a system that is sealed in its original carton. When you take the system home and open it up, you discover that it is not the same type of system as the model you were shown. A breach of an express warranty has occurred.

IMPLIED WARRANTIES

Implied warranties are warranties implied by the acts of the parties, by the nature of the transaction, or by the surrounding circumstances. These guarantees are given to buyers by operation of law. There are two types of implied warranties: (1) warranty of fitness for a particular purpose, and (2) warranty of merchantability.

Warranty of Fitness

A **warranty of fitness for a particular purpose** is created when the seller knows about a particular purpose for which the goods are needed. The seller advises the buyer in making a purchase and the buyer relies on the seller's knowledge and advice when selecting the proper goods. This warranty exists even when the seller is a nonmerchant if these conditions are present.

EXAMPLE 7 Katherine Eng, who knew little about paint, went to a paint store and told the proprietor that she wanted some paint to use on an outdoor concrete patio. The proprietor selected a gallon of paint from a shelf and told Eng that it would be perfect for that type of job. Eng bought the paint and painted the patio, following the directions on the can. Two weeks later, the paint washed off the patio during a heavy rainstorm. The paint store had breached the implied warranty of fitness for a particular purpose.

Warranty of Merchant- ability

Probably the most important warranty, as far as the consumer is concerned, is the **warranty of merchantability.** This warranty is given only by someone who is a merchant. A **merchant** is a person who deals in goods of the kind being sold in the ordinary course of business or who otherwise holds himself or herself out as having knowledge or skill pertaining to those goods.

EXAMPLE 8 Gail Simms bought a secondhand video cassette recorder from Kenneth Aborn. He had placed an advertisement for the VCR in the classified section of the newspaper. Aborn was not in the business of selling VCRs. The day after Simms bought the VCR, it stopped working. Simms would not have the benefit of the warranty of merchantability because Aborn was not a merchant.

Whenever a merchant sells goods, the merchant warrants that the goods are merchantable. To be **merchantable,** goods must (1) pass without objection in the trade under the contract description; (2) be fit for the ordinary purposes for which such goods are used; (3) be adequately contained, packaged, and labeled as the agreement may require; and (4) conform to the promises or statements of fact made on the container or label, if any.

EXAMPLE 9 If Gail Simms had purchased the video cassette recorder, in Example 8, from a local store instead of from Kenneth Aborn, she would have had legal recourse against the merchant for breach of warranty of merchantability. Even a secondhand VCR is not merchantable if it breaks down the day after someone buys it. It is not fit for the ordinary purpose for which VCRs are used.

Other examples of items that the courts have held to be nonmerchantable are the following: day-old chickens that had bird cancer; contaminated blood received in a blood transfusion; weed killer that also killed a farmer's squash; a boat engine that gave off excessive amounts of black smoke; a used car that was not reasonably fit for the general purpose for which it was sold (see Chapter 17); applesauce that was inedible because of poor taste and smell; contaminated cheese; and any food containing impurities, such as bits of wood, metal, or glass.

WARRANTY OF TITLE

Whenever goods are sold, the seller warrants that the title being conveyed is good and that the transfer is rightful. The seller also warrants that the goods shall be delivered free of any financial obligations (security interests or other liens) about which the buyer had no knowledge. This is called the **warranty of title.**

When stolen goods are sold to an innocent purchaser, the true owner, if discovered, is entitled to the return of the goods. The innocent purchaser's remedy is against the seller for breach of warranty of title.

EXAMPLE 10 Irving Grossman sold a diamond watch to Larry Bardley for $100. A short time later, Bardley had to give the watch to Bill Lardner, who offered proof that he was the true owner. The watch had been stolen from Lardner's room and sold to Grossman, who knew nothing of the theft. Because Grossman did not have good title, he could not transfer good title to Bardley. Grossman was, therefore, liable for breach of the warranty of title. Of course, Grossman may also sue the person who previously sold the watch to him for breach of the same warranty.

PRIVITY OF CONTRACT NOT REQUIRED

People who contract directly with each other are said to be in privity of contract. In the past, warranties existed only between people who were in privity of contract. To illustrate with an example that occurred years ago, a man purchased a can of salmon from a store. He took it home and served it to his family. His young son was injured from bits of metal that were in the salmon. When suit was brought on behalf of the son against the store for breach of warranty of merchantability, the son lost the case. He had not purchased the salmon.

The boy probably would have won the case if it had occurred today. Today, under the UCC, a seller's warranty extends not only to the buyer, but also to any person in the buyer's family or household. It also extends to the buyer's guest if it is reasonable to assume that a guest may use the goods. Sellers may not exclude this provision of the law. That is, a seller may *not* say, "These goods are warranted to the purchaser only."

EXCLUSION OF WARRANTIES

Sellers are allowed, under the UCC, to exclude warranties. In order to exclude or modify any implied warranty of fitness for a particular purpose, the exclusion must be in writing and must be conspicuous—that is, it must be written and presented so that it will be readily noticed by the buyer. The statement may simply say, ''There are no warranties that extend beyond the description on the face thereof.'' An implied warranty can also be excluded or modified as a result of the course of dealing that takes place between the two parties or in accordance with the custom of the marketplace (the general practice within a particular trade).

To exclude the warranty of merchantability, the word *merchantability* must be mentioned specifically. If the exclusion is in writing, the writing must be of the kind that can be easily noticed by the buyer. The warranty of title may not be excluded.

All implied warranties are also excluded by expressions such as ''as is,'' or ''with all faults.'' They are also excluded by other language that, in common understanding, calls the buyer's attention to the exclusion of warranties.

EXAMPLE 11 Teresa Quigley bought a computer desk for cash from a retail furniture dealer. The red sales tag attached to the desk read: ''Reduced from $198 to $75, sale final, with all faults.'' When the desk was delivered to Quigley's home, she found that the drawers stuck and that one side was badly marked and scratched. Quigley would have no recourse in most states. By the terms of the sale, she has assumed all risk as to quality. She is protected only by an implied warranty of title.

Protection for the Consumer

The Magnuson-Moss Warranty Act places limits on the exclusion of implied warranties to consumers. Under this federal law, if a seller makes a written express warranty to a consumer, the implied warranties cannot be disclaimed or excluded. This law also applies if the seller gives the buyer a service contract. Implied warranties may be limited to the length of time of the express warranty unless it is too short to be reasonable. However, if that is done, it is a limited warranty rather than a full warranty.

■ Some states have gone even further in protecting consumers by saying that implied warranties cannot be excluded when goods are sold to consumers. If the sale in Example 11 had taken place in Massachusetts, for example, Quigley might have had a remedy. That state does not allow sellers to exclude implied warranties when goods are sold to consumers. Other states have enacted similar laws regulating the exclusion of warranties.

REMEDIES FOR BREACH OF WARRANTY

Express and implied warranties usually concern either title or quality. If the title is not clear and if, for this reason, the buyer has to give up the goods to the true owner or to pay the true owner some money, the buyer has a claim against the seller for any amount he or she has paid out. This means, for instance, that if

---

■ This symbol indicates that there may be a state statute that varies from the law discussed here. Whenever you see this symbol, find out, if possible, what the statute in your state says about this point or principle of law.

A manufacturer who allows a piece of glass to be packaged in its ice cream can cause personal injuries. What warranty is breached? What remedies are available to the customer?

the true owner takes the goods, the buyer may recover the full purchase price of the goods.

When the breach of warranty refers to the quality of the goods, the buyer has the choice of various remedies. He or she may accept and keep the goods and may put in a claim for the damage suffered by the breach of warranty. If the buyer has not yet paid the price, he or she may make a proper deduction from it. It is important to note, however, that the buyer must notify the seller of any breach of warranty as soon as possible after it occurs. If the buyer fails to notify the seller within a reasonable time after discovering the breach, the buyer may lose the right to recover damages.

Legal Issues Nos. 1 and 4

If the buyer has not yet received the goods, he or she may refuse to accept them and may sue for damages suffered, if any.

The buyer may return the goods and receive a refund of the purchase price unless the seller fixes the defect. If the seller refuses to correct the problem or to accept the return of the goods or to return the money received for them, the buyer may hold the goods for the seller and sue for the purchase price plus incidental damages.

Suggestions for Reducing Legal Risks

1. Examine carefully all goods for sale on an "as is" basis. They ordinarily carry no express or implied warranties as to their quality.
2. As a merchant, be sure that your goods are of proper quality and are not harmful or adulterated. Customers have a right of action against both the seller and maker of defective goods.
3. Specify to the seller exactly what any goods you purchase are to be used for, and let the seller select the goods to be used for your specific purpose. Rely on his or her expert skill and knowledge of the goods.
4. When buying expensive goods by trade name for a special need, try to obtain an express warranty from the seller. Ask the seller to warrant that the goods will serve the purpose for which they are to be used.

5. When you are about to purchase goods that say "limited warranty" on them, read the warranty to find out what the limitation is.
6. Notify the seller immediately if you discover that there is something wrong with the goods you bought. If you fail to do this, you may lose your right to recover for breach of warranty.
7. Written warranties come with most major purchases, although this is not legally required. The protection offered by written warranties varies greatly, so it is important to compare warranties *before* making a purchase. Here are some questions to keep in mind when comparing warranties.
   a. What parts and repair problems are covered by the warranty?
   b. Are any expenses excluded from coverage?
   c. How long does the warranty last?
   d. What will you have to do to get repairs?
   e. What will the company do if the product fails?
   f. Does the warranty cover "consequential damages"? (Consequential damages not caused directly by the product, but as a consequence of the product's failure. For instance, the spoiling of food when a freezer fails is a consequential damage.)
   g. Are there any conditions or limitations on the warranty?

Language of the Law

Define or explain each of the following words or phrases:

express warranty
implied warranty
full warranty

limited warranty
warranty of fitness for
  a particular purpose

warranty of mer-
  chantability
merchant

merchantable
warranty of title

Questions for Review

1. What are the two kinds of warranties? How do they differ?
2. Describe three ways in which an express warranty comes about.
3. Why is it important to demand a warranty that is stated in clear, precise, and understandable language?
4. Why is it important to have warranties in writing and to insist that all oral promises be written down on the sales slip?
5. What protection is given to consumers by the Magnuson-Moss Warranty Act?
6. Explain how the implied warranty of fitness for a particular purpose comes about.
7. Who gives the warranty of merchantability? When is it given?
8. List the requirements that must be met for goods to be merchantable.
9. Explain how the warranty of title comes about.
10. Give three examples of items which the courts have held to be nonmerchantable.
11. Is anyone other than the buyer protected by warranties? Explain.

12. What does the exclusion of a warranty mean to the buyer?

13. May implied warranties be excluded when a consumer is given an express warranty?

14. Explain what happens if the buyer fails to notify the seller of a breach of warranty within a reasonable period of time.

Cases in Point

In each of the following cases, give your decision and state a legal principle that applies to the case:

1. The salesperson in a furniture store told Isak Weinberg that the table he was looking at was solid cherry. Weinberg purchased the table and discovered later that it was made of another kind of wood that had been stained to look like cherry. Does Weinberg have any legal recourse? Explain.

2. Relying on a statement by the sales clerk that it was the best on the market, Sonia Donaldson bought an exercise bike. Soon after buying it, Donaldson discovered that it was not the best on the market. In fact, two of her friends purchased bikes that were much better than the one she bought. Does she have any legal recourse against the store where she bought the bike? Why or why not?

3. James Cullen bought a used car from a car dealer. As part of the transaction, the dealer promised to put four new tires on the vehicle. One of the tires blew out shortly after Cullen had bought the car, while he was driving on an interstate highway. Cullen discovered that the tires on the vehicle were recapped rather than new. Does he have any legal recourse? Explain.

4. Pedro Gonzalez ordered a clock radio from a store catalog. The radio that was sent to Gonzalez was different from the one pictured in the catalog. On what legal grounds may he obtain relief against the store?

5. While eating a hamburger at a fast-food restaurant, Eva Duarte bit into a piece of green-colored wire that was mixed in with the lettuce on the burger. She received serious injuries from the mishap. Has the restaurant breached a warranty?

6. Roger Haley bought a car from a used-car dealer. Later, it was discovered that the same car had been stolen from Margarita Gomez. What law protects Gomez in this situation? What law protects Haley?

7. Ursula Hurkin, who knew little about furnaces, said to the proprietor of the Holland Heating Supply Co. that she wanted a furnace that was suitable to heat her new building. The supply company measured the building and selected a furnace for Hurkin, saying that it would be suitable for the job. The furnace turned out to be too small, however, and did not adequately heat the building. On what legal grounds may Hurkin obtain relief?

8. Lorenzo Aboud bought a used car from a private party. The next day, the engine of the newly acquired vehicle seized up and stopped running. Aboud learned that it had to be completely rebuilt. He claimed that the seller breached the warranty of merchantability. Do you agree?

9. After looking at several samples, a committee from the Austin School District chose a particular kind of classroom desk and ordered 120 of them for a new school addition. The desks that were delivered had a smaller writing surface than the sample shown to the committee. On what legal grounds may the school district obtain relief?

10. Jennifer Harrington purchased a new television set from a large discount store. The following words were printed in bold letters on the sales slip: "THE WARRANTY OF

MERCHANTABILITY IS HEREBY EXCLUDED.'' Packed in the box with the set was a written limited warranty from the manufacturer. Jennifer took the set home, unpacked it, and turned it on. It would not work. Does Jennifer have a claim against the store for breach of warranty of merchantability? Explain.

Cases to Judge

1. David Gentile received severe head injuries while playing in a high school football game. His helmet, which had been furnished by the school board, was 7 years old. Each year the school board had sent the helmet, along with other football equipment, to a reconditioning company for repair and post-season storage. Gentile brought suit against the manufacturer of the helmet and the reconditioning company for breach of warranty. Can the reconditioning company be held liable on that ground? Why or why not? *Gentile v. MacGregor Mfg. Co.*, 493 A.2d 647 (New Jersey)

2. Ross Herbolt bought an F-2 Gleaner Combine from Hillsboro Farmers Exchange. The written manufacturer's warranty that came with the combine included the following sentence: ''There are no warranties which extend beyond those expressly stated herein.'' Later, when problems developed, the seller argued that the warranty of merchantability was disclaimed by that sentence. Do you agree with the seller? Why or why not? *Allis-Chalmers Credit Corp. v. Herbold*, 479 N.E.2d 293 (Ohio)

3. Roy E. Farrar Produce Co. ordered boxes to be used for packing tomatoes from International Paper Co. Farrar requested that the boxes be the same type as those supplied to Florida packers for the shipping of tomatoes. It requested two sizes of boxes that would hold 20 and 30 pounds of tomatoes and would not collapse during shipping and storage. International Paper shipped 21,500 unassembled boxes to Farrar. They were not tomato boxes and were not the type used in Florida. They did not have adequate stacking strength and would not hold up during shipping. On what grounds may Farrar obtain relief? *International Paper Co. v. Farrar*, 700 P.2d 642 (New Mexico)

4. Mr. and Mrs. Calvert purchased a used GMC pickup truck from D & K Auto Sales. As part of the sales transaction, the Calverts signed a ''Used Vehicle Order.'' The order contained a declaration stating, ''Sold as is, no inspection.'' It also stated, ''I hereby make this purchase knowingly without any guarantee, expressed or implied, by this dealer, or his agent.'' The truck broke down 12 days after the Calverts bought it, due to a faulty engine. The Calverts brought suit against the seller for breach of warranty of merchantability. Will they recover damages? Explain. *Harper v. Calvert*, 687 S.W.2d 227 (Missouri)

5. Rufus Allen, d/b/a (doing business as) A & B Motors, acquired a used pickup truck in trade. Parsons asked about purchasing the truck. Allen told him that he had no knowledge of the truck's condition or quality but would sell it to him for $250. Parsons replied that he could not use the truck unless it had a valid inspection sticker on it. Allen said that if Parsons would do the necessary work to enable the vehicle to pass inspection, he would put a sticker on it. Parsons paid $100 down and agreed to pay the balance at $15 per week. He took possession of the vehicle and had work done on the lights and windshield wipers so that it would pass inspection. He took the truck to Allen several times for the sticker, but never received it. Some weeks passed, and Allen repossessed the truck because Parsons had not made the payments. Allen affixed an inspection sticker on the truck and resold it to another person. On what legal grounds does Parsons have a cause of action against Allen? Explain. *Allen v. Parsons*, 555 S.W.2d 522 (Texas)

Chapter 16

CONSUMER PROTECTION

Scene: The living room of the Chin residence. Mrs. Chin is talking with a salesperson.

Mrs. Chin: This is something I've needed for a long time.

Salesperson (*writing up an order*): It's the best vacuum cleaner on the market!

Mrs. Chin: I'm sure my husband won't mind if I buy it. He knows how much I need one of these.

Salesperson: Believe me, you can't go wrong with this. Sign right here (*handing her the order sheet*).

Mrs. Chin (*signing*): Will it take long to be delivered?

Salesperson: About 2 weeks.
(*Mrs. Chin lets the salesperson out just as the mail carrier arrives.*)

Mail carrier (*handing her some letters*): How are you, Mrs. Chin?

Mrs. Chin: Fine, thank you. I guess you don't have that package that I'm expecting.

Mail carrier: Here's a small package for you (*handing her a package from the mail pouch*).

Mrs. Chin: Oh, the one I'm expecting is quite large.

Mail carrier: That'll be delivered by truck. I only carry small items.

Mrs. Chin: Thank you.
(*She takes the mail into the kitchen, where Joe and his friend Tom are taking food out of the refrigerator. Dorothy is doing homework at the kitchen table.*)

Dorothy: What came in the mail, Mom?

Mrs. Chin: Mostly bills, except for this package. (*She opens the package.*) It's a box of greeting cards. I didn't order these. And look, there's a note asking me to return the cards if I don't want them. Well . . . (*tossing the package onto a table*) . . . when I get around to it . . . .

Mrs. Chin: I was hoping that Dad's birthday present would come today. I ordered it from that catalog over 6 weeks ago, and it still hasn't come. I'm beginning to get worried.

Dorothy: Maybe you should write to them.

Joe: We're going downstairs and work out on the rowing machine for a while.

Mrs. Chin: Okay, Joe.
(*In the basement, Joe is using his new rowing machine.*)

Tom (*looking on*): This is terrific!

Joe (*puffing*): Yeah, it was a nice present! (*CRACK! THUD!*) Oof!

Tom: What happened?

Joe: The pedal broke right off! I don't believe it!

Tom: You can probably sue them! I think there's a law called "product liability" that covers things that break down like this.
(*Upstairs, Mr. Chin enters.*)

Mrs. Chin: Honey! You're home early!

Mr. Chin: Yes. I thought I'd surprise you. (*He carries a large box into the kitchen.*)

Mrs. Chin: What's that?

Mr. Chin: Something for you. You can open it.

Mrs. Chin: What can it be? (*She opens the box.*) Oh, my! (*Her face turns red.*) A new vacuum cleaner!

Mr. Chin: I got it wholesale through one of our suppliers. It's the best one they make!

LEGAL ISSUES

1. May consumers return goods that they buy from a door-to-door salesperson?
2. When people receive in the mail goods that they did not order, must they return the goods or pay for them?
3. When consumers order goods by mail, must sellers send the goods to them within a particular time?
4. Do product liability laws cover products that break down but that do not cause injuries to people or property?

THE SPIRIT OF THE LAW

During the early part of this century, consumer protection law was practically nonexistent. Law students memorized the phrase *caveat emptor* (let the buyer beware). Very little protection, other than the contract law discussed in Unit 2, was available to consumers who bought faulty merchandise. Similarly, people who were injured by dangerous products usually had no recourse because they were not in privity of contract with manufacturers. Today, the power of consumers has increased, and the law has changed. Society has demanded that consumers be given protection and that manufacturers be held responsible for foreseeable injuries their products cause to people who use them. Now, the phrase that students often memorize is *caveat venditor* (let the seller beware).

In addition to protection by the laws of negligence (Chapter 4), fraud (Chapter 9), and express and implied warranties (Chapter 15), consumers are given legal protection against unfair and deceptive practices, false advertising, mail-order fraud, and defective products.

UNFAIR AND DECEPTIVE PRACTICES

Consumer protection laws are designed to protect consumers against unfair and deceptive acts or practices by sellers. A consumer, you will remember, is any person who purchases or leases goods, services, or property primarily for personal, family, or household use. An **unfair and deceptive act or practice** is one that misleads (or has the potential to mislead) consumers. Almost all states have now enacted some kind of unfair and deceptive trade practice law. Although state laws differ, all of them are more or less similar to the Federal Trade Commission Act, which has prohibited unfair and deceptive acts or practices for many years. In addition to individual remedies available to consumers, consumer protection laws allow state attorneys general to bring suit against violators.

Deceptive Pricing

It is an unfair and deceptive practice for a store to raise the price of an article with the intention of lowering the price later and claiming that the ''lower'' price is a bargain.

EXAMPLE 1 The Kut-Rate Stationery store purchased a quantity of ball-point pens for $2 each. The store normally sells such pens at 50 percent above cost, which would be $3 per pen. In this case, however, the store purposely put a $5 price tag on each pen, knowing that very few would sell at that price. A few days later, the store dropped the price to $3 and advertised, ''Terrific bargain! Ball-point pens! Formerly $5, now only $3!'' This is a deceptive practice because the bargain is not real. Three dollars is the store's regular price for the goods.

It is also deceptive and unlawful for a store to claim that prices are wholesale or are factory prices when this is not true. Sometimes stores will advertise that a product is being sold below the ''manufacturer's suggested list price'' or below the price printed by the manufacturer on the package. Such advertising violates the law if the manufacturer's suggested list price (or the price printed on the package) is not actually used by similar stores in that area. It is deceptive because it is not a valid price comparison.

Another deceptive practice is to advertise a two-for-the-price-of-one sale, or any similar alleged bargain, when there is really no bargain at all.

EXAMPLE 2 The Kut-Rate Stationery store put a price of $6 on ball-point pens that usually sell for $3. Shortly thereafter, the store advertised the pens at two for $6, saying, ''Two-for-one sale! Buy one and get one free!'' This practice is unlawful because customers are misled into thinking that they are getting a bargain when they really are not.

Referral Schemes

■ Sometimes, as a sales technique, the seller will ask the buyer for the names of friends who might also be interested in purchasing the product. This practice is termed a **referral scheme.** The seller promises to give the buyer a cash rebate or something for free if a certain number of the buyer's referrals also purchase the item. This type of scheme can be a deceptive practice if it depends on something happening that is very unlikely.

A common type of illegal referral scheme sometimes occurs when people have their houses remodeled (as with vinyl or other siding). Sellers sometimes say as a sales pitch that they will use the house as a model home. They promise the homeowner a commission on resulting sales. This is a deceptive practice because, more often than not in such a situation, the homeowner receives very little or nothing from the scheme.

Deceptive Service Estimates

■ A great many consumer complaints occur in the area of repairs and services. Sometimes these complaints are the result of misunderstandings between the customer and the party offering the repair service. Frequently, however, the complaints are the result of unfair and deceptive business practices.

It is unfair and deceptive to understate *significantly* the cost of repair services or to charge for repairs that were not authorized by the customer. It is also deceptive to tell a customer that repairs are necessary when they are not or to say that repairs have been made when that is not true.

EXAMPLE 3 Lois Ovadia's color television broke down. The repair shop estimated that the cost of the repairs would be about $75. Ovadia decided to have the work done. When she returned to pick up her television, she was presented with a bill for $175. This was a violation of the state consumer protection law.

In nearly all states, businesses must provide to customers, upon request, a written estimate of the cost of the anticipated repairs. Businesses must also tell customers the approximate time it will take to complete the job.

Door-to-Door Sales

Legal Issue No. 1

Sometimes fast-talking door-to-door salespersons convince consumers to buy things that they would not otherwise buy. Consumers often change their minds later, when sales pressure is no longer present and they have had a chance to think about the purchase more carefully. For this reason the law gives consumers 3 business days to cancel most contracts made with door-to-door salespersons. The law only applies to purchases of $25 or more made away from the seller's regular place of business. Thus, it often applies to consumer product "parties" given in private homes and to sales made in rented hotel rooms or restaurants.

Under the Federal Trade Commission (FTC) rule, the salesperson must inform you of your cancellation rights at the time you agree to the sale. The salesperson must also give you two copies of a cancellation form (one to keep and one to send), and a copy of your contract or receipt. The contract or receipt should be dated, should show the name and address of the seller, and should explain your right to cancel.

If you decide to cancel a door-to-door sale, sign and date one copy of the cancellation form. Then mail or hand deliver it to the address given for cancellation any time before midnight of the third business day after the contract date. Keep the other copy for your records. Proof of the mailing date is important, so you should consider sending the cancellation form by certified mail, even though the law does not require it. You do not have to give a reason for canceling.

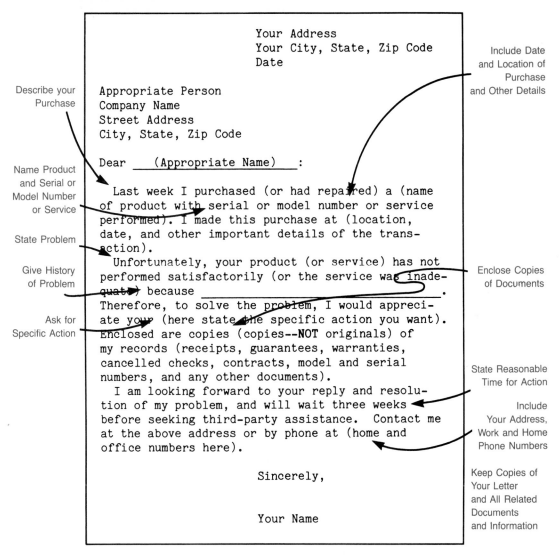

Describe your Purchase

Name Product and Serial or Model Number or Service

State Problem

Give History of Problem

Ask for Specific Action

```
                              Your Address
                              Your City, State, Zip Code
                              Date

Appropriate Person
Company Name
Street Address
City, State, Zip Code

Dear    (Appropriate Name)   :

   Last week I purchased (or had repaired) a (name
of product with serial or model number or service
performed). I made this purchase at (location,
date, and other important details of the trans-
action).
   Unfortunately, your product (or service) has not
performed satisfactorily (or the service was inade-
quate) because _____.
Therefore, to solve the problem, I would appreci-
ate you (here state the specific action you want).
Enclosed are copies (copies--NOT originals) of
my records (receipts, guarantees, warranties,
cancelled checks, contracts, model and serial
numbers, and any other documents).
   I am looking forward to your reply and resolu-
tion of my problem, and will wait three weeks
before seeking third-party assistance.  Contact me
at the above address or by phone at (home and
office numbers here).

                         Sincerely,


                         Your Name
```

Include Date and Location of Purchase and Other Details

Enclose Copies of Documents

State Reasonable Time for Action

Include Your Address, Work and Home Phone Numbers

Keep Copies of Your Letter and All Related Documents and Information

A complaint letter documents a problem and asks for specific relief. You may wish to send a copy of such a letter to a local consumer protection agency if you buy a defective product or receive poor service.

Under the FTC rule, the seller must do the following within 10 days:

1. Cancel and return any papers you signed.
2. Refund your money.
3. Tell you whether any product left with you will be picked up.
4. Return any trade-in.

This "cooling-off" rule does not apply to sales made totally by mail or telephone. Similarly, it does not apply to sales of real estate, insurance, securities, or emergency home repairs.

Fraudulent Misrepresentations

A **fraudulent misrepresentation** is any statement that has the effect of deceiving the buyer. It usually occurs when the seller misstates the facts about something that is important to the consumer.

EXAMPLE 4 When Kevin Conary bought his car, he was told by the used-car dealer that the engine had been completely rebuilt. Two months later the car broke down. Conary discovered that the engine had actually not been rebuilt. The dealer's statement was a fraudulent misrepresentation.

You will remember from Chapter 9 that someone who is defrauded has the choice of either getting out of the contract or suing in tort for money damages. In addition, consumers have the added protection of other remedies under the consumer protection laws.

Making false statements about the construction, durability, reliability, safety, strength, condition, or life expectancy of a product is a deceptive practice. It is also deceptive to fail to disclose to a buyer any fact that would cause the buyer not to enter into the contract.

FALSE ADVERTISING

The states, in general, have statutes that regulate false advertising. The FTC regulates false advertising on the national level. Congress has given the commission the power to issue **cease and desist orders** (orders to stop) to anyone using advertising that would mislead the public. Anyone who is ordered to stop using such advertising has the right to appeal to the federal court.

EXAMPLE 5 A company ran an advertisement that said, "Yes, it's true. There is a safe, harmless medicated liquid called Cleerex that dries up pimples overnight. . . . Many users report that they had a red, sore, pimply face one night and surprised their friends the next day with a clear complexion." A doctor testified at a hearing that Cleerex would dry up and remove pimples, but not overnight. The FTC ordered the company to stop running ads saying that Cleerex would cause pimples to disappear within any particular period of time. When the company appealed, the court ordered the company to stop running only that part of the ad that said that Cleerex would cause pimples to disappear overnight.

It should be pointed out, however, that the federal courts rarely overturn the orders of a regulatory agency such as the FTC. They usually do so only if the agency's orders are grossly unfair.

Advertising of Guarantees

Have you ever seen the words *guaranteed, satisfaction or your money back,* or *lifetime guarantee* in a newspaper, magazine, or television advertisement? A **guarantee,** as it is used here, is a promise or assurance of the quality or life of a product. As you will recall, such a guarantee is also known as an *express warranty*. The one who makes the guarantee is called the **guarantor.**

People often discover after purchasing a "guaranteed" product that the guarantee was not what they thought it would be. They often learn that there were limitations on the guarantee that were not mentioned in the advertisement.

EXAMPLE 6 Virginia Avadanian saw a hair-curling set advertised in the newspaper. The ad simply said that the set was guaranteed. Avadanian bought the set and used it for 6 months, after which time it broke down. When she returned it to the store, she was told that the guarantee had been for only 90 days.

It is meaningless to say merely that a product is guaranteed or warranted. The word *guarantee* (or *warranty*) is incomplete without other words describing precisely what the guarantee is. Even though the FTC encourages all advertisers to present their guarantees clearly, some do not.

The Magnuson-Moss Warranty Act, which is discussed in Chapter 15, authorizes the FTC to develop rules regulating the advertisement of guarantees and to enforce these guidelines. Under the FTC's guidelines, an advertised guarantee must disclose:

1. The product or part of the product that is guaranteed.
2. The specific characteristics of the product that are covered or not covered by the guarantee.
3. The time limit of the guarantee. (When a product is advertised as having a "lifetime guarantee," the meaning of *lifetime* must be stated in the ad—that is, it must be made clear whether the guarantee covers the lifetime of the product or the owner's lifetime.)
4. What, if anything, someone must do to make a claim under the guarantee.
5. How the person or company making the guarantee will settle any claims made—that is, whether the seller will repair the item, replace the item, or return the purchase price.
6. The identity of the person or persons making the guarantee. It is often not clear as to who makes the guarantee—the manufacturer or the retailer (sales outlet).

Advertising of Consumer Credit

Have you ever seen an ad that said, "No money down" or "36 months to pay" or "100 percent financing available"? Such statements alone, without further information, violate the federal Truth in Lending Act. Whenever sellers advertise that goods may be purchased on credit, they must disclose in the advertisement the exact cost of purchasing on credit. To purchase on credit is to buy something and pay for it later.

There are two ways that people can buy things on credit. One way is to open an account and buy things from time to time on account (on credit). This is called **open-end credit.** Open-end credit may be obtained by opening a charge account at a particular store or by using a credit card. Open-end credit is so called because people can keep adding to the amount they owe for as long as they keep making monthly payments. Interest is computed on the amount that is owed each month. The other way that people buy things on credit is called **closed-end credit.** This occurs when someone buys one item, such as a car or a piece of furniture, and agrees to pay for it later on an installment basis; the installments are usually monthly. Closed-end credit also occurs when someone takes out a loan and agrees to pay the money back at a later date. Credit is discussed further in Chapter 29.

```
              COMMONWEALTH OF MASSACHUSETTS

              DISTRICT COURTS OF MASSACHUSETTS

ESSEX, ss                        FIRST DISTRICT COURT OF ESSEX
                                 Civil Action No. 87-316

STEVEN GRAZIO, a minor, by    )
MATTHEW GRAZIO, his father    )
and next friend,  Plaintiff   )  PLAINTIFF'S INTERROGATORIES
                               )       TO BE ANSWERED
           v.                  )      BY THE DEFENDANT
                               )
WAYNE WILLIAMSON, Defendant    )


1.  What is your full name, age, residence, and occupation?

2.  Were you the operator of the vehicle which was involved
in the accident in which the plaintiff claims damages?

3.  If your answer to the above question is "yes," state:

     a.  The registration of the vehicle, giving state,
number, and year of registration.
     b.  The full name and address of the owner of the
vehicle.

4.  If there were any persons in the vehicle operated by
the defendant, state the number of such persons, and their
names and addresses.

5.  What was the speed of the vehicle operated by the
defendant at the exact point of the alleged accident?

6.  Describe in detail just what the defendant did in an
attempt to avoid the alleged accident?

7.  If the vehicle operated by the defendant was damaged as
a result of the alleged accident, describe in detail the
damages to the best of your ability, naming every part that
was so damaged.

8.  What part of the vehicle operated by the defendant was
in contact with the plaintiff's vehicle.

9.  Describe fully and in detail just how the alleged
accident occurred, in the order in which the events took
place.

November 15, 19--                _____
                                 Susan L. Powers,
                                 Attorney for Plaintiff
                                 28 Main Street
                                 Beverly, MA 01915
```

Interrogatories are questions posed by either party to a lawsuit. Grazio v. Williamson is an automobile negligence case. The same form would apply for product liability.

Advertising for Open-End Credit An advertisement for open-end credit must disclose the following:

1. The time period within which a customer must pay to avoid finance charges.
2. The method of computing the balance on which the finance charge is based.
3. The method of computing the amount of the finance charge, including any minimum charge.
4. The annual percentage rate.

EXAMPLE 7 Here is a proper advertising disclosure for open-end credit:

> 1. *No finance charge* is incurred if payment is received within 30 days from the closing date shown on your monthly billing statement.
> 2. If any purchase remains unpaid for 30 days from the closing date shown on the monthly billing statement, a *finance charge* at the periodic rate of 1½ percent per month of the total past-due balance will be imposed.
> 3. The *annual percentage rate* will be 18 percent.
> 4. The minimum monthly payment will be $10.

Advertising for Closed-End Credit An advertisement for closed-end credit must disclose the following:

1. The cash price.
2. The amount of down payment required or the fact that no down payment is required.
3. The number of payments, the amount of each payment, and the due dates or period between payments.
4. The annual percentage rate. (The exact term must be used.)
5. The **deferred payment price** (that is, the total cost to the buyer).

EXAMPLE 8 Here is a proper advertising disclosure for closed-end credit:

> 1. The cash price is $100. No down payment.
> 2. There will be 12 monthly installments of $9 each.
> 3. The annual percentage rate will be 14.5 percent.
> 4. The deferred payment price will be $108.

Bait and Switch Advertising

Bait and switch advertising is an alluring but insincere invitation to customers to buy a product or service that the advertiser does not really want to sell. The advertiser steers consumers away from buying the advertised product in order to sell something else. Usually, the other product is more expensive and is offered on a basis more advantageous to the advertiser. Be alert for this deceptive practice.

EXAMPLE 9 The Delray department store advertised an electronic correcting typewriter for $99.98. When Irma Bolanos Blanco went to the store to purchase the typewriter, the clerk discouraged her from buying it. The clerk pointed out all of the typewriter's faults and then demonstrated another typewriter, saying that it was a much better buy, even though it cost $299.95.

Bait and switch advertising is a violation of FTC regulations and of the laws of many states.

The following practices may be evidence of a bait and switch:

1. The refusal to show, demonstrate, or sell the advertised product.
2. Attempts to discourage customers by criticizing the advertised product.
3. Claims that advertised products are out of stock.

4. Refusal to promise delivery of advertised products within a reasonable period of time.
5. Demonstrations of products that are inferior to the advertised items.

SHOPPING BY MAIL

Legal Issue No. 3

The FTC has established rules that protect consumers who order goods by mail. Sellers must ship goods within the time that they say they will in their catalog or advertisement. If no time for shipment is stated, sellers must ship goods within 30 days after receiving an order. Buyers have the right to cancel orders and have their money returned if these time limits are not met. Sellers must notify buyers of any delay in shipment and give buyers a free means of answering, such as by sending them a postage-paid postcard. When buyers are notified of a delay in a shipment of goods, they may either cancel the order and get their money back or agree to a new shipping date.

Unordered Merchandise

Legal Issue No. 2

Have you ever received a package in the mail containing something that you did not ask for? Under both federal and state laws, consumers can consider such unordered merchandise as gifts. They can keep the items without paying for them.

Only two kinds of products can be sent legally through the mails without the prior consent of the consumer: manufacturers' free samples and merchandise mailed by charities asking for contributions. In the case of free samples, it is illegal for senders to attempt to get the items back or send bills for them. In the case of goods mailed by charities, the receiver may often feel a moral obligation to make a contribution or to return the goods, but the law does not require this.

PRODUCT LIABILITY

Legal Issue No. 4

Have you ever read a news story about an automobile maker who has *recalled* (called back) cars in order to repair defective parts—at no cost to the buyer? or about a seller or manufacturer who has recalled a particular food, drug, or other item because evidence has shown the product to be unsafe? Such recalls occur because manufacturers and sellers have **product liability**—that is, they are accountable (responsible) for the products that they market. A manufacturer or seller is responsible for injuries to consumers when he or she places a defective, unhealthy, or unsafe item on the market. This is true even if (1) the manufacturer or seller has not been negligent in the care, preparation, and sale of the product and (2) the user of the product is not the one who bought the item or entered into the contract with the manufacturer or seller. The protection against defective items not only covers the one who bought the items but anyone who comes into contact with the items and who may be injured by them.

People who are injured or who suffer property damage from a defective product may recover from the manufacturer or seller if they can prove all of the following:

1. The manufacturer or seller sold the product in a defective condition.
2. The manufacturer or seller was engaged in the business of selling the product.
3. The product was unreasonably dangerous to the user or consumer.
4. The defective condition was the proximate cause of the injury or damage.

What would an injured customer have to prove to succeed with a product liability claim against Acme Fold-A-Bed? (*ZIGGY, by Tom Wilson. Copyright © 1986, Universal Press Syndicate. Reprinted with permission. All rights reserved.*)

5. The defective condition existed at the time it left the hands of the manufacturer or seller.
6. The consumer sustained physical harm or property damage by use or consumption of the product.

The defective condition may arise through faulty product design, faulty manufacturing, inadequate warning of danger, or improper instructions for the product's use.

This consumer protection law is sometimes referred to as *strict liability*. This is because liability exists in such cases even though the manufacturer or seller has exercised all possible care in the preparation and sale of the product.

EXAMPLE 10   In 1986, the manufacturer of Tylenol capsules stopped producing the product in capsule form. The design of the capsule made it possible for someone to substitute its contents with poison. Not only was this a threat to public safety, it could also damage the company's excellent reputation and cause it to have to defend expensive product liability lawsuits.

Consumer Product Safety Act

The laws governing product liability were greatly expanded when Congress passed the federal **Consumer Product Safety Act** of 1972. This act says that a manufacturer or seller who places an item on the market must:

1. Test the quality and reliability (fitness) of the product before shipping it from the plant and placing it on the market.
2. Obtain proof that the product has been tested and is safe.
3. Have the capability to recall the product if the need should arise.
4. Take action on any valid complaints made by users of the product.

The penalty for violating this federal act is severe. A manufacturer or seller can face a civil fine of up to $500,000 and criminal penalties of up to a $50,000 fine and a 1-year prison term. In addition, separate tort actions for damages can be brought by those who are injured.

Food, Drug, and Cosmetic Act

One of the most important federal laws in the area of product liability is the federal **Food, Drug, and Cosmetic Act.** It prohibits the manufacture and shipment in interstate commerce of any food, drug, cosmetic, or device for health purposes that is injurious, adulterated, or misbranded.

A food or drug is said to be **injurious** if it contains any substance that may make it harmful to health. An **adulterated** food or drug is one that contains any substance mixed or packed with it to reduce its quality or strength below the prescribed minimum standards. A food or drug is **misbranded** if its labeling or packaging is false or misleading in any way. (These three terms may be applied similarly to cosmetics and to devices used for health purposes.)

The Food, Drug, and Cosmetic Act requires that packaged drugs bear the name and address of the manufacturer and a statement of the quantity or weight of the contents. Labels on nonprescription drugs must give the common name of the drug, if a trade name is used, and must give directions for the drug's use. Labels must also caution against any use that may be unsafe for children or harmful to the consumer in general. If the drug is to any degree habit-forming, the label must say so. The act prescribes criminal penalties for firms or individuals responsible for violations of this law, even if they were unaware of the adulterated or misbranded character of the goods involved.

The **Delaney Amendment** was added to the Food, Drug, and Cosmetic Act in 1958. It gives the federal government the right to remove from the market any food or food additive shown or believed to cause cancer in humans or animals. Using this amendment, the government has removed Red Dye No. 2 and cyclamate, an artificial sweetener, from the market.

The federal government also uses several other methods to discourage the sale of goods considered harmful to the public health. These include:

1. *Unusually high taxes.* For example, there are special excise taxes on liquor and tobacco.
2. *Labeling and packaging.* The Food and Drug Administration, to illustrate, issued regulations requiring warning labels and tamper-proof packaging of certain nonprescription drugs and cosmetics following the Tylenol poison capsule scare of the early 1980s.
3. *Outright prohibition.* For example, all cigarette advertising on television has been banned since 1971. Television advertising of liquor (not beer or wine) is also banned.

State and Local Laws

If goods are manufactured and sold within the boundaries of a state, the federal government has no control. For this reason many states have enacted their own product liability laws that apply to intrastate sales (sales within a state). For example, most states and local governments have their own pure food laws as well as health laws to protect the public. Nearly all states and localities license and regulate establishments that sell food. Most states also have meat-and-milk laws and laws regulating the processing and canning of food. All these laws were passed to protect the consumer.

CONSUMER PROTECTION ASSISTANCE

In order to make consumer protection legislation, such as laws covering product liability, easier to find and understand, the federal Office of Consumer Affairs was created in 1971. Its main goal is to help to develop and put into practice federal programs to aid the consumer. It may also take action on those individual consumer complaints that involve goods sold in interstate commerce.

Many state and local governments have also set up **consumer protection agencies** to investigate consumer complaints. Increasingly, also, private business is policing itself in an effort to protect consumers from those who engage in questionable practices. The Better Business Bureau is an example of a nongovernment agency at the local and state level that hears consumer complaints and tries to steer consumers to reliable business concerns.

Suggestions for Reducing Legal Risks

1. Be a careful buyer. Read every contract before you sign it.
2. Make sure that what a seller calls a bargain price really offers a saving over comparable items.
3. Realize that referral schemes are usually deceptive practices.
4. Be sure to get an estimate on repair and service work before having the work done. If the final cost is much higher than the estimate, the business doing the repair work is committing an unfair and deceptive act. Seek help from your nearest consumer agency.
5. Remember that a consumer has 3 business days to cancel a contract made with a door-to-door salesperson.
6. Shop around for the lowest rate of interest before borrowing money or buying things on credit. The annual percentage rate must be disclosed to you.
7. Be alert for signs of bait and switch advertising.

Language of the Law

Define or explain each of the following words or phrases:

unfair and deceptive actor practice	guarantor	product liability	adulterated
referral scheme	open-end credit	Consumer Product Safety Act	misbranded
fraudulent misrepresentation	closed-end credit	Food, Drug, and Cosmetic Act	Delaney Amendment
cease and desist orders	deferred payment price	injurious	consumer protection agencies
guarantee	bait and switch advertising		

Questions for Review

1. Explain the purpose of consumer protection laws.
2. Give three examples of deceptive pricing.
3. Is there any way to cancel a contract made with a door-to-door salesperson? Explain.
4. What must an advertised guarantee disclose?
5. Describe a bait and switch advertisement.
6. When buying goods by mail, what protection do consumers have?
7. How may a person treat unordered goods received through the mail?
8. What six things must a person who is injured from a defective product prove to recover from the manufacturer or seller?
9. Describe four requirements of manufacturers under the Consumer Product Safety Act.
10. What does the Food, Drug, and Cosmetic Act prohibit?

Cases in Point

In each of the following cases, give your decision and state a legal principle that applies to the case:

1. Joe Yablonski ordered a camera through the mail from the United Camera Supply Company. After waiting 40 days and not receiving the camera or hearing from the company, Yablonski asked for the return of his money. Must the company return his money even though they may now be ready to send the camera? Explain.
2. A cosmetics company sent by mail samples of a perfume to people who did not ask for them. Later the company sent bills for the perfume to those people who did not send them any money in return. Has the company violated the law? Explain.
3. Sherri Blustein ordered a vacuum cleaner for $490 from a door-to-door salesperson. The next day she learned that the same vacuum cleaner was available for only $390. Can she cancel the order made with the door-to-door salesperson? Explain.
4. Gino Romulo owned the Fun 'n' Play Toy Manufacturing Company. Before shipping a new toy, he failed to have the company test the safety of the new product. Juan Ramirez, 12 years old, was injured while playing with the toy because of a defect in its design. Do Juan or his parents have a cause of action against the Fun 'n' Play Toy Manufacturing Company? Explain.
5. Kelly Galeck brought her typewriter in for repairs at a local repair shop. The estimate for the repair bill was $60. When she received the bill, however, the actual cost for the repairs was listed as $120. Under the laws of most states, did the local repair shop do anything illegal? Explain.
6. Barbara MacFarlane bought a cassette player advertised as completely guaranteed in local newspapers across the country by a well-known manufacturer. However, the ad failed to say which parts of the cassette player were guaranteed, nor did it spell out how long the guarantee would last. Does this advertisement violate any guidelines of the FTC? Explain.
7. Cut-Rate Department Stores ran an advertisement in a local newspaper. It read: "Tremendous bargain! Brand name home movie camera, regularly priced at $999 now on sale for only $599." Judy Mitzner answered the ad only 2 hours after it appeared in the newspaper. When she arrived at the store, however, a sales representative told her that the movie camera was out of stock. She was also told that another, more dependable but higher-priced movie camera was available. The sales representative tried to convince her to buy it. Is there any evidence to suggest that Cut-Rate's advertising was illegal? Explain.

Cases to Judge

1. William Everett, Jr. was a member of the New Preparatory School hockey team. In a game against the Brown University freshman team, a hockey puck fractured his skull. His protective helmet was designed so that it could be adjusted for different-sized heads. When stretched, the helmet had gaps between the sections of high-impact plastic lined with shock foam. In the accident, the hockey puck penetrated the helmet through one of the gaps and caused the skull fracture. Can Everett recover damages from the manufacturer of the helmet under the theory of product liability? Explain. *Everett v. Bucky Warren, Inc.*, 380 N.E.2d 653 (Massachusetts)

2. Delores Bierlein made arrangements with Alex's Continental Inn to rent the ''Silver Room'' for her daughter's wedding reception. Bierlein paid a $200 deposit. Three months before the wedding, Bierlein notified the Inn that her daughter's fiancé had been transferred and that the wedding reception would have to be canceled. In her suit to recover the $200 deposit, Bierlein claimed that the Inn had not provided her with a proper receipt, required under that state's consumer protection law. The Inn argued that this was not a consumer transaction. Do you agree with the Inn? Explain. *Bierlein v. Alex's Continental Inn, Inc.*, 475 N.E.2d 1273 (Ohio)

3. Dr. and Mrs. Samovitz owned a vacant house. Mrs. Samovitz discovered one of the toilets overflowed when flushed. She called a plumbing firm, Luskin & Sons, which sent a plumber to the premises that day. The plumber was unable to clear the blockage. Another Luskin plumber met Mrs. Samovitz at the premises the following day, a Friday. He told Mrs. Samovitz that the main sewer line needed to be replaced. He prepared a contract for the work for $7,000, and Mrs. Samovitz signed it. Later in the day, Dr. Samovitz told Martin Luskin, of the plumbing firm, that he wanted to obtain some other estimates and not to do any work until Luskin heard back from him on Monday. On Sunday, the Samovitzes went to the premises and were shocked to find that Luskin had already started work. Dr. Samovitz refused to pay for the work. Was Mrs. Samovitz bound to the contract she signed? Why or why not? *Louis Luskin & Sons, Inc. v. Samovitz*, 212 Cal. Rptr. 612 (California)

4. Gaylan entered into a contract to buy a Cadillac Eldorado from Dave Towell Cadillac, Inc., for $23,263.83. Before taking possession of the vehicle, Gaylan asked about buying the Cadillac Fleetwood that was in the showroom. The parties negotiated, and it was agreed that Gaylan would buy the Fleetwood instead of the Eldorado for an additional $950. The Fleetwood had been advertised in a newspaper 2 weeks earlier for the price of $20,450, and Gaylan knew about that advertisement before purchasing the vehicle. Gaylan then sued Dave Towell Cadillac, Inc. for false advertising. How would you decide? *Gaylan v. Dave Towell Cadillac, Inc.*, 473 N.E.2d 64 (Ohio)

5. The Pine Grove Mobile Park rented lots to people who placed their mobile homes on them. The rental agreements used by Pine Grove required mobile-home owners to pay a 10 percent resale fee to Pine Grove whenever they sold their mobile homes to someone else who continued to keep the homes on the Pine Grove lot. Most mobile-home owners found it best to sell their homes on a lot. Mobile homes in that area had a much greater value on a lot than without a lot. They complained, however, about paying the 10 percent fee, which was sometimes as high as $1,200. The attorney general of that state claimed that the 10 percent resale fee charged by Pine Grove was an unfair and deceptive practice and should be stopped. How would you decide? *Commonwealth v. Decotis*, 316 N.E.2d 748 (Massachusetts)

Chapter 17

BUYING AND INSURING A CAR

Scene: The Chin residence. Joe and his friend Tom are looking at newspaper advertisements.

Tom: This looks like a good deal. A brand new car for $599 down and only $203.93 a month.

Joe: How many months do you have to pay?

Tom: The ad doesn't say.

Joe: Does it say how much interest you'll have to pay?

Tom: No. There's nothing about interest here at all.

Joe: Let's go over to that used-car lot on Broadway. We don't have to buy anything. We can just look around.
(A short time later, they are at the used-car lot.)

Tom (*kicking the tire of a car*): This one isn't bad. The sign says $2,988. I'll bet we could get it for $2,000.

Joe: I wonder if it has a warranty?

Tom: The sign doesn't say.
(A salesperson approaches.)

Salesperson: Can I help you boys?

Joe: What kind of warranty does this car have?

Salesperson: Thirty days, parts and labor. This car's a honey! It belonged to a retired couple that hardly ever drove it. See the mileage? It's only got 30,000 miles on it.

Joe: Do you mind if we take it for a spin?

Salesperson: No. Go right ahead. I'll get you the key.
(With Joe sitting on the passenger side, Tom drives the car out of the lot.)

Joe: How does it feel, Tom?

Tom: Not too bad. This looks like cruise control. Let's see how it works.

Joe (*opening the glove compartment*): Maybe the owner's manual is here. Yes. Here's the manual. I'll look up cruise control. Say, here's something interesting. (*He takes a yellow piece of paper out of the manual.*) It's a receipt for some work done on the car 6 months ago. It says the mileage was 97,000 miles.

Tom: What?
(At that moment, the car in front of them stops abruptly.)

Tom (*slamming on the brakes*): Watch out! The brakes are no good! (*CRASH!*)

(*The car Tom is driving smashes into the car in front of it, pushing in the bumper and denting the trunk. Tom's car is not damaged.*)

Tom: Are you all right, Joe?

Joe: Yeah, you weren't going fast.

Stranger from the car in front (*approaching Tom's car*): What's the matter? Didn't you see me stop?

Tom: The brakes are no good on this car! I don't own it. I'm just trying it out. It belongs to a car dealer.

Stranger: Look at that! It ruined the back of my car and didn't even scratch yours.

Tom: They don't make strong bumpers like this any more. Don't worry. The dealer's collision insurance will cover it.

Stranger: I sure hope so.

LEGAL ISSUES

1. Must a newspaper ad that states the monthly payment to buy a car also include other information about the cost of the car?
2. Must a used car on the lot of an auto dealership display any information about warranties relating to that vehicle?
3. Does the purchaser of an automobile have any legal protection against having the odometer (mileage meter) turned back?
4. Does the consumer have any protection against weak bumpers placed on automobiles by manufacturers?
5. Does collision insurance pay for damages to someone else's car?

THE SPIRIT OF THE LAW

You will probably buy several automobiles during your lifetime. If so, they will be among the most important and expensive purchases you will make. You may buy a new car or a used car, depending on your taste and on how much you can afford to pay. You can usually expect fewer problems when purchasing a new car, but you can also expect to pay for that luxury. If you buy a used car, you may save a large amount of money, but there will be a greater risk that the car will have something wrong with it.

The law that applies when you buy a car comes from several different sources. Since cars are considered goods, the Uniform Commercial Code (UCC) applies to their sale. If you buy a car for personal, family, or household purposes, both federal and state consumer protection laws may also apply to the transaction. In addition, if you finance the car, special laws regulate credit.

FINANCING A CAR

One of the first steps in buying a car is to determine how much you can afford to pay for one. This will depend largely on the amount of money you have saved, the amount you earn, the amount you owe to others, and your living expenses.

You will save money if you can pay cash, because you will not have to pay interest on a loan. Additionally, cash buyers are often in a better bargaining position to negotiate a lower purchase price by offering to pay cash immediately.

If you decide to borrow money to buy a car, remember that some lenders charge more than others for lending the same amount of money. You may be able to save a sizable amount of money by shopping around for credit and then borrowing where it is least expensive. To help you do this, a federal law called **Regulation Z** of the Truth in Lending Act requires lenders to disclose two important things to borrowers: (1) the finance charge (the actual cost of the loan in dollars and cents) and (2) the annual percentage rate (APR), the true rate of interest of the loan. With this information, you can compare the cost of a loan from different lenders. You can then make a wise decision and borrow from the least expensive lender. Regulation Z is discussed in more detail in Chapter 29.

Many people go heavily into debt because they buy things they really cannot afford. Paying off a purchase on a monthly basis seems easy enough at first. Then, before they realize it, the total monthly payments are more than they can afford.

EXAMPLE 1 Angie Perakis found a used car that she liked very much. She could not afford to pay for it all at once in cash, and the monthly payments under a 24-month payment plan were too high. She bought the car anyway and agreed to pay for it over a 36-month period instead. As a result, her monthly payments are smaller. However, the car broke down completely 2 years later and was not worth fixing. Angie then found herself in a position of having to pay for a car a full year after it was no longer of use to her. At the same time, she had to make payments on another car.

Be sure to examine closely automobile advertisements that allow you to buy a car by paying a certain amount each month. To help you to be fully informed, federal law requires that important disclosures be made to you in the advertisement. These include the cash price, the down payment required, the number of payments, the amount of each payment, the APR, and the deferred payment price (your total cost). With this information, you will know exactly how much the car will cost you if you decide to pay the monthly price that is advertised.

Legal Issue No. 1

Consumer Protection

A regulation passed in 1976 by the Federal Trade Commission (FTC) gives consumers protection when they buy certain goods, including automobiles, on credit.

EXAMPLE 2 Linda Amero bought a used car from a local dealer. She paid $500 down and signed a contract in which she promised to pay the balance of $3,500 plus interest in 24 monthly installments. The dealer received the $3,500 the same day by transferring the contract to a finance company by a prearranged agreement. Amero was then required to pay the finance company the monthly payments, including interest, for the following 24 months.

Federal law allows the advertisement of a general financing policy. Regulation Z of the Truth in Lending Law only requires lenders to advertise the total cost of a loan, if the purchase price is advertised.

Under the 1976 regulation, Amero can use any defenses against the finance company that she has against the car dealer. If something was wrong with the car when she bought it so that it was not fit for the ordinary purpose for which cars are used, the car was not merchantable (fit to be sold or resold). She could use breach of warranty of merchantability as a defense if she were sued by the dealer for the money. (Warranty of merchantability is discussed fully in Chapter 15.) She can use this same defense if she is sued by the finance company.

This rule does not apply if you borrow money to buy a car from a lending company that has no arrangement with the seller.

EXAMPLE 3 Deborah Maynard went to her local bank and borrowed $3,500 to buy a car. She agreed to pay the money back in 24 monthly installments at the current interest rate. With the borrowed money, she bought a car from a used-car dealer. The car broke down 2 days after she bought it. Maynard found that the car needed $1,000 worth of repair work. The car was not merchantable. She could use breach of warranty of merchantability as a ground for getting her money back from the dealer but not from the bank. There was no financing arrangement between the bank and the car dealer. She would have to pay back to the bank the full $3,500 plus interest.

Financing the purchase of a used car through a bank rather than through a car dealer may save money, but it is important to select the used car carefully.

WHERE TO BUY A USED CAR

A used car may be purchased from a used-car dealer, a new-car dealer, a private party, or a car-rental company. Sometimes a bank or loan company will sell repossessed cars—cars that have been claimed because someone did not keep up the payments.

Purchasing From a Dealer

A used-car dealer may have a larger selection of cars but may not have the facilities to service the car after you buy it. New-car dealers, on the other hand, often have used cars that they have taken in for trade, and they usually have service facilities. However, service generally costs more at a new-car dealer than it does at a small garage.

Implied Warranties When a car dealer sells a car, the dealer gives an implied warranty that the car is merchantable. This warranty basically means that the dealer warrants that the car is fit for the ordinary purposes for which cars are used. The warranty of merchantability is one of the most important aids that the law gives to people who purchase any kind of goods from merchants. Be careful that this warranty is not excluded or disclaimed by the dealer.

EXAMPLE 4 Maggie Natera purchased a used car from a dealer. The dealer wrote "as is" on the sales slip that Natera signed. Two days after she bought the car, its transmission broke down. Natera had no legal recourse against the dealer. The UCC, which governs the sale of automobiles, says that all implied warranties are excluded by expressions such as "with all faults" or "as is."

Another way that some dealers exclude implied warranties is by the use of formal, printed language on the front or back of the sales slip. The printing is usually in capital letters and says something similar to this: "*The implied warranties of merchantability and fitness for a particular purpose are hereby disclaimed.*" Implied warranties cannot be excluded when express warranties are made, under the Magnuson-Moss Warranty Act, discussed on page 200.

Some states do not allow merchants to disclaim or exclude implied warranties when they sell motor vehicles to consumers. They include Kansas, Maine, Maryland, Massachusetts, Mississippi, New York, Vermont, West Virginia, and the District of Columbia. If Maggie Natera, in Example 4, lived in New York, for example, the result might have been different. In that state, dealers must certify to customers that a vehicle "is in condition and repair to render, under normal use, satisfactory and adequate service upon the public highway at the time of delivery."

A good rule for a car buyer to follow is to read any papers before signing them. Some lawyers say that the buyer should never sign any paper which excludes warranties. The law gives buyers the right to such warranties; therefore, it is foolish for buyers to sign warranties away.

Express Warranties Another advantage of buying a used car from a dealer is that very often the dealer gives you a 30-day, 60-day, or 90-day guarantee. Sometimes this express warranty is for parts and labor; at other times it is for labor only. On some occasions it is a 50-50 guarantee in which the buyer pays for half of the parts and labor. Many careful buyers try to get an express warranty when they buy a used car from a dealer.

The Used Car Rule To help consumers make better decisions when buying used cars, the FTC established the **Used Car Rule** in 1985. The rule requires all used car dealers to place a large sticker, called a **Buyer's Guide,** in the window of each used vehicle they offer for sale. The guide states:

Legal Issue No. 2

1. Whether the vehicle comes with a warranty and, if so, what specific warranty protection the dealer will provide.
2. Whether the vehicle comes with no warranty—''as is''—or with implied warranties only.
3. That you should ask to have the car inspected by your own mechanic before you buy.
4. That you should get all promises in writing.
5. What some of the major problems are that may occur in any car.

Whenever you purchase a used car from a dealer, you should receive the original or an identical copy of the Buyer's Guide that appeared in the window of the vehicle you bought. The Buyer's Guide must reflect any changes in warranty coverage that you may have negotiated with the dealer. It also becomes a part of your sales contract and overrides any contrary provisions that may be in that contract.

Dealers are required to post the Buyer's Guide on all used vehicles, including used automobiles, light-duty vans, and light-duty trucks. A **used vehicle** is one that has been driven more than the distance necessary to deliver a new car to the dealership or to test-drive it. ''Demonstrator'' cars are covered by the rule. Motorcycles are not covered by it.

Purchasing From a Private Party

You might find the car you want at the lowest price if you buy it from a private party. You should, however, remember that there are certain risks in doing this. The implied warranty of merchantability is not given by a private party who sells a car or other item. This means that you must buy the car ''as is'' and will have no recourse if something is wrong with it. An exception occurs if the seller gives you an express warranty of some kind. For example, the courts have held that a statement by the seller that a car is in good condition and runs properly amounts to an express warranty which prevails over a further statement that the car is sold ''as is.'' There is also the possibility that the car may have been stolen or that a bank or loan company may have the right to **repossess** (take back) the car, regardless of who presently owns it.

You can best protect yourself by inspecting the car carefully, or by having it inspected by a mechanic before you buy it. Ask to see the certificate of title. Be sure that the person selling the car is the one whose name appears on the certificate. Look on the back of the certificate. Usually, the names of persons holding **security interests** in the car (the right to repossess it) are written on the back of the certificate. You should also go to the city or town clerk's office in the area in which the seller lives and ask if there are any security interests filed under the seller's name. (Security interests are explained in Chapter 30.)

A repossessed car purchased from a bank or finance company may be a good buy, at least from a financial standpoint. However, remember that no warranty, either express or implied, is given by the seller of such a car. For this reason, it is especially important to inspect the car carefully before you buy it.

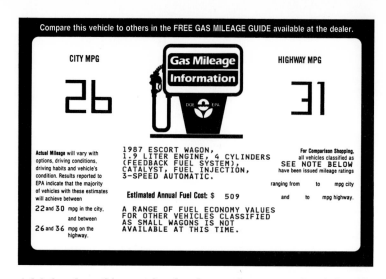

A label such as this must be placed on each new car when it is sold.

Purchasing From Lending or Car-Rental Companies

Car-rental companies often buy fleets of new cars each year and sell the cars when they are a year or two old. You may be able to buy such a car at a considerable saving. Keep in mind that such cars may have had heavy use and will probably have high mileage. On the other hand, rental cars usually have had regularly scheduled maintenance and come with a warranty.

BUYING A CAR—NEW OR USED

There are usually two steps to buying a car. The first is entering into a contract to buy the car. The second step is actually accepting the car (taking possession of it) and paying the purchase price. Both of these are important from a legal standpoint, regardless of whether the car is new or used.

The Contract to Buy

Under the UCC, a contract for the sale of goods valued at $500 or more must be in writing to be enforceable. Since cars are goods, and since most cars now sell for over $500, a contract for the purchase and sale of a car will usually be in writing.

When private parties enter into a contract, they can simply write on a piece of paper that one party agrees to sell and the other party agrees to buy the car. The contract must identify the car and must be signed by the party against whom enforcement is sought. It is also advisable to include the price of the car, although the UCC does not require it. All of this information can be placed on the check given for a deposit, if one is given. A deposit is not always required, but the seller has the right to require it as a condition of the contract.

When a contract is entered into between a private party and a dealer, the private party is usually at a disadvantage. The dealer asks the buyer to sign a printed form. There is generally a sentence on the front of the form, just above the buyer's signature line, saying that the buyer agrees to the terms on the reverse side. The back of the form very often contains a full page of terms that, with rare exceptions, favor the seller.

EXAMPLE 5 Maryann Hartigan signed a contract to buy a used car from a dealer for $2,500, minus a trade-in allowance of $1,000 on her old car. A few days later, when Hartigan went to pick up the car, she was told by the dealer that the trade-in allowance would be $800 instead of $1,000, even though her car was in the same condition it had been in when inspected by the dealer. Hartigan learned then for the first time that the contract she had signed stated that the trade-in could be reappraised at the time of the delivery of the car. Hartigan would be bound by the terms of the contract even if she had not read them before signing it.

Other terms are often found on the backs of contracts for the sale of an automobile. For example, the manufacturer of new cars may be allowed to change prices of cars and not be bound to the contract if the buyer does not agree to the new price. In addition, the manufacturer cannot be held to any time set for delivery of the car; yet buyers are penalized for being late in picking up the car when it is ready. The buyer may also have to agree to pay for the fee of the dealer's attorneys in the event the dealer sues the buyer for breach of contract.

Contracts with terms such as these are called **adhesion contracts** because in some cases buyers must sign and adhere to the contract exactly as it is written in order to make the purchase. Some courts have refused to enforce certain clauses in such automobile contracts, calling them unconscionable (too harsh and oppressive for the court to accept. See Chapter 7). This is not the general rule, however; most courts enforce such clauses in contracts. Some lawyers advise their clients not to sign this kind of contract unless the adverse clauses are crossed out.

Buying a Defective Car

Some cars, whether new or used, continually have things wrong with them after they are purchased. If a car has something major wrong with it, the buyer should notify the seller at once. The seller can be asked to fix it, to pay to have it fixed, or to give the buyer's money back. If the seller refuses, the seller (depending on the circumstances) may be liable for damages on any of the following grounds:

1. Breach of an express warranty, if a specific guarantee was made and was not kept.
2. Breach of warranty of merchantability, if the seller was a dealer and the car was not fit for the purpose for which it was sold.
3. Fraud or breach of an express warranty, if the seller made any statements of fact about the car that were not true.
4. Breach of the state consumer protection law, if the buyer purchased the car for nonbusiness use.

Revoking the Acceptance If a car that someone buys does not conform to the contract, the buyer may be able to revoke (take back) the acceptance, even after taking possession of the vehicle. This is allowed, under the UCC, if the nonconformance (defect) is serious and could not have been detected by the buyer. It may also be done in cases where the buyer was led to believe that the seller would fix a defect and the seller does not do so. The revocation must be made within a reasonable time after the buyer discovers the serious defect in the vehicle.

Other remedies that are available to a buyer when a seller breaches a contract are discussed on page 193 in Chapter 14.

Notifying the Seller About Defects If a buyer discovers something wrong with a car after using it for a short time, it is important that he or she notify the seller of the defect within a reasonable time. Failure to do so can cause the buyer to lose the right to recover damages for breach of an implied warranty. The buyer can also lose the benefits of an express warranty by failing to notify the seller of a defect before the warranty expires. Notification can be made in a number of ways. Notifying the seller by certified mail, return receipt requested, provides the buyer with proof that the seller was notified of the defect. Such proof is valuable if the matter ever becomes an issue in a legal proceeding.

State Lemon Laws

■ Many states have passed so-called ''lemon laws'' to protect consumers when they buy both new and used cars that are defective. In Massachusetts, for example, if a car does not pass the state's required inspection test and it will cost more than 10% of the purchase price to repair the car so that it will pass the test, the buyer can return the car and get back the money paid. As discussed under Implied Warranties, in New York, dealers must furnish customers with a certificate indicating that the vehicle ''is in condition and repair to render, under normal use, satisfactory and adequate service upon the public highway at the time of delivery.'' In addition, the vehicle must comply with the inspection requirements of the New York Vehicle and Traffic Law.

A majority of states have enacted new-car lemon laws. Under one such law, a ''lemon'' is defined as ''a substantially defective car that has been at a dealer's three times for the repair of the same defect or any combination of defects.'' The car must be no older than 1 year nor have exceeded 15,000 miles. A consumer may demand, in a letter to the dealer and manufacturer, the replacement of the defective part or parts or a refund on the purchase price. A refund is based on a formula that takes into account the use of the car. A dissatisfied consumer has 18 months to request arbitration, that is, have the complaint heard by a neutral party called an arbiter. If the seller or consumer is dissatisfied with the arbiter's report, it may be contested in court.

FEDERAL CONSUMER PROTECTION

Legal Issue No. 4

To assist consumers in buying cars, the federal government has enacted the Motor Vehicle Information and Cost Savings Act. Among other things, the act authorizes the Secretary of Transportation to establish bumper standards for passenger cars manufactured in or imported into the United States. Any owner of a passenger car who sustains damages as a result of a motor vehicle accident because a vehicle did not comply with a federal bumper standard may sue the car manufacturer for damages and attorney's fees.

Another feature of the act was to establish average fuel economy standards for motor vehicles. This part of the law caused the automobile industry to produce cars that use less gasoline. Automakers must reach a prescribed average of miles per gallon in the cars they sell or make each year. The law also requires a label to be placed on each new car when it is sold showing

1. The fuel economy for each vehicle.
2. The estimated annual fuel cost of operating the automobile.
3. The range of fuel economy of comparable automobiles.

This information allows you to shop around and select the car that gets the most mileage per gallon of gasoline for its type. Under the law, the estimated mileage disclosed by the manufacturer does not create an express or implied warranty.

Odometer Protection

Legal Issue No. 3

It is illegal for a car owner to turn back or disconnect the odometer (mileage indicator) of a car with the intent to change the mileage reading. The federal odometer law requires everyone who transfers an automobile, unless it is over 25 years old, to give the transferee a written mileage disclosure statement. This must be done whether the car is sold or given away. The disclosure statement must show the odometer reading at the time of the transfer. If the seller has reason to believe that the mileage reading on the odometer is incorrect, the disclosure statement must indicate that the actual mileage traveled is unknown.

When an odometer is repaired and cannot be adjusted to show the true mileage, it must be set at zero. The owner of the car must also attach to the left door frame a written notice showing the true mileage before the repair or replacement and the date that the odometer was set at zero.

Car buyers may sue people who violate this law and may recover three times the amount of the damages they suffered or $1,500—whichever is greater. However, they must prove that the violation was committed with the intent to defraud. In addition to the monetary fine, some states impose criminal penalties for violating this law.

Theft Prevention

In 1984, Congress passed the Theft Prevention Act. The purpose of this act is

1. To provide for the identification of certain motor vehicles and their major replacement parts to decrease motor vehicle theft.
2. To augment the federal criminal penalties imposed upon persons trafficking in (buying or selling) stolen motor vehicles.
3. To encourage decreases in premiums charged consumers for motor vehicle theft insurance.
4. To reduce opportunities for exporting or importing stolen motor vehicles and off-highway mobile equipment.

Lawmakers hope to enable law enforcement officials to prevent car thefts and to prosecute car thieves. By identifying major automobile parts with serial numbers, stolen goods can be traced more easily.

LEASING A CAR

An alternative to buying a car is leasing one. Although this is the most expensive way to obtain a car, it has become increasingly popular in recent years. A low down payment and smaller monthly payments are the principal advantages of leasing. It is especially advantageous for small business owners who do not want to tie up lines of credit by financing new cars. Leasing is also useful for young professional people who have high incomes but little or no savings accumulated. It is not the most desirable way for average consumers to obtain cars, because after making monthly payments, they own nothing and have nothing to trade in toward their next vehicle.

HAVING THE CAR REPAIRED

Because of the growing number of consumer complaints concerning automobile repairs, there is a trend toward requiring automobile repair shops to be licensed and registered by state and county governments. Laws are being adopted, on a state-by-state basis, requiring such things as repair estimates, advance disclosure of prices, and in some cases specific training for mechanics. Some states require automobile repair shops to be bonded. This protects the consumer. The bonding company is an insurer who must pay the consumer if the consumer suffers a loss as a result of fraud or any other wrongdoing on the part of the repair shop.

AUTO-MOBILE INSURANCE

Automobile insurance is designed to help pay for people's losses when they are involved in automobile accidents. Some states have compulsory automobile insurance laws that require all car owners to be insured for bodily injury liability and property damage. Other states have **financial responsibility laws.** These laws require car owners who are not insured to show proof that they can pay for the damages when they are at fault in an automobile accident. Such proof is usually given by posting a bond equal to the amount of damages sustained in an accident.

Kinds of Insurance

The principal kinds of automobile insurance are (1) bodily injury liability, (2) property damage liability, (3) collision, (4) comprehensive coverage, (5) medical payments, and (6) uninsured motorist insurance.

Bodily injury liability insurance protects the policyholder from claims or lawsuits for injuries or death caused by his or her negligent operation of a motor vehicle. In order to recover from the insurance company, the injured person must prove that the driver of the motor vehicle was at fault.

Property damage liability insurance provides protection when other people bring claims or lawsuits against the insured for damaging property of theirs, such as a car, a fence, or a tree. The person bringing the claim or suit must prove that the driver of the motor vehicle was at fault.

Legal Issue No. 5

Collision insurance pays for damage to the insured's own car. It does not matter who was at fault. The cost of collision insurance is much cheaper if the policyholder carries part of the risk. This can be done by having a deductible clause in the policy. For example, if the insured has a $200-deductible policy, he or she pays for the first $200 of any loss and the insurance company pays for any loss over $200.

Comprehensive coverage protects the insured when his or her car is lost or damaged because of fire, lightning, flood, hail, windstorm, riot, vandalism, and theft. In case of loss, the insurance company's liability is limited to the actual cash value of the damaged property at the time of the loss.

EXAMPLE 6 John Finch's car, which was covered by a comprehensive insurance policy, was stolen and presumed unrecoverable. Finch argued that the insurance company was liable for the replacement cost of the car. The company offered in settlement the actual cash market value of the automobile at the time of the theft. It was held that the insurance company was correct in its settlement.

TABLE 17-1
TYPES OF AUTOMOBILE INSURANCE

Kind of Insurance	What It Pays For
Bodily injury liability	Injuries to other persons if the insured is at fault.
Property damage liability	Damage to the car(s) or property of others if the insured is at fault.
Collision	Damage to the insured's car.
Comprehensive	Loss or damage to the insured's car caused by fire, flood, storm, theft, or vandalism.
Medical payments	Medical expenses incurred by anyone occupying the insured's car.
Uninsured motorist	Injuries to the insured if another is at fault and has no insurance or hits and runs.
No-fault	Injuries to other persons without regard to fault.

Medical payments insurance pays for medical (and sometimes funeral) expenses resulting from bodily injuries to anyone occupying the policyholder's car at the time of an accident. In some states it pays for the medical bills of all family members who are struck by a car or who are riding in someone else's car when it is involved in an accident.

Uninsured motorist insurance provides protection when the insured is injured in an automobile accident caused by another driver who is at fault and who has no bodily injury liability insurance to cover the loss to the injured party. This insurance also protects parties who are injured by a hit-and-run driver.

No-Fault Insurance

A relatively new type of automobile insurance that is now used in several states and is being considered by other states is **no-fault insurance.** No-fault insurance reduces the litigation necessary to recover damages from an accident. It also reduces the rights of an injured party to sue. Under this type of insurance, the insured's own insurance company pays the insured's own bills when he or she is in an automobile accident, regardless of who was at fault. This type of insurance is designed to reduce fraud and thereby decrease the cost of insurance. It also provides quicker payments to injured persons.

No-fault insurance varies from state to state. Under the Massachusetts plan of no-fault insurance the insurance company pays up to $2,000 to every person injured while occupying an insured car or to any pedestrian struck by such a car. It pays for medical, hospital, and funeral expenses, and for 75 percent of wage or salary loss, regardless of who was at fault. Benefits are not paid to persons whose injuries result from their own drunken driving or from driving under the influence of drugs. They are also not paid to persons injured while seeking to avoid arrest, committing a felony, or driving with the intent to injure themselves or others. The injured person may not sue the person at fault unless hospital and medical expenses exceed $500 or unless the injury caused death, loss of a limb or other body member, permanent and serious disfigurement, loss of sight or hearing, or a fracture.

What You Should Do in Case of an Accident

1. Stop immediately.
2. Give aid to the injured while exercising extreme care to avoid further injury. Call for help if anyone is injured. Do not move an injured person until a doctor arrives.
3. If you are driving a car that belongs to someone else and the owner is not with you, notify the owner at once.
4. Get the license number and the names of the driver, owner, and passengers of the other car. Give your name, address, and license number.
5. Get the names and addresses of all witnesses.
6. If a police officer is present, get his or her name and badge number.
7. Notify your insurance company as soon as possible. State statutes may require that you report the accident to some public official. This is especially true if the damage exceeds an amount specified by statute.
8. Give no information regarding the accident to anyone but your insurance company's representative or the police, except if local law requires otherwise. To anyone else, give only your license number, name, and address, together with the names and addresses of passengers in the car. You should also state whether you are the owner of the car. If the car is not yours, you should give the name and address of the owner.
9. Do not admit any responsibility.

Suggestions for Reducing Legal Risks

1. If you are going to borrow money to buy a car, shop around and find the lowest APR.
2. Try to get an express warranty from the person selling the car. Be sure that the warranty tells exactly what is covered and states what the seller will do if something goes wrong with the car.
3. If the seller is a dealer, do not sign a paper that says ''as is'' or ''with all faults,'' or that excludes the warranty of merchantability.
4. Never pick out a used car at night or on a rainy day. If possible, take the car to an unbiased mechanic and have it checked.
5. If you buy a car from a private party, check the back of the certificate of title to see if any security interests are listed. Also check the town or city clerk's office in the seller's area to see if there are any security interests on file.
6. Ask the seller for a written mileage disclosure statement.
7. Never sign a contract without reading it. Cross out anything you do not understand or do not agree to. Write into the contract anything that the seller promised you. Refuse to sign if the contract is not in your best interest.
8. Be sure to insure your car in accordance with the laws of your state. Investigate the various types of automobile insurance as thoroughly as practicable and choose the type (or types) that best suits your needs.

Language of the Law

Define or explain each of the following words or phrases:

Regulation Z
Used Car Rule
Buyer's Guide
used vehicle
repossess

security interests
adhesion contract
financial responsibility laws
bodily injury liability insurance

property damage liability insurance
collision insurance
comprehensive coverage insurance

medical payments insurance
uninsured motorist insurance
no-fault insurance

Questions for Review

1. If you borrow money to buy a car, what two important things must be disclosed to you under Regulation Z?
2. Why is it important to examine closely automobile advertisements that allow you to buy a car by paying a certain amount each month?
3. How do regulations of the FTC apply to consumers who buy things, such as automobiles, on credit?
4. Give two examples of the ways in which automobile dealers exclude implied warranties.
5. What precautions should you take when purchasing a car from a private party?
6. Why is it important to read the front and back of an automobile contract before signing it?
7. Why is it important to find out if someone else has a security interest in a motor vehicle that you intend to buy? Where can you find out whether or not someone else holds a security interest in a motor vehicle?
8. On what four grounds might a seller be liable for damages to a buyer if a car is defective?
9. What is the definition of a "lemon" under one state's new-car lemon law?
10. What three items must be on the label placed on new cars when they are sold?
11. Under the federal law, how much can a car buyer recover from a seller for illegally turning back an odometer?
12. Under financial responsibility laws, what proof must be shown by persons who are at fault in an automobile accident?
13. List six principal kinds of automobile insurance, and state the protection offered by each.
14. How does no-fault insurance differ from other kinds of insurance?

Cases in Point

In each of the following cases, give your decision and state a legal principle that applies to the case:

1. Dong Woo Cha was thinking of buying a car. At one used-car dealership, he was told that he could buy a particular car for only $100 per month. What other information would he need to compare the cost of that loan with loans from other lenders?
2. Herman Klein bought a used car from a car dealer. The dealer had arranged financing for the car with a local finance company. The car had a 30-day warranty. Two days after Klein bought the car, the engine gave out. The following day, the dealer filed for

bankruptcy and went out of business. Klein could not use the car. Must he pay the amount of the loan back to the finance company?

3. Would your answer be different in the preceding case if Klein had borrowed the money from a local bank before going to the car dealer to buy the car? Explain.

4. Elaine Carbajal test-drove a light-duty truck that was for sale at a used-car dealership. She noticed that the truck had no Buyer's Guide attached to it explaining warranties. When she asked the sales person about this, she was told that a light-duty truck was not covered by the used-car rule and did not have to have a Buyer's Guide attached. Was the dealer correct?

5. Roberta Claymore was in the process of buying a new car from a dealer. The salesperson made out the order for the car and asked Claymore to sign it. Claymore read the small print on the back of the order form and did not agree with some of the terms. What choices does she have, other than signing the form or refusing to buy the car?

6. John Lisi bought a used car from a dealer. The dealer wrote "as is" on the sales slip that Lisi signed. In addition, the Buyer's Guide that was given to him by the dealer was checked "AS IS—NO WARRANTY." The very next day, Lisi discovered that the car had a broken frame. Does he have any legal recourse against the seller? Explain.

7. Sara Marsh bought a used car from a private party. No statements whatsoever were made by the seller about the quality of the vehicle. That very night, Sara discovered that the car's engine had a cracked block. Does she have any legal recourse against the seller? Explain.

8. Anna Rodriguez bought a used car from a dealer. The Buyer's Guide that the dealer gave her was checked "IMPLIED WARRANTY ONLY." Two days later, Anna discovered that the car's engine had a cracked block. Does Anna have any legal recourse against the dealer?

9. Joseph Ahearn bought an automobile from A-1 Used Car Sales. When he looked at the odometer of the car, it showed that the vehicle had been driven 10,000 miles. Later, after Ahearn bought the car, he found evidence that the car's odometer had been turned back; it should have read 50,000 miles. Does Ahearn have any legal recourse?

10. Edmund Wicks took out an insurance policy on his automobile, providing for $10,000 property damage, $15,000 bodily injury liability to any one person, and $30,000 maximum for all persons involved in an accident. An accident occurred in which Wicks was at fault. Three persons in the other car suffered bodily injuries to the extent of $60,000. The other car was damaged to the extent of $4,000, and Wicks' car was damaged to the extent of $3,000. How much and to whom will Wicks' insurance company pay as a result of this accident?

Cases to Judge

1. Kevin Woods bought a used Pontiac from Robert Secord for $1,300. Both were private parties, and the sale took place at Secord's residence. Secord told Woods that the sale was "as is" and without guarantee. He also said that the car was in good condition and ran properly. The car broke down a few miles away from Secord's residence, even before Woods could reach home. After notifying Secord of the problem and receiving no relief, Woods sold the car for salvage for $600. Can Woods recover damages from Secord? Why or why not? *Woods v. Secord,* 444 A.2d 539 (New Hampshire)

2. In August, R.M. Burritt Motors, Inc. sold a used car to Lora Rice. The purchase agree-

ment stated in bold letters, which were clearly visible, ''AS IS—No warranty expressed or implied.'' Rice did not notice until the following October that the heater-defroster did not work, and the dealer refused to repair it free of charge. Under New York law, dealers must certify to customers that the vehicle ''is in condition and repair to render, under normal use, satisfactory and adequate service upon the public highway at the time of delivery.'' The law also states that vehicles ''must be equipped with a front windshield defrosting device in good working order.'' Did the dealer breach the New York law? Explain. *Rice v. R.M. Burritt Motors, Inc.*, 477 N.Y.S.2d 278 (New York)

3. A driver lost control of his car and left the roadway. The car traveled 187 yards along a ditch beside the roadway and then struck a tree. Between the time that the motor vehicle left the roadway and the time it struck the tree, the driver was ejected from the vehicle. He was killed when he hit the ground. The driver's blood alcohol content was more than 0.10 percent. His insurance policy excluded double-indemnity coverage to anyone killed while ''operating a vehicle'' with that percentage of blood alcohol. In interpreting the policy, the lower court held that the deceased was not ''operating the vehicle'' when he was killed. Do you agree? Why or why not? *American Nat. Ins. Co. v. Ybarra*, 690 S.W.2d 661 (Texas)

4. At the end of the model year, John W. Kohl agreed in writing to buy a specific, new automobile from Silver Lake Motors, Inc. Delivery was to take place at a later time. Silver Lake sold the car to someone else, however, and delivered a different one to Kohl. It did not have the same optional equipment on it as the other one, and its original transmission had been replaced because it was defective. Kohl had considerable trouble with the car. He sent Silver Lake a written demand for relief. The next year's models were available, and Silver Lake offered to exchange the car for a similar model. Kohl refused the offer, saying that it was not reasonable. Do you agree? *Kohl v. Silver Lake Motors, Inc.*, 343 N.E.2d 375 (Massachusetts)

5. Bayer took his car to Whitaker's auto repair shop for repairs. Whitaker took the car for a test drive, with Bayer seated in the passenger seat. During the test drive, a car operated by another person drove on the wrong side of the road and collided with Bayer's vehicle, injuring Bayer. Neither the Bayer vehicle nor the vehicle owned by the wrongdoer was insured. Whitaker carried insurance on his own vehicles, including uninsured motorist insurance. Can Bayer recover from Whitaker's insurance company under the uninsured motorist provision of the policy? Why or why not? *Bayer v. Travelers Indemnity Co.*, 267 S.E.2d 91 (Virginia)

Chapter 18

BAILMENTS

Scene: Joe and Dorothy are riding in Tom's car. Tom is driving.

Dorothy: I love your car, Tom.

Tom: Thanks, Dorothy. It's not bad for its age. I filled in the dents and gave it a coat of paint.

Joe: It's amazing what a paint job will do to an old car.

Dorothy: It's really impressive!

Tom: It's cheap to run, too. It's so old it burns regular gas instead of unleaded.

Dorothy: Joe, would you mind stopping at the Fotoshop for a minute? While I'm here, I might as well pick up my pictures. I left a film to be developed there over a year ago.

Joe: Are you kidding?

Dorothy: No. I didn't have the money until just now to pick it up.

Tom (*looking for a parking space*): There's no place to park around here.

Dorothy: Why don't you park in that parking garage. I'll pay for it.

Tom: I hate to pay to park, but if you don't mind paying . . .

Joe: She's loaded with money.

(*They park in the garage and receive a ticket from the attendant.*)

Dorothy (*at the Fotoshop counter*): I'd like to pick up this film, please. (*She hands a numbered ticket to the clerk.*)

Clerk (*looking through envelopes and files*): Oh, this ticket is over a year old! We don't keep films for more than a year. We just have no room for them.

Dorothy: Really?

Joe: See? I told you, Sis. You need to be more efficient.

Tom: She seems efficient to me! (*The three leave the Fotoshop and return to the parking garage.*)

Joe (*approaching Tom's car*): I thought you said that you fixed all the dents in your car?

Tom: I did!

Joe: Well, you've got a new one now.

Tom: Are you kidding? (*The three look at a large scratch and dent on the passenger side of the vehicle.*)

Joe: I think that the parking garage will pay to have that fixed.

Tom: Do you think so? It wasn't my fault!

Dorothy (*looking in her pocketbook*): Say, my wallet isn't here! I had it at the Fotoshop when I got out the ticket for my film.

Joe: You probably left it there. Why don't you go check it out while we show the garage attendant this dent.

Dorothy: Okay. (*She walks to the Fotoshop.*)

Clerk: Oh, you came back. A customer found your wallet on the counter, and I let him take it. He said that he'd look you up and return it to you.

Dorothy: Do you have his name?

Clerk: No. I don't know who he was!

LEGAL ISSUES

1. Do consumers have a duty to pick up items they leave with merchants (such as a film to be developed) within a certain time?
2. Is a parking garage owner responsible for damage done to a customer's car?
3. Does the finder of property on a store counter have the legal right to hold the property until the true owner is found?

THE SPIRIT OF THE LAW

People often place their property in the possession of others: a camera is left in a shop for repairs; an automobile is parked in a parking garage; a tool is loaned or rented. Naturally, such property may be damaged or lost. The law of bailments defines the rights and duties related to property not in the control of the owner. Generally, the law protects the rights of the owner without placing undue burdens on the person holding the property.

You may be a bailee or a bailor at this very minute. If you have in your possession something that belongs to someone else, you are a **bailee.** If someone else has some of your belongings in his or her possession, you are a **bailor.** A **bailment** exists any time personal property is in the rightful possession of and under the control of someone who is not the owner.

EXAMPLE 1 Robert Acker had a term paper to write for his English class and thought the paper would appear neater if it was typewritten. However, Acker did not own a typewriter. Harold Barr, a good friend of Acker's, had just purchased a new typewriter. Acker borrowed his friend's new typewriter. Was this a bailment?

Yes, it was a bailment. Acker was the bailee and Barr was the bailor. Even in this simple transaction, basic legal rights and duties exist.

A bailment is one of the most common business and personal transactions. It may be the simple act of borrowing a neighbor's vacuum cleaner, or borrowing a book from the school or public library, or depositing $1 million in bonds with a bank for safekeeping.

BAILMENTS WITH AND WITHOUT CONTRACTS

Most bailments in business transactions are based on contracts, but many bailments in personal relationships are not based on contracts. If the bailment agreement is supported by consideration, then a contract probably exists. But, if no consideration is present, then you know from your study of the laws of contracts that there can be no contract.

EXAMPLE 2   Barbara Bailey placed her mink coat in storage for the summer with the Cleveland Fur Salon. Bailey promised to pay the $45 service charge for storage. The Cleveland Fur Salon agreed to store the mink coat safely and return it to Bailey early in the fall. What would you call this transaction?

It would be a bailment, because the Cleveland Fur Salon has in its possession the coat belonging to Bailey. It would also be a contract because of the presence of consideration—Bailey's promise to pay the service fee of $45 in exchange for Cleveland's service.

EXAMPLE 3   George Popson offered the use of his motorcycle to his friend, Andrea Harvilla. This was a friendly gesture on Popson's part with no thought of repayment. Harvilla accepted Popson's offer and borrowed the motorcycle to ride to a neighboring town.

This would be a gratuitous—that is, a free—bailment, and no contract would be involved. By accepting a gratuitous offer, however, Harvilla made an implied promise to use the motorcycle with great care.

Sometimes there may be a bailment even when there is no agreement at all.

EXAMPLE 4   John Tracy found a watch lying on the sidewalk. He picked it up and put it in his pocket. He later advertised in the local paper to find the true owner. Was this a bailment?

Yes, it was a bailment. Tracy was the bailee because he had in his possession a watch that belonged to someone else. There was no contract. He had made no agreement with anyone.

MUTUAL-BENEFIT BAILMENTS

A **mutual-benefit bailment** is one in which both the bailor and the bailee receive some benefit. It is the result of a contract in which each party receives and gives some consideration. Some of the more common mutual-benefit bailments occur when people leave items with others (1) to be serviced or repaired, (2) to be stored, (3) as security for a loan, (4) out of necessity, and (5) because of a rental or lease agreement.

Leaving Items With Others for Service or Repair

Whenever someone leaves an item of personal property with another person to be repaired or serviced, a mutual-benefit bailment takes place. This type of bailment takes place whenever you take clothes to the cleaners, leave a car at a garage to be serviced, or leave any item with someone else to be repaired.

EXAMPLE 5 Suppose that you took your cassette recorder to a shop to be repaired. By implication you would be promising to pay the shop for its service. The shop would be promising to repair your cassette recorder satisfactorily. Your leaving the cassette recorder with the shop would be a bailment for the mutual benefit of you and the shop.

Leaving Items With Others to Be Stored

Sometimes people place things that they own in storage—that is, they leave their property with someone else who holds it for them until they want it back. Storage warehouses are designed for this purpose.

EXAMPLE 6 James and Janet Follain sold their house in Pennsylvania and moved to California. They were not sure exactly where they wanted to live and wanted to take their time in selecting a house. After placing their furniture in a storage warehouse, they lived in an apartment temporarily.

In this example, the warehouse company became the bailee of the Follains' furniture. It was the duty of the warehouse to store the furniture as required by the agreement made with the Follains. It was also the duty of the warehouse to exercise reasonable care in protecting the furniture against loss and damage, and to return the goods to the Follains (the bailors) on demand. In turn the Follains were required to pay all storage costs and to otherwise meet their obligations under their agreement with the warehouse.

Very short-term storage may also create a bailment. For example, when a customer delivers a coat to the checkroom attendant of a hotel or restaurant, a bailment takes place. In contrast, when a customer hangs a coat on a hook in a shop or restaurant, a bailment does not usually come about, because the shop or restaurant owner has no control over the property.

What kind of bailment is created when a car is parked by a paid attendant?

What are the duties of a moving company regarding the condition of the goods it delivers?

Legal Issue No. 2

Parking a Car in a Parking Lot Occasionally, people who park their cars in parking garages or lots find that the cars have been damaged or stolen when they return. In a situation of this type, it is important to establish whether the transaction was a bailment or simply an agreement to rent a parking space. If the transaction was a bailment, the bailee has the responsibility to use reasonable care in protecting the car from damage or theft. To prevent being liable in such cases, bailees must prove that they were not negligent. On the other hand, if the transaction was merely the rental of a parking space, the owner of the car must prove negligence on the part of the parking lot owner to recover for damage or theft by other persons.

The courts have held that a bailment takes place when a car owner surrenders the car keys to a parking lot attendant. Some courts have also held that a bailment occurs if the car owner must pass through a gate where an attendant stops and checks all cars leaving the premises. A bailment does *not* occur, however, if the owner of the parking lot has no control over the automobile that is parked there.

Leaving Items With Others as Security for a Loan

Many times, a bailment is coupled with the loan of money. The goods of the borrower in such a bailment are turned over to the lender to hold as security for the loan. This is a special type of transaction, but it is a bailment for the mutual benefit of both parties.

The property left as security is called the **pledge,** or **pawn.** The borrower is the **pledgor,** or bailor. The lender is the **pledgee,** or bailee. The pledgee may be a bank, a loan company, a credit union, a pawnbroker, or another person.

EXAMPLE 7 Nancy Seferis needed to buy a car. She had $1,500 in the bank that she had been saving to finance her college education. She felt that if she took $1,500 out of the bank to buy a car, she would never put it back. So she went to the bank and borrowed $1,500. The bank held her passbook as security for the loan. She had to pay interest on the loan, but her savings continued to earn interest while the bank held the passbook. The net cost of her loan was about 2 percent of $1,500 and her savings remained intact.

The passbook was the pledge. Seferis was the pledgor, and the bank was the pledgee in this transaction. Both Seferis and the bank benefited—Seferis achieved her goal, and the bank earned interest on the money that it lent to her.

Renting Goods From Others

Today it is common practice to rent goods that are needed only for a limited time. If you made a survey in your locality, you would probably find the following (and many other) items for rent by the day or by the week: video cassettes, floor sanders, power tools, lawn mowers, trucks, and power shovels. Paying for the use of another's goods is another type of mutual-benefit bailment.

EXAMPLE 8 Jacob Sorenson agreed to pay Martin Levy $800 if Levy would paint Sorenson's house. Levy agreed to do the job and decided that he could save time if he used a paint sprayer. He rented a paint sprayer from a local equipment rental company and completed the job in a very short time.

In the above transaction, Levy was the bailee of a good belonging to the rental company—that is, he was the bailee of the paint sprayer. He was obligated to pay for the use of the sprayer and to return it to the company in as good a condition as it was in when he received it. The rental company was the bailor and was obligated to give Levy a sprayer that was free of defects that might cause him injury. At the same time, a mutual-benefit bailment existed between these two parties because both of them benefited from the deal. The rental company received its rental fee and Levy received the right to use the sprayer temporarily without having to make a permanent investment in it.

Bailments by Necessity

A common type of mutual-benefit bailment, implied by law, is the **bailment by necessity.** This type of bailment occurs when a customer must give up possession of property for the benefit of both parties. This occurs, for example, when someone purchases a suit or dress and leaves his or her own clothing in a changing booth temporarily while being fitted. It also occurs when someone goes to a barber or beauty shop and gives up possession of a hat or other item of apparel so that the services can be performed. In such cases, the bailee is required to accept the other's property and to protect it with reasonable care.

GRATUITOUS BAILMENTS

Gratuitous bailments are of two types: (1) those in which the bailor lends the goods to the bailee for use without charge and (2) those in which the bailee takes possession of the goods for the bailor and keeps them safely without charge. When the bailor lends goods without charge, the bailment is for the sole benefit of the bailee. When the bailee cares for the goods without charge, the bailment is for the sole benefit of the bailor.

EXAMPLE 9 If your friend John Chiang lent you his microcomputer for a week, expecting nothing from you in return, the bailment would be for the sole benefit of the bailee (you). Chiang, in this case, would be the bailor.

EXAMPLE 10 If your friend Andrea Como, who was going away for a week, asked you to look after her dog as a personal favor while she was away, then a bailment for the sole benefit of the bailor would be created, provided that you agreed and took possession of the dog.

Lost Property

Legal Issue No. 3

One of the most common ways in which you may become an **involuntary bailee**—that is, a bailee who has made no agreement of any kind—is to find a lost article. As the finder, you are considered to be a bailee for the true owner. You have certain rights and duties in this capacity.

Misplaced Property   There is an exception to the rule that the finder holds the property until the true owner can be found. If the lost property is found on the counter of a store, or on a table in a restaurant or hotel, or on a chair in a washroom, or in some similar public or semipublic place, it is considered not to be lost but to have been misplaced. It is reasonable to suppose that the owner will recall where it was left and will return for it. For this reason the finder may not keep the article in his or her possession but must leave it with the proprietor or manager to hold for the owner. The proprietor must not knowingly allow misplaced property to be taken by anyone but the rightful owner. If the property is found in a corridor or in any other place that would indicate that it was not placed there intentionally, the finder may keep the article. It is not likely that the owner would recall where it was lost.

EXAMPLE 11   Alice Luster, a customer, found a purse in a fitting room of the Fashion Dress Shop. She gave the purse to the owner of the store. Later, when she learned that it had not been claimed, she sued the store for its return.

Luster could not regain possession of the purse. It was found in an area used only by customers of the shop. The proprietor owed the customers a duty to hold the property that was left there. The proprietor was therefore entitled to retain possession of the purse until it was claimed by the true owner.

Rewards and Reimbursement   Finders of lost property are entitled to any reward offered if they know about the reward when they surrender the property to its owner. However, if they learn about the reward after returning the lost article, they may not legally enforce the payment of the reward. If a reward has not been offered, the finder is nevertheless entitled to be reimbursed for any expenses incurred in returning the property to its rightful owner.

Local Ordinances   ■ It is wise to ask whether your state or your city has any special laws concerning lost articles. Some states and cities provide for the special handling of lost articles. These regulations differ considerably, but the general purpose of such regulations is to aid in restoring the lost article to its true owner. Local regulations may, for example, require you to advertise for the true owner or to deposit the article with a certain public official. Persons who have lost things would then have to go to that official.

Suppose that while you are walking down the street, you find a watch lying on the sidewalk. You pick the watch up and take it home with you. You have a duty to try to find the true owner, but you can use the watch as your own until the true owner is found.

RIGHTS AND DUTIES OF THE PARTIES

Both the bailor and the bailee have certain rights and assume certain duties. The greater duty is usually on the bailee because he or she has someone else's (the bailor's) goods. The bailee, however, is not absolutely responsible for any and all losses that might befall the goods. He or she must exercise the degree of care required by the particular facts of each bailment.

Rights and Duties of the Bailor

When a bailment takes place, the bailor has the right (1) to receive the services or money that was contracted for, (2) to have the goods protected from harm by the use of reasonable care, and (3) to have the goods returned when the job is done and payment is tendered. What is considered to be reasonable care varies in accordance with the goods involved. For example, the care required to store a fur coat would be different from that required to store a piece of maple furniture or a live animal.

Legal Issue No. 1

The bailor's duties are (1) to pay for services or storage costs, (2) to warn the bailee of any possible danger involved in handling the goods, (3) to give notice of any special care required, and (4) to pick up the goods within a reasonable time after they are ready unless they are to be delivered. (A bailor who fails to do this assumes the risk of the loss of the goods.)

Rights and Duties of the Bailee

Generally, the rights and duties of the bailee are closely related to (and in a sense the opposite of) those of the bailor. If the bailor, under the terms of a contract, has the right to receive service or money, the bailee has the duty to provide that service or money. Likewise, if the bailor has the right to have the goods protected from harm by the use of reasonable care, the bailee has the duty to protect those goods by using reasonable care.

The bailee's duty of care has changed in recent years. Formerly, three degrees of care were recognized in the law of bailments: great care, ordinary care, and slight care. In a bailment for the sole benefit of the bailee, the bailee was required to use *great care* and was responsible for *slight negligence*. In a bailment for the sole benefit of the bailor, the bailee was required to use only *slight care* and was responsible only for *gross negligence*. In a mutual-benefit bailment, the bailee was required to use *ordinary care* and was responsible for *ordinary negligence*.

Although some states still recognize the degrees of care as part of their bailment law, other states have done away with them. Instead, these other states hold that it is the duty of all bailees to exercise **reasonable care** under the circumstances. Reasonable care is the degree of care that a reasonable person would exercise to prevent the goods from being harmed. If the bailee fails to exercise the necessary care, he or she is regarded as negligent and is liable for any loss or damage to the goods.

The bailee must also comply strictly with the terms of the bailment. If the bailee violates the terms of the agreement in any way, the bailee becomes an **insurer,** one who is absolutely liable for any loss.

Bailees such as people who repair cars have a mechanic's lien on property in their possession. A **mechanic's lien** is a right to hold the goods until service charges are paid. Generally, if bailees are not paid for services rendered, permission must be obtained from a court before they can sell the goods. Additionally, if bailees give up possession of the goods, they lose the right to a mechanic's lien.

Liability of Tortious Bailees

A **tortious bailee** is one who wrongfully retains possession of the lost property of another or is knowingly in possession of stolen property. One who uses a bailed article for a purpose other than agreed upon or refuses to return property at the termination of the bailment may also be considered a tortious bailee. If you found a watch and knew who the owner was and refused to return it, you would be considered a tortious bailee. Tortious bailees are fully and unconditionally responsible for all damage that results to property in their possession. They are responsible regardless of the degree of care that they might exercise and regardless of the cause of the damage.

PROVING THE BAILEE'S NEGLIGENCE

Generally, when one person sues another for negligence, the plaintiff has the burden of proving that the defendant was negligent. For many years this rule was followed in bailment cases.

EXAMPLE 12 Ernesto Andrade left his car at a local garage to be repaired. His car was damaged in a fire at the garage. The garage refused to pay for the damage, claiming that it was not negligent. Under the law in existence at that time, Andrade had the burden of proving the garage's negligence in order to recover for his damages. This was very difficult for him to do because he was not at the garage when the fire occurred.

Recent decisions by state and federal courts have changed this rule in the case of bailments. Many courts now say that the burden of proof should rest on the party who is in the best position to determine what actually happened to the goods. The courts place the burden on the bailee to prove that he or she had exercised reasonable care if the goods were lost, damaged, or destroyed.

REMEDIES FOR BREACH OF BAILMENT RELATIONSHIP

As discussed previously, a person who holds the bailed property of another wrongfully or illegally is said to be a tortious bailee. The party injured by the acts of the tortious bailee may ask the court to take legal measures to have the tortious bailee return the property in question or pay the value of the property to its rightful owner.

If the injured party wants the property back, he or she may bring an action to **replevy** the goods—that is, the injured party may ask the court to have the goods returned. A *writ of replevin* is used to accomplish this.

If the injured party does not want the property back, he or she may sue the tortious bailee for conversion. If the injured party wins the case, the amount of damages awarded will be the fair value of the property at the time of the conversion. (The tort of conversion is discussed in Chapter 4.)

These two remedies may be used not only with reference to bailed property, but also with reference to personal property that is bought and sold under the law of sales.

TERMINATION OF BAILMENTS

Mutual-benefit bailments normally are terminated at the end of a period of time specified by the parties in their contract. The parties may also terminate the relationship by mutual agreement.

EXAMPLE 13 Harriet Stobbs rented a car for 4 hours at $6 per hour from the Reliable Car Rental Service. She was able to complete her business in just 3 hours, however. If she returns the car and the rental company agrees to charge her only for the 3 hours, the bailment would be terminated by mutual agreement.

Gratuitous bailments are terminated in a number of ways. They may be terminated automatically by completion of the use agreed upon or at the end of a time limit set by the bailor. If no specific time limit is set, the bailor may demand return of his or her property at any time. Death or insanity also ends a gratuitous bailment.

Suggestions for Reducing Legal Risks

1. When you take goods to be repaired, look for someone who not only has a good reputation but also has the physical facilities for protecting your goods.
2. If you store your goods for any length of time, it may be wise to protect them with insurance rather than to depend on the legal liability of the bailee for protection.
3. If you rent goods from someone, inspect them carefully before taking possession. Do not accept defective goods unless the defect is pointed out by the bailor before you take possession.
4. If you rent goods to someone, be sure that they are in good condition and safe to handle before you deliver them.
5. When a friend lends you something without charge, use the property with great care and only within the terms of the agreement.
6. If you lend goods to a friend, be sure to warn of any inherent dangers involved in the use of the goods. If the goods are not in first-class condition, be doubly careful to warn of any defects.
7. If you find a lost article, use all reasonable means to find the true owner. Investigate any special statutes or ordinances that might impose special duties on you. Some statutes impose a penalty on a finder who does not conform to statutory requirements.

Language of the Law

Define or explain each of the following words or phrases:

bailee	pledge	bailment by necessity	insurer
bailor	pawn	gratuitous bailment	mechanic's lien
bailment	pledgor	involuntary bailee	tortious bailee
mutual-benefit bailment	pledgee	reasonable care	replevy

Questions for Review

1. Give an example of a bailment that is based on a contract. Give an example of a bailment in which there is no contract.
2. If you take your radio to a repair shop, are you a bailor? What are your rights?
3. What duties do you owe to someone who services your radio in his or her shop?
4. Give an example of a mutual-benefit bailment.
5. How does a pledge differ from a bailment for storage?
6. What is the general degree of care that is required in a mutual-benefit bailment?
7. Explain how a bailment by necessity arises.
8. In what way does a gratuitous bailment differ from a mutual-benefit bailment?
9. If you lend a neighbor an article that is potentially dangerous to use, must you warn the neighbor of the possible danger?
10. Give an example of an involuntary bailment.
11. What are the rights of the finder of a lost article?
12. What are the remedies for breach of bailment?
13. When does a gratuitous bailment terminate?
14. When does a mutual-benefit bailment terminate?

Cases in Point

In each of the following cases, give your decision and state a legal principle that applies to the case:

1. Dwight Wade saw his neighbor Karen Warner trimming her hedge by hand. Wade took his power trimmer over to Warner and said, ''Use my trimmer if you wish.'' Warner accepted, but said nothing except, ''Thank you.'' Is there a bailment? a contract?
2. Suppose that, in question 1, Wade had said to Warner, ''I will let you use my power trimmer if you will trim my side of the hedge also,'' and she agreed. Would this be a bailment? Would it be a contract?
3. Donna Ryder rented a power saw from Salman Hardware. She left it out in the rain, and it was badly damaged. Will she have to pay for the damage done?
4. Victor Worth agreed to pasture Cecilia Tegler's cattle at an agreed weekly price. Is this a bailment? What degree of care is required in looking after the cattle?
5. Crystal Gorman lent her car to Manuel Galiano, giving him permission to drive to a neighboring town. On the trip the car was damaged in an accident through no fault of Galiano's. Must Galiano pay for the repairs?
6. Homer Dale borrowed a ladder from Wendy Conrad. When Conrad gave Dale the ladder, she told him that it was old and that some of the rungs might be rotten. Dale assured her that he would use it with care. The ladder broke while in use, and Dale was seriously injured. Could he sue Conrad because the ladder was unsafe?
7. Debby Chase offered to store Kirsten Burg's television set in her living room free of charge. In return Burg told Chase to use the set any time. Would this be a gratuitous bailment or one of mutual benefit?
8. If the television set in question 7 burned out a transformer while in use, would Chase have to replace it?
9. If Chase used the set without permission, would she have to replace the transformer?
10. Bunny Carlson found a dog. After making a reasonable effort to locate its owner, Carlson sold the animal to Alan Linder. About 6 months after Linder had purchased the dog, Opal O'Rourke, the true owner, saw the dog and demanded that Linder return it to her. Would Linder have to give the dog to O'Rourke?

Cases to Judge

1. Evelyn Palmenteri rented an apartment to Daoust and a friend. She told them that the refrigerator in the kitchen did not go with the apartment. She had made arrangements to have the refrigerator moved and was informed that it had been cleaned and defrosted. Because they wanted to begin decorating the apartment, Daoust and his friend offered to carry the recently defrosted refrigerator down the stairs. During the move, a large quantity of water escaped from the refrigerator causing Daoust to slip and fall down the stairs. The refrigerator fell on top of him, and he was seriously injured. Was this a mutual-benefit or a gratuitous bailment? What duty did the bailor have to inform the bailee of hidden dangers within the refrigerator? *Daoust v. Palmenteri*, 486 N.Y.S.2d 288 (New York)

2. Upon discovering that his transmission was leaking, Thompson took his automobile to Mr. Transmission, Inc., and asked to have the transmission seals replaced. He expected to pay the advertised fee of $69.95. When he returned for the car, he found that the transmission had been removed and disassembled, which was unnecessary for the replacement of the seals. He was told that the transmission had to be rebuilt or replaced. To get his car back, he paid $377 under protest for a replacement rebuilt transmission. After the rebuilt transmission was used for a time, it also began to leak. When Thompson took the car back for correction, the chair on which he was sitting in the manager's office collapsed under him, causing injuries. What type of bailment was involved in this case? What duty did the bailee violate? *Mr. Transmission, Inc. v. Thompson*, 328 S.E.2d 397 (Georgia)

3. Richard Noble ordered a stereo tuner from a store in Maine and directed that it be shipped to his apartment in Washington, D.C. The tuner was delivered to the apartment building by United Parcel Service. Paulette McLean, a receptionist at the building, received the tuner, signed a receipt for it, and placed it on a shelf in a small room next to her desk where packages for tenants were kept. Access to the room was limited. McLean and the night receptionist had keys to the door, which was kept locked, and there were bars on the windows. The tuner disappeared from the small room some time during the night. Is the owner of the apartment building responsible to Noble for the loss? Why or why not? *Bernstein v. Noble*, 487 A.2d 231 (Washington, D.C.)

4. L.S.R., Inc., sold a laser surveying unit to Frontier Contracting Co., Inc. Because the unit was not yet in production, L.S.R. temporarily provided Frontier with a prototype of the unit. A month later, the prototype was exchanged for a more expensive one. When it was delivered, Frontier's superintendent remarked that there had been attempts to break into their trailer at the job site. He added, however, that there was no need to worry, because he took the prototype home in the evenings. He also signed a slip which read, "You are responsible for loss or damage to this equipment until it is returned to L.S.R., Inc. and checked in by us. Value of above equipment $7,200.00." That night the unit was stolen from the construction trailer. What type of bailment did this case involve? What was the duty of care of the bailee? For whom would you decide? *Frontier Contracting Co., Inc. v. L.S.R., Inc.*, 330 S.E.2d 414 (Georgia)

Chapter 19

CARRIERS AND HOTELKEEPERS

Scene: The airport. Dorothy and Joe are saying good-bye to Mr. and Mrs. Chin.

Dorothy (*kissing her father*): Bye, Dad. Have a good time.

Joe (*kissing his mother*): Bye, Mom.

Mr. and Mrs. Chin: Good-bye, kids. Be good while we're gone! (*They board the plane. A distraught woman runs up to the gate.*)

Attendant: Can I help you, ma'am?

Distraught Woman (*puffing*): Yes. Did I make the plane?

Attendant: It doesn't leave for another 10 minutes.

Distraught Woman: That's a relief. (*She hands her ticket to the attendant.*)

Attendant: I'm sorry, ma'am. This plane is full. All the seats are taken.

Distraught Woman: But I have a reservation! I confirmed it yesterday!

Attendant: I'm really sorry, ma'am. You should have gotten here sooner. There is just nothing we can do for you.

Distraught Woman (*starting to leave*): I can't believe it! I've been bumped!
(*A disturbance can be heard in the distance. In a moment a police officer comes into view, dragging a man who is obviously very drunk.*)

Drunken Man (*shouting*): You can't take me off thish plane! (*hic*) I had a reserved seat! I'll shue you for this!

Officer: Come on, buddy. You've got to learn to leave other people alone.

Attendant (*calling the distraught woman*): Oh, Madam! Madam! We have a seat for you!
(*Four hours later, Mr. and Mrs. Chin enter the lobby of a hotel. They are carrying no luggage.*)

Mrs. Chin: Do you think the airline will ever find our luggage? I shouldn't have put my camera and jewelry in the suitcase. Those two things alone are worth about $2,000.

Mr. Chin: I'm sure they'll locate them.

Desk Clerk: May I help you?

Mr. Chin: Yes. We have reservations. Mr. and Mrs. Chin.

Desk Clerk: Oh, yes. Please fill out this card. You're in Room 2117. (*He signals to the bellhop, who is washing the lobby floor.*) The bellhop will take your luggage, sir.

Mr. Chin: The airline lost our luggage. They said it will probably come later.

Bellhop: You'll never get it, mister! I know them! And they won't pay you more than $75 for the lost luggage.

Mrs. Chin: Really? (*backing away*) Oops! (*She falls over the cleaning bucket that the bellhop had left behind her.*)

Mr. Chin (*helping her up*): Are you all right, dear?

Mrs. Chin: Oh! (*her hand on her back*) I think I hurt my back!

LEGAL ISSUES

1. Does an airline have any responsibility toward a ''bumped'' passenger?
2. May an intoxicated, disruptive person be denied passage on an air carrier?
3. Is an airline responsible for lost luggage only to the extent of $75?
4. Is a hotel responsible for injuries to guests caused by a hotel employee's negligence?

THE SPIRIT OF THE LAW

In Chapter 18, ordinary bailments were examined. They included situations in which people left their goods with others, either for a benefit or gratuitously. In this chapter, special types of bailments are discussed. They arise in two situations: (1) when goods are given to a common carrier to be transported and (2) when people leave their belongings at a hotel or motel. In addition to bailment questions, other important legal issues arise when carriers transport people and when hotelkeepers take in guests. Many of these important issues are also discussed in this chapter.

COMMON AND PRIVATE CARRIERS

A person or a company that undertakes to transport persons or goods or both for a consideration is called a **carrier.** Carriers are of two kinds—common and private.

A **common carrier** is a company or a person who undertakes to transport people or goods for hire. Common carriers are bailees because they are in temporary possession of goods belonging to others. They differ from other bailees in the following respects: (1) they are not free to choose their customers and must treat everyone in the same manner; (2) they are, for all practical purposes, insurers of the goods in their care; and (3) they are subject to specific government regulations. Examples of common carriers are railroads, express companies, steamship lines, trucking companies, and airlines.

Private carriers, sometimes referred to as *contract carriers,* haul goods for others under special arrangements. They do not claim to serve the public in general and are free to accept or reject any offers of transportation that are made to them. Private carriers are governed by the rules that we have already learned in our study of the bailee. The acceptance of merchandise by them creates a mutual benefit bailment. They are required to exercise ordinary care.

EXAMPLE 1 Your neighbor, Cassie Callaghan, has a truck. You employ her to transport a piano for you. In this transaction Callaghan is a private carrier and is governed by the rules of ordinary care. She may also do similar jobs for others, but this does not make her a common carrier as long as she leaves herself free to accept or reject any offers of transportation submitted to her.

REGULA-TION OF CARRIERS
Interstate Commerce Commission

All business concerns are more or less regulated by the general rules of law. Common carriers, however, are regulated by special laws.

If a carrier operates in more than one state, the quality of service, employee relationships, and other matters are governed by the **Interstate Commerce Commission,** often referred to as the **ICC.**

Schedule changes, whether for passenger or freight service, must have ICC approval. If the schedules filed by the carriers are not followed, the carrier may be called before the ICC for a hearing on a complaint, resulting either in a penalty or in a dismissal of the charge.

EXAMPLE 2 Rachel Shore found that the passenger train on which she wanted to travel was removed from the train schedule. When she complained to the station agent about the cancellation, the agent called her attention to a change-of-service notice which was posted on the station bulletin board. This notice indicated that the suspension of service was approved by the ICC. Shore had to accept the ICC ruling.

The ICC also has jurisdiction over trucks operating as common carriers between states. The drivers of such equipment must carry logbooks in their truck cabs showing the number of hours they have been driving, the points of departure and destination, trips made, and other information.

State Commissions

Almost all states have set up commissions that are responsible for the regulation of intrastate common carriers. (**Intrastate carriers** are those that operate within the boundaries of a single state.) Bus companies, short-line railroads, other public carriers, pipelines, and toll bridges come within their jurisdiction. Rulings of the state commissions, such as the Intrastate Commerce Commission and the Public Service Commission, as well as those of the ICC, may be appealed to the courts if they do not satisfy the complainants or the carriers.

EXAMPLE 3 The Blue Star Bus Line carried employees of Machines, Inc., to the plant. Regular schedules were followed under a franchise granted the bus company by the state. Without the approval of the state commission, Blue Star reduced the number of trips by 50 percent. The employees at Machines, Inc. would have the right to petition the state commission for redress and could even appeal to the courts if the commission's decision was not in their favor.

SHIPMENT OF GOODS BY COMMON CARRIERS

Common carriers are required to provide universal service—that is, the operators of common carriers must serve everyone who asks to be served. They must also treat everyone alike.

The liability of the common carrier for universal service is limited, of course, by the type of transportation that is offered and by the capacity of the carrier's equipment. Furthermore, the carrier is not compelled to transport goods without receiving the full scheduled compensation. Carriers are entitled to receive payment in advance, although they do not always insist on this right.

To treat everyone alike, carriers must charge the same rate to all persons and provide them with the same services under the same circumstances. They cannot charge a good customer a low rate and a poor customer a higher rate for the same transaction.

EXAMPLE 4 A public trucking company, operating between Minneapolis and Kansas City, charged a rate of $5.50 per 100 pounds on a certain type of merchandise shipped in lots of 1,000 pounds or over. The trucking company offered to give a 10 percent refund to a shipper who made heavy use of their services. This was a violation of ICC rules prohibiting preferential rates.

Common carriers have more responsibility than ordinary bailees for the property entrusted to their care. With some exceptions, they are insurers of all goods that they accept for shipment. They are not responsible for loss or damage to goods caused by (1) an **act of God** (an unforeseen natural disaster, such as a

A common carrier like Emery Worldwide must accept shipments from all customers. May Emery charge different customers different rates for the same transportation?

snowstorm, earthquake, tornado, flood, hurricane, or a fire caused by lightning); (2) an enemy at war with the United States; (3) the taking of goods by a public official; (4) the carelessness, or fault, of the person who shipped the goods; and (5) the spoilage of perishable goods.

A common carrier has two rights: (1) the payment of fees agreed upon for shipment and (2) the right of lien on all goods shipped for the amount of the shipping charges. This latter right ends when payment is received by the carrier. If the party to whom the goods are shipped does not pick up the goods within a reasonable time, the carrier may charge an additional fee, known as a **demurrage charge,** for storage.

PUBLIC CARRIERS OF PASSENGERS

Common carriers of passengers are those which serve the public in general. They are often called **public carriers** to distinguish them from carriers of goods. They include buses, railroads, airlines, taxicabs, ferries, and cruise ships.

Duties to Passengers

Public carriers have an obligation to accept all persons who may seek passage. There are, however, some exceptions. Public carriers may refuse passengers (1) when all available space is occupied or reserved, and (2) if they are disorderly, intoxicated, insane, or infected with a contagious disease. In addition, air carriers may deny passage to any person when, in the opinion of the carrier, it might jeopardize the safety of the flight. Air carriers may refuse to transport people who do not consent to a search of their person or property to determine whether they are unlawfully carrying a dangerous weapon, explosive, or other destructive substance.

Legal Issue No. 2

Carriers must either provide opportunities for refreshments on board the vehicle or must take regular stops so that passengers can buy refreshments.

Ejection of Passengers   A person may be ejected from a train or other conveyance for any reason that would have prevented the carrier from accepting the person as a passenger in the first place.

Perhaps the most common reason for ejecting a passenger is failure to pay the fare. The carrier is not compelled to carry a passenger without compensation.

Any person may be ejected if that person is a serious nuisance or danger to the other passengers or threatens the interests of the carrier. The carrier must exercise considerable caution in enforcing this rule, because ejecting a passenger without sufficient cause is a serious offense.

If a passenger is to be ejected, it must be done as gently as possible, and the vehicle must come to a complete stop. The passenger must be put off at a place where he or she will not suffer danger or serious privation.

EXAMPLE 5   Howard Anderson, while in a railway coach, started a disturbance that was displeasing to all and possibly dangerous to some. As the coach passed through a small town, the train slowed to about 5 miles per hour, and Anderson was ejected. He suffered an injury and collected damages from the railroad company. It was held that the train should have come to a full stop before Anderson was ejected.

Safety of Passengers A public carrier has a very high responsibility for the safety of its passengers. There are strict and specific requirements regarding the means to be employed for safeguarding them. The carrier is responsible for any damage or injury caused by failure to provide proper safeguards. The carrier is also responsible for harm arising from the torts of its employees. A public carrier has no responsibility for accidents caused by forces beyond its control, such as an act of God, legal intervention, or the acts of a public enemy. A **public enemy** is a person or group that attempts through violence to overthrow the government.

A public carrier is not liable if a passenger is harmed chiefly because of the passenger's own negligence or if the harm results from a violation of the carrier's reasonable rules.

The duty of a public carrier to a passenger, in most cases, ends when the passenger has reached the destination printed on the ticket and has left the premises of the carrier. An exception exists when a carrier has a continuing obligation for the care of its passengers, as in the case of a cruise ship. Here, the carrier has a duty to warn of dangers known to the carrier in places where the passenger may reasonably be expected to visit while on the cruise. This duty extends throughout the length of the voyage, and does not end at each port of call.

EXAMPLE 6 Mildred and Michael Kushner took a cruise ship to an island in the Caribbean. The members of the ship's crew knew that there were areas on the island where tourists were sometimes robbed. They did not warn the passengers of this danger. The Kushners were robbed while visiting an unsafe area on the island. The cruise ship had violated its duty to warn the Kushners of possible danger and was susceptible to a lawsuit for their injuries.

Must a passenger consent to standard security checks at an airport in order to board a plane?

The carrier must have a certain schedule and must follow this with reasonable accuracy. It must never leave a point of departure ahead of time, and it must use great efforts to reach each station on schedule. The carrier must give the passengers ample time to get on and off the vehicle. It must use great diligence in directing the passenger to get off at the proper destination indicated by the passenger's ticket.

Bumped Airline Passengers

When a flight is oversold, no one may be denied boarding against his or her will until airline personnel first ask for volunteers who will give up their reservation willingly in exchange for a payment of the airline's choosing. If there are not enough volunteers, other passengers may be denied boarding involuntarily in accordance with the airline's priority rules. Airlines are required to establish and publish priority rules for determining which passengers holding confirmed reserved space will be denied boarding on an oversold flight.

Legal Issue No. 1

Passengers who are denied boarding involuntarily, or "bumped," are entitled to a payment of **denied boarding compensation** from the airline unless (1) they have not fully complied with the carrier's ticketing, check-in, or reconfirmation requirements or are not acceptable for transportation under the airline's usual rules and practices; (2) they are denied boarding because the flight is canceled; (3) they are denied boarding because a smaller-capacity aircraft was substituted for safety or operational reasons; or (4) they are offered accommodations in a section of the aircraft other than that specified in their ticket at no extra charge.

Passengers who are denied boarding involuntarily must be given a written statement explaining the rules about bumping and describing the airline's boarding priorities. Those who are eligible for denied boarding compensation must be offered, in addition to alternate transportation, a payment equal to the sum of the face value of their tickets, with a $200 maximum. Furthermore, if the airline cannot arrange alternative transportation for the passenger, the compensation is doubled, with a $400 maximum. The alternate transportation must be scheduled to arrive at the passenger's destination or next stopover not later than 2 hours (4 hours for international flights) after the planned arrival time of the originally scheduled flight. (*Stopover* means a deliberate interruption of a journey by the passenger, scheduled to exceed 4 hours, at a point between the place of departure and the final destination.) Instead of the cash payment already mentioned, airlines may offer free or reduced-rate air transportation as long as its value equals or exceeds the cash payment requirement.

The airline must give each passenger who qualifies for denied boarding compensation payment by cash or check on the day and place the involuntary denied boarding occurs. If the airline arranges alternate transportation for the passenger's convenience that departs before the payment can be made, the payment must be sent to the passenger within 24 hours. The air carrier may offer free tickets in place of the cash payment. The passenger may, however, insist on the cash payment.

Acceptance of the compensation relieves the airline of any further liability to the passenger caused by its failure to honor the confirmed reservation. However, the passenger may decline the payment and seek to recover damages in a court of law or in some other manner.

NOTICE—OVERBOOKING OF FLIGHTS

Airline flights may be overbooked, and there is a slight chance that a seat will not be available on a flight for which a person has a confirmed reservation. If the flight is overbooked, no one will be denied a seat until airline personnel first ask for volunteers willing to give up their reservation in exchange for a payment of the airline's choosing. If there are not enough volunteers, the airline will deny boarding to other persons in accordance with its particular boarding priority. With few exceptions, persons denied boarding involuntarily are entitled to compensation. The complete rules for the payment of compensation and each airline's boarding priorities are available at all airport ticket counters and boarding locations. Some airlines do not apply these consumer protections to travel from some foreign countries, although other consumer protections may be available. Check with your airline or your travel agent.

This notice must be displayed where airline tickets are sold. It must also be printed on airline tickets.

EXAMPLE 7 Ralph Nadar, the consumer activist, made a reservation with Allegheny Airlines for a flight from Washington D.C. to Hartford, Connecticut, where he had a speaking engagement at a particular time. His reservation was confirmed. Upon arriving at the airport 5 minutes before the flight was to leave, he was told that he could not be accommodated because all the seats were occupied. Allegheny had overbooked the flight. The airline offered Nadar alternative transportation to Hartford via Philadelphia. Nadar rejected this offer, fearing that the plane connection, which allowed only 10 minutes between planes, was too close. Instead, he flew to Boston and had someone drive him to Hartford. Nadar brought suit against the airline for common-law fraud. He claimed that the airline had committed fraud by failing to disclose to him its overbooking practices. The U.S. Supreme Court held that he could bring suit against the airline for fraud.

Passengers' Baggage

Legal Issue No. 3

If a passenger checks baggage with the carrier or otherwise leaves baggage entirely within the carrier's control, the carrier becomes liable in the same manner as any carrier of goods. With the exceptions noted on pages 255 and 256, it is an insurer of the baggage. Technically and legally, **baggage** includes only such articles as the passenger intends for his or her own personal use. The fact that no extra compensation is given when baggage is checked is immaterial, although it is required that the checker must be a passenger.

Federal rules place limits on the liability of airlines for lost luggage. For travel wholly within the United States, the maximum liability of an airline for lost luggage is $1,250 per passenger. Excess valuation may be declared on certain types of articles. However, some carriers assume no liability for fragile, valuable, or perishable articles.

If the passenger carries his or her own belongings onto the carrier, the passenger has the main responsibility.

A **hotelkeeper** or **motelkeeper** is an individual, partnership, or corporation that offers rooms to transients for a price.* A **transient** (also called a *guest*) is one whose stay is more or less uncertain in length. A transient wishes to have temporary lodging rather than long-term lodging. Persons become guests when they enter a hotel with a definite intention to register.

A **roomer,** or **lodger,** is any person staying at a hotel, motel, or rooming house for a definite period of time. Thus the arrangement between a rooming-house keeper and a roomer is of a more permanent character than the relationship between a hotel or motel and a guest.

EXAMPLE 8 Rhoda Quezada was able to secure a comfortable room at the Mainliner Motel. After 3 days' residence, she decided that the Mainliner was ideally located for her business. She made arrangements to rent the room for 6 months at a special rate. Although Quezada was originally a transient guest, the new arrangement changed her status to that of a roomer, or lodger.

Responsibilities and Rights of Hotelkeepers

A hotelkeeper must serve all people who are able to pay for their lodging, assuming that rooms are available. This has been the rule of the law for hundreds of years. It dates back to a time in history when travel was not safe. Robbers and highwaymen abounded, and it was not safe to stay on the road overnight. Thus hotels, or inns, were places of refuge; and to refuse guests lodging was to leave them at the mercy of those who would rob them. Travel is comparatively safe today, but the genuine need for the convenience of overnight accommodations has caused the rule to remain.

EXAMPLE 9 Bob Freytag sought lodging at the Mainliner Motel but was refused. The clerk could give no reason for his refusal other than her personal dislike for Freytag's political affiliations. Freytag was a member of a minority political group that was holding a convention in the town at the time. Freytag could hold the motel liable for any damages that he might show had resulted from the motel's failure to accept him as a guest.

Rooming-house keepers, on the other hand, may accept or reject persons according to their own judgment. They may usually bargain as they see fit. Except for certain statutes in some states and provisions of the Civil Rights Act of 1964, rooming-house agreements are governed only by the general laws applying to contracts and personal behavior. The **Civil Rights Act of 1964** makes it a criminal offense for a hotelkeeper to refuse to give a room to anyone on the grounds of race, creed, or color.

Guest's Privacy A hotelkeeper must guarantee a guest's right of privacy in the room to which he or she has been assigned. Any interference with the guest's privacy by hotel employees or others gives the guest a right of action for invasion of privacy.

EXAMPLE 10 A few hours after occupying her room in the Mainliner Motel, Susan Smith was embarrassed by the appearance of a bellboy and an-

---

*In the discussion that follows, the laws discussed apply to motelkeepers and motels as well as to hotelkeepers and hotels.

other guest, who entered the room with a passkey. Investigation proved that the room clerk had negligently assigned Smith's room to another guest, who arrived at a later hour. Such entry would be an invasion of privacy, for which Smith could seek damages from the Mainliner Motel.

Security of Guest's Property With exceptions discussed below, hotelkeepers are held, up to an amount set by state statute, to be insurers of the guest's property. This includes all property brought into the hotel for the convenience and purpose of the guest's stay. In the event of a loss, the hotelkeeper may be held liable, regardless of the amount of care exercised in protecting the guest's property. Hotelkeepers are not strictly liable for the property of lodgers, however.

EXAMPLE 11 Edgar Mosby's room at the Mainliner Motel was entered by a thief, who stole two suits of clothing and valuable samples used in Mosby's business. The motel is responsible for the loss, although it was in no way negligent in its effort to protect Mosby's property.

An exception is made in the case of accidental fire in which no negligence can be attributed to the hotelkeeper. In such instances the hotelkeeper is not liable as an insurer. This provision includes fires caused by other guests at the hotel at the same time. Such persons, even though on other floors, are called **fellow guests.**

EXAMPLE 12 A fire broke out on the second floor of the Mainliner Motel. Although the fire was confined to that floor, several guests on the first floor reported losses to their property due to fire and water. The motel was able to prove that the fire had started from a cigarette dropped on a bed by one of the guests. Such careless smoking violated both a city ordinance and a rule of the motel. The motelkeeper was not responsible for the losses caused by the fire.

Most state statutes provide that the hotelkeeper must keep a safe place for storing valuables belonging to guests. If guests do not use the hotel safe, the hotelkeeper does not have the common-law liability of an insurer. It would be liable for loss only if the guest could prove the hotel negligent.

EXAMPLE 13 Isabel Salazar took a room at the Evergreen Hotel. She had in her possession a valuable diamond necklace, which was lost during the night. The hotel proved that there was a good lock on the door and that all reasonable precautions had been made to protect the hotel against thefts. On the basis of these facts, the hotel escaped liability because Salazar should have put her necklace in the hotel vault for safekeeping.

Guests are permitted to keep in their room valuables that they would ordinarily have on their person, such as a watch, cuff links, rings, and a reasonable amount of cash.

Guest's Comfort and Safety Hotels and motels must provide a minimum standard of comfort, safety, and sanitation. Minimum standards include reasonable heat and ventilation, clean beds, reasonably quiet surroundings, and freedom from disturbances by hoodlums, criminals, and persons of immoral character.

Legal Issue No. 4

Hotelkeepers are liable to their guests for injuries suffered as a result of negligence. While they do not insure guests against the risk of injury, they are required to use reasonable care. They must protect guests from injuries that can be reasonably anticipated. A basic element of this duty is the maintenance of the premises in a reasonably safe condition.

EXAMPLE 14 A section of carpeting in the hall outside Susan Smith's room had torn loose, and the motel housekeeper had neglected to make the necessary repairs for several days. Smith tripped over the torn carpeting, suffering painful injuries. The Mainliner Motel had been negligent and may be held responsible by Smith for damages resulting from the injury.

Hotel's Right to Payment Hotels may demand payment in advance, but frequently this right is waived for people with luggage. If the guest does not pay the bill, the hotel has a lien on whatever articles the guest has, with the exception of clothes worn. The lien entitles the hotel to hold these goods until the guest pays the bill. The hotel, however, loses its lien if it permits the guest to take the property away.

EXAMPLE 15 When Susan Smith completed her business and was about to leave the city, she discovered that she did not have sufficient cash to pay her bill at the Mainliner Motel. The motel would not accept a check and took possession of her luggage as security until the bill was paid. After cash had been wired to Smith by her firm, she paid the bill. This terminated the motel's right of lien on her property.

■ Except as otherwise provided in the statutes of a few states, a lien on the property of a roomer is not permitted. Perhaps the reason for this is that a roomer's arrangements are of a more permanent nature than a guest's, and the proprietor takes less risk of a roomer leaving without paying the bill.

Obligations of Guests

Guests may not give lodging to a visitor overnight without the express consent of the management. Since a visitor is not paying the hotel for accommodations, such a stay may well be considered petty theft.

A hotel is within its rights in preventing a person from entering the halls where guest rooms are located, unless the person wishes to see someone for a legitimate purpose.

When you wish to get a room at a hotel, you must register at the desk. This **checking in** is necessary for the records of the hotel and also makes it possible to locate you if you are called.

When you are ready to leave, you must check out. **Checking out** is turning in your key and giving up further claim to a room. Paying your bill to date does not necessarily mean that you are checking out. A record of a definite checking-out time is needed in order to settle any dispute as to when you departed from the room.

Suggestions for Reducing Legal Risks

1. If you are given a seat on an overbooked airline, consider giving up your seat in exchange for a profit on your ticket.
2. Always seek advice from knowledgeable people before going to deserted areas while visiting foreign places.
3. When shipping goods, always pack them carefully. If they are fragile or perishable in nature, give proper notice to the carrier of the need for special handling.
4. If you pay shipping charges in advance, always get a receipt for your money and file the receipt in a safe place. You may have to prove that charges were paid in the event that there is a dispute later.
5. If you are notified of the arrival of a shipment of goods, pick the goods up at once. This action will not only save you extra charges but will also protect you against possible loss, since the carrier remains an insurer for only a reasonable time after you receive notice.
6. If you wish to make the carrier an insurer of your baggage, you should check your baggage rather than carry it with you.
7. Always deposit your valuables in the hotel safe if you wish full protection. Also, lock your luggage when you leave your room. Hotel rooms are often burglarized by petty thieves.
8. Report any loss of valuables or any accidents incurred in the hotel promptly to the hotel management. Keep a record of the date, time, person to whom the report was made, and all other information needed to establish a legitimate claim for loss or damages.

Language of the Law

Define or explain each of the following words or phrases:

carrier	act of God	baggage	Civil Rights Act
common carrier	demurrage charge	hotelkeeper	of 1964
private carrier	public carrier	motelkeeper	fellow guests
Interstate Commerce	public enemy	transient	checking in
Commission (ICC)	denied boarding	roomer	checking out
intrastate carrier	compensation	lodger	

Questions for Review

1. How is a common carrier different from a private carrier?
2. What is the meaning of the requirement that common carriers must provide universal service?
3. On what five occasions is a common carrier not an insurer of goods that it accepts for shipment?
4. When may common carriers refuse to take passengers?
5. When may a passenger be ejected from a train or other vehicle?

6. At what point does the duty of a common carrier to a passenger end?
7. What must be offered to an airline passenger who is ''bumped'' from a flight?
8. On a carrier that is not an airline, what is the carrier's liability for a passenger's baggage? on an airline?
9. Does it make any difference whether the baggage is checked or carried by a passenger?
10. What is the difference between a hotel and a rooming house?
11. When, if ever, may a hotelkeeper refuse to accept a guest?
12. What are the basic responsibilities of hotelkeepers?
13. Under what circumstances does a guest have the right to an action for invasion of privacy against a hotelkeeper?

Cases in Point

In each of the following cases, give your decision and state a legal principle that applies to the case:

1. Marcia Ferguson purchased a ticket on an airline for a flight to a distant city. She complied with all of the carrier's ticketing, check-in, and reconfirmation requirements. When Ferguson went to board the plane, she was told that it was filled but that the carrier would arrange alternative transportation for her. Must the carrier do anything else for Ferguson in this situation?
2. As he walked toward the gate on the way to boarding a plane, Conrad Hale was asked to walk through an electronic detector. He refused to do so, claiming that it was an invasion of his privacy. The airline refused him passage on the plane. Was the airline within its rights?
3. Alton Davis shipped perishable goods by freight but did not give the carrier notice of the perishable nature of the goods. Will the carrier be liable if the goods spoil because of a delay in delivery?
4. Helga Kaiser enters a railroad station in a very intoxicated condition. She demands the right to buy a ticket and board the train. Must the carrier accept her as a passenger?
5. Miranda Irish was given the opportunity to check her baggage on her ticket and have it carried in the baggage car on her train. She refused to do so and carried her baggage with her on the train. Was the carrier an insurer of Irish's baggage?
6. A shipment of grain was lost when the lake steamer on which it was shipped collided with another boat and sank. Would the carrier's claim that the loss was caused by an act of God excuse the carrier from liability?
7. Merchandise shipped by Alberta Roman was destroyed in a train wreck. The railroad company was not negligent. Can Roman collect for damages from the carrier?
8. The Kroths owned and operated a rooming house. They decided to enter the hotel business and proceeded to accept transient guests. Did the Kroths take on new responsibilities? What are those responsibilities?
9. The Schwartzes were registered guests at the Oswego Hotel. They were keeping a large sum of money with them, even though a safe was provided by the hotel for the use of guests. If the money were stolen, would the hotel be held liable for the loss under most present-day state statutes? Would the hotel have been held liable under common-law rules?
10. Juanita Ojeda was a guest at a hotel for a period of 3 days. She attempted to leave without paying her bill. She said that her employer would pay the bill later. If Ojeda is employed by a reputable company, may the hotel claim a right of lien on her baggage?

Cases to Judge

1. A post-prom party for Bay View High School students was held at the Red Carpet Inn. Alcoholic beverages were served. John Rodriquez, a minor, became belligerent and violent after drinking alcoholic beverages. He struck Alonge, another student, in the face with a glass, causing him to lose the sight of one eye. Can Red Carpet Inn be held responsible for the injuries to Alonge? Explain. *Alonge v. Rodriquez,* 279 N.W.2d 207 (Wisconsin)

2. Edna Christensen had a confirmed reservation on flight 603 from Spokane to Seattle with Northwest Airlines. She was to connect in Seattle with Northwest Flight 87 to Honolulu, then transfer to Hawaiian Airlines Flight 502 to Hilo. Upon boarding Flight 603 in Spokane (and after having been assigned a seat on the plane) she was informed that her seat was already occupied and was denied the flight to Seattle. Other travel arrangements to Hilo were made for her by Northwest Airlines. She eventually arrived in Hilo approximately 1 hour and 38 minutes later than her originally scheduled arrival time. Can she successfully bring suit against the airline for the inconvenience that she suffered? Explain. *Christensen v. Northwest Airlines, Inc.,* 455 F. Supp. 492 (Hawaii)

3. Salvador Lorio and his wife and brother checked into the San Antonio Inn. They were informed by the desk clerk that an ice machine was located at the bottom of the stairs near their rooms. After depositing their luggage in their rooms, all three went downstairs for ice. The stairway was poorly lit, and the stairs were wet and slippery. When Salvador was on the last flight of stairs, he slipped and fell, injuring his back. He testified that there was a puddle of water at the foot of the stairway caused by the leaking ice machine. Water from the puddle had apparently been tracked up the stairs by other guests. Was the Inn responsible for his injuries? Why or why not? *Lorio v. San Antonio Inn,* 454 So. 2d 864 (Louisiana)

4. The Carlisles and the Albrights were passengers aboard the S.S. Dolphin on a 4-day cruise to Freeport and Nassau. Upon arriving in Nassau, the two couples rented a jeep and headed for the beaches. Following the advice of the ship's activities director, they traveled a perimeter road around the island until they discovered an isolated access road, which they took down to a secluded beach. On their return up the overgrown dirt road, they were ambushed by three masked gunmen who opened fire on them with shotguns. All four of them were wounded. Mr. Carlisle later died from a gunshot wound to the head. After the incident, the survivors learned from members of the ship's crew that other tourists and a member of the ship's crew had been victims of violent acts at various places on the island. Did the cruise ship line owe a duty to its passengers to warn them of dangers of which it is aware? *Carlisle v. Ulysses Line Ltd., S.A.,* 475 So. 2d 248 (Florida)

5. While staying at the Sonesta Beach Hotel, Sam Aniballi requested and was assigned a safe-deposit box. He signed a card, which the hotel kept. Two keys were needed to open the box, one held by the customer and the other by the hotel clerk. After the clerk left the room, Aniballi deposited a pouch into the box. He then called for the clerk, and the two people closed and locked the box. This procedure took place on three separate occasions. Aniballi was never given a receipt or other document of any kind for the items placed in the box. On the fourth occasion, the safe-deposit box was found to be empty— $85,000 worth of jewelry was missing. A hotel employee had stolen the jewelry by making an extra key to the safe-deposit box. The law of that state required a receipt to be given to guests for their valuables. It also limited the hotel's liability to $1,000 when the hotel gave a receipt. Is Aniballi's recovery against the hotel limited to $1,000? Explain. *Florida Sonesta Corp. v. Aniballi,* 463 So. 2d 1203 (Florida)

Virgil v. Kash N' Karry Service Corp.
484 A.2d 652 (Maryland)

Mrs. Irma Virgil was injured when a thermos bottle manufactured by Aladdin Industries, Inc. and sold by Kash N' Karry Service Corp. imploded while Mrs. Virgil was pouring milk into it. Mrs. Virgil brought suit against both the seller and the manufacturer for negligence, breach of express warranty, breach of implied warranty of merchantability, and strict liability.

THE TRIAL

Mrs. Virgil testified that she purchased the pint-size thermos while shopping at Kash N' Karry two or three months prior to the implosion. Every weekday morning she filled it with coffee and a little milk and took it to work, carrying it either by its handle or in a bag with her shoes. On Saturday mornings, she filled it with coffee and milk and carried it downstairs to the den, where she spent most of the day studying. Although the thermos bottle bore a label, "Easy To Keep Clean," there were no instructions as to how to clean the thermos and no indication that any normal manner of cleaning it might damage it. Mrs. Virgil described how she washed it, filling it at night with a mild solution of baking soda in warm water, then washing it the following morning with a bottle brush. She denied dropping the thermos or misusing, abusing or damaging it in any way. One morning, after pouring coffee into the thermos, she started to pour milk into it when it imploded, throwing hot coffee and glass into her face and injuring her eye. [She] presented no expert testimony to give any scientific explanation for the implosion. [The label on the thermos bottle recommended that the product not be used by children and advised potential users that the product contained glass.]

At the conclusion of the plaintiff's case, the trial judge granted the defendants' motion for directed verdict as to all claims. [This means that the court held as a matter of law that the plaintiffs could not win the case. The court told the jury that it must find in favor of the defendant.] [The court said]

that Mrs. Virgil had presented no evidence that the bottle was defective when purchased.

In granting [the] motion for directed verdict, the trial judge stated that he was "unable to discern that the thermos was not fit for the ordinary purposes for which it was intended. . . . " With regard to the claim based on strict liability, the trial judge found that Mrs. Virgil had failed to produce evidence that the thermos was defective when purchased, stating that "the passage of time increases the burden upon the claimant" and that "substantial time [had] elapsed between the purchase and the accident."

THE ARGUMENTS ON APPEAL

[Mrs. Virgil] contend[s] that the trial judge erred in directing the verdict. She claims there was sufficient evidence to warrant submission of the case to the jury on the issue of negligence in failing to warn of inherent danger, on the issue of breach of implied warranty, and on the issue of strict liability. [She] also contend[s] that the judge erred "in ruling as a matter of law that a period of three months from purchase to the accident increases the plaintiffs' burden of proof." There is no contention of error in the granting of the motion as to the claim for breach of express warranty.

QUESTIONS FOR DISCUSSION

1. What must Mrs. Virgil prove in order to recover under a theory of strict liability?
2. What must Mrs. Virgil prove in order to recover for breach of warranty of merchantability?
3. Why did Mrs. Virgil, in her appeal, not pursue the argument that there was a breach of express warranty?
4. Do you believe that the manufacturer of the thermos bottle was negligent in failing to warn of an inherent danger in the product?
5. Do you believe that there was enough evidence to allow the jury to decide this case?
6. If you were an appellate court judge hearing this case, what would be your decision?

CASE TO BRIEF

After reading *How to Write a Case Brief* on page 78, and examining the sample brief on page 80, write a brief of the following case:

Bernstein v. Sherman
497 N.Y.S.2d 298 (New York)

Plaintiff [Bernstein] purchased a used . . . Datsun 280 Z automobile from defendant [Sherman] for the sum of $1,300 and sues for $1,500 in damages arising out of a corroded frame which, about one month after the sale, caused an accident and became irreparably broken. After a trial before the court, the following facts were undisputed:

The vehicle was sold to plaintiff following an accident which caused front end damage. That fact was fully disclosed. Plaintiff was invited by defendant's agent, his daughter, Brenda, [who actually owned the car] to check out the condition of the car with the defendant's mechanic, who was also Brenda's mechanic. Because the car had been in an accident, plaintiff specifically asked the defendant's mechanic about the condition of the frame. She was told that it was in "good condition." Plaintiff did not avail herself of an opportunity to have the car inspected by her own mechanic.

Plaintiff alleged fraud or concealment by seller and/or his agent based upon the following evidence:

Newspaper stuffed into the frame above the front wheels with a tar undercoating which concealed the paper and also the true condition of the frame; defendant's mechanic's assurance that the frame was in "good condition," followed by defendant's preparation of a bill of sale which contained an "as is" clause; defendant's sale of the car to plaintiff only several months after it was purchased; two or three different reasons as to why defendant or Brenda was selling the car; Brenda's prompt acquiescence to a $200 reduction from the offering price without further negotiation; defendant's mechanic's having created the concealed condition, or having had the opportunity of discovering it during a brake repair job and again later, after Brenda's front end accident just prior to the sale of the vehicle to plaintiff.

The date on the portion of the newspapers which were admitted into evidence preceded by several months the date upon which defendant acquired the vehicle. Defendant denied knowledge of the concealed condition, but did not dispute the worthlessness of the vehicle following the detachment of the steering mechanism from the frame a month after the sale as the result of corrosion.

On the basis of all the evidence, the court finds and concludes as follows:

The proof was insufficient to establish actual fraud. Although the evidence raises a suspicion of intentional concealment, that claim, as well, must fail for the reason that plaintiff has not sustained her burden of proof by clear and convincing evidence. Defendant relies upon his "as is" provision in the bill of sale as a disclaimer of any warranties. However, as to the effect of that disclaimer, plaintiff contrasts the defective water pump which had to be replaced the day following the sale with the concealed corroded condition of the vehicle's frame.

Defendant's daughter and his mechanic were his agents. Through his daughter, defendant invited plaintiff, a young woman who appeared to be barely 20, to rely upon the representation of his mechanic that the frame was in "good condition." That representation was relied upon by plaintiff as part of the basis of the bargain. Although there were no implied warranties under [the] U.C.C. . . . for the reason that the seller was not a dealer or a mechanic, this court finds and concludes that the oral representation of seller's mechanic amounted to an express warranty under [the] U.C.C. at least to the extent that the frame was in "good condition." . . .

[The] U.C.C. provides in pertinent part: "Words or conduct relevant to the creation of an express warranty and words or conduct tending to negate or limit warranty shall be construed wherever reasonable as consistent with each other. . . ."

[The court held that the words "as is" did not necessarily conflict with the express warranty. Even if they did conflict, in view of the elements of haste, pressure, and an inequality of bargaining power, the words "as is" would be unconscionable in this situation and unenforceable. As a result of the defect, an accident occurred, and the plaintiff was fortunate to escape serious personal injury. The court also held the disclaimer of warranty invalid because it was against public policy.] The question of plaintiff's damages is a more difficult one. At the time of the mechanic's representation as to the "good condition" of the frame, it had apparently not yet become detached from the steering mechanism. Hence, that distressing event, which occurred a month after the sale, was, at the time of the sale, a matter of conjecture about the future. Conceivably, the frame could have lasted for six months or a year. What, if anything, an inspection by plaintiff's mechanic might have shown, is also as a matter of conjecture. However, . . . the doctrine of "caveat emptor" [let the buyer beware] is [not] completely dead. Under all of the circumstances, plaintiff assumed some risk about the future condition of her purchase. On the facts before the court, and with a view toward effecting "substantial justice" between the parties, judgment is hereby awarded to plaintiff in the amount of $650 together with disbursements of $3.67.

TRIAL PROCEDURES

PRETRIAL DISCOVERY

Under modern trial practice, the aim of the court is to make the facts of a case known to all parties involved before the trial begins. In this way, the issues that are in dispute become clearly recognized. In addition, the case takes less time to try and, many times, can be settled without even going to trial.

Methods used to bring facts out before the trial are called *methods of discovery*. The most common of these are depositions, interrogatories, requests for documents and other evidence, physical and mental examinations, and requests for admission.

A *deposition* is the examination of a witness under oath before the trial takes place. It is usually done in an attorney's office with attorneys for both sides present. Witnesses are examined and cross-examined. Their testimony is taken down by a stenographer and later transcribed. Sometimes, depositions are used in court to take the place of a witness's testimony when a witness is ill, has moved away, or has died. At other times they are used to attack the credibility of a witness if later testimony differs from that given in the deposition.

Another form of discovery allows either party to the suit to ask the other party a limited number of questions about the facts in the case. The questions, called *interrogatories*, must be in writing. In addition, they must be answered in writing within a certain time period. Failure to answer interrogatories on time can result in the loss of the case. Interrogatories are useful in learning about the other party's position in the case. They may also be used to impeach (call into question) a witness's testimony if it differs from the answers on the interrogatories.

Either party may file a written *request for admission* of the truth of any matter that is relevant to the case. Such a request must be answered under the penalties of perjury within a specified time period. *Perjury* is the crime of giving false testimony under oath. The answer must state (1) a denial of the matter; (2) a reason the answering party cannot truthfully admit or deny the matter; or (3) an objection, with reasons, to the request. If an answer is not filed, the matter is considered by the court to be admitted.

Sometimes, after discovery proceedings, the facts are so clear that there is no need for the case to go to trial. The winner of the case becomes obvious. In such a case, a party may make a *motion for summary judgment*. This is a request to the court that it find in favor of the person making the motion without further proceedings. If the motion is allowed by the judge, the trial ends. If the motion is not allowed, the trial continues.

THE CASE OF GRAZIO V. WILLIAMSON (continued from page 181)

In preparing the case for trial, Attorney Powers decided to ask Wayne Williamson a series of questions about the accident. She prepared the interrogatories shown on page 216 and filed them with the court. At the same time, she mailed a copy of the interrogatories to Attorney Rodriquez, Williamson's attorney. Under the law of that state, Williamson must answer the questions in writing within 45 days. The answers to the interrogatories must be signed by Williamson under the penalties of perjury. When the answers are prepared by Attorney Rodriquez and signed by Williamson, they will be filed with the court, with a copy sent to Attorney Powers.

LEGAL PRACTICUM

Assume that you are Wayne Williamson who is being sued by Steven Grazio. Your attorney has received the interrogatories shown on page 216, and has asked you to provide the answers to them. First, review the scene at the beginning of Chapter 4. Then write out the answers that you would give to each of the questions asked in the interrogatories.

OBTAINING A JOB AND BEING AN AGENT

UNIT 4

Chapter 20

CREATION OF AN AGENCY

In this unit you will meet Adam Cole and his sister Sara. Adam obtains and then loses a job at Mr. Phelps's appliance store.

Scene: The appliance store. Mr. Phelps is talking to Adam, an unemployed neighbor boy, and his sister, Sara.

Mr. Phelps: Adam, I'm going to lunch. Will you watch the showroom until I get back?

Adam: Sure, Mr. Phelps.
(*Just after Mr. Phelps leaves, a customer, Mrs. Taylor, enters the showroom.*)

Mrs. Taylor: Can you help me, young man?

Adam: Sure. What can I do for you, ma'am?

Mrs. Taylor: Well, I need a microwave oven. I'm buying it for my sister. Well, actually I'm buying it for my mother.

Adam: I don't understand.

Mrs. Taylor: Well, my mother asked my sister, Ruth, to buy the microwave for her. But Ruth got sick, so she asked me to go in her place.

Adam: Oh, I get it.

Mrs. Taylor: Anyway, Mr. Phelps told me someone would be here at noon to help me. I guess you're the one. Which do you recommend?

Adam: Gee, I don't know. Hey, Sis, which of these microwaves is the best?

Sara: Aunt Louise just bought one of those new Dynamite Micro 700s, so they're probably pretty good.

Mrs. Taylor: How much?

Adam: Let's see. The price tag says $320.

Mrs. Taylor: Not bad. My sister gave me $400. I can give you $320 and save $80 for myself. You've got yourself a deal, son.

Sara: Are you sure you can keep that money?

Mrs. Taylor: Why, of course I can, young lady. After all, I'm entitled to make a little profit when I work for someone.

Adam: Here's your receipt, ma'am.

Mrs. Taylor: Thank you. Make sure the microwave is delivered to my mother's apartment building today.

Here's the address. You can leave it with the doorman.

(*Mrs. Taylor leaves. Adam puts a "sold" sign on the microwave.*)

Sara: I don't think you should've done that.

Adam: Why not?

Sara: You don't work here, so you don't have any right to sell Mr. Phelps's property.

(*Mr. Phelps returns.*)

Mr. Phelps: Say, who put the "sold" sign on that microwave?

Adam: I did. I sold it to Mrs. Taylor.

Mr. Phelps: You what? You had no authority to do that.

Sara: Told you so.

Adam: She paid cash.

Mr. Phelps: Oh, then I guess it's okay. But why didn't she take it with her?

Adam: She wants it delivered. Here's the address.

Mr. Phelps: Okay. I'll call E & M Delivery. They deliver for all the appliance stores in town. All I have to do is give them the address, and they take care of the rest.

(*A little later, after E & M has picked up the microwave, the phone rings. Mr. Phelps answers it. When he hangs up, he seems very upset.*)

Mr. Phelps: This is terrible. Terrible.

Adam: What's wrong, Mr. Phelps?

Mr. Phelps: The E & M delivery truck had an accident. The truck driver ran a red light and hit a car, and now the guy in the car wants to sue the truck driver, E & M Delivery, and me, too.

Adam: Gee, he can't sue all of you, can he?

LEGAL ISSUES

1. Can someone who is not an employee bind a store owner to a contract?
2. Can a lawfully appointed agent appoint someone else to act for the principal?
3. Can an employer validate a contract made by someone who had no power to enter the contract in the first place?
4. Can a third party who is injured by a worker sue the person who hired that worker?

THE SPIRIT OF THE LAW

No one can be in two places at once. At times, however, each of us must get things done in two different places at the same time. Similarly, no one can be an expert in everything. Yet we frequently need something done that requires an expert's ability. How can we be in two places at once or accomplish things that require knowledge beyond our own? The legal system provides an answer to these and similar questions through the law of agency. An agency relationship allows us to act through other people to accomplish things that might otherwise be difficult or even impossible.

AGENCY AND SIMILAR RELATIONSHIPS

The term **agency** describes a relationship between two people in which one does something for the other under the other's authority. Agency relationships always involve at least two people. One party in the relationship is the original party who needs something done. Sometimes this original party is called the principal; at other times, employer, master, or proprietor. In all cases, however, this original party is the one who wants the act done. To accomplish this act, the original party will engage the services of a second party. Sometimes the second party is called the agent; at other times, employee, servant, or independent contractor.

Principal-Agent

In the principal-agent relationship, the original party is called the **principal,** and the second party is called the **agent.** The principal is the person who gives another person the authority to act for him or her. The agent is the one who carries out the wishes of the principal. The term *agency* refers to the relationship that exists between an agent and a principal. This is a very powerful relationship, because when the agent acts for the principal, it is legally just as if the principal were acting. Generally, we distinguish an agent from the other types of second parties by noting that the agent has the power to transact business in the place of the principal. So, for example, an agent would have the power to enter a contract on behalf of the principal. Some, but not all, agents are employees.

EXAMPLE 1 Patricia Piper asked Al Albrecht to sell her car while she was on vacation. Since Albrecht had the power to enter a contract on Piper's behalf, he was an agent. (**Note:** In all examples in the next two chapters, the principal's name will always begin with ''P,'' and the agent's name will always begin with ''A.'' Similarly, any third party, that is, someone who is outside the agency relationship, will have a name beginning with ''T.'' This naming system will help you identify the legal role of each character.)

Master-Servant

The terms *master* and *servant* are legal terms that are no longer used in our everyday language. Nevertheless, they are very helpful in identifying a specific type of two-party relationship. Often today we use the terms *employer* and *employee* instead. Keep in mind that the terms employer and employee are everyday terms that have no real meaning within the common law of agency. The difference between the master-servant relationship and other relationships is the power of the master to control the physical conduct of the servant. A **master** is a person who has the right to control the physical conduct of another. A **servant** is a person whose physical conduct in the performance of a task is controlled by another. If the servant (employee) also has the power to conduct business transactions for the master (employer), then the servant is also an agent. If the servant does not have this power (as in the case of a dishwasher or a chauffeur), then the servant is not an agent.

Craig Bell works for Buckeye Educational Systems, a manufacturers' representative organization that represents products from 12 different companies. Bell is not only the firm's sales representative to colleges, he is also the firm's main troubleshooter. As sales representative, he has the power to negotiate contracts for the firm. He is therefore both an employee and an agent. If his only job were to troubleshoot defective equipment, he would be an employee but not an agent.

Proprietor–Independent Contractor

In the proprietor–independent contractor relationship the original party is the proprietor and the second party is the independent contractor. The **proprietor** is the one who hires an independent contractor. An **independent contractor** is hired to perform a task for the proprietor but is not controlled by the proprietor in carrying out the task. When a homeowner hires a plumber to fix a sink, an independent contractor has been hired.

EXAMPLE 2 Pauline Paxton has just hired three new workers. One, Angela Andrews, will sell toys for the Paxtons' new toy company. The second worker is Sam Stanhope, who has been hired as Paxton's chauffeur. The third worker is Irwin Clark, a building contractor, who has been hired to repair the steps of the Paxtons' brownstone. Andrews is both an agent and a servant, since she has the authority to transact business according to the wishes of Paxton. Stanhope is a servant but not an agent. His conduct is controlled by Paxton and he cannot transact business for Paxton. Clark is an independent contractor, since Paxton has told him to fix the steps but has no control over how he does the repair work.

Why Are These Distinctions Important?

The distinctions among the relationships of principal-agent, master-servant, and proprietor–independent contractor are often very important. For example, a servant who is not an agent, as in the case of the chauffeur, cannot bind the master to a contract that the servant makes with a third party. Thus Stanhope would have no authority to buy a car for Paxton, no matter how much Paxton needed a new car.

The master-servant and proprietor–independent contractor relationships are especially important in tort law. As you will recall from the chapter on tort law (Chapter 4), all people are liable for their own torts. There are times, however, when the law will also hold the person who hired the **tortfeasor** (the person who committed the tort) liable for that tort. This is known as the principle of **respondeat superior** (let the master respond). If a master-servant relationship exists, the master can be held liable if the servant commits a tort while working for the master. The servant must, of course, be doing something within the scope of his or her job-related duties. In contrast, when a proprietor–independent contractor relationship exists, the proprietor cannot be held liable. The distinction is the element of control. Since the master can control the activities of the servant, the courts consider it fair to hold the master liable when those activities injure someone. On the other hand, since the proprietor cannot control the independent contractor, the courts consider it unfair to hold the proprietor liable.

TYPES OF AGENCY

For the moment we will concentrate on the principal-agent relationship. Basically, we can distinguish between types of agents on two bases: (1) the extent of their authority and (2) how the agents relate to one another.

Extent of Authority

The two types of agents distinguished on the basis of the extent of authority are *general* and *special* agents.

General Agent A **general agent** is a person who has been given authority to perform any act within the scope of a business. The general manager of a department store, for example, would be a general agent. General agents are sometimes called discretionary agents because they have the right to use their judgment or discretion in all matters pertaining to the agency.

EXAMPLE 3 Allen Ambrose was managing editor of the *Galion Eagle,* a small-town newspaper. When the space shuttle disaster occurred, Ambrose hired several new printers so the paper could put out an extra edition. When one of the presses broke down, Ambrose called a mechanic to repair the damage. As managing editor of the paper, Ambrose was granted the authority to make decisions like this and to bind the publisher (his employer) to these decisions.

Special Agent A **special agent** is employed to accomplish a specific purpose or to do a particular job. Sales representatives are special agents. They have authority to sell and pass title to specific goods sold, but that is the extent of their authority. They cannot buy in the principal's name, nor are they usually authorized to collect payment for goods unless they actually deliver the goods they have sold. Other special agents may be hired for these purposes.

How Agents Relate to Each Other

Agents may be classified as subagents, agent's agents, or coagents, depending on their relationships with other agents.

Subagents A **subagent** is an agent lawfully appointed by another agent. There are only certain situations when an agent has the legal ability to appoint a

A literary agent is a special agent who helps writers with the business aspect of publishing and promoting their work. Some special agents may exaggerate their importance. (*Drawing by M. Stevens. Copyright © 1986, The New Yorker Magazine, Inc.*)

subagent. For example, the principal could authorize the agent to appoint subagents. In addition, the power to appoint a subagent is recognized when business custom allows such appointments or when the tasks the subagent is to perform are routine. For example, it would be customary for the general manager of a hotel to hire desk clerks, bellhops, and doormen. It would also be perfectly legal for the general manager to hire someone to perform a routine task such as filing or answering the phone. Finally, an emergency situation might make the appointment of a subagent necessary.

Legal Issue No. 2

EXAMPLE 4 Andy Arden was appointed by Patricia Porter to buy a rare antique at an auction in Peru. On the way to Peru, Arden's plane was grounded in Florida by a hurricane. He found he could not contact Porter, who was vacationing on a cruise ship in the South Pacific. In desperation, Arden cabled an old friend in Peru, Stephen Spencer, who agreed to purchase the antique at the auction. Since this was an emergency, Arden had the authority to appoint Spencer as a subagent.

Agent's Agent   If an agent has no authority to appoint a subagent but does so anyway, he has not appointed a subagent at all. Rather, he has appointed an agent's agent. For instance, if in Example 4 there had been no hurricane, and Arden had simply decided to stay in Florida to improve his tan, then the hiring of Spencer would not have been authorized. Arden would have hired an agent's agent, not a subagent. The difference is significant because if Spencer were merely an agent's agent, he could not bind Porter to the contract. If Porter no longer wanted the antique, she would be free to reject the transaction. Arden, on the other hand, would still be bound by Spencer's contract. An **agent's agent** binds the agent who hired him or her, but not the principal.

Coagents   If a principal hires two or more agents, he or she has created coagents. **Coagents** are subject to the authority of the principal but are not subject to one another. All authority in this case flows from the principal to the agents.

TABLE 20-1
SELECTED AGENCY RELATIONSHIPS

Type of Agent	Creation	Liability
Subagent	Created by an agent, but only under conditions of authorization, custom, routine, or emergency.	Principal and agent liable for acts of subagent.
Agent's agent	Created by an agent in the absence of proper authority.	Agent liable for acts of agent's agent. Principal not liable.
Coagents	Created by principal.	Principal liable for acts of coagents. Coagents not liable for each other.

HOW AGENCY RELATION-SHIPS ARE CREATED

Normally an agency relationship is created by an agreement between the parties. This is not always the case, however. A person may give the impression that a second party is an agent, and the law may hold the original party liable. Sometimes an original party may accept unauthorized actions, thus ratifying them. Hence, agency relationships can be created by agreement or by operation of law.

By Agreement

Most agency relationships are created by agreement. These agreements are usually, but not always, contracts. If the agreement does not involve consideration, however, no contract exists.

EXAMPLE 5 Perry Porter was going to be married on Saturday. Since he had several errands to run, he asked his friend, Arnie Allen, to pick up his rented tuxedo and to buy the flowers for the wedding. Allen agreed to do these things for free. There was no consideration here, so there was no binding contract. Still, because Allen was authorized to carry out the transactions for Porter, an agency relationship existed.

Usually, the agency agreement does not have to be in any particular form. Like other contracts, an agency agreement is sometimes oral and sometimes written.

Many agency agreements are express, but others are implied. An **express agency agreement** is one that involves clearly stated terms of agreement. For example, if the parties draw up some sort of written contract, they have an express agency agreement. At other times, however, the parties have agreed to the agency by implication only.

EXAMPLE 6 Suppose that in Example 2 Sam Stanhope, the chauffeur, had a written agreement that said his only duty was to drive Paxton and her family around town. One morning, Paxton tells Stanhope, "I'm going away. Be sure to take care of the car." Paxton then leaves the country. Is Stanhope now an agent? Yes. Even though his original agreement was simply to act as chauffeur, Paxton's actions have implied that Stanhope now has the power to make certain types of contracts. These contracts might include arranging for maintenance, hiring mechanics, and buying gas in Paxton's absence.

By Operation of Law

Legal Issue No. 1

Agency relationships may be created automatically under law. Sometimes the law operates to create an agency relationship by circumstances; at other times it does so by specific statutory enactment.

Apparent Authority   When the law creates an agency relationship by circumstance, it is called **apparent agency** or **agency by estoppel.** The circumstances usually involve some sort of communication between the principal and a third party that leads the third party to believe that a nonagent is an agent. This situation is discussed in more detail in Chapter 21 under the topic of apparent authority.

EXAMPLE 7   In the opening of this chapter, Mr. Phelps had told Mrs. Taylor that someone would be in the store at noon to help her pick out a microwave. When she arrived, she found Adam. Because Mr. Phelps told Mrs. Taylor that someone would be in the showroom to help her pick out a microwave oven and because Adam was there when she entered, she could reasonably assume that Adam was Mr. Phelps's agent. Mr. Phelps would therefore be stopped from denying Adam's authority to sell Mrs. Taylor the microwave.

In this example, Mr. Phelps actually said something which led Mrs. Taylor to her erroneous conclusion. Agency by estoppel can sometimes arise by actions or appearances alone. For example, when a store opens, the owners are communicating to the public that salespeople will be present to help them. If an imposter enters and pretends to be a salesperson, the store will be liable for any loss incurred by an innocent third party who deals with the imposter.

By Statute   Sometimes the state legislature decides that certain circumstances justify creating agency relationships automatically by statute. Usually, the state has some special interest to protect by creating the agency relationship. For example, in many states the law requires corporations to appoint an agent who can be served with a complaint and summons in case the corporation is sued. If the appointed agent dies or leaves the state, the secretary of state automatically becomes the statutory agent of the corporation for service of process. The state has a special interest to protect here. It wants to make sure its citizens always have a way to sue a corporation that has injured them.

By Ratification   At times a person may act as an agent without the authority to do so. **Ratification** occurs if the principal, with full knowledge of the facts, accepts the benefits of the unauthorized act. The act is thereby approved or ratified.

EXAMPLE 8   In the opening skit, Adam Cole had no authority to sell the microwave oven to Mrs. Taylor. Once Mr. Phelps accepted Mrs. Taylor's money, however, he had ratified Cole's act of agency.

Legal Issue No. 3

A principal's failure or refusal to ratify the unauthorized act of an agent makes the agent personally liable to the third party.

Suggestions for Reducing Legal Risks

1. When you enter an agency contract, as either principal or agent, be sure the terms of the contract are clear, particularly with respect to the duties of the agent and the extent of the agent's authority.
2. When you work for someone else, make certain that the nature of the relationship is clear. Trouble may result if you think you are a servant and the other party thinks you are an independent contractor (or the other way around).
3. When you contract with independent contractors, make certain they know they are responsible for any liabilities they incur.
4. Use great care in appointing a general agent. Remember, it is usually to your advantage to limit an agent's authority to specific acts.
5. Remember that an agent's authority to appoint subagents is limited to four circumstances: agreement, custom, routine tasks, and emergency.
6. Remember that although most agency relationships are created by agreement, some come about by circumstance, by statute, and by ratification.

Language of the Law

Define or explain each of the following words or phrases:

agency	proprietor	special agent	apparent agency
principal	independent contractor	subagent	agency by estoppel
agent	tortfeasor	agent's agent	ratification
master	respondeat superior	coagent	
servant	general agent	express agency agreement	

Questions for Review

1. What solution does the law provide for a person who wants to enter a contract but cannot be present to do so?
2. What solution does the law provide for someone who wants to invest money in the stock market but does not have the expertise to choose the best stock?
3. What distinguishes an independent contractor from a servant?
4. How can you determine whether an employee is also an agent?
5. Give an example of a general agent.

6. Under what four circumstances can an agent lawfully appoint a subagent?
7. Name two ways agency agreements come into existence.
8. What do we mean by an agency by estoppel?
9. Give an example of an agency created by statute.
10. Why is it important to distinguish between a master-servant relationship and a proprietor–independent contractor relationship?

Cases in Point

In each of the following cases, give your decision and state a legal principle:

1. Ben Milner was employed by Lew Oswald in Lew's General Store. Whenever Oswald left the store, he told Milner to handle all business. Oswald refused to acknowledge Milner as an agent, however, claiming that only he himself had the power to make Milner an agent. Is Oswald correct? Why?

2. Mary Drouhard sold a set of antique dishes to Betty Sloane. Bruce Richards offered to deliver the dishes and collect the money for Drouhard as a personal favor. Was Richards an agent? Why?

3. Gary Sharp, an agent of the State Ranch Insurance Company, was in an automobile accident and could not run his insurance agency for 3 days while he was in the hospital. Sharp had his wife, Mona, run the office while he was recuperating. Was she an agent? If so, what kind of an agent? Why?

4. Jennifer Corsi appointed Beatrice Miller her agent to sign a contract to sell her stereo. What kind of agent is Miller?

5. Joanne Neptune hired Raymond's Royal Roofers to reshingle the roof of her home. Neptune told Raymond what she wanted done but left the details up to Raymond and his workers. While on Neptune's roof, one of Raymond's roofers dropped his tool box onto Ted Cafferty's new car, smashing the windshield. Is Neptune liable? Why?

6. Shaun Nyquist worked as an x-ray technician for Dr. Regina Ingram. Ingram trained Nyquist. The doctor was always present when Nyquist conducted an x-ray examination. One day, however, she told Nyquist that he was on his own. While Nyquist was x-raying a patient, the patient fell to the floor and broke his ankle. Is Ingram liable for Nyquist's negligence? Why?

7. Phil Nicholson hired Ted McGraw as general manager of the Nicholson Restaurant. In this capacity, McGraw booked the restaurant for a wedding reception on a Friday night. Nicholson got upset because Friday was the most lucrative night of the week. He canceled the reservations, claiming that McGraw had no authority to make such bookings. Is Nicholson correct? Why?

8. The O'Grady Department Store opened a new branch store. One day Jeffrey Hall was passing through the men's department when he was approached by Trish Houston, who mistook him for a sales clerk. Hall helped Houston pick out a suit for her boyfriend and wrote up the sale, but he pocketed the cash and left the store before Houston figured out what had happened. When she learned of Hall's deception, she demanded that O'Grady honor the sale. Is Houston within her rights? Why?

9. The Ohio General Assembly was upset by the incidence of out-of-state drivers having accidents in Ohio and leaving the state. Under such circumstances it was very difficult to serve such drivers with complaints and summonses. The General Assembly passed a statute appointing the secretary of state as statutory agent for service of process in such cases. Was Ohio within its rights in doing this? Why?

10. Henry Douglas worked as a gardener for Union State University. His only responsibility was to keep the campus lawns in good shape. One morning the university's old riding lawn mower finally broke for the last time. Since Douglas knew the governor was going to speak on campus that afternoon, he rushed down to the Green Grass Lawn Supply Company with a university purchase order and bought a new lawn mower. When Douglas's boss found out about the sale, he told Douglas to go ahead and mow the lawn but then to return the mower to Green Grass. When Douglas tried to give the mower back, Green Grass refused to take it. The university then refused to pay for the mower. Was the university within its rights? Why?

Cases to Judge

1. Nine people owned the Starlite Industrial Park. In an effort to sell the park, the owners appointed Mayer Greenberg as their exclusive sales agent. Greenberg was not authorized to appoint a subagent. Andy Skurski, a real estate broker, approached Greenberg, indicating that the Janitell brothers wished to purchase the park. After extensive negotiations, the Janitells told Skurski to accept Greenberg's terms. Skurski called Greenberg's office and talked to Staniek, who agreed to sell the property to the Janitells. When the deal fell through, Skurski sued the nine owners for his commission, claiming Staniek had acted as a subagent when he agreed to Skurski's acceptance. Is Skurski correct? *Estate of Greenberg v. Skurski,* 602 P.2d 178 (Nevada)

2. R. L. VanCleave, acting as the agent of J. W. Murchison, sold Murchison's oil rights to E. R. Kinabrew. When Murchison attempted to invalidate the deal, Kinabrew sued. Murchison claimed VanCleave was a special agent, not a general agent, and therefore had no power to transfer the oil rights. Murchison pointed to the writing which made VanCleave his agent. The document listed many powers, all dealing with the mineral rights to Murchison's land, but the specific type of transfer that VanCleave had made in this case was not mentioned. For his part, Kinabrew argued that VanCleave was a general agent because he had broad powers to deal with Murchison's mineral rights in any way he saw fit. Is Kinabrew correct? *First National Bank in Dallas v. E. R. Kinabrew,* 589 S.W.2d 137 (Texas)

3. Floyd Stigler agreed to sell 43 acres of land to Leon Hogg, Jr. for $1,418,332.76. Stigler's agent, Russell, delivered the deed to Hogg. Stigler gave Russell the power to subordinate Stigler's claim to the property to anyone from whom Hogg would obtain a loan to improve the property. When Hogg could not come up with the down payment, he got a loan from HNC Realty. To do so,

however, he first got Russell to subordinate Stigler's claim to HNC. This subordination meant that if Hogg defaulted, HNC and not Stigler could take the property. With the loan, Hogg paid Stigler the down payment. Hogg later defaulted on both his loan to HNC and his payments to Stigler, and HNC took the property. Stigler claimed that Russell had no power to subordinate his claim unless the loan was to improve the land. Since the loan was for the down payment and not land improvements, Stigler argued he had first claim to the property. HNC claimed Stigler had ratified Russell's subordination when he accepted the down payment. Is HNC correct? *Land Title Company of Dallas v. F. M. Stigler,* 609 S.W.2d 754 (Texas)

4. Polinski rented a house next to a building site. The general contractor at the building site was Atlanta Commercial Builders, Inc. Atlanta had hired a group of block masons as subcontractors. Atlanta told the masons where to lay the blocks and made out the work schedule for the masons. Atlanta also had the right to shift priorities, moving the masons from one part of the job site to another. One afternoon the masons left a warming fire unattended. Sparks from the fire ignited Polinski's house, destroying much of his property. Polinski sued Atlanta, claiming the masons were servants. Atlanta denied liability, claiming that the masons were independent contractors. Is Atlanta correct? *Atlanta Commercial Builders, Inc. v. Polinski,* 250 S.E.2d 781 (Georgia)

5. Mrs. Taylor was recuperating as a patient in Doctor's Hospital. While in her room, she was assaulted by an orderly who, although off duty, was wearing his hospital uniform. Taylor sued the hospital under the theory of respondeat superior. The hospital argued that intentional torts were beyond the scope of the orderly's duties. How would you decide? *Taylor v. Doctor's Hospital,* 486 N.E.2d 1249 (Ohio)

Chapter 21

AGENCY RELATIONSHIPS AND THEIR TERMINATION

Scene: The appliance store. Mr. Phelps has hired Adam Cole to work in the store.

Mr. Phelps: Adam, I have to see my accountant downtown. You handle all the business while I'm gone. Just don't let any sales rep talk you into buying anything, especially if he wants cash. I don't let my employees buy anything for cash. Remember that.

Adam: I understand, Mr. Phelps. (*After Mr. Phelps has left, a sales rep enters the showroom.*)

Sales rep: Say, you've got a real nice place here.

Adam: Thanks. Can I help you?

Sales rep: The question is, can *I* help *you*?

Adam: What do you mean?

Sales rep: I've got a load of 20 VCRs in my van that I have to let go for $50 apiece.

Adam: You're kidding! That's amazing.

Sales rep: Well, I've got a knack for business.

Adam: How can you make a profit selling VCRs for $50?

Sales rep: I not only make a profit, I make a 100 percent profit.

Adam: How can that be?

Sales rep: My last boss gave me $8,000 to buy 20 VCRs at $400 apiece. I found a guy who could sell them to me at half price. So I got 40 VCRs for $8,000 instead of only 20.

Adam: I'll bet your boss was happy.

Sales rep: Nah. He was sore because I gave him 20 VCRs and kept the other 20 for myself.

Adam: Maybe you shouldn't have kept them.

Sales rep: Why not? It was a good business deal. Now about those VCRs. You give me $1,000 in cash and you can have the lot. Then you sell them for $400 apiece and you make an 800 percent profit. Your boss will love you.

Adam: Okay.
(*Adam goes to the safe and returns with $1,000 in cash. The sales rep*

unloads the VCRs, takes the cash, and leaves. Mr. Phelps returns.)

Mr. Phelps: Where did all these VCRs come from?

Adam: I bought them from a sales rep.

Mr. Phelps: Not the guy I just saw driving away in that van.

Adam: That was him, alright.

Mr. Phelps: Oh, no. He's the guy I fired last week. He used $4,000 of my money to buy himself 20 VCRs and now I just bought them again.

Adam: Gee, I'm sorry, Mr. Phelps.

Mr. Phelps: That's okay. At least you didn't pay cash. I'll just stop the check.

Adam: Uh-oh!

Mr. Phelps: What's that supposed to mean?

Adam: I paid him $1,000 in cash.

Mr. Phelps: Adam.

Adam: Yes, Mr. Phelps?

Mr. Phelps: You're fired.

LEGAL ISSUES

1. How much real authority does an employee have when left in charge of a business?
2. If an agent is given money by a principal, must the agent account for all of that money?
3. May an agent who has been instructed to pay only by check use cash for a good deal that requires cash?
4. Do agents owe their first loyalty to themselves or to their principals?

THE SPIRIT OF THE LAW

The last chapter discussed the different techniques for creating agency relationships. These techniques were agreement and operation of law, including creation of apparent authority, statutory requirement, and ratification. Many factors, including the way an agency relationship begins, can determine the extent of the agent's authority. Regardless of their authority, however, all agents owe certain duties to their principals, and all principals owe certain duties to their agents. This chapter explores the extent of an agent's authority and the duties involved in the agency relationship. The chapter will conclude with techniques for the termination of an agency relationship.

TYPES OF AGENCY AUTHORITY

When agents act within the scope of their authority and contract with a third party on behalf of the principal, the contract that results is actually between the principal and the third party. The agent's authority may be actual or apparent.

Actual Authority

Actual authority includes the powers really given by the principal to the agent. Such actual authority may be expressed in words, or it may be implied from the nature of the relationship or the conduct of the parties.

Express Authority **Express authority** involves all the directions or commands that are detailed by the principal when the agency relationship is first created. These commands may be very general, as when a principal tells an agent, "Take care of my car while I'm gone," or very specific, as in the case of a complex, formal writing.

Implied Authority Naturally, it is impossible for the principal to mention every single act that the agent is allowed to perform. Listing all these acts in an agreement, whether the agreement is oral or written, would not only be cumbersome and wasteful, but also unnecessary. The law allows some actual authority to be implied from the express terms that create the agency relationship in the first place. Those powers that are implied from the express terms are included in the agent's **implied authority.**

EXAMPLE 1 Perry Patler's service station in Springfield had experienced a loss of business over the last few years. To remedy this situation, Patler hired Abe Applegate as his new general manager. When discussing their employment arrangements, Patler told Applegate that he wanted him to do a market analysis of Springfield. He told Applegate to use the market analysis to identify the community's need for any specialty services and to hire the necessary specialty people. He concluded by saying, "Make sure this station gets its share of the market." Applegate went to the Springfield Library and compiled the market analysis in Table 21-1.

The market analysis indicated that the service stations in the area were low in transmission and tune-up specialists. Using this data, Applegate hired Sal Salvatore as the station's new transmission and tune-up expert. He also decided to target the south side of town for an advertising campaign using billboards and handbills. In addition, he began a pick-up and drop-off service for south side customers. These decisions were made because the south side had experienced a 100 percent increase in population over the last 17 years and because two-thirds of the cars in Springfield were owned by residents of the south side.

If we analyze these transactions, we can easily distinguish between those activities that are included in Applegate's express authority from those actions that are included in his implied authority. Since Patler told Applegate to do a market analysis, Applegate has the express authority to make certain the study is done. Similarly, because Patler gave Applegate the power to hire specialists, he has the express authority to employ Salvatore. From the express authority to see that the station gets its share of the market, Applegate would also have the implied authority to begin the advertising campaign and the pick-up and drop-off service on the south side of town. Note that Patler never told Applegate, "You have the power to start a pick-up and drop-off service." However, he told Applegate to make certain the station was competitive. Since the pick-up and

Population (1987):	150,000 people—48,330 in the north, down 16% from 1970 Census; 101,700 in the south, up nearly 100% from 1970 Census.
Households (1987):	60,000 households, divided between 23,000 in the north and 37,000 in the south.
Persons/Household:	2.1 persons/household in the north 2.7 persons/household in the south (Note: In 1970, persons/household was 2.5 for both north and south.)
Income/Household:	$26,500 for the north side $31,000 for the south side
Total number of personal cars:	80,000, with 25,300, or 1.1/household, in the north, 54,700, or 1.45/household, in the south.
Total annual automotive service expenditures (not including gas):	$40,000,000

Service mix—General repair outlets (includes tire dealers and car dealers offering general service)—117
    Transmission specialists—3
    Alignment specialists—4
    Radiator specialists—5
    Muffler franchises—5
    Tune-up franchises—2
    Other specialists—5 (4 × 4, strictly one-make imports, etc.)
Total service bays (general shops)—412
Total service bays (specialists)—90
Total bays—502
Potential income per bay (total)—about $80,000/bay
Distribution of bays—(1970—60% north, 40% south)
                —(1987, 40% north, 60% south)

drop-off service is aimed at the bulk of the market, it will help Patler's station to be competitive. Applegate therefore had the power to institute it.

Sometimes a dispute arises as to what power can be implied from the express authority given the agent. The court draws the line by saying that implied authority must be "reasonably derived from the express power." What is reasonable in a given agency situation is determined by looking at the actions that are customarily performed by other agents in similar situations.

Legal Issue No. 1

EXAMPLE 2   If, in Example 1, Applegate had used Patler's money to buy himself a new suit and a new car, he would have acted beyond the scope of his implied power. Applegate might argue that the car and suit were necessary because he had to look nice when he went to the various advertising agencies in town and because he had to drive across town to get to those agencies. Such expenditures, however, are not customarily part of a service station general manager's authority.

Apparent Authority

In the case of actual authority, the agent receives real power from the principal because of what the principal has communicated to the agent. Consequently, the key to determining actual authority, express or implied, is to figure out what happened between the principal and the agent. In contrast, the key to understanding apparent authority is to focus on what happened between the principal and a third party. **Apparent authority** exists when the principal has somehow led a third party to believe that a nonagent is an agent. As discussed in Chapter 20, apparent authority is sometimes called agency by estoppel because the principal cannot deny that the nonagent acted on his behalf.

EXAMPLE 3   Pierre Perrault owned and operated a jewelry store in downtown Minneapolis. At a party one evening, he told Theresa Turner to come by his shop at 9 a.m. and that someone would be in the shop to sell her a diamond necklace. At 8:30 a.m. the next day, Perrault had to leave the shop to run several errands. Because his regular clerk was late, Perrault left his niece, Amy, at the shop "to keep an eye on things." When Turner arrived at 9 a.m., she assumed Amy was the clerk. Turner saw a necklace she liked. Amy sold it to her, and Turner left, a satisfied customer. When Perrault returned and found the necklace gone he became very upset, because he had promised the necklace to another customer. He called Turner, who refused to give the necklace back. In this case, Turner would be within her rights, because Perrault had created a situation in which she could reasonably believe that Amy had authority to sell the necklace. The apparent authority in this case is created because of something that Perrault said directly to Turner and because he left Amy in the shop.

AGENT'S DUTIES TO THE PRINCIPAL

The five duties that an agent owes to the principal are the duties of (1) obedience, (2) good faith, (3) loyalty, (4) accounting for all of the principal's money handled by the agent, and (5) exercising judgment and skill in the performance of the assigned work.

Obedience

Legal Issue No. 3

An agent must obey all reasonable orders and instructions within the scope of the agency agreement. If agents disobey instructions, they become liable to the principal for any loss that results. Even an agent who is not paid (a gratuitous agent) must follow instructions or become responsible for any loss resulting from a failure to do so.

Good Faith

An agency is a **fiduciary relationship,** a relationship based on trust. Principals often entrust their agents with their business, their property, their money, and

Adam Cole is Mr. Phelps's agent. What duties does he owe to his principal in considering an offer from a salesperson? Did Cole breach these duties in the scene on pages 282 and 283?

sometimes even their good reputation. This places a duty of special care on the agent. To have good faith simply means to deal honestly with the principal. It also requires the agent to notify the principal of all matters pertaining to the agency relationship.

Loyalty

Legal Issue No. 4

The agent must be loyal to the principal. **Loyalty** means acting in the principal's best interests at all times. Agents may not work for others who are in competition with their principals, nor may agents make deals that are advantageous to themselves at the expense of their principals. The only exception to these rules is when the principal knows the agent is also working for another principal or for him- or herself.

Duty to Account

Legal Issue No. 2

When an agent handles money for a principal, the agent owes a duty to account for every cent of the principal's money the agent handles. The **duty to account** means that the agent must keep a record of all money collected and paid out and must report this to the principal. The agent must also keep the principal's money separate from the agent's own money, keep it safe, and turn it over to the principal in keeping with the principal's instructions. If the agent commingles the principal's money with the agent's own so that it is impossible to tell how much belongs to the agent and how much belongs to the principal, the agent loses all claim to the money. The entire amount belongs to the principal.

Judgment and Skill

In performing work for principals, agents must use all the skill and judgment of which they are capable. They are not held liable for honest mistakes in judgment or for lack of skill when they have done the best they can.

EXAMPLE 4 Avery August was hired by Peggy Perkins to act as a financial counselor. Perkins entrusted August with $500,000 and told him to invest in the best stocks possible. August made a careful analysis of business trends and available stocks. In the end, he decided to invest in the Toth–Van Meader Chemical Company, a new company that was clearly one of the best investment opportunities at the time. One week later, a huge chemical gas leak at a Toth–Van Meader plant in Brazil injured thousands of people and destroyed millions of dollars worth of prime real estate. Toth–Van Meader stock fell, and Perkins lost much of her $500,000. August could not be held liable for this loss, because he had done the best he could. If, on the other hand, August had invested in Toth–Van Meader knowing that it was on shaky ground, he would have violated his duty to exercise judgment and skill. If he had invested in Toth–Van Meader because he was on the board of directors and knew the company needed the money, he would also have violated his duties of loyalty, good faith, and obedience.

DUTIES OF THE PRINCIPAL TO THE AGENT

It certainly would not be fair for the agent to have all the duties and no rights. For this reason, among others, the law imposes certain duties on the principal in dealing with the agent. The same duties are found in the employer-employee relationship. They include the duties of (1) compensation, (2) reimbursement, (3) indemnification, and (4) cooperation.

Compensation

An agent who is working for and on behalf of a principal is entitled to be paid for services rendered unless the agent is a **gratuitous agent,** an agent working for free. The principal must pay the agent any **compensation** (salary or wages) agreed upon in the contract. If no specific amount is set, a reasonable sum must be paid for any authorized acts performed by the agent for the principal.

Reimbursement and Indemnification

Agents are entitled to **reimbursement,** or repayment, when they are required to spend their own money for the principal's benefit. In addition, if an agent suffers a loss as a result of the principal's instructions, he or she is entitled to **indemnification,** that is, payment in the amount of the loss.

Cooperation

The duty of **cooperation** means that the principal, having given the agent the duty to perform certain tasks, must not interfere with the performances of those tasks. If the principal makes the agent's job difficult or impossible, the principal has breached the duty of cooperation. Sometimes this duty requires providing a safe workplace for the agent. At other times it may involve allowing the agent to operate without interference.

EXAMPLE 5 Phoebe Parkes hired Al Alvarez to be her agent in the door-to-door sale of Curren-Bartlett Cosmetics. Parkes told Alvarez that he would have exclusive rights to sell the Curren-Bartlett line in Willowick, Ohio. She also told Alvarez that to remain a Curren-Bartlett agent he would have to make a quarterly profit of at least $10,000. Later that month, Alvarez discovered that Parkes had also hired 22 other agents to sell Curren-Bartlett Cosmetics in Willowick. The high number of agents made it impossible for Alvarez to return $10,000 quarterly. Parkes had violated her duty to cooperate with Alvarez.

Canadian Tire Settles Suits Filed by Dealers Of 13 White Stores

By a WALL STREET JOURNAL *Staff Reporter*

TORONTO—Canadian Tire Corp. said it reached an agreement to settle lawsuits with 13 of 20 White Stores Inc. dealers.

The dealers, whose lawyers declined to comment on the settlement, had claimed in the suit filed in U.S. federal court in Texas that Canadian Tire's price-fixing practices prevented them from earning profits.

A spokesman for Canadian Tire, which owns White Stores, said costs of the settlement were included in a $66 million (Canadian) write-down that it reported last week for its fourth quarter. He declined to elaborate.

The dealers' lawyers previously said that the damages sought could amount to as much as $60 million (U.S.).

The Canadian Tire spokesman said minor issues are still to be resolved with the remaining seven dealers. Two other dealers recently dropped their lawsuits.

Canadian Tire is a wholesaler of auto accessories, hardware and home-improvement products, and the Wichita Falls, Texas-based White Stores sells automotive products. Canadian Tire recently sold most of its White Stores assets.

As principal, what duties did Canadian Tire Corp. owe to the 13 White stores? Which of these duties did Canadian violate here?

AGENTS AND THIRD PARTIES

The agent is the go-between who brings the contracting parties together and "stands in the shoes of the principal" in making the contract. If the agent represents a **disclosed principal,** one whose existence is known to the third party, the agent assumes no liability for the resulting contract. The principal assumes this responsibility.

There are two special situations, however, in which agents may be held liable. These are (1) when agents do not disclose their principal and (2) when agents wrongfully go beyond their authority.

When Principal Is Not Disclosed

An **undisclosed principal** is one whose identity is not revealed, even though the third party knows that the agent is acting for someone else. When the principal is undisclosed at the time of the contract and the third party later learns the identity of the principal, the third party has the option of holding either the agent or the undisclosed principal—but not both—to the contract.

EXAMPLE 6 Ann Armstrong managed a produce stand for Phil Prospect. Armstrong was very popular in town, so the business was named "Ann Armstrong's Produce Stand." Armstrong operated the business as though it were her own. The Terminal Tower Produce Market gave credit to the business. When the bills were not paid, the Terminal Tower Produce Market brought an action against Armstrong. Armstrong defended herself on the grounds that she was only an agent.

The Terminal Tower Produce Market could hold either Armstrong or Prospect responsible for the payment. Ordinarily, a creditor will choose to hold the principal responsible because the principal usually has more money. However, if Armstrong had more money than Prospect, the Terminal Tower Produce Market might elect to hold Armstrong responsible for the bills.

When Agents Wrongfully Exceed Their Authority

Agents bind their principals to contracts only when the agents act within the scope of their actual or apparent authority. When agents enter into contracts on behalf of principals without authority to do so, the agents themselves usually become liable for the contract.

EXAMPLE 7 The People's Printing Company told Anita Arnett to buy an electric typewriter for not more than $595. Arnett found that she could buy the typewriter for $425, which she did. She used the remaining $170 to buy a duplicating machine for the office. The employer refused to accept the duplicator, which Arnett had no authority to buy. Arnett would be required to pay the People's Printing Company $170. She could then either return the duplicator to the seller for a cash refund (if the seller allowed a refund) or keep the duplicator for herself.

TERMINATION OF AGENCY RELATIONSHIPS
Termination by Operation of Law

Nothing lasts forever—not even the most gracious and profitable agency relationship. Since most agencies are based on contracts, the ordinary rules for the termination of contracts apply to agencies. Agencies may be terminated by operation of law or by the acts of the parties.

An agency relationship will terminate by operation of law in the following circumstances: death of the principal or agent, bankruptcy, impossibility of performance, or subsequent declaration of illegality.

Death or Permanent Incapacity of Principal or Agent The death or permanent incapacity of the principal or of the agent will terminate an agency. This makes sense, since an ordinary agency is based on personal services. When death terminates an agency, third parties do not have to be notified, since the law assumes everyone knows about a person's death.

Bankruptcy The bankruptcy of the principal will also terminate an agency. Bankruptcy cancels all of the principal's ordinary contracts and gives title to the principal's property to a trustee for the benefit of creditors.

The bankruptcy of an agent will terminate the agency if the agent is required to use his or her own funds in conducting the business of the principal. If the agent is not using his or her own money, the bankruptcy will not prevent the agent from doing the job in the regular way, and there is no reason to terminate the agency.

Impossibility of Performance When the destruction of essential subject matter or the incapacity of the agent makes performance impossible the agency is terminated. For example, suppose that a real estate agent entered into an agreement to sell a house to a third party on behalf of the principal. Through no fault of the parties and without their knowledge, the house is destroyed before the contract is signed. The agency would be terminated because the essential subject matter of the contract, the house, has been destroyed, and performance of the contract would be impossible.

Subsequent Illegality   If, after an agency contract has been entered, the purpose of the agency is declared illegal, the agency is terminated by operation of law. If only part of the agent's required activity becomes illegal, only that part of the authority ends. The remaining authority to perform legal acts remains in effect.

Termination by Acts of the Parties

Most agency relationships are terminated when the parties have fully carried out their duties. The parties may also terminate their relationship by mutual consent even before the contract is fully performed. Moreover, certain acts by agents or principals may be enough to terminate a relationship.

Performance   If an agent is appointed to accomplish a certain result, the agency terminates when the result is achieved. In other words, when the job is done, the agency ends.

Mutual Agreement   As in contracts, the principal and the agent may mutually agree to terminate the agency. Termination may result from the passage of a predetermined time period. Or the principal and the agent may agree to end the relationship at any other time, even if the task is left undone or the time period has not yet elapsed.

Agent's Withdrawal   An agent may terminate the agency at any time by quitting the job or giving up the agency. However, if this involves a breach of contract, the agent may be liable for any damages suffered by the principal.

Agent's Discharge   The principal may terminate an agency at any time by discharging the agent. There are some limits on the authority of the principal to discharge an agent. When an agent has an interest in the subject matter of the agency, that agent is said to have an **irrevocable agency,** which cannot be discharged by the principal.

EXAMPLE 8   Pamona Pratt borrowed money from the Associated American Bank to remodel her office building. To secure the repayment of the loan, Pratt appointed Associated American as agent for the collection of rent from the tenants in the building. The understanding was that the rent money was to be applied to the repayment of the loan and that the agency would last until the loan was repaid. This agency would be irrevocable until the loan was fully repaid.

Notice to Third Parties

Third parties who have done business with the principal through the agent and third parties who knew of the agency relationship are entitled to notice of its termination. A principal who fails to notify third parties that the agency has ended may be liable for future acts of the agent.

EXAMPLE 9   Art Arbaugh, a salesperson, was discharged from Penrose Products, Inc., because of several misunderstandings with the sales manager. Shortly thereafter, Arbaugh visited one of Penrose's accounts and accepted a payment of $125 that the debtor expected Arbaugh to turn over to Penrose Products, Inc. No notice had been given to the debtor company concerning Arbaugh's discharge. If Arbaugh were to flee with the $125, Penrose Products, Inc., would have to give credit to its customer for the payment because of its failure to give notice.

The type of notice required depends on how the former business relations were carried on. There are three situations to be considered:

1. When the third party has given credit to the principal through the agent, the third party is entitled to actual notice. Notice by certified mail is perhaps the best way to give notice, because a receipt of the notice can be obtained from the post office.
2. When the third party has never given credit but has done a cash business with the agent or knows that other persons have dealt with the principal through the agent, notice by publication in a newspaper is sufficient.
3. When the third party has never heard of the agency relationship, no notice of any kind is required. The third party who is dealing with an agent for the first time has a duty to investigate and determine the exact extent of the agent's authority.

Suggestions for Reducing Legal Risks

1. Remember that when you create an agency with express terms, some implied authority will flow from those express terms.
2. Avoid situations where, in the role of principal, you may somehow inadvertently lead a third party to believe a nonagent is your agent.
3. When you are an agent, you owe the duties of obedience, loyalty, good faith, and judgment and skill to the principal. An agent must also account for all of the principal's money entrusted to his or her care.
4. When you are a principal, you owe the duties of compensation, reimbursement, indemnification, and cooperation to the agent.
5. Remember that agency relationships can terminate in two ways: by operation of law and by the acts of the parties.

Language of the Law

Define or explain each of the following words or phrases:

actual authority	fiduciary relationship	compensation	disclosed principal
express authority	loyalty	reimbursement	undisclosed principal
implied authority	duty to account	indemnification	irrevocable agency
apparent authority	gratuitous agent	cooperation	

Questions for Review

1. When agents act within the scope of their authority and contract with a third party on behalf of the principal, the contract that results is really between which two parties?
2. Give an example of an agent's express authority.
3. Give an example of an agent's implied authority.
4. What rule is used to govern the limits of implied authority?
5. What distinguishes actual authority from apparent authority?
6. The agent has certain duties to the principal. What are they?
7. The principal has certain duties to the agent. What are they?
8. What does termination of an agency agreement by operation of law mean?
9. Name the various ways in which an agency agreement might be terminated by the acts of the parties.
10. May an agent who has declared bankruptcy continue to serve as an agent? Explain your answer.

Cases in Point

In each of the following cases, give your decision and state a legal principle that applies to the case:

1. In the opening of this chapter, Adam Cole had been authorized to pay for merchandise by check only. Instead, he paid for some goods by cash. Clearly he violated his duty of obedience to Mr. Phelps. Suppose that the salesman had been legitimate and that it was customary in the appliance business to purchase by cash. Would Phelps then be bound by the contract?
2. Theodore Van Dine owed Oliver Wayne $320 for goods delivered to Van Dine's printing shop. Each month for the past 2 years Wayne had sent his collection agent, Kent Brewster, to Van Dine's to collect on Van Dine's account. Unknown to Van Dine, Wayne had recently fired Brewster. Nevertheless, Brewster continued to collect money from Wayne's customers, which he kept for himself. After Van Dine paid Brewster, did he still owe Wayne $320?
3. After discharging Brewster as his collection agent, Wayne hired Graham McDaniels to collect his accounts. McDaniels was new to the collection business and did not under-stand proper procedure. As a result, he placed the day's proceeds in his private bank account. The next day, when Wayne demanded his money, McDaniels realized he could no longer remember how much of the money in his account belonged to Wayne. Wayne demanded the entire amount. What would be the court's decision?
4. Shirley Jackson has been hired as Leo Anderson's literary agent to find a publisher for his books. When Jackson reads Anderson's latest manuscript, she realizes she has a best seller on her hands. She tells Anderson that the book is so bad no publisher would even want to read it, let alone publish it. She offers to pay him $200 for the manuscript. He agrees. Jackson then sells the manuscript to a book publisher for $100,000. What duties has Jackson breached? Explain.
5. Jay Hoffman was hired by Earl McKnight to negotiate the rights to certain oil land. Unknown to McKnight, Hoffman bought the rights for $100,000 and then sold the rights to McKnight for $500,000. Later, when McKnight found out about the deal, he demanded Hoffman's profits. Was McKnight entitled to recover $400,000?

6. The Millstern Advertising Agency has been hired by Aztron, Inc., to begin an advertising campaign. Part of the campaign involves placing 30 billboards on 30 different state highways, each one 10 yards from the roadway. Before the billboards are put in place, the state legislature passes a statute which requires all billboards to be set 50 yards away from the edge of all state routes. Millstern wants to continue with the campaign but Aztron says the agency has been terminated by operation of law. Has the agency indeed been terminated by operation of law?

7. Fred Salem worked as a sales representative for Pennrock Greeting Cards. He had an exclusive 3-year contract but quit after only 2 years. As a result of Salem's renunciation of the contract, Pennrock lost sales that amounted to $10,000. Can Pennrock recover that amount from Salem?

8. Mark Devolder is hired by a famous politician to negotiate a deal for the purchase of a seaside resort. The politician cautions Devolder not to reveal that he is acting as an agent. At the last minute, the politician cancels the deal. The seller of the land loses a great deal of money. He sues Devolder and recovers $70,000. Devolder asks the politician for the $70,000. The politician refuses. Is the politician liable for Devolder's loss?

9. On February 7, Lois Martin, acting as agent for Mack Bascom, sold Bascom's yacht to Murray George. Unknown to anyone connected with the deal, the yacht had sunk on February 6. Is the contract binding?

10. Yvonne Tribune gave Ronald Brothers authority to sell her comic book collection for $2,000. Brothers sold the collection for $2,500 and kept the additional $500 for himself. May Tribune, on learning of the facts, recover the $500?

Cases to Judge

1. The board of directors of Central Alaska Broadcasting Company voted to terminate the employment of one of its employees for heavy drinking. It directed Bracale, its president and general manager, to fire the employee immediately. Bracale refused to do so. The board of directors terminated Bracale's employment with the company for refusing to obey the board's instructions, even though there were 4 years remaining on his 5-year written contract. Was the board of directors within its rights in firing Bracale? Explain. *Central Alaska Broadcasting v. Bracale,* 637 P.2d 711 (Alaska)

2. An attorney was hired by the plaintiff to handle certain business transactions regarding the plaintiff's real estate. A dispute arose concerning the plaintiff's rights to the land. The attorney settled the dispute out of court without consulting the plaintiff. The plaintiff objected to the terms of the settlement and argued that the attorney had no implied or apparent authority to settle the dispute without consulting the plaintiff. Can an agent's express authority to represent a principal in matters concerning a tract of real estate imply the creation of the authority to settle any claims the principal has regarding that tract? Does the other party in the negotiation have the right to rely on the apparent authority of the agent to negotiate and settle the claim? *Ottawa County Commissioners v. Mitchell,* 478 N.E.2d 1024 (Ohio)

3. Acting in his capacity as a plant supervisor for the Lone Star Steel Company, Floyd Currey gave Shorty Jones a disciplinary pink slip. Upset, Jones followed Currey home and attacked him. Currey defended himself and, in the process, injured Jones, who then threatened to sue Currey. Currey immediately reported the incident to his supervisor and to the plant employee relations manager, who called in the plant attorney, Tarbutton, who interviewed Currey at length. When

Currey was sued, Tarbutton told him not to involve Lone Star. He promised Currey that Lone Star would pay all legal fees. When Lone Star refused to honor that promise and pay Currey's $3,675 bill, Currey sued the company. Currey argued that Tarbutton had apparent authority to make the promise of legal fees because the plant management had told all employees that Tarbutton was the plant attorney, empowered to deal with all legal matters. Lone Star management argued that they had never communicated to employees that Tarbutton had the power to promise payment of legal fees. Is Lone Star correct? *Currey v. Lone Star Steel Co.,* 676 S.W.2d 205 (Texas)

4. Michael Free, a geologist, was hired by Larry Milner, an attorney in the firm of Smith, Emerick, Milner and Colquhoun. Free was to restake some disputed mining claims allegedly owned by Milner's client, Wilma Helric. Free was told by Milner that Helric was the client. However, Milner also told Free to send Milner's firm the bill. When Free tried unsuccessfully to collect his fee directly from the law firm, Milner argued that since Helric was a disclosed principal, the law firm, as agent, had no liability to Free. In answer to this, Free argued that the law firm had assumed liability by indicating they would receive the bill. Is Free correct? *Free v. Helric,* 688 P.2d 117 (Oregon)

5. Marie Price orally authorized her nephew, Price Normile, to buy certain government bonds for her. The bonds were to be used to pay her estate taxes after her death. Soon thereafter, Price suffered a stroke. While she was in a coma, Normile purchased the bonds. After Price died, Normile tried to give the bonds to the government to pay for Price's estate taxes. The government refused to take the bonds, claiming that Price's comatose condition was a permanent incapacity that terminated Normile's agency. Normile claimed that Price's coma was a temporary condition that did not terminate the agency. He based this claim on expert medical testimony, which indicated that up until her death it was possible that Price could have recovered. Is Normile correct? *United States v. Will Price,* 514 F. Supp. 477 (Iowa)

Chapter 22

EMPLOYMENT CONTRACTS AND MINORS AND EMPLOYMENT

Scene: On his way home from the appliance store, Adam Cole meets his friend Eddie.

Eddie: Say, you really look down in the dumps. Is anything wrong?

Adam: I just got fired.

Eddie: Fired! I didn't even know you had a job.

Adam: I was working for Mr. Phelps in the appliance store.

Eddie: No kidding. Why'd he fire you?

Adam: He said he couldn't use me any more because he had to hire his nephew.

Eddie: That's too bad.

Adam: Yeah, especially since his employee handbook promises that no one who gets good evaluations would ever be fired.

Eddie: Did you get good evaluations?

Adam: The best. I only made one mistake all year.

Eddie: What was that?

Adam: I bought some VCRs I shouldn't have. Mr. Phelps had a good reason to fire me that time.

Eddie: You were fired before?

Adam: Yes. But he rehired me. I got his money back. In fact, he even gave me a raise for being so clever. After that, I followed all the rules in his employment handbook, but he still fired me.

Eddie: Too bad you don't have a union there.

Adam: What good would a union do?

Eddie: A union would make sure you had some sort of contract that would say you had a job for life.

Adam: Mr. Phelps would never go for a union.

Eddie: How do you know that?

Adam: I just know. He's real careful about who he hires and what he puts in their contracts. In fact, I've heard he's put some real crazy things in some of his workers' contracts.

Eddie: Like what?

Adam: Well, he made his bookkeeper sign a contract that said if he ever left Mr. Phelps's appliance store he would never work as a bookkeeper again anywhere in the state.

Eddie: That doesn't seem fair.

Adam: I know, but I guess he can do it.

Eddie: Well, maybe he can, but I still think it's terrible.

Adam: Yeah. Terrible for the bookkeeper and terrible for me.

Eddie: I'm awfully sorry you lost your job. You must be really upset after going through all that trouble to get a work permit.

Adam: Work permit?

Eddie: Sure, a work permit. You got a work permit at school, didn't you?

Adam: No.

Eddie: You're not 18 yet, are you?

Adam: No.

Eddie: Then you need a work permit to work.

Adam: No kidding.

Eddie: It's the truth.

Adam: Well, maybe it's a good thing I got fired after all.

LEGAL ISSUES

1. Does a statement in an employee handbook about hiring and firing bind an employer?
2. Do agreements between employers and unions guarantee employees employment for life?
3. Can an employer restrict the employment of a former employee after that employee has left his job?
4. Do minors always need work permits before they can get jobs?

THE SPIRIT OF THE LAW

As we have noted before, not all agents are employees, and not all employees are agents. Agents who do not receive compensation for their work are gratuitous agents and not employees. Those agents who do get paid, whether by salary, commission, or hourly wage, and who work under someone else's control are employees. If a person who works for another is compensated but does not have the power to transact business, then that person is an employee but not an agent. Regardless of agency or nonagency status, however, an employment agreement is a contract because each side promises to do something for the other party. The employee promises to work and the employer promises to provide compensation in return. Often in the past, the employer held a position of great power in negotiating the terms of the employment contract. Many employers abused that power at the expense of employees. To combat these abuses, the employees banded together into labor unions. Eventually, the union movement received governmental support through a variety of labor laws. This chapter will examine the changing nature of the employment contract and the evolution of labor laws. It will end with a look at agreements that restrict subsequent employment and labor laws that apply to minors.

THE EMPLOYMENT CONTRACT

Employment contracts can take many forms. An employment contract may be an oral agreement between an employee and an employer or a highly complex and detailed written agreement arrived at after much discussion between union and management. Naturally, contracts involving employment that will last longer than a year must be in writing under the Statute of Frauds. Beyond this requirement, however, many different kinds of contracts are possible. Regardless of whether a contract is oral or written, simple or complex, however, certain rules apply to its enforcement. Today, these rules are undergoing changes. The old doctrine of employment-at-will is gradually being replaced by a new doctrine known as wrongful discharge.

Employment-at-Will

In the past, most jurisdictions in the United States held to the doctrine of **employment-at-will.** This meant that an employer could fire an employee at any time for any reason. In fact, the doctrine went so far as to say that the employer did not even have to give a reason. Obviously, this doctrine gave a great deal of power to employers, who were reluctant to see it watered down in any way. They resisted the labor movement, which helped chip away at the doctrine. Today, those employees who work for businesses and belong to unions are protected by hiring and firing procedures built into their collective bargaining agreements. A **collective bargaining agreement** is a contract negotiated by the employer and the union, covering all issues related to employment. Such agreements will prevent the unfair discharge of employees. The employer will need some legitimate, employment-related reason, or **just cause,** for the release. For example, employees who were habitually late, were frequently absent, and did poor-quality work would be giving an employer just cause for their discharge. An employer could not, however, fire an employee just because he "didn't like his looks."

Generally, collective bargaining contracts also provide a **grievance procedure.** Under a grievance procedure, employees would have the right to appeal any employer's decision they felt violated just cause.

Naturally, even collective bargaining agreements do not guarantee employees lifelong employment. Often economic conditions will force layoffs or plant closings. When such events occur, some or all employees may lose their jobs. Still, most collective bargaining agreements will provide a negotiated procedure under which such layoffs will occur. In this way, employees are at least guaranteed that the layoffs will be handled in as fair a manner as possible, according to a negotiated procedure.

Legal Issue No. 2

However, many employees are not protected by unions and, as a result, do not have collective bargaining agreements or grievance procedures. While some

Under the doctrine of employment-at-will an employer may discharge a worker for any reason, or for no reason at all.
(*Drawing by Handelsman. Copyright © 1986, The New Yorker Magazine, Inc.*)

"*My leaving Wilkins & Jennings was perfectly amicable. They felt that I should be fired, and I agreed.*"

professional and executive employees may be able to negotiate their own contracts, most workers do not have that much power. Consequently, most employees would have no protection were it not for the evolving doctrine of wrongful discharge. While wrongful discharge is a very young doctrine, and while it is not fully developed in most states, it merits our attention because it represents an important trend in the law which may eventually completely replace employment-at-will.

Wrongful Discharge

The doctrine of wrongful discharge is not the opposite of employment-at-will. It does not guarantee lifelong employment regardless of performance. Such a doctrine would be impossible to enforce financially, ethically, and legally. Wrongful discharge, however, does attempt to provide employees with grounds for legal action against employers who discharge them unfairly. The courts have established three standards by which to judge the "wrongfulness" of a discharge, or firing. In general, the term **wrongful discharge** applies to a discharge that violates public policy, violates an implied contract, or violates an implied covenant. (A *covenant* is an agreement which is part of a larger contract.) An employee who is wrongfully discharged may sue the employer and collect damages and, perhaps, even be reinstated.

Public Policy If it can be demonstrated that the firing of an employee violated public policy, the discharged employee can recover compensatory and punitive damages in tort. Upholding **public policy** is a broad legal principle that says that no one should be allowed to do anything that tends to injure the public at large. For example, if an employee is fired for refusing to violate the law, such a discharge would be wrongful. Public policy encourages people to obey the law. Punishing someone for obeying the law would therefore violate public policy.

Note that the employees' rights in such cases do not arise from their contracts. It is the employer's duty not to violate public policy and cause harm or injury to employees or the public. Therefore an employer who causes harm commits a tort. It is on this basis that employees may be entitled to compensatory and sometimes punitive damages.

EXAMPLE 1   Edward Edelmann was ordered by his supervisor to remove the labels from several hundred drums containing poison. The supervisor planned to reuse the drums to ship other chemicals to a buyer. Edelmann refused because he knew removing the labels and reusing the drums would violate regulations set up by the Environmental Protection Agency (EPA). Edelmann was fired. Edelmann sued his employer for wrongful discharge and recovered damages because his employment termination violated public policy.

A discharge that violates public policy does not always involve an employee refusing to violate the law.

EXAMPLE 2   Ella Engels worked as a biochemist for the Toth–Van Meader Chemical Company. Although the FDA had approved a new drug created by Toth–Van Meader, Engels believed she had evidence that the drug was unsafe. She called a press conference during which she expressed her fears about the new drug. Later she was fired. Engels sued Toth–Van Meader for wrongful discharge. She won the suit because terminating an employee for warning the public of a danger violates public policy.

Implied Contract   An **implied contract** is not formally drawn and signed but comes into being through the statements and actions of the parties. Under the doctrine of implied contract, a discharge will be wrongful if the employer has implied that the employee will not be discharged without just cause. To determine whether this implication exists, the court will examine various company documents, including the policy and procedure manual, letters and memos sent to the employee, the employee's evaluation record, and so on. The object of this examination is to determine whether the employer implied that the employment relationship was something other than employment-at-will. If, for example, a company has a detailed evaluation process, and the employee has been consistently rated highly, then the discharged employee may have a good case demonstrating wrongful discharge. The implied contract need not be detailed, however. Even such seemingly neutral statements as "We welcome you as a lifelong member of our team" appearing in a policy manual or an employment offer may be interpreted as creating an implied contract.

Legal Issue No. 1

EXAMPLE 3   Erica Ervine was hired as a bookkeeper for the Karl Harmalian Corporation. Ervine was required to go through a probationary period of 6 months while she trained for the job. When the probationary period ended, Ervine was designated a "permanent employee." Each quarter all permanent employees were evaluated by their supervisors. Ervine always received the highest rating. When a new supervisor took over, he fired Ervine so that he could hire his nephew. Ervine sued the corporation for wrongful discharge. The court held that since Ervine had passed the probationary period, had been designated a permanent employee, and had been rated highly in the evaluation process, an implied contract existed indicating that she would not be terminated without just cause. Since no just cause had been shown for her termination, Ervine had been wrongfully discharged. Consequently, she could recover damages for lost wages and could even be reinstated if she so desired.

Implied Covenant This doctrine holds that in any employment contract there is an **implied covenant** (an implied promise) that the employer will be fair and honest in the treatment of employees. Unlike implied contract, the existence of an implied covenant does not depend upon a statement in a policy manual or a practice of evaluating employees. Rather, an implied covenant exists simply because the employment contract exists. This covenant does *not* guarantee that employees will be discharged only for good cause. In Massachusetts, for instance, an employer could fire an employee without good reason and not violate the implied covenant of fair dealing and honesty. A violation of fair dealing and honesty would have to involve cheating the employee out of some benefit which rightly belonged to the employee under the contract. The classic example of this type of cheating is seen in the case of commission employees (employees who are paid a percentage of their sales in addition to or instead of their regular salary).

EXAMPLE 4 Ella Ernst was to receive a 25 percent commission on all computer sales she made for her employer, the Clarkson Computer Company (CCC). Ernst made a $10,000,000 sale to the federal government. To avoid paying $2,500,000 to Ernst, CCC fired her, despite her record as a terrific salesperson. Ernst sued CCC in its home state of Massachusetts. The Massachusetts court held that CCC had violated an implied covenant of fair dealing and honesty in its contract with Ernst. Therefore Ernst was entitled to her $2,500,000 commission.

In this example, CCC violated the implied covenant because (1) it had no valid reason (good cause) to fire Ernst and (2) it fired her to keep the $2,500,000 legitimately owed to Ernst. If, however, no commission was due and Ernst was fired without good cause, no violation of the implied covenant of honesty and fair dealing would have occurred.

Collective Bargaining Contracts

As mentioned earlier in the chapter, in many industries, employment contracts are negotiated not by individuals but by groups of employees called bargaining units. A bargaining unit is usually a union that is selected by a vote of the employees. The union represents them in working out conditions of employment with their employers. This process, called collective bargaining, is now firmly established as a way of improving working conditions and industrial relations.

Government Control of Collective Bargaining

Many years ago, collective bargaining was held by the courts to be an illegal conspiracy. Attitudes changed, however, and the courts began to see that collective bargaining was a matter to be determined by employers and their employees. As time went on, the government began to encourage collective bar-

Sometimes the collective bargaining process fails to bring agreement with management and a strike results.

gaining. Still later, people came to think that the government should regulate and control the process somewhat.

The first federal law dealing with collective bargaining was the National Labor Relations Act of 1935, sometimes called the Wagner Act. The purpose of this act was to encourage collective bargaining, discourage certain unfair labor practices, and provide federal assistance in obtaining fair bargaining. The **National Labor Relations Board** was established to enforce the provisions of the act.

The Wagner Act also established guidelines for determining which employment concerns are mandatory subjects of collective bargaining. The act states that employees must negotiate on "wages, hours and conditions of employment." Subsequent court decisions have helped interpret what "conditions of employment" might include. Some employment concerns are not within the province of the collective bargaining. For example, business decisions that are at the very heart of an executive's ability to control the company, such as decisions on how to invest corporate funds, would be outside the scope of the collective bargaining process.

EXAMPLE 5 Wilma Durrell, chief executive officer of Collier-Ansen Laboratories, Inc., decided to discontinue a line of over-the-counter capsule medications that had been the subject of tampering. Several tampering incidents had resulted in customer deaths. Unfortunately, the discontinuation caused the shutdown of one of Collier-Ansen's manufacturing plants. The union claimed the decision to close the plant should have been submitted to collective bargaining. The court held that such a decision was clearly within business discretion of the corporate management team.

Many people felt that the Wagner Act gave too great an advantage to the union bargaining unit, and it was amended in 1947 by the Taft-Hartley Act.

This act tried to equalize the power of labor and management. It provided, among other things, for an 80-day "cooling-off" period. Under this provision, the President of the United States could postpone a strike for up to 80 days if the strike would endanger the nation's health or safety. During the 80-day period, federal mediators (referees) could meet with management (the employer) and labor (the employees) to try to end the dispute.

The Taft-Hartley Act made the closed shop illegal. A **closed shop** is a business in which a person must be a union member before being hired. A union shop is allowed under the act. A **union shop** is a business in which a worker must join the union within 30 days after being employed. Under the act, however, each state may pass right-to-work laws if it wishes. Such laws prohibit union shops.

The Wagner Act was amended further in 1959 by the Landrum-Griffin Act. This act was designed to stop corruption within unions. It gives many rights to union members and encourages them to take an active part in union activities.

Campbell Soup Reaches Accord With Union

TOLEDO, Ohio, Feb. 23 (AP) — Agreements signed by the Campbell Soup Company and a farm workers' union will end a labor dispute that dates to 1968, the union's president says.

Baldemar Velasquez, president of the Farm Labor Organizing Committee, based here, said Friday that agreements with Campbell included provisions for wage increases, medical insurance and paid holidays for 550 migrant workers who pick tomatoes and cucumbers.

An official of Campbell also expressed satisfaction with the pact.

The union said Campbell reached agreements earlier in the week with some 150 migrant workers at 20 tomato farms in Ohio and 400 workers on 12 cucumber farms in Michigan. Both agreements, which were signed by growers as well as Campbell and the union, go into effect at the start of the harvest seasons this summer.

The union had been pressing the company, with headquarters in Camden, N.J., since 1968 to support unionization of farm workers and involve the company in three-way contract negotiations with growers in the Middle West.

Collective bargaining agreements are not always reached easily. Sometimes, it takes a great deal of time to hammer out the details. Negotiations for this contract began in 1968 and were not completed until 1986.

1. Identify the collective bargaining unit for the farmers in this story.
2. What issues were involved in the collective bargaining negotiations?
3. Do these issues clearly belong within the Wagner Act's definition of **mandatory bargaining topics**? Defend your answer.
4. List several decisions that could be made by Campbell's executives that would not be proper subjects of negotiation.
5. If Campbell refused to bargain in good faith, to what government agency could the union leaders take their complaint?
6. Suppose the union had demanded a clause in the contract that said no farm workers could be hired by Campbell until they joined the union. Would such a clause be legal? Why or why not?

TABLE 22-1
LABOR LAW DEVELOPMENT

Statute	Purpose
National Labor Relations Act of 1935 (the Wagner Act)	Established the National Labor Relations Board to —Encourage collective bargaining —Discourage certain unfair labor practices —Provide federal assistance in obtaining fair bargaining
Taft-Hartley Act of 1947	Equalized the power of labor and management by —Establishing the 80-day "cooling-off" period —Making closed shops illegal —Allowing "right-to-work" acts
Landrum-Griffin Act of 1959	Designed to stop corruption within unions by —Giving rights to union members —Encouraging workers to participate in unions

Agreements Not to Compete

Some employers worry that workers will learn business secrets, quit, and then go to work for a competitor. To protect themselves, these employers will have their employees enter into restrictive employment covenants. In a **restrictive employment covenant** an employee promises not to work for anyone else in the same field or to open a competing business after leaving his or her current job for a specified number of years within a particular geographical area.

Limits on Restrictive Employment Agreements   Agreements not to compete are not favored by the courts because they tend to violate public policy by depriving people of their livelihoods and by limiting competition. As a result, restrictive employment covenants must be reasonably limited as to the type of work prohibited, the length of time involved in the prohibition, and the extent of the geographic area covered by the prohibition.

Legal Issue No. 3

EXAMPLE 6   Esther Eddington was a loan officer for Fairfax Savings and Loan Association, located on the east side of Cleveland. When Eddington began working for Fairfax, she signed an employment agreement that contained a restrictive employment covenant saying that she could not work in any capacity for another savings and loan association anywhere in the state of Ohio for 10 years after leaving Fairfax. Six months after leaving Fairfax, Eddington became a loan officer for the Sebastian Savings and Loan Association, located in Lakewood, Ohio, a suburb of Cleveland. Fairfax sued Eddington to prevent her from working for Sebastian. The court held the restrictive employment covenant to be unreasonable as to time, geographical area, and type of work. Eddington won the case. Six months was a reasonable length of time to refrain from working for a bank. Any time beyond that would be unreasonable.

Reasonable Protection for Employers   Some employers would suffer unfairly if competing firms managed to obtain inside information on their new products, processes, or inventions. (Such inside information is usually referred to as a **trade secret**.) Imagine a company spending millions of dollars on an industrial process, only to have an engineer quit and take the process to a competitor. While businesses are protected by patents and copyrights, the courts have also held that they can restrict their employees to some degree for further protection.

People employed by firms doing research and development and people who know trade secrets through their jobs may be kept from accepting a job with other firms doing the same work for a reasonable time after the end of their employment. These agreements are considered to be for the public good, since they protect employers who spend time, effort, and money in the development of new ideas. The same reasonable restraints as to geographical area, time, and type of work apply here also.

RESTRICTIVE EMPLOYMENT COVENANT

FOR GOOD CONSIDERATION, and in consideration of my being employed by Fairfax Savings and Loan Association, (Company), I, the undersigned, hereby agree that upon termination of my employment and notwithstanding the cause of termination, I shall not compete with the business of the Company, or its successors or assigns.

The term "not compete" as used in this agreement means that I shall not directly or indirectly work as a loan officer for a savings and loan association (or a business substantially similar to a savings and loan) which is in competition with Fairfax.

This restrictive employment covenant shall extend only for a radius of five miles from the present location of the Company, and shall be in full force and effect for six months, commencing with the date of employment termination.

Signed this seventh day of February, 1986.

Esther Eddington
Employee

This version of Eddington's restrictive employment covenant would be upheld by the court. Note the limitations on activity, location and time. Remember, to be valid, a restrictive employment agreement must be part of a larger agreement. This form would be added to a more complete employment contract.

MINORS AND EM-PLOYMENT

In the early days of the industrial revolution, children were often abused by employers as cheap labor. For example, some mine owners would use children deep in the mines because children could crawl into small cracks and crevices where adults could not go. Even though this work was difficult and dangerous the children were paid ridiculously low wages. The children could not refuse to do the work because jobs were often scarce and hard to keep. To prevent such abuses, laws were enacted to protect children who enter the labor force.

State Legislation

Child labor laws—laws that control the work that children are permitted to do—developed very slowly. In 1842, Massachusetts passed a law limiting the work of children under the age of 12 years to 10 hours per day. In the same year, Connecticut passed a similar law, but these two states were far ahead of their time. By 1880 only a few states had laws limiting the work of children in factories, and only one state had laws limiting the hours for children in "any gainful occupation." By 1930, 44 states had child labor laws dealing with nonmanufacturing occupations. In 1934, the annual Conference on Labor Legislation adopted a set of standards for state child labor legislation, and these standards have had a great influence on child labor laws.

In addition, many states specify certain types of activities that cannot be performed by minors on the job. Such prohibitions include working on or around dangerous machinery. These laws are designed to protect minors who, because of inexperience, might not completely appreciate the dangers involved.

Federal Legislation

The most forward-looking step in federal child labor laws was the passage of the child labor portion of the **Federal Fair Labor Standards Act** of 1938 as updated in 1974. This act prohibits the interstate or foreign trade shipment of any goods produced by factories in which "oppressive child labor" has been used within 30 days of the removal of the goods. The act also prohibits the employment of oppressive child labor in any enterprise engaged in commerce or in the production of goods for commerce. Oppressive child labor is defined in the act as any employment of minors under the age of 16 in any of the jobs covered by the act and the employment of minors under 18 in jobs declared by the Secretary of Labor to be especially dangerous.

Minors between 14 and 16 may be employed in jobs other than those covered by the act, but only if the Secretary of Labor determines that such employment does not interfere with their schooling. There are many exceptions to the minimum wage and maximum hours rules in the Fair Labor Standards Act. They include (1) children working in agriculture after school hours, (2) child actors, (3) children working for their parents in jobs other than manufacturing, and (4) children delivering newspapers.

The greatest contribution of the act probably has been the placing of some control of child labor under a federal agency that can study its operation.

Industry-Education Cooperation

Effective control of child labor requires the help of industry and schools. Laws alone cannot do the whole job. Many industries have their own child labor codes which restrict child labor to an even greater extent than the laws do. Other industries, however, conform only if the law requires them to do so.

Legal Issue No. 4

Education and the child labor problem are closely connected. One of the great evils of child labor is its interference with the education of children. Public schools work hand in hand with the enforcement officers of child labor acts. Work permits, for example, are often issued by the public school system. A **work permit** is a document that allows a minor below a certain age to work. The law varies from state to state regarding the issuance of work permits.

Suggestions for Reducing Legal Risks

1. Keep copies of your offer of employment, your employment manual, and your work evaluations. They may help prove an implied contract or an implied covenant in the case of wrongful discharge.
2. Do not violate the law or neglect your duties even under direct orders from your employer; you will be liable for your crimes. The law will protect you if your employer fires you for not breaking the law.
3. If you join a collective bargaining unit, be an active, responsible member. The employment contract the unit negotiates will bind you as well as your coworkers.
4. Abide by *reasonable* restrictive employment covenants.
5. Obtain a work permit if you are required to by the laws of your state.

Language of the Law

Define or explain each of the following words or phrases:

employment-at-will	public policy	closed shop	child labor laws
collective bargaining agreement	implied contract	union shop	Federal Fair Labor Standards Act
just cause	implied covenant	restrictive employment covenant	work permit
grievance procedure	National Labor Relations Board	trade secret	
wrongful discharge			

Questions for Review

1. What is meant by the doctrine of employment-at-will?
2. What advantages do employees have if they work for a company with a union that has a collective bargaining agreement?
3. What does the doctrine of wrongful discharge attempt to guarantee?
4. What does the doctrine of public policy mean?
5. Explain the difference between implied contract and implied covenant in relation to wrongful discharge.
6. How has the concept of collective bargaining evolved over the past few decades?
7. Are there some industries in your area in which employees are organized and their employment contracts are governed through collective bargaining agreements? If so,

name the collective bargaining unit repre-senting the employees.

8. What three limitations must be included in a legally binding restrictive employment covenant?

9. What exceptions to the Federal Fair Labor Standards Act permit minors between 14 and 16 years of age to work, even though the product of their labors may be sold in interstate commerce?

10. Give an example of a job, other than one described in this chapter, for which a court might enforce a restrictive covenant.

Cases in Point

In each of the following cases, give your decision and state a legal principle that applies to the case:

1. Elliot Mayer was employed as a biochemist at the Rayburn–St. James Pharmaceutical Company. Mayer was ordered by his superior to alter his test results on a new drug named Transgliceral Hydraziamine. Rayburn–St. James needed the FDA's approval to market the compound and thus improve the company's poor financial condition. Mayer refused to alter his test results and was fired as a result. Does Mayer have a case for a suit based on wrongful discharge?

2. Diane Harper was an engineer who worked at the Tyler-Gordon Aircraft Company. Tyler-Gordon developed sophisticated high-level bombers for the U.S. Air Force. Harper was part of an evaluation team which worked on a secret aircraft, the VN-22, and prepared it for a test flight. On the morning of the initial test, Harper believed that high-altitude turbulence might do damage to the bomber and refused to approve the flight. Her supervisor ordered her to OK the test flight. When Harper refused, she was fired. Does Harper have grounds for a suit based on wrongful discharge?

3. Luther McConnell had been an employee of Erin Publishing for 14 years when he was discharged for incompetence. Fourteen years earlier McConnell had passed his probationary period. On passing his probationary period, McConnell received a copy of a standard letter sent to all Erin employees. The letter welcomed McConnell and said, "You'll always have a home at Erin Publishing." All of McConnell's efficiency reports rated him as an outstanding employee. Does McConnell have grounds for a suit based on wrongful discharge?

4. Refer to the skit at the opening of Chapter 22. In your opinion, does Adam Cole have any grounds for a suit based on wrongful discharge? Explain your answer.

5. Suppose that the United States has been victimized by an outbreak of a new flu epidemic. The disease, while not deadly to most people, tends to incapacitate them for a week to 10 days. At the height of the epidemic, the workers at several pharmaceutical companies go on strike. Explain what options, if any, the President of the United States might have in such a situation.

6. Refer to the skit at the opening of Chapter 22. Would the clause in the bookkeeper's contract be enforced by the court? Explain your answer.

7. Edith Strickland, a tax accountant, employed Cindi Weikel as a tax preparer. It was specified in Weikel's employment contract that she would not work as a tax preparer for any competing tax accountant anywhere in town for a period of 10 years after she left Strickland's employ. Do you think the court would uphold this covenant?

8. Pete Malden, 14 years of age, worked on a neighbor's farm after school. Would his work be controlled by the Federal Fair Labor Standards Act?

9. Suppose that Pete Malden's family owned the local steel mill where Pete worked after school. What further information would you need to determine whether the Federal Fair Labor Standards Act applied?

10. Suppose that Pete Malden lived in the city and worked after school hours in his father's grocery store. Would the Federal Fair Labor Standards Act apply to his job?

Cases to Judge

1. When Annunzio Ferraro applied for a job at the Hyatt Regency Milwaukee he signed an application which stated that his employment at the hotel could be terminated at any time. After being hired, Ferraro was asked to read and sign the employee handbook. He did so. The handbook contained a number of provisions related to employee discharge. For instance, it stated that layoffs would be based on seniority. It provided different discharge procedures for different classes of employees. It set up a hierarchy of rule violations that could lead to discharge. Finally, it provided a procedure for discharge that included two warnings and a suspension before actual discharge. When Hyatt fired Ferraro it claimed the job application statement created an employment-at-will situation. Ferraro claimed that the handbook created an implied contract to discharge him only by the procedures contained in the handbook. Is Ferraro correct? *Ferraro v. Koelsch,* 368 N.W.2d 666 (Wisconsin)

2. Orville Fortune worked as a salesman for National Cash Register (NCR). His contract with NCR specifically characterized his relationship with the company as one of "employment-at-will." As a salesman, Fortune was entitled to a commission on any sales made in his territory. The commission was calculated according to the company's system of "bonus credits." Under this system, a salesman received a payment equal to 75 percent of the applicable bonus credits if the sale was made in his territory. He would receive the remaining 25 percent of the credits if the territory was still his at the time of delivery. NCR negotiated a $5 million sale with First National, a firm located in Fortune's territory. The value of the bonus credits amounted to $92,079.99. Fortune was designated as the salesman to be credited with the bonus. After receiving only 75 percent of the money, Fortune was fired. Since Fortune was an "employee-at-will," NCR claimed he could be discharged at any time. Fortune argued that since his firing coincided with the loss of a benefit due under the contract, the discharge violated an "implied covenant" of fair dealing and honesty. Is Fortune correct? *Fortune v. National Cash Register Co.,* 364 N.E.2d 1251 (Massachusetts)

3. Neil Bagge was only 17 when he got a job working on a construction site where dump trucks were in use. State law prevented anyone under 18 from operating any "motor vehicles of any description." Bagge's employer did not hire him to operate a dump truck. However, the employer did assign Bagge to work around and on a dump truck. Would such an assignment violate the state law forbidding minors to operate a motor vehicle on the job? What justification could the state legislature use for passing such a law? *Bagge's Case,* 363 N.E.2d 1321 (Massachusetts)

4. For two years, Cardinal Distributing and Peter Rabbit Farms, owned and operated by John Powell, grew 24 acres of beets, which were harvested by members of the United Farm Workers (UFW). Powell then decided he would no longer grow beets. The union, which acted as the farm workers' collective bargaining unit, was not informed of the decision until after it had been made. More-

over, Powell refused to submit the decision to collective bargaining, claiming it was a decision that lay exclusively within the business judgment of the farm's owner/operator. The UFW filed a complaint with the Agricultural Labor Relations Board, which decided that the decision should be part of the collective bargaining agreement. Powell appealed the decision to the California courts. On appeal, the UFW argued that while Powell had stopped growing beets, he had sublet 61 acres to another farmer, Sam Keosean, who grew beets and delivered those beets to Powell. The union therefore concluded that the decision had an impact on employment in such a way as to make it the proper subject of collective bargaining. Powell argued that he had no control over what Keosean grew. The beets, he said, were simply a rental payment for the acres. Therefore, Powell concluded, the decision was not a proper subject of collective bargaining. Is Powell correct? *Cardinal Distributing Company, Inc. v. Agricultural Labor Relations*, 205 Cal. Rptr. 860 (California)

5. When Donald Mokrynski was hired by the Coolidge Company, a mailing list broker, he signed a restrictive employment covenant in which he agreed not to work in a similar occupation anywhere east of the Mississippi for 2 years after leaving Coolidge. After leaving Coolidge, Mokrynski violated the agreement by opening his own mailing list brokerage. He argued that Coolidge could only restrict him from working as a catalog list broker for which he had been trained. He also argued that 2 years was too long because brokers changed lists every 6 months, and that a territorial limit that covered half the United States was unreasonable. Coolidge argued that they could limit Mokrynski's entire mailing list brokerage because he learned everything from them. The company claimed 2 years was not unreasonable because it would take a great deal of time to train a replacement. Finally, Coolidge argued that the territorial limit was reasonable since they solicited business throughout the entire area. Is Coolidge correct? *Coolidge Company, Inc. v. Mokrynski*, 472 F. Supp. 459 (New York)

Chapter 23

EMPLOYEE PROTECTION AND EQUAL OPPORTUNITY

Scene: Adam Cole has just arrived at home. He meets his sister, Sara.

Adam: Hi, Sara.

Sara: Hi, kid. What's wrong? You look upset about something.

Adam: I got fired.

Sara: What happened?

Adam: Nothing. Mr. Phelps just said he couldn't use me anymore and fired me on the spot.

Sara: Maybe he'll change his mind.

Adam: I doubt it. Mr. Phelps doesn't need much of a reason to fire someone. One time a guy reported that Mr. Phelps was storing some dangerous chemicals in his warehouse. Mr. Phelps fired him, too.

Sara: I didn't know you could do that.

Adam: Sure, a boss can fire anyone he wants.

Sara: No, I mean I didn't know you could report stuff like that. Who do you report it to?

Adam: I don't know. The police, I guess.

Sara: I'd like to find out, because some crazy stuff has been happening at the plant.

Adam: What kind of crazy stuff?

Sara: Well, they're using some outdated equipment that's ready to fall apart. Someday someone's going to get hurt.

Adam: Well, if they get hurt, then they can just sue the boss.

Sara: Maybe, but that's not all. They want to make us work 60 hours a week without paying overtime.

Adam: That's not fair.

Sara: I'll tell you something else that's not fair. Do you remember that new guy I told you about?

Adam: That guy from the west side?

Sara: That's the one. Well, I found out he's getting more money than I get, and we're doing the same job.

Adam: Did you ask your boss why?

Sara: Sure. He said it was because he's a family man.

Adam: Well, then maybe it's okay. At least you've got a job.

Sara: That's true. Say, maybe you should file for unemployment compensation.

Adam: What's that?

Sara: When you're fired, they pay your salary, with no strings attached.

Adam: No kidding.

Sara: Nope. Come on, I'll drop you off at their office on my way to work.

Adam: Will I need a social security number?

Sara: I don't know. Probably.

Adam: Then you better drop me off at the social security office first.

Sara: You mean you don't have a social security number?

Adam: Mr. Phelps said I didn't need one because he paid me in cash.

Sara: I'm beginning to think it was a good thing you got fired from that place.

Adam: Maybe you're right, Sara. Maybe you're right.

LEGAL ISSUES

1. Does the law allow workers to report dangerous or unhealthy conditions? If so, where would a worker go to file such a complaint?
2. Can a worker who is hurt on the job sue the company?
3. Is it against the law to pay females less than males for the same work?
4. Are there laws regulating overtime pay and providing compensation for workers who are laid off?

THE SPIRIT OF THE LAW

The last chapter introduced a number of federal and state laws that deal with the regulation of labor. Labor laws, however, are not limited to protecting the integrity of the employment contract. In the early years of the industrial revolution, the employer was in a position to demand a great deal from his workers for very little in return. The employer was in complete control of the workplace. After workers organized to demand better treatment, the government stepped in, passing laws that regulate employment conditions, provide worker benefits, and guarantee equal employment opportunity.

LAWS REGULATING EMPLOYMENT CONDITIONS

For purposes of discussion, employment conditions can be divided into two areas: the actual physical situation in which the employee must work and the compensation received by the employee. The federal government has stepped into both areas to protect workers.

The Occupational Safety and Health Administration

The **Occupational Safety and Health Administration (OSHA)** was established by the federal government to ensure safe and healthy working conditions for workers throughout the country. Under the Occupational Safety and Health Act, which created OSHA as an agency responsible to the Department of Labor, the government has set up standards that employers must meet.

All employers who own businesses affecting interstate commerce are covered under this statute. One employer not covered is the government, federal, state, or local.

To make certain that employers follow health and safety regulations, OSHA inspects the workplace and tries to make sure no hazards exist. However, OSHA must not be thought of as a police force for labor and industry. Its resources are severely limited, and it cannot conduct many random inspections. Generally, businesses are inspected in response to complaints from employees. Such complaints must be made in writing at a local OSHA office by the employee or someone representing the employee. In addition, OSHA will inspect a business when a death or disaster has occurred. Businesses in high-risk industries are also frequently inspected. Even under these circumstances, OSHA officials must first ask permission from the employer to inspect the plant. If the employer denies permission, the OSHA official must secure a warrant before entering the premises.

Legal Issue No. 1

Under the statute, it is possible for the Secretary of Labor to penalize an employer for violating safety standards. Moreover, OSHA may also ask a federal court to issue an injunction forcing the employer to discontinue the hazardous practice. Naturally, the employer can contest the findings.

EXAMPLE 1 David Selkirk is a bindery worker employed at Merrill Printing, Inc. For several weeks, Selkirk has been working near a hoist that is not operating properly. Selkirk believes the hoist may malfunction and dump tons of equipment on the employees who work beneath it. He files a complaint with OSHA. After the OSHA official leaves the plant, Mr. Merrill finds out Selkirk filed the complaint. Merrill fires Selkirk.

The firing would be illegal. Employers are forbidden to fire a worker for filing a complaint with OSHA. OSHA makes every effort to conceal the identity of workers who file complaints. However, if an employer uncovers the identity of the complainant and then fires him or her for that reason alone, the employer has opened himself to further action by OSHA, including a potential lawsuit.

To help inform people around the country about safer working conditions, OSHA also has education and training programs. Regional offices of OSHA have been established in 52 locations throughout the United States.

Wage Laws

Laws dealing with wages and hours are another example of society's interest in you and your job. The hardships of the Great Depression of the 1930s strengthened the feeling that the government must, in the interest of public health and safety, set minimum standards for wages and working conditions. This led, in 1938, to the passing of the **Federal Fair Labor Standards Act,** also known as the **Wage and Hour Law.**

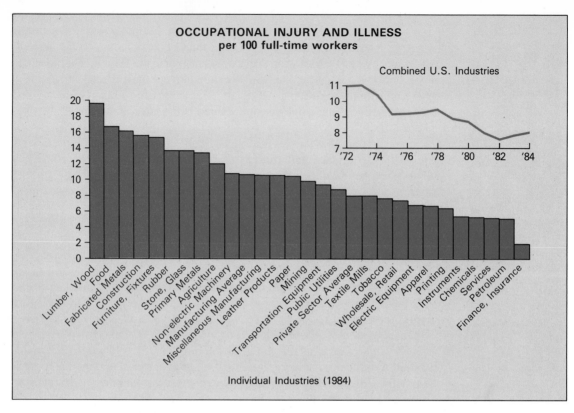

OCCUPATIONAL INJURY AND ILLNESS
per 100 full-time workers

Combined U.S. Industries

Individual Industries (1984)

Occupational injury and illness vary greatly by industry. A worker in a lumber mill is about ten times more likely to be hurt on the job than an insurance clerk is. Since 1972, however, industrial injuries overall have decreased greatly. OSHA regulation and increased awareness of job health and safety contributed to this trend.

Legal Issue No. 4   *Federal Fair Labor Standards Act*   The chief provisions of the Federal Fair Labor Standards Act are (1) a minimum hourly wage rate, (2) time-and-a-half pay for all overtime work in excess of 40 hours per week, and (3) control of child labor (discussed in Chapter 22).

Originally, the federal law covered only workers who produced goods for shipment in interstate commerce. Amendments have broadened the definition of interstate commerce to provide coverage for many more workers, including certain hospital, retail, hotel, restaurant, and school employees. Exempted from the minimum wage and overtime provisions of the act are employees of small local retail or service establishments (gross sales less than $250,000 annually) and employees of certain seasonal amusement or recreational businesses. Also exempted are outside salespeople and executive, administrative, and professional employees.

Legal Issue No. 3   *Equal-Pay Rule*   In 1964, Congress passed the Equal-Pay Act as an amendment to the Fair Labor Standards Act. This amendment, known as the **Equal-Pay Rule,** states that employers engaged in interstate commerce must pay women the same rate of pay as that paid to men holding the same type of job. This law covered the same employees that were subject to the minimum-wage laws mentioned previously. In 1972, the Equal-Pay Rule was extended to executives, administrative and professional employees, and outside salespeople. The Equal-Pay Rule does, however, have its limitations. It requires equal pay for men and women who are performing the same work. It does not require equal pay for "comparable work" (work that is different but requires a similar level of training, skill, and effort).

LAWS PROVIDING WORKER BENEFITS

The law not only protects workers while they are on the job but also helps workers who have retired and those who have been injured or disabled while working. The law even provides assistance to workers who have lost their jobs. The three areas covered here include social security, unemployment compensation, and workers' compensation.

Social Security

Today, **social security** is the nation's basic method for providing income when family earnings stop or are reduced because of retirement, disability, or death. Nine out of ten workers in the United States are earning protection under social security.

The basic idea of social security is a simple one. During working years, employees, their employers, and self-employed people place money into special trust funds. (The social security money is taken directly out of employees' paychecks.) When earnings stop or are reduced because the worker retires, dies, or becomes disabled, monthly cash benefits are paid from these funds to replace part of the lost earnings. Money from these funds also helps to pay the hospital bills of workers and their dependents after the workers reach 65 years of age.

Each person who applies for one is given a social security number. It may be obtained at any time after birth. The same number is used throughout the person's lifetime. The Social Security Administration, the Internal Revenue Service, and certain other federal agencies use social security numbers in their programs. Other organizations may use the number for record keeping purposes, but they cannot see official social security records. Social security records, which contain a lifetime count of a person's earnings, are kept secret.

Employers must keep records that contain, among other things, the social security number of each of their employees. A system has been developed, called the **notify employer procedure**, which helps employers get social security numbers for new employees who do not have numbers. Under the system, employers may ask employees who are about to start work to get a receipt from the social security office to show that they have applied for a number. The employee may begin work, and the employer is notified directly by the Social Security Administration of the employee's number as soon as it is issued.

People of all ages may, under certain circumstances, receive social security payments. Retired workers; disabled workers; spouses and children of retired and disabled workers; spouses, children, and certain other dependents of deceased workers; certain divorced wives of male workers; and certain surviving divorced widows of deceased male workers often receive social security benefits.

Be a Social Security

expert Which of the following statements are true?

1. Social Security provides retirement income to older people.

2. Social Security helps pay health care costs for retired and long-term disabled people.

3. Social Security offers protection for the young worker.

All three statements are *true*.

Many young workers question the value of Social Security. Are they getting their money's worth? They know Social Security pays retirement benefits, but retirement is a lifetime away. What are they getting for their Social Security tax dollars today? If you are a young worker in a job covered by Social Security, you're getting valuable protection that is available today—long before retirement.

But I'm young, single, & healthy

No one—especially a young worker—anticipates a serious illness, accident, or injury.

Unfortunately, the risk of disability hangs over all of us. What would you do if you were to become disabled? With Social Security, you have disability insurance to protect you.

Disability insurance covers you if you become severely disabled and your medical evidence indicates that you cannot work for a year or longer. Monthly payments start after an initial waiting period of 5 full months. Disability benefits are payable anytime before age 65. Your monthly checks continue for as long as you're disabled. Not only that, if you receive disability benefits for 24 months, you're

Social Security benefits are not limited to retirement. Many young people are eligible, too.

Unemployment Compensation

Jobs are not always plentiful. When people have no jobs, they cannot buy goods. When goods are unsold, the factories that make goods shut down, and more people are out of jobs. To overcome this vicious cycle and to provide for the families of people who are out of work, we have **unemployment compensation.** Unemployment compensation is a system of government payments to people who are out of work to provide them with support until they find another job.

Legal Issue No. 4

A section of the Social Security Act provides for a joint federal and state system of unemployment compensation. According to the Federal Unemployment Tax Act, each state operates its own unemployment compensation system, subject to certain conditions made by the federal government. The following are some of the general features of state unemployment compensation systems:

1. They are administered through public employment offices that try to find jobs for the unemployed.
2. Benefits are paid only to those who truly desire work and cannot find it.
3. Workers are disqualified if they refuse suitable work without cause, have been discharged for misconduct, or have quit a job without "good cause."
4. Workers also may be disqualified for a limited period if their unemployment arises out of a strike or lockout. Individual states determine the period of a worker's disqualification.

The amount a worker receives varies from state to state. However, the following fundamental principles are found in almost all state unemployment compensation insurance systems.

1. The benefit is related to the worker's rate of pay.
2. The benefit is related to family need.
3. The benefit is not large enough to remove the incentive to work.

There is an appeal process built into the unemployment compensation system. Employees who believe they have been denied compensation for unjust reasons may contest the decision by filing an appeal.

EXAMPLE 3 David Winston worked as a sales representative for Eyetech, Inc., a firm that functioned as a manufacturers' representative between manufacturers of protective eye gear and local businesses. Winston decided to leave Eyetech and start his own business as an eye gear manufacturers' representative. He gave his 2 weeks' notice. After 1 week, his boss, Fred Baxter, discovered Winston's plan and fired him. When Winston applied for unemployment compensation, he was told he was not qualified for benefits because he had quit his job. Winston appealed the decision, arguing that he had been fired by Mr. Baxter. His appeal was heard and a reversal granted. Winston was entitled to benefits beginning at the date of his firing and continuing for the length of time authorized under the statute or until he obtained another job.

While most appeals are resolved at the first level, as Winston's was, some can end up climbing as high as the state supreme court or even, in rare cases, as high as the U.S. Supreme Court.

Workers' Compensation

Legal Issue No. 2

With the advent of the industrial revolution, employment-related injuries became commonplace, but the law provided little protection for workers who were injured or disabled on the job. The only recourse that injured employees had was to sue their employers.

Unfortunately, the law gave employers an ample arsenal of defenses to use against employees. Employers could, for example, argue that the injured em-

TABLE 23-1
UNEMPLOYMENT COMPENSATION
APPEAL RIGHTS (IN OHIO)

When you file an application for unemployment compensation or a claim for benefits, you will receive written determination(s) of your eligibility. If you disagree with any of these determinations, you have the right to appeal. There are seven levels of appeal:

1. Request to administrator for reconsideration
2. Appeal to the Board of Review
3. Further appeal to the Board of Review
4. Appeal to a Court of Common Pleas
5. Appeal to a Court of Appeals of Ohio
6. Appeal to the Supreme Court of Ohio
7. Appeal to the United States Supreme Court

In Ohio, unemployed workers who feel they have been unjustly disqualified from unemployment compensation have a right to appeal the decision. The system of appeals varies among states. While Ohio provides seven levels of appeal, other states may provide more or fewer.

ployee had assumed the risk of injury when he or she took the job in the first place. Or, if circumstances were right, they could protest that the worker was negligent and had caused the injury. Finally, employers could often escape liability if a fellow employee was responsible for the worker's injury. This last defense is known as the "fellow servant rule."

With all these defenses at their disposal, employers rarely lost suits brought by employees. However, when employers did lose, they lost in a big way. The worker sometimes won damage awards so large that the offending business was placed in severe financial jeopardy.

Faced with this unfair situation, various state legislatures responded by creating their own workers' compensation systems. Under workers' compensation, both sides gave up some rights in exchange for a more systematic and a far more equitable method of settling disputes over worker injuries.

The employee gives up the right to sue the employer, while the employer gives up the right to use the defenses mentioned above. In exchange, the employee receives a guarantee of compensation for injuries, while the employer receives a guarantee that he will not be sued by his employee.

All 50 states now have some form of workers' compensation. A state **workers' compensation** system is an insurance system which makes payments to workers who are injured on the job. Generally, a state workers' compensation system takes one of three forms. One form provides a fund operated only by the state government. In this situation employers pay into a state-controlled fund. When employees suffer injuries, they apply to the state to receive their benefits. In another form of workers' compensation insurance, all companies are required to carry workers' compensation insurance but have the option of contributing to a state fund or purchasing such insurance from a private insurer. In the third system all employers are required to purchase workers' compensation insurance from private insurers.

A few states also allow employees to sue an employer if the injuries result from an intentional tort. Thus, the worker has two sources of recovery, one under workers' compensation and one in litigation. Recently, some courts have expanded the definition of intentional tort. One court, in Ohio, for instance, has defined intentional tort as "an act committed with the knowledge that such injury is substantially certain to occur." This means more workers than ever before have the option of recovering workers' compensation and also suing in tort.

EXAMPLE 4 Sherry Calloway worked as an engineer at a nuclear power plant run by the Volker Electric Power Corporation. Calloway suspected that the nuclear reactor was leaking dangerously high levels of radiation. She complained to her supervisor, who repeatedly told her that everything was safe. Calloway and several other workers developed radiation poisoning. Evidence indicated that the managers of Volker Electric knew of this leak and did nothing to warn or protect the employees. A few states would hold this to be intentional conduct and would allow the employees to recover workers' compensation and to sue in tort. However, since no specific intent to injure was involved, most states would not characterize this as an intentional tort. They would, instead, label it negligence. If the action is labeled negligence, the injured employees could recover workers' compensation but could not sue the employer in tort.

Often, even when workers are allowed to sue in tort, their awards are offset by an amount received under workers' compensation. A few states even have a special intentional tort fund from which such awards are paid. This system preserves the benefits bestowed by workers' compensation on both employers and employees. The worker can sue in tort to recover extra compensation for an intentional wrong. Employers are protected from huge awards because they have already contributed to the workers' compensation fund.

LAWS REGULATING EMPLOYMENT OPPORTUNITIES

Over the last three decades, government has also attempted to make the law as fair as possible in the area of employment opportunities. **Title VII** of the Civil Rights Act of 1964 prohibits employment discrimination based on sex, race, color, religion, or national origin. In general, all employers of 15 or more people are covered by the act. Employees who believe they have been discriminated against can file complaints with the **Equal Employment Opportunity Commission (EEOC).** Under Title VII, discrimination can be committed in one of two ways: disparate treatment or disparate impact.

Disparate Treatment

The most obvious and direct way that businesses discriminate is through **disparate treatment.** Under disparate treatment, the employer intentionally discriminates against an individual or a group belonging to one of the protected categories. For example, an employer who holds a general policy that declares "We do not hire women engineers" would be practicing discrimination through disparate treatment.

May a police force require that all officers be 5′8″ or taller? Under what aspect of Title VII could such a rule be challenged?

Employers have a defense against a challenge of disparate treatment, called *business necessity*. If the employer can show that the qualification is a business necessity, the discrimination may be justified. For example, a requirement that all applicants for a job modeling women's bathing suits be female would be a business necessity. There is an exception to this general rule. A business necessity defense can never be used to justify deliberate discrimination based on race.

Disparate Impact

Disparate impact is a more subtle type of discrimination. In contrast to disparate treatment, disparate impact is unintentional. Discrimination through **disparate impact** occurs when an employer has a policy which on the surface seems neutral but which has a disparate or unequal impact on members of one or more of the protected groups. For instance, an employer who hires only people over 6 feet tall might be guilty of unintentional discrimination under the doctrine of disparate impact. Although the criterion might seem neutral on the surface, it would exclude women disproportionately and would thus have an unfair impact on their employment opportunities.

Employers have a defense against a charge of disparate impact that is known as *bona fide occupational qualification (BFOQ)*. If the employer can show that a qualification is required to perform the job, then it may be permitted despite its disparate impact on one or more of the protected groups. For example, a requirement that all job applicants have a Ph.D. in nuclear physics for a job as a nuclear research scientist might have a disparate impact on one or more of the protected groups. However, if the Ph.D. is a BFOQ, it will be allowed.

Recently some people have argued that Title VII should be used to make up for some shortcomings in the Equal-Pay Rule, especially in the area of comparable work. **Comparable work** is work that requires skill, training, and effort of a level similar to those required by another job. For instance, one might argue that a registered nurse does work comparable to that of an engineer.

The Equal-Pay Rule requires equal pay for equal work but does not require equal pay for comparable work. Title VII, however, makes no such distinction. In fact, Title VII is supposed to eliminate *all* unjustifiable discrimination in the workplace. Consequently, some people make a strong case when they argue that Title VII outlaws any practice which would allow different pay for two jobs that are comparable in worth. The courts have rejected this argument, however.

EXAMPLE 5 A union representing state workers sued the state of Washington, claiming that its policy of paying workers in traditionally "male" jobs 20 percent more than workers in traditionally "female" jobs violated Title VII of the Civil Rights Act. The women worked as secretaries and clerical workers. The men were primarily maintenance and sanitation workers. The union argued that the work of the women was "comparable" to the work of the men. Therefore, the union concluded, the women should be paid at the same rate as the men. The court, however, rejected the union's comparable-worth arguments. The court found no disparate treatment, since disparate treatment requires intent, and no intent to discriminate was demonstrated here. The court found no disparate impact, since the wages were not set by an isolated employment decision. Rather, the wages resulted from a long, complex analysis which took into consideration a multitude of factors including budget proposals, statutory enactments, executive actions, agency hearings, administration decisions, and marketing surveys.

Other Types of Employment Discrimination

In recent years, the government has recognized that discrimination in employment can take place beyond the protected categories mentioned above. This realization prompted the passage of two congressional acts, the Age Discrimination in Employment Act and the Rehabilitation Act.

Age Discrimination The **Age Discrimination in Employment Act** prohibits employment agencies, employers of 20 or more employees, and labor unions of more than 25 members from discriminating on the basis of age. This act forbids discrimination against any person between the ages of 40 and 70 in hiring, firing, promotion, or other aspects of employment. Of course, this law does not apply if age is a true job qualification, as in the modeling of junior miss fashions.

Discrimination Against the Handicapped Employers that participate in government contracts must take affirmative action to employ and promote qualified handicapped persons. This is required by the **Rehabilitation Act of 1973**. Instead of requiring companies to set up goals and timetables, the act seeks to have employers meet the individual needs of handicapped persons.

Suggestions for Reducing Legal Risks

1. As an employee you have the right to file a complaint with OSHA if you know of unsafe conditions where you work. Your employer cannot retaliate against you if you do file such a complaint.
2. Many jobs are covered by the Federal Fair Labor Standards Act, which provides for a minimum hourly wage rate, time-and-a-half for all overtime work in excess of 40 hours per week, and equal pay for men and women doing the same work.
3. Social security benefits of one form or another may be available to you before retirement.
4. If you lose your job, you may be eligible for unemployment compensation.
5. If you are injured on the job, you are entitled to be compensated for your injuries under your state's workers' compensation program, whatever form that system may take.

6. Title VII of the Civil Rights Act of 1964 prohibits employment discrimination based on sex, race, color, or national origin.
7. Federal law also forbids age discrimination (involving workers between 40 and 70) and discrimination against the handicapped.

Language of the Law

Define or explain each of the following words or phrases:

Occupational Safety and Health Administration (OSHA)
Federal Fair Labor Standards Act
Wage and Hour Law

Equal-Pay Rule
social security
notify employer procedure
unemployment compensation

workers' compensation
Title VII
Equal Employment Opportunity Commission (EEOC)

disparate treatment
disparate impact
comparable work
Age Discrimination in Employment Act
Rehabilitation Act of 1973

Questions for Review

1. Generally, what businesses receive inspection visits from OSHA?
2. What happens if an employer refuses to allow an OSHA official to enter?
3. What are the chief provisions of the Federal Fair Labor Standards Act?
4. What is the purpose of the Equal-Pay Rule?
5. What is the purpose of the Social Security Act?
6. How are a worker's benefits determined under unemployment insurance?
7. What rights do employers and employees give up under workers' compensation laws?
8. Explain the three forms of state workers' compensation insurance systems.
9. What are the two types of discrimination outlawed under Title VII of the Civil Rights Act of 1964?
10. Identify the organizations which are regulated by the Age Discrimination Act. What workers are protected by this act?

Cases in Point

In each of the following cases, give your decision and state a legal principle that applies to the case:

1. Wilma McAtee was chief executive officer of Nortex International, a chemical engineering corporation that specialized in the development of high-grade rocket fuel. Douglas Sweeney, a Nortex engineer, believed that several operations in the main plant were endangering workers. Sweeney filed a detailed complaint with OSHA. When an OSHA official arrived at the plant, McAtee refused to allow him to enter. Was McAtee within her rights? What would happen next?

2. McAtee later learned that Sweeney was the one who filed the complaint with OSHA. McAtee called Sweeney into her office and fired him for "blowing the whistle" on Nortex. Is McAtee within her rights in discharging Sweeney? Explain.

3. In January, Lydia Truell was hired by Oxotech Petroleum as a research scientist at a salary of $45,000 per year. In March, Oxotech hired Gary Carr to do essentially

the same job Truell did. In fact, the two of them had very similar experience and worked side by side. One day Truell discovered that Carr had been hired by Oxotech at a starting salary of $52,000. Does the law have any provisions covering this sort of inequity?

4. Lou Hines was employed by a small neighborhood grocery store as a clerk. He said that the amount of his wages should be determined by the Fair Labor Standards Act. Was he correct? Explain your answer.

5. Alec Bennett was employed as a night watchman for the Northbrook Pipe Company. He decided after only 2 weeks of work that he did not like the working conditions at Northbrook, so he gave his boss 2 weeks' notice and quit. Although the local newspaper had a daily listing of no less than 12 security job openings, Bennett decided he needed a vacation and did not apply for any of these jobs. Instead, Bennett went to his local state unemployment office and applied for unemployment compensation. Is Bennett eligible for unemployment compensation? Explain your answer.

6. Linda McGuire worked for the Lomas-Perrin Aircraft Corporation as a construction worker. One day she was working on a scaffold that had not been properly positioned by her fellow worker, Edwin Malin. As a result of Malin's negligence, McGuire fell and broke her leg. She had not been wearing the required safety harness at the time of the incident, but she claimed that she could not wear the harness and reach the area that needed repair. Under common-law rules, before workers' compensation laws, what would McGuire's legal recourse have been?

7. Looking back at the last question, assume that McGuire sued her employer. What arguments under common law could McGuire's employer, Lomas-Perrin, have raised in its defense?

8. Donna Lansing applied for a job as an accountant with the Eurograef Financial Network. She was told that Eurograef had a strict policy that women were hired as secretaries only. The company never hired women as either accountants or executives. If Lansing files a complaint with the EEOC, which of the two discrimination theories would form the basis of her claim? Explain.

9. Franklin Vasques was employed as a maintenance worker for New Jersey Air. He wanted to apply to become a flight attendant but was discouraged from doing so by a supervisor who told him that the company only hired people who had taken home economics classes in high school or who had been members of Future Stewardesses of America. If Vasques files a complaint with the EEOC, which of the two theories of discrimination would form the basis of his claim? Explain.

10. Robert Patton worked as an accountant for the Marquois-Hansen Financial Corporation. At 55, Patton developed problems with his eyes which required him to use a special lamp installed at his desk and to take frequent breaks. The condition also required his relocation to an office with a window. Upon learning of the changes that would have to be made, Patton's supervisor fired him and hired a younger person. What law or laws might protect Patton in this situation? Explain.

Cases to Judge

1. Pamela White was hired by Inside Radio/Radio Only, Inc. as a newsletter editor. The company told her that she would have to work about 10 hours overtime per week once in a while. The original estimate of her total work week was 50 hours. After several assistants quit, White was forced to put in more than 80 hours per week. This went on for 4

months. During that time, she had to do the work of the assistants and had to create the newsletter manually. She was forced to work long hours and had to skip meals. She ended up with nutritional problems, a mild case of depression, and a more severe case of nervous exhaustion. Eventually, White quit her job and filed for unemployment compensation. Should she receive benefits? Explain. *Inside Radio/Radio Only, Inc. v. Board of Review,* 498 A.2d 793 (New Jersey)

2. Jim Foster was employed by the Xerox Corporation for 12 years. Part of his duties required him to work around machinery containing large amounts of arsenic. Although executives at Xerox knew about the effects of working around arsenic, Foster was not advised of these dangers. Eventually, Foster developed arsenic poisoning. Although he did not recognize the disease, he did tell his supervisor about his symptoms. No one in the company revealed to Foster that his symptoms might have resulted from the arsenic. Xerox also withheld the fact that the longer he worked around the arsenic, the worse the disease would become. Eventually Foster's physician diagnosed his illness. Can Foster recover workers' compensation and sue Xerox in tort? *Foster v. Xerox Corporation,* 219 Cal. Rptr. 485 (California)

3. As part of its state retirement system, the state of Wyoming required state employees who were 65 years old to apply for yearly extensions of their employment. Six state workers, Anderson, Bosshardt, Chessbrough, Kautholz, Nelson, and Ventling, filed complaints with the EEOC. Do the state workers have a cause of action against Wyoming? Should the state workers win their case? *EEOC v. The Wyoming Retirement System,* 771 F.2d 1425 (10th Circuit)

4. Prior to the passage of the Civil Rights Act of 1964, the Duke Power Company had practiced overt discrimination against blacks by preventing them from being hired in any way except as common laborers. After passage of the act, the company instituted two aptitude tests. In order to be hired into any department but labor and in order to be promoted out of the labor department, employees had to score at a certain level. Thirteen black employees denied promotion because of low test results argued that the tests should be discontinued as discriminatory because (1) they bore no direct relationship to the work done in the other departments and (2) they had a disparate impact on blacks. The company argued that the tests were neutral and were therefore not forbidden under the act, and that it had no intent to discriminate and should therefore not be held in violation of the act. Is the company correct? *Griggs v. Duke Power Co.,* 91 S.Ct. 849 (United States)

5. When Dorothy Francoeur found out she was being paid about $6,000 less than her male predecessor, Edward Russin, had been, she filed a complaint with the EEOC alleging a violation of the Equal-Pay Act. Her employer, Corroon and Black Co., argued that Francoeur's duties as personnel manager and office administrator were substantially different from Russin's duties as office manager. Russin had been primarily responsible for equipment, furniture, and office relocation, while Francoeur was responsible for personnel matters such as hiring, firing, testing, and training. The company did, however, admit that some duties overlapped. Francoeur argued that this overlap of duties and the fact that she had been hired as Russin's replacement entitled her to the same salary Russin had received. Is Francoeur correct? *Francoeur v. Corroon and Black Co.,* 552 F. Supp. 403 (New York)

CASE TO DISCUSS

Jones v. VIP Development Co.
472 N.E.2d 1046 (Ohio)

This case comprised three separate cases that were consolidated on appeal. We will consider two of these cases. Both involved injured workers who collected workers' compensation and then sued their employers for intentional torts.

In the first case, John Jones and Douglas Pridemore, who were employees of VIP Development Co., received injuries while working at a VIP construction site. Jones and Pridemore were working on a sewer line when the boom of an excavator they were operating touched a power line. The resulting surge of electricity severely injured both men. Jones and Pridemore argued that VIP knew about the power lines but made no effort to remedy the situation or to warn them of the danger. The plaintiffs claimed that this lack of action amounted to intentional conduct, making VIP liable.

In the second case, several employees of Snow Metal Products became sick because of toxic fumes in the air at the plant. When the employees complained to management, they got no results. Gradually their conditions worsened. Again they complained to management, who assured them that the plant was safe. Finally, when a number of the workers became sick on the job, the plant was shut down. Part of the plant was never reopened because of the toxic damage to the area. The workers collected workers' compensation but then sued Snow Metal in tort, alleging intentional conduct.

THE TRIAL

Jones and Pridemore never made it to trial. The lower court held that, as a matter of law, once the employees had collected workers' compensation, they could not sue their employers even for an intentional tort. The Snow Metal Products employees were successful at the trial level. They were awarded $43,000 in compensatory damages and $5,000 in punitive damages. However, the appeals court reversed the decision. This appellate court held, however, that if the employees could have proven intent, they could have maintained their suit. Both cases were appealed to the Ohio State Supreme Court.

ARGUMENTS ON APPEAL

Two issues were presented on appeal. The first issue was whether the conduct of the employers was intentional. The employers argued that an intentional tort requires a specific intent to injure. From their point of view, neither a failure to warn (in Jones) nor the failure to notify the employees of a chemical danger (in Snow Metal Products) could be construed as an intent to hurt someone. If anything, they claimed, the conduct was negligent, nothing more.

The employees all argued that an intentional tort does not require a specific intent to injure. Rather, an intentional tort is committed if the *"actor proceeds despite a perceived threat of harm to others which is substantially certain, not merely likely, to occur."* The failure to warn about the power lines or the toxicity in the plant both involved a substantial certainty of harm.

The second issue was whether workers who had already received workers' compensation should be allowed to recover additional damages in a tort suit. The employers argued that such a stand destroys the foundation of the Workers' Compensation System. The system, they argued, is based on a compromise in which workers give up the right to sue in exchange for the certainty of receiving some benefits. By allowing workers to receive both benefits and damages in a tort suit, the court would be encouraging workers to label every action that injures them as "intentional." The employers contended that this would create a glut of valueless cases and undermine the system.

The employees argued that employers must be held accountable for intentional torts. Otherwise what is to stop them from committing intentional misdeeds? For example, what would prevent an employer from lying about dangerous fumes, if it can never be sued? This would be a "green light" to employers, allowing a flood of intentional misdeeds.

Note: Jones v. VIP was decided in favor of the employees. Two years later, the state legislature in Ohio passed a law to counteract the effects of that decision. The new statute allows employees who have been intentionally injured by their employers to sue in tort. However, any award won by an employee is offset by the amount the employee received under worker's compensation. In addition, the amount of any award is determined not by the court but by the Industrial Commission which administers worker's compensation in Ohio. Moreover, a one million dollar limit was placed on any award. In any event, the award is not paid by the employer, but by a new intentional tort fund. This fund also pays attorneys' fees and court costs for employers. Finally, the statute redefines intentional tort. The statute uses the employees' suggested definition as noted in the italics above. However, the legislature redefined "substantially certain" to mean acting with "deliberate intent to cause an employee to suffer injury."

QUESTIONS FOR DISCUSSION

1. Review intentional torts and negligence in Chapter 4. Which of the intentional tort definitions above seem to be most accurate?
2. Should the workers be forced to choose between worker's compensation or a lawsuit?
3. Is it fair to offset a damage award by the amount received under worker's compensation? Justify this policy.
4. Is it fair to set up a fund that pays damage awards, fees, and costs for employers who commit intentional torts? Explain.
5. Will the new Ohio law cause an increase in intentional misconduct and worker injuries?
6. What are some strong economic arguments for the legislature to make this new law?

CASE TO BRIEF

After reading How to Write a Case Brief on page 78, and examining the Sample Brief on page 80, write a brief of the following case:

Valley View Cattle Company v. Iowa Beef Processors, Inc.
548 F.2d 1219 (5th Circuit)

Valley View Cattle Company conducted negotiations in Hereford, Texas, with Louie Heller for the sale of 259 head of cattle. Heller took possession of the cattle on January 29 and immediately made arrangements to have them shipped to the Iowa Beef Processors' plant in Emporia, Kansas, where they arrived the next day. On January 30, after receiving the cattle, IBP advanced approximately 90% of the estimated dressed price to Heller. On January 31, after the cattle had been slaughtered, IBP sent Heller a check for the balance due him. Valley View billed Heller for the purchase price but his checks were not honored. On February 12 some of Heller's creditors filed an involuntary bankruptcy petition against him, and later he was [judged] bankrupt.

Valley View filed this diversity suit against IBP in the Northern District of Texas seeking to recover the value of the 259 head of cattle . . . .

All issues were resolved in favor of Valley View, and the trial court entered a $113,649.41 judgment for Valley View . . . . IBP appeals. We affirm on the grounds that the trial court did not abuse its discretion in denying IBP's motion for new trial and that there was sufficient evidence in support of the jury's finding that Heller purchased the cattle in question as the agent of IBP.

Under Texas law, "[t]he relation of agency is a consensual relation existing between two persons, by virtue of which one of them is to act for and in behalf of the other and subject to his control." The relationship of agent and principal is created either by express or implied contract or by operation of law. Thus, the existence of an agency relationship may be implied from the conduct of the parties.

On this appeal IBP argues that there was insufficient evidence from which a consensual agency arrangement between it and Heller can be inferred and that, to the contrary, the evidence demonstrates conclusively that Heller was an independent dealer buying for his own account and dealt with Valley View in that capacity. Valley View points to evidence which circumstantially tends to show that Heller was not an independent dealer but was an order buyer acting as the agent of IBP and vested with actual or implied authority. Therefore, we review the evidence tending to show the existence of agency, ...

(1) Heller was IBP's only regular buyer in the South Plains area of west Texas. IBP had at least some control over the choice of area in which Heller could buy cattle to be shipped to IBP.

(2) It was understood between Heller and IBP what kind of cattle IBP was interested in. Heller called IBP almost every day to find what IBP would pay for dressed cattle and how many head IBP wanted. Thus, IBP controlled size, quality and quantity purchased by Heller . . . .

(3) Although no evidence of the exact volume of Heller's dealings with IBP was introduced, . . . it is apparent that these dealings constituted a large percentage of Heller's total business. . . .

(4) IBP regularly advanced to Heller, at his request, a large portion of the . . . price of the cattle, and in [this case] advanced 90%. . . .

(5) Dealers normally pay cattle sellers within 48 hours after the cattle are weighed. Heller customarily paid his sellers by check written on the weekend for purchases made during the week.

(6) Heller consistently paid "top dollar" among cattle buyers in the South Plains and helped to hold the market price up. Inferentially, an independent dealer buying for his own account could not regularly do this and survive.

(7) Heller leased railroad cars for the sole purpose of shipping cattle to IBP's Emporia, Kansas, plant. Plaintiff's expert witness, Holly Toler, stated this practice was consistent with his conception of an order buyer.

(8) IBP's daily conversations with its packer buyers were similar to its instructions to Heller.

(9) Heller billed IBP with invoices on which, below his name, was printed "LIVESTOCK DEALER" and "ORDER BUYER."

(10) During a price freeze in 1973, IBP was unable to sell to its customers and make a suitable margin. At IBP's instruction . . . Heller made an unusually large purchase of cattle and shipped them directly to IBP customers in his name.

(11) Though not in connection with the instant transaction, Heller had told Cox (owner of Valley View) and Moss (operator of the feed lot . . .) that he bought cattle for IBP.

There is, on the other hand, considerable evidence which tends to prove that Heller dealt with Valley View as an independent dealer.

(a) The cattle bought by Heller from Valley View . . . were invoiced to him, the feed lot's scale tickets showing weight of the animals named him as buyer, and he paid with his own checks.

(b) At times Valley View had sold cattle to IBP's salaried packer-buyers, and these had been paid for by IBP checks.

(c) On Valley View's books the transaction was shown in Heller's name.

(d) The cattle were shipped by rail, and the bill of lading showed Heller as shipper. No documents sent with the cattle showed IBP where they had been bought.

(e) On February 20, Valley View made a book entry charging off Heller's bad checks as "Bad debt—James Heller."

(f) Valley View claimed against Heller's Packers & Stockyards Act surety bond, asserting that he was the purchaser of the cattle, and against Heller's bankrupt estate, and partially recovered from both. . . .

The body of evidence gravitates in two different directions. It tends to establish that, with respect to his purchases of cattle destined for IBP, Heller gave the appearance of an independent dealer and Valley View dealt with him as though he were an independent dealer. But this evidence does not obviate the possibility that, by arrangement express or implied between IBP and Heller, Heller was actually authorized to serve as IBP's agent in buying cattle. The special arrangements between them, and the other evidence, some of which we have outlined, permitted a jury to draw that inference. . . .

The most persuasive evidence to us is the combination of advances by IBP and delayed payments by Heller (Heller often paid later than the period prescribed by the Packers & Stockyards Act), so that in effect cattle bought by Heller were being paid for by IBP's funds channeled through Heller's bank account. The arrangement permitted Heller to buy in greater quantities than a dealer operating in the usual manner would have been able to buy. Advances to Heller averaged around $7,000,000 for a month or slightly more than a month. There was evidence that the packing industry as a whole does not engage in the practice of making advances. Also the arrangement between IBP and Heller gave IBP considerable actual control over Heller's activities . . . .

As jurors we might have reached a different verdict. But we do not sit a thirteenth juror. The evidence was sufficient to take the case to the jury on actual and implied authority, the jury has decided that, and there it must end. We need not discuss the other issues.

AFFIRMED.

TRIAL PROCEDURES

BEGINNING THE TRIAL— SELECTING THE JURY

If a case cannot be settled after the pretrial discovery phase, the clerk of the court places the case on the calendar, or court docket, for trial. The *court docket* is simply a list of the cases which are to be tried, in the order in which they are to be tried.

On the day set for trial, the judge calls the court to order and, in a jury trial, has a jury drawn from a pool of jurors made up of citizens who have been called to serve as jurors. The jury's job is to determine the facts of the case and to apply the law to those facts. Obviously, the jury's role is critical to the outcome of the trial.

To ensure a fair trial, jurors should not be biased or prejudiced. Jurors are biased if they would tend to favor either the plaintiff or the defendant. They are prejudiced if they would tend to decide the outcome of the case before considering the evidence. A method has been built into the jury selection process to help select jurors who are not biased or prejudiced. The method involves the questioning of jurors before the trial begins. The judge supervises the attorneys' questioning of each juror selected from the pool. The judge and the attorneys try to determine the following:

1. Are the jurors related to any party in the lawsuit?
2. Do the jurors have any interest in the case?
3. Have the jurors expressed or formed an opinion in the case?
4. Do the jurors have any bias or prejudice that would affect their ability to evaluate the facts?

Determining whether a juror will be biased or prejudiced is not as easy as it sounds. Attorneys must not only think about such things as the juror's background, education, experience, relationships, attitudes, and employment, but must also consider how the jurors will relate to one another as a group.

If an attorney can present a good reason indicating that a potential juror would be biased or prejudiced, he or she can challenge the juror, that is, ask the court to dismiss that juror from the panel. This is called a *challenge for cause*. There is no limit to the number of challenges for cause that each attorney may have. Sometimes attorneys cannot show cause but still want certain jurors dismissed from the jury. They may do this by exercising their *peremptory challenges*. These are challenges to jurors without any reasons given. Unlike challenges for cause, the number of peremptory challenges is limited. Some states permit as few as two for each party; others allow as many as six. Federal courts allow three peremptory challenges for each party.

A new person is selected (by lot) from the jury pool to take the place of each juror who is challenged. Finally, by agreement or when all challenges are exhausted, the jury selection process is complete, and the trial is ready to begin.

THE CASE OF GRAZIO v. WILLIAMSON (continued from page 269)

The clerk of the court has called the case for trial, and jurors have been selected by lot from the jury pool to hear the case. You will remember that the case involves a teenage driver who swerved to avoid hitting a squirrel, damaging a parked car. The defendant's attorney attempts to determine if one particular juror dislikes animals or is prejudiced towards teenage drivers by asking the following questions:

Q. Mrs. Schmidt, what would you say is the cause of most automobile accidents?
A. I would say that teenage drivers cause most accidents.

Q. Have you had any teenagers of your own?

A. No, but my sister does. They give her nothing but trouble.

Q. Have you ever had any pets?

A. No. I don't go for animals.

Q. What about wild animals, like squirrels? Do you like them?

A. No way! We had squirrels in our attic once—what a mess they made! I don't have any love for squirrels, I'll tell you.

When the attorney asked the court to excuse Mrs. Schmidt from the jury, the judge agreed, and Mrs. Schmidt was replaced by another juror. The attorney had successfully challenged her for cause, that is, her prejudice against teenagers and animals.

LEGAL PRACTICUM

In the beginning of Chapter 23 (page 311), Sara Cole's boss paid a male worker more than he paid Sara, even though they were doing the same work. After talking to Adam, Sara decided to complain to her union. The union investigated and found that Sara's situation was not an isolated incident, but part of a widespread practice. The union brought suit against the company. Imagine that you are the attorney for Sara's union. List the characteristics you would like jurors to have and the characteristics you would like to avoid. Then switch sides and do the same for the company. Once you have done this, formulate questions that will help you examine the jurors to reveal bias and/or prejudice.

THINKING ABOUT MARRIED LIFE

UNIT
5

Chapter 24

MARRIAGE FORMALITIES AND RESTRICTIONS

In this unit you will meet Melanie Klein, age 22, her fiancé David Green, age 23, Melanie's sister, Debra, age 15, and her brother, Steven, age 17. Debra feels she is ready for marriage too. This has Melanie and Steven worried.

Scene: The Klein residence. Melanie is having an argument with her sister, Debra, in the den.

Debra: I don't care what you say, Melanie! I'm going to marry Alan even if he is 24 and I'm only 15! You know that I'm very grown up for my age. It's better to marry than to just move in together, and I want to be a real wife!

Melanie: You can't get married without Mom and Dad's permission anyway.

Debra: I can too! Alan said we can elope!

Melanie: Debra, teenage marriages have a low success rate. Listen to me! Wait until you're older. Finish school and get more education like David and I are doing. You know how much you respect Pauline and Mark! They're waiting until they finish college before they get married.

Debra: Yes, I know that they're waiting, but they have to go to another state to marry because they're first cousins. They won't even be legally married here and can't even come back to this state to live!

Melanie: That doesn't matter. They'll be happy anyway. Someone told me that first cousins are related by infinity—so it should last a long time. (*Steven, the girls' brother, knocks on the door.*)

Debra: Yes?

Steven: It's me, Steven. Can I come in?

Debra: Sure (*opening the door*), come on in.

Steven: Debra, there's something I just found out that you should know about. That guy you're going with— you know, Alan—lived with a girl for a year, and she's claiming to be his common-law wife. She says that he's the father of her child too.

Melanie: Oh, no!

Debra (*stunned*): You must be kidding!

Steven: No I'm not. I heard it from

someone who lives in Alan's apartment house and knows them both.

Debra: It can't be true! Alan's very honest! He wants to marry me!

Steven: He can't marry you if he's already married. That's polygamy! Anyway, you're too young to get married.

Debra: I am not! I'm not too young!

LEGAL ISSUES

1. Can a 15-year-old girl marry without her parent's consent?
2. Is a marriage between first cousins allowed?
3. What is the legal name for the relationship of blood relatives such as first cousins?
4. What is a common-law marriage? Is it ever recognized as legal?
5. What is the name and legal effect of the state of having two spouses at one time?

THE SPIRIT OF THE LAW

Throughout history, public policy has looked favorably upon marriage as being a stabilizing force in the life of the family. Public policy has been opposed to people living together outside of wedlock. Along with creating rights and duties, as all contracts do, the marriage contract creates a condition in which the parties' rights and duties are governed by law rather than by agreement. Marriage partners have the right to receive economic support from each other when necessary. They are responsible for each other's debts in payment for the necessities of life. They have legal rights to a portion of each other's property in the event of death and sometimes in the event of separation or divorce. Their children are entitled to their custody and support and, in some cases, a portion of their property upon death. Marriage also brings with it the duty of faithfulness.

THE ENGAGEMENT CONTRACT

When a couple of proper age and capacity become engaged, a bilateral agreement containing all the elements of a contract takes place. There is an agreement containing consideration (promising to give up one's legal right to remain single) between two parties who have capacity to contract, by mutual consent and for a legal purpose. Under common law, if one of the parties failed to go through with the marriage, the other party could sue for damages caused by breach of the marriage contract.

EXAMPLE 1 John Olivito asked Joyce Waldie to marry him, and Waldie accepted. A few months later, before they were married, Waldie changed her mind and called off the engagement. If the parties lived in a state which still follows the common law on this point, Olivito could sue Waldie for any damages he suffered because of the breach of contract.

■ Most states have passed statutes which no longer allow suit to be brought for breach of the marriage contract. In addition, according to court decisions in some states, the man is entitled to the return of the engagement ring on the theory that it was a gift contingent (dependent) upon the marriage taking place. If the marriage does not occur, the gift is not made. Courts have allowed the woman to keep the ring in cases in which the man has broken the engagement.

AGE AT WHICH PERSONS MAY MARRY

Under common law, a male had the capacity (legal ability) to marry at the age of 14 and a female at the age of 12. These ages were called the **ages of consent** to marry. The marriage of a person under the age of 7 was absolutely void. If such a marriage took place, it would have no legal effect whatever, and anyone could raise the issue before a court. A marriage of a person over the age of 7 but under the age of consent (14 for a male, 12 for a female) was voidable. The marriage was valid unless a party to the marriage took some kind of court action to have the marriage **annulled** (made void). No one else could attack the validity of the marriage.

■ Modern statutes in the United States have established ages at which young people can become married if one of their parents gives permission. In some states, the permission of the court as well as a parent is required if the person is below a certain age.

EXAMPLE 2 Joseph Bontorno, who was 25 years old, wanted to marry Joyce Bell, who was 13 years of age. Under the law of their state, which was Massachusetts, the couple could marry only if permission were granted by Bell's parents and by the probate court judge. If her parents or the judge denied permission, the couple would have to wait until Bell was 18 to become married.

Before 1971 the laws of many states provided that persons could get married without a parent's consent at the age of 18 if a female and 21 if a male. In 1971 the Twenty-Sixth Amendment to the U.S. Constitution allowed persons to vote at the age of 18. That change in the law caused most states to change their marriage laws, allowing both males and females to marry at the age of 18 without their parents' consent.

The custom of treating males and females differently with respect to age is coming to an end. For example, Utah had a law which held that males under 21 and females under 18 were minors so far as being entitled to receive support from their parents. In 1975 the U.S. Supreme Court held the statute to be unconstitutional because it treated males and females of the same age differently. (See Table 24-1.)

Legal Issue No. 1

■ This symbol indicates that there may be a state statute that varies from the law discussed here. Whenever you see this symbol, find out, if possible, what the statute in your state says about this point or principle of law.

TABLE 24-1
MARRIAGE INFORMATION

State	With Consent		Without Consent		Blood Test Required*	Wait for License	Wait after License
	Men	Women	Men	Women			
Alabama (b)	14	14	18	18	Yes	None	None
Alaska	16(m)	16(m)	18	18	No	3 days	None
Arizona	16(g)	16	18	18	Yes	None	None
Arkansas	17	16(h)	18	18	Yes	3 days	None
California	18(g)	18	18	18	Yes	None	None
Colorado	16	16	18	18	Yes	None	None
Connecticut	16	16(j)	18	18	Yes	4 days	None
Delaware	18	16(k)	18	18	No	None	24 hours (c)
District of Columbia	16	16	18	18	Yes	3 days	None
Florida	17	17	18	18	Yes	None	None
Georgia	16(g)	16(g)	18	18	Yes	None (k)	None
Hawaii	16	16	18	18	Yes	None	None
Idaho	16	16	18	18	No	None	None
Illinois (a)	16	16	18	18	Yes	None	1 day
Indiana	17(k)	17(k)	18	18	Yes	72 hours	None
Iowa	—(k)	—(k)	18	18	No	3 days	None
Kansas	—(k)	—(k)	18	18	No	3 days	None
Kentucky	—(k)	—(k)	18	18	Yes	3 days	None
Louisiana (a)	18(k)	16(h)	18	16	Yes	None	72 hours
Maine	16(h)	16(h)	18	18	No	5 days	None
Maryland	16	16	18	18	None	48 hours	None
Massachusetts	—(k)	—(k)	18	18	Yes	3 days	None
Michigan (a)	16	16	18	18	Yes	3 days	None
Minnesota	16(e)	16(e)	18	18	None	5 days	None
Mississippi (b)	17(l)	15(l)	21	21	Yes	3 days	None
Missouri	15	15	18	18	None	3 days	None
Montana	15	15	18	18	Yes	None	3 days
Nebraska	17	17	18	18	Yes	2 days	None
Nevada	16(h)	16(h)	18	18	None	None	None
New Hampshire (a)	14(e)	13(e)	18	18	No	3 days	None
New Jersey (a)	16(g)	16(g)	18	18	Yes	72 hours	None
New Mexico	16	16	18	18	Yes	None	None
New York	14(e)	14(e)	18	18	No(f)	None	24 hours

PRE-MARITAL AGREE-MENTS

Sometimes, before they are married, people enter into written agreements concerning the real and personal property they will own during their marriage. They set forth in the agreement how their property interests will be disposed of in the event the marriage comes to an end, either by death or divorce. A **premarital agreement,** also called an **antenuptial** or **prenuptial agreement,** is an agreement between prospective spouses made in contemplation of marriage and to be effective upon marriage. In making a premarital agreement, the parties

TABLE 24-1 (Continued)
MARRIAGE INFORMATION

State	With Consent		Without Consent		Blood Test Required*	Wait for License	Wait after License
	Men	Women	Men	Women			
North Carolina (a)	16	16	18	18	Yes	None	None
North Dakota (a)	16	16	18	18	Yes	None	None
Ohio (a)	18	16	18	18	No	5 days	None
Oklahoma	16	16	18	18	Yes	None	None
Oregon	17	17	18	18	Yes	3 days	None
Pennsylvania	16	16	18	18	Yes	3 days	None
Rhode Island (a) (b)	14	12	18	18	Yes	None	None
South Carolina	16	14	18	18	None	24 hours	None
South Dakota	16	16	18	18	No	None	None
Tennessee (b)	16	16	18	18	Yes	3 days	None
Texas	14(k)	14(k)	18	18	Yes	None	None
Utah	14	14	18	18	None	None	None
Vermont (a)	16	16	18	18	Yes	None	5 days
Virginia (a)	16	16	18	18	No	None	None
Washington	17	17	18	18	(d)	3 days	None
West Virginia	16	16	18	18	Yes	3 days	None
Wisconsin	16	16	18	18	Yes	5 days	None
Wyoming	16	16	19	19	Yes	None	None
Puerto Rico	18	16	21	21	Yes	None	None
Virgin Islands	16	14	18	18	None	8 days	None

Note: This table gives marriageable age, by states, for both males and females with and without consent of parents or guardians. In most states, the court has authority to marry young couples below the ordinary age of consent, where due regard for their morals and welfare so requires. In many states, under special circumstances, blood test and waiting period may be waived.

*Many states have additional special requirements; contact individual state. (a) Special laws applicable to nonresidents. (b) Special laws applicable to those under 21 years; Ala., bond required if male is under 18, female under 18. (c) 24 hours if one or both parties resident of state; 96 hours if both parties are nonresidents. (d) None, but both must file affidavit. (e) Parental consent plus court's consent required. (f) Test for sickle-cell anemia required for people who are not of the Caucasian, Indian, or Oriental race. (g) Statute provides for obtaining license with parental or court consent with no state minimum age. (h) Under 16, with parental and court consent. (i) If either under 18, wait 3 full days. (j) If under stated age, court consent required. (k) If under 18, parental and/or court consent required. (l) Both parents' consent required for men age 17, women age 15; one parent's consent required for men 18 to 20 years, women ages 16 to 20 years. (m) Parental and court consent required if 14 or over, but under 16.

Source: The World Almanac and Book of Facts 1986, Newspaper Enterprise Association, Inc., 200 Park Ave., New York, New York, 10166.

must be honest in the statements they make to each other. In addition, they must fully disclose their assets to each other.

A premarital agreement must be in writing and signed by both parties. Although the laws from state to state vary, in general, parties to a premarital agreement may contract with respect to:

1. The rights and obligations of each of the parties in any of the property of either or both of them and wherever acquired.

2. The right to buy, sell, manage, and control real and personal property.
3. The disposition of real and personal property upon separation, divorce, death, or some other event.
4. The change or elimination of support.
5. The making of a will.
6. Ownership of and benefits from life insurance policies.

Prenuptial Agreement

Agreement made this 10th day of June, 19-- between Joseph Taft of 1273 Holly Lane, Amesburgh, PA, and Susan Jacobs, of 299 Oak Lane, Amesburgh, PA.

Whereas a marriage is shortly to be solemnized between the parties hereto:

Whereas Susan Jacobs now owns a large amount of property and expects to acquire from time to time additional property under a trust established by her uncle, Henry Jacobs;

Whereas Joseph Taft has agreed that all of the property now or in the future owned by Susan Jacobs, or her estate, shall be free of all rights that he might acquire by reason of his marriage to her.

It is agreed as follows:

1. Susan Jacobs shall have full right and authority, in all respects the same as she would have if unmarried, to use, enjoy, manage, convey, mortgage, and dispose of all of her present and future property and estate, of every kind and character, including the right and power to dispose of same by last will and testament.

2. Joseph Taft releases to Susan Jacobs, her heirs, legal representatives, and assigns, every right, claim and estate that he might have in respect to said property by reason of his marriage to Susan Jacobs.

IN WITNESS WHEREOF the parties have hereunto set their hands and seals the day and year first above written.

_____Joseph Taft_____

_____Susan Jacobs_____

Married people have certain economic rights and duties, which a prenuptial agreement may exclude.

MARRIAGE FORMAL-ITIES

Although attitudes toward marriage have changed in recent years, public policy continues strongly to favor the institution of marriage. **Public policy** is that aspect of the law which makes unenforceable or illegal those acts considered harmful to the public good. Thus it is a crime in most states for an unmarried man and woman to live together openly and continually ''as man and wife'' over a period of time. The period of time varies from state to state. The name of the crime may also differ depending on the state. In some states it is known as ''lewd and lascivious cohabitation''; in others it is called ''illicit cohabitation'' or living in adultery and fornication.

Common-Law Marriage

Legal Issue No. 4

In England, under the common law, no formal ceremony was necessary to bind the parties in wedlock. All that was required was that the parties agree between themselves that they were married. No witnesses were required, and the agreement could be either oral or in writing.

■ All but 13 states in the United States today consider the common-law marriage to be contrary to public policy and do not allow it. Those jurisdictions (areas) which still recognize this type of marriage are Alabama, Colorado, the District of Columbia, Georgia, Idaho, Iowa, Kansas (where it is a misdemeanor), Montana, Ohio, Oklahoma, Pennsylvania, Rhode Island, South Carolina, and Texas.

With a few exceptions, the states that recognize the **common-law marriage** require the following elements:

1. The parties must agree, by words in the present tense, that they are husband and wife.
2. The parties must cohabit—that is, they must dwell together (for no particular time period) in the same place as husband and wife.
3. The parties must hold themselves out to the world as being husband and wife so that the public recognizes their marital status.

A few states do not regard the last two elements as essential to a valid common-law marriage.

A common-law marriage properly entered into in a state which recognizes it will be regarded as valid in any other state.

EXAMPLE 3 George Desjardine and Jacqueline Kelly say to each other that they are married. They cohabited in the state of Rhode Island and introduced themselves as husband and wife to people they met. They did not have a marriage ceremony. Later they moved to Massachusetts, which does not recognize the common-law marriage. That state would regard them as being legally married because the Rhode Island law, which allows the common-law marriage, was properly followed.

In Pennsylvania, the state's minimum age to marry (16 with the court's permission) does not apply to common-law marriages. However, the common law rules affecting people under the age of 7 are still in effect.

Proxy Marriage

A **proxy marriage,** which is recognized in some states, requires a ceremony, but one or both of the parties to the marriage are absent and are represented by an agent who acts on their behalf. In most states, a proxy marriage is void as against public policy; nevertheless, all states will recognize it as valid if it was valid in the state or country where it was performed.

Ceremonial Marriage

From early colonial times, a ceremony, officiated by a cleric or magistrate, was required to become married. Today, a majority of the states require a marriage to be **solemnized** (performed by a ceremony). No particular form of marriage ceremony is required, as long as the parties declare in the presence of a person who has authority by state law to solemnize marriages that they take each other as husband and wife. Courts have held that a marriage that is properly solemnized is valid even though a marriage license was not obtained before the ceremony.

Marriage Banns ■ Under common law, in order to give persons who might oppose a marriage the opportunity to object, notices of a forthcoming marriage were required to be published and posted. These notices were called **marriage banns.** Instead of the requirement that marriage banns be published, most states today have a waiting period before a license is issued. This period varies from 24 hours to 7 days, depending on the state. Recently, some states have done away with the waiting period altogether.

There are several reasons for the waiting-period requirement. The man and woman may need time to reconsider their decision to marry. In addition, a waiting period may allow evidence of fraud, force, or jest to be uncovered. As with marriage banns, it gives interested parties, such as the parents of the prospective marriage partners, the opportunity to object on other grounds.

Blood Tests   A blood test to determine the presence or absence of syphilis, a dangerous disease, is required before a marriage license can be issued in most states. Under a typical statute, if syphilis is found and is in the noncommunicable stage, both parties are informed of the nature of the disease and the possibilities of transmitting such infection to the marital partner or to their children. If syphilis is found and is in the communicable stage, a marriage license is not issued. (Syphilis in the noncommunicable stage cannot be readily transmitted from one person to another. In the communicable stage, it can be transmitted more readily, in most instances through sexual contact.)

■ In some states the doctor who gives the blood test must also certify that the female (if within childbearing age) has been tested and found immune to rubella (German measles) infection. If the female refuses the test, the doctor must advise her of the risks of contracting rubella during childbearing years and of the immunizing vaccine available to eliminate or protect against such risks.

EXAMPLE 4   William Nolan and Lynn Bryant decided to get married. They went to the town clerk's office in their town and filled out an application for a marriage license. They were told that they would have to wait at least 3 days before a marriage license could be issued and that they would have to go to a doctor to have their blood tested.

USE OF MAIDEN NAME

Under common law, people may use any name as long as they do not do so to commit fraud. The use of the husband's surname (last name) by a wife came about through custom. It was not required at common law. Following this lead, many states allow women to continue to use their maiden name or hyphenate it with their husband's surname even after they are married. Some states, however, take the position that a married woman takes her husband's surname as a matter of law.

VOID MARRIAGES

The law says that certain types of marriages are illegal from the start. These include marriages between relatives and marriages by one party to two or more other people—that is, bigamous or polygamous marriages.

Marriage Between Relatives

■ By statute in many states, marriage between certain persons who are related by **consanguinity** (blood) and **affinity** (marriage) are prohibited and are, therefore, void. Many of the states base their law on the common law which made it illegal to marry certain relatives. The table on page 340 shows which relatives it was illegal to marry under the common law.

If a person did marry any of these relatives in violation of the law, the marriage would be void and any children born of the union would be illegitimate. Under the common law, it would be illegal to marry a person related by affinity even after the relationship ends, as by death or divorce.

Legal Issue No. 3

EXAMPLE 5   Frank and Susan Sargent, whose marriage lasted for 6 months, were divorced. Susan later fell in love with Frank's father, a widower. In a state which follows the common-law rule, they could not marry.

TABLE 24-2
CONSANGUINITY AND AFFINITY

Consanguinity (Related by Blood)	Affinity (Related by Marriage)
Mother or father	Stepmother or stepfather
Grandmother or grandfather	Step-grandmother or step-grandfather
Daughter or son	Stepdaughter or stepson
Granddaughter or grandson	Step-granddaughter or step-grandson
Aunt or uncle	Mother-in-law or father-in-law
Sister or brother	Grandmother-in-law or grandfather-in-law
Niece or nephew	Daughter-in-law or son-in-law
	Granddaughter-in-law or grandson-in-law

Marriage to these relatives is prohibited by common law.

Legal Issue No. 2

The marriage of first cousins is allowed under the common-law rule. Many states, however, prohibit marriages between first cousins. Almost half the states have no prohibition against marriage of persons related by affinity.

Bigamy and Polygamy

Legal Issue No. 5

A marriage that is contracted while either party is already married is void in all states unless the prior marriage is ended by annulment. **Bigamy** is the act of having two spouses at the same time. **Polygamy** is the act of having more than two spouses at the same time. Any children born of a man and woman whose marriage is void are illegitimate. Both bigamy and polygamy are crimes under the laws of every state in this country.

■ In some states, if one of the parties entered into the marriage in good faith without knowing that the other party was already married, the second marriage may become valid on the death or divorce of the partner to the first marriage.

Language of the Law

Define or explain each of the following words or phrases:

age of consent	common-law mar-	marriage banns	affinity
annulled	riage	consanguinity	bigamy
premarital agreement	proxy marriage		polygamy
antenuptial or prenuptial agreement	solemnized		

Questions for Review

1. Explain the legal issues involved when people become engaged to marry.
2. At what ages did boys and girls have the capacity to marry under common law?
3. How does the age of consent affect the capacity of parties to marry?
4. Explain the public policy of most states regarding common-law marriage.

5. What are the three elements usually required in order to have a common-law marriage?
6. What is the law regarding proxy marriages?
7. What form of marriage ceremony is required in most states today?
8. What do most states now have in place of marriage banns?
9. Why is a blood test required in most states before a marriage license can be issued?
10. What is done, under a typical statute, if the blood test determines that a person applying for a marriage license has syphilis?
11. Under the common law, what would be the result if a person married an uncle or aunt? if a person married a first cousin?
12. What is the law regarding bigamy? polygamy?

Cases in Point

In each of the following cases, give your decision and state a legal principle that applies to the case:

1. Paul Sessions asked Ellen Throckmorton to marry him and at the same time placed a diamond ring on her finger. Throckmorton accepted. Three months later, Throckmorton broke off the engagement. Sessions threatened to sue Throckmorton for breach of contract. Can he do so?
2. In the preceding case, Throckmorton refused to return the engagement ring, saying that she had a right to keep it under the law. Was she correct?
3. James and Mary lived together as husband and wife for 20 years in the state of Vermont. They agreed with each other that they were husband and wife and presented themselves to others as being married. They had never gone through a marriage ceremony. When James died without leaving a will, Mary claimed that she should inherit from his estate because she was his common-law wife. Do you agree?
4. Ernest Lemon and Juanita Guarnieri wanted to be married at the seashore. Guarnieri said that the sun, sands, and waves could solemnize their marriage and that no member of the clergy or other official would be necessary. Would this marriage be legally solemnized? Explain.
5. When Thomas Emerson and Denise Inge went to the doctor's office before getting married, Emerson told the doctor that he did not need a blood test because he had donated a pint of blood the week before. Was Emerson correct?
6. Shirlee Spencer fell in love with her Uncle Henry and wanted to marry him. Would their marriage be valid? What would be the legal status of any children born of the marriage?
7. When Anna and Lawrence were married, Anna wanted to continue to use her maiden name. Lawrence objected, saying that the law required Anna to use his surname. Anna took Lawrence to court over this issue. How would you decide?
8. William Lyons, who was 22 years old, wanted to marry Alice Galo, who was 14 years old. They both lived in the state of Massachusetts. Both of Galo's parents refused to give their permission for the marriage. Can Lyons and Galo become legally married?
9. Before they were married, Phyllis and Robert entered into an oral premarital agreement. They agreed that if their marriage should come to an end, Phyllis would own the furniture and Robert would own the car. Is the agreement enforceable?
10. James and Josephine were married. Five years later, Josephine discovered that James had never gotten a divorce from his first wife, Wanda, who was still living. Is the marriage between James and Josephine valid?

Cases to Judge

1. When they became engaged, Charles Gill gave Dianne Shively an engagement ring worth approximately $3,620. Less than a month later, Shively told Gill that she would not marry him because she was not ready for marriage. Is Gill entitled to the return of the ring? Why or why not? *Gill v. Shively,* 330 So. 2d 415 (Florida)

2. Two months after her divorce from Bobby Gunter, Gloria Gunter married Edward Peters. She thought that Peters was divorced. She learned later, however, that he was still married to his fourth wife and that he had deceived her into thinking he was divorced. What legal wrong did Peters commit? What is the legal effect of Gunter's marriage to Peters? *Gunter v. Gunter,* 418 N.E.2d 149 (Illinois)

3. Hilaria Cabrera went through a ceremonial religious marriage with Louis Chavez in Mexico. Later, she immigrated to Texas, where she met Benjamin T. Franklin. She and Franklin agreed to be husband and wife, cohabited, and held each other out to others as husband and wife. She then sought a divorce from Franklin. Was the common-law marriage to Franklin valid? Explain. *Franklin v. Smalldridge,* 616 S.W.2d 655 (Texas)

4. Ernest Davis married Precious Black in a ceremonial wedding performed by a minister. There is no evidence that a marriage license was ever issued or recorded, however. A question arose as to whether or not the marriage between Davis and Black was valid. How would you decide? Explain. *Wright v. Vales,* 613 S.W.2d 850 (Arkansas)

5. Mary Jolley sued George Jolley, claiming that he was her common-law husband. They were married in 1965 and divorced in 1970. After the divorce, Mary and George continued to live together and presented themselves to others as being husband and wife in the state of Ohio, which allows the common-law marriage. She now claims that they are married. George denies it. How would you decide? *Jolley v. Jolley,* 347 N.E.2d 557 (Ohio)

Chapter 25

RENTING AN APARTMENT

Scene: Melanie and David, who are to be married in 3 weeks, are looking for an apartment. They stop their car in front of a two-family house.

Melanie: I'm so tired. Every apartment we've seen so far has been either too expensive or too run down.

David: Or already rented.

Melanie: I can't get over that place where the owner said he never rented to young couples because they might have children.

David: Yeah. And how about the one who wouldn't allow dogs. Rusty never bothered anyone. He's just a big, lovable softie.

Melanie: Well, I guess some people don't like Great Danes.

David (*knocking on the door*): This place looks pretty good from the outside.

Owner (*opening the door*): Hello.

David: Hello. We'd like to look at the apartment that you advertised for rent.

Melanie: Is it still available?

Owner: Yup. Come on in. There are two apartments upstairs. The one on the right is vacant. I'll show it to you.

(*On the way up, Melanie stumbles and David grabs her.*)

Owner: Watch out for that broken stair! A couple of nails came out. I'm going to fix it next week. Here you are (*unlocking the door*). Take a look around.

Melanie: This is pretty.

David: I don't like that light fixture.

Owner: This place never stays empty long.

David: Is it okay to have a dog?

Owner: Sure. I like little critters as long as they don't bark too much.

Melanie: Rusty isn't . . .

David (*interrupting*): Rusty's very quiet.

(*David and Melanie decide to take the apartment.*)

Owner: I'll need a security deposit and the first and last month's rent.

David: Do we need to sign a lease?

Owner: No way. I don't bother with that written stuff.

(*Later, the couple are married and have moved into the apartment.*)

David: It's nice to have our own little place.

Melanie: It's wonderful! That new light fixture is just perfect. You did such a good job wiring it in that it looks as though it has always been here. I wonder if we should have thrown out the old fixture, though. (*A month later, David and Melanie are sitting in the dark with candles burning.*)

Melanie: That was mean of the landlord to shut off our electricity, just because he doesn't like Rusty.

David: I didn't like him calling Rusty an elephant, either.

Melanie: He said that he's going to keep the light fixture and our security deposit too—all on account of Rusty!

David: I'm going downstairs and tell him a thing or two! (*He rushes out the door, down the stairs, and trips on a loose floorboard.*) Oof! Oooh! I think my leg's broken!

LEGAL ISSUES

1. Is it against the law to refuse to rent to people who might have children in the future?
2. Must the rental of an apartment be evidenced by a writing or may it be oral?
3. May landlords shut off a tenant's electricity?
4. May landlords keep a security deposit because they do not like a tenant's dog?
5. Who owns the fixtures that are built in by the tenant—the landlord or the tenant?
6. Who is responsible for injuries caused by a defect in a common stairway of an apartment building—the landlord or the tenant?

THE SPIRIT OF THE LAW

Real property is the ground and anything permanently attached to it. Thus real property includes land, buildings, growing trees and shrubs, and even the air space over the land. Things that are not real property are called **personal property.** They are generally things that are movable. A tree growing in the ground, for example, is real property; if the tree is cut down, it becomes personal property. Bricks that are used for building houses are personal property. Once a building is built out of them, however, they become real property. Real property may be owned outright, or it may be rented. In this chapter, we discuss renting real property. In the next chapter, we discuss owning it.

If you rent real property, you are a **tenant.** If you own real property and rent it to someone else, you are a **landlord.** The law that deals with the relationship between the two is known as the law of landlord and tenant. Most of the legal problems involved in landlord-tenant relationships can be anticipated in advance and properly provided for by contract.

The contract you make with your landlord, called a **lease,** is one of the most important of your everyday agreements. In a lease, the tenant is known as the **lessee;** the landlord, as the **lessor.** The lease needs your most careful attention. A knowledge of the legal problems involved, plus forethought and planning, is very important.

TYPES OF TENANCIES

Tenants actually own an interest in the real estate they possess. The interest which they own is called a **tenancy.** The principal kinds of tenancies are (1) a tenancy for years, (2) a periodic tenancy, (3) a tenancy at will, and (4) a tenancy at sufferance.

Tenancy for Years

A **tenancy for years** is a right to occupy property for a stated period of time. It may be for 1 year, 2 years, 5 years, or even as much as 99 years. It could also be for 1 week, 1 month, or 6 months. However long the period, the time when the tenancy will come to an end must be clearly established. A tenancy for 100 years or more has the effect of transferring the property outright to the tenant so that he or she owns it absolutely. For this reason, we occasionally see 99-year leases for business or industrial property. States that follow the common-law rule require a tenancy for years to be in writing to be enforceable because it is a transfer of an interest in real property.

Periodic Tenancy

A **periodic tenancy** is a tenancy which continues for successive periods until one of the parties ends it by giving proper notice to the other. It is called a *periodic tenancy* because the period of time does not have to be for 1 year. It can be a tenancy from week to week, a tenancy from month to month, or a tenancy from year to year. If proper notice to end the tenancy is not given, the tenancy continues on for another period. The notice requirement differs from state to state, but it is often the period between rent days. The **rent day** is the day on which the rent is due.

EXAMPLE 1   Albert Kingston agreed to rent Zenas Clark's house for the price of $7,200 a year. Nothing else was mentioned. Neither party stipulated the length of time of rental. This situation would be a year-to-year tenancy and would continue as long as Kingston paid the rent and stayed in possession.

EXAMPLE 2   If Kingston had agreed to rent Clark's house for 1 year at a rental of $7,200 for the year, it would be a tenancy for years. In this case, the period of time—that is, 1 year—is clearly stated. At the end of the year, the tenancy automatically comes to an end.

It is important to distinguish between these two tenancies. When a tenant maintains occupancy after the term of a lease has ended, the tenant is said to be "holding over." If the tenant from year to year holds over, even for 1 day into the second year, he or she automatically renews the obligation for the entire second year. In a tenancy for years, if the tenant holds over, he or she may be a tenant at sufferance. This will be discussed below. Some courts will consider this new arrangement with the landlord as a monthly agreement, and others consider it as a renewal of the lease for 1 year.

Tenancy at Will

A **tenancy at will** is an interest in real property that continues for an indefinite period of time. No written agreement is required to create this tenancy, and it may be terminated by either party giving the proper statutory notice. In some states, the notice must be no less than 30 days from the next rent day.

EXAMPLE 3 Wilma Hockensmith agrees to rent Eli Shaffer's home for $600 per month and moves in. The agreement is oral, and nothing is said about the length of the contract. This is a tenancy at will. Either party may end the tenancy at any time he or she wishes by giving proper notice to the other party.

Tenancy at Sufferance

A **tenancy at sufferance** arises when a tenant wrongfully remains in possession of the premises after the tenancy has expired. It often comes about at the expiration of the term of a tenancy for years or when a tenancy at will has been properly terminated by giving notice and the tenant remains in possession. A tenant at sufferance is also called a **holdover tenant.** The tenant is a wrongdoer, having no interest in the property. A tenant at sufferance is not entitled to notice to vacate but is liable to pay rent for the period of occupancy.

EXAMPLE 4 Edwina Robson's lease specified that she was to occupy the apartment for 1 year, starting July 5. One month before the lease expired, Robson was notified by the landlord that the lease was not going to be renewed. She did not try to find another apartment and stayed on after July 5. Robson then became a tenant at sufferance.

A periodic tenancy or a tenancy at will may come about, instead of a tenancy at sufferance, if a landlord accepts rent from a tenant whose tenancy has expired.

EXAMPLE 5 Suppose, in Example 4, that Robson sent the landlord a check for rent for the month following the end of the lease. The landlord cashed the check. This act by the landlord renewed Robson's tenancy, and Robson could remain even though the landlord had others waiting for a vacancy.

To be on the safe side, the parties should provide in the lease itself what the effect of holding over shall be.

▍THE LEASE

The agreement between a lessor and a lessee, called a lease, creates the landlord and tenant relationship. It provides the tenant with exclusive possession and control of the real property of the landlord. Since it is a contract, the general rules of contract law apply to it.

In some states, a tenancy for a year or less can be oral. If the tenancy is for more than 1 year, the Statute of Frauds requires that it be in writing. In other states, a tenancy for a definite period of time, no matter how short, must be in writing to be enforceable. If no time is stated, however, it may be oral.

Legal Issue No. 2

Like a marriage contract, a lease contains a number of covenants. What are they?

Remember: It can be very dangerous to buy a standard lease form and fill in the blanks without careful study; the parties signing may find themselves bound in ways that neither of them intended.

Covenants in a Lease

A lease contains many promises, called **covenants,** which the parties agree to follow. Some of the most common convenants are discussed below.

Legal Issue No. 3

General Covenants The basic right the tenant wants is possession and a continued occupancy free from interference or annoyances. The landlord wants rent and possession of the property in good condition at the term's end. Every lease contains covenants providing for these things.

Decoration and Repairs The landlord has no obligation to decorate or maintain the premises unless it is so provided in the lease, or by statute or local ordinance. The landlord must, however, make those repairs necessary to keep the premises fit to live in. This obligation is known as the **implied warranty of habitability.** Basically the tenant owns the property for the stated period and has the obligation to maintain the premises and make repairs that are not the obligation of the landlord.

If you were to rent only a small apartment in a large building, you would have control of your apartment only. The landlord would have control of the entry, stairs, halls, basement, and so on. It would be the landlord's implied duty to maintain these parts of the premises.

You should always have a complete understanding with your landlord on these points before you sign a lease. The safest thing to do is to get everything written into the lease and not leave anything to be implied.

■ There are also some state statutes and local ordinances that relate to the maintenance and repair of multiple-family dwellings. The health and safety of its citizens are important to the state.

The tenant must return the premises to the landlord in as good a condition as the tenant received it, reasonable wear and tear excepted. Anything more than reasonable wear and tear is called **waste.** If the tenant has been guilty of waste, the tenant must pay the landlord for the damage done. Sometimes the landlord may deduct payment for such damages from the tenant's security deposit (see below).

EXAMPLE 6   While renting a house in Public Circle, Connie Zentner placed an electric heater in one of the rooms. Because the thermostat in the heater was out of order, the heater became red hot and burned a hole in the floor. This damage was not the result of ordinary wear and tear. Zentner will be held responsible.

Assignment and Subletting   An **assignment** of a lease occurs when a tenant transfers the remaining period of time that a lease has to run to someone else. A **sublease** occurs when a tenant transfers part of the term of a lease but not the remainder of it to someone else.

EXAMPLE 7   The Olsons held a 3-year lease on a house in Vinnet. The house was near a college campus where their daughter went to school. One summer, while the lease was still in effect, the Olsons went on vacation. A friend of theirs, John Bennis, had been hired by the college for the summer. The Olsons sublet their house to Bennis and his family. In the fall, the Olsons returned to their house, and Bennis and his family moved back to their permanent home.

If the landlord does not want the tenant to assign or sublet the property, there must be a covenant to that effect in the lease. Otherwise, the tenant may either assign or sublet the property to someone else. When this happens, however, the original tenant is still responsible to the landlord for the rent.

Recent cases in some states have held that an implied covenant of good faith and fair dealing exists in every commercial lease (a lease of business property). Under this rule, landlords may not withhold their consent to the sublease or assignment of commercial premises without a good reason.

Renewals   A tenancy for years ends absolutely at the expiration of the stated period unless there are provisions in the lease or statutory provisions to the contrary. It would be a hardship on either party if neither knew what the other was going to do prior to the end of the term.

■ To prevent this hardship, many states have statutes that require each party to give notice to the other a specified time before the end of the term. It is also quite common to have a provision pertaining to renewals written into the lease itself.

Security Deposit   ■ Frequently, the landlord will require a money deposit as security for the payment of rent or repairs for damages done by the tenant. This

security deposit often is equal to 1 or 2 months' rent. Whether the security deposit may be used as rent is determined by the landlord. Some states require that the landlord pay interest on the security deposit.

Legal Issue No. 5   **EXAMPLE 8**   Paul Malone leased an apartment from Julie Madden for 1 year. The lease provided that Malone was to deposit security equal to 2 months' rent with Madden and that the money was (1) to be applied to the payment of

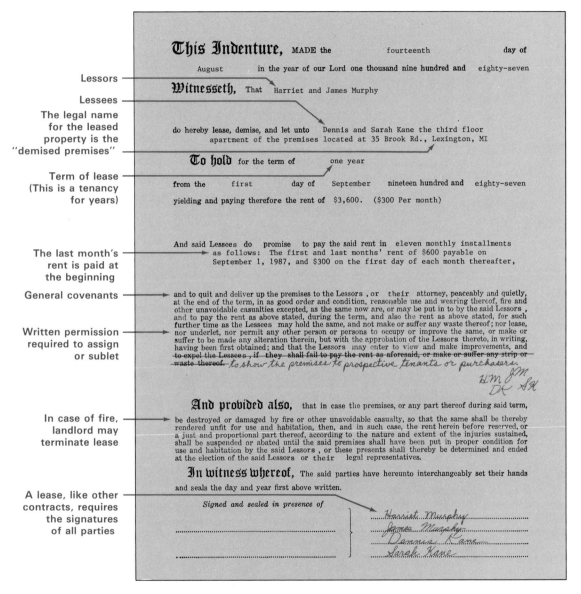

This Indenture, MADE the   fourteenth   day of
August   in the year of our Lord one thousand nine hundred and   eighty-seven

Witnesseth, That   Harriet and James Murphy

do hereby lease, demise, and let unto   Dennis and Sarah Kane the third floor apartment of the premises located at 35 Brook Rd., Lexington, MI

To hold for the term of   one year

from the   first   day of   September   nineteen hundred and   eighty-seven

yielding and paying therefore the rent of $3,600.   ($300 Per month)

And said Lessees do   promise   to pay the said rent in   eleven monthly installments as follows: The first and last months' rent of $600 payable on September 1, 1987, and $300 on the first day of each month thereafter,

and to quit and deliver up the premises to the Lessors , or their attorney, peaceably and quietly, at the end of the term, in as good order and condition, reasonable use and wearing thereof, fire and other unavoidable casualties excepted, as the same now are, or may be put in to by the said Lessors , and to pay the rent as above stated, during the term, and also the rent as above stated, for such further time as the Lessees may hold the same, and not make or suffer any waste thereof ; nor lease, nor underlet, nor permit any other person or persons to occupy or improve the same, or make or suffer to be made any alteration therein, but with the approbation of the Lessors thereto, in writing, having been first obtained ; and that the Lessors may enter to view and make improvements, and to expel the Lessees , if they shall fail to pay the rent as aforesaid, or make or suffer any strip or waste thereof. *to show the premises to prospective tenants or purchasers.*

HM JM DK SK

And provided also, that in case the premises, or any part thereof during said term, be destroyed or damaged by fire or other unavoidable casualty, so that the same shall be thereby rendered unfit for use and habitation, then, and in such case, the rent herein before reserved, or a just and proportional part thereof, according to the nature and extent of the injuries sustained, shall be suspended or abated until the said premises shall have been put in proper condition for use and habitation by the said Lessors , or these presents shall thereby be determined and ended at the election of the said Lessors or their   legal representatives.

In witness whereof, The said parties have hereunto interchangeably set their hands and seals the day and year first above written.

Signed and sealed in presence of

....

....

Harriet Murphy
James Murphy
Dennis Kane
Sarah Kane

Margin labels:
Lessors
Lessees
The legal name for the leased property is the "demised premises"
Term of lease (This is a tenancy for years)
The last month's rent is paid at the beginning
General covenants
Written permission required to assign or sublet
In case of fire, landlord may terminate lease
A lease, like other contracts, requires the signatures of all parties

A standard form such as this one is often used to prepare a lease. The terms of the lease may be changed before signing by agreement of the parties. Handwritten changes should be initialed by the parties. Study the lease carefully before signing it.

the last 2 months' rent, (2) to be applied by Madden to any unpaid rent, or (3) to be used to repair any damage caused by Malone during his occupancy of the premises.

Legal Issue No. 4   This would not be Madden's money, and she could not use it as her own. She must keep the money safely to be used as provided. In addition to a security deposit, some landlords also require the last month's rent to be paid at the beginning of the tenancy.

Destruction by Fire   Modern statutes usually provide that if the property is destroyed by fire, the lease is terminated. The termination is usually left up to the parties, however. If the landlord wishes to rebuild and the tenant wishes to continue, they may do so.

Termination of the Lease   By its very nature, a tenancy for years comes to an end at the termination of the specified term. The lease is a contract, and the parties may provide for any other methods of termination. For example, tenants whose employment may oblige them to move to another locality on short notice may obtain from their landlords an agreement that if such a move becomes necessary, the lease will come to an end. This provision is especially important to military personnel who, because of their induction into service or call to duty, must relinquish their leases.

BREACH OF LEASE AND REMEDIES

Like other contracts, a lease may be terminated if the parties commit a breach. The most common form of breach by a tenant is the failure to pay rent; the most common breach by the landlord is the failure to provide some service as stipu-

---

NOTICE TO TERMINATE TENANCY AT WILL

DATE _____   TIME _____

To: _____

   It being my intention to terminate your tenancy you are hereby notified to quit and deliver up at the expiration of that _____ of your
MONTH OR WEEK
tenancy which shall begin next after this date, the premises now held by you as my tenant, namely:

_____

_____

_____

_____

_____

_____
Landlord or Agent

Legal notice must be given to terminate a tenancy at will.

lated in the lease. The law gives the landlord the remedy of eviction for a tenant's breach; the tenant also has remedies if there is a breach by the landlord.

Eviction

As was mentioned previously, a tenant has the right to **quiet enjoyment** of the premises that he or she rents. Thus the tenant has the right to undisturbed possession of the property. However, the tenant has this right provided that she or he pays the rent, does not commit continual waste, and does not otherwise violate the provisions of the lease. If the tenant does any of these things, the landlord may bring an action, known as a **dispossess proceeding,** to evict the tenant. An eviction occurs when the landlord, through court action, is given the right to deprive the tenant of physical possession of the premises. To evict the tenant, however, the landlord must first obtain a court order allowing the landlord to remove the tenant. The law generally does not give the landlord the right to self-help—that is, the right to remove the tenant by himself or herself. The court will generally appoint a sheriff or other authorized officer to carry out the order. If the landlord wants to collect back rent, in most states a separate action must be brought for the money due. Some states also permit the landlord to attach a lien to the tenant's property for any rent owed. However, the landlord must use judicial process to keep a tenant's property.

Constructive Eviction

Legal Issue No. 3

Constructive eviction occurs when the landlord breaches his or her duties under the lease. Constructive eviction may take place if the landlord deprives the tenant of heat, gas, light, electricity, or some other fundamental service that was called for under the lease. When constructive eviction occurs, the tenant may consider the lease terminated, leave the premises, and stop paying rent. Deciding whether or not a constructive eviction has occurred, however, is usually a matter for a court.

Legal Issue No. 4

RECENT LANDLORD-TENANT LAWS

Until recently, most laws governing the landlord-tenant relationship were highly favorable to the landlord. This is not surprising, since many of these laws derive from feudal times when the feudal lord (landlord) was really an absolute master over the property he owned and over the people he allowed to live and work on it. The trend in recent years, however, has been to pass laws which have given more rights and protection to tenants.

Habitability

■ Recent legislation in some states allows the tenant to pay rent to the court, instead of to the landlord, if the premises are not fit for human habitation and violate the sanitary code. In some states the tenant, after giving notice to the landlord, can correct the defect at his or her own expense and withhold rent up to the amount of the expense. Thus in states that allow such action, the tenant is allowed some measure of self-help.

Rent Control

■ Rent control laws have been enacted in many large communities because of the housing shortage, which tends to cause a rapid increase in rental rates. **Rent control laws** are laws which place limits on the amount of rent that may be charged by the landlord. They also may provide for procedures to be followed before a tenant may be evicted. Such laws differ from place to place.

Antidiscrimination Laws

In selecting tenants and in all other aspects of their business, landlords are bound by various antidiscrimination statutes. Laws such as the Civil Rights Act place special emphasis on human needs and rights.

■ In nearly all states it is against the law for a landlord to refuse to rent or lease property to any person because of race, religious creed, color, national origin, sex, age, ancestry, or marital status. It is also against the law to refuse to rent to anyone because he or she is a veteran, a member of the armed forces, a blind person, or a person who at present has no children but who might have children in the future.

Legal Issue No. 1

TORT LIABILITY

When someone is injured on rented or leased property, the person who is in control of that part of the premises where the injury occurs is generally responsible if the injury is caused by negligence. The landlord is often responsible for injury caused by a defect in the common areas over which the landlord has control, such as hallways, stairways, and so on. Likewise, the tenant is often responsible for injury caused by defects in the portion of the premises over which the tenant has control.

Legal Issue No. 6

EXAMPLE 9 Paul Malone invited guests to visit him at his apartment. One of the guests was injured when she tripped over a loose floorboard in a hallway that was used by the occupants of several different apartments. Julie Madden, the owner of the building, will probably be responsible for any damages suffered by the injured person. If the accident had occurred inside Malone's apartment, he would be responsible if he were found negligent.

REMOVAL OF FIXTURES BY A TENANT

One of the most troublesome problems that arises in the leasing or purchasing of real property is in regard to fixtures. **Fixtures** are items of personal property that have become attached, annexed, or affixed to real property. They become part of the real property and, unless otherwise agreed, belong to the landlord. The two following examples are typical of the interpretations placed on articles that are classified as fixtures.

Legal Issue No. 5

EXAMPLE 10 Phil Torrey rented a house from Alex Tower. Torrey did not like the electric-light fixtures in the house, so he replaced them with some of his own. At the end of his tenancy, Torrey insisted that the new fixtures were his and that he would remove them and take them with him. Tower, however, contended that they had become part of the real property and could not be removed.

EXAMPLE 11 Paul Snyder bought a house from Louise Valle. When Snyder looked at the house before he made his offer, there were attached to the house window shades, storm windows, awnings, a dishwasher, and a stove. When Snyder took possession, he found that Valle's former tenant had removed all these items. The tenant claimed that they were all items of personal property that she could remove and take with her.

There is no absolute answer to either one of these problems. In deciding lawsuits growing out of problems of this kind, courts usually consider the following things: (1) whether or not it can be removed without damage to the building, (2) whether or not it was specially made to fit the particular building, and (3) the intention of the parties at the time the attachment was made.

EXAMPLE 12 Tom Brill had built several bookshelves in his apartment with written permission of the landlord. When Brill moved, the landlord permitted him to remove the shelves, with an obligation to fill in any holes left by the nails or screws used to attach the shelves to the wall.

When fixtures are installed in such a way that their removal would definitely deface the appearance of a room or building, the fixtures become part of the real property and may not be removed.

EXAMPLE 13 Besides the bookshelves, Brill received permission to install a breakfast nook, building it into the room in such a way as to make it an integral part of the room itself. This installation would be considered real property, and Brill would have no right to remove it at the expiration of his lease.

Trade fixtures are those items of personal property brought upon the land by the tenant which are necessary to carry on the trade or business to which the land will be devoted. Contrary to the general rule, trade fixtures remain the personal property of the tenant or occupier of the land and are removable at the expiration of the term of occupancy.

Remember: Never attach any item of personal property to real property until you have an agreement with the landlord allowing you to remove it. Make sure that there is complete understanding with all parties who might be concerned before any attachment is made. Usually, tenants may remove things they attach if they can do so without damage to the real property. When you make an offer to buy real property, write into your offer every item that you expect to go with the house, no matter how small.

Suggestions for Reducing Legal Risks

If you plan to rent or lease an apartment:

1. Negotiate a written lease that will be entirely satisfactory to you. Try to anticipate your future needs and desires.
2. Read and reread the lease. Do not sign it until you understand it thoroughly.
3. It is wise to record the lease at the registry of deeds if it involves property of considerable value with a high rental charge.
4. If you may be called on to move to another community before the expiration of the lease, have a definite understanding about subletting or assigning the lease.
5. Have a definite understanding as to the effect of holding over.
6. Be sure that you understand the effect of default in rental payment on the due date.

Language of the Law

Define or explain each of the following words or phrases:

real property	tenancy	covenants	quiet enjoyment
personal property	tenancy for years	implied warranty of	dispossess proceeding
tenant	periodic tenancy	habitability	constructive eviction
landlord	rent day	waste	rent control laws
lease	tenancy at will	assignment	fixtures
lessee	tenant at sufferance	sublease	trade fixtures
lessor	holdover tenant	security deposit	

Questions for Review

1. What does real property include?
2. What is the difference between a tenancy for years and a periodic tenancy?
3. Who is a tenant at sufferance? What are the rights of a landlord in relation to such a person?
4. When a tenant holds over without a specific covenant in the lease covering this possibility, how may the landlord interpret this act?
5. List several covenants or specific agreements that you would insist on having in a lease if you were to rent a house or apartment.
6. What is the difference between the assignment and subletting of a lease?
7. How does an implied warranty of habitability affect the rights and duties of the landlord and tenant?

8. How is a lease terminated?
9. What are the exceptions, if any, to the tenant's right to quiet enjoyment of rented premises?
10. When does a landlord have the right to evict a tenant? Under what circumstances may a landlord be found guilty of constructive eviction?
11. How do recent laws regarding habitability, rent control, and antidiscrimination affect the rights of tenants?
12. Who is responsible when someone is injured because of a defect in an apartment house stairway?
13. In deciding a case that involves a dispute over the ownership of a fixture, what factors should a judge take into consideration?

Cases in Point

In each of the following cases, give your decision and state a legal principle that applies to the case:

1. Ann Bixler rented an apartment for $500 a month. She did not sign a lease, and nothing was said about the length of her stay in the apartment. Can she end the tenancy any time that she wishes?
2. Earl Moylan signed a 1-year lease for an unfurnished apartment. The apartment was

in very bad condition, and Moylan assumed that the landlord would repair it and put it in a habitable condition. When the day arrived for Moylan to take possession, he found that nothing had been done to the apartment. May Moylan force the landlord to make needed repairs?
3. Patricia Hopkins owned a six-family house that was fully rented. The tenants complained that the hallway was not properly lighted and that the front steps were broken

and in dangerous condition. Hopkins refused to make repairs, contending that it was the responsibility of the tenants to do so. If the tenants attempt by court action to force Hopkins to make the necessary repairs, will they succeed?

4. Sandra Klinger rented a house to Karl Seltzer for 10 months at a monthly cost of $500. After 3 months, Seltzer moved, claiming that he had never signed a written lease and was not, therefore, liable to Klinger. Klinger sued for the rent for the remaining 7 months during which the house remained unoccupied. Whose claim will be upheld?

5. Damon Rhodes leased a house for 1 year. When his lease expired, he said nothing but continued to pay the rent and occupy the premises for 3 more months. Rhodes then moved and refused to pay any more rent after he moved. The landlord was unable to lease the house for the balance of the year. Does the landlord have a claim against Rhodes for additional rent?

6. Helen Morse signed a 3-year lease for Samuel Land's house at a yearly rental of $4,800 which was payable monthly in advance. After living in the house for 1 year, Morse assigned her unexpired lease to Jane Meeker and notified Land. Meeker failed to pay the rent for 3 months. Was Land legally entitled to collect from Morse?

7. Ralph Yager signed a 1-year lease for an apartment in the Executive Suites. During the winter, ice and snow piled up over the front entrance to the building and the janitor made no effort to remove it. Yager slipped and fell on the ice, suffering serious injury to his back. He sued the landlord for his injuries. The landlord defended herself, saying that she had no responsibility to clear ice and snow from the premises. What will be the outcome of this case?

8. Evelyn Romero rented an apartment in an apartment house from Wilbur Russo for 1 year at $350 a month, subject to termination by either party by giving 60 days' written notice. Nothing was said in the lease about painting and repairs. A small fire in Romero's apartment smoked up the woodwork and walls so that the apartment needed redecorating. Romero sought to have Russo redecorate the apartment. Russo refused. Can Romero force Russo to redecorate?

9. The elevator in Russo's apartment house was declared unsafe by a public official responsible for inspecting apartment houses. This forced Romero and her family to climb 16 floors to their apartment. Russo refused to replace the elevator. Because Romero had a heart condition, her doctor advised her to move. Romero moved out 1 week after the elevator was declared unsafe, and Russo sued Romero for 2 months' rent. Do you think Russo will succeed?

10. Arnold Schepp leased a house and lot for 2 years from Karen Tracy. Nothing was said in the lease about subletting the property. Three months later, Schepp was temporarily transferred by his employer to another city, so Schepp sublet the house to Marilyn Shell, who had two children. Tracy tried to restrain Schepp from subletting to Shell because she was afraid the children might damage the property. Do you think that Tracy can restrain Schepp from subletting? Is Schepp still liable to Tracy for the rent?

Cases to Judge

1. Sorrells rented a single-family dwelling house from Pole Realty Company. When eviction proceedings were brought against her for nonpayment of rent, Sorrells claimed that there had been a breach of the implied warranty of habitability. Pole Realty Company argued that the warranty of habitability does not apply to the rental of single-family

residences. Do you agree? Explain. *Pole Realty Co. v. Sorrells*, 417 N.E.2d 1297 (Illinois)

2. The Kings leased a residential dwelling from a partnership called JA-SIN. The lease agreement provided that the tenants were to "take good care of the house" and "make, at their own expense, the necessary repairs caused by their own neglect or misuse." A guest of the Kings, Sharon Ford, tripped on a loose tread on one step while descending an outside stairway and sustained personal injuries. Who was responsible, the landlord or the tenant? Give a reason for your answer. *Ford v. JA-SIN*, 420 A.2d 184 (Delaware)

3. A porch was located across the hall from Crowell's third-floor apartment. It was not part of the apartment, and the only access to it was through a hall window. At the inception of the lease, Crowell had told the landlord that he might use the porch in the summertime, but the landlord made no reply. On December 31, Crowell held a New Year's Eve party at the apartment. Shortly after midnight, he went out on the porch to get some air. When he put his hands on the railing, it gave way, and he fell to the ground. Was the landlord responsible for Crowell's injuries? Explain. *Crowell v. McCaffrey*, 386 N.E.2d 1256 (Massachusetts)

4. Lolita Pentecost rented an apartment from M. W. Harward, an apartment manager. According to Harward, Pentecost did not pay her rent. Pentecost alleged that Harward forcefully evicted her and her two children and, in addition, kept all her furniture and possessions. Harward claimed that he kept Pentecost's possessions because she did not pay the rent. Can a landlord forcefully evict a tenant and keep the tenant's possessions for nonpayment of rent? Explain. *Pentecost v. Harward*, 699 P.2d 696 (Utah)

5. Thelma Dixon entered into a long-term lease under which she rented a commercial building to Kenneth Hamilton for 24 years at $375 a month. A term of the lease required Dixon's consent to sublease the premises. Four years after signing the lease, with Dixon's consent, Hamilton sublet the premises to Donald Wolf for $750 a month for the first 5 years and $1,500 a month after that. Eight years later, Wolf sold his business to Jong Kap Park and Ki Jha Park. Dixon refused to consent to Hamilton's sublease to the new business owners without negotiating new terms, and Hamilton refused to negotiate. Must Dixon accept the Parks as her tenants and continue to receive $375 a month? Why or why not? *Hamilton v. Dixon*, 214 Cal. Rptr. 639 (California)

Chapter 26

BUYING A HOUSE

Scene: Melanie and David are sitting in their car in front of a house with a "For sale" sign on the front lawn.

David: We're a little early. The broker should be along soon.

Melanie: We're really lucky. Not many people have an aunt like your Aunt Florence to leave them enough money for a down payment on a house.

David: She always did have a soft spot for me.

Melanie: This house is cute.

David: Yes. It is nice. And the property around here is well kept up. That garage next door looks brand new.
(*A car drives up and stops behind their car.*)

Broker (*getting out of the car*): I see you found it alright. Isn't this a beauty? Come on, I'll show you the inside. (*They walk into the house.*)

Broker: You're going to love this place. It's got three bedrooms, a modern kitchen, and a nice little yard. Best of all, there's a little apartment over the garage that you can rent out to bring in some extra money.
(*After looking through the house, David and Melanie decide to buy it.*)

Broker: You won't be sorry. This house is the best buy I've had in a long time. Sign right here, and the house is yours.

David: Shouldn't we have our lawyer look at this contract before we sign it?

Broker: You can if you want, but I won't guarantee that the house will still be available. I just sold the house next door to a young couple yesterday.

Melanie: What kind of deed will we get?

Broker: Oh, the best kind. It's called a quitclaim deed.

David: Will the house be in both our names?

Broker: It sure will. You'll own it as tenants in common. That way, if one of you should pass away, the other will own it outright.
(*Two months later, David is measuring the length of the front yard with a tape measure. A car stops in front of the house, and a man gets out.*)

David: Hello.

Building Inspector: Hello. My name is Andrew Bacon. I'm the building inspector in town. I saw your "Apartment for Rent" sign.

David: Yes. We have an apartment for rent over the garage.

Building Inspector: I hate to tell you this, but you can't rent an apartment here. This part of town is zoned for single families only.

David: Really? We didn't know that.

Building Inspector: Sorry. (*He drives off*)

Jeff (next-door neighbor) (*approaching*): Hi David! How's everything?

David: I just found out that we can't rent our apartment over the garage.

Jeff: Is that right?

David: And I've just measured my front yard, and it doesn't seem to come out right. My deed says that our front yard is 150 feet, so I measured it. I started from the boundary over there, and 150 feet goes 2 feet into your garage.

Jeff: Are you sure? They built my garage on part of your land?

David: It looks that way.

LEGAL ISSUES

1. Is it important to have a lawyer check an agreement to buy a house before signing?
2. Is a quitclaim deed the best kind of deed to have?
3. What does owning property as tenants in common mean?
4. Do people always have the right to rent out an apartment in their house?
5. Can someone gain title to another's real property by placing a garage on it?

THE SPIRIT OF THE LAW

The purchase of a house is frequently the largest single business transaction that a person ever makes. From the initial signing of the purchase and sale agreement to the ultimate taking of title, many legal issues are involved in the transaction. Among other things, the type of mortgage to be used must be decided on; zoning laws should be examined if the house is a multifamily dwelling; title to the property must be checked to be sure that it is clear; easements and restrictions should be examined closely; and the type of deed must be chosen. If co-ownership is involved, a decision must be made as to the best way of taking title. Because of the complexity of the transaction, the purchase of a house is a time when many people find it beneficial to obtain the services of a competent attorney.

ARE YOU READY TO BUY?

There are both advantages and disadvantages to owning a house. One of the major advantages is that the value of real estate has increased rapidly in recent years. Consequently, people are often able to sell their houses at a profit after owning them for a number of years. Some people are able to sell their houses for two to three times the amount they originally paid for them. Another advantage is that homeowners can deduct real estate taxes and interest paid on their mortgage from their federal income tax if they itemize their deductions. People who rent houses or apartments cannot do this. Disadvantages of owning a house include the inconvenience and cost of upkeep and the inability to move about easily and quickly if the need arises.

The first steps in buying a house are to determine whether you can afford one and, if so, the price range that you can afford. One way to accomplish these things is to go to a bank that loans money to home buyers. A bank officer can give you an idea of the amount of down payment you will need and the approximate amount you can borrow, based on your income. One guideline followed by some federal government agencies is that the mortgage payment for a house (principal, interest, and real estate taxes) must not exceed 28 percent of the monthly income before taxes. In addition, monthly debt payments must not exceed 36 percent of income.

EXAMPLE 1   Peter and Margaret King had a combined income of $25,000 per year. They had no outstanding debts. Depending on their bank's requirements and property taxes, they might qualify for a mortgage of $50,000, at 12 percent interest, payable over 30 years. Their monthly mortgage payment would be $515.

Another rule is to limit your monthly housing expenses (including mortgage payments, taxes, heat, utilities, and repair and maintenance costs) to 1 week's pay. Keep in mind that these rules are general ones and do not apply to every individual situation.

ACQUIRING OWNERSHIP

Most property is bought and sold through real estate brokers. Buyers and sellers can deal directly, but finding a buyer for your property when you really want to sell or finding the right property when you want to buy is sometimes a problem. The broker, in most cases, is an agent of the seller. If you are the buyer, you should make it clear before you buy that the broker is to look to the seller for the commission. Whether the buyer and the seller get together by themselves or through a real estate broker, the same general procedure is followed in closing the transaction.

Contract of Sale

Once you have found a house that you want to buy, the next step is to enter into a purchase and sale agreement with the seller. A **purchase and sale agreement** is a written statement of the rights and duties of both parties to the contract. Under the Statute of Frauds, which was discussed in Chapter 11, a contract for the sale of an interest in real property must be in writing to be enforceable. Real property, as you recall, is the ground and anything permanently attached to it. Thus, when you buy a house, you usually buy real property. In some areas of the country it is possible to buy a building and rent the ground underneath. In such a case, the building is treated as personal property rather than real property.

The purchase and sale agreement is probably the most important instrument in the entire transaction of selling and buying a house. If you wish to have legal protection when you buy a house, you should see a lawyer before you sign the purchase and sale agreement. Often the broker will present you with a standard printed purchase and sale agreement and ask you to sign it. The agreement may contain terms that benefit the other party to the contract but not you. A lawyer can change the agreement or draft a new one for you so that it provides the protection you need when buying real property.

From the Office of:

OFFER TO PURCHASE REAL ESTATE

TO_____
     (Seller and Spouse)

_____

_____

                                              Date_____

The property herein referred to is identified as follows: ....
....
....
I hereby offer to buy said property, which has been offered to me by_____
_____ as your Broker, under the following terms and conditions:

                                                 CHECK ONE:

1. I will pay therefore $_____ , of which
     ☐ Check, subject to collection
     ☐ Cash
   (a) $..................... is paid herewith as a deposit to bind this Offer
   (b) $..................... is to be paid as an additional deposit upon the execution of the Purchase and Sale Agreement
                            provided for below.
   (c) $..................... is to be paid at the time of delivery of the Deed in cash, or by certified, cashier's, treasurer's or
                            bank check.
   (d) $.....................
     _____
   (e) $..................... Total Purchase Price
2. This Offer is good until _____ A.M./P.M. on _____ 19_____ , at or before which time a copy hereof shall be signed by you, the Seller and your (husband) (wife), signifying acceptance of this Offer, and returned to me forthwith; otherwise this Offer shall be considered as rejected and the money deposited herewith shall be returned to me forthwith.
3. The parties hereto shall, on or before _____ A.M./P.M. _____ 19_____ , execute the Standard Purchase and Sale Agreement recommended by the Greater Boston Real Estate Board or any form substantially similar thereto, which, when executed, shall be the agreement between the parties hereto.
4. A good and sufficient Deed, conveying a good and clear record and marketable title shall be delivered at 12:00 Noon on _____ 19_____ , at the appropriate Registry of Deeds, unless some other time and place are mutually agreed upon in writing.
5. If I do not fulfill my obligations under this Offer, the above mentioned deposit shall forthwith become your property without recourse to either party.
6. Time is of the essence hereof.
7. The initialed riders, if any, attached hereto are incorporated herein by reference. Additional terms and conditions, if any:
....
....

NOTICE: This is a legal document that creates binding obligations. If not understood, consult an attorney.
        In the event of any disagreement between the parties, the Broker may retain said deposit pending instructions mutually given by the Seller and the Buyer.

                                      SIGNED
WITNESS my hand and seal.   _____
                                                 Buyer
                                                 _____
                                                 Buyer

                                      ADDRESS   PHONE NO.
This Offer is hereby accepted upon the foregoing terms and conditions and the receipt of the deposit of $_____ is hereby acknowledged at _____ A.M./P.M. on _____ 19_____ .
    WITNESS my (our) hand(s) and seal(s).

_____   _____
Seller (or spouse)   Seller

RECEIPT FOR DEPOSIT

_____ 19_____

    Received from_____ the sum of $_____ as deposit under the terms
and conditions of above Offer.   Buyer

                                                 _____
                                                 Broker

COPYRIGHT© 1962   All rights reserved. This form may not be copied or reproduced in whole
GREATER BOSTON REAL ESTATE BOARD   or in part in any manner whatsoever without the prior express written
REVISED 1978, 1985, 1986   consent of the Greater Boston Real Estate Board.

This form creates a valid, binding, enforceable contract when signed by the offeror and offeree. Who is the offeror—the buyer or the seller? Who is the offeree? *(This form has been made available by courtesy of the Greater Boston Real Estate Board and is protected by copyright laws.)*

If you decide not to have a lawyer represent you, it is important that you read the agreement carefully. Cross out anything that you do not want to be in the agreement. Write in anything that you wish to have included. All this must be done before you sign it. The other contracting party (the seller) should be asked to initial any changes that you make.

Buyers should include clauses in the agreement which ensure that the seller will give clear title and the agreement will be canceled and all deposits refunded if the buyer is unable to obtain a loan to purchase the property: The seller should be required to provide a certificate stating that the house is free of termites. The parties should also be in agreement as to how taxes, water and sewer charges, utility bills, transferable insurance policies, and rents (if there are tenants) will be divided between them on the date when the ownership of the property is transferred.

Co-ownership of Real Property

Legal Issue No. 3

Real property may be owned by one person alone or by two or more persons together. There are three principal ways that people can own real property with others. They are tenancy in common, joint tenancy, and tenancy by the entirety. **Tenancy in common** is a type of co-ownership in which a person's heirs inherit that person's share of the property upon death.

EXAMPLE 2 Wendy Chow, Beverly Rojas, and Mark Rojas owned a parcel of real property as *tenants in common*. Chow died. Her one-third share of the property was inherited by her husband and two children. After Chow's death, each heir owned a one-ninth interest in the property as tenants in common with the Rojases, who each still owned a one-third interest in the property.

When two or more people own real property in **joint tenancy,** however, the surviving *joint tenants* own all the property when a co-owner dies.

EXAMPLE 3 If Wendy Chow, Beverly Rojas, and Mark Rojas, in Example 2, had owned the property as joint tenants instead of tenants in common, there would have been a different result. After Chow's death, the entire property would have been owned by the Rojases as joint tenants. Chow's husband and children would have received no interest in the property.

A **tenancy by the entirety** may be held only by a husband and wife. It is based on an old common-law doctrine which held that a husband and wife are regarded, in law, as one. In theory, each spouse owns the entire estate, which neither can destroy by any separate act. The husband, however, has the entire control over the property. This means that he alone has the right to enter the premises as well as to receive the rents and profits from it. Upon the death of one spouse, the property is owned outright by the surviving spouse. The advantage of this type of ownership is that the property cannot be taken away from one of the spouses, even by a court, unless both spouses are sued together.

EXAMPLE 4 Harry and Wanda Quinn owned their residence as tenants by the entirety. Mrs. Quinn was involved in an automobile accident which injured another driver. Suit was brought against Mrs. Quinn but not against Mr. Quinn.

Their residence could not be taken from them in court even if Mrs. Quinn was held to be responsible, because the couple owned the property as tenants by the entirety.

Some states have modernized this law to give women and men equal rights to possession of the property as well as to the rents and profits from it when they own it as tenants by the entirety. Other states have done away with this type of ownership altogether.

Deeds

A **deed** is a formal written instrument which transfers ownership of real property. The parties to a deed are the **grantor** (the one who gives the deed) and the **grantee** (the one to whom the deed is given). Title passes (is transferred) to the buyer the moment the deed is signed and delivered to the buyer. Although not necessary to pass title between the seller and the buyer, the buyer's lawyer will record the deed in the proper public office. The recording gives notice to the public that the buyer now owns the property. Other people cannot claim ownership after the deed is recorded.

Types of Deeds There are two basic types of deeds, although each type may have several specialized forms. The **quitclaim deed** is used to transfer whatever interest the seller may have in the property but does not warrant that he or she has any interest. It merely releases a party's rights to the property.

EXAMPLE 5 Janet Dubois learned that several years ago the seller of the house she had purchased had given a neighbor the right to cut across the rear of the property. Dubois did not wish to continue this practice. In return for a small consideration, the neighbor gave up his right by signing a quitclaim deed.

A **warranty deed** not only passes title to whatever interest the seller has in the property, but also warrants that the seller's title is good. This warranty is the personal promise of the seller that the title is good and that, if this later proves to be untrue, the seller will make good any loss that the buyer suffers.

Legal Issue No. 2

Mortgages

Very few people have enough money in cash to pay the full purchase price at the time they buy a house. They must borrow the money from such places as banks, credit unions, mortgage companies, and insurance companies or from private parties. Lenders of money need to have **security**—some way of getting their money back in case the borrower does not pay. A mortgage is used for this purpose. A **mortgage** is an instrument by which the person who borrows money (the **mortgagor**) pledges property to the lender (the **mortgagee**) as security for a loan. If the mortgagor does not pay the money back according to the terms of the agreement, the mortgagee can have the pledged property sold. This is done under court supervision and is called a **foreclosure.** The money received at the sale is used to pay the loan. If the mortgagor pays the money back as agreed, the mortgage is discharged, and the homeowner owns the property outright.

Types of Mortgage Loans There are various types of mortgage loan plans available. The **conventional loan** is a loan made strictly between the lender and the borrower with no government agency involved. Such a loan usually requires a sizable down payment, and interest rates vary from one lender to another. You may be able to save money by shopping around for the lowest interest rate when you get this kind of loan.

VA-guaranteed loans are made to eligible veterans by private lenders such as banks and other lending institutions. The Veterans Administration (VA) guarantees repayment of 60 percent of the outstanding balance of the loan. This guarantee encourages private lenders to loan money to veterans. Depending on the lender, sometimes a down payment is required, whereas other times it is not. The VA will make direct loans to eligible veterans in areas of the country where there is a shortage of money available for home loans.

The federal government also helps people finance their home purchases through the Federal Housing Administration (FHA), which is a part of the U.S. Department of Housing and Urban Development (HUD). Under the HUD/FHA system, a home buyer makes a small down payment and obtains a loan from a bank, a building and loan association, a mortgage company, an insurance company, or another government-approved lender. The loan is insured by HUD/FHA. Lenders are protected in case borrowers do not pay, which makes it easier for home buyers to obtain mortgage loans.

Because of high mortgage interest rates in recent years, various forms of creative financing have come into being. A **flexible-rate mortgage** has a rate of interest which changes according to fluctuations in a reference index to which it is tied. A **graduated-payment mortgage** has a fixed interest rate during the life of the mortgage; however, the monthly payments increase over the term of the loan. A **balloon-payment mortgage** is one which has relatively low fixed payments during the life of the mortgage followed by one large final (balloon) payment. Other creative financing devices include mortgage assumption (takeover) by the buyer, a second mortgage taken back by the seller, and a **wraparound mortgage** (all-inclusive mortgage) which includes existing mortgages by "wrapping around" old loans. (See Table 26-1.)

EXAMPLE 6 Joan Ackley wishes to borrow $100,000 to expand her business. She owns a valuable building on which there is an existing first mortgage of $50,000 at 8 percent interest. Ackley does not wish to disturb this mortgage because the interest rate is so low. Henry Baker agrees to loan Ackley $150,000 at 11 percent. Baker will give Ackley only $100,000 cash, however, and take over her payments on the $50,000 first mortgage. Ackley will pay $150,000 plus interest back to Baker over the life of the loan. The mortgage that Ackley gives Baker is called a wraparound mortgage because it includes the first mortgage in its payment plan.

Passing of Title

The **closing date** is the date on which the purchase price will be paid and the title (ownership) will be transferred. The seller signs and delivers the deed to the buyer. This date is contained in the purchase and sale agreement.

The thing to be done before the closing date is for the buyer to be satisfied that the seller has a good title to the property. This is done by means of a **title search.** The attorney making the title search provides the buyer with an **abstract of title** containing a history of the property. It lists all previous **encum-**

brances (claims of others) and evidence of their settlement, all present liens and encumbrances, unpaid taxes, and other matters of importance to the security of the buyer.

TABLE 26-1 SOME METHODS OF FINANCING A HOUSE	
Type	Description
Fixed-Rate Mortgage	Fixed interest rate, usually long-term; equal monthly payments including principal and interest until debt is paid in full.
Flexible-Rate Mortgage	Interest rate changes are based on a financial index, resulting in possible changes in monthly payments, loan term, and/or principal. Some plans have rate or payment caps.
Balloon Mortgage	Monthly payments based on fixed interest rate; usually short-term; payments may cover interest only with principal due in full at term end.
Graduated-Payment Mortgage	Lower monthly payments rise gradually (usually over 5 to 10 years), then level off for the duration of term. With flexible interest rate, additional payment changes possible if index changes.
Shared-Appreciation Mortgage	Below-market interest rate and lower monthly payments, in exchange for a share of profits when property is sold or on a specified date. Many variations.
Assumable Mortgage	Buyer takes over seller's original, below-market rate mortgage.
Seller Take-back	Seller provides all or part of financing with a first or second mortgage.
Wraparound Mortgage	Seller keeps original low rate mortgage. Buyer makes payments to seller who forwards a portion to the lender holding original mortgage. Offers lower effective interest rate on total transaction.
Rent with Option	Renter pays "option fees" for right to purchase property at specified time and agreed-upon price. Rent may or may not be applied to sales price.

EXAMPLE 7   Henry Mischel, the purchaser of a recently completed house, requested his attorney to do a title search. The search disclosed that an unpaid judgment had been recorded against the seller in connection with an automobile accident in which the court had found him guilty of negligence. Mischel's attorney insisted that the seller pay off the judgment before Mischel accepted a deed to the property.

The abstract itself does not prove ownership. The lawyer who presents the abstract of title is not insuring the title; he or she is merely giving you an opinion that the title is good. If you want title insurance, you must go to a title insurance company. **Title insurance** pays the property's value in the event a prior claim is uncovered.

Assuming that the title is found to be good, the parties get together on the day set for the final closing and the seller delivers to the buyer the deed to the property.

Settlement Costs   The Real Estate Settlement Procedures Act (RESPA), a federal law, will give you protection if you apply for a home loan and it is approved. When you apply for a loan, the lender must give you a copy of a booklet that explains the real estate settlement procedure. Soon after you apply for the loan, the lender must also give you an estimate of the costs you will incur in obtaining it. Later, a uniform settlement statement must be filled out which will show you in detail the exact cost of the settlement. You have a right to see the completed form on the day before the closing if you wish. The lender must also give you a truth-in-lending statement showing the true costs of the interest and finance charge on the mortgage loan. (Truth-in-lending is discussed in more detail in Chapter 16.)

Inheritance and Adverse Possession

There are ways to gain title to real property other than by deed. One of them is by **inheritance.** When someone dies owning real property other than as a joint tenant or tenant by the entirety, title to the property passes automatically to the deceased person's heirs. No deed is necessary. All that is required is that the deceased person's estate be probated (officially recognized by a court). This is discussed in Chapter 39. Another way to gain title to real property is by **adverse possession.** This occurs when one or more people, who do not really own the property, take possession of it for a continuous length of time. The time period, which differs from state to state, ranges from 10 to 21 years. The continuous possession by others, one after the other, without interruption by the real owner, is counted to make up the time period. The possession must be open, not secretive, with a claim that it is being done rightfully.

Legal Issue No. 5

EXAMPLE 8   Bruce and Jennifer Lue bought a house and lived in it for 25 years. After all that time, they discovered that the property line ran through the middle of their house. Their next-door neighbor actually owned the land under half their house. A mistake had been made when the house was built. The Lues could petition the court to obtain title to the land under their house by adverse possession.

LIMITATIONS ON REAL PROPERTY RIGHTS

If you are the owner of real property, you have certain rights to that property. Basically, these are (1) the right to use the property during your lifetime, (2) the right to exclude others from using it, (3) the right to leave the property to your heirs when you die, and (4) the right to sell the property to someone else during your lifetime. However, some limitations on your use may be imposed by law or may arise out of contracts.

Limitations Imposed by Law

Your use of property is limited by laws enacted at the federal, state, and local levels of government. Generally speaking, these laws are designed to protect the rights of the general public and to promote the general welfare.

Protection Against Nuisance and Zoning Laws The use you make of your land may have an effect on other people. If this use seriously damages the property of your neighbors or otherwise violates their rights, you may be prevented by law from continuing it.

EXAMPLE 9 Don Peters owned a house on a city lot in a middle-class neighborhood. He decided to raise chickens in his backyard for food and as a hobby. His neighbors objected strongly, claiming that such a project would lower the property value of their street.

The neighbors would have every right to object. Peter's action would in law be called a **nuisance,** which can be defined as an annoyance that does harm. To determine whether a given use of property is legally a nuisance is difficult; it is necessary to examine the facts of each case. Loud noises, constant vibrations, smoke, dust, obnoxious odors, and the like are said to be nuisances, as are the loud playing of a television set late at night, bright lights on a lawn, or unsanitary conditions on the property. Persons subjected to such things may seek removal of the nuisances in courts of equity.

EXAMPLE 10 Sally Clayton directed a local dance band which often conducted rehearsals at the Clayton home late at night. Residents in the neighborhood asked Clayton to stop the band practice at a reasonable hour. When she refused to do so, her neighbors entered a complaint in a court of equity. The final result was an injunction which required the band to end its rehearsals by 11 p.m.

The value of all the property in a given neighborhood will be kept at a higher level if all the property is used in about the same way. It is for this reason that most cities or towns have **zoning laws,** which prescribe the use that may be made of property in specified areas. One area, for example, might be zoned for one-family houses only, another for multiple-family dwellings, and another for stores.

Legal Issue No. 4

EXAMPLE 11 The Lingenfelters purchased a new home. Shortly after moving into the new residence, they learned that a private land developer had purchased 5 acres of adjoining property and planned to build a new shopping center. The Lingenfelters reviewed the zoning laws of the area and discovered

A nuisance is an annoyance that causes harm. Courts of equity can order the discontinuance of a nuisance. *(ZIGGY, by Tom Wilson. Copyright © 1986, Universal Press Syndicate. Reprinted with permission. All rights reserved.)*

that commercial construction of any kind was prohibited within a 20-block area. The land developer would probably be denied a construction license because of the zoning restriction.

When a new zoning law is enacted, it does not apply to existing uses of the property. They are called **nonconforming uses** and may continue to exist. Had the zoning law in Example 11 been adopted after the developer had developed the land, it would have been allowed as a nonconforming use.

Health and Public Safety Regulations City ordinances or town bylaws dealing with health and public safety may include fire-prevention laws; required inspections of plumbing, electric wiring, heating equipment, and general soundness of construction; and regulations dealing with public health. This right of government to regulate the use of real property for the public welfare, morals, and health is known as the government's **police power.**

Eminent Domain The right of the government (federal and state) to take private land with or without the consent of the owner for public use is called the right of **eminent domain.** It is under this right of eminent domain that private land can be taken for such things as public buildings, highways, school buildings, power projects, housing projects, parks, and many other public uses. The private owner is paid for the land taken. Usually, a price can be agreed on by the two parties. If they cannot agree, an action in court is begun; then the court must determine the value.

Air Rights   Before the start of the air age, landowners had exclusive possession of property from the surface up to the sky and down to the center of the earth. The exclusive right to the airspace above the ground has been limited by court decisions in the interest of aviation, permitting free navigation of the air without fear of trespass actions. Today, owners are said to own all the airspace above their land over which they have reasonable control. This is usually interpreted to be only a few feet above the highest structure.

Subterranean and Riparian Rights   The exclusive rights of an owner below the land surface, or **subterranean rights,** are still said to extend to the center of the earth. Property owners sometimes sell subterranean rights if their property is in an area where mines or wells are operated.

The rights of a person through whose lands a natural watercourse runs are known as **riparian rights.** The owner of such land may use the water and may build a wharf and have access to navigable water. However, he or she does not have title to the water or to the fish that swim in the water. Thus the owner may not pollute waters flowing through the land, or divert streams from their natural channels to the harm of landowners, or otherwise unreasonably lessen the flow of water in the streams. If the stream is not navigable and does not adjoin navigable waters, the owners of the land on each side have title to the soil to the middle of the stream.

EXAMPLE 12   The Franklin Tool Corporation drew water for manufacturing use from a stream that flowed through its property. Siefert, who owned property farther upstream, dammed the stream, cutting off all flow into the plant's property. The corporation secured an injunction against Siefert, requiring her to remove the dam and stop interfering with the natural flow of the stream.

When water freezes, the ice is considered to be a part of the land and belongs to the owner of the land adjoining the stream. Owners on opposite banks of the same stream have ownership of the ice to the midpoint of the stream unless their deeds state otherwise.

Limitations Arising Out of Contract

In addition to limitations on the use of property imposed by law, there are also various limitations that arise out of contracts. These contractual limitations include restrictions contained in the deed to property and provisions (such as easements or licenses) contained in separate contracts.

Restrictions in the Deed   Restrictions in deeds may require that all the houses in a given tract of land cost not less than a certain amount to build, that all houses be set not less than a specified number of feet from the street, or that they all have basements. Such restrictions are possible when all the land so restricted originally belonged to one person.

EXAMPLE 13   Tom Olivo owned a 40-acre farm located at the city limits. He decided to subdivide his farm into building lots and sell them to prospective builders. He laid out streets and blocks, dividing each block into building lots.

Since he owned all the lots, he could sell them subject to any building restrictions he wished. These restrictions would be written into the deed of each lot sold. He knew that prospective buyers would pay a higher price for the lots because of the protection offered by the restrictions.

Easements and Licenses   An **easement** is a right to make some use of land belonging to another. Most often it is a right to cross someone else's land at a particular place. It may also be a right to erect poles and suspend power lines over land or to lay pipelines beneath the surface. An easement is a property interest, and once established, it cannot be terminated without the consent of the owner of the right. Usually, it is a right that is bought and paid for, either in money or by some other consideration.

EXAMPLE 14   A driveway extended from the street between the property owned by the Hestons and that owned by their neighbors. By consent of both parties, one-half the driveway was constructed on Heston's land and one-half on the neighbor's land. Therefore, each owner had an easement in a part of the other's land in the use of this driveway. Neither could close off his or her part of the driveway without affecting the rights of the other.

A **license** is a right to do something on the land of another that would otherwise be unlawful. A good example would be hunting or fishing or the painting of a sign on a farmer's barn. A license does not convey a right or interest in the land; it merely grants the right to use the land in the manner and for the purpose agreed upon by the owner.

SPECIAL TYPES OF HOME OWNERSHIP

There are certain types of home ownership which are regulated, at least in part, by special laws. Mobile homes, cooperative apartments, and condominium apartments are examples of these special types of home ownership. The laws governing these types of home ownership are discussed below.

Mobile Homes

■ Mobile homes represent a sizable portion of the dwellings in this country. Mobile homes are less expensive to purchase than ordinary houses and cost less to keep up. They usually can be sold quickly and easily. Unless placed on permanent foundations and given other special treatment, mobile homes are said to be personal property and therefore do not come within the jurisdiction of real estate tax boards.

Most states have passed legislation requiring special fees to be paid by mobile-home residents. These fees, in addition to the usual highway license, provide income from the mobile-home owners for use in providing schools and other services enjoyed by all citizens. The ownership of mobile homes and the operation of mobile-home parks are regulated by state statutes.

Cooperatives

Cooperative ownership of apartment houses begins with the formation of a corporation which builds or buys an apartment building with a number of living units. The corporation usually places a mortgage on the land for the purpose of constructing the building. Prospective tenants purchase shares of stock, and thus the capital necessary to complete the apartment building is raised. The purchase of a specified number of shares gives a prospective tenant the right to a **proprietary lease,** which is a long-term lease issued by the corporation. Such a lease gives the tenant all the usual rights of ownership. The tenant has the right of possession of the apartment, for which the tenant makes regular payments to the corporation of a share of the operating expenses, mortgage debt and reduction, and taxes. The amount levied against each tenant is determined by the number of shares of stock held. The large apartments are held by those owning a greater number of shares. Tenants provide their own electrical appliances, floor coverings, and interior maintenance.

The disadvantage of cooperative apartments is the possibility of mortgage foreclosure, in which case the tenant may lose some rights. In such a case, a receiver is appointed for the operation of the apartment project for the benefit of the mortgagee, and each tenant is required to pay either a share of the mortgage or the full rental for the apartment as a means of paying off the mortgage.

Condominiums   Another kind of apartment ownership is the **condominium.** Each owner purchases a unit and receives a deed that gives that person absolute ownership of the apartment unit that has been purchased. The owner also receives an undivided interest or share in the ownership of those parts of the ground and structure that are not under the supervision or care of one individual. These include the roof, stairways, yard, swimming pool, elevators, heating system, and the like.

The owner of a condominium has a legal status similar to that of a home or cooperative owner. He or she has exclusive ownership of a unit and, with certain restrictions, may decorate and occupy the premises as desired. The advantage of a condominium over a cooperative is that the owner is not faced with the possibility of foreclosure affecting the entire building. The only foreclosure that might threaten a condominium owner would be of a mortgage covering his or her own investment, which is always under that person's own control and not affected by limited occupancy of other units or by faulty management.

Suggestions for Reducing Legal Risks

If you plan to purchase a house:

1. Carefully examine the property before entering into a contract to determine whether the property will meet your present and future needs. Obtain the advice of an expert if necessary. Do not be in a hurry.
2. Get the advice of your attorney as to legal restrictions, covenants, zoning laws, or easements that could interfere with the use of the property.
3. Have your attorney examine the owner's title for possible defects, recorded liens, recorded leases, unpaid taxes, mortgages, or other encumbrances.
4. Consult your attorney as to the way the deed should name the owner if both husband and wife are owners. This is very important in case of later divorce, sale, or death.
5. If payment of the loan is to be in installments, carefully read the note and mortgage to determine the effect of a default in payment.
6. Record the deed as soon as possible.

Language of the Law

Define or explain each of the following words or phrases:

purchase and sale agreement
tenancy in common
joint tenancy
tenancy by the entirety
deed
grantor
grantee
quitclaim deed
warranty deed
security

mortgage
mortgagor
mortgagee
foreclosure
conventional loan
VA-guaranteed loans
flexible-rate mortgage
graduated-payment mortgage
balloon-payment mortgage

wraparound mortgage
closing date
title search
abstract of title
encumbrances
title insurance
inheritance
adverse possession
nuisance
zoning laws

nonconforming uses
police power
eminent domain
subterranean rights
riparian rights
easement
license
proprietary lease
condominium

Questions for Review

1. Give two advantages and two disadvantages of owning a house.
2. What is the first step in buying a house?
3. Describe a guideline followed by some federal government agencies in determining the mortgage payment for a house.
4. Why is the purchase and sale agreement important?
5. What kinds of clauses might a buyer wish to include in an agreement to purchase a house?
6. How does a buyer make certain that the seller has good title to real property?
7. What kind of protection does the Real Estate Settlement Procedures Act give to a person who purchases real estate?
8. Does a warranty deed guarantee that you will get a good title to the property? Explain.
9. What is the difference between joint tenants and tenants in common as a form of co-ownership?
10. Explain the advantage of a husband and wife owning property as tenants by the entirety.
11. How may a person gain title to real property by adverse possession?
12. Does a deed give you absolute rights to do as you please with your property? Explain.
13. Are mobile homes considered real property? Explain.
14. What advantage does a condominium offer over a cooperative in multifamily dwellings?

Cases in Point

In each of the following cases, give your decision and state a legal principle that applies to the case:

1. Joseph DiRito owned a parcel of real property with Oskar Henrich as tenants in common. Henrich died. Who owned the property after his death?

2. Horace and Inez Atkinson owned their residence as tenants by the entirety in a state that still follows the old common-law doctrine on that subject. One day, Mr. Atkinson refused to allow Mrs. Atkinson to enter the premises. Was Mr. Atkinson within his legal rights?

3. Kerr bought 10 acres of land bordering on a river from Sandra Adams, who gave a quitclaim deed to the land. Later, Kerr discovered that a former owner of the land had sold and assigned the water rights to the land to an industrial plant, thereby defeating Kerr's plans for using the property. Kerr sued Adams for damages. Can Kerr recover?

4. Edgar Volmer, a contractor, made an agreement with Edward White to build a brick building at the rear of White's house to be used as an automobile repair shop. Before the building was started, a city ordinance was passed making it illegal to operate such a business in that particular area. Was this contract terminated by the passage of this ordinance?

5. Ezra Prindle entered into a written contract to purchase a house and lot from Joanne Sanders for $80,000. Before the closing date arrived, Prindle saw a better house which he could buy for $70,000, so he notified Sanders that he had changed his mind. If Prindle refuses to purchase the house, what are Sanders's legal rights?

6. Two years after Ramirez started raising pigs on her property, the neighborhood in which she lived was rezoned. The new zoning law prohibited the raising of pigs and other specified animals. Must Ramirez stop raising pigs?

7. The Harding Social Club purchased a house adjoining the Community Church. Equip-ment was installed in the house for the entertainment of members, including a public-address system to be used for dances. The members held regular dances every Wednesday evening, during which time the church held midweek services. The music was so loud that the church service had to be called off. May the church stop the operation of the public-address system by its neighbors?

8. Jane Kinder entered into an agreement to purchase a building lot in a new development. The deed contained a provision that any house built on the lot must cost at least $100,000. Kinder wanted to build a $75,000 house. Can Kinder be restrained from building the $75,000 house?

9. Samuel Carr lent $18,500 to Hans Dahl, receiving from Dahl a note for that amount secured by a mortgage on his house. The note was not paid at maturity, and Carr foreclosed on the realty. The property brought only $15,000 when sold under order of the court. What may Carr do to collect the $3,500 still due him? If the property at the foreclosure sale had brought more than the amount due Carr, to whom would the money remaining after Carr was paid belong?

10. Bob Welter had a $5,000 properly recorded mortgage on real estate owned by Marjorie Mestler. Mestler sold the property to Quincey Monroe. Did Welter still have a mortgage on the property?

Cases to Judge

1. Ronald and Mary Kennedy owned a 4,600-acre farm as joint tenants. Mr. Kennedy died without a will, owing a large amount of money to creditors. The question arose as to who owned the land after Mr. Kennedy's death. If his estate (his heirs) owned the land, the creditors could reach it; otherwise, they could not. How would you decide? Explain. *In re estate of Kennedy,* 369 N.W.2d 63 (Nebraska)

2. Edward Desmond, who was in his eighties, signed a warranty deed which would transfer his house to his daughter Elizabeth Lenhart. He placed the deed in his safe-deposit box and told Lenhart that he wanted her to have the house when he passed on. Later, when Desmond was injured in an automobile accident, Lenhart opened the safe-deposit box to obtain insurance papers. Some time after that, Desmond discovered that the deed had

been taken from the box and recorded at the registry of deeds. He testified that he did not give the deed to his daughter and that he did not intend her to have title to the property before his death. Did title pass to Lenhart? Why or why not? *Lenhart v. Desmond,* 705 P.2d 338 (Wyoming)

3. Yolanda Blakely bought some real property, improved it, and leased it to Reider and Dolores Kelstrup for 5 years. During the lease period, Blakely deeded the property to a trust. That deed was recorded. Later, the trust deeded the property back to Blakely. That deed, however, was not recorded. When their lease expired, the Kelstrups refused to vacate the premises, and Blakely brought suit to have them evicted. The Kelstrup's claim that Blakely does not own the property because the deed from the trust to her was not recorded. Do you agree? Why or why not? *Blakely v. Kelstrup,* 708 P.2d 253 (Montana)

4. George Woodruff owned a lot of land in Beatrice, Nebraska. For about 7 years, he planted a vegetable garden on the vacant lot next door, with permission of the owner. At some point after that, he placed a fence between the two lots. The fence, however, was placed about 3 feet beyond the property line, on the vacant lot. He planted some rosebushes on his side of the fence and a row of cedar trees on the line appearing to be a continuation of the fenceline. Is it possible for Woodruff to obtain title to the 3-foot strip of land next to his lot? *Hadley v. Ideus,* 374 N.W.2d 231 (Nebraska)

5. Helen M. Norcross agreed in writing to sell her house to Mr. and Mrs. Steven R. Simon. The house had a $27,000 mortgage on it. The written agreement stated that the buyer "is to pay the sum of $27,000 of which $100 have been paid this day, $26,900 balance in cash on delivery of said deed." This was followed by the words: "It is agreed between the parties that the purchasers shall assume and agree to pay the balance due on the existing mortgage with Cape Cod Cooperative Bank as part of the consideration of this sale." The buyers claim that the agreement means that the price of the house is $27,000—the amount of the mortgage. The seller claims that it means that the price of the house is $54,000—the cash plus the mortgage. How would you decide? *Simon v. Norcross,* 353 N.E.2d 789 (Massachusetts)

Chapter 27

FAMILY INSURANCE PROTECTION

Scene: The Green home. Melanie and David are about to have dinner with their next-door neighbors, Liz and Jeff.

Melanie: It's great to get together with you guys.

Liz: You wouldn't believe what happened while you were away yesterday.

Melanie: What happened?

Jeff: We had a fire in the neighborhood and a shoot-out!

Melanie: A shoot-out?

Jeff: Yeah. The police had a warrant out for the arrest of Mrs. Winslow's son—she lives up the street, you know.

David: Yes. I know her.

Jeff: Well, when her son saw the police in front of his house, he started shooting out the window at them.

Melanie: I don't believe it!

Liz: He wounded two police officers, and they finally killed him.

Melanie: Oh my! What a shame. Poor Mrs. Winslow!

Jeff: And later in the day, Bill and Betty's house across the street caught on fire.

Liz: Yes. Bill had started their grill on the back porch, and he went in the house for a minute, and when he came out, the porch was on fire.

David: Did it do much damage?

Jeff: It ruined the porch and damaged the kitchen quite a bit.

Melanie: I hope their insurance will cover it.

David: Bill and I were talking about our fire insurance coverage just last week. He said that his house was insured for about half its value.

Melanie: Oh that's good. It will cover their fire damage then.

David: Say, I just remembered something. I loaned Bill our VCR last week. I wonder if it got burned up?

Jeff: Your homeowner's insurance should cover that. I wouldn't worry.

Liz: It looks as though we need a lot of insurance coverage in this neighborhood.

Jeff: You can say that again! Life insurance, fire insurance, shoot-out insurance!

Liz: Don't be funny, Jeff.

David: Speaking of life insurance, I don't know whether it's better to get term insurance or whole life insurance.

Jeff: I think term insurance is best. I heard that it builds up a loan value that you can borrow from.

David: Are you sure of that?

Melanie: Dinner's almost ready. I can smell the steak cooking.

David: I hope you're watching it!

Jeff: I've got an idea! Why don't Liz and I take out life insurance on your two lives, and you two take it out on ours. That way, if you get killed in a shoot-out, we can collect.

Liz: Oh, Jeff, don't joke about that.

Melanie: That poor Mrs. Winslow. I hope she had insurance on her son's life.

LEGAL ISSUES

1. Is an entire loss covered (up to the face value of the policy) when a house is insured for half its value?
2. Does a homeowner's policy cover damage to personal property left at someone else's house?
3. Can people borrow money on a term insurance policy?
4. Can people take out life insurance on anyone they want to?
5. Is an insurance company liable if the insured is killed while trying to avoid capture by the police?

THE SPIRIT OF THE LAW

Our lives are filled with risks. These risks include loss of property, loss of health, loss of jobs, and the loss of our very lives. The purpose of insurance is to spread the losses among a greater number of people.

Insurance is a highly regulated business activity governed by the laws of each state. Ordinary contract law, discussed in Unit 2, forms the basis for the interpretation of insurance policies. Agency law plays an important role when insurance is purchased through an agent or broker. The law of torts, criminal law, personal property law, and bailments often determine an insurance company's responsibility in paying insurance claims. Over the years, many rules of law have developed to address the legal issues raised in the insurance field.

INSURANCE TERMS

Insurance may be defined as a contract whereby one party, known as the insurer, agrees to reimburse another if the latter suffers a specified monetary loss. Certain terms are common to most forms of insurance. The most important of these terms are as follows:

The **policy** is the written statement containing the insurance agreement.

The **policyholder** is the owner of the insurance policy.

The **insured** is the person whose life or property is insured.

The **premium** is the amount paid periodically by the insured for insurance.

The **risk** is the event insured against, such as fire, theft, or death.

The **insurer** is the party that issues the policy, collects the premium, and assumes the risk.

The **binder** is an oral or written statement putting the insurance into force until the regular policy can be issued. As a matter of fact, insurance is usually considered as being in effect as soon as the application is accepted by an authorized agent of the insurance company.

The **beneficiary** is the person who is to receive **indemnification** (payment) under the policy. Except in life insurance, the beneficiary is usually, but not always, the insured.

EXAMPLE 1 The Merchants Bank loaned Grace Gardner $4,800 for the purchase of a sports car. Gardner signed an installment note, and the bank took out insurance on Gardner's life to protect its investment. Gardner was the insured; the insurance company was the insurer; the Merchants Bank was the beneficiary of the policy. The bank received a binder from the agent of the insurance company and later received a regular policy. The policy would provide coverage until the loan was totally repaid. Thus, if Gardner were to die before repaying the loan, the Merchants Bank would recover the balance due from the insurance company.

When a premium is not paid, the policy is said to have **lapsed.** This does not mean that the policy is not good; it means that the company may, at its option, void the contract. Generally, the company will require the insured to take a physical examination (in case of life insurance) in addition to paying the premium due before a lapsed policy can be reinstated.

The period allowed after the premium is due and before the policy will lapse for nonpayment of the premium is called **days of grace.** The time period varies but is usually 30 or 31 days.

EXAMPLE 2 All Town Insurance Company mailed a premium notice to one of its policyholders whose premium was due on May 1. The premium was not received by May 1. In that particular state, All Town must allow a 30-day grace period during which time the policy would remain in force. The policy could not be canceled during this period without the insured's consent.

The **cash surrender value** of an insurance policy is the amount that the policyholder will receive if he or she decides to cancel the insurance. The cash surrender value of whole life insurance increases with the age of the policy.

The **loan value** of an insurance policy is the amount that the policyholder may borrow from the insurance company. The loan value increases with the age of the policy if the policy provides for this feature.

The **insurable interest** is the financial interest that the policyholder has in the person or property that is insured.

A **valued policy** is one in which the amount to be paid by the insurance company is definitely stated.

An **open policy** is one in which the amount to be paid by the insurance company is to be determined when the loss occurs.

INSURABLE INTEREST REQUIRE-MENT

Legal Issue No. 4

A person cannot take out insurance unless she or he has an insurable interest in the person or property that is insured. In the case of life insurance, the policyholder must be in the position of suffering a loss if the insured dies. The insurable interest need be present only when the policy is first issued.

EXAMPLE 3 You lend $1,000 to a friend, to be repaid at the end of 3 years. You now have an insurable interest in your friend's life to the extent of $1,000 for a 3-year period. You should be able to get an insurance policy on your friend's life for $1,000 if your friend can pass the required physical examination and meet all the other requirements.

The close relationship that exists between a husband and wife or between parents and their children creates an insurable interest. The requirement of insurable interest is different in life insurance contracts as compared to fire insurance contracts. In life insurance contracts, you must have an insurable interest at the time the policy is taken out. In fire insurance, you must have an insurable interest at the time of the loss.

EXAMPLE 4 A house owned by Fred Quinn was insured against fire. Quinn sold the house to Thomas Clark. Quinn had paid a premium to All Town Insurance Company which would have continued the policy in force for 7 more months subsequent to the sale. One month after the sale, the house burned to the ground and Quinn sought to collect on the policy. All Town did not have to pay because Quinn did not have an insurable interest in the house at the time of the fire. His interest ceased when he sold the house to Clark.

If, in Example 3, your friend repaid the loan at the end of 3 years, you would no longer have an insurable interest in his life. However, if you continued to pay regular premiums on the insurance contract, the insurer would have to pay the amount of the policy on your friend's death.

LIFE INSURANCE

The essential feature of life insurance is the promise by an insurance company that it will pay the beneficiary a stated amount, called the **face value,** in case of the death of the insured. The amount the beneficiary actually receives upon the death of the insured is called the **proceeds.** It usually includes interest added to the face value of the policy. In addition to this essential feature, life insurance policies often contain other provisions. Some policies contain a **double indemnity** clause. In the event of the accidental death of the insured, the beneficiary receives double the amount of the face value of the policy. The policy may also provide for the payment of a monthly sum to the insured if he or she becomes totally disabled. There is often a **waiver of premium** provision, which means that premiums do not have to be paid as long as the insured is disabled.

Most policies have a provision permitting the policyholder to reserve the right to change the beneficiary. If this provision is not in the policy, the beneficiary may not be changed.

Premium rates are based on the age of the insured at the time the policy is issued. If people lie about their age and thereby obtain a lower premium rate, the insurance, in most cases, will not be void. Instead, the insurance company is required to pay only the amount of insurance that could be purchased by the premiums figured on the basis of the true age of the insured.

Legal Issue No. 5

Most policies provide that the insurance company is not liable if the insured is killed while trying to avoid capture by the police. They also state that the insurer will not pay if the insured commits suicide within a specified time, usually 1 or 2 years, after the policy is issued. After the specified time period, however, the insurer will have to pay in the event of suicide. In addition, the beneficiary of a life insurance policy who intentionally causes the death of an insured forfeits all rights he or she may have under the policy.

The ordinary laws of infancy, which were discussed in Chapter 8, apply to a minor's contract of life insurance, except as changed by state statute. Many states have statutes that permit minors to enter into legally enforceable contracts for life insurance which cannot be avoided by the minor.

If the insurer has been misled in issuing the policy by false statements of the insured, the policy may later be canceled. It would be unjust, however, to allow the insurer to collect premiums for many years and then, upon the death of the insured, refuse to pay because of some small misrepresentation. For this reason, most policies provide that after a specified number of years—usually 2 or 3— the policy becomes incontestable. This means that the insurer must pay, regardless of former defenses that might have been good prior to the expiration of the contestable time period. Many states provide for an incontestability clause by statute.

EXAMPLE 5 Arthur Lindsley applied for a $50,000 ordinary life insurance policy but did not disclose that he had suffered severe injuries during combat in Viet Nam which had seriously affected his heart. He made a misrepresentation when questioned on these matters, and the policy was thereafter issued. Four years later the insured died, and the misrepresentation was offered by the company as a defense against paying the policy. Since the policy had been in force for more than 2 years, such a defense was not admissible and the policy had to be paid.

Kinds of Life Insurance

Some people want protection only. Others are interested chiefly in investment. Between these two extremes, we have people who want both protection and investment in varying degrees written into one policy. These are the main reasons so many kinds of policies are offered.

Term insurance is insurance which is issued for a particular time period, usually 5 or 10 years. The time period is known as the term. Term insurance is the least expensive kind of life insurance. This is so because term policies have no cash surrender value or loan value, as others do. Term insurance offers protection alone, in contrast to ordinary life insurance (discussed below), which combines protection with a savings plan. Also, at the end of each term, unlike ordinary life insurance, the premium is raised. This is so because the insured is older and, therefore, is a greater risk.

A modified form of term insurance is **decreasing term insurance.** The premium stays the same from year to year, but the amount of protection (death benefit) decreases over the years. This type of policy is widely used to cover the outstanding balance of a home mortgage.

Ordinary life insurance, which is also known as **straight life** or **whole life insurance,** requires the payment of premiums throughout the life of the insured. Upon the insured's death, the beneficiary is paid the face value of the policy. This type of insurance gradually builds up a cash surrender value which the policyholder may withdraw if he or she decides to discontinue the insurance. It also gradually builds up a loan value. For these reasons, ordinary life insurance has both protection and investment features.

Limited-payment life insurance provides that the payment of premiums will stop after a stated length of time—usually 10, 20, or 30 years. The amount of the policy will be paid to the beneficiary upon the death of the insured, whether the death occurs during the payment period or after. Such a policy makes it possible for persons to complete the premium payments on their policies while they still have a high earning power. The cash surrender value of a limited-payment life policy is much greater than that of an ordinary life policy.

EXAMPLE 6 Ann Caro took out a policy that provided that she should continue paying premiums until she was 60 years old. From that time on, she would not have to pay any premiums, and the amount of the policy would be payable to her beneficiary. This is an example of a limited-payment life policy.

Endowment insurance provides protection for a stated time, generally 20 to 30 years. The face of the policy is paid to the insured at the end of the agreed period, or if the insured dies during the period, the full amount is paid to the beneficiary. The premium is higher because the policy builds up its cash value more rapidly.

EXAMPLE 7 Don Ray purchased a $10,000 twenty-year endowment policy naming his wife as beneficiary. He died after the policy had been in force only 3 years. It was held that his wife was entitled to the face value of the policy, $10,000. If he had lived until the policy had been in effect for 20 years, the insurance company would have paid the $10,000 to him.

An **annuity** is not really life insurance. Rather, it is a guaranteed retirement income which a person secures either by paying a lump-sum premium or by periodically paying a set amount to an insurer. The insured may choose to receive an income for a certain fixed number of years, with a beneficiary receiving whatever is left of the annuity when the insured dies. The insured, however, may choose to receive payments as long as he or she lives and, upon death, will lose whatever is left of the annuity.

EXAMPLE 8 William Lotz, 50 years old, had no dependents. He made an agreement with an insurance company to pay $100 a month for the next 15 years, at which time he would begin drawing an annual amount based on his deposits plus interest. This is an example of an annuity. If Lotz should die sometime within the 15-year period, his heirs would collect only the accumulation based on the provisions of the contract.

Accidental death and dismemberment insurance provides benefits when the insured is killed in an accident or loses the use of both hands, both feet, one hand and one foot, sight in both eyes, one hand and sight in one eye, or one foot and sight in one eye. Commonly, if one hand or one foot or the sight in one eye is lost, the policy provides for payment of half the full benefit. Insurers often include a maximum payment clause, but such limits on liability are open to jury interpretation.

HEALTH INSURANCE

Because of the high cost of medical care, it is of increased importance for people to have some kind of health insurance. Many employers provide group health insurance plans as part of the benefits to their employees.

Hospitalization insurance provides benefits to cover the cost of staying in a hospital. Blue Cross coverage is a well-known example of this kind of insurance. Hospital insurance pays for room and board, medical services and supplies, and nursing care in a semiprivate hospital room for a particular number of days.

Medical and surgical insurance pays for doctors' and surgeons' bills when the insured becomes ill or has to have an operation. Blue Shield coverage is a well-known example of this type of insurance. Many medical and surgical insurance policies place limits on the amount that the insurance company will pay for particular kinds of treatment.

Major medical insurance pays for large hospital and medical bills resulting from serious and prolonged illness. This insurance commonly contains a **deductible clause** requiring the insured to pay an initial amount before the insurance company will pay anything. In addition to paying the deductible, the insured will often be required to pay a small percentage of the amount owed.

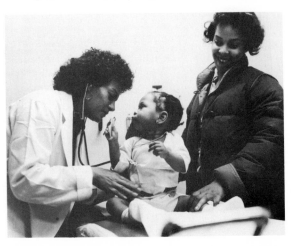

Health insurance helps pay for medical care.

Disability income insurance pays benefits to the insured when he or she is either totally or partially disabled. **Total disability** occurs when a person is unable to perform normal job duties for a year or longer. **Partial disability** occurs when a person is unable to perform one or more of the basic duties of a job but is able to perform some of the duties.

FIRE INSURANCE

Fire insurance is a contract in which the insurer promises, for a stated premium, to pay the insured a sum not exceeding the face amount of the policy if a particular piece of real or personal property is damaged or destroyed by fire. Even before a policy is issued, a written or even an oral binder is valid and may make fire insurance effective. The policy covers losses to specific property located at the place stated in the policy. The policy itself becomes effective as soon as the application is accepted by the insurer, even though the insured has not yet paid the premium.

A fire insurance policy covers loss resulting directly or proximately (very closely or almost directly) from an unfriendly fire. An **unfriendly,** or **hostile, fire** is one that becomes uncontrollable or escapes from the place where it is supposed to be. A bonfire or a fire in a furnace is a friendly fire unless it gets beyond control.

EXAMPLE 9 Anna Kornilov, while starting a fire in her living room fireplace, accidentally dropped her glasses into the fire. Recovery for loss of the glasses would not be permitted. Had embers fallen from the fireplace to the rug and damaged it, however, a recovery would be allowed for that damage.

Damages to property resulting from attempts to put out a fire or from theft or breakages in attempting to remove insured goods to a safer location are **proximate results** of the fire and are covered by the insurance policy. The same is true of damage due to soot, smoke, water, or heat from a nearby burning building. The standard New York and New Jersey policies, however, expressly provide that losses by theft from the insured premises during a fire are not covered by the contract of insurance.

Coinsurance Clauses

Legal Issue No. 1

Under a **coinsurance-clause policy,** the insurance company expresses the relationship between the insurance a client wishes to carry and the actual value of his or her property as a fraction. The client receives this fractional part of a loss as an indemnity payment. Thus, if a house valued at $100,000 is insured for $60,000, only 60,000/100,000, or three-fifths, of the loss can be recovered by the insured, since only three-fifths of the value of the property was insured.

EXAMPLE 10 Suppose Alma Laski's summer house, valued at $20,000 and insured for only $12,000, had a fire loss of $10,000. Under the provisions of the coinsurance-clause policy, Laski would receive only $6,000:

$$\frac{12,000}{20,000} \text{ of } \$10,000 = \$6,000, \text{ amount recoverable}$$

Under an **80 percent coinsurance-clause** policy, a house must be insured for at least 80 percent of its value for the owner to receive full reimbursement for a loss. The insurance company will pay that part of a loss that the insurance carried bears to 80 percent of the value of the property. Thus, if a house valued at $100,000 is insured for only $60,000, only

$$\frac{\$60,000}{80 \text{ percent of } \$100,000} \quad \text{or} \quad \frac{\$60,000}{\$80,000} \quad \text{or} \quad \frac{3}{4}$$

of the loss can be recovered by the insured, since only three-fourths of 80 percent of the value of the property was insured. If $80,000 insurance had been carried, the full loss up to $80,000 could have been collected from the insurance company, since this amount is 80 percent of the value of the property.

The 80 percent clause in a policy does not mean that 80 percent of the value of the property is the maximum amount collectible. If the property is insured for its full value, the full amount of the loss could be collected.

Homeowner's Policies

Many of the leading insurance companies offer a combination policy known as the **homeowner's policy.** This policy covers protection for all types of losses and liabilities related to home ownership. Among the kinds of protection covered are losses from fire, windstorms, and related damage; burglary; vandalism; and injuries of other persons while they are on the property. Homeowner's policies are issued in which the insured and his or her family are protected not just on the premises, but anywhere in the world and for almost any cause. The rates are much lower than they would be if each protection offered were covered by a separate policy.

EXAMPLE 11 All Town Insurance Company sold a homeowner's policy to Sam Mackin. During a vacation, Mackin learned that his house had caught fire and was extensively damaged. After the fire, other losses resulted from vandalism and theft. All these risks were covered in one policy, and Mackin had much less difficulty computing his losses than he would have if he had carried separate policies covering each specific loss with different insurers.

Policy Provisions

If there was any willful misstatement of any facts concerning the risks involved or the interest of the insured in the property, the policy is declared void.

EXAMPLE 12 Barbara Rukowski took out a fire insurance policy on her home. She concealed from the insurance agent the fact that she planned to open a small dry-cleaning plant in her basement. The policy would be void, and Barbara could recover nothing if a fire happened after the cleaning plant was installed.

If the policy covers personal property, the company is not liable for any loss if the property is removed from the premises specified in the policy.

EXAMPLE 13 Betty Farnese obtained a fire insurance policy which included coverage of personal property in her house. She loaned a chair from her

Homeowner's insurance provides protection for all types of losses related to home ownership.

Legal Issue No. 2

living room to Jack Smith for a special occasion. While the chair was at Smith's house, the house was damaged by fire, and the chair was destroyed. Farnese's policy would not cover the chair while it was in Smith's home because it had been removed from the premises specified in the policy.

Provision is made for the cancellation by either party on proper notice. If the insurer requests the cancellation, the proportion of the premium which has not been used (the **pro rata amount**) is returned to the insured. However, if the insured requests such an action, the premium to be returned is determined by using a short-term rate table. The amount of the premium returned in this case will be less than the pro rata amount.

Many homeowners have more than one insurance policy on their houses. In such a case, an insurer will pay no greater percentage of the total loss than is represented by that insurer's policy in proportion to the total insurance carried by the insured. Different insurance companies prorate (divide proportionately) the loss among themselves. The insured can recover the amount of his or her loss only once.

Riders, or Endorsements

If the coverage offered by a standard policy does not give you all the protection you desire, additional coverage is available. These provisions for additional coverage are called **riders,** or **endorsements.** They are written on special additional blanks and usually are pasted to your basic policy. The most common of these special contracts are called **extended** or **special-extended coverage endorsements.** Such endorsements ordinarily provide for protection against losses resulting from windstorm, hail, explosion, riots and other civil commotions, aircraft, vehicles, smoke, and often water.

There also may be special endorsements providing for the assignment of the policy to a mortgage holder when the insured places a mortgage on his or her house as well as for the added cost of increased hazards such as longer periods of vacancy and the storing of inflammable materials.

OCEAN AND INLAND MARINE INSURANCE

Marine insurance is one of the oldest types of insurance coverage, dating back to the Venetian traders who sailed the Mediterranean. **Ocean marine insurance** covers ships at sea. **Inland marine insurance** covers goods that are moved by land carriers such as rail, truck, and airplane. Inland marine insurance also covers such items as jewelry, fine arts, musical instruments, and wedding presents. Customers' goods in the possession of bailees, such as fur-storage houses and dry cleaners, are also covered by inland marine insurance.

A **floater policy** is one which insures property that cannot be covered by specific insurance because the property is constantly changing in either value or location. A **personal property floater,** for example, covers personal property in general, wherever located.

Suggestions for Reducing Legal Risks

1. Because a copy of the application is usually made a part of the insurance policy, any misstatement is an invitation for trouble and possible expense later when trying to force the settlement of an insurance claim. Therefore, be accurate and complete in your application statements.
2. Beware of inexpensive policies sold through the mail, unless you know that these policies have been approved for sale in your state by your state insurance department or commission.
3. Life insurance companies usually require proof of age before final settlement is made on their policies. To save time and expense to your heirs, it is wise to affix to your policies before your death a copy of your birth certificate.
4. Since you may desire to change the beneficiary someday, check your policy to make sure that it provides for this possibility.
5. Follow the written instructions of the insurance company for reporting a loss, an accident, or a claim; otherwise, the company may decline to settle.

Language of the Law

Define or explain each of the following words or phrases:

insurance
policy
policyholder
insured
premium
risk
insurer
binder
beneficiary
indemnification
lapsed policy

days of grace
cash surrender value
loan value
insurable interest
valued policy
open policy
face value
proceeds
double indemnity
annuity
waiver of premium

deductible clause
total disability
partial disability
unfriendly, or hostile, fire
proximate results
coinsurance-clause policy
80 percent coinsurance-clause policy

pro rata amount
riders, or endorsements
extended or special-extended coverage endorsements
floater policy
personal property floater

(continued)

TYPES OF INSURANCE:

term	endowment	medical and surgical	homeowner's policy
decreasing term	accidental death and	major medical	ocean marine
ordinary, straight, or	dismemberment	disability income	inland marine
whole life	hospitalization	fire	
limited-payment life			

Questions for Review

1. What is the purpose of insurance?
2. What is the effect of a binder?
3. What are the rules regarding insurable interest for a life insurance policy? a fire insurance policy?
4. What might result if you make a false statement when you take out insurance?
5. Explain briefly five types of life insurance.

6. Explain the difference between hospital insurance and medical and surgical insurance.
7. Explain *total* and *partial disability*.
8. What is meant by an *actual hostile fire*?
9. Describe the protection given by a homeowner's policy.
10. How does ocean marine insurance differ from inland marine insurance?

Cases in Point

In each of the following cases, give your decision and state a legal principle that applies to the case:

1. Nicholas Albee decided to take out life insurance on his best friend's life. He did this because he knew that if his best friend died, he would be depressed and would need to take a long vacation to recover. The money from his friend's insurance policy would pay for the vacation. May Albee insure his friend's life for this purpose?
2. Elena and Mark were about to be married. The wedding invitations had been sent out, and a great many wedding gifts had arrived at the bride's home. Fearful that the gifts might be stolen while they were away on their honeymoon, Elena and Mark decided that they should place insurance on the wedding gifts. What kind of insurance could be obtained for this purpose?
3. Victor Cleary insured his house for $32,000 under a fire insurance policy that contained an 80 percent coinsurance clause. The house was worth $80,000. An accidental fire occurred in the house causing $10,000 worth of damage. How much money will Cleary receive from the insurance company?
4. Keith Keneston, a single minor, took out an insurance policy on his own life, naming his mother as beneficiary. He reserved the right to change the beneficiary in accordance with the terms of his policy. Ten years later, Keneston married and changed the beneficiary to his wife. Upon his death, both his wife and his mother claimed the insurance. To whom must the insurance company pay the insurance?
5. On May 1, Sally Hilton, in an application for life insurance, stated that she had never been treated for tuberculosis. The policy was issued. Eighteen months later, Hilton died of tuberculosis. On finding that Hilton had been treated prior to filing the application for insurance, the company refused to pay the beneficiary the face value of the policy. Does the insurance company have the legal right to refuse?
6. An insurance policy was issued on the life of a person who was killed 6 months later

while participating in an attempted bank robbery. The insurance company refused to pay the face of the policy to the named beneficiary. May it legally do so?

7. Meade Kalter stated in his application for life insurance that he was 22 years of age, when, in fact, he was 28 years old. After paying the premiums for 5 years, he died. At the time of Kalter's death, the insurance company discovered the correct age of Kalter and refused to settle on the policy, claiming that this was a material misrepresentation. Will the insurance company have to pay the claim?

8. May Ling insured her stock of goods under a standard fire policy. Later, she removed her stock to another warehouse but did not notify the insurance company of the change. The second warehouse burned, destroying Ling's merchandise. Can Ling collect on her insurance policy?

9. Hannah Gedrow carried fire insurance on her furniture, which was damaged by water used by firefighters in dousing a fire in Gedrow's house. Was Gedrow entitled to collect from the insurance company for damage to the furniture?

10. Marilyn Herbert had fire insurance on her house, which was damaged by the collapse of a nearby burning building. Was Herbert entitled to collect from her insurance company for the damage?

Cases to Judge

1. In July, Angeline Browning went to an insurance agent and told him that she owned a home and was "going to will the house over" to the person with her, Shirley Brewton, and her husband John Brewton. Fire insurance was placed on the property in the Brewtons' name, and the Brewtons paid the premium. Mrs. Browning died without a will the following December. Her five sisters inherited the property. The house burned down a month later. Are John and Shirley Brewton entitled to the insurance proceeds? Why or why not? *Brewton v. Alabama Farm Bureau Mutual Casualty Insurance*, 474 So. 2d 1120 (Alabama)

2. In an application for life insurance, Larry Puccia stated that he had not, within the last 5 years, consulted any physician for any reason. He was issued the insurance. He died the next year of a brain tumor. The insurance company then learned that on two occasions in the year prior to filling out the application he had been medically treated for pain in the arm and unsteady gate. Must the insurance company pay the amount of the policy to the beneficiary? Explain. *Puccia v. Farmers and Traders Life Insurance Co.*, 428 N.Y.S.2d 78 (New York)

3. A $10,000 life insurance policy was issued to Chester Henrikson Sr. on the life of his son, Chester Henrikson Jr. For the first 9 years of the policy's life, young Chester's mother and father were listed as "first beneficiaries" of the policy. Chester Sr. then had his wife's name removed as a beneficiary of the policy. Two years later, Chester Sr. was found guilty by a jury in Wyoming of the voluntary manslaughter of his son, Chester Jr. Is Chester Sr. entitled to the proceeds of the insurance policy? Why or why not? *New York Life Insurance Co. v. Henriksen*, 415 N.E.2d 146 (Indiana)

4. William Galindo Jr. received a broken neck while playing in a high school football game and, as a result of that injury, is a quadriplegic; that is, he cannot use his arms or legs. The high school had an accident insurance policy which paid the following: $10,000 for the loss of both hands or both arms and $10,000 for the loss of both feet or both legs. The policy also contained the following words: "Maximum Dismemberment Benefit $10,000." Is Galindo entitled to insurance proceeds? If so, how much? Explain. *Galindo v. Guarantee Trust Life Insurance Co.*, 414 N.E.2d 265 (Illinois)

Chapter 28

DIVORCE AND ITS LEGAL CONSEQUENCES

Scene: The Greens' backyard. Melanie is talking over the fence with her next-door neighbor, Liz.

Melanie: This sunshine makes me want to stay out here in the garden all day.

Liz: It sure is making the weeds grow. Have you heard the latest gossip?

Melanie: No, tell me!

Liz: Bill has left Betty and the twins and moved to Alaska.

Melanie: Bill split up with Betty? I would never have thought that would happen. How long has Bill been gone?

Liz: Just a week or so. I guess the fire in their house was too much for them to handle. The rumor is that Betty is going to file for a divorce on the grounds of desertion next week.

Melanie: Really? Isn't she rushing things a bit? Maybe he'll come back. How could he leave those beautiful twins? Why, he took care of them more than Betty did after the fire.

Liz: That's true. Betty went back to work, and Bill stayed home to fix up the house and care for the twins.

Melanie: I don't understand what's going on these days. So many people are getting divorced.

Liz: Either that or having their marriages annulled.

Melanie: Whatever—isn't an annulment the same as a divorce?

Liz: I'm not sure.
(*Six months later, Melanie meets Betty at the supermarket. The twins are sitting in the grocery carriage.*)

Melanie: Hi Betty. The twins are growing so big that I hardly recognized them.

Betty: Well, you had better take a good look at them now because they may not be here for long.

Melanie: What do you mean? Are you moving?

Betty: No, I'm staying right where I am, but Bill is trying to get custody of the twins. He claims that I'm an unfit mother because I've gone back to work. I thought that mothers always have the right to the custody of their children.

Melanie: I don't know how the courts decide things like that. Anyway, I doubt if you have to worry. Everyone knows that you're a good mother.

Betty: Thanks, Melanie. I appreciate that.

Melanie: Does Bill send you anything for support?

Betty: That's another problem. Bill says that he won't pay the support payments that the judge ordered if he doesn't have custody of the twins.

How can I force him to pay support payments when he's way up in Alaska?

Melanie: I see what you mean.

Betty: Well, the twins are getting restless. I guess I'd better finish my shopping. It's nice to see you, Melanie.

Melanie: Thanks Betty. It's good to see you, too. Good luck!

LEGAL ISSUES

1. Can someone file for a divorce on the ground of desertion 2 weeks after his or her spouse has left home?
2. What is the difference between a divorce and an annulment?
3. Do mothers always have the right to the custody of their children?
4. What is the most important factor in determining who gets the custody of children?
5. Does the law provide a method for obtaining support payments from spouses who live out of state?

THE SPIRIT OF THE LAW

Divorce laws, which vary from state to state, set forth the grounds for divorce and provide for the custody and support of children. Divorce laws also determine the allowance or disallowance of alimony and establish guidelines for the distribution of marital property. Probate and family courts in the various states have jurisdiction to enforce these laws.

Legal Issue No. 2

A marriage comes to an end in any of three ways: (1) the death of one of the parties, (2) annulment, and (3) divorce. An **annulment** is a declaration by the court that the marriage was never effective; it was void from the beginning. A **divorce,** however, is a declaration by the court that a valid marriage has come to an end. Although the law of most states recognizes the possibility of divorce, public policy generally tries to discourage it. Also, some people, for strong moral and religious reasons, feel that divorce is wrong. The purpose of this chapter is not to argue the merits or demerits of divorce, but simply to present the law as it now exists in this country.

ANNULMENT

You have learned from your reading of Chapter 9 that people who are induced by fraud to enter into contracts may get out of them if they wish. It is this same theory that allows certain marriages to be annulled. A marriage contract can be set aside if it was induced by fraud.

The most common frauds that are grounds for annulment are:

1. Being under the age allowed by state law to marry (under common law, the minimum age to marry was 14 for a boy and 12 for a girl).
2. Not having the intent to marry (such as going through a marriage ceremony as a joke).
3. Secretly intending never to have children.
4. Concealing pregnancy by someone other than the husband.
5. Concealing incurable venereal disease.
6. Suffering from mental illness at the time of the marriage.
7. Being impotent (unable to have sexual relations).

Another ground for an annulment is duress. This occurs when someone is forced to marry against his or her will.

GROUNDS FOR DIVORCE

The grounds (basis) for a divorce are different in each state. Table 28-1 (on pages 392–393) shows the laws in each state. The most common grounds for divorce are (1) breakdown of the marital relationship (commonly called no-fault), (2) adultery, (3) mental or physical cruelty, (4) desertion, (5) alcoholism or drug addiction, (6) nonsupport, (7) conviction of a felony, and (8) impotency.

No-Fault Divorce

The acceptance of the idea of a divorce without fault has now become widespread. Almost all states have what is commonly called a **no-fault divorce law,** which eliminates the need to prove that one party is at fault when seeking a divorce. All that must be proved, under the law of most states, is that the marriage relationship has broken down.

■ States give different names to the breakdown of the marriage relationship. Some call it **irretrievable breakdown;** others call it **irreconcilable differences.** In New Hampshire, for example, a divorce may be granted without further regard to the fault of either party on the ground of irreconcilable differences which have caused the **irremediable** (incurable) **breakdown** of the marriage. Under the law of that state, a spouse, in most instances, cannot introduce evidence in court of misconduct by the other spouse if a no-fault divorce is sought. A no-fault divorce is called a *dissolution* in some states.

A few states, such as Nevada, have for many years allowed divorce on the ground of **incompatibility.** One spouse does not have to prove that the other spouse is at fault. All that is required is evidence which indicates that the couple have a personality conflict so deep that there is no chance for a **reconciliation** (a return of friendship).

Some states require that the parties live apart from each other for a period of time before the divorce is allowed. In New York, for example, the parties must either enter into a separation agreement approved by the court or one of them must obtain a **judicial separation** (whereby the court allows the couple to live separate and apart). A divorce may then be granted after the husband and wife have lived apart for 1 year.

Reconciliation bureaus have been established in some states in an attempt to reunite couples and save marriages. Certain states have established procedures for couples to seek reconciliation. In Connecticut, for example, either spouse may submit a request for reconciliation. The county Clerk of Court then orders the parties to meet at least twice a week with a marriage counselor. If either party refuses to meet with the counselor, no further action is taken on the case for a period of 6 months.

A few states allow a no-fault divorce if one of the parties first obtains a **limited divorce** (judicial separation). The **absolute divorce** (final divorce) is allowed at the end of a waiting period.

Adultery

Adultery is a voluntary sexual relationship involving a married person and someone other than his or her spouse. It is a crime in many states in addition to being a ground for divorce.

Because of its private nature, adultery is most commonly proved by **circumstantial evidence** (evidence that is indirect). It is often proved by showing that the person charged with adultery had (1) the opportunity to commit adultery and (2) the inclination or tendency to do so. This is generally sufficient for a court to grant the complaining party a divorce. However, if criminal adultery is to be proved, a much greater degree of proof must be presented by the prosecution. This is so because it must be proved, beyond a reasonable doubt, that the person committed the crime.

EXAMPLE 1 A husband sought a divorce from his wife in Illinois on the ground of adultery with a man who roomed in the same house with them. There was evidence that a sexual relationship between the husband and wife had not existed for many years. The wife often visited barrooms and went on dates with other men. The court granted the divorce, saying that both the opportunity and the inclination to commit adultery existed.

In Example 1, if the wife had been charged with the crime of adultery, the evidence would not have been enough. To convict someone of a crime, the state must prove the defendant guilty beyond a reasonable doubt.

Cruelty

Until the introduction of no-fault divorce laws, cruelty was probably the most common ground for divorce. The requirements to obtain a divorce because of cruelty are similar throughout the country. Generally, there must be actual personal violence that endangers the life or health of a spouse and that makes living together unsafe or unbearable. Usually, more than one act of violence is required, although in some instances a single act may be enough.

EXAMPLE 2 A drunken wife once struck, knocked down, and beat her husband during an argument. The husband had bruises on his back, throat, arms, and legs. The court allowed the divorce even though there was only a single act of violence.

Cruelty may be established without proving actual physical contact if a spouse is threatened with bodily harm. Sometimes it is possible to obtain a divorce because of mental suffering alone without physical violence or the threat of physical violence.

In such a case, it must be proved that the mental suffering damaged the health of the spouse.

EXAMPLE 3 A wife persisted in going out with other men against the objections of her husband. Her conduct caused his health to become very poor. The court granted a divorce on the ground of cruelty, even though there was no physical violence.

Desertion

Legal Issue No. 1

Desertion is the unjustified, voluntary separation of one spouse from the other, for a period of time set by law, with the intent of not returning. In most states, the time period is one year.

EXAMPLE 4 A wife left her husband because he got drunk once or twice a week and beat her. The husband would not be able to use desertion as a ground for divorce because the wife had a good reason for leaving him.

Usually, the deserting spouse leaves home. On some occasions, however, both spouses stay at home and live in different rooms. In older cases the courts have also held that the refusal of a wife, without just cause, to live at the residence of her husband is desertion by the wife. This occurred, for example, when the husband went to another state to get a job and the wife refused to follow. More recent cases do not follow this reasoning.

In all cases, the marital relationship must cease for the entire time period established by state law. If the marital relationship resumes, even for 1 day, the time period must begin over again. In addition, the one seeking the divorce must want his or her spouse to return. He or she cannot consent to the other spouse's absence.

Alcoholism or Drug Addiction

Habitual intoxication, either with alcohol or drugs, is a ground for divorce in most states. The habit must be confirmed (well established), persistent, voluntary, and excessive. It is the abuse of alcohol or drugs, rather than the mere use of them, that is a ground for divorce.

Nonsupport

■ In the past, nonsupport could be used as a ground for divorce only by the wife and only in states that recognized it. In recent years, however, more and more states have begun to allow the husband to use nonsupport as a ground for divorce.

The person seeking the divorce must show that the party had the ability to provide economic support and willfully failed to do so. In some states, the person seeking the divorce must ''grossly or wantonly and cruelly'' refuse or neglect to provide suitable support.

EXAMPLE 5 A wife sought a divorce from her husband on the ground of nonsupport. During their marriage, the couple had lived with the wife's parents, who supported them. The court refused to grant the divorce, saying that the wife at no time suffered or was ill because of lack of support by the husband.

TABLE 28-1
GROUNDS FOR DIVORCE*

Jurisdiction	Residence Time Requirement	Adultery	Cruelty	Desertion	Alcoholism	Drug Addiction	Impotency	Nonsupport	Insanity	Felony and/or Imprisonment	Marriage Breakdown†
Alabama	6 mos.	✔	✔	✔	✔	✔	✔	✔	✔	✔	✔
Alaska	None	✔	✔	✔	✔	✔	✔		✔	✔	✔
Arizona	90 days										✔
Arkansas	3 mos.	✔	✔	✔	✔		✔	✔	✔	✔	
California	6 mos.								✔		✔
Colorado	90 days										✔
Connecticut	1 yr.	✔	✔	✔	✔			✔	✔	✔	✔
Delaware	6 mos.										✔
District of Columbia	6 mos.	✔									
Florida	6 mos.								✔		✔
Georgia	6 mos.	✔	✔	✔	✔	✔	✔		✔	✔	✔
Hawaii	3 mos.										✔
Idaho	6 wks.	✔	✔	✔	✔			✔	✔	✔	✔
Illinois	90 days	✔	✔	✔	✔	✔	✔			✔	
Indiana	6 mos.						✔		✔	✔	✔
Iowa	1 yr.										✔
Kansas	60 days										✔
Kentucky	180 days										✔
Louisiana	1 yr.	✔	✔	✔	✔	✔		✔		✔	
Maine	6 mos.	✔	✔	✔	✔	✔	✔	✔	✔		✔
Maryland	1 yr.	✔	✔	✔			✔		✔	✔	
Massachusetts	1 yr.	✔	✔	✔	✔	✔	✔	✔		✔	✔
Michigan	180 days										✔
Minnesota	180 days										✔
Mississippi	6 mos.	✔	✔	✔	✔	✔	✔		✔	✔	✔
Missouri	90 days										✔

TABLE 28-1 (Continued)

Jurisdiction	Residence Time Requirement	Adultery	Cruelty	Desertion	Alcoholism	Drug Addiction	Impotency	Nonsupport	Insanity	Felony and/or Imprisonment	Marriage Breakdown†
Montana	1 yr.										✓
Nebraska	1 yr.										✓
Nevada	6 wks.								✓		✓
New Hampshire	1 yr.	✓	✓	✓	✓		✓	✓		✓	✓
New Jersey	1 yr.	✓	✓	✓	✓	✓			✓	✓	
New Mexico	6 mos.	✓	✓	✓							✓
New York	1 yr.	✓	✓	✓						✓	
North Carolina	6 mos.	✓					✓		✓		
North Dakota	1 yr.	✓	✓	✓	✓	✓	✓	✓	✓	✓	✓
Ohio	6 mos.	✓	✓	✓	✓		✓		✓	✓	✓
Oklahoma	6 mos.	✓	✓	✓	✓		✓	✓	✓	✓	✓
Oregon	6 mos.										✓
Pennsylvania	6 mos.	✓	✓	✓			✓		✓	✓	
Puerto Rico	1 yr.	✓	✓	✓	✓	✓	✓		✓	✓	
Rhode Island	1 yr.	✓	✓	✓	✓	✓	✓	✓		✓	✓
South Carolina	3 mos.	✓	✓	✓	✓	✓					
South Dakota	None	✓	✓	✓	✓	✓		✓		✓	✓
Tennessee	6 mos.	✓	✓	✓	✓	✓	✓	✓		✓	✓
Texas	6 mos.	✓	✓						✓	✓	✓
Utah	3 mos.	✓	✓	✓	✓	✓	✓	✓	✓	✓	
Vermont	6 mos.	✓	✓	✓				✓	✓	✓	
Virginia	6 mos.	✓	✓	✓						✓	
Washington	None										✓
West Virginia	1 yr.	✓	✓	✓	✓	✓			✓	✓	✓
Wisconsin	6 mos.										✓
Wyoming	60 days										✓

*As of January 1, 1986.   †Grounds for a no-fault divorce.

In addition to proving grounds for divorce, the complainant must file suit in the jurisdiction that is his or her home and must have lived in that jurisdiction for the "residence time requirement."

| **Conviction of a Felony** | Most states allow a divorce if either party is convicted of a felony, an infamous (disgraceful) crime, or a crime of moral turpitude (one that is morally wrong). The New York statute allows a divorce if either party to a marriage is in prison for a period of 3 or more consecutive years after the marriage. The Massachusetts statute allows a divorce if either party is sentenced to 5 years or more in prison. (See Table 28-1.) |

DOMICILE AND RESIDENCE REQUIREMENTS
Domicile

In order for a court to hear a case, it must have the authority to do so. Such authority is called jurisdiction. In a divorce case, jurisdiction is based on domicile. The person asking for the divorce must be domiciled within the geographic area over which the court has jurisdiction.

A **domicile** is a person's principal place of abode (home). It is the place to which, whenever a person is absent, he or she has the present intent of returning. A domicile cannot be abandoned or surrendered until another is acquired. Persons may have several residences, but they can have only one domicile at any given time.

At common law, a wife had no capacity to acquire a domicile of her own. Her domicile was that of her husband. In modern times, however, the courts have held that a wife may acquire a domicile separate from that of her husband. The husband usually must be guilty of some marital wrong which will justify the wife's living apart from him.

Members of the military are presumed to retain the domicile of their home state unless they are able to prove otherwise.

Residence Requirements

A **residence** is a place where a person actually lives, or resides. It may or may not be that person's domicile.

EXAMPLE 6 Kathleen Horak, while attending college, lived in a dormitory in California (her residence). She spent the summer working at Yellowstone National Park in Wyoming (another residence). Her domicile during this entire period, however, was her home in Kansas because it was her principal place of abode and it was her present intent to return there to live at some future time.

In addition to requiring that persons seeking divorces be domiciled in their jurisdiction, most states have particular residence requirements.

EXAMPLE 7 Myrna Zelin lived with her husband in Arizona. When marital difficulties arose, she left Arizona and went to live with her parents in New Mexico. Upon seeking a divorce in that state, she was told that she would have to live in New Mexico for at least 6 months before bringing the divorce action.

The residence requirements vary from 6 weeks in Idaho and Nevada to 1 year in many states. Court decisions in Massachusetts, Rhode Island, and Wisconsin held that a 2-year residence requirement is unconstitutional. It had the effect of restricting the right of interstate travel. See Table 28-1 (on pages 392–393) for the residence requirements of the various states.

OUT-OF-STATE DIVORCE

Sometimes people go to another state or country to get a divorce. They usually do so either because they do not have grounds for divorce in their own state or because they want an immediate divorce without a long waiting period. Many people have gone to Nevada to get a divorce because of its relatively short waiting period (6 weeks) and because a divorce may be obtained on the ground of incompatibility. Mexico, at one time, attracted people who wanted a quick, easy divorce. Even a mail-order divorce was legal there. The laws were amended some years ago, however, to end such practices. Haiti and the Dominican Republic are popular sites today for quick, easy divorces. A divorce there, however, may not be recognized as valid in all states of the United States.

ALIMONY

Alimony (from the Latin meaning ''sustenance,'' or ''nourishment'') is an allowance made to a divorced person by his or her former spouse for support and maintenance. In former years it was awarded to the wife only. Today the majority of states allow alimony to be awarded to either spouse, dependent on the discretion (judgment) of the court. The Massachusetts statute, for example, reads: ''Upon a divorce or upon a petition at any time after a divorce, the court may order either of the parties to pay alimony to the other.'' The allowance is usually in the form of a payment of money at regular intervals. However, it can be a lump-sum payment. Alimony is not intended as a penalty against the person who is ordered to pay it.

Temporary alimony is alimony granted to one of the spouses while he or she is waiting for a divorce or separate support action to be completed. It is sometimes called **alimony pendente lite,** (pen′dentē′ lītē) meaning ''alimony pending a lawsuit.''

Usually, a spouse will not be awarded alimony in the event that he or she is found to have been at fault during the marriage.

EXAMPLE 8 Stephen Gagne obtained a divorce from his wife on the ground of cruelty. The court did not order him to pay alimony. His wife's misconduct during the marriage (being cruel to her husband) eliminated her entitlement to an award of alimony.

There is no fixed rule for determining the amount of alimony. It depends on the judgment of the court. Such factors as the spouse's income and earning capacity, financial resources, future prospects, current obligations, the number of dependents, and the number of former and/or subsequent spouses are taken into consideration. Also considered are the spouse's situation in life, earning capacity, separate property, contribution to the other spouse's property, age, health, obligations, and number of dependents. Some states refuse to award alimony to a spouse who has sufficient wealth or income to provide for his or her own support.

In most instances, the court reserves the right to modify the alimony award at a later date. Under many state laws, if the court does not reserve the right to do so, the award of alimony must stand and cannot be changed after the expiration of the appeal period. Some states allow an alimony award to be modified by mutual agreement of the parties.

The remarriage of a spouse who is receiving alimony does not necessarily end the former spouse's obligation to pay it. Usually, however, the court will change its order relative to alimony in such a circumstance. In most states, the death of either party ends the obligation to pay alimony. The laws of a few states authorize the deceased husband's estate to continue paying alimony after the husband's death.

CUSTODY AND SUPPORT OF CHILDREN

Legal Issue No. 4

Under the common-law rule, which was initially followed in the United States, a father was entitled to the custody of his minor children along with their services. He, in turn, was obligated to support them if able. If a court deprived the father of the custody of his children, he was no longer obligated to support them. Today, by statute, most states require fathers to contribute to the support of their minor children, even if they do not have custody of them. Under the Child Support Enforcement (CSE) Program of the Social Security Act, systems have been developed in each state to collect child-support payments for families who are eligible for *Aid to Families with Dependent Children (AFDC)*. This

VISITATION GUIDELINES FOR SEPARATED PARENTS

The behavior of parents has a great influence on the emotional adjustment of their children. The following visitation guidelines have been found to be helpful in achieving meaningful visitation:

A. The children should be available at the time agreed upon for the visitation. A parent who is visiting should arrive on time so as not to keep the children waiting.

B. From time to time you may need to adjust your visitation schedule. If one parent has made plans with the children or if the children themselves have made plans which conflict with the visitation rights, you should be reasonable adults and work out the problem together. The spiritual well-being, health, happiness and safety of your children should be a prime consideration of both parents.

C. Not keeping a visit without notifying the other parent may be construed by the child as rejection. As soon as you realize that you will not be able to keep a scheduled visit, you should notify the other parent immediately. Not to do so will cause inconvenience to your child as well as to the other parent and prevent either of them from planning a different activity.

D. The visit should not be used to check on the other parent. The children should not be pumped for this kind of information. They should not be used as spies. Often in the child's mind, the parents hate each other, and if this belief is reinforced the child will feel uncomfortable at the time of the visitation. In his mind, if he does anything to please the visiting parent, he may invite outright rejection by his other parent. He feels he has already lost one parent and is fearful of losing the other. For this reason parents should show mutual respect for each other.

E. Do not use your visitation period as an excuse to continue arguments with your former spouse. Do not visit your children if you have been drinking.

program gives aid to needy families in which one parent has died, is continuously absent from home, is permanently disabled, and in some cases, is unemployed. The law provides for a federal and state parent locator service to assist local welfare departments in obtaining information on the whereabouts of any absent parent when such information is to be used in the enforcement of child-support obligations. The locator service has access to records of the Social Security Administration, the Department of Defense, the Internal Revenue Service, and other federal government agencies.

Welfare of the Child

Under the law today, the welfare of the child is the most important consideration in determining who is to have custody of the child. Such factors as the child's physical, emotional, social, spiritual, and economic needs are considered. If the child is very young, the court also considers the child's need for motherly love and care.

Generally, one of the parents takes custody of the children unless the right to custody has been lost because of improper conduct. Custody may also be awarded to a nonparent, but only when both parents have been found to be

---

VISITATION GUIDELINES FOR SEPARATED PARENTS (Continued)

F. Do not make extravagant promises to your children with respect to visits which you know will not take place. Such promises which are not kept result in a loss of trust and respect for you by your children.

G. Visitation should be pleasant not only for the children, but for both parents whenever possible. The visits should not take place only in the children's home. The visiting parent may wish the children to visit in his or her home overnight, or may want to plan an enjoyable outing.

H. Often the visiting parent questions where he or she will take the children on the visits and what should be planned in the way of amusement for them particularly if they are young children. Activities may add to the pleasure of a visit, but most important of all is the parent's involvement with the children. A giving of yourself is more

important than material things you may give your children. The visit is one of the few times that the visiting parent has personal contact with the children and for that reason it should be a meaningful time for both the parent and the children.

I. Visitation is a time for the parent and the children to be with each other, to enjoy each other and to maintain positive relationships. Having other people participate may dilute the parent-child experience during visitation. Also, it may appear to the children that the parent does not have time for them, and that he does not care enough to give them his undivided attention during visitation.

J. After a visit, the child may be confused and have anxieties, and both parents should make every effort to discuss the problems and agree on ways to deal with them.

Massachusetts Bar Foundation, Parents After Separation: Guidelines for Visitation. These guidelines were issued as a public service and do not constitute legal advice.

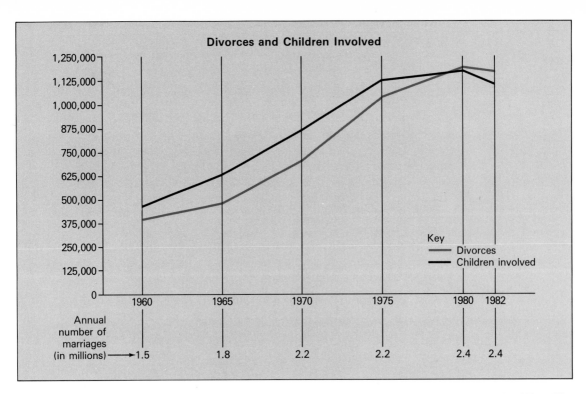

Divorces and Children Involved

Key
— Divorces
— Children involved

Annual number of marriages (in millions) → 1.5   1.8   2.2   2.2   2.4   2.4

Since 1960, the number of annual divorces rose from 393,000 to over 1 million. The number of children involved in a divorce each year rose from 463,000 to over 1 million. The average divorce in the 1980s involves one child. Today, approximately 2.4 million marriages occur annually, as do 1.2 million divorces.

Legal Issue No. 3

unfit. Husbands or wives can sometimes obtain custody by mutual agreement. **Joint custody**—the awarding of custody of children to both parents jointly—is becoming more common each year. Many people believe this helps not only the children, but the parents as well. Both parents are more likely to remain interested in the children, and the responsibility of raising children is more evenly shared under a joint custody arrangement.

Uniform Support Laws

Legal Issue No. 5

Every state in the United States has enacted the Uniform Reciprocal Enforcement of Support Act. Under the act, a support order of one state will be enforced in every state. The court order is enforced by the state, not by the **custodial parent** (the parent with custody).

EXAMPLE 9 George and Linda Fernandez were divorced in Kansas. The court ordered George to pay $75 a week in support of their children. George later moved to Missouri. If George were to stop making payments, Linda could go to court in Kansas and inform the court of that fact. The Kansas court would then notify the court in Missouri which has jurisdiction over the area where George is living. He would be summoned by the Missouri court to explain his failure to make the payments. In such cases, the court in one state has the power to enforce the order of the court in another state.

MARITAL PROPERTY

The marital property laws in most states are based on the early feudal system of England which is part of our common law (see page 4). Under this early law, any property brought into the marriage by a spouse remains the property of the spouse who originally owned it. Similarly, anything earned, inherited, or received as a gift by a spouse during the marriage remains the property of the spouse who earned or received it. Nine jurisdictions do not follow the common-law rule on this point. They are Arizona, California, Idaho, Louisiana, Nevada, New Mexico, Texas, Washington, and the Commonwealth of Puerto Rico. They are known as **community property jurisdictions.** Their laws provide that the wealth accumulated during marriage generally belongs equally to both spouses regardless of which spouse received it.

Regardless of whether they follow the common law or community property theory, most states now have laws providing for some form of equitable distribution of marital property when a couple is divorced. **Equitable distribution laws** allow judges to distribute property equitably (fairly) between the husband and wife regardless of who has title to the property. In dividing the property, judges consider such things as the age and individual earning power of each spouse, the length of the marriage, and the contributions of each spouse to the marriage, including the value of homemaking services. Because of the large amount of discretion given to judges in dividing marital property when couples are divorced, it is often difficult to predict the outcome of any particular case.

Language of the Law

Define or explain each of the following words or phrases:

annulment
divorce
no-fault divorce laws
irretrievable break-
  down
irreconcilable differ-
  ences

irremediable break-
  down
incompatibility
reconciliation
judicial separation
limited divorce
absolute divorce

adultery
circumstantial evi-
  dence
desertion
domicile
residence
alimony

temporary alimony
alimony pendente lite
joint custody
custodial parent
community property
  jurisdictions
distribution laws
equitable

Questions for Review

1. Explain the difference between an annulment and a divorce.
2. Name the most common grounds for an annulment.
3. Why do people sometimes go to another state or country for a divorce?

4. List the most common grounds for a divorce.
5. In general, what are the requirements for obtaining a divorce on the ground of cruelty?
6. Must a person who seeks a divorce on the

ground of desertion want his or her spouse to return at some time in the future?

7. Why have some states established reconciliation bureaus?

8. List some of the factors that are generally considered by the court in determining the amount of alimony that is to be granted.

9. What factor is most important to consider today when determining who shall have custody of the children of a man and a woman who are getting a divorce?

10. Explain the purpose of the Uniform Reciprocal Enforcement of Support Act.

Cases in Point

In each of the following cases, give your decision and state a legal principle that applies to the case:

1. Dorothy Mah lived in a state that had enacted a no-fault divorce law. When her husband sued her for divorce, she claimed that he could not get one because she had done nothing wrong during the time they were married. Is Dorothy correct?

2. Mike Siegel obtained a divorce from his wife, Eileen, on the ground of adultery on her part. Eileen sought alimony from Mike. Was the court likely to award alimony to Eileen? Explain your answer.

3. Raymond and Rebecca Waymer were divorced, and Rebecca was granted custody of their children. Raymond felt that he should not have to contribute to his children's support because he did not have custody of them. Might the court order Raymond to help support their children?

4. Henry Gamble and Gloria Markheim were divorced. Gamble was ordered to pay $100 a week toward the support of their children. Gamble moved to another state and stopped making support payments. Can Markheim enforce the court order?

5. Jean Hinckley, whose domicile was in Michigan, wanted a divorce from her husband, Philip. She was planning to spend a month vacationing in Florida that winter anyway and thought it would be a good idea to get a divorce while she was there. Could she do so?

6. Mabel Pincus was found guilty of first-degree murder and was sent to prison. Her husband, Carl, wanted a divorce but did not think he could be granted one because Mabel had been a good wife to him. Does he have grounds for divorce? Explain.

7. Carl Rezk and Barbara McIntosh decided to get married as part of a joke they were going to play on their parents. When their parents learned about the marriage, they asked the court to annul the marriage. Would the court grant an annulment? Explain.

8. Paul Romanowicz married Carol Bettencourt. At the time of the marriage, both parties were in good health. However, a year later Carol became mentally ill. Can Paul have the marriage annulled?

9. Conrad Milton wanted an overnight divorce from his wife, Agnes. He did not want to wait the time period required in his state for obtaining a divorce. He decided to fly to Mexico to get an overnight divorce. Would Conrad be successful?

10. Emily Banks believed that her husband, Eugene, had committed adultery. She knew that he often went alone to a barroom and left in the company of another woman. She also knew that he often went to the other woman's apartment. When she threatened to divorce him on the ground of adultery, he claimed that she could not prove beyond a reasonable doubt that he had committed adultery. Thus, he claimed, she could not get a divorce on that ground. Do you agree? Why or why not?

Cases to Judge

1. Francis and June Connor were divorced. Although Francis was permanently and totally disabled and unable to support himself, the lower court ordered him to turn over his half of their house to June as alimony. Francis appealed the decision and asked the appellate court to order his former wife, June, to pay him alimony. Should the appellate court reverse the lower court's decision? Why or why not? *Connor v. Connor,* 372 So. 2d 130 (Florida)

2. Judith and Carroll Gowins were married in Louisiana. Two years later, after graduating from Louisiana Tech, Carroll received a commission from the U.S. Air Force. The couple lived in various places during their 16 years of marriage, including South Dakota and Alabama. Carroll rose to the rank of lieutenant colonel. They were then separated. Carroll always listed Louisiana as his home state and paid Louisiana state income taxes. While living in Alabama, he obtained visitation rights to see his children at his parents' home in Louisiana. The question arose as to which state was his domicile. How would you decide? Why? *Gowins v. Gowins,* 466 So. 2d 32 (Louisiana)

3. Thea Curless filed for a divorce against her husband, Timothy, asking for custody of their two children, aged 13 and 10. The court granted the divorce, finding that both parents were fit and proper persons to have the care and custody of the children. During the trial, the children expressed preference to stay with their mother. The court, however, awarded custody of the children to the father with rights of visitation and temporary custody to the mother when the father is working away from the family home. The mother appealed. What is the most important consideration in determining who is to have custody of the child under the law today? *Curless v. Curless,* 708 P.2d 426 (Wyoming)

4. Kenneth Graham worked for a railroad. When he was transferred to a location about a hundred miles from home, he asked his wife, Hazel, to move there with him. She said that she would wait until the school year was over, but suggested that he take the family's camper near the job and live in that. He did so. For the first 2 or 3 months, he returned home on his days off. After that, however, he came home only once a month or once every 2 months. He closed out their checking account because Hazel had overdrawn the account several times. Kenneth then sued Hazel for a divorce on the ground of extreme and repeated mental cruelty. Could he obtain the divorce on that ground? *Graham v. Graham,* 358 N.E.2d 308 (Illinois)

5. Valerie and Bazil Wallace were divorced, and both were judged fit parents. Valerie was granted custody of their two children. The court said that Valerie could not take the children outside that particular county except for summer vacations, to allow Bazil visitation rights. Fifteen days after the divorce, Valerie married an Englishman and moved to England, taking the children with her. Bazil asked the court to change its order and to award custody of the children to him. How would you decide? *Wallace v. Wallace,* 358 N.E.2d 1369 (Ohio)

Tapley v. Peterson
489 N.E.2d 1170 (Illinois)

Donald and Shirley Nowak purchased their house on Water Street, Cahokia, Illinois, in 1955. Directly behind their lot was a large parcel of land owned by Dimitrious James. To the left of their lot was a 50-foot-wide strip of land, also owned by James. In 1963, James built a drive-in theater on the large parcel of land. He placed a 6-foot-high stockade fence between the drive-in and the backyards of the houses along Water Street to separate them from the drive-in theater. The fence went along the Nowaks's backyard and the back of the vacant 50-foot-wide strip next door. The Nowaks built a garage on the left rear corner of their lot and a driveway leading to it from Water Street. They used the driveway continuously. James did not use the 50-foot-wide strip next door. In 1984, the Nowaks sold their property to the plaintiff (Tapley), and James sold his drive-in property to the defendant (Peterson). Shortly thereafter, it was discovered that Nowak's driveway crossed over part of James's 50-foot-wide strip of land. This suit was filed on December 4, 1984, by Tapley, the new owner of the Nowaks's property, to establish title to the land under the driveway by adverse possession. (The period for establishing title by adverse possession is 20 years in Illinois.)

THE TRIAL

Dimitrious James testified that construction of the theater began in 1963 and that the theater opened on February 7, 1964.

Donald Nowak testified that he thought that the garage and driveway "might not have been built until a year or so after the opening of the drive-in."

Shirley Nowak testified, in part, as follows:

Q. In relation to when the drive-in was built or finished, can you tell us when the garage was built?

A. Right at about the same time to the best of my recollection.

Q. Would you say that the garage was there before the fence was put up?

A. Before the drive-in fence was put up?

Q. Yes, the drive-in fence, excuse me.

A. I think so.

Q. Now, when the garage was put up, was the driveway constructed at the same time?

A. Yes.

. . .

Q. Mrs. Nowak, did this drive-in movie provide speakers for the neighbors?

A. Yes, they did.

Q. Did they put those speakers in when they were building the drive-in?

A. Yes.

Q. Where is the speaker located on your property?

A. It is located—let's see. At the back of the lot near really close to the garage.

Q. Do you know if this speaker was placed in after your garage was there?

A. I would think it would have had to have been.

Her cross-examination included the following:

Q. As you sit here today, Mrs. Nowak, do you know for sure when that garage was constructed?

A. I can't tell you positively, no. In my best recollection it was there when the drive-in was completed but that is recollection.

The lower court held that the plaintiff had established title by adverse possession to the land bounded by the driveway.

THE ARGUMENTS ON APPEAL

The defendant argues that Mrs. Nowak's recollection of the garage and driveway construction was contradicted by her husband; therefore, the trial court's finding must be reversed. The defendant claims that the plaintiff failed to show by strict, clear, and unequivocal evidence that the disputed area was possessed adversely for the required 20-year period.

In rebuttal, the plaintiff points to the findings of the lower court judge:

The Court has closely considered the content of the testimony by Mr. and Mrs. Nowak and their demeanor on the stand. The Court finds that the testimony of Mrs. Nowak was sufficiently convincing to meet the burden of proof required by an adverse possession case, and that the testimony of Mr. Nowak did not sufficiently rebut her testimony to deny plaintiffs' claim.

QUESTIONS FOR DISCUSSION

1. How does one gain title to real property by adverse possession?
2. When do you believe the period of adverse possession began and ended in this case?
3. Who has the stronger argument, the plaintiff or the defendant? Why?
4. If you were the appellate court judge hearing this case, for whom would you decide? Why?

CASE TO BRIEF

After reading *How to Write a Case Brief* on page 78 and examining the sample brief on page 80, write a brief of the following case:

Lensey Corp. v. Wong
403 N.E.2d 1066 (Illinois)

This is an appeal from a money judgment entered in a forcible entry and detainer [eviction] suit to recover rent and possession of a leased single family residential dwelling. Peter Wong, the tenant, filed an answer and an affirmative defense based on breach of an implied warranty of habitability.

At trial, Mrs. Ivy Wong testified that she and her husband moved into the house on January 25. There were many problems with the house: the foundation leaked; the kitchen and bathroom faucets leaked; the doors and locks were not properly fitted; there was a one-inch gap between the bottom of the front storm door and the door sill; the stairs to the second floor had weak spots; the light switch in the pantry had a short in it; and the front and rear porches were sagging and lacked support. Requests to Lensey Corporation for repairs were ignored or the repairs were poorly made. On [the following] May 16, notice was sent to Lensey that rent would be withheld unless proper repairs were made.

Harold Sedrel, chief housing inspector for the city of Rock Island, and Joe Woods, a housing inspector, testified that many housing code violations were found during an inspection on May 17. Lensey was informed of the violations and asked to correct them by July 23. Sedrel also testified that prior inspections of the house had shown numerous violations. If the Wongs moved out of the house, it would be a violation of the housing code to re-rent the premises before the violations were corrected.

Leonard Dalkoff, president of Lensey, testified that many repairs had been made but because the Wongs were frequently absent from the home, repairmen were unable to gain entry for the purpose of making further repairs.

No evidence of the fair market rental value of the premises was presented by either party. The trial court found that there was no implied warranty of habitability in leases of single family dwellings and that an entire month's rent was due. The court awarded Lensey judgment in the amount of $225.00 and possession of the premises within thirty days.

On appeal, Wong raises the following issues: (1) whether the implied warranty of habitability applies to the lease of a single family residential dwelling; (2) whether the tenant's obligation to pay rent is dependent on the landlord's compliance with the implied warranty of habitability, thereby allowing the tenant to withhold rent when the warranty of habitability is breached; (3) whether the trial court's finding that full rent was due was against the manifest weight of the evidence.

. . .

[The appellate judge cited these cases in deciding to reverse the lower court decision:]

In 1972 [the Illinois] supreme court held [in Spring v. Little] that a warranty of habitability is implied in all contracts, whether written or oral, governing the tenancies of occupants of multiple unit dwellings.

In 1979 the First District considered whether the implied warranty of habitability should be extended to leases of single family dwellings in [Pole v. Sorrels] and found that the holding [in Spring v. Little] as to implied warranty of habitability was also applicable to the leases of single family dwellings. . . .

Wong has asked us to further extend the contractual analysis of the landlord-tenant relationship to allow general contract remedies to tenants, including the right of rent withholding.

The Illinois Supreme Court [in Spring v. Little] refused to alter the long established rule that liability for rent continues so long as the tenant retains possession of the premises regardless of the landlord's breach of warranty. The court did not, however, preclude [rule out] the tenant from attempting to prove that damages suffered as a result of the breach of warranty equalled or ex-ceeded the rent claimed to be due. We believe this to be the proper rule.

Wong also argues that the decision of the trial court was contrary to the manifest weight of the evidence. We need not consider this issue since we have recognized that implied warranty of habitability applies to the leasing of single family dwellings. A reversal of the trial court's decision is necessary, since it is evident that such warranty was breached. At the trial court level there was no evidence presented as to the fair market rental value of the premises and it is necessary that this case be remanded for the purpose of making the determination of rental value after receiving evidence on the question.

For the reasons stated above, the judgment of the trial court is hereby reversed and the cause remanded for hearing consistent with this opinion.

Reversed and remanded.

TRIAL PROCEDURES

THE OPENING STATEMENTS

The first step in the trial, after the jurors have been selected, is the opening statement of each attorney. It is at this time that the attorneys for each side tell the judge and jury about the case and what they intend to prove. The plaintiff's attorney makes an opening statement first, followed by the defendant's attorney. In some states, the defendant's attorney may elect to postpone making the opening statement until after the plaintiff's evidence has been presented.

Opening statements include: (1) a short summary of the facts, (2) an indication of the burden of proof required (see page 571), (3) a description of the evidence that will be introduced, (4) an opinion of the law involved, and (5) a statement of what the attorney expects will be the outcome of the trial.

THE CASE OF GRAZIO v. WILLIAMSON (continued from page 329)

After the jury has been selected, the judge tells the plaintiff's attorney to make her opening statement. Attorney Powers stands and addresses the judge and jury:

May it please the court, ladies and gentlemen of the jury: My name is Susan Powers. I represent Steven Grazio, the plaintiff in this case. The purpose of this opening statement is to tell you about the evidence that we will present. This will give you a clear picture of the events that occurred and help you to see how each piece of evidence fits into the whole picture.

The evidence will show that on April 10, 19—, my client, Steven Grazio, was visiting his friends Mike and Sue DeFazio. He had parked his car in front of their apartment on North Street. While inside the apartment, Steven and his friends heard the screech of brakes and the sound of crashing metal and broken glass. They ran outside, and saw that a car, driven by the defendant, Wayne Williamson, had smashed into Mr. Grazio's parked car. Witnesses will testify that the first thing that Mr. Williamson said after the accident was that a squirrel had run out in front of him and that he couldn't hit the squirrel. I am sure you will agree, after hearing the evidence, that a reasonably prudent person would not run into someone's car to avoid hitting a squirrel. Without question, this was a negligent act.

On the basis of this evidence, we will ask for a

verdict in an amount sufficient to compensate Mr. Grazio for the damages done to his car. Thank you.

Next, Attorney Rodriguez, the defendant's attorney, makes an opening statement to the jury as follows:

May it please the court, ladies and gentlemen of the jury: My name is George Rodriguez. I represent Mr. Williamson, who is the defendant in this case. As you have been told, these opening statements are for the purpose of assisting you in understanding the evidence, and not for arguing the case. My opponent, Attorney Powers, has told you about some of the evidence that will be presented to you. You know that Mr. Grazio is suing my client, Wayne Williamson, for damages to Mr. Grazio's automobile. We do not deny that Mr. Grazio's car was damaged. Nor do we deny that Mr. Williamson drove the car that struck Mr. Grazio's car. We deny, however, that Mr. Williamson drove in a negligent manner. A competent witness, who was a passenger in the car, will testify that Mr. Williamson drove in a very competent manner.

Furthermore, the evidence will show that the real cause of the accident was not Mr. Williamson's negligent driving, but rather, Mr. Grazio's own violation of the law. You will hear evidence showing that Mr. Grazio's automobile was parked in front of a fire hydrant. Had the car not been parked there, in violation of the law, no damages would have occurred.

I ask you to wait until you hear all of the evidence before making your decision. At that time, I will ask you to return a verdict in favor of the defendant. Thank you.

At the conclusion of the opening statements, the attorneys present their *cases in chief*. This means that each attorney calls witnesses and introduces any other type of evidence that is available to prove the case.

LEGAL PRACTICUM

At the beginning of Chapter 25, David was injured when he tripped on a loose floor board on the stairway of the apartment building where he lived. The owner of the building had no insurance to cover David's injuries and refused to give David any money towards his medical bills and other losses. Imagine that you are an attorney representing David in a suit against the apartment owner. Write an opening statement that you would give to the jury at the beginning of the lawsuit. Before writing the opening statement, refer to the discussion of tort liability in Chapter 25 (page 352), and the discussion of negligence in Chapter 4 (page 60).

USING YOUR
PURCHASING POWER

UNIT
6

Chapter 29

BORROWING MONEY AND BUYING ON CREDIT

This unit touches on the lives of Carlos and Inez Rodriguez, a newly married couple who live in a small second-floor apartment.

Scene: Carlos enters the apartment. It is February 14.

Carlos (*stamping the snow from his boots*): Inez! I'm home!

Inez (*running to greet him*): Oh, honey, I've been waiting for you to come home! How was your first day back at work?

Carlos: Turn around and close your eyes. I've got a surprise.

Inez: For me (*turning around, smiling*)?

Carlos: Happy Valentine's Day! (*He slips a heart-shaped diamond pendant necklace over her head.*)

Inez (*opening her eyes*): Oh, Carlos, you're so romantic.

Carlos: It was on sale. It only cost $499.

Inez: I just love it, but where did you get the money? You've been laid off work for so long.

Carlos: I put it on the credit card.

Inez: Oh, did you find your credit card?

Carlos: No, I still haven't found it, but I borrowed your card this morning so that I could surprise you.

Inez: That was sweet of you, honey. It was worth going through all that trouble to get my own credit card. I'll never forget the hassle they gave me. They wouldn't consider my part-time job in figuring my income, and they said I couldn't use my maiden name—but that's okay. I like being called Mrs. Rodriguez.

Carlos: You couldn't have a better name!

Inez: Honey, are you sure that we can afford this necklace? I read that the APR on the credit card is 19.8 percent, and we haven't made a payment on the furniture for two months.

Carlos: For you, we can afford anything.

Inez: Oh, Carlos, you're so thoughtful.

Carlos: What does APR mean?

Inez: I'm not sure, but it has something to do with interest.

Carlos: Did the mail come yet?

Inez: Oh, I forgot to tell you. There's a letter for you from Aunt Angelica and something that looks like a bill.

Carlos (*finding the mail and opening an envelope*): Look at this, Inez, Aunt Angelica heard that I was out of work and sent us a check for $100.

Inez: Really? What a wonderful aunt. She is so generous!

Carlos: She sure is (*opening the other envelope*). Say, this is a bill for the credit card that I lost. Somebody has been charging things on our card! We paid it up last month, and there are charges here for $1,697! None of them are ours!

Inez: Oh, no! Let me see that. (*There is a knock on the door.*) I'll get it. (*She goes to the door and opens it.*)

Stranger (*putting his foot inside*): Mrs. Rodriguez?

Inez: Yes.

Stranger (*moving into the room with an associate*): We're from the furniture store. We're here to take back the furniture that you bought.

Carlos (*approaching*): What's the trouble, honey?

Inez: These people are here to take our furniture.

Stranger (*moving even further into the room*): Sorry, you're behind in your payments. We have to take the furniture back.

Carlos: Get out of here! You're not taking anything!

Stranger: Look here, buddy, you wouldn't want your pretty wife to get hurt would you?

Carlos (*stepping in front of the strangers*): Inez, call the police, quick!

Stranger: Let's get out of here! (*They leave.*)

(*Later that evening.*)

Inez: Carlos, where did you put the check from Aunt Angelica?

Carlos: On the table near the door.

Inez: It's not here. I can't find it anywhere.

Carlos: It must be around somewhere.

LEGAL ISSUES

1. May creditors refuse to consider income obtained from part-time employment when extending credit?
2. May a married woman use her maiden name when applying for credit?
3. What is the meaning and purpose of APR?
4. To what extent is a credit cardholder liable when a card is lost?
5. May force and threats of bodily harm be used by someone attempting to repossess goods?

THE SPIRIT OF THE LAW

"Buy now and pay later" is a saying that expresses an important aspect of the American way of life. Almost everyone uses credit in one form or another today. People borrow money from banks, finance companies, credit unions, automobile companies, and private parties. They use credit cards extensively. They have charge accounts and pay for expensive items on installment plans. As a result, there are many laws which regulate the borrowing and lending of money and the purchasing and selling of goods and services on credit.

THE MEANING OF CREDIT

When people buy on credit, they are given the right to pay later for the things that they buy instead of having to pay for them immediately. It usually costs more to buy something on credit. This extra cost is known as a finance charge, or interest. The party who sells the goods on credit or lends the money is called the **creditor.** The party who buys the goods on credit or borrows the money is called the **debtor.** There are a number of ways that people may obtain credit. Credit is divided into two classes: open-end credit and closed-end credit.

Open-End Credit

A common way to obtain credit is to open a charge account at a place of business. The seller gives the buyer permission to buy goods or services and to pay for them later. The seller sends the buyer a bill each month showing the amount that is due. Interest is usually added to the bill if there is an outstanding balance (an amount still owed from last month's bill). Some stores encourage customers to keep an outstanding balance all the time and simply to pay a small amount each month. This is called a **revolving charge account.** Such a practice is costly for the buyer because interest must be paid each month on the outstanding balance. The yearly amount of interest often exceeds 18 percent.

In order to identify their charge-account customers, businesses commonly give them credit cards. A **credit card** is a card, plate, coupon book, or other device used to obtain money, goods, or services on credit. The most common kind of credit card is made of plastic and contains the name and account number of the cardholder (the person to whom the card was issued). It usually has some means of identifying the cardholder, such as a place for the cardholder's signature.

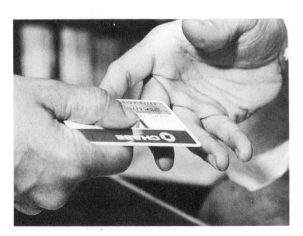

A credit card is an example of open-end credit.

Credit cards are also issued by banks and other companies that are in the business of loaning money. These organizations make arrangements with businesses that agree to extend credit to cardholders. The issuing company handles the billing and collection procedures, receives the interest that is charged, and suffers all losses caused by people who do not pay. Some well-known companies that issue such cards are MasterCard, Visa, Diners Club, and American Express.

Charge accounts and credit cards are examples of open-end credit. **Open-end credit** is credit that can be increased by the debtor, up to a limit set by the creditor, by continuing to purchase goods or services on credit. The customer may pay the balance owed in full or in installments (several partial payments), and interest may be charged on the unpaid balance.

Closed-End Credit

Another common way to obtain credit is to buy something, such as a car or a set of furniture, and pay for it in monthly installments. Very often, in such cases, the seller takes a security interest in the goods. This is done to protect the seller's rights to the property if the buyer stops making payments. Security interest is explained below. People also obtain credit by borrowing money from a lending institution, which is an example of closed-end credit. **Closed-end credit** is credit that is extended only for a specific amount of money. It cannot be increased by making future purchases.

Usury

■ Most states put limits on the amount of interest that may be charged by anyone who extends credit. Usury, which was discussed in Chapter 10, is the charging of a greater amount of interest than is allowed by law. Usury is generally a criminal offense, and very often the law provides that such loans do not have to be paid back by the debtor.

▌BORROWING ▌MONEY

The first step in borrowing money from a lending institution is to fill out a loan application. This is followed by an interview with a loan officer. The importance of this interview cannot be overemphasized, because it is on the basis of the interview that many loans are made. The following are some important considerations that determine whether or not a loan will be made:

1. The borrower must be a good risk. He or she must have a good reputation for paying bills and a genuine desire to pay debts when they are due.
2. The borrower must have a job or other source of regular income. Sometimes the nature of the job and its permanence are more important than the amount of the wages.
3. The regularity of income, the amount of debts, the property owned, and the savings the borrower has accumulated are all important considerations.
4. The borrower must be competent to contract. The number of persons dependent on the borrower for support is considered. However, the lender may not discriminate against any person on the basis of sex or marital status.

■ This symbol indicates that there may be a state statute that varies from the law discussed here. Whenever you see this symbol, find out, if possible, what the statute in your state says about this point or principle of law.

5. What the money is to be used for, the length of time required to repay it, and the security that can be offered are all important factors to be considered.

After the application is filed and the applicant is interviewed, the lender will usually require a little time to check references and credit. If these prove satisfactory, the loan will ordinarily be made within a day or so.

Small loans are usually repaid in monthly installments. For some loans, the full amount of the loan is turned over to the borrower, and the amount of the interest is added to each month's installment payment. For other loans, the loan is **discounted**—that is, the amount of the interest is subtracted from the amount of the loan at the time the loan is approved and the borrower receives only the difference. If, for example, the amount of a 1-year loan is $1,000 and the interest is to be 15 percent, the borrower would receive $850, the amount less the discount.

Interest is charged in different ways by different institutions. Banks usually charge interest by the year and generally use the discount method, whereas small loan companies usually charge their interest by the month on the unpaid balance. All maximum interest rates are fixed by state statute for each type of loan.

Secured Versus Unsecured Loans

Lenders make loans on the basis of the good character, credit standing, and ability of the borrower to pay. Often, when a borrower's credit rating is poor or has not yet been established, a lender will accept another person, called a **cosigner** or **surety**, to agree to pay the loan if called upon to do so. Even then the lender takes the risk that the cosigner will not pay the loan back when it is due. Also, it is not easy to find someone who will agree to pay back another person's loan.

A better way for a lender to have assurance that a loan will be paid back is to give a secured loan. A **secured loan** is one in which creditors obtain an interest in something of value, called **collateral,** from which they can be paid if the debtor does not pay. The interest that is given to creditors is known as a **security interest.** An **unsecured loan** does not have this important feature.

EXAMPLE 1 Jill Stone wishes to buy an automobile and must borrow money to do so. She is a recent high school graduate, just beginning her first full-time job. Naturally, since she has never borrowed money from a commercial source, she has not yet established a credit rating. Nevertheless, she may be able to obtain financing by giving the lender a security interest in the car she buys as security for the loan. Before making a decision, she has decided to compare the interest rates offered by car dealers and banks to be sure that she borrows the money at the cheapest rate of interest.

Secured loans are governed by the Uniform Commercial Code. A security interest is created by a written agreement, called a **security agreement,** which identifies the goods and is signed by the debtor. The lender or seller who holds the security interest is known as the **secured party.**

The rules governing security interests are highly complex and differ with consumer goods, inventory, equipment, and farm products. In some instances, a **financing statement** (a written notice that a security interest exists) must be filed by the creditor in the city or town clerk's office and in the office of the state secretary. This system protects people when they buy items of personal property from others. They can check at the public office to make sure there are no security interests on the items before buying them.

Rights of Secured Party ■ If a debtor does not pay, the secured party has the right to **repossess** (take back) the goods. This repossession must be accomplished without breaching the peace (causing a disturbance); if the debtor refuses to surrender the goods, legal process must be used to obtain them. After obtaining the goods, the secured party may either keep them (with some exceptions) or sell them. The sale may be a public sale (an auction) or a private sale as long as the terms of the sale are reasonable. If the goods are consumer goods and the debtor has paid 60 percent of the cash price or more, the secured party cannot keep the goods. They must be sold. The debtor is entitled to receive any surplus of a sale after expenses have been paid, the debt has been satisfied, and any other security interests have been paid off. The debtor is entitled to be notified of any such sale and, in most cases, has the right to purchase the goods back.

Legal Issue No. 5

TRUTH IN LENDING

To protect the consumer who buys things on credit, the federal government has passed a law called the Truth in Lending Act. Under Regulation Z of this act, specific rules must be followed by people who extend credit to consumers.

Regulation Z

The purpose of Regulation Z is to let borrowers and consumers know the exact cost of obtaining credit. With such information, people can compare different sources of credit. They can shop around for credit in the same way that they shop for anything else and can save money by obtaining it at the cheapest cost. This regulation applies whenever credit is extended to people for personal, family, household, or agricultural purposes. It does *not* apply to an extension of credit of over $25,000, except in the case of real estate transactions. Similarly, it does not apply to credit extended to businesses or corporations or to anyone for business or commercial purposes. (See also Chapter 17, page 226.)

EXAMPLE 2 Peter Martinez purchased an automobile for his personal use at a cost of $4,400. He paid $400 down and agreed to pay the balance of $4,000 in monthly installments over a 2-year period. This transaction was governed by Regulation Z. The regulation would not apply if Martinez had purchased the automobile for business purposes.

Regulation Z also regulates the use of credit cards and sets limits on the amount of money people must pay when their credit cards are used without authority. In addition, it provides a procedure for settling disputes over billing errors on certain types of accounts.

Required Disclosures

Under Regulation Z, anyone issuing credit must disclose two things before completing the transaction: (1) the finance charge (the actual cost of the loan in dollars and cents), and (2) the annual percentage rate (the true rate of interest computed according to a special formula).

FEDERAL TRUTH IN LENDING DISCLOSURES
Loan

Lender (Creditor)....Friendly Bank and Trust Co.

.........700 East Street, Little Creek, USA.........
Address: No. and Street, City, State and Zip Code

Borrower ....Lisa Stone.........

.........300 Maple Avenue, Little Creek, USA.........
Address: No. and Street, City, State and Zip Code

Co-Borrower ....none.........

.........Address: No. and Street, City, State and Zip Code

ANNUAL PERCENTAGE RATE The cost of your credit as a yearly rate.	FINANCE CHARGE The dollar amount the credit will cost you.	Amount Financed The amount of credit provided to you or on your behalf.	Total of Payments The amount you will have paid after you have made all payments as scheduled.	
12 %	$ 675.31	$ 5000.00	$ 5675.31	

Your payment schedule will be: "E" means an estimate

Number of Payments	Amount of Payments	When Payments Are Due	Or as Follows:
1	$262.03 E	Monthly beginning	6/1/XX
23	$235.36	7/1/XX	

Late Charge If a payment is not paid in full within...5 business...days from the due date shown above, you will pay a late charge of $5 or 10% of the payment, whichever is less.

Prepayment If you pay off early, you ☐ May ☒ Will not have to pay a penalty
☐ May ☐ Will not be entitled to a refund of part of the finance charge.

Security You are giving a security interest in:
☒ the goods or property being purchased.
☐ (brief description of other property) 19XX model automobile
serial number VL123456789

See your contract documents for any additional information about nonpayment, default, any required repayment in full before the scheduled date, and prepayment refunds and penalties.

You will receive a form like this if you borrow $5,000 for 24 months at 12 percent per annum interest. How much will the loan cost? *(Forms may be purchased from Julius Blumberg, Inc., NYC 10013, or any of its dealers. Reproduction prohibited.)*

Legal Issue No. 3

The **finance charge** is the total dollar amount you pay to use credit. It includes interest costs and sometimes other costs, such as service charges, insurance premiums, and appraisal fees. The **annual percentage rate (APR)** is the percentage cost (or relative cost) of credit on a yearly basis. This is your key to comparing the cost of credit from different lenders, regardless of the amount of credit or how long you have to repay it. The APR is very often greater than it might appear at first glance.

EXAMPLE 3 Suppose you borrow $100 for 1 year and pay a finance charge of $8. If you can keep the entire $100 for the whole year and then pay it all back at once, you are paying an APR of 8 percent. But, if you repay the $100 and the finance charge (a total of $108) in 12 equal monthly installments of $9 each, you don't really get to use $100 for the whole year. In fact, you get to use less and less of that $100 each month. In this case, the $8 charge for credit amounts to an APR of 14.5 percent.

The APR is computed by the use of a complicated mathematical formula. However, tables used by Federal Reserve Banks make it easy to determine the exact APR on any loan.

EXAMPLE 4   Before purchasing the car in Example 2, Peter Martinez asked the car dealer what the APR would be to finance the purchase through the dealer. The dealer said that it would be 7.9 percent. Martinez then inquired at a bank and found that the APR there would be 12 percent. He saved money by borrowing from the car dealer instead of financing the purchase through the bank. (Note: Some car dealers raise prices to recover the finance cost.

Method of Calculating the Finance Charge

Creditors who extend open-end credit use various systems to arrive at the balance on which they determine finance charges. Some creditors add finance charges after subtracting payments made during the billing period. This is called the **adjusted-balance method.** Other creditors give you no credit for payments made during the billing period. This is called the **previous-balance method.** Still other creditors add your balances for each day in the billing period and then divide by the number of days in the billing period. This is known as the **average-daily-balance method.** Table 29-1 shows examples of the three billing systems.

As Table 29-1 shows, the finance charge varies considerably for the same balance owed and amount of payment. Under the Truth in Lending Act, creditors must tell you the method they use to calculate the finance charge. In addition, they must tell you when finance charges begin on your credit account so that you will know how much time you have to pay your bills before a finance charge is added.

Advertising of Credit

As discussed in Chapter 17, the law also regulates the advertising of credit terms. The law says that if a business mentions one term of credit in its advertising, such as the amount of the down payment, it must mention all other important terms, such as the number of payments and the amount of each payment.

TABLE 29-1
THREE METHODS OF CALCULATING FINANCE CHARGE

	Adjusted Balance	Previous Balance	Average Daily Balance
Monthly Interest Rate	1½ percent	1½ percent	1½ percent
Previous Balance	$400	$400	$400
Payments	$300	$300	$300 (payment on 15th day)
Interest Charge	**$1.50** ($100 × 1.5 percent)	**$6.00** ($400 × 1.5 percent)	**$3.75** (average balance of $250 × 1.5 percent)

CREDIT CARDS

A customer may obtain a credit card by filling out an application form and sending it to the company that issues the card. If the application is approved, the company will send the customer a card. It is against the law for companies to send out credit cards to people who have not asked for them, except for the purpose of replacing old cards with new ones.

Lost or Stolen Cards

Legal Issue No. 4

One of the major problems with credit cards is that they can be easily lost, stolen, or used by people who have no authority to use them. In such cases, the law places the principal loss on the issuing company, believing that the company is in a better position to prevent the unauthorized use. Cardholders are not responsible for any unauthorized charges made after the company has been notified of the loss, theft, or possible unauthorized use of the card, and even then, customers are responsible only for the first $50 of any unauthorized charges.

EXAMPLE 5 Susan Miltiades lost her purse containing a credit card that had been issued to her by Golden's Department Store. A week after discovering the loss, she notified the store. By then, someone had charged a purchase of $175 with the credit card. Miltiades will have to pay $50 to the store for this unauthorized purchase. If she had notified the store before the purchase was made, she would not have to pay the store anything.

Notification of loss, theft, or possible unauthorized use of a credit card may be made by telephone, letter, or any other means. It becomes effective when received by the store or, if delayed, when it would have ordinarily been received.

Customers are not responsible even for the first $50 of unauthorized charges if the company fails to provide them with a description of a means of notifying the company of loss or theft of the card. In addition, customers are not responsible for the first $50 of unauthorized charges unless the credit card contains some method to identify the customer, such as a signature or photograph. Card issuers must also notify cardholders in advance of the potential $50 liability.

EQUAL CREDIT OPPORTUNITY

Credit is a basic tool for both businesses and individuals. Without access to credit, many people would be prevented from buying homes, making major purchases, or starting and running businesses. Consequently, the Equal Credit Opportunity Act of 1975 was passed to prevent discrimination against credit applicants because of gender, marital status, age, religion, race, national origin, or receipt of public assistance income. People must be considered equally for credit and be judged on the same basis—their ability to repay their debts.

Applying for Credit

The following rules apply when people ask for credit:

1. Creditors may not ask people their sex, race, national origin, or religion.
2. Creditors may not, on the basis of sex or marital status, refuse to grant a separate account to a person who qualifies for credit.
3. With some exceptions, creditors may not ask a person's marital status; how-

ever, they may ask to what extent a person's income is affected by alimony or child support obligations. People do not have to disclose income from alimony or child support payments if they will not be relying on that income.

4. In addition, people may not be prohibited from using their given names (their name at birth) or a combined last name when applying for credit.

Legal Issue No. 2

EXAMPLE 6 Donna O'Keefe worked for 5 years and developed a good credit rating while she was still single. After she married, she continued working and applied for a charge account in her maiden name at Golden's Department Store. The store could not prohibit her from using her maiden name and probably could not ask her if she was married.

Evaluation of the Application

The following rules apply when creditors evaluate applications:

1. Creditors may request and consider information about a person's spouse only when the spouse will be using or will be liable for the account or when the spouse's income is being relied upon.
2. Alimony, child support, and maintenance payments must be considered as income to the extent that such payments are likely to be consistently made.
3. Creditors may not consider the race of the people in the neighborhood where a person wants to buy or improve a house with borrowed money.

Hilbert's Department Store
Credit Division
234 Third Street
Cincinnati, OH 70239

To whom it may concern:

Under the Equal Credit Opportunity Act, I request that you report all credit information on this account in both names.

_____
ACCOUNT NUMBER

ACCOUNT NAMES: *PRINT OR TYPE*

FIRST	MIDDLE	LAST
FIRST	MIDDLE	LAST

STREET, NUMBER, APT.

CITY, STATE, ZIP

SIGNATURE OF EITHER SPOUSE

Credit Histories for Married People. If you get married and want to establish a credit history in your own name, simply write your creditors and request it. Creditors have an obligation to provide the history in both names when accounts are shared. As a sample of what you should say, you can use this format.

4. Creditors may not consider an applicant's age (with certain exceptions such as minority).
5. Creditors may not discount a spouse's income because of sex or marital status or discount income obtained from part-time employment.
6. Creditors may not ask about applicants' childbearing plans.

Acceptance and Rejection

The following rules apply to the acceptance or rejection of credit applications:

1. Creditors must inform applicants whether the application was accepted or rejected within 30 days of its filing.
2. When an application for credit is denied, creditors must also provide, upon request, the reasons for the denial within 60 days.
3. With certain exceptions, creditors may not close an account because of a change in marital status, unless there is evidence that a person is unwilling or unable to repay.

EXAMPLE 7 Ronald and Colleen Perry, while married, experienced financial difficulty. They bought too many things on credit, got behind in their payments, and established a very poor credit rating. Their financial problems eventually led to a divorce. A few years later, Ronald paid off his debts, obtained a better-paying job, and became financially sound. This would be sufficient evidence that his past credit record should not be used against him.

FAIR CREDIT REPORTING

The Fair Credit Reporting Act, passed by Congress in 1970, is another consumer protection device provided by the government. This act prohibits the abuse of a very valuable asset of consumers—their credit.

The Fair Credit Reporting Act deals with unfavorable reports issued by credit bureaus. These reports, which often contain much personal data, character studies, and so on, are frequently issued to insurance companies, businesses, or prospective employers. When rejecting an applicant, the company must supply the applicant with the source of its credit report, thus giving such a person the right to challenge the report. The applicant then has an opportunity to offer and support his or her side of the story.

The Fair Credit Reporting Act also provides that the credit reporting agency must tell you the nature of the information that they have on file for you. If the information is incorrect or incomplete, you have a right to correct the report and provide supporting information to prove your contentions. If the report is proved inaccurate, the reporting agency must delete it and send deletion notices to businesses and others who have received reports containing the wrong information. In cases of mistaken reports, you have a right to know who received your credit record in the past 6 months. If the report was given to companies in which you were seeking employment, you must be advised of the distribution of such incorrect information during the past 2 years.

EXAMPLE 8 George Keegan was a successful business owner in Minnesota. He and his family moved to Arizona because of his wife's health. When Keegan tried to get a job, he had no luck. After he applied to many firms and was turned away from each one, he found out that a credit bureau in Arizona had received incorrect information that he had a very undesirable personal life which included incidents of wife beating and disorderly conduct. Keegan had the right to find out the source of this incorrect information. He also had the right to support his side of the story and to correct the mistaken information.

FAIR CREDIT BILLING

Occasionally, people receive bills which they dispute, that is, which they believe are in error. To assist the consumer when this happens, the federal government has passed the Fair Credit Billing Act. This law establishes a procedure for the prompt handling of billing disputes in the case of open-end or revolving charge accounts. Under the act, when consumers believe an error has been made on a bill, they should notify the creditor in writing within 60 days after the bill was mailed. The notice should state the creditor's name and account number, the suspected amount of error, and an explanation of why the consumer believes there is an error. The creditor must acknowledge the consumer's letter within 30 days. In addition, the creditor must conduct a reasonable investigation and either explain why the bill is correct or correct the mistake within 90 days. While waiting for an answer from the creditor, consumers do not have to pay the amount of money in dispute, but they still must pay all parts of the bill not in dispute.

While a bill is being disputed, creditors may not threaten to damage the consumer's credit rating or report the consumer as delinquent to anyone. However, creditors are permitted to report that a consumer is disputing a bill.

DECEPTIVE BILL COLLECTING

Legal Issue No. 5

The federal government and some states have laws protecting consumers against certain kinds of harassment and deceptive bill-collection practices. It is a violation of the Federal Trade Commission Act for a creditor to use any deceptive means to collect debts or to obtain information about debtors. Creditors may not use forms, letters, or questionnaires for the purpose of collecting debts unless they state that they are for that purpose. Further, as discussed in Chapter 12 (page 169), a creditor who was assigned a debt is subject to the debtor's defenses against the original creditor.

In 1977, the U.S. Congress also enacted the Fair Debt Collection Act. This act makes it a federal offense for debt collectors to threaten consumers with violence, use obscene language, or contact consumers by telephone at inconvenient times or places in an effort to collect a debt. Other parts of the law prohibit debt collectors from impersonating government officials or attorneys, obtaining information under false pretenses, and collecting more than is legally owed. A **debt collector** is anyone, other than a creditor or creditor's attorney, who regularly collects debts for others. A debt collector must stop contacting a consumer when notified in writing to do so. Consumers may sue a debt collector for violating this law.

■ In some states it is also against the law to inform a debtor's relatives, employer, or other close associates about a debt in order to obtain payment. Additionally, collection letters may not be sent in such a way that the envelopes indicate that a debt is owed. Some of these laws are designed not only to prevent unfair collection practices, but also to protect debtors from undue embarrassment and invasion of privacy.

Suggestions for Reducing Legal Risks

1. Being able to borrow money is important in both personal and business relationships. Build a reputation for meeting financial obligations. To do otherwise invites financial and legal risks in future emergencies.
2. Be very accurate and completely honest in filing the application for the loan. Misstatements of any kind can lead to future difficulties.
3. Use credit cautiously. Avoid excessive debt. A good question to ask yourself is "Will I still be making payments for this after I no longer use it?" If your answer is yes, you probably should not buy it.
4. Take advantage of the Truth in Lending Act. Before you buy on credit or borrow money, look for the finance charge and the APR. They must be disclosed to you. With this information, you will know the exact cost of obtaining credit and will have a method for comparing credit costs.
5. Shop for credit the same way that you shop for merchandise. Shop at more than one place, and look for the lowest APR.
6. If your credit card is lost, stolen, or used without authority, notify the card issuer immediately by telephone and then follow up by letter. Keep addresses and forms for notifying credit issuers in a place that is separate from where you keep your credit cards.
7. If you are denied credit because of a bad credit report and wish to question it, ask for the name and address of the credit reporting company. Arrange for an appointment with that company to go over your file. You have a right to take someone of your choice with you if you wish. Ask to have any incorrect information in your file reinvestigated and removed unless it can be verified. If a dispute cannot be resolved, you have a right to have your version of the dispute placed in the file.

Language of the Law

Define or explain each of the following words or phrases:

creditor	discounted	financing statement	previous-balance
debtor	cosigner or surety	repossess	method
revolving charge	secured loan	finance charge	average-daily-balance
account	collateral	annual percentage	method
credit card	security interest	rate (APR)	debt collector
open-end credit	unsecured loan	adjusted-balance	
closed-end credit	security agreement	method	
	secured party		

Questions for Review

1. Name several ways in which people use credit today.
2. What is the purpose of Regulation Z? Under what act is this regulation found? When does it apply?
3. What are the two things, under Regulation Z, that anyone issuing credit must disclose before completing the transaction?
4. What should someone do if his or her credit card is lost, stolen, or used without author-

ity? To what extent is a cardholder liable in such a case?

5. If a business mentions one term of credit in its advertising, what else must it also do?
6. Why was the Equal Credit Opportunity Act passed?
7. What are four rules that apply when people ask for credit?
8. What rights does a secured party have if a debtor fails to pay back what is owed?

9. What legislative act deals with unfavorable reports issued by credit bureaus? What act deals with billing errors?
10. In what circumstances must repossessed consumer goods be sold instead of being kept by the secured party?
11. Name three deceptive bill-collecting practices that are prohibited under the Federal Trade Commission Act.

Cases in Point

In each of the following cases, give your decision and state a legal principle that applies to the case:

1. An automobile dealer advertised, "Own a brand-new car for only $500 down." Did this ad fulfill the requirements of the law?
2. Dianne Bilandic purchased a truck for her rug-cleaning business for $3,500. She paid $500 down and agreed to pay the balance in monthly installments over the next 3 years. Does Regulation Z apply to her purchase?
3. Alice Montero went to buy a car from a used-car dealer. The dealer said, "We'll finance the car for you. The finance charge will be the same wherever you go anyway because Regulation Z requires it to be." Should Montero believe the dealer?
4. Yi Chung Hak had an open-end credit account with a store, charging the items he purchased and paying a small amount each month toward the bill. The store disclosed to him that it used the previous-balance method of calculating finance charges. Was this the most beneficial method to Hak?
5. Beverly Kirkland received a bill from High Fashion, Inc., a nationwide chain store, which she believed contained an error. She had returned a $65.99 item the day after purchasing it, but the return was not shown on the bill. She immediately wrote to the store, giving her name, account number, and an explanation of the error. Is the store legally required to respond to Kirkland?
6. Owing to illness, Mary and Frank Costello

were 4 months behind on the payments for their living room furniture. Two representatives of the finance company came to their house and attempted to break in the door in order to repossess the furniture. Was the finance company within its rights?
7. David Cutler's pocket was picked in the subway. The thief got away with his wallet which contained his credit cards, including one issued by Tyler's Department Store. Cutler failed to notify the store of the loss of the credit card. The next month, he received a bill for $210 for an unauthorized purchase from the store. How much of the bill will he have to pay?
8. Mary Peguero was recently married. When she went to a bank to take out a loan, the loan officer asked her if she planned to have a child in the next few years. Mary refused to answer and was denied the loan. Did the bank officer break the law?
9. Ellen Rothstein had always paid her bills on time. Because of a computer error, she was given a poor credit and character rating. Several firms refused to give her credit, citing her poor rating with the credit reporting agency. Could Rothstein take any legal action?
10. Eric Forsstrom lost his job and ran up several high bills with his credit cards. When he was unable to pay, he began to receive repeated telephone calls day and night from a debt collector asking for payment. Could Forsstrom stop the phone calls?

Cases to Judge

1. Donna and Joseph Kish contracted with Todd Van Note, doing business as Cowboy Pools, to have a swimming pool built in their backyard for $5,500. Cowboy Pools had an arrangement with a bank for the financing. The following statement was included at the bottom of the installment contract: NOTICE— ANY HOLDER OF THIS CONSUMER CREDIT CONTRACT IS SUBJECT TO ALL CLAIMS AND DEFENSES WHICH THE DEBTOR COULD ASSERT AGAINST THE SELLER. Cowboy Pools installed a different pool from the one it had contracted to install. Because of poor excavation work, the fiberglass pool cracked during the early stage of construction. Cowboy Pools attempted several unsuccessful patch jobs, but the pool could never be used. The Kishes made five payments to the bank, totaling $504.30, but they refused to pay more. They won their suit against Cowboy Pools, but a question arose as to whether the bank must return the $504.30. Must it do so? Why or why not? *Kish v. Van Note,* 692 S.W.2d 463 (Texas)

2. A fire caused extensive damage to a mobile home owned by Robert and Sharon Rowland. The Rowlands sold the burned-out mobile home to Lyle and Ann Anderson, who bought it for the purpose of repairing and reselling it rather than living in it. As part of the transaction, the Andersons took over the Rowlands's loan. Is the loan to the Andersons covered by the Truth in Lending Act? Why or why not? *Anderson v. Rocky Mountain Federal Savings and Loan,* 651 P.2d 269 (Wyoming)

3. Stewart and Marjory Selmans applied to the Manor Mortgage Company for a loan of $23,000, apparently to be used for personal purposes. They were told that if they incorporated, they would be given a loan. (Under the law in that state, money could be loaned to corporations at a higher rate of interest than to individuals.) The Selmans formed a corporation, received the loan, and then had the corporation dissolved. Does the transaction fall within Regulation Z of the Truth in Lending Act? Explain. *Selman v. Manor Mortgage Co.,* 551 F. Supp. 345 (Michigan)

4. Still Associates, Inc., sold a new pickup truck to Charles J. Lavoie on credit. Lavoie signed three papers giving a security interest to Still Associates. On all of these papers, the serial number of the truck was listed as No. 1161-702088. It should have been No. 1161-702080. A year later, before the truck was completely paid for, Lavoie sold the truck to Kenneth F. Murphy. Murphy had no knowledge of the security interest held by Still Associates on the truck. Still Associates, Inc., then sued Kenneth F. Murphy for the value of the truck. Murphy claimed that he should win the case because the financing statement that he signed did not identify the truck properly. How would you decide? *Still Associates, Inc., v. Murphy,* 267 N.E.2d 217 (Massachusetts)

5. Frank Byrd purchased a Ford Torino from Bassett Ford, Inc. The lender, Ford Motor Credit Company (FMCC), took a security interest in the automobile. Approximately 34 months later, Craig, a repossession agent, contended that the payments were late. Craig requested that Byrd go to Bassett Ford to review the records. Byrd drove there in the Torino. While Byrd was at Bassett Ford arguing that his payments were not late, his vehicle was removed and locked up.

   Byrd brought suit against FMCC, claiming that FMCC had fraudulently lured him to Bassett Ford to repossess the vehicle without his knowledge and consent, through stealth and trickery. FMCC contended that a secured party has on default the right to take possession of collateral without judicial process if this can be done without breach of the peace. Should FMCC's arguments be accepted? Why? *Ford Motor Credit Co. v. Byrd,* 351 So.2d 577 (Alabama)

Chapter 30

KINDS OF NEGOTIABLE INSTRUMENTS

Scene: The Rodriguez apartment. Carlos arrives home from work and is greeted by Inez.

Carlos (*after a warm hug*): Here it is, honey (*holding a check in his hand*), my first paycheck since I've been back to work.

Inez: Oh, let me hold it. We've waited a long time for this.

Carlos: I'd frame it and put it on the wall if we didn't need the money.

Inez (*reading out loud the words on the check*): Pay to the order of Carlos Rodriguez $322.78. This is better than an unemployment check. Why does it say draft on the top of the check?

Carlos: I don't know, and I don't care as long as the check's good and I don't get drafted into the service.

Inez: Oh, they wouldn't do that to us! Say, there's no date on this check.

Carlos: Let me look at it (*taking the check*). Say, you're right. I wonder if it's any good?

Inez: It must be. Do you think we can pay something to the furniture company? The owner called again this morning about getting a payment.

Carlos: I sure wish we could pay him, but we have so many other bills. We've got to make a payment on your credit card so we won't ruin your credit.

Inez: It would be great if we could collect the money that Julio owes you. It must be almost due. I remember that we were making our wedding plans when you loaned him the money. That was about a year ago.

Carlos: You're right. It was about a year ago. Let's look at the promissory note that he gave me. I'll get it. (*Carlos leaves the room and returns with a piece of paper.*) Here it is. The whole paper is written in his handwriting. It says, "One year from date, I, Julio Rueda, promise to pay to the order of Carlos Rodriguez the sum of $1,000 with interest at the rate of 12 percent per annum." It's not due for another month. Say, I just realized . . . he didn't sign it! This is no good!

Inez: I wouldn't worry. You can trust Julio. He'll sign it the next time he comes over. Anyway, I'd trust him even if he didn't put it in writing.

Carlos: You know, the amount he owes me is about the same amount that we owe the furniture company. Wouldn't it be great if Julio could sign a paper that would transfer his debt directly to the furniture company.

Inez: That would make the furniture company happy.

Carlos: I think I'll write out a few checks right now. I can mail them on the way to work early tomorrow morning.

Inez: Hadn't you better deposit your paycheck first?

Carlos: I'll just postdate the checks a few days. That way they can't cash them until my check clears.

Inez: I didn't think it was legal to do that.

1. Is a draft necessarily the same thing as a check?
2. Is a check void if it has no date on it?
3. May a signature on a negotiable instrument be written into the text instead of at the bottom?
4. Is there a type of negotiable instrument that can be used to transfer debts?
5. Does the law allow people to postdate checks?

THE SPIRIT OF THE LAW

Throughout history there has been a need to transact business without carrying around large sums of money. There has also been a need to borrow money in order to buy things now and pay for them later. The **law of commercial paper** (also called the **law of negotiable instruments**) has been developed in recognition of these needs. This law is part of the Uniform Commercial Code (UCC), which is discussed in Chapter 14.

The term *negotiable* means "capable of being transferred by indorsement or delivery." The term *instrument* is the legal name for a written document. Thus a **negotiable instrument** is a written document that may be transferred by indorsement or delivery, giving special legal rights to the transferee. Indorsements are explained in Chapter 32. There are three basic types of negotiable instruments: drafts (including checks), notes, and certificates of deposit.

DRAFTS

A **draft** (also known as a **bill of exchange**) is an order for the payment of money drawn by one person on another. There are three parties to a draft. The one who draws the draft (that is, the one who orders the money to be paid) is called the **drawer.** The one who is ordered to pay the money is called the **drawee.** The one who is to receive the money is known as the **payee.**

Drawees, although ordered to do so, are not required to pay money unless they have agreed to pay it. They do this by writing the word *accepted* on the paper (usually the front) and signing their name. A drawee who has done this is called an **acceptor.**

The draft developed during the Middle Ages when it was the custom of merchants to hold international trade fairs. Merchants at first carried gold and silver with them as they traveled from one fair to another buying goods. They were in constant danger of being robbed, however, and needed a safer and more convenient method of exchanging their gold and silver for the goods they bought. A system was developed by which merchants could deposit their precious metals with goldsmiths or silversmiths for safekeeping. When the merchants bought goods, instead of paying for them with gold or silver, they simply filled out a piece of paper, known as a bill of exchange. The bill of exchange ordered the goldsmith or silversmith to give a certain amount of the precious metals to the person who sold the goods. That person would then take the bill of exchange to the goldsmith or silversmith and receive payment.

Drafts Used to Transfer Debts

Legal Issue No. 4

Business people often use drafts to transfer debts from one party to another. Suppose, for example, that A owes $500 to B and that B owes $500 to C. If A could somehow pay C directly, both debts would be paid. This can be done with a draft. B can draw a draft ordering A to pay the $500 to C. If A agrees to pay C by writing *accepted* and signing the face of the draft, A will be obligated to pay $500 to C.

A **sight draft** is a draft that is payable as soon as it is presented to the drawee for payment. A **time draft** is a draft that is not payable until the lapse of a particular time period stated on the draft.

Trade Acceptances

A **trade acceptance** is a draft used by a seller of goods to receive payment and also to extend credit. It is often used in combination with a bill of lading, which is a receipt given by a freight company to someone who ships goods. A seller ships goods to a buyer and sends a bill of lading, with a draft attached, to a bank in the buyer's city. The draft is drawn by the seller ordering the buyer to pay the money either to the seller or to someone else. If it is a sight draft, the buyer must pay the draft immediately to receive the bill of lading from the bank. If it is a

---

> $ 500.00   April 1,   19 XX
> On June 1, 19XX ————————————————————— Pay to
> the order of _Henry Collins_ ————————————————
> Five Hundred and 00/100 ————————————————— Dollars
>
> Value received and charge the same to account of
> To _Jason Amsler_ ——————— } _Susan Barrett_
> No._____ }

In this time draft, Barrett (the drawer) orders Amsler (the drawee) to pay Collins (the payee) $500. The draft may be presented to Amsler for acceptance before June 1, or for payment on June 1.

| | Benton _____, Illinois, | December 2, | 19 -- |

To William Hayes _____

Williamsburg, Virginia _____

On sight _____ **pay to the order of** ------Doris Polanski----------

the sum of Five hundred and 00/100------------------------------------- DOLLARS

Doris Polanski

Present through:

Williamsburg Bank _____

Who is the drawee of this trade acceptance? Who is the payee?

time draft, the buyer must accept the draft (sign the front of it) to receive the bill of lading from the bank. The freight company will not release the goods to the buyer unless the buyer has the bill of lading.

EXAMPLE 1 Doris Polanski, of Benton, Illinois, wishes to ship goods valued at $500 to William Hayes, in Williamsburg, Virginia. Polanski receives an order bill of lading from the railway company. She makes out a sight draft for $500, payable to herself and drawn on Hayes. The draft is attached to the bill of lading, and both are sent to a designated bank at Williamsburg. Before Hayes can obtain the bill of lading, he must pay the bank. The bank will then give it to Polanski. The trade acceptance for this example is shown above.

Checks

Legal Issue No. 1

Legal Issue No. 5

The most common kind of draft in use today is the ordinary check. People put money in the bank and then order the bank to pay it to others by writing out checks. The difference between a check and other drafts is that a check is always drawn on a bank. Also, a check is always payable on demand. Persons cannot write out checks to be paid at later dates except by postdating them. **Postdating** a check is putting a later date on the check than the date on which it is being written. This is allowed under the UCC. A more detailed discussion about the writing of checks appears in the next chapter.

▌NOTES

A **note** (often called a **promissory note**) is a written promise by one person, called the **maker,** to pay money to the payee. When two persons sign a note, they are called **comakers.** Notes are used by persons who loan money or who extend credit as evidence of debt. An advantage of using a note is that such an instrument can be negotiated (transferred) to other people without much difficulty.

There are various types of notes. A **demand note** is one that is payable whenever the payee demands payment. A **time note** is one that is payable at a future date that is written on the face of the note. An **installment note** is one that is paid in a series of payments. This latter type of note is often signed by people who borrow money to buy a car or a house.

```
$ 400.00                    Tyler, Texas,              May 4, 19 --

Sixty days                                I
                                after date   promise to pay to

the order of --------------Thomas Ryan------------------------------

Four hundred and 00/100------------------------------------ DOLLARS

at  The Liberty National Bank

Value Received

No.  55    Due  July 3, 19--      Diane Cosenzo
```

A note promises payment at a future date.

EXAMPLE 2 Kathy Gerlach bought a car from Laura's Used-Car Exchange for $2,000. She paid $200 down and signed a note promising to pay the balance to Laura's Used-Car Exchange in monthly installments over a 2-year period with interest at the rate of 18 percent per year. Laura's Used-Car Exchange, in order to get its money immediately, negotiated the note to the Ace Finance Company, which took it for a small service charge. Gerlach will have to make her monthly payments to the holder of the note—that is, to the Ace Finance Company.

CERTIFI-CATES OF DEPOSIT

A **certificate of deposit** is an acknowledgment by a bank of the receipt of money and a promise to pay the money back on the due date, usually with interest. Certificates of deposit generally pay more interest than regular savings accounts because the depositor cannot draw the money out of the bank before the due date of the certificate without paying a penalty. People who have certificates of deposit can obtain money very easily by negotiating the certificates to other people or by pledging them as security for a loan.

EXAMPLE 3 Nena Holyfield wanted to put $1,000 in the bank and, at the same time, obtain the highest interest rate possible. Upon investigation, she found that a 5-year term deposit certificate would pay the most interest. She deposited $1,000 in the bank, and the bank gave her a certificate of deposit that was to become due in 5 years. If she were to need the money before that time, she could either negotiate the certificate to someone else or pledge it as security for a loan.

REQUIRE-MENTS OF NEGOTIA-BILITY

To be negotiable, an instrument must satisfy certain formal requirements that are outlined in the UCC. It has been said that negotiability is entirely a matter of form and that an instrument, to be negotiable, must stand on its own. By this it is meant that within the borders of the instrument itself, all the information needed to determine whether it is negotiable must be present. A negotiable instrument must (1) be in writing, (2) be signed by the maker or drawer, (3) contain an unconditional promise or order (4) to pay a certain sum in money, (5) be payable on demand or at a definite time, and (6) be payable to order or bearer.

In Writing

The promise, or order, to pay must be in writing. An oral promise, no matter how specific it may have been, cannot be negotiated. The writing may be handwriting, typewriting, printing, or any other means of writing. The person who writes his or her name on it as the maker or drawer of the instrument is liable on it.

Signed by the Maker or the Drawer
Legal Issue No. 3

A promissory note must be signed by the maker. A draft must be signed by the drawer. A signature may be any mark that is placed on the instrument with the intention of its being a signature. The signature may be either written at the bottom or into the text, such as ''I, John Carico, promise to pay . . . ''

Unconditional Promise or Order

The promise in the note, or the order in the draft, must be unconditional. If either is qualified in any way, the instrument is not negotiable.

EXAMPLE 4 Scott Sullivan's uncle gave him a promissory note for $100. The note was complete and regular in every way except that written on it was the statement, ''Payable only on Scott Sullivan's graduation from high school.''

This is a valid promise to pay, and if Scott graduates from high school, his uncle will owe him $100. The note is not negotiable, however, and never can be. It is conditioned, or dependent, on Scott's graduation. Even if Scott is graduated and meets the condition, the note is still not negotiable because on its face it is conditional. Statements requiring that certain things be done or that specific events take place prior to payment make the instrument a simple contract rather than negotiable paper.

Definite Sum of Money

A negotiable instrument must be payable in a sum certain of money. Usually it can be payable in any money that has a known or established value. An instrument payable in a foreign currency or any medium of exchange accepted by a domestic or foreign government is negotiable.

Definite Time of Payment

The time at which the instrument is payable must be definite, or the instrument must be payable on demand. An instrument payable only upon an event whose occurrence is uncertain is not payable at a definite time.

EXAMPLE 5 If Sullivan's uncle had given him a note which was worded ''payable 30 days after my death,''the note would not be negotiable because it was not payable at a definite time.

If the instrument is payable on demand or at sight, it must be presented for payment within a reasonable length of time.

Words of Negotiability

To be negotiable, the instrument must say, ''to the order of'' or ''to bearer.'' These are the **words of negotiability.** If such words are omitted, the instrument is not negotiable.

EXAMPLE 6   Suppose that the note given to Sullivan did not contain the condition mentioned in Example 4. It read only ''I promise to pay Scott Sullivan . . . '' without the words *order* or *bearer*.

The implication is that the uncle would pay Scott but no one else. Thus the instrument would not be negotiable.

In the case of a draft, the drawee must be named or indicated with reasonable certainty. If an instrument named the drawee as ''National Bank, New York'' and there were several National Banks in New York City, the paper would be nonnegotiable because the drawee was not named with sufficient definiteness.

NONESSEN-
TIALS

Certain things may be omitted without destroying the negotiable character of the instrument. Some of these are (1) the date,* (2) the consideration, or value, given by the maker or the drawer, (3) the place where the instrument is drawn, and (4) the place where it is payable.

DELIVERY
OF NEGO-
TIABLE IN-
STRUMENTS

A negotiable instrument—unlike other contracts—must be delivered to be effective. A negotiable instrument is delivered when the one who issues it transfers ownership and voluntarily gives up possession of it to a new owner. If the instrument is in circulation, however, it is presumed to have been properly delivered until evidence is introduced to prove that it was not. An instrument is in circulation when it is negotiated to another party by the holder.

EXAMPLE 7   Robert McIntosh fully executed a promissory note payable to Rodney Hough and left it lying on his (McIntosh's) desk. Hough came in when McIntosh was out, took the note, and carried it away with him. If Hough later brought an action against McIntosh to collect the note, the very fact that this note had been fully executed and was in circulation would be evidence of proper delivery. McIntosh, however, would be permitted to introduce evidence to show that Hough took the note wrongfully and that there was no legal delivery.

If Hough had properly negotiated the note to the Exchange Bank, which had no notice of the wrongful taking, and the Exchange Bank had brought an action for its collection, the bank could collect it. McIntosh would not be permitted to use the defense of improper delivery against the bank. The proper negotiation would eliminate this defense.

Suggestions for Reducing Legal Risks

1. Consider paying an obligation with a negotiable instrument, because the canceled instrument serves as a receipt for the payment.
2. Consider accepting a negotiable instrument in payment when the buyer is unable to pay cash immediately, because it gives the holder an instrument that can be readily converted to cash.

Legal Issue No. 2   *An instrument's negotiability is not affected if it is undated, antedated, or postdated. If an instrument is undated, the date agreed upon may be inserted by the holder. If it is antedated or postdated, the time it is payable is determined by the date stated, making the instrument payable on demand or at a fixed period in the future.

3. Prepare all your negotiable instruments carefully using ink, a typewriter, or a check protector so that it will be difficult or impossible for them to be altered by a future holder, finder, or thief.
4. If you have to hold negotiable instruments for a period of time until maturity, keep them safe from loss, theft, fire, or destruction.

Language of the Law

Define or explain each of the following words or phrases:

law of commercial paper (law of negotiable instruments)
negotiable instrument
draft
bill of exchange

drawer
drawee
payee
acceptor
sight draft
time draft

trade acceptance
postdating
note
promissory note
maker
comaker

demand note
time note
installment note
certificate of deposit
words of negotiability

Questions for Review

1. What are two reasons for the development of the law of commercial paper?
2. Name the three basic kinds of negotiable instruments.
3. Name the parties to a draft. What is the most common type of draft?
4. Explain the difference between a sight draft and a time draft.
5. Distinguish between a note and a certificate of deposit.

6. Name the six requirements of a negotiable instrument.
7. Does the signature of the maker of a note always have to be in handwriting? Explain.
8. What is meant by an unconditional promise to pay a certain sum?
9. Explain what is meant by *words of negotiability*. Must all negotiable instruments contain words of negotiability?

Cases in Point

In each of the following cases, give your decision and state a legal principle that applies to the case:

1. Percy Zelig owned the Country Coin Shop, which specialized in rare coins, stamps, gold and silver bars, and other collector's items. In exchange for a loan of $10,000, Percy gave a promissory note to Kimberly Tate which read: "In 60 days, I promise to pay to the order of Kimberly Tate $10,000 worth of silver bars. [Signed] Percy Zelig." Is the note negotiable?
2. John Alverado wrote out a check to Donna Leone for $75 and, by mistake, omitted the date. Leone claimed that the check was not negotiable. Is she correct?

3. In place of a paycheck, Janet Wilson accepted an IOU from her employer which said, "I owe you $150." Wilson offered the IOU as payment for her grocery bill. Do you think the grocery-store owner would be likely to accept this type of payment? Why?
4. Stanley Stevens, who lives in California, sent a check to Lynda Bundy, who lives in New York. Can Bundy reasonably expect that the laws relating to the collection of the check will be the same in both states?
5. Is this a negotiable instrument? Explain. On May 20, 19—, I promise to pay Glen Cooper one hundred dollars.
   [Signed] Cynthia Howell
6. Is the following a negotiable instrument? (See next page.) Explain why or why not.

I promise to pay to the order of Henry Lloyd two hundred dollars when he completes the painting of my house.

[Signed] Judd Lindsay

7. Helen Grisley offered Diane Termain a promissory note for $100 for merchandise purchased. Although the terms of the sale provided for payment with a 30-day note, Termain refused to accept the note because it had been written in pencil. Could the holder of the note have collected the $100 in 30 days had she accepted it in payment?

8. Dorothy Crochett executed a promissory note for $200 payable to the order of Sal Domingo 5 days after the next full moon. If all other essentials are present, is the note negotiable?

9. Is the following note a negotiable instrument?
Portland, Oregon, May 6, 19—
On the twenty-first birthday of Ella Horowitz, I promise to pay to her, or to her order, five hundred dollars.

[Signed] Merton Cass

10. Pierre Monet gave Attorney Carl Pierce, of Beverly, Massachusetts, a promissory note in exchange for legal services. The note read, "I promise to pay to the order of Carl Pierce, in or within 60 days, the sum of 500 French francs." Is the instrument negotiable?

Cases to Judge

1. As part of an alimony settlement, T. Jay Seale III signed a promissory note for $5,000 payable on a specific date to the order of "myself." In addition to signing the note on the front, Seale indorsed it and delivered it to his former wife, Ann Saint Seale Turney. When the note became due, he refused to pay it, and the question arose as to whether or not the note was a negotiable instrument. How would you decide? Why? *Turney v. Seale,* 473 So. 2d 855 (Louisiana)

2. In a suit against Dominic Loweth, Philip N. Fazio introduced into evidence the following written instrument dated November 15: "This is to certify that I borrowed $15,000 from Philip N. Fazio on this day to be returned within 10 days." This was followed by what appeared to be the signature of Loweth. Fazio claimed that the instrument was negotiable. Do you agree? Explain. *Fazio v. Loweth,* 490 N.Y.S.2d 859 (New York)

3. Sandra A. McGuire signed the following note as part of a business transaction: "For value received, Thomas J. McGuire and Sandra A. McGuire, husband and wife, do promise to pay to the order of Pascal L. Tursi and Rebecca L. Tursi of 110 Curtis Lane, Moorestown, N.J. and of The Green Mountain Inn, Stowe, Vt. the sum of Sixty-Five Thousand Dollars ($65,000)." Is the note a negotiable instrument? Why or why not? *P. P. Inc. v. McGuire,* 509 F. Supp. 1079 (New Jersey)

4. In exchange for legal services rendered to her by the law firm of Westmoreland, Hall, and Bryan, Barbara Hall wrote the following letter: "I agree to pay to your firm as attorney's fees for representing me in obtaining property settlement agreement and tax advice, the sum of $2,760, payable at the rate of $230 per month for twelve (12) months beginning January 1, 1970. Very truly yours, Barbara Hall Hodge." Was the letter a negotiable instrument? Explain. *Hall v. Westmoreland, Hall, and Bryan,* 182 S.E.2d 539 (Georgia)

5. Jon and Rita How gave the Fulkersons a postdated check for $2,000 as their acceptance of an offer to sell a trailer park. The Fulkersons claimed that no contract came into existence because the postdated check created a qualified acceptance. Is the negotiability of an instrument affected by the fact that it is postdated? Explain. *How v. Fulkerson,* 528 P.2d 853 (Arizona)

Chapter 31

WRITING CHECKS

Scene: The Rodriguez apartment. There is a knock on the door.

Inez (*opening the door*): Hi Julio! How are you?

Julio (*entering*): Hi Inez! Today's your lucky day!

Carlos (*walking into the room*): Julio! It's good to see you!

Julio: This is the day you've been waiting for! Here's a check for the amount that I borrowed from you, plus interest!

Inez (*taking the check*): That's great, we can sure use it! I'll put this in a safe place so we won't lose it. (*She opens the buffet drawer and lifts up some papers.*) Carlos! Look what I found! That check from Aunt Angelica that we lost. It was under these papers in the drawer!

Carlos: Oh, am I glad to hear that! That check must be about seven months old. I thought for sure that it was stolen.

Julio: I told you that this was your lucky day!

Inez: You know, if I hadn't told Aunt Angelica that we lost that check she never would have known. She never reconciles her bank statement.

Julio: I don't either.

Inez: You should, you know.

Julio: I never have. Is it important?

Carlos: It is if you don't want your checks to bounce. Will you be able to go to the bank tomorrow, Inez?

Inez: Yes. I'll deposit both checks.

Carlos: While you're there, why don't you cash the paycheck that I got today. I'll indorse it right now.

Julio: Well, I've got to go.

Carlos and Inez: Thanks Julio!

Julio: Okay. See you later!

Inez: I'll write a check for the last payment to the furniture company. It'll be good to have that taken care of. It's only $125.

Carlos (*the next evening, talking with Inez*): Were you able to cash the paycheck today?

Inez: The bank wouldn't cash it for me. They said that I'd have to wait a few days for it to clear, so I just deposited it.

Carlos: We should sue that bank! I think they have to cash it!

Inez: They wouldn't take Aunt Angelica's check, either. They called it a stale check, or something. (*Two weeks later, Inez is trying to reconcile the bank statement.*)

Carlos: What a month this was. First the bank wouldn't cash my paycheck, then Julio's check bounced.

Inez: This thing won't balance! There's something wrong somewhere! (*She looks through the canceled checks.*) Carlos, according to the check stub, that check you wrote to the furniture company was for $125.

Carlos: That's right.

Inez: Look at the canceled check. It's in your handwriting, and its written for $425.

Carlos: Really? (*Looking at the check*) You're right! That furniture company must have raised the check I wrote!

LEGAL ISSUES

1. For what legal reason is it important to reconcile a bank statement as soon as possible after receiving it?
2. May a bank be sued by a person for not cashing that person's paycheck?
3. Must a bank honor a check that is 7 months old? What is such a check called and why?
4. What may be the legal consequences of writing a bad check?
5. Who must bear the loss when a bank pays a raised check?

THE SPIRIT OF THE LAW

The check is the most common kind of negotiable instrument in use today. Millions of dollars change hands daily by means of checks, eliminating the need for people to carry large sums of cash around with them. Checks provide a relatively safe method for sending money through the mail. They also provide automatic receipts for the people who write them.

OPENING A CHECKING ACCOUNT

A checking account is opened by depositing money in the bank and signing a signature card. The bank then agrees to pay money out, up to the amount on deposit, when ordered to do so by the depositor. A **check** is a draft drawn on a bank and payable on demand. It orders the bank to pay unconditionally on demand a definite sum of money to the bearer or to the order of a specified person. If the bank refuses to pay a check when there are sufficient funds on deposit, it is a breach of contract with the depositor. The depositor may sue the bank for any damages actually suffered as a result of the breach.

EXAMPLE 1 Donna O'Grady had $300 on deposit in her checking account. She wrote out a $250 check and mailed it to the Ace Camera Company for the purchase of a camera. The camera usually sold for $310 but was on sale that week for $250. O'Grady's bank refused to pay the check, and the Ace Camera Company refused to send her the camera. By the time the matter was straightened out, the sale was over, and O'Grady had to pay $310 for the camera. She could sue the bank for $60 (the difference between the sale price and the actual cost of the camera), plus interest and court costs.

Legal Issue No. 2

Only the depositor has the right to sue the bank for failing to pay a check. In Example 1, the Ace Camera Company could not sue the bank because the bank made no agreement with the company to pay the check. The bank's agreement to pay is with the depositor only. An exception to this rule occurs with a certified check, as discussed later in this chapter.

Legal Issue No. 3

A bank may refuse to pay a check that is more than 6 months old without incurring liability to the depositor. Such a check is known as a **stale check.** If the bank elects to pay a stale check, however, it may charge the amount to the customer's account.

A bank may charge any properly payable item against its depositor's account. The bank may not charge items, however, such as postdated checks, that are not properly payable. If it does, the depositor has a claim against the bank for the amount improperly charged.

Parties to a Check

The parties to a check are the same as the parties to a draft. The person who writes the check is called the drawer. The bank that is ordered to pay the money is called the drawee. The one to whom the check is made payable is called the payee.

WRITING CHECKS

Checks are usually written on regular printed forms provided by the bank, but such forms are not required. As long as the instrument follows the requirements set forth by law, it will be legally considered a valid instrument.

EXAMPLE 2   Charles Hurd, a debtor from a nearby town, stopped at the offices of the Lotus Loan Company to make a payment. He had forgotten his checkbook, and the company had no blank checks available. Hurd wrote out a check on a piece of 8½- by 11-inch typing paper, taking care to include the requisites of negotiability and the coded number assigned to him by his bank for identification. This would constitute a valid check when signed and delivered by Hurd.

Avoidance of Negligence

It is important to write checks so that they cannot be changed easily or signed by a forger. Drawers are responsible for altered or forged checks only if their negligence contributed to the **alteration** (change) or forgery. It would be negligent to write a check in such a way that a forger could easily raise the amount by inserting additional words and figures next to those originally written.

EXAMPLE 3   Delores Gomez wrote out a check for $6 payable to Donald Kozak. The check was written in such a way that it could easily be altered. Donald lost the check. His cousin, James, found it and altered it so that it was payable to him in the amount of $160. He negotiated it to another person. The bank paid $160 to the holder, who was innocent of any wrongdoing and had given value for the check. Gomez would be responsible for paying the $160 because her negligence in writing the check contributed to its alteration.

NO. 3   55-293 / 212

June 23   19 — —

PAY TO THE ORDER OF *James Donald Kozak* $*160*⁰⁰⁄₁₀₀

One Hundred Sixty and ⁰⁰⁄₁₀₀   **DOLLARS**

Delores Gomez

CENTER TRUST COMPANY
RED BANK, NEW JERSEY 07701

⑆0212⑉0293⑆ 0243⑈0677⑊

NO. 3   55-293 / 212

June 23   19 — —

PAY TO THE ORDER OF *Donald Kozak* $*6*⁰⁰⁄₁₀₀

Six and ⁰⁰⁄₁₀₀   **DOLLARS**

Delores Gomez

CENTER TRUST COMPANY
RED BANK, NEW JERSEY 07701

⑆0212⑉0293⑆ 0243⑈0677⑊

Notice how easily the top check could be altered from $6.00 to $160.00. Notice also how another name could easily be added. Writing a check in the manner shown in the lower check lessens the likelihood that it will be altered.

Gomez could have avoided responsibility for the alteration mentioned in Example 3 if she had followed a few simple rules.

When handwriting a check, place the figures very close to the dollar sign and keep them close together. Always start at the extreme left when writing amounts of money in words, and draw a wavy line in any part of the space not needed for the amount. This line should be drawn to prevent someone from putting in additional words and figures to raise the value of the check. Write the name of the payee close to the words *Pay to the order of* and fill in all unused space with a wavy line.

Be sure that the figures are the same as the written amount. If there is a difference and the bank pays the check, it will usually honor the written amount. Under the Uniform Commercial Code, words take precedence over figures except that if the words are ambiguous, the figures can be the deciding factor. The bank can be held responsible for paying the incorrect amount.

Sign your name last, and make your signature look as much as possible like the one on the bank signature card. Never sign a blank check. Never cross out or change a check once it has been written. If you make a mistake, write a new check and tear up the spoiled one. Write the word *void* on the check stub, or in your checkbook, to keep your records accurate.

Bad Checks

A **bad check** is one issued against a bank balance that is insufficient to cover or against a bank in which the drawer has no funds. Most states have statutes making it larceny for persons to issue checks drawn on banks in which they have no funds. Some states make it an offense for persons to issue checks on banks in which they have insufficient funds. The payee has the obligation to inform the drawer of the nonpayment of the check.

Legal Issue No. 4

Failure of the drawer to make full payment of the check within the number of days allowed by statute will serve as presumption of guilt. It will be presumed that the drawer issued the check with full knowledge of all facts and with the intent to defraud.

EXAMPLE 4   The Lotus Loan Company received Renee Millard's check for $125, due on an installment note. After it was deposited, the check was returned to Lotus with the notation "Insufficient Funds." Lotus's collection department sent a certified letter to Millard, notifying her of the matter and of her responsibilities under the bad-check law. If Millard were to fail to make the check good, a criminal complaint might be lodged against her through the state's prosecuting attorney.

Bad-check laws are effectively used as a means of collection. When notified that they are subject to prosecution, most persons make every effort to pay the creditor the amount of the check.

FORGED CHECKS

A **forged check** is a check signed by someone other than the drawer and without authority. If a bank pays a forged check and the drawer was not negligent, the bank must bear the loss. It is the duty of the bank to know the signatures of its depositors. The bank must also bear the loss of the amount added if a check is changed from the original amount to a higher amount. This altered check may be referred to as a **raised check.**

Legal Issue No. 5

EXAMPLE 5   Henry Greer applied for a $250 loan from the Lotus Loan Company and received its check for that amount. He raised the amount to $2,500, presented the check to a bank for payment, and received the money. Greer was guilty of forgery, having had the intent to defraud Lotus by making an alteration and by creating for it a liability that had not existed before. The bank must suffer the loss unless it can recover the money from Greer.

Legal Issue No. 1

The depositor has the responsibility of notifying the bank of a forgery within a reasonable time after receiving the monthly bank statement containing the canceled checks. Failure to give notice will relieve the bank of liability. For this reason, it is important to reconcile your bank statement as soon as possible after receiving it. The **reconciliation of a bank statement** is brought about by comparing a check-stub balance with the bank statement balance to be sure that they agree. Usually it is necessary to take into consideration **outstanding checks,** that is, checks that you have written but that have not yet been returned to the bank.

EXAMPLE 6 In Example 5, Lotus would have had an obligation to inform the bank at once after discovering that the $250 check had been raised. Any unreasonable delay in giving this information to the bank would relieve the bank of liability.

Customers have 1 year to discover and report to the bank unauthorized signatures or alterations on the face of a check. They have 3 years to discover and report to the bank any unauthorized indorsements on the check. After that time, the bank is not liable.

CERTIFIED CHECKS

Because of the possibility of checks being returned for insufficient funds, people are reluctant, sometimes, to take ordinary checks. In contrast, they will usually take certified checks. This is so because certified checks are guaranteed by the bank on which they are drawn. When a check is **certified,** the bank on which it is drawn agrees to pay it whenever it is presented for payment. The bank cashier stamps "Certified" across the face of the check, together with the date and the signature of a bank official. The cashier takes the money out of the depositor's account at the time the certification is made. A careful person would request a certified check when involved in a business transaction with a stranger rather than accept an ordinary check.

EXAMPLE 7 Robert Buterbaugh contracted to sell some expensive machinery to Allstate Equipment Company. Because Buterbaugh did not know Allstate, he required a certified check before releasing the machinery. By doing this, he was assured of obtaining the money due him unless, of course, the bank that certified the check became insolvent (unable to pay debts).

STOPPING PAYMENT OF A CHECK

The drawer of a check may change his or her mind before the check is presented for payment and may order the bank not to pay it when presented. The bank is bound by this **order to stop payment** and has no right to pay the check after such an order is given. If the bank fails to heed the order and cashes the check, it is liable for any loss suffered by the drawer who ordered the payment stopped.

An oral stop-payment order is binding on the bank only for 14 calendar days unless confirmed in writing within that period. A written order is effective for only 6 months unless renewed in writing.

EXAMPLE 8 Ramona Alvarez applied for a loan from the Lotus Loan Company, offering as a credit reference a letter bearing the signature of one of the city's leading business executives. Lotus granted the loan, issued a check for the amount of the loan to Alvarez, and then learned that the reference letter was a fraud. It had not been written by the person whose name was used. Lotus issued a stop-payment order to the bank on Alvarez's check. Since Lotus had a

The drawer is liable for the checks he writes. *(Copyright © 1985, Universal Press Syndicate. Reprinted with permission. All rights reserved.)*

"Why don't you write more clearly? You left a $200 tip."

good and valid reason for issuing such an order, it will be free of liability for damages in any action by Alvarez.

If you stop payment on a check given in payment of an amount actually owed, you still owe the amount of the debt and can be sued for it. Also, you cannot avoid liability on a check even by stopping payment on it if it gets in the hands of a *holder in due course*. A holder in due course is one who takes the instrument for value, in good faith, and without notice that anything is wrong with it. Such a holder is explained further in Chapter 33.

The death of the drawer of a check does not revoke the authority of the bank to pay an item until the bank knows of the fact of death and has a reasonable opportunity to act on it. Even with knowledge, a bank may for 10 days after the date of death pay or certify checks drawn on it prior to that date unless ordered to stop payment by a person claiming an interest in the account.

EXAMPLE 9 On April 1, Sam Harding made out several checks and mailed them at once to various creditors in payment of their bills. On the evening of the same day, Harding died. When the checks were presented for payment during the next few days, Harding's bank paid them. The bank had a right to do so.

SPECIAL KINDS OF CHECKS

Special kinds of checks have been developed for use in particular situations. Some of these checks are traveler's checks, money orders, cashier's checks, and bank drafts.

Traveler's Checks

Traveler's checks are drafts drawn by a reliable financial organization. They may be purchased from banks and other institutions. For a person who travels extensively, traveler's checks are a particularly convenient and safe form in which to carry money. They are safe because anyone finding or stealing them cannot use them. Only the purchaser who signed the checks when they were bought may cash them. If the purchaser loses them, they will be replaced.

When a purchaser wishes to cash one of the checks, the purchaser signs it a second time in the presence of the payee. Traveler's checks are more acceptable than personal checks, are easily negotiable, and are accepted virtually all over the world.

Money Orders

Money orders, both postal and express, are acceptable in situations where a personal check would not be honored. Whether or not money orders are issued by banks, they serve as checks. They may not be as freely transferable as other credit instruments are because they may be negotiated by indorsement only once.

A bank money order offers the customer who purchases it the convenience of showing the customer's name on the face of the instrument. It also provides the customer with a numbered stub or carbon-copy receipt.

Cashier's Checks

A **cashier's check** is a check that is drawn by a bank upon itself. No matter where a cashier's check is sent by the bank or by a customer who purchases it from a bank, it must be returned to that bank for final payment.

Bank Drafts

A **bank draft** is a check drawn by a bank against funds which that bank has on deposit with another bank. People will often take a bank draft or a cashier's check when they will not take someone's personal check because they have faith that a bank will honor its own check.

ELECTRONIC BANKING

A special way to bank, called **electronic fund transfers (EFTs),** uses computers and electronic technology as a substitute for checks and other paper forms of banking. In response to the growing use of EFTs, Congress passed the Electronic Fund Transfer Act. The law covers these common EFT services:

1. Automated teller machines (ATMs) or 24-hour tellers are electronic terminals which permit you to bank at almost any time of the day or night. Generally, you insert a special EFT card and enter your own secret personal identification number (PIN) to withdraw cash, make deposits, or transfer funds between accounts.

EXAMPLE 10 On her way home from work, Janie Codwise realized she had no money for the weekend. The bank was closed, but she had her bank cash card with her. She inserted the card into an automated teller machine outside the front door of the bank. Then, using a number keyboard, she entered her code and pressed the buttons for a withdrawal of $50. The cash was dispensed automatically from the machine, and Codwise's bank account was electronically debited for the $50 cash withdrawal.

2. Pay-by-phone systems permit you to telephone your bank (or other financial institution) and instruct it to pay certain bills or to transfer funds between accounts. Only plans arranged in advance with your bank, however, are covered by the law.

3. Direct deposits or withdrawals allow you to authorize specific deposits such as paychecks and social security checks to your account on a regular basis. You can also arrange to have recurring bills such as insurance premiums and utility bills paid automatically. The law only applies, however, if you have authorized the transaction in advance. The law does not apply to payments you make directly to your own bank, such as mortgage payments.

4. Point-of-sale transfers let you pay for retail purchases with your EFT card. This is similar to using a credit card with one important exception: the money for the purchase is immediately transferred from your bank account to the store's account.

When you use an EFT, the federal law gives you no right to stop payment. Once you make the transaction, you can't change your mind. If your purchase is defective or if your order is not delivered, it is up to you to resolve the problem and get your money back—just as if you had paid with cash. An exception exists when you have arranged in advance for bills to be paid regularly out of your account. In this case, you can stop payment by notifying the bank within 3 business days before the scheduled transfer. This right to stop payment does not apply to bills you owe your bank, such as loan payments.

The Electronic Fund Transfer Act contains provisions to help deal with bank errors. Each time you initiate an EFT at a terminal (automated teller machines or point-of-sale transfers), you must receive a written receipt. Periodic statements must also be issued for all EFTs. You have 60 days from the date a problem or error appears on your periodic statement or terminal receipt to notify the bank. After being notified, the bank has 10 business days to investigate and tell you the results. If the bank needs more time, it may take up to 45 days to complete the investigation—but only if the money in dispute is returned to your account. At the end of this investigation, if no error is found, the bank can take the money back. If you fail to notify the bank within 60 days, the bank has no obligation to conduct an investigation.

If your EFT card is lost or stolen, you must notify the bank within 2 business days after discovering that the card is missing. You will then lose no more than $50 if someone else uses your card. If you don't notify the bank within 2 business days and your card is used, you can lose as much as $500, or even more if 60 days have elapsed.

Suggestions For Reducing Legal Risks

1. Never use a pencil to draw a check unless you plan to cash it immediately in your bank. Even then it is better to use ink. It would be very difficult for you to prove forgery in case an altered check had been drawn in pencil. The bank would be relieved of liability without adequate proof of forgery.

2. A check drawn payable to "Cash" or "Bearer" or indorsed in blank can be cashed by anyone. Use these forms only when you plan to cash a check immediately in your bank.

3. Use ink to draw and fill in all blank spaces on a check, note, or draft, so that nothing can be added to or inserted before or following your writing of the instrument. You take a serious risk in permitting anyone to have a signed instrument that leaves blank the payee or the amount. Any holder may legally fill in these blanks and negotiate the instrument.

4. If an error is made in drawing a negotiable instrument of any kind, do not attempt to correct it. Mark it "Void" or destroy it.

5. To avoid possible loss, cash all checks as soon as possible after receipt, because unreasonable delay in presentment is calculated from the date of the check rather than the date of last negotiation.

Language of the Law

Define or explain each of the following words or phrases:

check	raised check	order to stop pay-	cashier's check
stale check	reconciliation of a	ment	bank draft
alteration	bank statement	traveler's checks	electronic fund trans-
bad check	outstanding checks	money orders	fers (EFTs)
forged check	certified		

Questions for Review

1. List three reasons why the check is the most common kind of negotiable instrument used today.

2. Can a person who holds a check insist that a bank cash it? Why?

3. Discuss the liability of the depositor and the bank for forged checks and stale checks.

4. Name and identify the three parties to a check.

5. How does a bank certify a check? What does the bank promise when it does so?

6. Who may present a check for certification to the bank?

7. List several ways to avoid negligence when writing checks.

8. When is a customer most likely to use (a) a traveler's check, (b) a money order, (c) a cashier's check, and (d) a bank draft?

9. Explain the difference between an oral and a written stop-payment order.

10. Describe your right to stop payment when you use an EFT.

11. List four common EFT services that are covered by the Electronic Fund Transfer Act.

12. What is the meaning of a point-of-sale transfer under the Electronic Fund Transfer Act?

13. When using an EFT, how many days do you have to notify the bank when an error appears on your statement or receipt? How soon must the bank investigate and tell you the results?

14. If your EFT card is lost or stolen, how soon must you notify the bank? Even then, how much might you lose if someone else uses your card?

Cases in Point

In each of the following cases, give your decision and state a legal principle that applies to the case:

1. Paul Jones received from his bank a statement of his account and his canceled checks. Among them he found a check for $50 on which his name had been forged. Could Jones hold the bank liable for $50?
2. Nancy Hudson received a check from Harvey Grant for $500. For no very good reason, the bank refused to pay it. Can Hudson sue the bank? Does she have a claim against Grant? Explain.
3. In case 2 above, does Grant have a claim against the bank?
4. Margareta Droz wrote out a check for $25 payable to "cash" in such a way that it could be easily altered. She cashed the check at a local store, receiving $25. The assistant manager of the store raised the check to $225 and gave it to a supplier in payment for goods. Droz's bank paid the full amount of the check and charged $225 to her account. Must she pay $225? Explain.
5. On October 1, Leah Laskevitch discovered that she had overlooked cashing a check that she had received in May of that year. Thinking that the check was worthless, she threw it in the wastebasket. Should she have done so? Explain.
6. Rita Schena wrote out a check for $300 payable to Norma Zangari. When Zangari received the check, she had it certified by the bank on which it was drawn. She then gave the certified check to the Sawyer Appliance Company as partial payment for a television set that she purchased. Is Schena liable if the check is not paid?
7. In case 6 above, would your answer be different if Schena had had the check certified? Why or why not?
8. Ken Chong arranged with a bank to have his telephone bill paid automatically out of his bank account under an EFT system. A month after receiving his November telephone bill, Chong noticed a long-distance charge that he had not made. He told the bank to stop payment on the bill. Must the bank do so? Explain.
9. Late one evening, after banking hours, Dale Mills used her EFT card to withdraw $100 from her bank account. Her next bank statement showed a withdrawal of $1,000 rather than $100. She notified the bank of the error immediately. Two weeks later, the bank informed her that it was still looking into the situation and that it needed more time to complete its investigation. Must the bank return the $900 that it withdrew from Mills's account?
10. George Suderberg requested his bank to stop payment on a certified check that he had drawn. The bank refused to do so, although the check had not been presented for payment at the time that the request was made. Was the bank justified in its refusal to honor Suderberg's request?

Cases to Judge

1. Emmett E. McDonald, representing an estate, wrote out a check to himself as follows: "Pay to the order of Emmett E. McDonald $10075.00 Ten hundred seventy five Dollars." The bank paid McDonald $10,075, which was stated in figures on the check, and he absconded with the money. The estate sued the bank to recover the $9,000 difference between the amount written in words and the amount written in figures. For whom would you decide? *Yates v. Commercial Bank and Trust Co.,* 432 So. 2d 725 (Florida)

2. On September 14, David Siegel drew and delivered a $20,000 check to Peter Peters, postdated to the following November 14. Peters immediately deposited the check in his own bank. Siegel's bank overlooked the date and deducted the money on September 17 from Siegel's account. Does Siegel have a valid reason to bring suit against his bank? Explain. *Siegel v. New England Merchants National Bank,* 437 N.E.2d 218 (Massachusetts)

3. Morvarid Paydar Kashanchi and his sister, Firoyeh Paydar, had a savings account at Texas Commerce Medical Bank in Houston, Texas. They had no prearranged plan with the bank to make telephone withdrawals. Someone without authority telephoned the bank and caused $4,900 to be withdrawn from their bank account. Kashanchi claims that this transaction is governed by the Electronic Fund Transfer Act. Do you agree? Why or why not? *Kashanchi v. Texas Commerce Medical Bank, N.A.,* 703 F.2d 936 (5th Circuit)

4. In payment for services rendered, one of Stewart's clients gave him a check for $185.48 which had been drawn by the client's corporate employer and made payable to the order of the client. Although properly indorsed by the client, the drawee bank flatly refused to cash the check for Stewart. The bank acknowledged that the check was good, that is, that there were sufficient funds in the account. Can Stewart sue the bank for refusing to honor the check? Why or why not? *Stewart v. Citizens & National Bank,* 225 S.E.2d 761 (Georgia)

5. Ussery, a former convict, was hired by Nu-Way Services, Inc., as its night manager. Part of his duties entailed obtaining parts from parts companies. Nu-Way's president, on several occasions, dated and signed checks and filled in the names of the payees, leaving the amounts blank for Ussery to fill in later. Ussery substituted his name for the name of the payee on seven of the checks and cashed them. He also obtained access to the company's checkbook and removed some checks. Over a 6-month period, he wrote out and cashed 43 checks on which he named himself as payee and forged the company president's signature. No one in the company examined the monthly bank statement or canceled checks for forgeries or alterations nor compared the checks with the company checkbook. Is the drawee bank liable to Nu-Way Services, Inc., for paying the forged checks? Why or why not? *Nu-Way Services, Inc. v. Mercantile Trust Co.,* 530 S.W.2d 743 (Mississippi)

Chapter 32

TRANSFERRING NEGOTIABLE INSTRUMENTS

Scene: The Rodriguez apartment.

Inez: Carlos, the mail's here! There's a letter from the furniture company. The rest are just ads. Oh, here's a letter from Aunt Angelica!

Carlos (*entering*): I wonder what the furniture company wants now. I told them that I was going to notify the police if they didn't make good on that check they raised.

Inez (*opening an envelope*): Oh, Carlos, look! Aunt Angelica sent us another check to replace the one that we lost.

Carlos: She's so nice! (*He opens another envelope.*) This is a letter from the president of the furniture company apologizing for raising our check. He says that they fired the employee who did it. There's a $300 check enclosed with the letter. It's made out to both of us.

Inez: Wow! Two checks in one day! (*There is a knock at the door.*) I'll get it (*opening the door*). Oh, Julio! Come in.

Julio: Hi Inez! I'm sorry about that bounced check. I thought I had enough in the bank to cover it.

Inez: That's okay. It's easy to make that mistake. That's why I reconcile my bank statement each month.

Carlos: How're things, Julio?

Julio: I sold my car, and the buyer gave me this check, and I want you to have it. It's all yours. (*He hands the check to Carlos.*)

Inez: Are you sure the check's good? Who is Maria Reynolds?

Carlos: I think you have to indorse this check.

Julio: As I said, Maria Reynolds bought the car and made out this check. I'll sign the back. (*He writes his name on the back of the check.*) Well, I've got to run—I wanted to give you the check right away.

Carlos: Thanks, Julio, that was nice of you. See you later. (*Julio leaves.*)

Inez: Isn't this amazing! One minute we're broke, and the next minute we've got three checks. What shall we do with them?

Carlos: Why don't we cash the $100 check and put the other two in the bank.

Inez: That's a good idea. I'll cash Aunt Angelica's check at the grocery store tomorrow and put the other two checks in the bank. Her check is made out to you. Why don't you indorse* it over to me.

Carlos: Okay. (*He writes on the back of the check "Pay to the order of Inez Rodriguez [signed] Carlos Rodriguez."*) I guess we both have to indorse this furniture company check.

(*He writes on the back of that check "Pay to the order of First Bank and Trust Company for deposit only," and they both sign under that.*)

Inez (*the next evening*): I'm usually so careful when I go shopping.

Carlos: Don't blame yourself, honey, it wasn't your fault. It could have happened to anyone.

Inez: I'm sure that my pocketbook was in the shopping basket. I left it for just a second to get some potato chips and when I came back, the pocketbook was gone. We lost all three checks.

Carlos: It will work out somehow.

LEGAL ISSUES

1. Can a negotiable instrument indorsed simply with the payee's name be cashed by anyone?
2. Does a special indorsement such as "Pay to the order of Inez Rodriguez" prevent others from cashing a check?
3. Can anyone cash a check indorsed "Pay to the order of First Bank and Trust Company for deposit only"?

THE SPIRIT OF THE LAW

Commercial paper may be passed freely from one person or business to another in the same way as money. It is done by a method called negotiation. **Negotiation** is the transfer of an instrument in such a way that the transferee becomes a holder. A **holder** is a person who is in possession of an instrument that is payable either to the person holding it or to the bearer.

EXAMPLE 1 Rita Terenzi made out a check payable to the order of Paul Codinha. Terenzi gave the check to Paul's brother, Frank, and told Frank to take the check home and give it to Paul. Even though Frank held the check in his hands, he was not a holder because the check was not made payable to him or to the bearer.

*This text uses the spelling preferred in legal writing: *in*dorse, meaning to sign the back of a negotiable instrument. The more common *en*dorse is preferred in non-legal writing.

When the maker of a note or the drawer of a draft executes the instrument and hands it to the payee, the instrument is said to be **issued.** At this point, there has been no negotiation. There is simply an ordinary contract between the maker (or drawer) and the payee. The instrument is **negotiated** when the payee transfers it in the proper manner to another holder. From this time on, any transfer in the proper manner to a subsequent holder is a further negotiation of the instrument.

NEGOTIATION OF BEARER INSTRUMENTS

A **bearer instrument,** often called **bearer paper,** may be negotiated by delivery only. The payee simply hands it to the holder with the intention of passing title to the holder, and the instrument is said to have been negotiated. A common bearer instrument is a check made payable to the order of ''cash'' or ''bearer.'' The Uniform Commercial Code (UCC) states that either of these words makes the instrument a bearer instrument.

EXAMPLE 2 Henry Wheeler purchased two football-game tickets from Molly Prince. Wheeler handed Prince a check made payable to the order of ''cash.'' The check had been given to him by someone else. This delivery constituted the proper negotiation of a bearer instrument to a holder.

NEGOTIATION OF ORDER INSTRUMENTS

Instruments that are payable to someone's order, such as ''Pay to the order of,'' are called **order instruments,** or **order paper.** They are payable only when the payee orders them to be paid. The payee gives this order by a process called *indorsement.* Order instruments may be negotiated only by indorsement followed by delivery.

EXAMPLE 3 If, in Example 2, Henry Wheeler had paid for the tickets by a check made payable to Molly Prince, the check would be an order instrument. If Prince used the check to pay for groceries at the corner grocery store, there would be no negotiation until Prince indorsed the check and handed it to the grocer.

Kinds of Indorsements

An instrument is **indorsed** when the holder writes his or her name on it, thereby indicating the intent to transfer ownership to another. Indorsements may be written in ink, made on a typewriter, or even stamped with a rubber stamp. For convenience, the indorsement is usually placed on the back of the instrument. To be acceptable, the indorsement must be written for the entire amount stated on the instrument.

EXAMPLE 4 Guarantee Loan Company receives numerous checks each day from persons making payments on their loans. To simplify and make uniform the indorsements of checks for deposit, the cashier uses a rubber stamp containing Guarantee's indorsement.

There are four principal types of indorsements. They are (1) blank indorsements, (2) special indorsements, (3) restrictive indorsements, and (4) qualified indorsements. Each of these indorsements fulfills a special purpose.

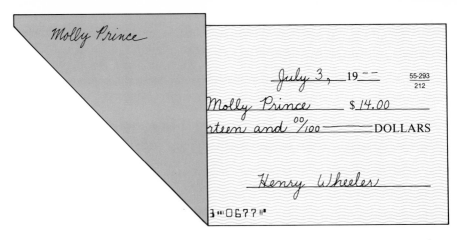

A blank indorsement consists of the signature of the payee. It should be used only at the bank teller's window because it turns order paper into bearer paper.

Legal Issue No. 1

Blank Indorsement A **blank indorsement** is an indorsement made by the simple act of turning the instrument over and signing it on the back. By doing this, the payee on an order instrument is in effect saying, "From now on this instrument may be paid to anyone." Once indorsed in blank, the former order instrument is now a bearer instrument. It requires no further indorsement to pass title, so it can be further negotiated by delivery only. It is not safe to put this type of indorsement on an instrument that is carried around or put in the mail. If the instrument is lost or stolen and gets into the hands of an innocent holder for value, the new holder may recover on it. It is best to use this only at a bank teller's window.

When an instrument is made payable to a person under a misspelled name or a name other than that person's own, he or she may indorse in the incorrect name or in the correct name, or in both. Signatures in both names may be required by a person paying or giving value for the instrument.

EXAMPLE 5 In Example 3, the check given to the grocer was indorsed in blank and is now a bearer instrument. It could be further negotiated by delivery only. If the grocer were to attempt to negotiate it to a wholesaler, however, the wholesaler would be wise to demand the grocer's indorsement even though the indorsement is not necessary for negotiation. The wholesaler knows the grocer, but not Prince or Wheeler. If the bank were to refuse to pay for the check when presented with it, the wholesaler would then expect the grocer to pay for it.

Remember: Any bearer instrument may be indorsed to add the security of the transferor's signature, even though an indorsement is not necessary for a proper negotiation of a bearer instrument.

Special Indorsement A **special indorsement** (also called an **indorsement in full**) is an indorsement made by first writing on the back of the check an order to pay to a specified person and then signing the instrument. When indorsed in this manner, the instrument remains an order instrument and must be indorsed by the specified person before it can be further negotiated.

EXAMPLE 6 Suppose Charles Ingersoll had borrowed money from the Guarantee Loan Company to repay a debt which he owed to Mary Ganz, who lived in another city. Fearing that the check might get lost or stolen in the mail, Ingersoll indorsed it ''Pay to the order of Mary Ganz [signed] Charles Ingersoll.'' This indorsement would provide protection to the parties if the check were to fall into the hands of a dishonest person.

Restrictive Indorsement A **restrictive indorsement** is one in which words have been added, in addition to the signature of the transferor, that limit the use of the instrument. A restrictive indorsement does not prevent further transfer or negotiation of the instrument. However, prior to further transfer, it must be used for the purpose stated in the indorsement.

The indorsement *For deposit only* is a frequently used restrictive indorsement. A check indorsed in this way may not be cashed. A restrictive indorsement can be in either special or blank form, depending on the needs of the indorser.

EXAMPLE 7 Sharon Clausewitz received her monthly paycheck at the end of the month. She knew it would not be convenient for her to deposit the check for several days. To protect herself fully, she indorsed it ''For deposit only— Sharon Clausewitz.'' This is a restrictive indorsement. If the check were to be stolen or lost, the only thing that could possibly be done with the check by any subsequent possessor would be to deposit it to Clausewitz's bank account.

Banks often use restrictive indorsements when they send checks through the collection process. They do this by stamping *Pay any bank* or *For collection only* on the back of each check.

In the opening of this chapter, Carlos and Inez received three checks. How was each indorsed? What kind of indorsement would you have recommended?

SPECIAL INDORSEMENT	FULL RESTRICTIVE INDORSEMENT	FULL QUALIFIED INDORSEMENT
Pay to the order of Janice Wellitts *Norton Harms*	*Pay to the order of Amesbury Trust Company for deposit only* *Norton Harms*	*Pay to the order of Basil Greenburg without recourse* *Norton Harms*

Qualified Indorsement   A **qualified indorsement** is one in which words have been added to the signature that limit or qualify the liability of the indorser. The indorsement, however, transfers title to the instrument. This form of indorsement is frequently used when the business paper is backed by a mortgage security or by collateral. In case of default by the maker, the indorsee is compelled to look for payment of the paper to the securities rather than to the indorser. The indorser is relieved from liability on the paper by writing the words *without recourse* above his or her signature. The indorsement can be in either blank or special form.

EXAMPLE 8   Joan Wilson held a note signed by William Bradford in the amount of $500. Wilson knew that Bradford did not have the money and that he probably could not pay the note for 6 months and might not be able to pay the note at all. For this reason, she sold the note to Jerry Ward for $400 and indorsed it ''Without recourse—Joan Wilson.'' By this indorsement, she passed title to the note to Jerry Ward, but she did not agree to pay it if Bradford fails to do so. (Of course, Ward was not bound to accept the note as payment from Wilson. Because he did, however, he took all risks of collection from Bradford.)

The holder of an instrument who negotiates it by a qualified indorsement, or by delivery only if it is a bearer instrument, does warrant (1) that the instrument is genuine, (2) that he or she owns it, (3) that all prior parties had the capacity to contract, and (4) that he or she has no knowledge of anything wrong with the instrument. No agreement is made that the instrument will be accepted or paid when presented.

Accommodation Indorsement

An **accommodation indorsement** is used to help someone else by guaranteeing payment of the instrument. It is usually an indorsement in blank, although under special circumstances it might be any of the other forms illustrated and described. An accommodation indorser signs an instrument only to assist some other party and does so to add the security of his or her credit to the instrument.

EXAMPLE 9   Warren Walker wished to borrow money from the First National Bank. Walker was known to be honest, but he did not have any property to pledge as security for the loan. His friend, Irene Wilkinson, owned valuable property and was known to be financially sound. Wilkinson agreed to indorse her name on the back of the note and assume responsibility for its payment, just for Walker's accommodation. The bank then loaned the money to Walker.

Wilkinson would be an accommodation indorser and is liable for the payment of the note just as if she had negotiated it to the bank herself. Having indorsed the note as an accommodation without receiving any consideration, Wilkinson, of course, is not liable to the accommodated party (Walker). She is liable, however, to all subsequent holders, just as if she were a regular indorser.

Forged Indorsements

A **forged indorsement** is not a valid indorsement at all. Anyone who takes an instrument after a necessary indorsement has been forged does not acquire title and is not a holder. An order instrument requires the indorsement of the person to whose order the instrument is made payable. It may be made by that person or by someone else on that person's behalf (an authorized agent), but not by someone acting without authority. Anyone who pays an instrument on which there is a forged indorsement is liable to the true owner for the amount of the instrument.

WARRANTIES OF INDORSERS

To encourage people to accept negotiable instruments from others, a system of implied warranties is part of the law. An indorser who receives consideration for an instrument makes five warranties (guarantees) to subsequent holders of the instruments:

1. The indorser warrants that he or she has good title to the instrument.

EXAMPLE 10   The Guarantee Loan Company accepted a check from Josephine Chester in payment of her account. The check contained a blank indorsement by Hannah O'Leary. The loan company discovered that Chester had found the check on the street and that a stop-payment order had been issued by the real owner, Hannah O'Leary. Chester, by her indorsement, had warranted that she was the true owner of the instrument. She may be held liable on this warranty for any loss suffered by the loan company.

2. The indorser warrants that all signatures are genuine or authorized. If a signature is forged, the indorser may be held responsible to a subsequent holder for payment of the instrument.

3. The indorser warrants that the instrument has not been materially altered.

4. The indorser warrants that no defense of any party is good against the indorser. If the instrument is dishonored for a valid, legal reason, the holder can still recover against the indorser.

EXAMPLE 11   Evelyn Dove, who was 17 years old, gave a $350 personal check to Max Horvitz in payment for a second-hand moped. She used the moped for 1 day, decided she didn't want it, and stopped payment on her check. Two days after that, Horvitz indorsed the check she had given him and cashed it at his bank. He was then notified by Dove that she was disaffirming her contract to buy the moped. When the check was returned to Horvitz's bank because of the stop-payment order, the bank could recover the $350 from Horvitz. By indorsing the check, he warranted to the bank that no defense (including that of minority) was good against him.

A qualified indorser warrants only that the indorser has no knowledge of any defense.

5. The indorser warrants that he or she has no knowledge of any insolvency (bankruptcy) proceeding instituted with respect to the maker, acceptor, or drawer of an unaccepted instrument.

Warranties arising from or connected with the transfer of negotiable instruments are transferred to every subsequent holder if the transfer is by indorsement. If the transfer is by delivery alone, the warranty applies to the immediate transferee only.

EXAMPLE 12 In payment for cleaning services, Harry Adams gave William Bell a $50 check which was written properly so that it could not be easily altered. Nevertheless, Bell altered the check to $500. Bell then indorsed the check and gave it to Mary Carlson in payment for a debt. Carlson indorsed the $500 check and deposited it in her bank account. Adams's bank deducted $500 from his account instead of $50, the amount actually written. Later, when the alteration was discovered, Adams was entitled to the return of the $450 from his bank. Adams's bank could recover the $450 from either Carlson's bank, Carlson, or Bell, if they are given proper notice, based on their warranty that the instrument had not been materially altered. Similarly, Carlson's bank can recover from either Carlson or Bell, and Carlson can recover from Bell, for the same reason.

CONTRACT OF INDORSERS

Unless an indorsement states otherwise (as by such words as *without recourse*), every indorser agrees to pay any subsequent holder the face amount of the instrument if it is dishonored by the maker or drawee. This is known as the indorser's secondary liability and is explained in Chapter 33.

Suggestions for Reducing Legal Risks

1. Do not accept negotiable instruments from a stranger without taking all possible precautions to verify his or her correct identity. Try to have the stranger personally identified by someone you know.
2. If this is impossible, request a number of items of identification showing the stranger's signature. Compare these signatures carefully with a signature made in your presence. Recent letters addressed to the party delivered through the post office will ordinarily verify his or her most recent address. Insist that the person indorse the instrument and place his or her address under the indorsement. If still in doubt about the person's identity, do not accept!
3. Examine all negotiable instruments carefully to determine whether they contain words of negotiability. If they are bearer instruments, request that the persons offering the instruments indorse them before you accept.

Language of the Law

Define or explain each of the following words or phrases:

holder	order instrument, or	special indorsement,	qualified indorsement
issued	order paper	or indorsement in	accommodation
bearer instrument,	indorsement	full	indorsement
or bearer paper	blank indorsement	restrictive indorsement	forged indorsement

Questions for Review

1. When is a negotiable instrument issued?
2. When is a negotiable instrument negotiated?
3. How may a bearer instrument be negotiated?
4. How may an order instrument be negotiated?
5. Why is a blank indorsement unsafe if the instrument is carried in the holder's pocket or sent through the mails?
6. What is required to further negotiate an instrument that is indorsed with a special indorsement?
7. Give an example of a frequently used restrictive indorsement.
8. What words are written above the indorser's signature in a qualified indorsement?
9. Explain the purpose of an accommodation indorsement.
10. What is the effect of a forged indorsement?
11. Explain the purpose of implied warranties made by indorsers who receive consideration for negotiable instruments.
12. Describe the contract made by every indorser unless the indorsement states otherwise.

Cases in Point

In each of the following cases, give your decision and state a legal principle that applies to the case:

1. Michael Reed found a check payable to Irene Lupi on a downtown street. Is Reed a holder? Why or why not?
2. Suppose in the situation described in case 1 above that the check that Reed found had been indorsed in blank by Irene Lupi. How would your answer differ?
3. Suppose in the situation described in case 1 above that the check that Reed found had been indorsed by Irene Lupi with a special indorsement to Charles MacLean. How would your answer differ?
4. Suppose in the situation described in case 2 above that Reed indorsed the check and cashed it at a bank. On what *two* legal grounds does the bank have recourse against Reed if the check does not clear?
5. What kind of indorsement should a holder use in each of the following situations?
   a. A check is mailed to a bank for deposit.
   b. The holder is not sure of the financial responsibility of the maker of a note or other instrument he or she had received for value.
   c. A note is given to a contractor for work to be done on a house.
   d. A check is presented for payment and is indorsed at the teller's window and in the teller's presence.
6. Angela Guitterez refused to accept a check from Dutch Edwards because it was indorsed with a rubber stamp. She contended

that to be valid, all indorsements on a check must be written in ink. Was her contention correct?

7. At various times, Henry Selby, a merchant, indorsed the following checks and notes. Identify each type of indorsement.
   a. A note payable to the order of Henry Selby was indorsed on the back, "Henry Selby."
   b. Selby received a check that carried Lisa Norwood's indorsement on the back, "Without recourse, Henry Selby."
   c. Selby transferred a check that he had received from a customer to Murray, after indorsing the check, "Pay to the order of Fran Murray, Henry Selby."
   d. Selby sent several checks to the bank, indorsed as follows: "Pay to the Ridge National Bank for deposit only, Henry Selby."

8. Maureen Bennett was the maker of a $400 note, and Angus Campbell was the payee. Campbell transferred the note to Mark Farrell by a qualified indorsement. Farrell sold it to the City Bank, using a blank indorsement. Because of a lack of funds, Bennett refused to pay the note when it was properly presented to her by the City Bank. The bank gave proper notice of dishonor. Does the City Bank have any claim against Campbell? Does the City Bank have any claim against Farrell?

9. Alma Becket, a store owner, cashed a check for a customer. Becket indorsed the check in blank and cashed it at her bank. Later, the bank returned the check to Becket because the signature of the drawer had been forged. On what legal ground is Becket liable to the bank for payment?

10. In order to obtain a loan from a bank, Karen Kuhns needed the signature of someone known to be reliable. Gene Kleinberg indorsed the note, and Kuhns obtained the loan. On the due date, Kuhns failed to pay, and the bank sought to recover from the indorser. Kleinberg claimed that he received nothing for his signature and therefore could not be held liable. Is he right?

Cases to Judge

1. Holland Farms wrote out a check payable to the order of La Sara Grain Company in the amount of $62,000. The check was indorsed by La Sara Grain Company "For deposit only" and taken to the bank by the company's general manager, Harold Jones. The bank deposited $40,000 of the check into Jones's personal account and $22,600 into La Sara Grain Company's account. Does La Sara Grain Company have recourse against the bank for the loss of the $40,000? Explain. *La Sara Grain v. First National Bank of Mercedes,* 673 S.W.2d 558 (Texas)

2. Humberto Decorators, Inc., a general contracting firm, renovated the Restaurant Argentino Tango, Inc., for an agreed price of $27,415. When the work was completed, a check for the agreed price was given to the restaurant by the Plaza National Bank as part of the proceeds of a loan. The check was payable to the order of Humberto Decorators, Inc. Instead of delivering it to the contractor, the restaurant deposited the check in its own bank account at the Plaza National Bank. Humberto Decorators, Inc., never received the money. May it recover the money from the bank? Why or why not? *Humberto Decorators, Inc. v. Plaza National Bank,* 434 A.2d 618 (New Jersey)

3. Alan D. Smathers and his wife, Josephine, signed two promissory notes payable to the order of Alan's father, John H. Smathers. After the death of John, the unindorsed notes were in the possession of another daughter-in-law, Joy I. Smathers, who claimed that John had given them to her husband, who had subsequently died. Joy contends that she is a holder of the notes. Do you agree with

her contention? Why or why not? *Smathers v. Smathers,* 239 S.E.2d 637 (North Carolina)

4. The plaintiff indorsed its checks by placing its name, Palmer & Ray Dental Supply, Inc., on the back with a rubber stamp. An employee of the plaintiff took the checks to the bank, cashed them, and kept the money. The plaintiff sued the bank for cashing the checks, arguing that the bank was required to deposit the money in the plaintiff's bank account. Do you agree? Why or why not? *Palmer & Ray Dental Supply, Inc. v. First National Bank,* 477 S.W.2d 954 (Texas)

5. Cecil Garcia borrowed $25,000 from the Rio Grande Valley Bank and received a cashier's check for that amount payable to himself. He indorsed the check, "Pay to the order of Lucy N. Casarez, Cecil Garcia" and delivered it to Lucy N. Casarez. She indorsed the check "Pay to the order of Albuquerque Fence Co., Lucy N. Casarez" and handed it to Blas Garcia, thinking he worked for the fence company. Blas Garcia, without any authority (he did not work for the fence company), indorsed the check "Alb. Fence Co." He gave the check back to Cecil Garcia, who signed his own name under the words "Alb. Fence Co." and cashed the check at the Rio Grande Valley Bank. Casarez claims that the bank owes her the money. How would you decide? Explain. *Casarez v. Garcia,* 660 P.2d 598 (New Mexico)

Chapter 33

COLLECTING NEGOTIABLE INSTRUMENTS

Scene: The police station. Inez is talking with the officer at the desk.

Police officer (*handing Inez her pocketbook*): Whoever stole this must have been scared off. Some children found it in a grocery cart not far from the store where you reported it lost.

Inez (*looking through the pocketbook*): Everything seems to be here—my driver's license, credit card, even the three checks we just received—they're all here!

Police officer: You're very fortunate. Most stolen pocketbooks that we find are completely empty.

Inez: I want to thank those children and give them a reward.
(*The Rodriguez apartment, 3 weeks later.*)

Inez: It didn't surprise me a bit to have that check that Julio gave us bounce. He should have gotten cash when he sold the car to a stranger—especially when he sells a junk car to a kid.

Carlos: I think it was the kid's father who talked her into returning the car. I would have done the same thing if I were him.

(*There is a knock on the door.*)

Inez: I'll get it. (*She opens the door.*) Julio! We were just talking about you this minute!

Julio (*entering*): Hi guys! How's everything?

Carlos: Did you know that the check you gave us bounced?

Julio: What? Are you kidding?

Carlos: No! The bank returned it with a stop-payment notice attached. I called that Maria Reynolds girl who made it out and found out that she's a minor. Her father won't let her keep that junk car of yours.

Julio: This is the first I've heard of it. When did you call her?

Carlos: About 10 days ago.

Inez: I don't think we're ever going to get that money you owe us.

Julio: Why don't you sue the girl I sold the car to? She's not supposed to stop payment on a check like that!

Inez: We should sue you, Julio! You indorsed that check before you gave it to us.

Julio: Don't worry, I'll pay you.

Carlos: The bank must think we're weird! They returned two of our checks on the same day—yours and Aunt Angelica's.

Julio: Did her check bounce too?

Inez: Of course not, Julio! She stopped payment on it when she heard that it was stolen. That was the second check of hers that we lost, you know.

I don't think she's going to give us any more checks. She doesn't think we're too responsible.

Julio: You can probably sue her for stopping payment.

Carlos: Are you kidding? She gave us those checks out of the goodness of her heart! Is that all you can think about Julio—sue, sue, sue?

LEGAL ISSUES

1. May minority be used as a defense by a drawer of a check against a holder in due course?
2. Can an indorser of a dishonored check be held responsible when notified of the dishonor 10 days later?
3. May a person who received a check as a gift be a holder in due course of the instrument?

THE SPIRIT OF THE LAW

We saw in Chapter 32 that negotiable instruments are easily transferable from one person to another. They are also readily collectible from the various people who transferred them. This is so because, with some exceptions, people who transfer negotiable instruments are held liable on the instrument either absolutely or conditionally. In addition, holders in due course of instruments are given even more rights to collect than their transferors had. Holders in due course are not subject to personal defenses of any party. They also take the instrument free from all claims to it by any person.

THE HOLDER IN DUE COURSE

A **holder in due course** is a holder who takes the instrument for value, in good faith, and without notice of any defects: There must be no notice that the instrument is overdue or has been dishonored; in addition, there must be no notice of any defenses against or claim to the instrument on the part of any person. A payee may be a holder in due course.

Essential Requirements

A person may be a holder in due course only if the following requirements are fulfilled:

Holder To be a holder in due course, the person in possession of the instrument must first be a holder. This means that the instrument must have been issued or indorsed to that person or to that person's order or to bearer or in blank.

Value A person must give value for an instrument to be a holder in due course. Persons give value for instruments when they give the consideration that was agreed upon or when they accept instruments in payment of debts.

Legal Issue No. 3 **EXAMPLE 1** Ann Price received a $25 check from her Aunt Gertrude as a graduation gift. Ann was not a holder in due course of the check because she did not give value for it.

Good Faith To be a holder in due course, the holder must take the instrument in good faith. **Good faith** simply means "honesty in fact."

Without Notice To be a holder in due course, a holder must not have notice of any claim or defense to an instrument or notice that an instrument is overdue or has been dishonored. A holder has notice of a claim or defense if the instrument bears visible evidence of forgery or alteration. The same is true if the instrument is so incomplete or irregular as to make its legal acceptance doubtful. Notice of a claim or defense is also given if the holder notices that the obligation of any party is voidable.

EXAMPLE 2 Hank LeBel, owner of LeBel's furniture store, sold Joanne Barr a table after telling her that it was made of solid cherry. LeBel knew that the table was actually made of hard pine. Barr paid by check. LeBel indorsed the check and gave it to a supplier who was in the store at the time of the transaction and knew of the fraud. Because of this knowledge, the supplier did not become a holder in due course of the check.

If the purchaser of a draft has notice that the draft has been presented for acceptance and has been dishonored, he or she is not considered to be a holder in due course.

A Holder Through a Holder in Due Course

Any person, other than the payee, who derives title to an instrument through a holder in due course receives all the various rights of a holder in due course. Such a person is said to be a holder through a holder in due course.

EXAMPLE 3 Peter Vincent wrote out a check to Nena Holyfield, who was a holder in due course. Holyfield indorsed the check and gave it as a gift to her friend, Deborah Madden. Madden is not a holder in due course because she did not give value for the instrument. However, she has the rights of one because she is a holder through a holder in due course.

DEFENSES TO NEGOTIABLE INSTRUMENTS

At times a party called on to pay an instrument may try to prevent payment by raising defenses against the holder. Two kinds of defenses are recognized: personal and real. Only the latter may be used against a holder in due course.

TABLE 33-1
SOME OF THE MOST COMMON PERSONAL DEFENSES*

Breach of Contract	One of the parties to a contract has failed to do what he or she has previously agreed to do.
Failure of Consideration	One of the parties to a contract has failed to furnish the agreed consideration.
Lack of Consideration	No consideration existed in the underlying contract for which the instrument was issued.
Fraud in the Inducement	The drawer or maker of an instrument is persuaded to enter into a contract because of a misrepresentation of some fact regarding the item purchased.
Lack of Delivery of a Negotiable Instrument	A payee forcibly, unlawfully, or conditionally takes an instrument from a maker or drawer. The maker or drawer did not intend to deliver the instrument.
Payment of a Negotiable Instrument	The drawer or maker of an instrument has paid the amount of the instrument.

*Holders in due course are not subject to these defenses.

Personal Defenses

When a negotiable instrument in proper form is negotiated to a holder in due course, all personal defenses are cut off—that is, people cannot use personal defenses against a holder in due course.

A **personal defense** is a defense that arises because of some improper act or omission by a party to the instrument. These are the same acts or omissions that would create a defense to a simple contract.

The most common personal defenses are such things as breach of contract, lack of consideration, duress, fraud, nondelivery of a complete or an incomplete instrument, and anything else that would be a good defense to the enforcement of an ordinary contract. (See Table 33-1.)

EXAMPLE 4   Joseph Hartmann sold his sports car to Kristina Reid for $700. In order to make the sale, Hartmann told Reid that the brakes had been relined 2 weeks earlier; however, this was not a true statement. Reid gave Hartmann a check for $700. The next day, after taking the car home, Reid learned that the brakes had not been relined. She stopped payment on the check. Hartmann, however, had indorsed the check in blank and had given it to Eugene Gately, a holder in due course. Gately could collect the full $700 from Reid. Even though Reid was defrauded, she cannot use that defense against a holder in due course.

It is risky to sign a check or other negotiable instrument without filling it out completely. If such an instrument is lost or stolen, the finder or thief could fill in any amount or other information and negotiate it to someone else. It would have to be paid by the person who signed it, regardless of the amount that was filled in, if it reached the hands of a holder in due course. This same danger exists when someone signs an instrument, gives it to someone else, and tells that person to fill it out.

EXAMPLE 5 Timothy Kahn owed Clem Nugent $75 for work Nugent had done on Kahn's car. Without taking time to fill in a check, Kahn merely signed the check, saying to Nugent, "You fill in the check; I'll be on my way." Nugent made out the check for $125 instead of for the amount owed. It was then negotiated to an innocent third party, who presented it for payment at Kahn's bank. Kahn would be responsible to the holder for the full amount of the check, although he has a right of action against Nugent for the loss suffered.

The law provides that the loss should fall on the party whose conduct in signing blank paper has made the fraud possible, rather than on the innocent purchaser.

Consumers Given Protection   In the past, the law which gives special protection to holders in due course was sometimes unjust to people who bought things on credit.

EXAMPLE 6 Gale Scotina purchased a stereo set from a local store. She paid no money down and signed a contract in which she promised to pay for the set in 24 monthly installments. (The contract was a promissory note and was immediately negotiated to a finance company to whom Scotina would have to pay the money.) Two months later, the stereo stopped working. The store refused to repair the set and would not take it back.

If this had occurred before 1976, the law of most states would have required Scotina to pay the finance company the full amount of the note. The fact that the stereo set did not work is a personal defense and could not be used against the finance company because the finance company was a holder in due course.

In 1976, the Federal Trade Commission (FTC) ruled that holders of consumer credit contracts are subject to all claims and defenses that the buyer could use against the seller. Thus, if the situation described in Example 6 were to occur today, Scotina's defense that the stereo had stopped working could be used against the finance company even though it is a holder in due course. The rule also applies when a seller sends people on a regular basis to a particular finance company or bank to arrange for purchases on credit. However, the rule only applies to sales of consumer goods or services for personal, family, or household use. It does not apply to sales of goods for commercial use.

Real Defenses   If the instrument itself is defective, the defect is called a **real,** or **absolute, defense,** and it is good against everyone, even a holder in due course. A real defense is a defense that is directed against the instrument itself. The contention

TABLE 33-2
SOME OF THE MOST COMMON REAL DEFENSES*

Infancy	The maker or drawer of the instrument was a minor.
Illegality	The underlying contract for which the instrument was issued was illegal.
Duress	The instrument was drawn against the will of the maker or drawer because of threats of force or bodily harm.
Fraud as to the Essential Nature of the Instrument	A false statement was made to the maker or drawer about the nature of the instrument being signed.
Bankruptcy	An order for relief was executed by the federal court which ended all the debtor's outstanding contractual obligations.
Unauthorized Signature	Someone wrongfully signed another's name on an instrument without authority to do so.
Material Alteration	The amount of the instrument or the payee's name was changed wrongfully after it was originally drawn by the maker or drawer.

*Holders in due course are subject to these defenses.

Legal Issue No. 1

is that no valid instrument ever came into existence; therefore, the instrument could not be real or genuine. Some types of real defenses are forgery, material alteration, minority, fraud as to the essential nature of the instrument, illegality, and bankruptcy. (See Table 33-2).

A person cannot be required to pay a negotiable instrument unless that person's signature appears on the instrument. Therefore, if a person's signature is forged, that person is not liable on the instrument even to a holder in due course. Likewise, an instrument that has been materially altered may not be enforced except in the original way it was written.

EXAMPLE 7 The Gotham Loan Company issued a $5,000 check on an automobile loan. John Barton altered the check to $8,000, indorsed it, and presented it for payment to an out-of-town bank. When the check was returned to Gotham's own bank for collection, it refused to honor it, noting the alteration. If Gotham was sued by the bank that cashed the check, it would have an obligation to pay only the amount for which the check was originally drawn, $5,000.

There are two kinds of fraud: fraud in the inducement and fraud as to the essential nature of the instrument. Fraud in the inducement occurs when someone is persuaded to enter into a contract because of a misrepresentation (false statement) of some fact regarding the item being purchased. This kind of fraud is a personal defense and cannot be used against a holder in due course. Fraud as to the essential nature of the instrument occurs when someone makes a false statement as to the nature of the instrument being signed. This kind of fraud is a real defense and can be used against anyone.

EXAMPLE 8 Carmen Carento, who could not speak English, was told by John Borash that the paper she was signing was a receipt. It was actually a promissory note. Carento would not have to pay the instrument even if it got into the hands of a holder in due course.

PARTIES WITH PRIMARY LIABILITY

Primary liability is an absolute liability to pay. A party with primary liability has promised to pay the instrument without any reservations of any kind. There are two parties who have primary liability. They are (1) the maker of a promissory note and (2) the acceptor, if any, of a draft. Each of these parties has personally promised to pay the obligation represented by the instrument without reservation. When there are comakers on notes, they have primary liability and are considered makers regardless of whether they receive any consideration.

PARTIES WITH SECONDARY LIABILITY

Secondary liability is a liability to pay only after certain conditions have been met. There are two types of parties who may have secondary liability for the payment of an instrument. They are (1) the drawer of a draft (a check, you will remember, is the most common kind of draft) and (2) the indorser or indorsers of either a note or a draft.

The conditions that must be met before either the drawer or the indorser has liability to pay are as follows: (1) The instrument must be properly presented to the primary party or drawee and payment must be demanded, (2) payment must have been refused by the primary party or be impossible (this refusal is called **dishonor**), and (3) notice of this refusal must be given to the secondary party within the time and in the manner prescribed by law.

Presentment for Payment

In order to be sure that a **secondary party** (drawer or indorser) will be liable on an instrument, the holder must make proper **presentment for payment** unless excused. This means that the holder must present the instrument to the maker or drawee and ask for payment. If such presentment is not made at the proper time, all indorsers are discharged from their obligation. They will not have to pay the holder of the instrument. In addition, if such presentment is not properly made and the drawee cannot pay because of insolvency (inability to pay debts), the drawer is discharged from all obligation.

Time for Presentment Presentment must be made on the date that the instrument is due. If there is no due date stated on the instrument, presentment must be made within a reasonable time after the maker or drawee became liable on it. The definition of a reasonable time for instruments other than checks will vary according to the circumstances. A reasonable time for a check is 30 days with respect to the liability of the drawer and 7 days with respect to the liability of an indorser.

DIRECT REDUCTION
MORTGAGE NOTE

Account No. ....

$ ....50,000.00..........   April 14, ...19 XX

FOR VALUE RECEIVED we jointly and severally, promise to pay to

Paul J. Kelleher

or order the sum of ....Fifty Thousand ($50,000)---------------------------------------.......... Dollars

in or within ....twenty-five.......... years from this date, with interest thereon at the rate of ....12........ per cent per annum, payable in monthly installments of $ ....526.62.......... on the ....first.......... day of each month hereafter, which payments shall first be applied to interest then due and the balance thereof remaining applied to principal; the interest to be computed monthly in advance on the unpaid balance, together with such fines on interest in arrears as are provided.

With the right to make additional payments on account of said principal sum on any payment date.

Failure to pay any of said installments within thirty (30) days from the date when the same becomes due, notwithstanding any license or waiver of any prior breach of conditions, shall make the whole of the balance of said principal sum immediately due and payable at the option of the holder thereof.

The makers, endorsers and guarantors or other parties to this note, and each of them, severally waive presentment, notice and protest.

Signed and sealed in the presence of

Charles E. Jones   *Carl Pierce*

                                                Sylvia Pierce

The holder of this note does not have to make proper presentment or give proper notice to hold secondary parties liable because presentment, notice, and protest are waived.

Legal Issue No. 2 · **EXAMPLE 9** Joanne Lawler made out a check to Doris Madden for $100. Madden indorsed the check and cashed it at a grocery store near her home. The store kept the check for 8 days before taking it to the bank. If the check did not clear, the store could not hold Madden liable on the instrument. She would not have to pay it because the store did not present the check to the bank within a reasonable time to hold an indorser responsible.

The party from whom payment is demanded can request to see the instrument. If payment is made, the instrument must be handed over then and there. This is important because if the party paying does not get the instrument back, it might show up later in the hands of a holder in due course, and the holder would have to pay it again.

Presentment for Acceptance

There are a few instances where the holder of a draft must make **presentment for acceptance** in addition to making presentment for payment. For example, if a draft reads, ''30 days from sight Pay to the Order of . . . ,'' it must be presented for acceptance to establish the beginning of the 30-day time period. The holder must ask the drawee to accept the draft by writing the word *accepted* across the front of the draft and signing it. In most circumstances, however, the holder of a draft can choose either to make presentment for acceptance or not and can hold secondary parties liable in either case.

Dishonor by Maker or Drawee

A negotiable instrument is considered to be dishonored if it is not accepted when presented for acceptance or if it is not paid when presented for payment. It is also considered to be dishonored if the presentment has been excused and the instrument is past due and unpaid.

EXAMPLE 10 A note was presented to Stanley Fowler for payment on the due date. Fowler refused to pay, claiming that it was a forgery. If this claim were true, the holder of the note would have to proceed against the indorsers on their implied warranties in order to secure payment. The note is considered dishonored because of Fowler's refusal to pay it.

Notice of Dishonor and Protest

If an instrument has been dishonored, the holder must give notice of the dishonor, within a specified time, to the drawer and to the indorsers. Unless notice is excused, any indorser who is not given notice within the specified time is discharged. A drawer who is not given notice within the specified time is discharged if the drawee cannot pay because of insolvency.

Unless excused (see Waivers below), a protest is necessary to charge the drawer and indorsers of a draft drawn or payable outside the United States. A **protest** is a formal, written certificate of dishonor made by a person authorized to certify dishonor by the law of the place where the dishonor occurred.

Time and Method of Giving Notice Notice of dishonor (and protest, if necessary) must be given by the holder before midnight of the third business day after the occurrence of the dishonor. If the holder is a bank, notice must be given before midnight on the day of the dishonor. Notice may be given in any reasonable manner. It may be oral or written. Written notice is considered to be given at the time it is sent rather than when it is received.

EXAMPLE 11 The Gotham Loan Company mailed notice of dishonor on a notice that had been presented to Eleanor Chin and dishonored the same day. The notice was mailed to the three indorsers whose names appeared on the instrument. Although the notice was properly directed, two of the indorsers later claimed that they had never received the notice and sought to be discharged from their liability on their warranties as indorsers. The court ruled that as long as the notices had been correctly stamped, addressed, and deposited with the post office, the indorsers would be considered to have been served with notice.

Waivers

Often an instrument has words on it which say that presentment, notice of dishonor, and protest are waived. In such cases, none is required. The holder is also excused from making presentment and from giving notice and protest if the person to whom these things should be given cannot be found. Holders who are late in making presentment or giving notice and protest are excused only if the delay is caused by circumstances beyond their control.

DISCHARGE OF NEGOTIABLE INSTRUMENTS

There are two aspects to the discharge of negotiable instruments that need to be considered: the discharge of the instrument itself and the discharge of the individual parties involved.

A negotiable instrument itself is discharged in the following ways: (1) by payment at or after maturity, (2) by the principal debtor's becoming the holder of the instrument at or after maturity, or (3) by the intentional cancellation of the instrument by the holder. A fourth method of discharge is to release a secondary party to the instrument, that is, a person with secondary liability.

A secondary party to an instrument may be discharged by any action of a holder that would tend to change the nature of the obligation originally assumed by the secondary party. This original obligation might be changed by specifically releasing the secondary party, either by canceling his or her name from the instrument or by canceling the name of a prior party.

EXAMPLE 12 Pamela Popovich was the third indorser on a note that she delivered to Jeffrey Wilkins for value. Wilkins, prior to further negotiation, crossed out the name of an indorser ahead of Popovich's name. Popovich was thus relieved of all liability because her right to depend on one whose name was valid at the time the instrument transferred was denied.

The obligation of a secondary party may also be changed if the holder extends the time of payment.

EXAMPLE 13 The maker of the note informed Wilkins, when the note was presented for payment, that he would pay the note if he could be given an additional 30 days. If Wilkins agreed to the extension of time, Popovich and all other indorsers on the note would automatically be discharged.

Suggestions for Reducing Legal Risks

1. Do not sign a check or other instrument without filling it out completely.
2. If the seller arranges your financing for the purchase of a product that proves to be defective, stop making payments unless the defect is corrected.
3. Consider the risks involved before accepting a negotiable instrument from a minor.
4. Be on the lookout for forged or altered instruments.
5. Never extend the time of payment on notes you hold that are secured by indorsements.
6. In case of the dishonor of a negotiable instrument, give immediate notice of the dishonor to all indorsers and drawers.
7. Keep a calendar of the maturity dates of all negotiable instruments held so that prompt and proper presentment can be made when the instruments become due.

Language of the Law

Define or explain each of the following words or phrases:

holder in due course
good faith
personal defense
real, or absolute,
  defense

primary liability
secondary liability
dishonor

secondary party
presentment for pay-
  ment

presentment for
  acceptance
protest

Questions for Review

1. What are the requirements for a person to be a holder in due course?
2. How does a person become a holder through a holder in due course? What are the rights of a person who becomes a holder in such a way?
3. Name three personal defenses that would not be good against a holder in due course.
4. How does the 1976 FTC ruling about holders in due course help consumers?
5. Name three real defenses that are good against a holder in due course.
6. What is meant by *proper presentment?*
7. When is a negotiable instrument dishonored?
8. If an instrument has been dishonored, what must the holder do in order to recover from an indorser?
9. Under what circumstances would the holder be excused from giving notice of dishonor to prior indorsers or to a drawer?

Cases in Point

In each of the following cases, give your decision and state a legal principle that applies to the case:

1. Hunter Roberts gave his sister a promissory note for a birthday gift. When the note became due, Roberts refused to pay it, claiming that he had received no consideration for it. What are the rights of the parties? Suppose Roberts's sister had transferred the note, for value, to another person who presented it for payment. Would your answer be the same?
2. Jack Donley, a minor, gave his $100 note to Eleanor Gage, in payment for a radio. Gage transferred the note to Joyce MacKay, a holder in due course. Donley refused to pay the note when it was properly presented for payment by MacKay. What defense, if any, did Donley have against MacKay?
3. Tom Harrison bought an automobile from the Acme Motor Company. In payment of the $600 purchase price, Harrison gave the seller $100 in cash and his negotiable promissory note for $500 payable in 90 days. The Acme Motor Company indorsed the note and sold it to the Broadway Bank. If Harrison did not pay when the note was presented to him for payment, would the Acme Motor Company have to pay? Could the bank hold the motor company responsible without first demanding payment from Harrison?
4. If, after Harrison had failed to pay the note when it was presented to him on the due date, the Broadway Bank failed to give notice to the Acme Motor Company for 1 week, could the motor company then be held responsible?

5. Suppose in the preceding case that Harrison asked the Broadway Bank for a 30-day extension of time and that the bank extended the time of payment for an additional 30-day period. Could the bank then hold the motor company responsible if Harrison did not pay at the end of the extended time?

6. While walking along the sidewalk of the main street in her town, Helen Johnson found a check that was made payable to Jane Arakawa. Johnson forged Arakawa's signature and cashed the check in a local store. Is the store a holder in due course of the check?

7. Edward Lee employed Howard Jackson, a real estate broker, to buy a tract of land for him. Lee gave Jackson $1,000 in cash and a $1,000 note to be used as a down payment on the property. Jackson indorsed and transferred the note to Sam Hull, a holder in due course. Hull sued on the note when payment was refused. Lee's defense was that Jackson had betrayed his trust by not using the note as directed. Explain this defense.

8. Steve Atkins forged the name of Joanne Newman, a well-known merchant, to a $500 note. He then negotiated the note to William Kester, an innocent purchaser, for value. Kester sued Newman when payment was refused at maturity. Will Newman be required to pay the note?

9. Diane Hatfield was the holder of a negotiable note signed by Louis Simion as maker. Hatfield did not present the note to Simion for payment until 1 week after it was due. Simion then contended that he was relieved of liability by the delay in presenting the note for payment. Do you agree?

10. Louise Torelli presented a note to Duke Fairfax for payment on the due date. Fairfax had become insolvent and could not honor the note. There were four indorsers on the note, and Torelli gave notice of dishonor to the indorser immediately ahead of her. That indorser failed to give notice to the other indorsers. If Torelli cannot collect from the indorser to whom notice was given, may she then proceed against each of the others for payment?

Cases to Judge

1. Robert Phelps, who worked for Jet Service Company, was given two paychecks, one for $454.49 and the other for $350.05. He indorsed the two checks and cashed them at a grocery store. Both checks were returned by the bank to the grocery store marked "Insufficient funds." The store brought suit against Phelps for the amount of the checks. A question arose as to whether the grocery store notified Phelps of the dishonored checks before bringing suit. What notice must the grocery store give Phelps to hold him liable on the checks? *Brannons No. Seven, Inc. v. Phelps,* 665 P.2d 860 (Oklahoma)

2. John and Beverly Girner executed a $5,000 promissory note payable to the order of First Realty Corporation. The note was to be paid in monthly installments. First Realty transferred the note to Imran Bohra in exchange for property. At a time when the note was 6 months past due, Bohra transferred the note to his attorney in exchange for legal services. The attorney was told that the note was past due. Is the attorney a holder in due course? Why or why not? *Richardson v. Girner,* 668 S.W.2d 523 (Arkansas)

3. Richard K. Pemberton forged indorsements on company checks totaling $480,000 and deposited them in his personal bank account. He then wrote a check on his personal account for $250,000 and used it to purchase a cashier's check for the same amount. Pemberton flew to Las Vegas, Nevada, indorsed the check, and gave it to the Hotel Riviera in

exchange for gambling markers. The hotel held the check in its safe until Pemberton had finished gambling. (In Nevada, as in many other states, a negotiable instrument to pay a gambling debt is void.) When Pemberton left town, the hotel deposited the $250,000 cashier's check into its account. The check was returned unpaid due to the forgeries. The Hotel Riviera claims that it was a holder in due course of the check. Do you agree? Why or why not? *Hotel Riviera, Inc. v. First National Bank and Trust Co.,* 580 F. Supp. 122 (Oklahoma)

4. Charleston Corporation gave a check for $8,500 to Financial Universal Corporation. Financial deposited the check in the National Bank of Georgia. National presented it for payment to the Mercantile National Bank at Dallas. That bank found insufficient funds in Charleston's account to pay the check. It re-turned the check to the National Bank of Georgia but sent it to the wrong address. Financial now claims that Mercantile gave improper notice of dishonor to the National Bank of Georgia. Do you agree? Explain. *Financial Universal Corporation v. Mercantile National Bank,* 683 S.W.2d 815 (Texas)

5. Carolyn Brazil wrote a check to a contractor who agreed to make certain improvements on her home. She wrote the check in reliance on the contractor's false representation that the materials for the job had been purchased. They, in fact, had not been purchased. Brazil had the bank on which the check was drawn stop payment on it. Another bank, which cashed the check and became the holder in due course of the instrument, attempted to recover the amount of the check from Brazil. Can it do so? Explain. *Citizens National Bank v. Brazil,* 233 S.E.2d 482 (Georgia)

CASE TO DISCUSS

Walker Bank & Trust Co. v. Jones
672 P.2d 73 (Utah)

Betty Jones opened a VISA and a Master Charge account with Walker Bank & Trust Co. Credit cards were issued, at her request, to Jones and her husband in each of their names. On November 11, Jones informed the bank, by two separate letters, that she would no longer honor charges made by her husband on the two accounts. The bank immediately revoked both accounts and requested the return of the credit cards. Under the terms of the credit card agreements, accounts could be closed by returning all outstanding credit cards to the bank.

Despite numerous notices of revocation and requests for surrender of the cards, Mr. and Mrs. Jones retained the cards and continued to make charges against the accounts. It was not until March 9 that Betty Jones finally relinquished the credit cards to the bank, and then only after a bank employee visited her place of employment. At the time she surrendered the cards, the balance owing on the VISA and Master Charge accounts was $2,685.70. Betty Jones refused to pay the balance owed.

THE TRIAL

At any time during the pleading stage of a lawsuit, either party may make a *Motion for Summary Judgment*. This is a motion asking for an immediate decision by the court based on the pleadings that have been filed. This procedure is designed to dispose of suits when there is no real issue of fact for a judge or jury to decide. Sometimes *affidavits* (sworn statements) of witnesses are also filed with the court. After a Motion for Summary Judgment is filed, the judge reviews the pleadings and affidavits and hears the arguments of the attorneys. If there appears to be no important issue of fact, the judge makes a ruling that no trial is necessary and decides the case on the pleadings.

Because there was no dispute over the facts in this case, the trial ended after the pleading and discovery stage. The court allowed a motion for summary judgment in favor of the bank.

THE ARGUMENTS ON APPEAL

Jones appealed the decision by the lower court judge. She contends that her liability for the unauthorized use of the credit cards by her husband is limited to $50. She claims that since she requested the credit cards for herself and her husband, she alone was the "cardholder." In addition, she claims that her notice to the bank stating that she would no longer be responsible for charges made by her husband rendered any subsequent use of the cards by her husband unauthorized.

The bank contends, however, that the $50 maximum liability rule does not apply. The bank claims that Jones's husband's use of the cards was at no time "unauthorized use" within the meaning of the statute. Section 1602 of the U.S. Code defines "unauthorized use" as "use of a credit card by a person other than the cardholder who does not have actual, implied, or apparent authority for such use and from which the cardholder receives no benefit." The bank maintains that Jones's husband clearly had apparent authority to use the cards, inasmuch as his name was printed on them and his signature was written on them.

QUESTIONS FOR DISCUSSION

1. How does the law protect cardholders against the unauthorized use of credit cards?
2. What is the meaning of *apparent authority*?
3. Do you believe that Jones's husband had apparent authority to use the credit cards even after she revoked the authority by writing to the bank? Explain.
4. If you were an appellate court judge hearing this case, for whom would you decide? Why?

CASE TO BRIEF

After reading *How to Write a Case Brief* on page 78, and examining the sample brief on page 80, write a brief of the following case:

Lewis v. Marsh
489 N.E.2d 1269 (Massachusetts)

When the defendant debtor, Marsh, purchased a mare, she did so with funds which, at least in part, she borrowed from the plaintiff creditor, Lewis. In so doing, Marsh signed a promissory note on June 6, . . . the same date she bought the mare from a third party, which provided that, in the event of a default, Lewis would be entitled to "full possession, custody, and ownership of the animal described above, to be seized, removed, sold, traded, or otherwise used to satisfy this debt." The total amount of the debt was three hundred dollars. Marsh defaulted on her payments, but Lewis took no immediate action in respect to the mare, referred to by the parties as "Annie." Annie gave birth to a filly, "Star," and Lewis, almost a year after the default, made claim to Annie and Star under the terms of the note. Marsh surrendered Annie but said no to Star. On a complaint brought in the Superior Court, Lewis sought possession of Star and compensation for Marsh's use and enjoyment of Annie and Star subsequent to her default. The judge dismissed the complaint. . . . We affirm.

1. Lewis has no right of possession of Star, and all counts of her complaint concerning the filly were properly dismissed. It is Lewis's contention that when Marsh failed to meet her payment obligations under the terms of the note, title to Annie vested immediately in her (Lewis). Because Annie was then pregnant, Lewis concludes that title to Star also vested at that time.

If Lewis is not a secured creditor, and in her brief she eschews [denies] that status, then her only claim to Star would be to satisfy any judgment on the note that she might obtain. Even then, Lewis would not have a right to specific property belonging to Marsh, who could satisfy a judgment with money rather than part with Star.

Like it or not, Lewis must accept her status as a secured creditor. By the very allegations of the complaint and the terms of Marsh's note attached to the complaint, Marsh gave Lewis an interest in Annie to secure payment on that note. The note, therefore, is a security agreement and Lewis a secured creditor. . . . As a secured party,

Lewis's rights to Annie, who has been surrendered to Lewis, are set out in [the Uniform Commercial Code (UCC)].

Whether Lewis also has a right to Star depends upon the terms of the security agreement (the note) and not on Annie's pregnancy at the time of Marsh's default. Lewis's right of possession is limited to the collateral specified in the security agreement. . . . The note was secured by "the animal described above." That description reads: "an angelo-arab horse, a brown mare of approximately 15 hands, purchased this date from" the identified third party. This description is neither general nor inclusive. Rather, it is particular and limited. . . .

Although the complaint does not reveal whether Annie should be viewed as a consumer good or a farm product, . . . that fact is irrelevant to our conclusion. The distinction would be material only were we first to conclude that Lewis had a right to Star. . . .

2. As Lewis had no right to Star, her claim for compensation for Marsh's use and enjoyment of the filly fails. Construing the complaint as favorably as we can in Lewis's favor, we do not see how she is entitled to be compensated for Marsh's use of Annie after her default on the note. By Lewis's own allegations, she told Marsh that Marsh could keep Annie until she (Lewis) wanted her. In view of Lewis's rights to Annie under [the UCC,] and her permissive statements to Marsh concerning retention of Annie, the claim of unjust enrichment was properly dismissed. . . .

3. Marsh seeks an award of counsel fees under [a law awarding fees when a frivolous appeal is made]. An appeal should not, however, be tarred as frivolous because it presents an argument that is novel, unusual or ingenious, or urges adoption of a new principle of law or revision of an old one. . . . Although we are inclined to think that the parties should have been able, without litigation, to settle their dispute, which could be viewed as insignificant (Marsh alleges in her brief that at the time the action was brought, there was twenty-five dollars, at most, due and owing on the total debt of three hundred dollars) when compared to other cases pending in the courts of the Commonwealth, we do not think the matter sinks to the level considered by the court in Allen [another case cited by the court]. Therefore, we deny Marsh's request.

Judgment affirmed.

TRIAL PROCEDURES

THE CLOSING ARGUMENTS

After both attorneys have rested their cases, they present their closing arguments. The plaintiff's attorney is first, followed by the defendant's attorney. Each attorney summarizes the evidence and suggests reasons why the judge or jury should find in favor of his or her client.

Closing arguments include: (1) a summary of the evidence most favorable to the party presenting it; (2) a review of the witness's testimony and other evidence, outlining the strengths of your own side and the weaknesses of the opposing side; (3) a reminder of the burden of proof, including a statement as to how you have satisfied this burden (or how your opponent has not); and (4) an explanation of how the law applies to the facts that have been presented.

THE CASE OF GRAZIO v. WILLIAMSON (continued from page 405)

The witnesses for both sides have been examined and cross-examined by the attorneys. All of the evidence has been introduced. The attorneys have rested their cases. It is now time for the attorneys to give their closing arguments. Attorney Powers, the plaintiff's attorney, speaks to the jury first:

May it please the court, ladies and gentlemen of the jury. Soon, it will be your duty to decide this case based on the evidence that you have heard. Before you begin your deliberations, I would like to say a few words to you about the evidence.

It is clear, from the testimony, that the defendant, Wayne Williamson, drove the car that smashed into Mr. Grazio's car. It is also clear that Mr. Grazio's car was parked, unattended, next to the curb. You have heard the testimony of the defendant that a squirrel ran out in front of his car and that to avoid hitting the squirrel, he swerved to the right and smashed into Mr. Grazio's unattended parked car.

The basic question then, that you must decide, is quite simple. Was Mr. Williamson negligent in swerving to avoid the squirrel? To put it another way, would a reasonably prudent person swerve

into a parked car simply to avoid hitting a squirrel? I have no doubt that you will say "no" to this question. It is a negligent act to smash into a parked car simply to avoid hitting a squirrel. As you consider the evidence, I ask that you find in favor of the plaintiff for the damage to his car in the amount of $3,000. Thank you.

Next, the defendant's attorney, speaks:

Ladies and gentlemen of the jury, if it please the court: You have heard my colleague, Miss Powers, summarize the facts of this case. She pointed out, correctly, that one of the questions you must decide is whether or not a reasonably prudent person would have swerved the car to avoid hitting a squirrel. The answer to this question is not easy. I think the first reaction of most people today is to try to avoid killing live, helpless animals whenever possible—especially animals, like squirrels, that do others no harm and bring pleasure to our lives. Remember, too, that squirrels run fast! Mr. Williamson had to react almost instinctively when the squirrel ran in front of his car. In my opinion, it is not a negligent act to swerve away from something, instinctively, that comes into one's path.

One further point that was obviously overlooked by my colleague in her closing argument: The plaintiff's car was parked in front of a fire hydrant! Not only is it illegal to park in front of a fire hydrant, it is also a negligent act! If the car had not been parked in front of the hydrant, there would have been no accident!

I am confident that you will render a fair and just verdict and find against the plaintiff, in favor of the defendant, Wayne Williamson. Thank you very much for your consideration.

LEGAL PRACTICUM

In the skit at the beginning of Chapter 29, a stranger put his foot in the door of Carlos' and Inez' apartment, attempting to repossess their furniture. The stranger made threats but left when Carlos told Inez to call the police. Assume that Carlos and Inez brought charges against the furniture store for violating the Fair Debt Collection Act. Assume, also, that you are an attorney representing the plaintiffs in the lawsuit. Refer to page 418 and write a closing argument for your case.

STARTING A BUSINESS
UNIT
7

Chapter 34

SOLE PROPRIETORSHIP AND PARTNERSHIP

In this unit you will meet Jennifer, Ernie, and Sally, three young people beginning their business careers. They are ambitious and enterprising, but they have to learn about the law through experience.

Scene: Jennifer, Ernie, and Sally are talking in Sally's new pet shop. The shop is located in Sally's basement.

Jennifer: So this is the new pet shop.

Ernie: Sure is. How do you like it?

Jennifer: Looks terrific. But Sally, why did you open it up in your basement? Why not get a storefront on Main Street?

Sally: It's a lot cheaper this way. I don't pay any rent.

Jennifer: I guess that's a good idea. I just didn't know the zoning laws would let you open a store in a residential neighborhood like this one.

Sally: Well, nobody's stopped me yet, so it must be okay.

Jennifer: I don't know about that. My friend Kara tried to open a store in her garage, but she couldn't get a license or a zoning change.

Sally: License?

Jennifer: Sure, you need a license to open a store.

Sally: Well, I don't know about those things.
(Just then a customer enters. Sally walks over to the customer. Jennifer and Ernie continue the conversation.)

Jennifer: I think you had better look into the zoning laws. A boss like that who doesn't know anything about the law can get you into big trouble.

Ernie: You mean like the trouble you're in.

Jennifer: You better believe it. Did you hear the latest?

Ernie: No, what?

Jennifer: I'm being sued.

Ernie: Sued? For what?

Jennifer: Wait 'til you hear this. You remember how I went to work for Pat when he opened that video store?

Ernie: Sure, you let him use your garage.

Jennifer: Right. Well, he owes a lot of money to people, and they say I owe it too because I'm his partner.

Chapter 34: Sole Proprietorship and Partnership   **471**

Ernie: I didn't know you were Pat's partner.

Jennifer: I'm not. I didn't sign any kind of agreement.

Ernie: Then you're not a partner.

Jennifer: Well, they claim I'm a partner because I shared in Pat's profits.

Ernie: That doesn't seem like enough to make you a partner.

Jennifer: That's what I said, but no one listens to me.

Ernie: My brother had problems with his partners once.

Jennifer: What kind of problems?

Ernie: They were always using business cars for personal trips. One guy even drove across the country to see his girlfriend.

Jennifer: Well, I would think that partners would be allowed to use the business car, wouldn't you?

Ernie: I don't know. All I know is that it sure made my brother mad.

Jennifer: Did he do anything about it?

Ernie: I'll say; he gave one of the cars to his son.

Jennifer: Well, I guess that fixed those guys.

Ernie: Maybe. But it also busted up the partnership. Say, where are you going in such a hurry?

Jennifer: Over to Pat's. Maybe if I use his car, he'll get mad enough to bust up our partnership.

Ernie: Good luck.

Jennifer: Thanks.

LEGAL ISSUES

1. Does a sole proprietor have to check any laws before opening a business?
2. Is a partnership agreement needed to set up a partnership?
3. Is it possible for someone to become a partner even if that person has no intention of becoming a partner?
4. Can partners use partnership property for personal reasons?
5. Can partners sell or give away partnership property without getting the consent of the other partner?

THE SPIRIT OF THE LAW

Calvin Coolidge once said, "The business of America is business." Whether or not President Coolidge was accurate in his assessment, the fact remains that all Americans are touched by business in one way or another. Most Americans are employed in business, and all must purchase goods and services from business people. Businesses come in a variety of forms, from the simple sole proprietorship, such as the corner grocery, up to gigantic multinational corporations, such as Exxon or Ford. Each business entity has its own characteristics, its advantages and disadvantages, and its individual legal rules. The object of this unit is to examine each of these entities. This chapter begins with sole proprietorships and moves through general and limited partnerships. Later chapters explore the formation and operation of the corporation.

SOLE PROPRI- ETORSHIPS

The **sole proprietorship** is a form of business that is owned and operated by one person. It is the most common kind of business and the easiest to establish. Usually, people choose to become sole proprietors because they feel they can handle the business by themselves or with only a few workers. Generally, sole proprietors either have enough money of their own to run the enterprise or feel little money is needed to start operating.

Creation and Operation

The major advantage of a sole proprietorship is that the owner/operator has total control of his or her business. Another advantage of a sole proprietorship is that there are few formal requirements to meet when opening such a business. To make sure that he or she knows about these formal requirements, a new sole proprietor should always seek guidance as to state laws and local ordinances when beginning a business. Some local areas may require a license to engage in certain kinds of businesses. Other areas may have zoning ordinances which prohibit businesses in certain parts of the city. Also, some states do require a formal filing when a proprietorship begins. In addition, many states require owners to file a certificate when the sole proprietor chooses not to use his or her own name in the name of the business.

Legal Issue No. 1

EXAMPLE 1 Sam Patterson decided to go into the dry-cleaning business. After some thought, he decided he needed a catchy and novel name for his new enterprise. Accordingly, he labeled his new firm the "Dry by Night" Dry Cleaning, Inc. After being in business for a year, Patterson had some trouble collecting on the account of a local corporate client that owed him several thousand dollars in back cleaning bills. When Patterson decided to sue, he discovered that under the laws of his state, he was banned from suing in court because he had not filed his fictitious name with the city clerk's office. He also found out that he could not label a sole proprietorship "Inc." because that term could only be used by corporations. By filing properly and dropping the abbreviation "Inc." from the firm's name, Patterson could bring his suit.

The major disadvantage of a sole proprietorship is its unlimited liability. In other words, the sole proprietor is personally liable for all the debts of the business and for the negligent acts of his or her employees. Many people who own sole proprietorships eventually incorporate the business to avoid unlimited liability.

Other disadvantages of the sole proprietorship include the fact that money is much more difficult to raise than it would be in a partnership with several contributors or in a corporation with many contributors. This limitation also makes expansion difficult. Another shortcoming in using this form of business enterprise is that the sole proprietor must be a "jack-of-all-trades." Unless the new owner can afford to hire a lot of help, he or she must be manager, buyer, sales representative, bookkeeper, personnel director, secretary, and public rela-

Sole proprietorships come in many shapes and sizes. *(Drawing by Lorenz. Copyright © 1986, The New Yorker Magazine, Inc.)*

"Is that with or without goat cheese?"

tions director all in one. This problem alone stops a lot of people from opening a sole proprietorship. Finally, the sole proprietorship will end when the proprietor dies. Those people who would like to see their firm continue for the benefit of their heirs should consider another form of business enterprise.

Relationships With Consumers and Employees

Legal Issue No. 1

Since most, if not all, sole proprietorships engage in buying and selling, sole owners should become familiar with laws regarding consumer sales and consumer protection. Information can be obtained by writing to the appropriate state official, usually either the state attorney general or the state secretary of state.

When a sole proprietor begins to hire employees, his or her business responsibilities become more complex. For example, the sole proprietor will have to contact the Internal Revenue Service to obtain a tax identification number. In addition, the owner should contact the social security office. State laws regulating minimum wage payments, workers' compensation, and unemployment compensation should also be consulted. Requirements in these areas will vary from state to state.

GENERAL PARTNER-SHIPS

Partnership law is largely found in the **Uniform Partnership Act (UPA)**. Most states have adopted at least some of the provisions of the UPA. A **general partnership** is defined by the UPA as ''an association of two or more persons to carry on a business for profit.''

Creation of a General Partnership

Legal Issue No. 2

A general partnership is created when two or more competent parties combine their money, labor, or skills for the purpose of carrying on a lawful business. They will share the profits and losses arising from the undertaking. General partnerships can be formed in one of three ways: (1) by contract or agreement, (2) by proof of existence, or (3) by estoppel.

Creation by Contract The formation of a general partnership by contract requires a valid agreement between the interested parties. Such a contract is usually entered into by express agreement, although it may be implied. An express agreement may be either oral or written. However, under the Statute of Frauds, if the partnership is to last more than a year, it must be evidenced by a writing. Following the same principle, a partnership which is formed to sell, buy, or lease real property also should be evidenced by a writing. The partnership agreement is known as the **articles of copartnership.**

There are so many possible points of difference between partners that the agreement should be clearly and fully set down in writing. Some of the important items to be covered are (1) the parties to the agreement, (2) the specific nature, scope, and limits of the business, (3) the duration of the business, (4) the amount of the original investment and what will be done about future investment, (5) provisions regarding salaries, withdrawal of funds, interest on investment, and the division of profits, and possibly, (6) some mention of the terms under which a partner may withdraw from the business.

Creation by Proof of Existence Sometimes a partnership can be created simply because of the way that two or more people conduct business with one another. This is called **partnership by proof of existence.** Such a partnership exists regardless of what label has been given to the venture and regardless of the intent of the parties. The UPA provides for such a situation, giving the courts a list of characteristics which determine whether a partnership has begun.

Legal Issue No. 3

The sharing of profits is at the top of this list. According to the UPA, if two or more people share the profits of a business venture, it will be very difficult for them to deny that the partnership exists. However, there are exceptions to this rule. A person may receive a share of the profits and not be declared a partner if the share is paid (1) in repayment of a debt, (2) as wages to an employee or rent to a landlord, (3) as an annuity to the widow or widower of a deceased partner, (4) as interest on a loan, or (5) as consideration for the sale of the goodwill of a business.

EXAMPLE 2 Perry Parisi opened a restaurant called Perry's Pit Stop Shop. He had little interest in the business but felt it would be a good investment. Parisi hired Paula Pearson to take care of all the details of the work. Most of the time, Parisi was absent from the premises, leaving Pearson in charge. Pearson took care of all the details of running the business. Parisi showed up on Fridays to collect his share of the profits and to give a few general instructions about the coming week's menu. Each week Pearson drew her own pay according to an agreement with Parisi which said he got 60 percent of the profits and she got 40 percent. This process continued for 5 years. At the end of that period, Parisi decided to discontinue the restaurant. Pearson claimed she was a partner and the court agreed, saying that not only had she shared in the profits on a weekly basis for 5 years, but she had also contributed two valuable assets to the partnership, her time and expertise.

Creation by Estoppel **Partnership by estoppel** occurs because someone says or does something that leads a third party to believe that a partnership exists. This type of partnership is not a real partnership. It is a way the court has of preventing injustice.

EXAMPLE 3 Pearl Panay and Pearce Porter were partners in an electronics firm. The firm needed a loan quickly or it would be forced to close down at a tremendous loss to both Panay and Porter. Unknown to Panay, Porter prevailed on his friend, Raymond Stanhope, to accompany Porter to the bank. Stanhope cooperated in a charade designed to mislead the bank's loan officer, Ted Thomas, into believing that Stanhope was a partner in the electronics firm. Since Thomas knew Stanhope had a solid credit rating, he extended credit to the firm. When the firm defaulted, Thomas could hold both Porter and Stanhope liable. Stanhope would be "estopped" from denying his participation in the partnership in obtaining the loan.

Note in the preceding example that a real partnership was not created. Stanhope has none of the partnership rights that come with a true partnership.

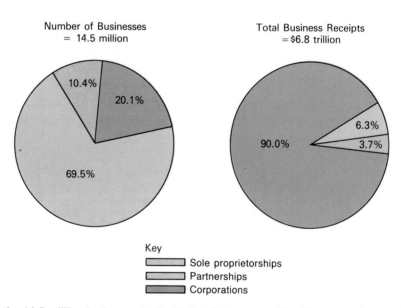

TYPES OF BUSINESSES
and Their Revenues

Number of Businesses
= 14.5 million

10.4%

20.1%

69.5%

Total Business Receipts
= $6.8 trillion

6.3%

90.0%

3.7%

Key
Sole proprietorships
Partnerships
Corporations

Of the 14.5 million businesses in the United States, over 10 million are sole proprietorships. Sole proprietorships account for only 6.3 percent of business receipts, however (about $430 billion). How do partnerships and corporations compare?

TABLE 34-1
TYPES OF PARTNERS

Kind of Partner	Participation in the Business	Relationship to the Public	Degree of Liability
General	Active	Known	Unlimited
Secret	Active	Unknown	Unlimited
Silent	Not active	Known	Unlimited
Dormant	Not active	Unknown	Unlimited
Limited (or Special)	Not active	Known	Limited

Types of Partners

There are five kinds of partners—general, secret, silent, dormant, and limited. Each of these partners is a co-owner of the business and has some liability for the debts of the firm.

Every partnership must have at least one general partner. In most firms, all the partners are general partners. A **general partner** takes an active part in the management of the firm and is publicly known as a partner. A general partner has unlimited liability for the firm's debts.

A **secret partner** is a general partner who is active in the management of the firm but whose connection with the firm is kept secret from the public. A secret partner also has unlimited liability for the firm's debts.

A **silent partner** is a general partner who takes no active part in the management of the firm. A silent partner is known publicly as a partner and has unlimited liability for the firm's debts.

A **dormant partner** is a general partner who takes no active part in the management of the firm and whose connection with the firm is kept a secret from the public. A dormant partner, however, has unlimited liability for the firm's debts.

A **limited partner** is one whose liability does not extend beyond that partner's investment. This liability arrangement is known as a limited partnership. (Limited partnerships are discussed in detail later in this chapter.) (See Table 34-1.)

Partnership Property

Since certain rights and limitations arise in relation to partnership property, it is important to be able to distinguish between the property that belongs to the partnership and the property that belongs to individual partners. Sometimes it is easy to determine that a particular piece of property belongs to the partnership. If the property is contributed directly to the partnership when the partnership is created, it is obviously partnership property. The UPA also makes it clear that partnership property includes any property that is bought with partnership money. At other times the question of whether a certain piece of property belongs to the partnership or to an individual partner is more difficult to answer. In such a situation, other indicators are available to help make this determination. For example, a court may ask the following questions: Has the partnership consistently used the property? Has the partnership listed the property in its account books? Has the partnership improved or repaired the property? Has the partnership paid expenses involving the property? Has the partnership paid taxes on the property? The more of these questions that can be answered "yes," the more likely the court will decide the property belongs to the partnership.

Property Rights of Partners

As noted earlier, it is important to distinguish between partnership property and nonpartnership property because certain rights occur in relation to partnership property. These rights include the right to use partnership property, the right to manage the firm, and the right to share in the profits of the firm.

Legal Issue No. 4

Legal Issue No. 5

The Right to Use Partnership Property Partners are co-owners of all real and personal property included in the partnership. This means that partners can use the property for partnership business. The property cannot, however, be used for nonpartnership business unless the other partners give their permission. This co-ownership, dubbed **tenancy in partnership** by the UPA, gives rise to other limitations. For example, a partner cannot, on his or her own, transfer ownership of the property. Also, the property cannot be taken by a partner's personal creditors. Moreover, when a partner dies, the rights to the partnership property go to the other partners.

EXAMPLE 4 Pete Petrone, Pat Paris, and Portia Phelps were partners in the Phoenix Fashion Center, which owned several personal computers as partnership property. In a matter not involving partnership business, Phelps was sued by Sherry Summers. When Summers won the suit and could not collect any money from Phelps, she attempted to have the computers seized. The court would prevent such a seizure because the computers are not the individual property of Phelps. However, if the judgment had been against the entire partnership, then the computers could be seized to answer for the judgment debt.

The Right to Manage the Firm Each partner has a right to share in the management of the firm. Unless it is provided in the partnership agreement, each partner has an equal voice in management and may bind the partnership business on any matter that is within its scope. In case of a disagreement about an ordinary business matter, the decision of the majority is final. If there is an even number of partners and the vote is split, then no decision can be made and the status quo is maintained. If such deadlocks continue, the only logical alternative is to end the partnership.

The Right to Share in the Profits Unless there is an agreement to the contrary, partners share equally in the profits, regardless of their contribution to the firm's capital or the time devoted by each to the business. This right can be assigned to others. In addition, this right passes to the partners' heirs. It also includes the right to an accounting at the end of the partnership.

Duties of Partners

Partners must be able to trust each other. Each partner is an agent of the other partners and has duties comparable to those of an agent. Partners must (1) always act in good faith and in the best interests of the firm, (2) be loyal to the firm and put the firm's interest ahead of self-interest (this is the partner's fiduciary duty to the partners and the partnership firm), and (3) always use their best skill and judgment in looking after their firm's affairs. Since each partner is an agent for the firm, each may bind the firm by any act that is part of the firm's business. Any act of a partner that is not part of the firm's business is not binding on the firm. Similarly, a change in basic policy in the conduct of the partnership affairs, such as the sale of the entire business, requires the consent of all the partners.

Liability of Partners

Partners have unlimited liability for all the debts of the partnership that are incurred while they are partners, even to the extent of their personal assets. Partners are always liable to the other members of the firm for their share of the firm's debts. Partners share losses in the same proportion that they share profits. If one partner is forced by creditors to pay all the firm's debts, that partner, in turn, has a right against the other partners for the payment of their shares.

In addition, partners are jointly liable with their copartners on contracts entered into by any member of the firm acting within the actual or apparent scope of the firm's business. **Joint liability** means that in the event of a lawsuit, all the partners must be sued together. Partners are jointly and *severally* (separately) liable for torts committed within the scope of the firm's business. This means that an injured party has the choice of suing all the partners together or one or more of them separately. This is the biggest single drawback to the partnership form of business organization. One partner, who may be completely innocent, can be held financially responsible for the wrongdoings of other partners.

EXAMPLE 5 Phil Lane was a dormant partner with Tom Piper in a trucking firm. In the course of a delivery to Thompson Lumber, Piper crashed into the warehouse, which collapsed and injured Thompson. Thompson could sue Lane for damages to his person and property.

Dissolution of a Partnership

The **dissolution** of a partnership is a change in the relationship of the partners which occurs when any partner stops being associated with the business. This is to be distinguished from the winding up of the business. When a partner dies or voluntarily withdraws from the firm, the firm is dissolved. The firm also may be dissolved by court decree. The partners then are no longer carrying on as co-owners of a business for profit. Dissolution occurs immediately, that is, at the moment that one partner ceases to be associated with the firm. The business operations, however, cannot be stopped on a moment's notice. It takes time to wind up the firm's affairs and bring the firm formally to an end. During this winding-up period, the partners are not carrying on a going business.

Effects of Dissolution Dissolution does not necessarily bring the business to an end. If partners are added or withdrawn and the other partners want to continue in business together, there must be an accounting of the old firm's affairs. New financial arrangements must be made with regard to the new firm. A new agreement must be drawn up regarding the conduct of the new firm. Public notice must usually be given in order to relieve retiring partners from liability on any new debts created by the new firm.

Distribution of Assets An accounting of the firm's financial affairs is necessary to determine how the firm's assets are to be distributed. If the business is continued, however, the remaining partners leave their share in the firm and continue as before.

The liabilities of the firm are paid in the following order: (1) those owing to creditors other than partners, (2) money lent by partners to the firm, (3) the original money paid into the partnership by each partner, and (4) the surplus owed to the partners.

If the firm is insolvent, all the assets go to pay the creditors; in addition, individual partners are liable for any unpaid balance that the sale of the assets will not cover. If both the firm and one or more partners are insolvent, the firm's creditors have first claim on the partnership assets, but the personal creditors of the individual insolvent partners have first claim on the insolvent partners' personal assets.

LIMITED PARTNER-SHIPS

A **limited partnership** is defined by the *Revised Uniform Limited Partnership Act* (RULPA) as "a partnership formed by two or more persons . . . having one or more general partners and one or more limited partners." Limited partners are investors only. They contribute cash or other property to the business and

Limited partnerships offer people the opportunity to invest their money without having to participate in the management of the firm. If Cencom of Missouri II fails, what is the limit of the liability of each limited partner?

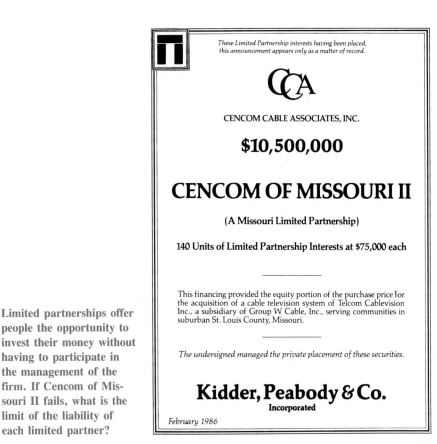

These Limited Partnership interests having been placed, this announcement appears only as a matter of record.

CCA

CENCOM CABLE ASSOCIATES, INC.

$10,500,000

CENCOM OF MISSOURI II

(A Missouri Limited Partnership)

140 Units of Limited Partnership Interests at $75,000 each

This financing provided the equity portion of the purchase price for the acquisition of a cable television system of Telcom Cablevision Inc., a subsidiary of Group W Cable, Inc., serving communities in suburban St. Louis County, Missouri.

The undersigned managed the private placement of these securities.

Kidder, Peabody & Co.
Incorporated

February 1986

share in the profits. They have no voice in managing the partnership and their name may not appear in the partnership name. A limited partner's liability does not extend beyond that partner's investment. Limited partnerships are subject to more stringent formalities than general partnerships. A limited partnership must file a certificate of limited partnership with the appropriate state or county office. The limited partnership name also must indicate that it is a limited partnership. These requirements are necessary to warn third parties of the limited liability that certain partners possess. Limited partners must be very careful not to become too involved in managing the firm. This is so because a limited partner may become a general partner by exercising too much control over management. When this happens, the partner loses the protective mantle of his or her limited liability. The limited partner also could lose limited liability if the certificate is not filed or is filed incorrectly.

In terms of liability, the limited partnership falls between the general partnership, in which all owners have unlimited liability, and the corporation, in which all owners have limited liability.

Suggestions for Reducing Legal Risks

1. When forming a sole proprietorship, make certain to check all applicable licensing laws and local zoning ordinances. If you are using a fictitious name, check filing requirements.
2. When dealing with consumers, check applicable state sales laws and consumer protection laws. When hiring employees, check applicable state and federal laws.
3. Before joining a partnership, discuss details of the operation of the business. Make certain written articles of copartnership are drawn up and agreed to by all partners.
4. Avoid business situations that might make you a partner inadvertently. Also, if you are a partner, avoid situations that might mislead third parties to believe that a nonpartner is a partner.
5. Keep careful track of partnership property. Also, use partnership property for partnership purposes only.
6. When entering a limited partnership, make certain the certificate of limited partnership is filed with the appropriate state or county office.
7. To retain limited-partner status, refrain from exercising too much control over the management of the limited partnership.

Language of the Law

Define or explain each of the following words or phrases:

sole proprietorship	partnership by proof	secret partner	tenancy in partner-
Uniform Partnership	of existence	silent partner	ship
Act (UPA)	partnership by estop-	dormant partner	joint liability
general partnership	pel	limited partner	dissolution
articles of copartnership	general partner		limited partnership

Questions for Review

1. Why would an individual decide to form a sole proprietorship rather than a partnership or a corporation?
2. What disadvantages can you see in using the sole proprietorship form of business?
3. Briefly explain three situations which might require a sole proprietor to know something about the law.
4. What advantages can you see in having a partnership agreement in writing?
5. Name three exceptions to the rule that profit sharing is proof that a partnership exists.
6. Name some important items that should be included in a partnership agreement.
7. What are some of the ways to determine whether property belongs to the partnership or to an individual partner?
8. What are the duties that partners owe to one another?
9. What are the rules for the distribution of a firm's assets when the firm goes out of business?
10. Why must a limited partner be careful not to become too involved in managing the firm?

Cases in Point

In each of the following cases, give your decision and state a legal principle that applies to the case:

1. As a sole proprietor, Larry Frome decided to open a drug store. He has hired Roy Suiter to work as a pharmacist because Suiter took chemistry in high school. Frome figures he will not have to pay Suiter as much as he would have to pay a real pharmacist. Frome has also decided to name his drug store the Best Pharmacy Incorporated. What legal problems do you see in Frome's plan?
2. Ben Cole owned and operated a ranch on the outskirts of Dallas. His three sons, Joe, Jim, and Jerry, worked the ranch with Ben all their lives. Ben was heard frequently to remark, "This will all be yours when I'm gone." The boys received a fixed salary each month. When Ben died, the boys discovered that he had willed the ranch to their sisters, Jane and Joan. They contested the will, claiming that the ranch was partnership property. Are the brothers correct?
3. Nancy Myers had her law office in the Brown and Brown Law Office Building. Brown and Brown was a very prestigious law firm. To help her business, Myers had business cards printed which read "Nancy Myers of the Brown and Brown Law Office." When Samuel Brown, one of the Brown partners, discovered what Nancy had done, he laughed and told her she was very clever. Relying on the information on Myers' business card, Bob Wash loaned Myers $5,000. When Myers did not pay the money back, Wash sued Myers and the Brown partnership. Who will be liable to Wash for the money Myers owes? Explain.
4. Terry Warwick was a partner in the general partnership of Warwick, Grimes, and Austin. Warwick bought a new car to get her to and from work. One day, the partnership truck broke down and Warwick used her own car to make deliveries. The partnership truck was not repairable, so the partners continued to use Warwick's car. Warwick used her own money for gas and repairs. She also continued to make the car payments out of her own pocket. When the partnership broke up, the other partners claimed the car was partnership property. Were the partners correct?
5. Using personal funds, Sandy Hill, a partner, paid the electric bill owed by the partnership. Is the partnership liable for reimbursing Hill?

6. Ruth Drummond, a general partner, was in charge of purchasing all merchandise for her partnership. A manufacturer gave Drummond 10 percent commission on the goods she purchased from him for the partnership. When the other partners learned about the commission, they demanded that Drummond turn over all the money to the partnership. Were the partners correct in their demand?

7. Max Massie was a general partner in the construction firm of Massie, Briggs, and Yates. While operating a forklift one afternoon at a construction site, Massie collided with a limousine owned by the mayor. The mayor sued not only Massie, but also Yates and Briggs. Yates and Briggs argued that Massie was at fault, so the mayor had no cause of action against them. Were they correct?

8. Douglas Maker was convinced by Irene Gale to join Gale's limited-partnership venture. Maker was assured that all he would have to do was contribute $1,000. Gale promised him a share in the profits in return for his investment. Several months later, Maker was served with a summons and a complaint naming him as a defendant in a suit against Gale's partnership. Was Maker in danger of losing his personal property?

9. Alan Gallagher and Norma Kendall each contributed $20,000 when their partnership began. At one point, the venture was in serious trouble, so Gallagher lent the partnership $10,000. Eventually the partnership was dissolved. After the creditors were paid, $50,000 remained in the assets. Kendall claimed each of them should receive $25,000. Was Kendall correct? Explain.

10. Howard Olen asked Clare March to become a limited partner in Olen's auto parts business. March would agree only if she was granted the power to choose the firm's general manager. Reluctantly, Olen signed a contract giving March the exclusive right to hire and fire the general manager. When the partnership failed to make an important delivery of several thousand parts to Jack Sutton's auto dealership, Sutton sued both Olen and March. March denied that she was a general partner. Was March correct? Explain.

Cases to Judge

1. Louis Covalt and William High were partners in a business which leased a warehouse and office space to Concrete Systems, Inc. (CSI). Covalt wanted the partnership to raise the CSI's monthly rent from $1,850 to $2,850. High, who was also one of the owners of CSI, refused to agree to the rent increase. Covalt brought suit against High, alleging that High had breached his fiduciary duty to the partnership by placing his own interests as owner of CSI above the interests of the partnership. How would you decide this case? *Covalt v. High,* 675 P.2d 999 (New Mexico)

2. George and Clarence Simandl jointly operated a combination gas station, delicatessen, and magazine stand. The two brothers carried on the business together and shared profits and losses for 40 years until George's death. All building permits were issued in both brothers' names. Both George and Clarence signed all contracts involving the business. When George died, his wife, Albina, carried on the business in his place. When Clarence died, his sister (also his executrix), Lillian, claimed all the property was in Clarence's estate. Albina disagreed, contending that a partnership had existed and that she was entitled to a share of the assets. Is Albina correct? *Simandl v. Schimandle,* 445 N.E.2d 734 (Ohio)

3. Robert and William Palmer owned and operated a partnership called Palmer Brothers. The partnership involved a ranch on which the brothers raised cattle for sale. In 1981, Robert died. The dispute involved a check-

ing account, into which partnership funds were deposited and from which partnership debts were paid. Also involved in the dispute were the livestock and a brokerage account in William's name. William claimed the checking account was his personal property due to a formality in the way the account was opened. He also claimed that the livestock was his alone because it was branded under a brand registered to William *or* Robert. Finally, he claimed that the brokerage account was his because it was in his name alone. Robert's wife, Constance, argued that the checking account was partnership property despite the formality in opening the account because all funds in the account came from the operation of the business. She also noted that the cattle were bought with partnership funds and used for partnership property. Finally, she argued that all the money invested in the brokerage account came from the partnership business. Since Constance herself was not a partner, why is she concerned about characterizing this property as partnership property? Is she correct? *In Re Estate of Palmer,* 708 P.2d 242 (Montana)

4. Charles Schlichenmayer sold cattle to Melinda Luithle's husband, who paid for the cattle with a worthless check. After Melinda's husband died, Schlichenmayer brought suit against Mrs. Luithle to recover the lost money. He claimed she had created the appearance of being a partner and was thus stopped from denying her partnership under the doctrine of partnership by estoppel. Schlichenmayer offered the following evidence: Mrs. Luithle frequently met her husband at the cattle sales ring after she had left her own job in a retail store. In addition, she had been present when Schlichenmayer had discussed the sale with her husband. Mrs. Luithle argued that she had been present at the sales ring and during the discussion of the sale to Schlichenmayer simply because she was waiting for her husband to go home. Did Mrs. Luithle's action create a partnership by estoppel? *Schlichenmayer v. Luithle,* 221 N.W.2d 77 (North Dakota)

5. Eddie Stewart, vice president of Exclusive International Pictures, Inc., contracted with K. A. Green, president of the Radio Picture Show Partnership. Under terms of the contract, Stewart was to have the exclusive right to promote a film entitled *The Radio Picture Show*. Subsequently, Green breached the contract with Stewart, and Stewart sued. After filing the suit, Stewart learned that a Texas limited partnership called 3622 Limited, headed by John Brown, was a limited partner in the Radio Picture Show Partnership. Stewart amended his complaint adding 3622 Limited as a defendant. The Radio Picture Show Partnership had never filed a certificate of limited partnership. Brown argued that neither he nor anyone associated with 3622 Limited had ever exerted any management control over the Radio Picture Show Partnership and that they had, therefore, retained their capacity as a limited partner. Is Brown correct? *Radio Picture Show Partnership v. Exclusive International Pictures, Inc.,* 482 N.E.2d 1159 (Indiana Appeals)

Chapter 35

THE CORPORATION

Scene: Jennifer and Ernie have just met in front of Jennifer's apartment. Ernie has just delivered a pizza to a tenant in the building.

Jennifer: Say, Ernie, what happened to your pet shop job?

Ernie: Well, it turns out you were right. Sally didn't have a license, and she violated zoning regulations by having a business in a residential area. The city shut her down.

Jennifer: So you got a job delivering pizzas.

Ernie: Better than that. Lew and Dan and I started our own business.

Jennifer: You opened a pizza shop?

Ernie: No, we started a pizza delivery service.

Jennifer: Say, that's a great idea. So you and Lew and Dan are partners.

Ernie: No way. Not after all that trouble my brother had with his partners. We decided to start a corporation instead.

Jennifer: A corporation?

Ernie: Sure, that way if we're sued or something, the corporation takes care of it.

Jennifer: What's the name of this corporation of yours?

Ernie: United Pizza Service. Only we use UPS for short.

Jennifer: Isn't there already a company called UPS?

Ernie: Sure, that's the beauty of it. We get a lot of their business by mistake.

Jennifer: I didn't know you could do that.

Ernie: Sure. It's called beating the competition.

Jennifer: Didn't the people you filed with tell you you can't use another company's name or initials?

Ernie: What people?

Jennifer: The people you filed your incorporation papers with.

Ernie: What papers?

Jennifer: Ernie, you can't just get up one morning and decide to be a corporation. There are certain formalities you have to go through.

Ernie: I didn't know that.

Jennifer: You could get in trouble pretending to be a corporation.

Ernie: I better tell Lew and Dan. So long.

Jennifer: Good luck.

Ernie: Thanks.

(*Several months later, Ernie and Jennifer meet in a restaurant downtown. Ernie is waiting tables.*)

Jennifer: What happened to United Pizza Service?

Ernie: Don't mention that name.

Jennifer: Why not?

Ernie: Because it got me in big trouble.

Jennifer: Did you file the right papers?

Ernie: We tried, but they wouldn't let us use UPS as our initials.

Jennifer: So what name did you use?

Ernie: None. They also wanted a filing fee.

Jennifer: Really?

Ernie: And we had to appoint some sort of statutory agent. I didn't understand that part.

Jennifer: Sounds like legal mumbo jumbo to me.

Ernie: You don't know the half of it.

Jennifer: What do you mean?

Ernie: Lew bought a delivery truck when we were pretending to be UPS. Well, when we decided we didn't want to incorporate, we tried to give the truck back. We told the truck dealer there was no corporation so he never had a real contract with anyone.

Jennifer: Sounds reasonable.

Ernie: Not to the court. The judge said we couldn't deny we were a corporation, even though we really weren't.

Jennifer: That doesn't make any sense.

Ernie: Since when does the law make sense?

Jennifer: Oh yeah, I see what you mean.

LEGAL ISSUES

1. What sort of formalities must be followed to begin a corporation?
2. Can one corporation use the name of another corporation in doing business?
3. What is the function of the statutory agent?
4. Can people who pretend to be a corporation be held accountable to creditors as if they were a corporation?

THE SPIRIT OF THE LAW

Although partnerships and sole proprietorships are excellent forms of organization for many small businesses, they have their limitations. Perhaps their most obvious limitation is the inability to command large amounts of money and property. The best solution to the problem of raising large amounts of money and property quickly is the corporation. A corporation can have literally thousands of shareholders (owners) contributing to the capital of the corporation.

DEFINITION OF CORPOR-ATION

A **corporation** is "an artificial person created by statute." In a partnership, the partners themselves are important. The partners have the legal life and capacity and are liable for the debts of the firm. A corporation, however, is given a life and existence of its own, separate and apart from that of the individual members. It is this new "legal person" created by the state that does business, makes contracts, creates debts, has the liability for paying them, can sue and be sued in its own name, and acquires and disposes of personal and real property. A corporation does all the things that a natural person might do if he or she were engaged in the same kind of business. One of the most attractive features of a corporation is the limited liability of the shareholders (owners). Shareholders, unlike partners or sole proprietors, can lose only their initial investment in the corporation. Their personal property is not subject to actions brought by corporate creditors.

TYPES OF CORPORA-TIONS

Corporations may be classified as public or private corporations, stock or non-stock corporations, and domestic or foreign corporations. **Public corporations** include incorporated political units, such as towns, villages, cities, school districts, and the like. **Private corporations** may be classified as profit or non-profit corporations. **Profit corporations,** private corporations organized for the purpose of making money, are found in nearly every major field of economic activity—the transportation, mining, manufacturing, business, financial, and service fields. These corporations are regulated by the laws of the state in which they operate. If they are engaged in interstate commerce, they are also regulated by federal regulations. Any corporation formed for business purposes is operating for a profit and has a capital stock. A bank, a railroad, and a trading firm are **stock corporations.**

Non-profit corporations, such as the Red Cross, are formed for educational, religious, charitable, or social purposes. A non-profit corporation in which membership is acquired by agreement rather than by acquisition of stock is also

TYPES OF CORPORATIONS

PUBLIC	PRIVATE	
	Domestic: incorporated in the state Foreign: incorporated in another state	
Incorporated Political Units	For Profit (Stock Corporations) Business Corporations	Non-Profit (Non-Stock Corporations) Religious Educational Social Charitable

A corporation may be domestic or foreign, public or private, for profit or non-profit.

a **nonstock corporation.** Many non-profit fraternal organizations are nonstock corporations.

Corporations also may be classed as domestic and foreign. In the state in which it is incorporated, the corporation is considered a **domestic corporation.** In all other states in which it may operate, the corporation is considered a **foreign corporation.**

FORMATION OF A CORPO- RATION

A corporation cannot come into existence by itself. It must be organized by natural (actual) persons who take the necessary steps to bring it into legal existence. Each state has its own law, generally patterned after the Model Business Corporation Act, under which a corporation must be organized. These laws set forth the exact steps that must be taken in order to form the new corporation.

Original Appointment of Statutory Agent

The undersigned, being at least a majority of the incorporators of _____
(Name of Corporation)

_____ , hereby appoint _____ to be statutory agent
(Name of Agent)

upon whom any process, notice or demand required or permitted by statute to be served upon the

corporation may be served.

The complete address of the agent is: _____
(Street)

_____ , _____ County, Ohio _____ .
(City or Village)   (Zip Code)

Date: _____   _____
(Incorporator)

_____
(Incorporator)

_____
(Incorporator)

Instructions

1) Profit and non-profit articles of incorporation must be accompanied by an original appointment of agent. R.C. 1701.04(C), 1702.04(C).

2) The statutory agent for a corporation may be (a) a natural person who is a resident of Ohio, or (b) an Ohio corporation or a foreign profit corporation licensed in Ohio which has a business address in this state and is explicitly authorized by its articles of incorporation to act as a statutory agent. R.C. 1701.07(A), 1702.06(A).

3) The agent's complete street address must be given; a post office box number is not acceptable. R.C. 1701.07(C), 1702.06(C).

4) An original appointment of agent form must be signed by at least a majority of the incorporators of the corporation. R.C. 1701.07(B), 1702.06(B).

Most states provide forms such as this one to help promoters incorporate properly. What is the function of a statutory agent? Why is a corporation required to have one?

The Incorporation Process

Legal Issue No. 1

Legal Issue No. 2

The persons who actually organize the corporation are called **promoters,** or **incorporators.** One of the first steps the promoters take is to choose a corporate name. Usually, the words *corporation, company,* or *incorporated* must appear somewhere in the corporate name. Also, the corporation cannot choose a name that some other corporation already uses or a name that would confuse the new corporation with one already in existence. Even in situations where a specific state does not prohibit the use of similar names, the court will prevent such duplication if confusion or unfair competition results. Often the secretary of state's office can tell promoters if a name has been taken. It is also possible to reserve a name. Usually, however, there is a small fee for this service.

The promoters must also obtain initial capital for the corporation. **Capital** is the money and property that a corporation needs to carry on its business. They do this by convincing people to invest in the new corporation. These new investors will pledge to buy a certain number of **shares** (units of ownership) when the corporation is formed. The promoters also must negotiate contracts for the as yet unborn corporation. For example, it may be necessary to lease office and warehouse space as a preliminary step in preparing the way for the new corporation. Finally, the promoters must draw up and file the **articles of incorporation.** Generally, this can be done by obtaining a form from the office of the secretary of state. The articles of incorporation include the name, object, duration, capital structure, place of business, and proposed directors of the corporation to be formed. The articles are then submitted to the secretary of state for approval. Along with the articles of incorporation, the promoters will appoint a person who will serve as statutory agent for service of process. The **statutory agent** is available to receive a complaint and summons if the corporation is involved in litigation. Finally, when the articles are filed, the promoters must pay the appropriate filing fees. Some states also require that the new corporation have a minimum amount of capital on hand, usually between $500 and $1,000, before starting business. The articles, once approved by the secretary of state, become the corporation's **charter,** or **certificate.** A charter is a corporation's official authorization to do business in the state.

Legal Issue No. 3

Incorporation Problems

If all the preceding steps are followed, then the corporation comes into existence, carrying with it all the powers and privileges due its new status. A legally formed corporation which has complied with all incorporation formalities is known as a **de jure corporation.** (De jure [dē·juŕ·ē] means ''lawful.'') Sometimes, however, problems occur that disrupt the incorporation process. At other times, people fail to incorporate and yet act as if they were incorporated. To deal with these problems, the court has developed two doctrines: de facto corporation and corporation by estoppel.

De Facto Corporation Sometimes it happens that the promoters, while making a good-faith attempt to incorporate, inadvertently make an error in filing or fail to complete the process. Technically, if the incorporation process has not been completed, the corporation does not exist legally. In other words, there is no de jure corporation. However, as long as the incorporators made a bona fide (good-faith) attempt to incorporate under an existing state incorporation law, and as long as the corporation has acted like a corporation by exercising some corporate power, few people can attack its existence. The law says that although the corporation does not exist under the law (de jure), it does exist in fact (de facto). We call this type of corporation a **de facto corporation.** A de facto corporation may be compelled by the state to cease operation. When the corporation has complied with proper statutory incorporation procedures, it can once again resume operation. However, an outsider could not sue a shareholder directly, because the shareholder's limited liability remains intact under the de facto doctrine.

EXAMPLE 1 Randall Kayser, Lloyd Gordon, and Curtis Beal hired Allen Dalton, an attorney, to draw up and file their incorporation papers. Dalton did so and had all three incorporators sign the articles, ostensibly creating KGB, Incorporated. Dalton's office was being moved that week, and in the process, the incorporation papers were lost and, therefore, were never approved by the secretary of state. Nevertheless, KGB acted as if it were a corporation, establishing a corporate headquarters along with a chemical plant nearby. When one of KGB's chemical dumps caused damage to Wayne Maloney's property, he filed suit against KGB. When Maloney's attorney discovered that KGB had never been incorporated, he filed suit directly against Kayser, Gordon, and Beal, claiming that since no corporation existed, they were personally liable. Since Kayser, Gordon, and Beal had made a good-faith attempt to incorporate, and since KGB had exercised corporate power, the doctrine of de facto corporation would protect them from personal liability. Kayser, Gordon, and Beal would also have a cause of action against Dalton should they suffer any loss due to his negligence in not completing the filing properly.

Sometimes the doctrine of de facto corporation is used when a corporation has temporarily lost its corporate status. For instance, if a corporation fails to pay its annual taxes to the state or fails to file an annual report with the state, the secretary of state may temporarily withdraw the corporation's charter until the taxes are paid or the report filed. If the corporation continues to operate despite its defunct status and then tries to escape contractual liability, the courts will often use the de facto doctrine to prevent injustice.

EXAMPLE 2 Devon Industries, Inc., failed to pay its annual taxes for 2 years in a row. As a result, its corporate status was withdrawn until it paid the back taxes. Despite the loss of Devon's corporate status, Maury Chandler, president of Devon, continued to operate the business. During this time, he entered into several contracts with Conroy-Mitchell, Inc. Unfortunately, the contracts proved impossible to fulfill. After Devon's corporate status was returned, Chandler informed Conroy-Mitchell that the contracts were void. Conroy-Mitchell sued to recover the money it had lost on the canceled contracts. Chandler argued that Devon Industries had not been a corporation when the contracts were made. Therefore, he said, the contracts were void. The court took a different view. Using the de facto doctrine, the court held Devon liable to Conroy-Mitchell. Since there had been a bona fide attempt to incorporate under an existing state incorporation law and an extensive use of corporate power, Devon Industries continued as a de facto corporation until it was returned to its former de jure status. Note that in this case the doctrine of de facto corporation is actually used *against* the corporation. In previous examples, it was used to protect the owners against third parties attempting to hold the owners personally liable.

Some states have abandoned the doctrine of de facto corporation. The rule in these states is relatively simple and straightforward. If a certificate of incorporation has been issued by the state, the corporation exists. If it has not been issued, the corporation has no legal or factual status.

Corporation by Estoppel Even states that have abandoned the de facto doctrine still use the estoppel doctrine. Like other estoppel doctrines, corporation by estoppel stops people from denying the existence of a corporation. **Corporation by estoppel** usually occurs when some party has been willing to treat a group of people as if they were a corporation, generally reaping some sort of benefit from the relationship. When this happens, the court will not allow that party to deny the existence of the corporation because to do so would be unfair.

EXAMPLE 3 Joyce Radcliffe was prevailed upon by Kathy Ulrich to become a shareholder and the chief executive officer of a newly formed corporation, Comtech, Inc. Unknown to Radcliffe, Ulrich had never filed the articles of incorporation with the secretary of state. In fact, Ulrich had made no attempt to file the articles. Nevertheless, for a period of 6 months, Comtech carried on operations as if it were incorporated. As part of its business, Radcliffe, acting for Comtech, purchased office furniture and supplies from Marham, Inc. Eventually, Comtech collapsed. When Marham discovered that no articles of incorporation had ever been filed, the company sued Radcliffe directly, attempting to hold her personally liable. Under these circumstances, Radcliffe would be protected. Since Marham had been willing to deal with Comtech, it would be "estopped to deny" Comtech's corporate existence.

Note in the preceding example that the doctrine of estoppel does not create a corporation beyond the transaction between Comtech and Marham. It is used as a solution to that individual problem and has no effect beyond that decision. It is also interesting to note that it is possible to reverse the doctrine of estoppel and turn it against those who held themselves out as a corporation when, in fact, they were not a corporation.

Legal Issue No. 4

EXAMPLE 4 In Example 3, in another case, Ulrich attempted to deny that Comtech had made any contracts with several suppliers. Ulrich's argument was that Comtech had never existed and so the contracts with the suppliers were invalid. Therefore, Ulrich argued, the remaining assets could not be tapped to pay those debts. Ulrich would be "estopped to deny" the existence of the corporation and would have to accept the validity of the contracts.

Piercing the Corporate Veil

As noted earlier, one of the primary advantages of forming a corporation is that the shareholders do not lose anything beyond their initial investment. Nevertheless, there are times when the courts will punch through the barrier and hold shareholders personally liable. This doctrine, known as **piercing the corporate veil,** is usually called on by the court when the owners have used the corporation as a facade to defraud or commit some other misdeed. Still, there are times when a shareholder inadvertently creates a situation which calls for the courts to pierce the corporate veil. This may occur when the shareholder is careless in maintaining the separate existence of the corporation.

Small Corporations   Owners of small corporations are very susceptible to losing their protected status because they often fail to keep appropriate records or hold appropriate meetings. Often the shareholders also fail to keep corporate assets (furniture, automobiles, office equipment, and so on) separate from their individual assets. Perhaps worst of all is the failure to keep enough money in the corporate treasury, so that, in effect, the corporation cannot operate on its own. Remember that a corporation is a legal entity with an identity separate from the shareholders. If the shareholders do not keep enough money and property in a corporation, then the corporation will be unable to establish its own identity. (Such a corporation is said to be **undercapitalized.**) In such a situation, the court may declare the undercapitalized corporation the alter ego (''other self'') of the shareholders and hold them personally liable.

EXAMPLE 5   Frank Underwood went through all the proper steps to incorporate his travel agency, Planetary Travel, Inc. Underwood was careless in keeping Planetary's books. In addition, he failed to hold directors' meetings and kept almost no money in the corporate treasury, transferring all funds to his own personal account. Eventually, Planetary collapsed, leaving several very unhappy creditors who sued Underwood directly, asking the court to pierce the corporate veil and declare Planetary to be Underwood's alter ego. The court complied.

Parent/Subsidiary   Although small companies are most susceptible to piercing the corporate veil, large companies also can fall victim to this doctrine. Usually this happens when the parent corporation has established a subsidiary. A **subsidiary** is a corporation owned and operated by another corporation, usually called the **parent corporation.** Parent corporations establish subsidiaries for a variety of reasons. For example, a corporation may want to engage in a project that is somewhat risky. Because of the risk, the corporation may want to hide its involvement in the project. It may, therefore, open a subsidiary to experiment in the project without endangering its reputation.

Of course, there are also some unjust reasons for establishing subsidiaries. Suppose, for example, that a corporation needs a large quantity of capital quickly. It could set up a subsidiary, sell stock in the subsidiary, and then syphon off the capital generated by the sale until the subsidiary collapses. Such an operation would constitute a fraud, because innocent investors would be pouring their funds into a corporation that has no existence of its own. In a fraudulent situation like this, a court would find it very easy to pierce the corporate veil, because the subsidiary never has a chance to become a freestanding entity. Even in legitimate situations, however, the court may pierce the corporate veil if the subsidiary is not really separate from the parent corporation. The court looks at essentially the same things it looks at in the case of the

TABLE 35-1
ADVANTAGES AND DISADVANTAGES OF PROPRIETORSHIP, PARTNERSHIP, AND CORPORATION

Type of Organization	Advantages	Disadvantages
Proprietorship	All profits are retained by the owner. Control of the company is unified. Taxation is less than that of a corporation. A proprietorship can adapt to a variety of situations. A proprietorship can often obtain family assistance. Responsibility is focused on one individual.	Capital is limited. The owner must bear all losses. The owner has unlimited liability. Management of the organization is concentrated. Expansion is difficult. Legally and actually, the proprietorship is destroyed by the death of the proprietor.
Partnership	More capital is available than is available for a proprietorship. Partners share the losses of the organization. A partnership is easier to expand than a proprietorship. More credit is available to a partnership than to a proprietorship. There is more opportunity for each partner to specialize. Supervision is better than that usually found under a proprietorship.	The death of a partner dissolves the partnership. Profits are divided between the partners. Each partner has unlimited liability. Bickering between partners can result in the collapse of the organization. A mutual agency is established.
Corporation	A large amount of capital is available. The continuity of the life of the corporation is ensured. The liability of the corporation is limited to corporate assets. A corporation is able to employ specialists in a variety of fields. A corporation is legally separate from its owners.	Corporations are usually subject to double taxation and other special taxes. Government regulation of corporations is extensive. The charter is restrictive. Organizing a corporation is more difficult than organizing a partnership or a proprietorship.

small corporation to determine whether the subsidiary is independent. However, in the case of the parent/subsidiary relationship, the interlocking nature of the control would be somewhat different.

EXAMPLE 6 Camron, Inc., ran a chain of international hotels known as the Camron-Monarchy Hotels. Balton, Inc., a subsidiary of Camron, operated maintenance at all Camron-Monarchy Hotels. One evening a boiler in the basement of the New York Camron-Monarchy Hotel exploded, causing a fire that injured several hotel patrons. When the plaintiffs sued Balton and Camron,

Camron argued that the operation and care of the boiler was the responsibility of Balton, Inc., which Camron characterized as an independent contractor. In looking at the evidence, the court discovered that Balton had no business other than to service Camron's hotels. The court also found that Balton was listed as a division of Camron, was undercapitalized, was financed by Camron, shared the same board of directors as Camron, and was operated by executives on the Camron payroll. As a result of these findings, the court had no problem piercing the corporate veil and holding Camron liable along with Balton.

Suggestions for Reducing Legal Risks

1. Remember that the incorporation process is a formal procedure that requires strict adherence.
2. Before submitting a corporate name during the incorporation process, check with the secretary of state's office to make certain the name has not been used by another corporation.
3. Remember to be as detailed as possible in completing the articles of incorporation before submitting them to the secretary of state's office. Also remember to appoint a statutory agent for service of process and to check to determine if your state requires a certain amount of start-up capital.
4. Be prepared to pay a filing fee for the incorporation process.
5. Be aware that faulty incorporation does not always open incorporators to unlimited liability. Doctrines such as de facto corporation and corporation by estoppel may protect incorporators.
6. Avoid establishing a corporation for fraudulent purposes.
7. Also, after establishing a corporation, make certain the corporation maintains a separate and distinct existence. To this end, make certain the corporation is properly capitalized and that corporate formalities are followed.

Language of the Law

Define or explain each of the following words or phrases:

corporation	nonstock corporation	shares	corporation by estoppel
public corporation	domestic corporation	articles of incorporation	piercing the corporate veil
private corporation	foreign corporation	statutory agent	
profit corporation	promoters, or	charter, or certificate	undercapitalized
stock corporation	incorporators	de jure corporation	subsidiary
nonprofit corporation	capital	de facto corporation	parent corporation

Questions for Review

1. Distinguish between public and private corporations.

2. Distinguish between foreign and domestic corporations.

3. Name the tasks performed by promoters in the incorporation process.
4. Explain the limitations involved in choosing a corporate name.
5. List the data contained in the articles of incorporation.
6. What is the purpose behind requiring a corporation to appoint a statutory agent?
7. Explain how the doctrine of de facto corporation protects shareholders. Are there any circumstances under which de facto corporation would not protect the shareholders?
8. Explain how the doctrine of corporation by estoppel protects shareholders.
9. Explain how the doctrine of corporation by estoppel can be used against shareholders.
10. Under what circumstances might a court decide it is necessary to pierce the corporate veil and hold individual shareholders liable?

Cases in Point

In each of the following cases, give your decision and state a legal principle that applies in each case:

1. Trans Global Concerts, Inc., when sued by Glenn Stanhope, stated that it could not be sued because it was an artificial person created by law. Is this argument a good defense?

2. Ethel Holmes, Chris MacLeod, and Alicia Stevens decided to incorporate their printing business, naming it HMS, Inc. All three incorporators signed the articles of incorporation drawn up by their attorney, George Kitchel, who assured them that the articles would be approved with no difficulty. Because of a misunderstanding between Kitchel and a coworker, the articles were never filed. When William Blake was injured by an HMS delivery truck, he sued Holmes, Macleod, and Stevens directly as individuals because the incorporation papers were never filed. What legal theory could Holmes, MacLeod, and Stevens use to protect themselves? Explain.

3. In the opening of the chapter, Ernie, Lew, and Dan bought a delivery truck while acting as United Pizza Service, Inc. When they decided to return the truck, they argued that since there was no corporation, the truck dealer had no contract with anyone. The court did not accept this argument. What doctrine did the court use to hold Ernie, Lew, and Dan liable for the truck payments? Explain.

4. Lorraine Haley, Randy Hager, and Dean Madison decided to incorporate their detective agency. However, since none of them knew anything about corporate law, they failed to follow the usual corporate formalities. Nevertheless, they sold stock to Darrell Lovett and persuaded Lovett to become an officer in the firm. Lovett purchased a computer for the detective firm. When the computer company discovered that no corporation existed, it attempted to hold Lovett personally liable for the amount due on the computer. What doctrine can Lovett use to protect himself? Explain.

5. Alice Pryor and Jessica Tunney operated their business for several years as a partnership. Pryor convinced Tunney that it would be a good idea to convert the business to a corporation. Tunney agreed, so they changed the name of the firm to Pryor and Tunney, Inc. They did nothing further, although they told their customers and creditors that they had formed a corporation. What would their legal status be if they were involved in a tort-based lawsuit?

6. Dennis Tharp and Merle Coffman decided to incorporate. They have decided to call their corporation Ford Motors because such a well known name would attract a lot of business. They drew up their articles of incorporation and included the name, object,

duration, capital structure, and place of business. They then took the articles and attempted to file them with the attorney general's office. Explain at least three mistakes that Tharp and Coffman made in their incorporation attempt.

7. Martin Greenlawn, Gladys Chilcote, and Lillian Brunner attempted to incorporate their flower shop, calling it The Hearts and Flowers Florist Shop, Inc. The articles were filed with the secretary of state's office. Neither Greenlawn nor Chilcote nor Brunner were told about naming a statutory agent. Through an oversight, the secretary of state's office still issued a charter. Eventually, the secretary of state's office discovered the error. Does Hearts and Flowers exist as a corporation despite the error? What action can the state take at this point?

8. Byron Cabell formed a corporation named Cabell, Inc. All the proper legal formalities were followed in the formation process. Nevertheless, Cabell failed to keep enough money in the corporate treasury to support the independent operation of the corporation. He also failed to hold any directors' meetings or to keep corporate records. Finally, he did not separate his business property from his personal property. If a creditor discovers the poor financial status of Cabell, Inc., and decides to sue Cabell as an individual, will the creditor succeed? What theory will the creditor use to hold Cabell personally liable?

9. The directors of Bibliotech, Inc., have decided to raise funds to save their failing business by creating a subsidiary and selling shares to unsuspecting investors. Unknown to the investors, all the subsidiary's money will go directly into the treasury of Bibliotech. When the subsidiary fails, will the investors have any cause of action against Bibliotech? Explain.

10. Jane Spiegle made a contract with the Southwest Galaxy Broadcasting Company for the sale of Spiegle's new science fiction TV pilot. Unknown to Spiegle, Southwest Galaxy's parent corporation, National Galaxy, was conducting negotiations with Frank Butler, who also had a science fiction pilot for sale. National Galaxy bought Butler's idea. Southwest Galaxy then told Spiegle that the deal was off. By the time Spiegle was notified of the breach of contract, it was too late to sell the idea to any other broadcasting company. Shortly thereafter, Southwest Galaxy went out of business. Does Spiegle have any legal recourse at this point in time? Explain.

Cases to Judge

1. Legal Aid Services, Inc., was incorporated as a non-profit organization providing free legal services for the poor. Four years later, American Legal Aid, Inc., was incorporated. American Legal Aid, Inc., functioned as a legal insurance corporation selling memberships to subscribers. After American Legal Aid had engaged in an extensive selling campaign, Legal Aid Services discovered that many people were confusing the two entities. The confusion of the two corporations hurt Legal Aid Services' image and threatened its sources of funding. Consequently, it filed action for an injunction prohibiting American Legal Aid from using the words *legal aid* in its corporate name. Should Legal Aid Services be granted the injunction? *American Legal Aid, Inc. v. Legal Aid Services, Inc.,* 503 P.2d 1201 (Wyoming)

2. Ira Adler, Frank Billitz, and J. Daniel Quinn devised a promotional scheme known as "Woody Hightower." The idea was to hire a performer to live in a mobile flagpole perch for 9 months to break the Guinness World Record for flagpole sitting. Adler, Billitz, and Quinn planned to send "Woody Hightower" on promotional tours at fairs, concerts, and shopping malls. To protect them-

selves, the three business people decided to incorporate. For this purpose, they hired Paul Wartzman, of Wartzman, Rombro, Rudd, and Omansky, a law firm in Baltimore. The corporation had been in operation for several weeks when Wartzman discovered that Hightower Productions had been improperly incorporated. As a result, Adler, Billitz, and Quinn could not sell stock until the correction was made. The correction and ensuing delay was so expensive that Adler, Billitz, and Quinn had to shut down operations. In the process, they lost $170,508.43. They sued Wartzman to recover this amount. Should Adler, Billitz, and Quinn recover? *Wartzman v. Hightower Productions,* 456 A.2d 82 (Maryland)

3. Thomas Dunham, Charles Elliott, and Charles Shamburger bought a Beech Baron B-55 airplane. Eight months later, the articles of incorporation for Jackson Air Taxi, Inc., were drawn up and notarized, but they were never delivered to the secretary of state. Dunham and Elliott then met with a vice president of Mount Olive Bank and secured a loan of $28,000 for Jackson Air Taxi, Inc. The next week the articles were finally sent to the secretary of state. He rejected them, however, for certain filing irregularities. Eventually, the filing was straightened out. However, in the meantime, Jackson Air Taxi had fallen on hard times. When Jackson did not pay its debt to Mount Olive, the bank sued the corporation. The court awarded the plane to Mount Olive to satisfy the debt. Dunham, Elliott, and Shamburger, however, argued that the promissory note in the name of Jackson Air Taxi was invalid because Jackson Air Taxi's certificate of incorporation had not yet been filed and was, in fact, subsequently disallowed. Since the corporation did not exist at the time the contract was made, the corporation's debt to Mount Olive was void. Is this argument correct? *Mount Olive Bank v. Jackson Air Taxi, Inc.,* 356 So. 2d 1090 (Louisiana)

4. Henry Zimbelman and Floyd Knox created Balto Industries. After 3 years, the corporation was terminated by the state because it did not file its yearly report nor pay its annual taxes as required by law. Despite the termination, Knox and Zimbelman continued to operate the business. During this time, Zimbelman diverted corporate funds into his own account. He was later charged with felony theft. Zimbelman argued that the corporation had ceased to exist in 1972 as a result of its termination by the state. Thereafter, he and Knox were outright co-owners of the business. As a co-owner, the money diverted to his account was actually his own and did not belong to the nonexistent corporation. Therefore, he concluded, he could not be guilty of theft. Is he correct? *People v. Zimbelman,* 572 P.2d 830 (Colorado)

5. Thomas E. Kelly and Associates (TEKA) entered into a contract with RRX Laboratories. Under terms of the contract, TEKA was to supply RRX with software to be used in RRX's medical laboratories. Shortly after contracting with RRX, Kelly formed Lab-Con, Inc. Kelly transferred all TEKA's assets, licenses, and software to Lab-Con. TEKA received nothing in return. After numerous attempts, RRX could not get the software to work properly. Consequently, it sued TEKA, Lab-Con, and Kelly, asking the court to pierce the corporate veil and hold Lab-Con liable for TEKA's breach of contract. RRX also asked the court to hold Kelly personally liable. RRX argued that TEKA was completely controlled by Kelly. Kelly was the only officer, director, and stockholder in TEKA. No employees worked for TEKA, and no stockholder meetings were ever held. Additionally, RRX demonstrated that TEKA was badly undercapitalized. Kelly argued that he had not acted in bad faith. Should the court pierce the corporate veil to reach Kelly and/or Lab-Con? *RRX Industries, Inc. v. Lab-Con, Inc.,* 772 F.2d 543 (9th Circuit)

Chapter 36

CORPORATE OWNERSHIP

Scene: Jennifer and Ernie meet unexpectedly in the lobby of a professional building complex downtown.

Jennifer: Say, Ernie, what are you doing down here?

Ernie: Doing something right for a change.

Jennifer: What's that supposed to mean?

Ernie: Well, remember how my last two business ventures got me in big trouble?

Jennifer: You mean the pet shop and the United Pizza Service? Sure, I remember both those great ideas.

Ernie: Don't be funny. I'm through with that fly-by-night stuff for good.

Jennifer: So what are you up to now?

Ernie: Investments.

Jennifer: Investments?

Ernie: Sure, I take most of my salary now and buy shares of stock in big, reputable companies.

Jennifer: How does that make you money?

Ernie: Well, when the company makes a profit, I get it.

Jennifer: All of it!

Ernie: No, just what I'm entitled to because of my shares. It's called my dividend.

Jennifer: Sounds impressive.

Ernie: Yeah, I thought so too. I just bought twenty shares of common stock in Kaplan Industries.

Jennifer: What's common stock?

Ernie: That's stock for common, everyday people like you and me.

Jennifer: Oh.

Ernie: Yep. This common stock has a par value of $20 per share.

Jennifer: Par value? What's that?

Ernie: I'm not sure, but I think it has something to do with golf.

Jennifer: Golf?

Ernie: Sure, Kaplan makes sports equipment.

Jennifer: Well, I guess that makes sense.

Ernie: Only I think Kaplan should get involved in nuclear energy.

Jennifer: Nuclear energy?

Ernie: Sure. That's where the big money is.

Jennifer: Well, I don't think they'll listen to you.

Ernie: They have to. I can vote the directors out of office if I want to.

Jennifer: All by yourself?

Ernie: No, I have to get some other votes from other shareholders. That's called getting their proxy.

Jennifer: Sounds painful. What if they don't want to give you their proxy?

Ernie: Then I'll just sue the corporation.

Jennifer: Sue your own corporation?

Ernie: Sure, it's done all the time. If you don't like the president of the company or something like that, you just go ahead and sue.

Jennifer: Sounds too easy.

Ernie: When you're a big tycoon like me, things come easy.

Jennifer: Ernie.

Ernie: Yeah?

Jennifer: Good luck.

LEGAL ISSUES

1. What is par value stock?
2. What is common stock?
3. Are shareholders entitled to dividends every time a company makes a profit?
4. Can one shareholder vote for another shareholder by using a proxy?
5. Can shareholders sue their own corporation if they do not like the president?

THE SPIRIT OF THE LAW

Although we speak of a corporation as something that really exists, actually no one ever saw a corporation and no one ever will see one. It is really an imaginary, legal concept—an artificial ''person'' created by the state with many of the rights, powers, duties, and abilities of a natural person. To function as a legal person and to be in business, a corporation needs capital. As you will recall, capital is the money and property that an organization needs to carry on its business. Capital is obtained by selling units or shares of stock. The owners of these shares, known as **shareholders,** become members of the corporation. An owner's interest in a corporation is represented by transferable shares of **stock.** When shareholders purchase stock, they obtain certain rights. Among these rights is the right to receive a return on their investment when the corporation makes a profit. This return is known as a dividend. Shareholders also have certain voting powers because, as owners, they have a right to participate in management to a limited degree. If shareholders want to participate more directly in management, they need to acquire more shares or they need to acquire the voting rights of other shareholders. Other methods of having an effect on the voting process include shareholder proposals, pooling agreements, and voting trusts. If all else fails, shareholders can bring suit against or on behalf of the corporation. These are some of the ideas we shall explore in this chapter on corporate ownership.

TYPES OF STOCK

There are different kinds of stock issued by corporations. Stock may be par value stock, or it may be no par value stock. It may also be common stock, preferred stock, or treasury stock. In addition, it may be watered stock.

Par Value Stock

Legal Issue No. 1

Where the value of the stock is stated in the articles of incorporation, the stock is said to be **par value stock.** Thus, if a share of stock is said to have a par value of $100, then $100 was paid to the corporation for the share. If par value stock is issued by the corporation for less than the stated par value, the stockholder owes the corporation the difference between the par value and the price that the stockholder paid for the stock. On the other hand, the stockholder who has paid par value for his or her stock may later sell or transfer it at any price he or she wishes.

No Par Value Stock

Sometimes stock is issued as **no par value stock.** Such stock does not have any stated value. The corporation can sell no par value stock for any price it chooses, and the purchaser cannot be held for any additional purchase price. However, most states require that corporations make known to the public the amount of money actually raised by the sale of no par value stock. This, again, is for the protection of the future creditors. Since creditors can look only to the corporation for payment, they have the right to know about the financial condition of the corporation.

Common Stock

Legal Issue No. 2

The most usual form of stock issued by a corporation is **common stock,** which represents the interest of the stockholders in the net worth of the corporation. Common stock does not guarantee to its holders the right to profits. The return is based on the earnings of the corporation and is usually the amount remaining after the holders of preferred stock have received the amount guaranteed them. The control of a corporation, as evidenced by the voting power of the stockholders, is in the hands of the holders of the common stock.

Preferred Stock

Preferred stock gives to the owner some special privileges not given to holders of common stock. The usual privileges are (1) the right to have their investment returned first in case the corporation ends, and (2) the right to have a certain rate of income paid to them before any of the profits are distributed to holders of common stock in the form of dividends. Usually, no voting rights go along with preferred stock. It is possible, however, for a corporation to grant preferred shareholders some limited voting rights. Nevertheless, full voting rights can be vested in only one type of stock. This rule allows the corporation to issue additional stock and obtain additional capital without upsetting the voting balance. Buyers would be motivated to buy preferred stock even though it lacked voting rights because they would receive a return on their investment before common shareholders.

Treasury Stock

Legally issued stock that is repurchased by the corporation or presented to it as a gift is called **treasury stock.** Only surplus funds may be used for the purchase of treasury stock. The stock may be resold at a reasonable price agreed on by the board of directors. Dividends are not paid on the stock while it is held by the corporation.

To overcome sales resistance, a corporation may guarantee to repurchase the stock from subscribers upon request. Such stock becomes treasury stock. When a corporation has financial problems, stockholders sometimes donate a portion of their shares as treasury stock. These shares are then resold in order to assist in refinancing the firm.

Watered Stock

Stock issued for insufficient value or for no value at all is called **watered,** or **discounted, stock.** Stock is said to be watered or discounted when it is issued as a bonus, when it is issued as fully paid but actually at less than its par value, or when it is issued for property or for services greatly overvalued. If a corporation becomes insolvent (owes more than it owns), creditors of the corporation can recover from owners of watered stock the true value that should have been paid by the owners. (See Table 36-1.)

TABLE 36-1
STOCK DIFFERENCES

Based on Value	Distinguishing Characteristics
Par Value	Value of stock stated in articles of incorporation
No Par Value	Stock with no stated value

Based on Dividends and/or Voting Rights	Distinguishing Characteristics
Preferred Stock	Right to receive dividends first; right to first return of investment on dissolution; usually no voting rights
Common Stock	Right to receive dividends after preferred holders have been paid; usually full voting rights

Based on Corporate Control	Distinguishing Characteristics
Treasury Stock	Legally issued stock repurchased by the corporation
Watered Stock	Stock issued for less than par value often in exchange for overvalued property or services; owner may be liable for difference between par value and value rendered at issuance

EXAMPLE 1 McFarland Industries, Inc., transferred $70,000 worth of stock to Sarah Barnes in exchange for property valued at $35,000. Creditors of McFarland could recover the additional $35,000 from Barnes should McFarland become insolvent.

▌DIVIDENDS

Dividends are profits distributed to the stockholders. They are generally payable when the board of directors declares them payable. A dividend must be a given percentage or a fixed amount for each share.

EXAMPLE 2 During its second year of operation, Enveen Petroleum, Inc., earned a profit which enabled the board of directors to declare a $20,000 dividend to its holders of common stock. Each share of common stock would be entitled to an amount determined by dividing the total number of shares of common stock into the $20,000 to be distributed.

Legal Issue No. 3

A dividend can be declared only from profits or from earned surplus. However, directors do not have to declare a dividend even when the corporation has made a profit. If the directors feel the best interests of the company require retaining the profits, they need not declare a dividend. When a dividend is declared, however, it becomes a liability of the corporation, and payment of this dividend can be enforced by the stockholders. The dividend belongs to the stockholders, who are the owners of record on a date set down by the board. A dividend is usually in the form of cash or stock.

EXAMPLE 3 During the Brooktech Corporation's fifth year of operation, a new venture into solar energy resulted in a tremendous increase in profits for the company. As a result, the board of directors declared a dividend to all shareholders of record on February 28. Everyone owning Brooktech shares on February 28 will participate in the dividend, even though they might sell their stock before the dividend is actually distributed.

▌STOCK
▌PURCHASES

A purchaser of stock may possibly buy the stock directly from the corporation or from individual owners of stock.

Purchase by Original Subscription

All stock is originally sold by the corporation itself. At the time the corporation is being organized, the promoters seek subscriptions from interested persons. These **stock subscriptions** are contracts to take stock when the corporation completes its organization and is authorized by the state to sell stock to the public. These subscriptions are similar to any contract to sell, and the subscribers do not become stockholders until the organization is completed and stock certificates are issued to them. The corporation may continue to sell shares after its incorporation is complete, up to the number of shares authorized in its charter.

Stock Transfers

Like any other form of personal property, stock may be transferred or assigned. To be binding on the corporation, however, the transfer must be recorded on the

A stock certificate is proof of ownership of shares of a corporation. Is it a negotiable instrument?

corporate books. The ownership of the stock certificate is essential to owning an interest in the corporation. The law provides that stock ownership is demonstrated by possession of a stock certificate displaying the possessor's name or indorsed to the possessor. Such a person is the legal owner with the power to sell or otherwise dispose of that certificate in any way he or she feels fit.

OPERATION OF A CORPORATION

Ownership of an interest in a corporation is acquired by the purchase of shares of stock. The number of shares you own indicates the extent of your ownership. As the owner of shares of stock, you are a stockholder, or shareholder, and have a right to share in the management, but in a special way. You may attend an annual meeting of shareholders and vote for the directors of your choice. Once elected, the board of directors has the right to manage the company for the next year.

It is the duty of the **directors** to control the overall general policy of the corporation. Immediately after their election, the directors meet to organize the board and to select officers. The **officers** are entrusted with the everyday operation of the company. The directors meet at stated times throughout the year for the purpose of giving general directions to the officers, checking on the general welfare of the corporation, and declaring dividends if any have been earned. Unless directors are also officers, they take no part in the active operation of the business.

The officers have the responsibility of running the business. They, in turn, hire employees and manage the firm as the directors' general agents. In the following discussion, we will use the term *managers* or *management* when referring to officers and directors. Also remember that majority shareholders

```
                    AFFIDAVIT OF LOST STOCK CERTIFICATE

        The undersigned, being of lawful age, first being duly sworn, on
oath states:

1.      That the undersigned is the record owner of 500 shares of common
stock of Toth-VanMeader Chemical Company (Corporation).  The stock appears on
the books and records of the Corporation as certificate number (5293).

2.      The undersigned has made a due and diligent search for the stock
certificate but has lost or misplaced it.  The undersigned warrants and
represents that the stock certificate has not been sold, pledged or
transferred.

3.      As an inducement for the Corporation issuing a duplicate
replacement certificate, the undersigned agrees to fully indemnify the
Corporation for any claim of ownership by any asserted owner or holder of the
original shares.

        Signed under seal this ninth day of September, 19XX.


                                        Catherine Louise Corsi


State of Ohio
County of Cuyahoga                               September 9, 19XX


        Then personally appeared Catherine Louise Corsi who acknowledged the
foregoing, before me.


                                        Mary Peter
                                 Notary Public
```

Stock ownership is demonstrated by possession of a stock certificate displaying the possessor's name or indorsed to the possessor. Consequently, the location of stock certificates is of vital importance. If a stock certificate is lost, the corporation must be informed using an affidavit such as this one.

can and often are directors of the corporation. Frequently, officers are also majority shareholders. In fact, most officers own some stock in the corporation. Thus, although different labels are used here, these people are often one and the same.

SHARE-HOLDER CONTROL

Shareholders who are unhappy with the way the managers are running the corporation have several alternatives available. One alternative is, of course, to sell their shares and buy shares in another corporation. This is not always desirable or even economically feasible. For example, if the value of the stock has fallen, then selling would mean a loss to the shareholder, who would prefer to realize a profit on the original investment. Of course, the shareholder could attempt to convince managers to alter their behavior by changing a decision or dropping a policy that the shareholder finds objectionable. If such an approach is unfeasible, however, the shareholder may have to resort to the two most powerful tools in his arsenal: the power to vote and the right to sue.

Shareholder Voting Power

One way for the shareholder to alter the policy of a corporation is to vote in a new board of directors. The new directors would then, presumably, hire new officers who would be more sympathetic to the dissident shareholder's position (**dissident,** or **insurgent, shareholders** are those shareholders who challenge management). Naturally, dissidents could aim at electing themselves to the board with the objective of later naming themselves as officers. Of course, the shareholder may not own enough shares to have an effect on the election. If the shareholder finds that she or he does not have enough shares to make a difference, she or he can always attempt to purchase more shares to strengthen her or his position. If the shareholder can buy a majority of the shares, then she or he can control the next election. This process is referred to as a **takeover bid.** If the shareholder intends to reorganize the corporation by ousting the present management team, it is generally referred to as an **unfriendly takeover bid.**

If the shareholder does not have enough capital to mount the necessary takeover bid, or if that shareholder cannot find enough shares available for sale, then other alternatives are available. These alternatives include proxy voting, shareholder proposals, pooling agreements, and voting trusts.

Proxy Voting If a shareholder does not own enough stock to elect his or her own board of directors, he or she can ''solicit the proxies'' of other shareholders. A **proxy** is the right to vote another shareholder's stock. The **proxy solicitation process** occurs when the dissident shareholder asks other shareholders if they will transfer their votes to him or her. The more proxies the dissident obtains, the greater his or her voting power becomes. Naturally, majority shareholders representing and often including management also can engage in this proxy solicitation process. This often sets up a battle called a **proxy contest** between the insurgents and the majority shareholders representing management. Proxy solicitations involving large, publicly held corporations are closely regulated by the Securities and Exchange Commission (SEC). SEC regulations require both dissidents and majority shareholders to send written proxy solicitations to shareholders. These written proxy solicitations must include certain information specified in the regulations. Some of this information includes: (1) background data on corporate directors or nominees to corporate directorships, (2) the amount of stock owned by directors and officers, (3) executive compensation, (4) potential conflicts of interest, and (5) the identities of the dissidents. In addition, the SEC specifically forbids including any false or misleading information in the solicitation or excluding any material (extremely important) information that would be needed by shareholders. Finally, the regulations say that the written proxy solicitation must be submitted to the SEC at least 10 days before it is sent to shareholders.

Legal Issue No. 4

EXAMPLE 4 Phil Winfrey, a dissident shareholder in the Brin-Midland Corporation, vigorously opposed a management decision to discontinue the corporation's role of providing a sophisticated guidance system for the space program. Since Winfrey clearly did not have enough stock of his own to outvote management, and since he did not have enough capital to buy a sufficient number of shares to increase his voting power, he decided to launch a proxy solicitation campaign. In preparing his written proxy solicitation, Winfrey neglected to mention that he owned a company that sold component parts to Brin-Midland for use in the guidance system. The management of Brin-Midland discovered Winfrey's plan and filed a complaint in federal court asking for an

Graphic Scanning Inc. Faces Fight By Group To Oust Its Directors

By a WALL STREET JOURNAL Staff Reporter

WASHINGTON — A shareholder group led by Lafer Amster & Co., a New York brokerage concern, said it plans to mount a proxy contest to oust Graphic Scanning Corp.'s board.

The group, which holds the equivalent of a 12.6% stake in the Teaneck, N.J., telecommunications concern, said in two Securities and Exchange Commission filings that it opposes an agreement between Graphic Scanning and its chairman, Barry Yampol. The accord provides for Mr. Yampol to acquire interests in some of the loss-plagued company's businesses.

The group said it believes the agreement "is illegal and grossly unfair to stockholders" other than Mr. Yampol.

Two members of the group also filed a suit in federal court in New York alleging that Mr. Yampol and four Graphic Scanning directors embarked on an illegal scheme to systematically "strip" the company of certain assets. The suit seeks a permanent injunction barring the defendants from selling Graphic Scanning's assets outside the ordinary course of business until a stockholders meeting is held.

According to the findings, the group also filed a complaint in a Delaware court asking it to compel Graphic Scanning to hold an annual meeting to elect directors.

Graphic Scanning declined to comment.

The company, which also has been plagued by regulatory troubles, said last month that it had struck an agreement under which Mr. Yampol would buy interests in some of its businesses. Graphic Scanning also has promised severance payments to certain top executives if the company is acquired or its businesses sold and their jobs are terminated.

1. Identify the dissident shareholder group in the story.
2. What formalities will the dissident shareholders have to go through to fulfill SEC requirements regarding their proxy solicitations?
3. What tactics will the management group use to defeat the dissidents' action?
4. What other voting options are available to the dissidents?
5. Is the suit filed by the dissidents direct or derivative?
6. Would the Business Judgment Rule or the Fairness Rule be used by the court to judge the conduct of the managers?

injunction to prevent Winfrey from mailing his proxy solicitation. Brin-Midland was successful in stopping Winfrey. The court declared that Winfrey's sale of component parts to Brin-Midland for the space program was a material fact that had to be included in the solicitation before it could be mailed to shareholders.

Shareholder Proposals A **shareholder proposal** is a method of exerting shareholder influence that falls short of a proxy solicitation but which allows a dissident shareholder the opportunity to affect the running of the corporation. Under SEC rules, certain shareholders of large, publicly owned corporations can compel management to include their proposals on the agenda of any shareholders' meeting. As long as the written proposal follows the timing and length requirements of the SEC, and as long as it is about an issue that involves all shareholders, management must include the proposal. Still, managers have a great deal of leeway here. If, for example, they feel the proposal is out of line because it involves a personal attack or something outside corporate business, they can reject the proposal. However, all rejected proposals must be reported to the SEC, along with an explanation of the rejection.

EXAMPLE 5 Jane Cummings owned 1 percent of Applied Eurotec stock. She felt a change in the bylaws of Applied Eurotec was needed to allow common shareholders more access to the board of directors. Cummings gave management a 500-word proposal 120 days before the annual shareholder meeting. Because Cummings had met all SEC guidelines and because her proposal involved all shareholders, the board had to include it on the agenda of the next shareholders' meeting.

Pooling Agreements **Pooling agreements,** also called **shareholder agreements** or **voting agreements,** involve a group of shareholders who join together and agree to vote the same way on a particular issue. Pooling agreements differ from proxies in that individual shareholders still retain control of their own votes. Generally, pooling agreements are upheld by the court, usually under ordinary contract rules.

Voting Trusts A **voting trust** is the most powerful voting tool available to shareholders. Under the terms of a voting trust, shareholders transfer their voting rights to a trustee. Sometimes the trustee is a shareholder member of the trust, and sometimes the trustee is an outsider. The voting trust is generally irrevocable (cannot be changed) for a specified period of time. Although there are limits to the duration of a voting trust, those limits are usually quite long. Most state limits run from 10 to 21 years. Voting trusts must be in writing and must be filed with the corporation. Shareholders retain all other rights in relation to the stock, including the right to receive dividends. (See Table 36-2.)

Shareholder's Right to Sue

Legal Issue No. 5

Shareholders have another right which has recently become more and more popular. This is the right to sue management to compel a change in direction or to force management to rescind a decision. Two types of suits are available to shareholders: direct and derivative suits. When faced with either type of suit, the courts have various standards which measure the performance of managers.

TABLE 36-2
SHAREHOLDER VOTING POWER

Voting Power	Definition
Proxy	One shareholder votes in place of another; regulated by SEC.
Shareholder Proposal	One shareholder adds proposal to annual shareholders' meeting agenda; regulated by SEC.
Pooling Agreement	Shareholders agree to vote the same way; each retains own stock.
Voting Trust	Right to vote shares turned over to a trustee; usually irrevocable; time limit: 10 to 21 years.

The two most prominent standards involve management's duty of loyalty and its duty of due care.

Direct Suits   A **direct suit** is brought by shareholders who believe they have been deprived of a right that belongs to them simply because they are shareholders. For example, shareholders have a right to vote, the right to receive dividends, and the right of access to corporate records. If shareholders have been denied any of these rights, considered an integral part of the status of shareholder, they can bring a direct suit to make up for any loss they have suffered.

Derivative Suit   A **derivative suit** involves a peculiar approach to the law which allows shareholders to sue corporate management on behalf of the corporation. In other words, a derivative suit is not based on a direct injury to shareholders. Rather, the suit is based on an injury to the corporation. The shareholders' right to sue is derived from the injury to the corporation, hence the label *derivative*.

Derivative suits are more difficult to bring than direct suits because certain prerequisites must be met before the shareholder is eligible. One prerequisite is that the shareholder must exhaust internal remedies. In other words, before bringing suit, the shareholder must attempt to resolve the dispute by communicating directly with the board of directors and with other shareholders. If these internal remedies do not work, then the shareholder can bring the derivative suit on behalf of the corporation. Generally, if the shareholder wins the suit, then management must pay damages to the corporation. The shareholder also would be entitled to reimbursement for the money he or she spent on the lawsuit.

EXAMPLE 6   Charles Herrera was a shareholder in the Hybritrust Corporation. Herrera discovered that the chief executive officer of Hybritrust, Ron Sloan, had the corporation purchase large tracts of overvalued real estate. Herrera later found out that the real estate had been owned by Sloan's wife. After exhausting internal remedies, Herrera brought a derivative suit asking the court to compel Sloan to transfer his profits on the real estate deal into Hybritrust's treasury.

MANAGEMENT DUTIES

The preceding example introduces an interesting question. When faced with a shareholder suit, how are the courts to measure the performance of management? Courts use several standards, but the two most common involve the duty of due care and the duty of loyalty.

Duty of Due Care

The **duty of due care** means that corporate managers must exercise proper skill and good judgment in running the corporation. Generally, the court will explore the issue of due care by asking whether the managers would have acted the same way if the matter in dispute had involved their own personal interests. The standard is an objective one, based on reasonable care. Naturally, a manager is not expected to be either Superman or Wonder Woman. However, he or she is required to be just as careful with corporate business as he or she would be with his or her own money and property. The rule usually employed to articulate this concept is the Business Judgment Rule. Under the **Business Judgment Rule,** if a manager has acted in good faith and has done nothing illegal, then his or her decision will stand. (See Table 36-3.)

Duty of Loyalty

A different situation arises if the manager has somehow personally benefited from a corporate decision. Such a transaction is immediately suspect, since all managers owe a duty of loyalty to the corporation and its shareholders. The **duty of loyalty** requires managers to put the interests of the corporation above their own interests. Thus, when managers enter contracts with the corporation or when managers take opportunities which the corporation could have taken itself, a different standard is used to judge their behavior. The rule used is known as the Fairness Rule. The **Fairness Rule** requires that managers be fair to the corporation when they are self-dealing. How fairness is measured is, of course, problematical at best. At a minimum, it requires corporate managers to disclose all material information when they enter contracts with the corporation. It also requires them to offer opportunities to the corporation before they take

TABLE 36-3 A CORPORATE MANAGER'S DUTIES		
Duty	Definition	Rule
Duty of due care	Corporate managers must exercise proper skill and good judgment.	Business Judgment Rule says corporate decisions stand if legal and made in good faith.
Duty of loyalty	Corporate managers must place the interests of the corporation above their own interests.	If a corporate manager benefits from a deal, the duty of loyalty is called into question and the Fairness Rule is used.

advantage of those opportunities themselves. Beyond these simple guidelines, however, fairness is a relative standard that must be judged on a case-by-case basis.

Suggestions for Reducing Legal Risks

1. When you buy stock, make certain that you know what type of stock you are purchasing, because different types of stocks give shareholders different rights.
2. When, as a shareholder, you are dissatisfied with management decisions, explore all avenues of shareholder voting control, including proxies, shareholder proposals, pooling agreements, and voting trusts.
3. If you are entering a proxy contest, make certain that you pay close attention to SEC regulations.
4. When, as a stockholder, you are dissatisfied with management decisions, you can also explore the possibility of filing a shareholder suit.
5. If filing a shareholder derivative suit, make certain to exhaust internal remedies first. Direct suits do not require this step.

Language of the Law

Define or explain each of the following words or phrases:

shareholder
stock
par value stock
no par value stock
common stock
preferred stock
treasury stock
watered, or discounted, stock
dividends

stock subscription
directors
officers
dissident, or insurgent, shareholders
takeover bid
unfriendly takeover bid
proxy

proxy solicitation process
proxy contest
shareholder proposal
pooling agreement, shareholder agreement, or voting agreement
voting trust
direct suit

derivative suit
duty of due care
Business Judgment Rule
duty of loyalty
Fairness Rule

Questions for Review

1. What is the most usual type of stock issued by a corporation?
2. A corporation is generally controlled by holders of which type of stock? Explain how this control is evidenced.
3. What are the usual preferences given to holders of preferred stock?
4. From what sources can a person purchase shares of stock?

5. Distinguish between the directors and the officers of a corporation.
6. What alternatives are open to shareholders who are unhappy with the way the managers are running the corporation?
7. How does the SEC monitor the proxy solicitation process?
8. In addition to proxy voting, what other voting strategies are open to shareholders?

9. Explain the distinction between a direct suit and a derivative suit brought by the shareholders of a corporation.

10. Explain the Business Judgment Rule. Explain the Fairness Rule.

Cases in Point

In each of the following cases, give your decision and state a legal principle that applies to the case:

1. Ralph Braden was a stockholder in the Perrin-Norton Aerospace Corporation. For several years, Braden received no dividends. He was particularly upset because a friend of his, Tom Foster, who also owned Perrin-Norton stock, received payments each year for the last 5 years. What type of stock did Braden probably own? To increase his chances of receiving a return on his investment, what type of stock would you recommend Braden buy? Explain.

2. Tammy Rouse owned 60 shares of Ogintech International, Inc. Ogintech declared a dividend payment on March 17 to be mailed to shareholders on March 21. Rouse sold her 60 shares to Chad Washington on March 19. When the dividend arrived on March 24, Washington claimed it belonged to him, since he now owned the stock. Is Washington correct in his claim?

3. David Woodward bought 100 shares of common stock in Cornell-Waltey, Inc. He is extremely unhappy with a recent policy change which calls for the closing of several plants in the Northeast. Woodward believes the change will cause a loss of profits and a drop in his yearly dividends. What options are available to Woodward besides exercising his voting power or bringing a suit against the corporation.

4. Aurora Serna was a minority shareholder in International Biotech, Inc. The Biotech board of directors decided to commit several hundred million dollars to oceanic farming. Serna believed this was a singularly foolish idea and was afraid she would lose her multimillion dollar investment. She did not want to sell her stock because, if she did so, she would lose a great deal of money. On the bright side, Serna is an extremely wealthy woman with a seemingly endless bankroll. Explain the options available to Serna.

5. Kate Stowe believed that her investment in the Lauderbaugh Media Group, Inc., was threatened by several extremely risky investments by the chief executive officer. Lacking the capital to mount a successful takeover bid, Stowe decided to begin a proxy contest. Her first step was to send telegrams to all the Lauderbaugh shareholders she knew personally, asking them for their votes. When the directors of Lauderbaugh discovered what Stowe had done, they filed a complaint with the SEC. On what grounds might the Lauderbaugh management have complained about Stowe's actions?

6. When stock in Howell Petroleum was priced at $30 a share, Raymond Ziegler bought 100 shares. Since that time, Howell Petroleum stock has dropped in value to an all-time low of $5 per share. Ziegler is convinced that the cause of the drop is Howell's hiring of Klaus Miller as chief executive officer. Ziegler and Miller have had a personality conflict for years, and since Ziegler cannot stand Miller, he naturally blames Miller for all Howell's problems. In an attempt to set things right, Ziegler submits a shareholder proposal to the Howell board of directors calling for Miller's removal from office. Will the board be compelled to present this proposal at the next shareholders' meeting?

7. Vanessa Rae Sanders, Gary Fox, and Mary Lepley were minority shareholders in the Lexington Steel Corporation. To consolidate their power, they decided to form a voting trust which would last for 40 years. To keep the agreement secret from management, they decided not to put the deal in writing and not to tell anyone at corporate headquarters. Have Sanders, Fox, and Lepley formed a valid, binding voting trust? Explain.

8. Jake Fuller owned several hundred shares of stock in Janson-Phillips Technical Regeneration, Inc. Janson-Phillips had not declared a dividend for 5 years, despite enormous profits. The management of Janson-Phillips consistently promised dividends, yet just as consistently failed to deliver. Upset by this turn of events, Fuller decided to sue the corporation, demanding a payment of dividends. When Fuller told his plan to Todd Fairfield, one of the directors, Fairfield told him that he could not sue until he had exhausted internal remedies. Is Fairfield correct? Explain.

9. Oberlander Film Processing, Inc., was engaged in the recovery of silver from used negatives. Patricia Robinson was chief executive officer of Oberlander. Robinson also owned a photography studio which sold used negatives to Oberlander. Justine Shepherd, a shareholder in Oberlander, discovered that Robinson was overcharging the corporation for the used negatives. When she went to the board of directors and the other shareholders and demanded an investigation, her pleas fell on deaf ears. As a result, Shepherd brought suit to compel Robinson to return her exorbitant profits to the corporation. What type of suit did Shepherd bring? What rule will be used to judge Robinson's conduct? Why?

10. Barbara Kessler was the chairman of the board and majority stockholder of the Cutler City Crusaders, a professional football team. The Crusaders played their games in an open-air stadium owned by the Crusaders corporation. Brian Otto was a minority shareholder in the Crusaders who believed that the Crusaders should construct a domed stadium. Otto contended that the open-air stadium was causing the Crusaders to lose money because attendance disappeared when the cold winter weather arrived. Kessler disagreed, stating, "Football is meant to be played outdoors." Otto brought suit to compel the construction of the domed stadium. What standard will be used to judge Kessler's decision?

Cases to Judge

1. Mills, an Autolite shareholder, complained that a proxy solicitation sent by management contained false information. He took his case to federal court, where an appeals court eventually ruled against him. The appeals court admitted that the statements were false, but said that as long as management could show that the shareholders would have voted for them anyway, then the vote would stand. Mills argued that a false proxy solicitation is illegal regardless of the outcome of the vote. He took his argument to the U.S. Supreme Court. Should the Court rule in his favor?

Mills v. Electric Autolite Co., 396 U.S. 375 (United States)

2. Charlotte Horowitz was angry about a shareholder vote that had amended the charter of the Martin Marietta Corporation. Horowitz claimed that management's proxy solicitation had not told shareholders that several lawsuits had been filed against them. When Horowitz took the matter to court, the managers, including Thomas Pownall, argued that the suits were not important enough to be included in the proxy solicitation. Horowitz argued that the suits were important

because they showed that someone had questioned the managers' competence and integrity. Is Horowitz correct? *Horowitz v. Pownall*, 616 F. Supp. 250 (Maryland)

3. Several shareholder derivative suits were brought by shareholders against the officers and directors of Public Service Company of New Hampshire. The purpose of the suit was to block the construction of a nuclear power plant. Only one of the shareholders, Robert Markewich, had attempted to exhaust internal remedies. Markewich had written several letters to the board, complaining about the cost of the plant. The board denied him a personal appearance at the board meeting and said they planned to proceed with the project. Markewich sent another letter indicating his intent to sue. The board indicated to Markewich that they had referred the matter to their attorney and would discuss it at an upcoming meeting. Markewich did not wait for a response, but filed the suit. Was Markewich's letter a sufficient demand on directors so that he had exhausted internal remedies? *Seidel v. Public Service Company of New Hampshire*, 616 F. Supp. 1342 (New Hampshire)

4. Several Marathon Oil shareholders were convinced that they had been cheated by management's agreement to merge Marathon Oil with U.S. Steel. Two of these shareholders, Irving and Charlotte Radol, brought a direct suit against the directors of Marathon. The Radols claimed that the directors had received promises from U.S. Steel that they would retain their jobs after the merger. The Radols argued that since the directors personally benefited from the deal, the Fairness Rule should be used to judge their conduct. The directors argued the desire to retain their jobs did *not* qualify as a breach of loyalty. Thus they concluded that the Business Judgment Rule should be used to gauge their behavior. Are the directors correct? *Radol v. Thomas*, 772 F.2d 244 (6th Circuit)

5. Norman Reisig, a shareholder in Normat Industries, Inc., became suspicious when the president of the company, Matthew Carter, indicated continuing delays in the construction of a condominium project which was Normat's primary business. Reisig's suspicions deepened when he discovered that the buildings were only 65 percent completed and that the company owed more than $25,000 in construction fees despite a recent $200,000 loan. Further investigation revealed that Carter had used the $200,000 to pay for personal expenses, including entertainment. Reisig brought suit, claiming Carter had breached his duty of loyalty to the company. Is Reisig correct? *Normat Industries, Inc. v. Carter*, 477 So. 2d 783 (Louisiana)

Chapter 37

GOVERNMENT REGULATION AND CORPORATE EXPANSION

Scene: Outside Ernie's apartment. Ernie is sitting on his front steps shaking his head in disgust. Jennifer approaches.

Jennifer: You look like you've got trouble again.

Ernie: Trouble is my middle name.

Jennifer: What happened this time?

Ernie: All my investments went up in smoke!

Jennifer: Oh no, and you were so sure of things.

Ernie: Too sure.

Jennifer: Well, what went wrong?

Ernie: Do you remember that Kaplan Industries stock I bought?

Jennifer: Sure, Kaplan makes sports equipment.

Ernie: Kaplan doesn't make sports equipment.

Jennifer: What do they make?

Ernie: That's just the point. They don't make anything.

Jennifer: How can that be?

Ernie: They're a phoney company. They don't exist. That stock sale was a big fraud.

Jennifer: Oh, no.

Ernie: Oh, yes.

Jennifer: Isn't there some way to check on those things?

Ernie: Nope. You just have to take their word for it.

Jennifer: That's too bad.

Ernie: You're telling me. I lost a bundle on that deal. But I lost more on the Digitech deal.

Jennifer: Digitech?

Ernie: Boy, did I goof there. I bought stock at $30 a share and now it's worth $5.

Jennifer: That's horrible. I'll bet you were mad.

Ernie: I was furious, especially since it was all because some guy on the inside knew more than the rest of us.

Jennifer: I don't understand.

Ernie: Some vice president knew that Digitech was going to lose a big government contract, so he told all his friends and they sold their stock and everybody panicked. It was crazy. Digitech stock fell like a rock.

Jennifer: I don't think that's fair.

Ernie: It's business. It doesn't have to be fair.

Jennifer: Still, you'd think the government would do something about it.

Ernie: Oh, the government does plenty. Only everything they do hurts my bankroll!

Jennifer: Like what?

Ernie: Like coming down hard on Applied Techtronics.

Jennifer: Who's that?

Ernie: My other big investment.

Jennifer: What did they do wrong?

Ernie: Search me. Something about interlocking directorates.

Jennifer: Sounds to me like you've had your fair share of bad luck.

Ernie: There's more.

Jennifer: More?

Ernie: The construction company that was making me such a big dividend merged with another company and nobody even asked me.

Jennifer: Can't you do something?

Ernie: Sure.

Jennifer: What?

Ernie: Go back to being a waiter. At least there I got tips that were worth something.

LEGAL ISSUES

1. Is there any government mechanism in place for helping investors learn about stocks *before* they invest?
2. Is there any law to prevent a company "insider" from cashing in on "inside information" about the company's stock?
3. Is there any law against interlocking directorates?
4. Do shareholders have to be consulted before one company merges with another?

THE SPIRIT OF THE LAW   In Chapter 36 we examined the operation of a corporation and discussed the various techniques available to shareholders for participating in that operation. Many of these devices are also designed to curb the power of corporate managers. Sometimes, however, the activities of a corporation cannot be effectively controlled by the shareholders. In fact, sometimes even the shareholders are willing participants in some unjust or illegal activity. When this occurs, it is up to some third party to step into the fray. This task, quite naturally, falls to the government. In this chapter we discuss some of the techniques the government uses to regulate corporate activities. One activity that is especially in need of regulation is the process of corporate expansion. The chapter ends with a look at this timely topic.

THE POWER TO REGULATE BUSINESS

The federal government derives its power to regulate business from the **commerce clause** of the U.S. Constitution. This clause states that Congress shall have the power to regulate commerce "among the several states." Under this clause, the federal government has the power to regulate interstate commerce.

The Securities and Exchange Commission

After the stock market crash of 1929, many experts identified one cause of the disaster as the sale and purchase of worthless securities which led many people to invest large amounts of money all to no avail. To combat this problem, Congress passed the Securities Act of 1933 and the Securities Exchange Act of 1934. The primary purpose of these acts is to protect investors by keeping them informed of the true nature of the securities in which they invest and by providing a mechanism to discover fraud and unfair manipulation. The independent regulatory agency that carries out this function is called the **Securities and Exchange Commission (SEC).**

Definition of a Security The SEC regulates the sale of all securities sold in interstate commerce as well as all stock exchanges doing an interstate business. The Securities Act of 1933 defines a **security** as a money investment which expects a return solely because of another person's efforts. Calling a security by another name does not change its essential nature.

EXAMPLE 1 The directors of Kemp-Calloway Petroleum were concerned about falling oil prices and a severe drain on their reserve capital. Ruth Barberton, the chief executive officer of Kemp-Calloway, devised a scheme whereby the firm would sell off tracts of land in its oil fields under a series of land contracts. In return, the purchaser of each land contract would be entitled to a return on his or her investment based on the year-end profits in proportion to the amount of land he or she owned. The SEC claimed each land investment was a security and thus fell under its jurisdiction. The court held that when the people bought the land, they intended to make a profit on their investment. Because this profit was derived solely from the efforts of others, the investment was, indeed, a security, not a simple land purchase.

Legal Issue No. 1

Registration Requirements As stated earlier, one of the most crucial functions of the SEC is to inform potential investors about the true nature of their investment opportunities. One way this is accomplished is through the registration requirement. Under this requirement, any company that falls under SEC jurisdiction must file a registration statement and a prospectus with the SEC before it can offer securities for sale. The **registration statement** includes details about the securities and about the business making the offer. The **prospectus** contains a condensed view of the information in the registration statement. The prospectus is given to investors. The corporation cannot offer its stock for sale until the SEC has approved the registration statement. This approval, how-

"Futures on pork bellies" are contracts to buy and sell hogs at a guaranteed price at some future date. Future contracts can be resold. Such investments are highly risky, since a small change in the expected price of hogs can cause a very large change in the value of the future contract. Would the purchase of a future be considered a "security" to the SEC? What would you expect to find in the "info kit" offered by the Chicago Mercantile Exchange?

New options soothe the savage beast.

Pork belly futures are not easy to tame. But now you can trade them with total control of the amount you have at risk. Introducing options on pork belly futures contracts, at the Chicago Mercantile Exchange.

Pork bellies have always been the ultimate test for the trader. No futures contract you can name moves faster. So, if your judgement is good, if your timing is right, pork bellies can pay off about as quickly as any investment around.

Options on pork belly futures let you protect yourself while you participate. Because they limit the amount you have at risk. (All futures and options are for people who can afford risk.)

And the combination of futures and options gives you a whole new set of strategies. Helps you make the most of most every market situation.

Get the whole story. Call The Merc for our free info kit: Heads you win, Tails you win.

CHICAGO MERCANTILE EXCHANGE

ever, simply means that the corporation has supplied all the information required by the SEC. It is not an endorsement of the security by the SEC.

EXAMPLE 2 Global Ocean Engineering and Farming, Inc., presented a registration statement to the SEC which indicated that Global Ocean intended to offer stock for sale. The registration statement indicated that Global Ocean intended to establish a domed city on the floor of the Atlantic Ocean. The city would serve as a mining and farming base and would eventually become a resort area. Global Ocean admitted that the technology to build the submerged city did not presently exist and that it was not likely to exist within the next 50 years. The registration statement also indicated that, for this and other reasons, the investment was very risky. In addition, the registration statement admitted that the firm had no engineers on their payroll but was actually staffed by science fiction writers. Despite all of this, the SEC approved Global Ocean's registration statement. The primary purpose of the SEC's registration requirement is to ensure that true information gets to investors. The SEC does not decide the value of a particular stock offering. In this case, the facts behind Global Ocean ought to speak for themselves.

A violation of the registration statement requirements by failing to file or by filing false information is punishable by fines and imprisonment. In addition, the SEC and the injured investors can bring suit. The SEC also can seek an injunction to stop an offering already in progress. An *injunction* is a court order which stops someone from doing something. In addition, the SEC has certain administrative remedies available.

The registration process just outlined applies only to **new stock issues.** (A new stock issue is the first time new stock is offered for sale.) The SEC also functions as a watchdog over trading on the stock exchange. It also regulates other corporate activities, including proxy solicitations (see Chapter 36) and insider trading.

Insider Trading Another objective of the SEC is to make certain that trading in securities is as open and aboveboard as possible. Thus the SEC seeks to shortcircuit any attempt by insiders (corporate managers, officers, majority shareholders, and so on) to use "inside information" to profit personally. This process is known as **insider trading.** Under SEC regulations, insiders who have important knowledge about some material aspect of a stock sale must either make that knowledge public or refrain from trading in the stock themselves and from giving the inside information to a select few individuals. A material aspect is, of course, something of extreme importance to the sale.

Legal Issue No. 2

EXAMPLE 3 Russell Sturgeon was chief executive officer of Atavatron Industries. As chief executive officer, Sturgeon knew that Stimens, Inc., the company's primary customer, was about to obtain an enormous government project. The project meant that Atavatron would sell millions of dollars of equipment to Stimens. As a result, Atavatron would have to open three new plants and hire over 2,500 employees. Naturally, Atavatron stock would sky-rocket in value on the stock exchange. Before the news of Stimens' contract became public, Sturgeon bought hundreds of shares of stock in Atavatron at incredibly low prices. Moreover, he urged his family and friends to do likewise. Under these circumstances, Sturgeon is clearly violating the SEC's prohibition against insider trading.

A violation of insider trading regulations can result in a severe fine. The maximum criminal penalty is $100,000. Damages, however, can be a lot more, since whatever amount investors lose can be tripled when damages are awarded by the court.

Antitrust Laws

During the late 1800s, many large corporations in the United States formed huge trusts that gained control of entire industries. These trusts were called **monopolies** because they had no competition. The Sugar Trust, formed in 1887, is a well-known example. In 1890, the Sherman Antitrust Act was passed by Congress in an attempt to stop the formation of monopolies. This act stated: "Every contract, combination . . . or conspiracy in restraint of trade or commerce among the states . . . is hereby declared to be illegal." It did not make any specific activities illegal; instead, it allowed the courts to decide in this regard.

EXAMPLE 4 Four large milk distributors entered into an agreement to sell milk at a price to be determined by a committee appointed by them. When one of the distributors, Star Dairies, cut the price to customers, the other distributors sought to recover damages because Star Dairies had violated the agreement. It was held that this agreement was not enforceable because it resulted in an illegal monopoly.

The Sherman Antitrust Act halted the growth of monopolies for a short period of time. However, a decision by the U.S. Supreme Court had the effect of encouraging the growth of monopolies once again. The Court held that contracts or combinations would be illegal only if they formed an "unreasonable restraint of trade."

In order to strengthen the Sherman Antitrust Act, Congress passed the Clayton Act in 1914. Unlike the Sherman Antitrust Act, the Clayton Act made specific practices illegal. It became illegal, for example, to sell the same goods to one company for less than the price charged to another company if the effect was to lessen competition. It also became illegal to sell goods on the condition that the buyer would not buy products from the seller's competitors. The practice of requiring buyers to purchase certain undesirable goods in order to buy more desirable merchandise became illegal. In addition, interlocking directorates were outlawed. **Interlocking directorates** occur when two or more competing companies are controlled by the same board of directors. Mergers of corporations, if the effect was to lessen competition, also became illegal.

Legal Issue No. 3

Theodore Roosevelt earned the name "trust buster" because he opposed "bad trusts," those which used their size to impose unreasonable business practices. Today's laws offer specific rules aimed at uniform enforcement to maintain a competitive marketplace.

At the same time that Congress passed the Clayton Act, it also passed the Federal Trade Commission Act. This act was initially designed to protect business firms from the wrongful acts of another business firm. The act stated: "Unfair methods of competition in commerce are hereby declared unlawful." The Federal Trade Commission Act does not define an unfair method of competition; instead, it allows the courts to determine unfair practices on an individual basis. The act also created the **Federal Trade Commission (FTC).** The job of this agency is to investigate alleged unfair methods of competition and to prevent businesses from violating the Federal Trade Commission Act.

In 1936, Congress again made changes in the law by passing the Robinson-Patman Act. This act made it illegal for companies to sell goods at lower prices to high-volume purchasers without offering the same discount to smaller purchasers.

EXAMPLE 5 A small, independent grocery store bought 2 cases of canned tomatoes from its supplier. On the same day, a large chain store on the same street bought 100 cases of the same brand of tomatoes from the same supplier. Under the Robinson-Patman Act, the supplier could not charge the chain store less money for each case of tomatoes than it charged the small store.

The Robinson-Patman Act is not limited to discrimination in pricing. In general, under the act, sellers are charged with the responsibility of treating all buyers equally. Any special frauds, such as preferential delivery schedules that help one seller and hurt others, have been outlawed.

EXAMPLE 6 Westbury-Moritz always made certain that the ELKO Corporation received its oil shipment from Westbury-Moritz before any of its competitors. When Rossini, Inc., discovered that it had lost several customers due to this discriminatory practice, it filed suit against Westbury-Moritz claiming a violation of the Robinson-Patman Act. The court agreed and awarded damages to Rossini.

The Federal Trade Commission Act was amended in 1938 (the Wheeler-Lea Amendment) and again in 1975 to provide protection to the consumer as well as to the business person. The act now says: "Unfair methods of competition in or affecting commerce, and unfair or deceptive acts or practices in or affecting commerce are hereby declared unlawful." The FTC was also given the power to make rules and regulations. These rules and regulations state specific activities that are considered to be unfair and deceptive.

Racketeer-Influenced and Corrupt Organizations Act

One federal statute which has become increasingly more powerful over the last few years is the Racketeer-Influenced and Corrupt Organizations Act (RICO). To respond to what it perceived as a crisis in corporate activity, Congress passed RICO in 1970. The crisis that troubled Congress was the entry of criminal elements into ordinary corporate ventures. To counteract this troubling trend, RICO made it a violation of federal law to get involved in any business venture through "a pattern of racketeering activities." Although *racketeering activities* sounds sinister, such activities are really quite commonplace. A pattern of racketeering activities requires at least two separate violations of law. For example, one mail-fraud violation and one wire-fraud violation would constitute a pattern of racketeering activities. With such a broad interpretation of racketeering activities, many actions that might have gone unpunished have become subject to federal suits. The government can bring suit under RICO. This category includes state, county, and local government. Also, private individuals can bring RICO suits. The advantages of bringing a suit under RICO include triple damages and the possibility of being awarded attorney's fees.

EXAMPLE 7 The Melrose-Ziegler Financial Network fraudulently induced several hundred investors to purchase real estate in Antarctica for the avowed purpose of establishing a geothermal power plant to provide electric power for the southern coast of Australia. The offer to purchase came through several mailings. In addition, numerous phone calls were made and hundreds of telegrams were sent to the investors. When the fraud was uncovered, the investors brought suit against Melrose-Ziegler under RICO. They collected triple damages and were awarded attorney's fees. Melrose-Ziegler had violated mail-fraud and wire-fraud statutes. These violations brought their case under the jurisdiction of RICO.

Other Federal Statutes

Several other federal statutes have gained prominence over the last few years, as the government exerts more influence over the operation of corporations and other business ventures. These statutes include the Currency Transaction Reporting Act and the Foreign Corrupt Practices Act.

The Currency Transaction Reporting Act Under the Currency Transaction Reporting Act, all financial institutions are required to report to the Internal Revenue Service (IRS) whenever a client deposits, withdraws, transfers, or otherwise handles coins or currency that amount to $10,000 or more. The form used in this reporting process is known as a **currency transaction report (CTR).** A CTR includes the identity of the agent who dealt directly with the bank in the transaction, the identity of the principal, and what the agent actually did at the bank. If the Currency Transaction Reporting Act is violated, criminal sanctions can result and the money involved could be confiscated by the government. The avowed purpose of this act involves the government's function as "watchdog" of business activity. The government wants to keep a close eye on corporations and corporate executives to keep them responsible and to avoid, as much as possible, even the appearance of impropriety. The problem with this law and others like it is that simple things that most people would not see as illegal activities may actually be illegal.

EXAMPLE 8 At 9 a.m. on a Monday, Aaron Boyd, vice president of Sunyoger Used Antique Cars, withdraws $4,000 cash from the company's account at Preston Financial Bank (PFB). Later that day, Boyd is given a once-in-a-lifetime offer to purchase a vintage 1964 Mustang from Basil Whitmore. However, Whitmore demands $7,000 in cash by 3 p.m. that day to finalize the deal. Boyd withdraws the $7,000 cash from PFB.

Although Boyd withdrew the cash on two separate occasions that day, the bank must still file a CTR within 15 days since the amount of the two transactions exceeds $10,000. Failure to file a CTR would violate the Currency Transaction Reporting Act.

A bank may exempt certain established depositors with existing accounts at the bank from the CTR filing requirement. Some of these exceptions include depositors who operate retail stores, sports arenas, amusement parks, and restaurants. Transactions by the government may also be exempted. However, some institutions, such as car dealerships, can never be exempted. Finally, although the primary duty to file CTRs lies with the financial institution, an individual will violate federal law if he or she falsifies information on a CTR or prevents a CTR from being filed.

The Foreign Corrupt Practices Act   The Foreign Corrupt Practices Act was passed by Congress in 1977. The act imposes strict accounting standards on corporations that have factories and offices in foreign countries. The objective of these strict accounting procedures is to make it virtually impossible for corporate executives to hand out bribes to foreign government officials and foreign executives without detection. The act was passed by Congress in response to what the government perceived as a crisis caused by the proliferation of bribery in foreign nations.

CORPORATE EXPANSION

Corporations rarely stay the same size forever. Either they grow and expand, or they shrink until they disappear or are absorbed by some larger, usually healthier enterprise. Like all other corporate ventures, corporate expansions are carefully scrutinized from within and from without. The chief methods of corporate expansion include merger, consolidation, asset acquisition, and stock acquisition.

Merger and Consolidation

Merger and consolidation really amount to the same thing today. However, some distinctions are still evident. In a **merger,** the acquired company agrees to "merge" into another corporation. In a **consolidation,** however, both former corporations disappear and a new corporation is created. In both mergers and consolidations, approval must be obtained from both boards and both groups of shareholders. Generally, a two-thirds majority of the shareholders is required, although under some state statutes the requirement can go as high as four-fifths. Those shareholders who dissent are entitled to be paid for their stock if they desire to pull out of the new venture. Often, dissenters are required to give written notice of their dissent before a vote is taken. One reason for this requirement is that the cost of purchasing the dissenters' stock must be taken into consideration as part of the cost of the merger. Most states will scrutinize mergers for fairness. Sometimes the state will set aside a merger as unjust. Another disadvantage of a merger is that, unlike asset acquisitions, debt flows to the new or surviving corporation. Moreover, other liabilities can flow to the new corporation. Some of these liabilities include potential suits for product defects or for toxic waste dumps.

Legal Issue No. 4

TABLE 37-1
CORPORATE EXPANSION TECHNIQUES

Expansion Format	Definition	Requirements	Liabilities
Merger and Consolidation	In merger, one company "merges" with another; in consolidation, two companies merge and a new company results.	Approval by boards and shareholders of both corporations.	Debts and product liability flow to the new or surviving company.
Asset Acquisition	One corporation buys all the property of another corporation.	Approval by board and shareholders of acquired company.	Debt usually does not flow to the buyer; product liability may flow to the buyer.
Stock Acquisition (Takeover)	One corporation (the suitor) makes a tender offer to the shareholders of another company (the target); if enough of the target shareholders accept and sell, the suitor takes control of the target.	Approval of enough shareholders to give the suitor control.	Debt and product liability flow to the suitor.

Asset Acquisition

Asset acquisition is one of the easiest and most efficient methods of corporate expansion. An **asset acquisition** involves one corporation purchasing all or most of the assets of another corporation. The assets generally include the entire property of the corporation. The only formality required is the approval of the acquisition by the shareholders and the board of directors of the corporation which is selling its assets. Approval is not required of the other corporation's shareholders. One advantage to asset acquisition is that, in general, no liabilities are transferred from the seller to the buyer. There are, however, three situations in which liabilities can be transferred from the seller to the buyer. First, the buyer can agree to assume some or all of the liabilities of the seller. Second, if the asset acquisition is actually a merger or a consolidation, then the new or the surviving company will assume the liabilities. Third, if the buyer is actually a continuation of the seller, the old liabilities fall to the buyer. Finally, if the asset acquisition is a sham designed to escape old liabilities, those liabilities will fall to the buyer.

EXAMPLE 9 Jay Elston, Curtiss Hunter, and Morris Moore were majority shareholders and directors of Gametech, Inc. Since Gametech was hopelessly in debt, Elston, Hunter, and Moore formed the Techgames Corporation and sold all Gametech's assets to Techgames. Gametech then filed for bankruptcy. When Strategy, Inc., a creditor of Gametech, found out that Techgames had been formed to cheat Gametech creditors, it sued Techgames. Elston, Hunter, and Moore argued that old liabilities do not flow to the buying corporation in an asset acquisition. The court disagreed, holding (1) that Techgames is a mere continuation of Gametech and (2) that Techgames was formed as a sham to cheat creditors. Techgames owed the money to Strategy, Inc.

Stock Acquisitions

Stock acquisitions are often called takeover bids. In a takeover, one corporation buys enough shares in another corporation to control that corporation. (The buyer is often called a **suitor**, whereas the other corporation is frequently referred to as the **target**.) One major advantage of the takeover is that it is very economical. The suitor does not have to purchase all the target's stock, but just enough to control the election of directors. Another attractive feature is that the suitor can ignore an unfriendly board and go directly to the shareholders with a tender offer. Generally, the **tender offer** (which is an offer to buy the stock of the target in exchange for cash or stock in the suitor) is made at an amount above the current market value of the stock. The point is to make the sale as attractive as possible to motivate shareholders to sell. Takeover bids are strictly controlled by the Williams Act, an amendment to existing federal securities statutory law. Under the Williams Act, whenever a suitor makes an offer to acquire more than 5 percent of a target, SEC requirements click into place. These requirements hold that the suitor must file a statement with the SEC stating (1) where the money for the takeover originates, (2) why the suitor is

When one company acquires another, an appraisal company is often hired to find the value of the target company.

purchasing the stock, and (3) how much of the target the suitor owns already. The objective of the Williams Act is to make certain that shareholders know the qualifications and intentions of a takeover bidder.

Often, a takeover bid may be difficult. Alerted to the possible loss of their jobs, the target's managers often launch a counterattack designed to defeat the takeover bid. The result is often a long, hard-fought battle for control of the corporation. For instance, to make the prize a little less attractive, management may sell one or more of the most lucrative subsidiaries of the firm. This process, known as ''selling the crown jewel'' in the corporate treasury, makes the corporation less attractive to the takeover bidder. Another tactic is for management to offer all shareholders except the takeover bidder a higher price for all outstanding shares. This tactic has come under fire, however, as a violation of some implicit provisions of federal law. Perhaps the most popular technique of counterattack against an unfriendly takeover is for management to invite a **friendly suitor,** or a **"white knight,"** to come to its rescue. In this scenario, another corporation outbids the hostile bidder. The white knight pledges to keep the same management team.

EXAMPLE 10 Brin-Gaef Pharmaceutical faces a takeover bid by Fibertronics, Inc. The managers realize that Fibertronics intends to reorganize the entire structure of Brin-Gaef and that they will, more than likely, lose their positions. Several of the managers favor selling Radtech Industries, a subsidiary of Brin-Gaef. The sale will make Brin-Gaef a less attractive target for Fibertronics. Unfortunately, the sale also will reduce Brin-Gaef's overall worth after Fibertronics has been discouraged. Another option would be to offer to buy shares from all other shareholders at a rate somewhat higher than Fibertronics' $71 bid. This practice, however, is of questionable legal merit. Finally, the managers invite another corporation, Eurocorp, to enter the battle, outbid Fibertronics, and thus save Brin-Gaef and the managers' positions within the corporation.

Suggestions for Reducing Legal Risks

1. Whenever you plan to invest money in a new stock issue, remember to read the prospectus carefully. Remember that the SEC does not endorse securities; it only ensures that the proper information is available to investors.
2. If you are ever in an insider position within a corporation, never use inside information in the sale or purchase of stock. Such a move violates SEC regulations.
3. Remember that federal antitrust laws cover a wide range of activities that might not ordinarily seem like monopoly activity.
4. Be aware that federal legislation policing corporate activities is becoming more and more powerful. The latest additions include the Racketeer Influenced and Corrupt Organizations Act, the Currency Transaction Reporting Act, and the Foreign Corrupt Practices Act.
5. Remember that corporations can expand in a number of ways. Chief methods of expansion include: asset acquisition, merger, consolidation, and stock acquisition (takeover bids).

Language of the Law

Define or explain each of the following words or phrases:

commerce clause
Securities and Exchange Commission (SEC)
security
registration statement

prospectus
new stock issues
insider trading
monopoly
interlocking directorates

Federal Trade Commission (FTC)
currency transaction report (CTR)
merger
consolidation

asset acquisition
suitor
target
tender offer
friendly suitor, or "white knight"

Questions for Review

1. What is the legal source of the government's power to regulate business?
2. What problem prompted Congress to pass the Securities Act of 1933 and the Securities and Exchange Act of 1934? What is the primary purpose of these acts?
3. Does the SEC endorse the sale of securities? Explain your answer.
4. What alternatives are available to an "insider" who gains some important inside knowledge affecting the sale of his or her company's stock?
5. Why did Congress find it necessary to amend the Sherman Antitrust Act with the Clayton Act?

6. Name some activities that qualify as racketeering activities under the Racketeer Influenced and Corrupt Organizations Act.
7. What is the purpose behind the reporting requirements of the Currency Transaction Reporting Act?
8. Name some of the advantages of the asset-acquisition technique of corporate expansion.
9. Name some of the advantages of the stock-acquisition (takeover) technique of corporate expansion.
10. Name some of the tactics available to management to stop an unfriendly takeover bid.

Cases in Point

In each of the following cases, give your decision and state a legal principle that applies to the case:

1. Ilsa Garthwaite owned and operated Futuregraphics, Inc., a fashion design business which specialized in developing avant-garde clothing for the super rich. Garthwaite proposed that four of her best clients sponsor each of her seasonal lines of clothing. She suggested that they each contribute $1 million. Each sponsor received a return on his or her contribution based on Futuregraphic's profits that year. Does Garthwaite's sponsorship scheme qualify as a security? Explain.

2. Edward Durrell, vice president of research and development at Angstrom Airlines, learned that Angstrom planned to open several dozen new air routes, including a number of low-fare routes to Europe and South America. Realizing that news of this would cause Angstrom stock to climb, Durrell bought several hundred shares. He also advised several other personal friends to do the same. Are Durrell's actions legally permissible? Explain.

3. Shel Morgan and David Lipinon were competitors in the auto parts business. Since they had the only two auto parts stores in the county, they agreed to divide the terri-

tory, raise the prices on their auto parts, and no longer compete. Morgan breached the agreement, gave cut-rate prices on some of his parts, and began to sell to service stations all over the county. Could Lipinon sue Morgan for breach of contract? Explain why this is a consumer problem.

4. Joy Drury owned a small grocery store. She asked one of her suppliers what the cost would be for a particular brand of breakfast cereal. The supplier said the price would be $32.50 for 1 case, but that if she bought 10 cases, as a chain store had done that week, the price would be $30.50 per case. Has any law been violated? Explain.

5. Sylvia Youngblood was president of Zikron Pictures, a fledgling film company having great difficulty raising money. Youngblood contacted a number of investors by mail and by phone and sold them each 100 percent interest in Zikron's next motion picture. At the end of Youngblood's sales campaign, Zikron had $100 million in its treasury. Youngblood used only $10 million to produce the worst film she could find, knowing it would fail and the investors would lose all their money. What course of action could the investors pursue in this situation?

6. In a monumental asset acquisition, Randall Motors, Inc., purchased all the auto parts factories belonging to the Palamo Motors Corporation. Palamo used the capital to pay off several hundred million dollars in debts and then went out of business. The Spender Steel Company still had a claim against Palamo for $700,000 in past-due accounts. When the directors of Spender learned of Randall Motors' asset acquisition, they tried to collect the $700,000 from Randall. Will Spender succeed in this attempt? Explain.

7. In the opening of this chapter, the construction company in which Ernie owned stock merged with another company. Ernie claims no one notified him about the proposed merger until after the merger was completed. Is this likely to happen when two corporations merge? Explain what the usual procedure would be and how shareholders would be involved in the merger.

8. Mallory-Atwood Pharmaceuticals, Inc., merged with the Sackville-Kazin Chemical Company. All the proper formalities were followed, shareholder approval was obtained, and the state declared the merger fair to all those involved. The surviving corporation was Sackville-Kazin. Several months after the merger, one of Mallory-Atwood's over-the-counter stomach remedies had to be recalled due to a defect in its chemical formula. Injured consumers have decided to sue Sackville-Kazin. Would such a lawsuit be permitted by the courts?

9. Swallow and Ascot Books, Inc., a large publisher of children's books, owned 3 percent of the stock in Pyatt, Inc., a leading publisher of comic books. Swallow and Ascot decided to make a tender offer for several million shares in Pyatt. Should the takeover bid be successful, Swallow and Ascot will own 7 percent of Pyatt's stock. Would any federal law govern this transaction? What information should be reported?

10. Feldman Advertising, Inc., has recently made a generous tender offer to the shareholders of Abel and Ingalls Advertising. The management of Abel and Ingalls fears that the Feldman group will reorganize Abel and Ingalls and that they will lose their jobs. What strategies are available to the management of Abel and Ingalls to counteract the Feldman takeover bid?

Cases to Judge

1. Vincent Chiarella worked for a financial printing firm. In this capacity, he had daily access to inside financial information involving corporate deals. Chiarella used this inside information to make shrewd stock investments. In this way, he made more than

$30,000. When the SEC found out about Chiarella's scheme, they prosecuted him for willfully using inside information in the purchase of stock in violation of SEC regulations. Chiarella admitted his scheme but denied that he was an "insider" because he had no connections with any of the companies. Since he was not a director, manager, officer, or major shareholder, he was, in effect, an outsider and thus had not violated the law. Is Chiarella correct? *United States v. Chiarella*, 588 F.2d 1358 (2d Circuit)

2. The Centex-Winston Corporation had a contract with the Edward Hines Lumber Company (Hines) to purchase lumber for resale after being hired to construct homes. Hines consistently failed to deliver Centex-Winston lumber orders on time. The delays were caused by Hines' practice of giving preferential treatment to several of Centex-Winston's competitors. Centex-Winston sued Hines, claiming that preferential delivery schedules violated the type of unfair competition banned by the Robinson-Patman Act. Is Centex-Winston correct? *Centex-Winston Corporation v. Edward Hines Lumber Co.*, 447 F.2d 585 (7th Circuit)

3. To avoid government scrutiny of several monetary transactions, Edgar and Manuel Puerto told Perla Abaroa, a teller at Merchants Bank of Miami, to file false currency transaction reports (CTRs). Instead, Abaroa decided she would not file any CTRs at all. When the Puertos were tried for violating the Currency Transaction Reporting Act, they argued that it was the bank's duty to file the CTRs. The law, they contended, was aimed at controlling bank activity, not the activity of individual clients. Were the Puertos correct? *United States v. Puerto*, 730 F.2d 627 (11th Circuit)

4. Raymond Leannais was injured while operating a coil slitter machine manufactured by the Forte Equipment Company. All of Forte's assets had been purchased by Cincinnati, Inc., in an asset acquisition. The agreement expressly limited Cincinnati's liability for injuries caused by Forte equipment. The limit covered a 5-year period. Cincinnati argued that since the purchase of Forte was a pure asset acquisition, no liability followed from Forte to Cincinnati except that liability expressly accepted by the contract. Since Leannais was injured a year after the 5-year period ended, Cincinnati concluded that it was not liable. Is Cincinnati correct? *Leannais v. Cincinnati, Inc.*, 565 F.2d 437 (7th Circuit)

5. Irwin Lampert, Leonard Levy, and Paul Scuderi purchased more than 12 percent of General Aircraft's stock. Since the purchase topped 5 percent, they filed the necessary forms with the SEC as required by the Williams Act. In the form, they stated that the purpose of their purchase was investment alone. For the next year, however, Lampert, Levy, and Scuderi caused a great deal of trouble for the management of General Aircraft. Eventually, they engineered a change in the composition of the board of directors so that the three of them had more influence on corporate decision making. They then entered a proxy contest challenging management for total corporate control. Management filed a complaint, claiming that the Williams filing had been fraudulent because their purchase of the stock had not been for investment purposes. The complaint asked the court to order Lampert, Levy, and Scuderi to amend their filing and to stop buying shares or soliciting proxies until the amendments had been properly processed. Should the court order be granted? *General Aircraft Corporation v. Lampert*, 556 F.2d 90 (1st Circuit)

CASE TO DISCUSS

United States Football League v. National Football League
634 F. Supp 1155 (New York)

The United States Football League (USFL) sued the National Football League (NFL) to obtain injunctive relief and damages. The USFL claimed that the NFL had violated the Sherman Antitrust Act because it had created a monopoly in professional football by engaging in certain activities that prevented the USFL from succeeding as a competitive league. The complaint lodged against the NFL contained a lengthy list of activities that the USFL alleged were antitrust violations. Remember that the Sherman Antitrust Act does not make any specific activities illegal. Instead, it allows the courts to decide such issues. The court in this case had to interpret whether certain activities by the NFL violated the act. The two activities we will focus on here are (1) preventing USFL teams from gaining access to suitable stadium facilities and (2) monopolizing the nationwide market for qualified professional football officials.

To counteract both claims, the NFL filed motions arguing that, given the facts and the law, there was no need to take either issue to trial. The question in both situations is whether the NFL's activities in regard to the "stadium leases" and the "game officials" amounted to conduct prohibited by the Sherman Antitrust Act.

THE ARGUMENTS

The Stadium Related Claims The USFL alleged that the NFL engaged in certain illegal practices designed to prevent any USFL clubs from gaining access to appropriate stadium facilities. Since this activity involved a direct attempt to eliminate the USFL as a competitor in pro football, the USFL argued that the activity violated antitrust law. The USFL pointed out that wherever it sought a stadium, the NFL brought pressure on local government officials to prevent any USFL stadium contract. The USFL further argued that this pressure involved threats by the NFL to pull NFL clubs out of any city that leased a stadium to the USFL. The USFL also claimed that the NFL told cities without NFL clubs that they would never get an NFL club if they leased a stadium to the USFL. The USFL concluded that such threats, aimed at eliminating competition, violated the Sherman Antitrust Act.

The NFL countered this position by arguing that in each situation it did nothing more than present its position to the government agency in control of the stadium. Such statements, the NFL claimed, were made to a governmental body exercising its governmental function. Therefore, the NFL's presentations to these government agencies were protected by the First Amendment guarantee of free speech. In response, the USFL urged the court to adopt an exception to this free speech argument. The USFL wanted the court to limit free speech involving a government agency when that agency is engaged in a purely business related matter and when that speech is aimed at eliminating competition.

The Game Officials Claim The NFL has 107 officials on its payroll. Each year the league hires approximately six new officials to replace those who have left. To be hired, a new official must have ten years of experience. Five of these years must be at the college varsity level. Approximately 1,400 to 1,500 officials in a nationwide pool fulfill these requirements. Contracts made between the NFL and its officials contain restrictive employment covenants which explicitly forbid those officials from working for any other football league while employed by the NFL unless that work is authorized by the NFL commissioner. Accordingly, the NFL would not allow any NFL officials to work for the USFL even during the NFL's off-season in spring. The NFL alleged that such springtime activity would interfere with the officials' duties during the NFL's off-season training program. Since all pro football officials work exclusively for the NFL, the USFL concluded that the NFL had monopolized the market. Such a market monopoly, the USFL said, violated antitrust law.

The NFL counterattacked this position by arguing that the USFL had not properly defined the market of game officials. The market should not be limited to officials working for the NFL. Rather, the market should include all college officials with ten years experience, including five years at the college varsity level. Since the USFL can draw officials from this same pool, and since the pool consists of approximately 1,400 to 1,500 officials, the NFL argued that it controls less than 10 percent of the market, and concluded that control of less than 10 percent of a market is not a monopoly.

QUESTIONS FOR DISCUSSION

1. Should the court allow the NFL to talk to government officials when the objective of that talk is to create a monopoly by denying the USFL access to adequate stadium facilities? Why or why not?

2. Should the court adopt the USFL's proposed free speech limitation? Why or why not?

3. Should the court uphold the restrictive employment covenant which forbids NFL game officials from working for any other football league while employed by the NFL? Why or why not?

4. Should the market of professional game officials be limited to those officials who presently work in that capacity or should the market include those eligible for that work? Defend your answer.

5. Do you think 10 percent of a market is sufficient to establish a monopoly? If not, speculate on what percentage control of a market would be sufficient to establish the existence of a monopoly.

CASE TO BRIEF

After reading *How to Write a Case Brief* on page 78 and examining the sample brief on page 80, write a brief on the following case:

Apicella v. PAF Corporation
479 N.E.2d 315 (Ohio)

PAF Corporation ("PAF") was incorporated in April 1967, to engage in various real estate transactions. Five hundred shares were authorized at $100 per share. Theodore G. Poulos, Michael Fornaro, Jr., and Peter Apicella each purchased two shares. No other shares have been issued. Apicella, Fornaro and Poulos elected themselves as directors and elected Poulos as President, Fornaro as Vice President, and Apicella as Secretary and Treasurer. Poulos and Fornaro are brothers-in-law.

PAF purchased property located at 527 South Green Road in South Euclid. In September 1967, PAF leased its property to Arrow Builders Supply Co. ("Arrow") for five years at $400 per month. Arrow had an option to renew the five-year lease at an annual rental to be negotiated between the parties. The record is devoid of any further lease agreements or evidence of negotiations, but Arrow has remained on the property since August 1972, on a month-to-month basis at $500 per month. Theodore Poulos and his wife own Arrow and executed the original lease agreement on Arrow's behalf as president and secretary, respectively. Peter Apicella was an employee of Arrow until May 1981.

In June 1968, Euclid Railroad Company ("Euclid Railroad") leased the property to the rear of PAF's property to PAF. PAF agreed to sublet this land, collect the rent from the sublessees, and remit fifty percent of the gross rents collected to Euclid Railroad. The lease-management agreement further provided that the term of the lease could be extended to encompass the term of any of the subleases negotiated by PAF. The lease-management agreement was executed on behalf of Euclid Railroad by Lillian Fornaro, president, and Theodore Poulos, secretary-treasurer.

When Lillian Fornaro died in 1975, her heirs terminated the lease-management agreement, but PAF was not formally notified of the termination. Euclid Railroad's property was continually used, as well as PAF's property, as a means of ingress and egress.

In May 1981, in connection with his intention to change positions and begin work with another company, Apicella was advised by letter to obtain certain documents in order to determine the value of his interest in PAF. Apicella gave a copy of this letter to Poulos who admitted that this was the first notice in writing that he had received regarding Apicella's opposition to PAF's rental policy. Letters dated October 8 and December 15, 1981, were later sent to Poulos demanding an examination of the books and records of PAF.

On February 16, 1982, Apicella filed a shareholders' derivative action against PAF, Poulos, Fornaro and Arrow, alleging, *inter alia,* that PAF leased its property for an inadequate rental fee and that PAF failed to obtain fees from sublessees for the ingress and egress over PAF's property. Defendants denied Apicella's allegations and raised the affirmative defenses of laches, estoppel and the statute of limitations.

Trial commenced on January 20, 1983. During plaintiff's testimony, when the court learned that plaintiff was still trying to discover evidence of mismanagement regarding Euclid Railroad, the court decided to appoint a referee to take evidence and prepare a report for the court. On March 7, 1983, the referee issued his report. Plaintiff and PAF objected to the referee's report. On September 7, 1983, the trial court entered judgment for PAF in the amount of $44,813.50 for damages suffered from July 1, 1981 to the present; ordered that Apicella be permitted to examine the books and records of PAF; and ordered that Apicella recover his litigation expenses, the amount of which were to be determined at a subsequent hearing.

On September 28, 1983, the court issued a Supplemental Order which awarded Apicella $16,352.65 as fees and expenses ($15,000 for attorney fees); awarded the referee $1,800; increased Arrow's rent to $1,625 per month effective October 1, 1983; and ordered costs to be borne by Poulos and Fornaro.

All parties timely appealed. We will address appellants' assignments of error first.

Appellants' first assignment of error is that:

"The trial court erred as a matter of law in finding that defendants Poulos and Fornaro breached their fiduciary duties as officers and directors to PAF Corp."

It is well-established "that directors of a corporation occupy a fiduciary relationship to the corporation and its shareholders and are held strictly accountable and liable if the corporate funds or property are wasted or mismanaged. . . ."

A director must perform his duties in good faith and in a manner he reasonably believes to be in the best interests of the corporation.

Contracts or transactions allegedly involving self-dealing or interlocking dominant directors on both sides are neither void nor unenforceable *ipso facto,* but will be closely scrutinized.

The Ohio statute provides, in relevant part, that:

"(A) Unless otherwise provided in the articles or the regulations:

"(1) No contract or transaction shall be void or voidable with respect to a corporation for the reason that it is between the corporation and . . . any other person in which one or more of its directors or officers are directors, trustees, or officers, or have a financial or personal interest, or for the reason that one or more interested directors or officers participate in or vote at the meeting of the directors or a committee thereof which authorizes such contract or transaction, if in any such case . . . (c) the contract or transaction is fair as to the corporation as of the time it is authorized or approved by the directors, a committee thereof, or the shareholders. . . ."

Therefore, when a shareholder acting on behalf of the corporation in a shareholders' derivative action, alleges mismanagement as a result of interlocking dominant directors on both sides of a contract or transaction resulting in harm to the corporation, the burden of proof is on the directors to show that the contract or transaction is fair to the corporation. . . .

In the present case, the evidence demonstrates that Poulos and Arrow benefited from the unreasonably low monthly rental fees to the detriment of PAF and its shareholders. In addition, PAF was harmed by the lack of enforcement of the lease-management agreement to the extent of the uncollected monies. The trial court did not err when it concluded that appellants breached their duties to PAF and its shareholders since appellants failed to show that the rental agreement with Arrow and the inaction with regard to the lease-management agreement were fair to PAF. Therefore, appellants' . . . assignment of error is overruled.

TRIAL PROCEDURES

INSTRUCTIONS TO THE JURY

Juries are composed of ordinary people who are not experts in law. Therefore, in all jury trials someone has to explain the law to the jury. The judge, as the trial's impartial referee, delivers these *jury instructions*. Attorneys from both sides may offer suggestions about the instructions to assist the judge with this process. Ultimately, however, the final *charge to the jury*, is up to the judge.

Jury instructions are not always easy to give, even for a judge. The judge must explain the law in terms that non-lawyers will understand, yet he or she must not dilute the law so much that the instructions become inaccurate. Since jury instructions are so important and because they are so difficult, they are often challenged on appeal.

THE CASE OF GRAZIO v. WILLIAMSON (continued from page 469)

The attorneys have given their closing arguments to the jury. It is now time for the judge to instruct the jury as to the law it must apply to the facts in the case. The judge's instructions are as follows:

Ladies and gentlemen, it is now time for me to tell you about the law that you must apply to this case. I instruct you that negligence is the failure to do that which a reasonably prudent person would have done under the same circumstances and conditions. In determining whether the defendant was negligent in this case, you must ask yourself whether or not a reasonably prudent person would swerve into a parked car to avoid hitting a squirrel. If you think a reasonably prudent person would do this, you must find that the defendant was not negligent. Similarly, if you think a reasonably prudent person would not do this, you must find that the defendant committed a negligent act.

You are further instructed that violation of law is evidence only of a negligent act which that law was intended to prevent. Now, it is important for you to realize that the law prohibiting parking in front of fire hydrants was not intended to prevent automobile accidents. Instead, it was designed to make fire hydrants easily accessible to fire trucks. You may not therefore, as a matter of law, consider the plaintiff's parking in front of the fire hydrant as evidence of negligence on the part of the plaintiff. It could be used as evidence if the car were parked too far away from the curb, but that did not happen in this case.

Another element of negligence that must be proved is damages. You must determine the amount of damages suffered by the plaintiff in dollars and cents. This is computed by finding the difference between the fair market value of the car before the accident and the fair market value after the accident.

Finally, the burden is on the plaintiff to prove that the negligent act, if there was one, caused the damages to the plaintiff's car. You must decide, ladies and gentlemen, from the preponderance of the evidence (that is, the evidence of the greatest weight) whether the defendant's act was negligent and, if so, whether it caused the damages to the plaintiff's car. The decision is now in your hands.

After instructing the jury about the law, the judge tells the bailiff to escort the members of the jury to the jury room for their deliberations. (This case continues on page 561.)

LEGAL PRACTICUM

Look back to the opening of Chapter 37. You will recall that a construction company in which Ernie owned stock had just merged with another company. Ernie had not been consulted. You know now that under the law, in such a situation, shareholders must be consulted. Assume that Ernie learns this fact and decides to sue the managers of the construction company. The basis of his suit is that the shareholders were not consulted prior to the merger. Your job, in a few short paragraphs, is to write the jury instructions for Ernie's lawsuit. Begin by telling the jury what a merger is, and then explain shareholder rights when a merger is about to take place. Use the preceding instructions as a pattern and make certain you review the law on mergers in Chapter 37. (Assume that Ernie's state requires a two-thirds shareholder majority to approve a merger.)

LOOKING TOWARD
LATER LIFE

UNIT
8

Chapter 38

PENSIONS, SOCIAL SECURITY, AND HEALTH CARE

This unit introduces the Henderson family—John and Sylvia and their 16-year-old daughter, Kathleen.

Scene: John is cooking supper as Sylvia arrives home. Kathleen is doing homework at the dining-room table.

John: Hi dear. How was your interview?

Sylvia: Wonderful! I got the job!

John: That's great!

Kathleen: Congratulations, Mom!

John: When do you begin?

Sylvia: They want me to start right away, but I told them I have to give a month's notice where I work now.

Kathleen: Will you be doing the same kind of work?

Sylvia: No, it's a better job. I'll begin as a supervisor. It's a young company, so there should be lots of room for advancement. They were impressed with the fact that I have a college degree.

John: I knew that would make a difference.

Kathleen: How's the pay?

Sylvia: My starting salary will be $27,000—that's $5,000 more than I make now! And the benefits are good, too. They have a noncontributory pension plan, among other things.

Kathleen: Is that important?

Sylvia: The one I have now is contributory.

John: You must have almost 6 years of pension benefits saved by now.

Sylvia: Yes, and I hope I don't lose them by changing jobs.

John: I hope not. Speaking of pensions, what do you say that we retire when I'm 55?

Sylvia: That's a good age to retire— that's just 15 years from now. Imagine, Kathleen will be on her own then, and I'll be 52—doesn't that sound ancient?

John: We can live on a South Sea island and forget about shoveling snow in the winter.

Kathleen: That's a good idea! I'll come and visit you at Christmas.

Sylvia: With your social security check and my pension we should do all right.

John: The important thing is that we're in good health. So many people retire when it's too late to enjoy themselves.

Sylvia: Like Mr. Kulak across the street. He worked hard all his life and collapsed a week after he retired.

John: Do the doctors think he'll make it?

Sylvia: I don't think so. He's being kept alive by machines. He just lies there in a coma.

John: I want to be sure that doesn't happen to me. If I ever reach that stage, I don't want to be kept alive by machines with no chance left for a good life.

Kathleen: Probably you should do something about it now rather than wait until the time comes.

Sylvia: I wonder what we could do about that.

LEGAL ISSUES

1. Is there an important difference between contributory and noncontributory pension plans?
2. Do workers have guaranteed rights in their pension benefits?
3. May workers transfer pension benefits from one job to another?
4. Can a worker retire and receive social security benefits at the age of 55?
5. In the event of terminal illness, is it possible to make a legally binding statement in advance directing the withholding of life-sustaining measures?

THE SPIRIT OF THE LAW

While most people gain personal satisfaction from the work they do, they naturally look forward to retiring and enjoying the fruits of their labors. To ensure a comfortable retirement, individuals must plan and save. Employers often help by offering pension plans. Private insurance can guarantee an income at retirement or in case of disaster. The government provides social security, a kind of public insurance program. Retirement investments involve hundreds of billions of dollars and the rights of millions of people. Laws governing retirement income and health care in old age affect us all.

PRIVATE PENSION PLANS

A **pension plan** is any plan, fund, or program that provides income to employees after they retire. There is no law that requires employers to set up pension plans other than social security for their employees; nevertheless, the number of private pension plans has increased considerably in recent years.

There are many kinds of private pension plans. A **single-employer plan** is one in which money is set aside and held by a single employer for the benefit of its employees when they retire. Under a **multiemployer plan,** many different employers give money to a central fund for the benefit of their employees when they retire. The central fund is usually managed by a group of people, known as

Legal Issue No. 1

trustees, who are given the job of taking care of the fund. Some plans are contributory; others are noncontributory. A **contributory pension plan** requires the employee to pay part of the cost of the plan. **Noncontributory pension plans** are financed entirely by the employer. In the United States, most **covered workers** (workers covered by private pension plans) participate in noncontributory plans.

Until 1974, the government did not attempt to regulate private pension plans. Before that time, many injustices took place.

EXAMPLE 1 Frank Polanski worked for the same company for 38 years. The company had its own pension plan, and Polanski looked forward to receiving a pension of $600 a month, in addition to social security, upon his retirement at the age of 65. However, Polanski lost his job a year before he was to retire. He also lost his entire pension because he was not employed by the company when he reached the age of 65.

The Pension Reform Law of 1974

To eliminate injustices that were occurring under many private pension plans, Congress passed the Employee Retirement Income Security Act of 1974 (ERISA). This act places many controls on the management of pension funds and gives certain rights to workers who have the benefits of private pension funds. It also gives some rights to workers who are not covered. Some of the rights are explained below.

Legal Issue No. 2

Vesting The **vesting** of retirement benefits is the act of giving a worker a guaranteed right to receive a future pension. The worker will receive the pension regardless of whether he or she is working under the plan at the time of retirement. Under Frank Polanski's retirement plan discussed in Example 1, benefits did not vest (become legally guaranteed) until an employee reached the age of retirement. Polanski would not have lost his benefits under ERISA because they would have vested sooner. The law requires all pension plans to have minimum vested benefits. Beginning in 1989, all pension plans must vest after 5 years on the job.

Legal Issue No. 3

Portability **Portability** is the ability to transfer pension benefits from one job to another. Persons wishing to take their vested benefits with them when they leave a company may do so. They may transfer benefits from one company's pension plan to the plan of another company, or from one company's pension plan to an individual retirement plan (IRA), or from an IRA to a company plan.

Participation An employee may not be left out of a retirement plan if he or she has reached the age of 21 and has completed at least 1 year of service. A plan, however, may require all workers to have 3 years of service in order to join if the workers' interests will become fully vested at the end of 3 years.

Make personal investments carefully. Pensions and social security benefits together may not provide an adequate retirement income. *(ZIGGY, by Tom Wilson. Copyright © 1986, Universal Press Syndicate. Reprinted with permission. All rights reserved.)*

Termination Insurance Under the Pension Reform Law, pension plans are insured by a government insurance agency. If a pension fund runs out of money before everyone in the plan has received all of his or her benefits, the governmental agency will pay benefits of up to $750 a month.

Funding All pension plans must be properly funded. Enough money must be set aside to pay benefits to the people who are expected to receive them.

Individual Retirement Accounts (IRAs) Individual workers may set up individual retirement plans of their own if they wish. A maximum of $2,000 a year ($2,250 for a married couple with one working and one nonworking spouse) may be set aside for retirement purposes. This amount is not subject to federal income taxes during the year that it is earned. It acts as an incentive for people to save money for their retirement (by avoiding taxes) rather than to depend solely on social security. There is, however, a 10 percent tax penalty imposed for withdrawals made before the age of 59½.*

Prudent-Person Rule Persons who manage pension funds are required to act with the care and skill that a **prudent person** (a wise and careful person) who is familiar with such matters would use under the circumstances. Such persons are known as fiduciaries. A **fiduciary** is a person who acts for another's benefit in a position of trust. Fiduciaries must file annual reports with the Secretary of Labor. The pension fund must be **audited** (checked by independent accountants) each year to be sure that all the money is properly accounted for.

*At the time of this writing, tax reform legislation under consideration by Congress may change or eliminate IRAs.

SOCIAL SECURITY

Social security is the basic method used in the United States to provide income to people when their regular income stops because of retirement, disability, or the death of someone who had provided them with income.

EXAMPLE 2 Mrs. Lola Gerber was 42 years old when her husband was killed in an automobile accident. He had been fully insured under social security. The couple had one dependent child (a son), who was 10 years old at the time of the accident. Mrs. Gerber will receive benefits until her son is 16. Payments will then cease until Mrs. Gerber reaches age 65, or age 60 if she is willing to accept reduced benefits.

Social security provides the following kinds of benefits: retirement insurance, survivors insurance, health insurance (Medicare), black lung benefits, disability insurance, and supplemental security income (SSI).

Legal Issue No. 4

People can now retire at the age of 65 and receive full retirement benefits. They can retire at the age of 62 and receive reduced benefits. The age for full benefits will gradually increase to 67 between the years 2000 and 2022 for those retiring after the turn of the century. Early payments at age 62 will still be available then, but the reduction will be somewhat larger than now.

People can receive social security benefits if a severe physical or mental impairment prevents them from working for at least a year or is expected to result in their death. Payments start with the sixth full month of disability and continue for as long as the person is disabled.

EXAMPLE 3 At the age of 38, Henry Walsh suffered injuries which totally disabled him. He applied to the local social security office for benefits provided by the federal disability insurance provision of the act. Proof of total disability would entitle Walsh to benefits after 6 months of disability to be paid monthly until he reaches the age of 65, when he is automatically covered by social security.

Workers are considered disabled and entitled to benefits under the social security law if they have a physical or mental condition which prevents them from doing any substantial, gainful work and which has lasted (or is expected to last) for at least 12 months. They are also considered disabled if they have any condition that is expected to result in death.

To be eligible for social security benefits, workers and self-employed people must pay into the fund for at least 40 quarters of a year. This is equal to 10 years of contributions to the fund. The 40 quarters need not necessarily be consecutive quarters.

If you do not have a social security number, if you have forgotten your number, or if you have lost your card, you should apply for a new one. Complete Form SS-5, which is available at any social security office or post office. You will be asked to identify yourself with a driver's license or with some other proof. You will also need evidence showing when and where you were born. If you were not born in the United States, you will be asked to prove either that you are a U.S. citizen or that you are an alien legally permitted to work in the United States.

FORM SS-5 – APPLICATION FOR A SOCIAL SECURITY NUMBER CARD
(Original, Replacement or Correction)

MICROFILM REF. NO. (SSA USE ONLY)

Unless the requested information is provided, we may not be able to issue a Social Security Number (20 CFR 422.103(b))

INSTRUCTIONS TO APPLICANT ▶	Before completing this form, please read the instructions on the opposite page. You can type or print, using pen with dark blue or black ink. Do not use pencil.

		First	Middle	Last
NAA NAB **1**	NAME TO BE SHOWN ON CARD	Lisa	Anne	Codwise
	FULL NAME AT BIRTH (IF OTHER THAN ABOVE)	First	Middle	Last
ONA	OTHER NAME(S) USED			

STT **2**	MAILING ADDRESS	(Street/Apt. No., P.O. Box, Rural Route No.) 35 Beachbluff Ave.

CTY STE ZIP	CITY Anytown	STATE Maine	ZIP CODE 04102

CSP **3**	CITIZENSHIP (Check one only)	SEX **4**	ETB **5**	RACE/ETHNIC DESCRIPTION (Check one only) (Voluntary)
	☑ a. U.S. citizen	☐ Male	☐ a. Asian, Asian American or Pacific Islander (Includes persons of Chinese, Filipino, Japanese, Korean, Samoan, etc., ancestry or descent)
	☐ b. Legal alien allowed to work	☑ Female	☐ b. Hispanic (Includes persons of Chicano, Cuban, Mexican or Mexican-American, Puerto Rican, South or Central American, or other Spanish ancestry or descent)
	☐ c. Legal alien not allowed to work		☐ c. Negro or Black (not Hispanic)
	☐ d. Other (See instructions on Page 2)		☐ d. North American Indian or Alaskan Native
			☑ e. White (not Hispanic)

DOB **6**	DATE OF BIRTH	MONTH 3	DAY 18	YEAR 66	AGE **7**	PRESENT AGE 17	PLB **8**	PLACE OF BIRTH	CITY Anytown	STATE OR FOREIGN COUNTRY Maine

MNA **9**	MOTHER'S NAME AT HER BIRTH	First Luella	Middle Spinney	Last (her maiden name) Allen
FNA	FATHER'S NAME	First Hubert	Middle Emerson	Last Codwise

PNO **10**	a. Have you or someone on your behalf applied for a social security number before?	☑ No	☐ Don't Know	☐ Yes

If you checked "yes," complete items "b" through "e" below; otherwise go to item 11.

SSN PNS PNY	b. Enter social security number	c. In what State did you apply?	What year?

NLC	d. Enter the name shown on your most recent social security card	e. If the birth date you used was different from the date shown in item 6, enter it here.	MONTH	DAY	YEAR

DON **11**	TODAY'S DATE	MONTH April	DAY 8	YEAR 83	**12**	Telephone number where we can reach you during the day	HOME 555-5432	OTHER

ASD WARNING: Deliberately providing false information on this application is punishable by a fine of $1,000 or one year in jail, or both.

13	YOUR SIGNATURE *Lisa Anne Codwise*	**14**	YOUR RELATIONSHIP TO PERSON IN ITEM 1 ☑ Self ☐ Other (Specify)
	WITNESS (Needed only if signed by mark "X")		WITNESS (Needed only if signed by mark "X")

DO NOT WRITE BELOW THIS LINE (FOR SSA USE ONLY)		DTC	SSA RECEIPT DATE _____
☐ SUPPORTING DOCUMENT- EXPEDITE CASE ☐ DUP ISSUED	SSN ASSIGNED OR VERIFIED SSN	NPN	
		BIC	SIGNATURE AND TITLE OF EMPLOYEE(S) REVIEWING EVIDENCE AND/OR CONDUCTING INTERVIEW.
DOC	NTC CAN		
TYPE(S) OF EVIDENCE SUBMITTED		☐ MANDATORY IN PERSON INTERVIEW CONDUCTED	DATE
			DATE
	IDN ITV	DCL	

Form **SS-5**

You may obtain a social security number by filing a form like this.

If you change your name, you should go to the nearest social security office and ask to have your records changed. Your new card will contain your new name and your old number. You will keep the same social security number your entire life. This is to ensure that you receive credit for every job you will have.

Supplemental Security Income

A program, called **Supplemental Security Income (SSI),** was established by the federal government in 1974. SSI is designed to provide additional cash benefits each month for needy people who are either aged, blind, or disabled.

To be eligible for benefits under this program, an individual may not own assets (except for those mentioned below) that are worth more than $1,800; the limit for a married couple is $2,700. An individual may, however, own a house, a car of up to $4,500 in value, household goods or personal effects of up to $2,000 in value, and life insurance of up to $1,500. In addition, no limit is placed on the value of a car that is used for transportation to a job, to go for treatment for a special medical problem, or if it has been modified for use by a handicapped person.

EXAMPLE 4 Patricia Morrison, a widow, was 68 years old. She was retired and lived on her social security benefits. She owned her house. She also owned a car that was worth about $1,000 and had $2,000 in a bank account. She would not be eligible for SSI because her assets (the money in her bank account) were more than $1,800.

Cash benefits are paid monthly to people who qualify for SSI. The benefits are reduced, however, by any income the individual or couple receives. However, the first $20 of unearned income (such as dividends or interest) each month and the first $65 of earned income each month do not count toward reducing the monthly benefit.

Medicare

Since 1966, nearly all Americans 65 years of age and over have been eligible for two kinds of health insurance protection under social security: (1) hospital insurance and (2) additional voluntary medical insurance. These are known as the **Medicare** provisions of social security.

The purpose of hospital insurance is to help pay the bills when a person is hospitalized. The program also provides payments for nursing care and other services in a skilled nursing facility after hospitalization, outpatient hospital diagnostic services, and home health services.

The purpose of medical insurance is to help pay bills for doctors' services and for a number of other medical items and services not covered under the hospital insurance program.

The medical insurance program is voluntary. Those eligible decide whether to enroll for protection under the medical insurance program. They can have this important added protection at a low cost ($17.90 monthly) because the federal government will pay an equal amount toward the cost.

LEGAL ISSUES IN HEALTH CARE

Medicare has become a vital component of most people's health care plans because of the extraordinary rise in health care costs over the last few decades. This unprecedented increase in costs has been caused by a number of interrelated factors. One factor is the great advances that have been made in medical science. These advances have resulted in treatments that have allowed us to extend life beyond limits previously thought impossible to surpass. Another cause is the tendency of health care providers to pass on increased costs, including the rise in the costs of medical malpractice insurance, on to the patient and the patient's family.

These two causes are closely related to each other. Moreover, both have been the cause and the effect of other larger and more complex legal and medical issues which all of us may encounter at some time in our lives.

Consent to Health Care

Patients receiving health care have the right to know about the tests and treatments administered to them. This right imposes on the treating physician a corresponding duty to inform the patient and obtain the patient's consent before proceeding with the treatment or the diagnostic technique. This duty is the duty to seek and obtain the patient's consent. There are two types of consent: general consent and informed consent.

General Consent **General consent** is given the moment that patients voluntarily step into the hospital setting. When patients enter this setting, they are giving permission for whatever routine procedures will be needed to make a diagnosis or to administer treatment.

Informed Consent If a diagnostic test or a treatment will involve any danger, the treating physician is required to get the patient's informed consent before proceeding. The physician obtains the patient's **informed consent** by telling the patient in advance about the treatment and the risks involved. The physician is also obligated to tell the patient about the alternative methods that are available. Informed consent must be in writing. A written, signed informed consent form is presumed valid by the court. This means that the patient who contests the issue of consent will have to prove that he or she did not really consent despite the written form and the presence of his or her signature. It is also important to remember that informed consent can be taken back at any time. In other words, patients are allowed to change their minds, and health care professionals must respect that decision.

Continuation of Treatment

Sometimes a patient is so seriously ill that nothing will cure his or her illness or injury. In such situations, the best the physician can hope to do is prolong the patient's life. At this point, a decision must be made whether or not to terminate treatment. This is a very difficult decision to make morally and legally. Hospitals, physicians, nurses, and other health care professionals have struggled with the problem for decades. No final answer exists now. One trend, however, is to base the decision to continue treatment on whether there is a reasonable chance the patient will recover. If the prospect for such a recovery is virtually nonexistent, then it is likely that treatment will be discontinued.

While many hospitals have not addressed this issue, those which have generally provide a definite mechanism for making such determinations. Most of these procedures require several physicians to come to the same conclusion to discontinue treatment. Most procedures also involve waiting periods to ensure that no mistake has been made. They also involve consultation with the patient's family and require the consent of those family members. Unfortunately, many hospitals have not adopted set procedures to follow. Consequently, without set procedures, the processes for making these decisions vary widely.

Some patients remain in an irreversible coma with no hope of recovery. They are kept alive with feeding tubes. Some hospitals refuse to remove the feeding tubes; others will do so only with a court order. A recently revised code of ethics of the American Medical Association states that physicians may stop providing food and water to comatose patients (those in a coma) after considering the wishes of the patient and the patient's family.

The Living Will

Legal Issue No. 5

One solution to this dilemma is the living will. The **living will** is a document which makes an advance statement directing the withholding of life-sustaining measures in the event of terminal illness or injury. It also may appoint someone to tell others what to do in the event of a serious medical emergency if the patient has lost the ability to make the decision personally. A person who has been in an accident and is in a coma with no chance of recovery would be in this type of situation.

The majority of states have enacted living will laws, making them legally binding. Even in those states which do not recognize living wills legally, they may have a moral effect on the physician and the family because the living will indicates the patient's intent when there is no other way to determine that intent. (See Table 38-1).

TABLE 38-1
LIVING WILL LAWS

1976	California
1977	Arkansas, Idaho, Nevada, New Mexico, North Carolina, Oregon, Texas
1979	Kansas, Washington
1981	Alabama
1982	Delaware, Vermont, District of Columbia
1983	Illinois, Virginia
1984	Florida, Georgia, Louisiana, Mississippi, West Virginia, Wisconsin, Wyoming
1985	Arizona, Colorado, Connecticut, Indiana, Iowa, Maine, Maryland, Missouri, Montana, New Hampshire, Oklahoma, Tennessee, Utah

Medical technology allows doctors to prolong the lives of patients who will probably never recover. Consequently, the legislatures of many states have addressed the issue of a patient's right to die.

Living Will Declaration

INSTRUCTIONS
Consult this column for help and guidance.

To My Family, Doctors, and All Those Concerned with My Care

I, _____, being of sound mind, make this statement as a directive to be followed if I become unable to participate in decisions regarding my medical care.

This declaration sets forth your directions regarding medical treatment.

If I should be in an incurable or irreversible mental or physical condition with no reasonable expectation of recovery, I direct my attending physician to withhold or withdraw treatment that merely prolongs my dying. I further direct that treatment be limited to measures to keep me comfortable and to relieve pain.

You have the right to refuse treatment you do not want, and you may request the care you do want.

These directions express my legal right to refuse treatment. Therefore I expect my family, doctors, and everyone concerned with my care to regard themselves as legally and morally bound to act in accord with my wishes, and in so doing to be free of any legal liability for having followed my directions.

You may list specific treatment you do not want. For example:

Cardiac resuscitation
Mechanical respiration
Artificial feeding/fluids by tubes

Otherwise, your general statement, top right, will stand for your wishes.

I especially do not want: _____

_____

_____

_____

_____

_____

You may want to add instructions for care you do want—for example, pain medication; or that you prefer to die at home if possible.

Other instructions/comments: _____

_____

_____

Proxy Designation Clause: Should I become unable to communicate my instructions as stated above, I designate the following person to act in my behalf:

Name_____

Address_____

If you want, you can name someone to see that your wishes are carried out, but you do not have to do this.

If the person I have named above is unable to act in my behalf, I authorize the following person to do so:

Name_____

Address_____

Sign and date here in the presence of two adult witnesses, who should also sign.

Signed:_____Date:_____

Witness:_____Witness:_____

Keep the signed original with your personal papers at home.
Give signed copies to your doctors, family, and to your proxy.

A living will may follow this form. What legal effect does such a document have in your state?

Refusal of Treatment

All the preceding situations involve patients who cannot make decisions for themselves and who cannot be cured. What about patients who can think for themselves and who cannot be cured? What about patients who can think for themselves and decide to refuse treatment for religious or other reasons? Can the court order treatment despite the patient's own wishes? Usually, the answer to this question is ''No.'' Many courts maintain that people can refuse treatment. The courts base this decision on the belief that a person has the right to decide what will be done to his or her own body. This right is based on the constitutional right of privacy. Often, if the case involves refusal on religious grounds, the issue also involves First Amendment religious rights. Nevertheless, this is not the final word on such matters. Courts have held that the government may force treatment if the government can demonstrate that it has a stronger interest that overrules the patient's right to privacy. For example, if the patient can be cured and still refuses treatment, many courts will order treatment. The courts believe that the government has a duty to protect life that is even greater than the patient's right to be left alone.

Suggestions For Reducing Legal Risks

1. Your nearest social security office will be glad to answer questions and provide booklets and pamphlets which describe the various social security laws.
2. Aged, blind, and disabled people with limited means may be entitled to SSI benefits, even if they are not receiving them at present.
3. Be sure to find out about a pension plan's provision for vesting. Once your benefits vest, you will always be entitled to them.
4. If you do not have a pension plan where you work, or if you are self-employed, consider establishing your own individual retirement fund. The money set aside for this purpose is not subject to federal income taxes when it is earned.
5. Remember that as a patient in a health care setting, you have certain rights, including the right to informed consent.
6. As a patient you also have the right to expect health care professionals to act with your best interests at heart. If a health care professional does not live up to the appropriate standard of care and you are injured as a result, you may be entitled to damages.

Language of the Law

Define or explain each of the following words or phrases:

pension plan
single-employer plan
multiemployer plan
trustees
contributory pension
 plan

noncontributory pen-
 sion plan
covered workers
vesting
portability
prudent person

fiduciary
audited
social security
Supplemental Secu-
 rity Income (SSI)

Medicare
general consent
informed consent
living will

Questions for Review

1. How does a noncontributory pension plan differ from a contributory pension plan?
2. What benefits does social security provide?
3. What law was passed in 1974 to prevent the occurrence of injustices in private pension plans?

4. Explain the difference in the amount of money a person retiring at age 62 instead of age 65 receives from social security.
5. When are workers considered to be disabled under the Social Security Act?
6. Who may receive benefits under the Supplemental Security Income (SSI) program?
7. Name and describe the two kinds of health insurance provided by Medicare.
8. What right to knowledge about their medi-

9. How does general consent differ from informed consent?
10. Describe the general basis for deciding whether to terminate health care treatment.
11. What mechanism do hospitals provide for making a decision to discontinue treatment?
12. What is the purpose of a living will?
13. When might a court order medical treatment against a patient's wishes?

Cases in Point

In each of the following cases, give your decision and state a legal principle that applies to the case:

1. After working for Datatech Corporation for 10 years, Harry Bailey took a similar position with another company. Datatech had a noncontributory pension plan for its employees. When Bailey left Datatech, the company notified him that his pension benefits terminated completely. Does Bailey have any legal rights? Explain.
2. Morrison Baking Corporation established a pension plan for its employees. In hopes of making a large profit, the company's general manager invested the pension funds in a highly speculative oil stock. The stock's price fell sharply and was eventually sold for a huge loss. Did the corporation violate the employees' legal rights? Explain.
3. Harriet Shaw, who was 21 years old, obtained a job with Crawford Insurance Company as a computer operator. The company had a pension plan which allowed employees to participate after completing 1 year of service. After working for 1 year, Shaw was denied participation in the pension plan because she was not yet 25 years old. Were Shaw's legal rights violated? Explain.
4. Ann Tamma entered the hospital voluntarily with a serious illness. Because she was so ill, she was not asked to sign a treatment consent form when she was admitted. Routine procedures were followed by doctors, and other hospital employees in diagnosing

her illness. Tamma later brought suit against the hospital, arguing that she had not consented to these routine procedures. How would you decide? Why?
5. Celia Soloway was admitted to a hospital with a coronary artery disease. After being informed of the risks involved, including the possibility of death, she signed a consent form authorizing the doctors to perform open heart surgery. On the morning of the operation, she changed her mind and decided against having the operation. The doctors, however, went ahead with the operation because she had signed the consent form. She died on the operating table. On what legal grounds might suit be brought on her behalf against the hospital?
6. After lapsing into a coma, Jack Regan's father, Henry, was kept alive for 2 years on life-support systems. He died without regaining consciousness. Jack wanted to be sure that if he became terminally ill, life-sustaining measures would not be used in vain to keep him alive. Is there any legal recourse available to Jack in this situation?
7. Darius Pelzer had a small income from property he had inherited, and he preferred to live on that income rather than work. After he was past 65 years of age, however, inflation made it difficult for him to live on his income. He made application for benefits under old-age, survivors, and disability insurance. Would he get the benefits? Why?
8. Heidi Schwartz was 56 years old when her

husband, who was covered by social security, died in an accident. Her two children were 23 and 25 years of age. Would Mrs. Schwartz be able to receive monthly social security payments immediately?

9. Mark Tarn had a nervous breakdown at the age of 34 and was told by his doctor that he could not work for 6 months. Would he qualify for social security benefits?

10. Linda Gomez, 45, became totally disabled and received a small social security pension. She owned a house and also had a life insurance policy that had a cash surrender value of $1,400. Her personal effects were valued at $5,000, and she had $1,200 in the bank. If her monthly income were small enough, would she qualify for SSI?

Cases to Judge

1. Carmen Ciciretti filed his application for retirement benefits under the Social Security Act. He died 10 days later. The Social Security Administration, unaware of his death, sent him a check for $677.60. The executor of Ciciretti's estate (the person named in his will to handle his affairs) returned the check to the Social Security Administration and asked for a check made payable to him as the executor of the estate. Instead of doing that, the Administration sent a check to Ciciretti's wife in Italy, who had not lived with him for over 50 years. Was the Social Security Administration correct in sending the check to Ciciretti's wife instead of to the executor of his estate? *(Guarino v. Celebrezze,* 336 F.2d 336 (3d Circuit)

2. Ms. Franklin, 45 years old and claiming to be an executive secretary, was involved in an automobile accident in which she sustained a sprain and a whiplash injury to her neck. She applied for disability benefits under social security, claiming that she could not return to her former job because it required her to keep her neck in a fixed position for long periods of time. Evidence in the case was introduced to show that although she might not be able to work as an executive secretary, she could perform other types of secretarial and clerical work. Should Ms. Franklin be considered eligible for disability payments under social security? Explain your answer. *Franklin v. Secretary of Health, Education and Welfare,* 393 F.2d 640 (2d Circuit)

3. Oscar Troupe, who worked as a furniture mover, stopped working after injuring his back while lifting a piano. Following the injury to his back, Troupe started taking more drugs, which he had been taking earlier to relieve leg and back pains. Two years later, he was hospitalized for detoxification and was enrolled in a methadone treatment program. When he stopped using drugs, his leg and back pains increased, and he began receiving treatment for his injury. He applied for disability insurance and SSI under the social security law, but his application was denied. In his appeal to the federal court, the question arose as to when workers are considered disabled and entitled to benefits under the social security law. How should this question be answered? *Troupe v. Heckler,* 618 F. Supp. 248 (New York)

4. Bertha Colyer suffered a heart attack. When the paramedics arrived on the scene, they revived her. However, Bertha had been without oxygen for 10 minutes. As a result, she suffered brain damage. When she was admitted to the hospital, she was placed on a respirator in a coma. Two physicians agreed that the likelihood of her recovering any significant amount of brain function was extremely small. They also agreed that she would probably die within a short time if removed from the respirator. Bertha's husband, who had been appointed her guardian, asked the court to allow the respirator to be disconnected. He claimed that using this extraordinary means to keep his wife alive, even though she was in a coma, violated her rights of privacy. How do you think the court ruled? Explain. *In re Colyer,* 660 P.2d 738 (Washington)

Chapter 39

WILLS AND INTESTACY

Scene: The living room of the Henderson residence. Sylvia, John, and their daughter, Kathleen, are talking.

Sylvia: It was a blessing that Mr. Kulak passed away. He was in a coma for almost 2 weeks before he died.

John: At least he didn't suffer, and the doctors took him off the machines when they knew there was no longer any hope. It must be hard for his daughter, Martha, though, after losing her mother just a year ago.

Kathleen: She's doing okay. I went over to see her this morning, and we had a long talk. She's the only one left in their family now. Did you know that she was adopted?

Sylvia: No, I didn't. Her mother never told me.

John: I hope she doesn't have any difficulty inheriting from her father's estate, being adopted.

Kathleen: She told me today that her father didn't have a will. He was going to have one made as soon as he retired, and he just never got around to it. It all happened so fast.

Sylvia: A lady in the grocery store told me that if you die without a will, the state takes everything. I hope that doesn't happen to Martha—after Mr. Kulak worked so hard all those years.

Kathleen: I hope not.

Sylvia: Speaking of wills, John, you and I don't have wills.

John: I had a will once—years ago—before we were married. I have no idea what happened to it.

Sylvia: You probably left everything to your old girlfriend.

Kathleen: That would be something, Dad, if you died, and your old girlfriend inherited everything.

John: I wonder what ever happened to her. She was nice looking. Her name was Stella.

Kathleen: Stella?

Sylvia: All the more reason you should have a will.

John: The last I heard of her, she owned a furniture store and was married to somebody named Lance Linsky.

Sylvia: There's a lawyer in the building where I work. I think I'll stop in to see him tomorrow about getting our wills made out.

John: That's a good idea. I hope you don't have some old boyfriend in mind to leave things to.

Sylvia: No. I'm going to leave everything to you, John, because I love you, and if you're not alive, everything will go to Kathleen.

Kathleen: Whenever you're ready, Mom. I'll be the first witness!

LEGAL ISSUES

1. From whom do adopted children inherit?
2. Does the state take the property of a person who dies without a will?
3. Does subsequent marriage have any legal effect on a will made prior to the marriage?
4. Is a surviving spouse given any legal protection when omitted from a deceased spouse's will?
5. What is the legal effect of a beneficiary under a will being a witness to that will?

THE SPIRIT OF THE LAW

People often pass away owning property of one kind or another. Unless the property is owned jointly with someone else, a special procedure must be followed to distribute the property to other people who are still living. This procedure varies somewhat depending on whether or not the deceased person (the **decedent**) left a will.

If the decedent left a will, the will must be **probated,** that is, proved and allowed by the court. If the decedent died without a will, the law of the state where the decedent was domiciled at death determines who will inherit the property. In either event, the property is distributed under the supervision of the court.

LEAVING A WILL

A **will** is a document that is drawn up and signed by persons during their lifetime providing for the distribution of their property upon their death. Each state has its own laws setting forth the requirements for making a will.

EXAMPLE 1 Allan Tuthill's Aunt Margaret liked him very much. Many times during her lifetime she had said to him in the presence of other people, "When I die, I want you to have my house." She died without leaving a will, however. Would Allan get the house?

No. It would become a part of the aunt's estate and would go, along with the rest of her estate, to her legal **heirs** (those who inherit by right of relationship).

Capacity of the Testator and Testatrix

The capacity of the testator or the testatrix is one of the most important considerations in determining the validity of any will. **Testator** is the name given to a man who makes a will; a woman who makes a will is called a **testatrix.*** In general, any person who has reached the age of adulthood (18 in most states) and is of sound mind may make a will.

Soundness of Mind Some wills are questioned or challenged on the basis of the soundness of the deceased's mind at the time of execution of the will. Testators must have sufficient mental capacity to understand the nature and extent of their property. In addition, testators must have sufficient understanding to know who would be the natural objects of their bounty. They must also be of sound enough mind to know that they are signing a will.

EXAMPLE 2 Edward Mullins called for an attorney during his last illness and dictated to the attorney the provisions that he wished to have included in his will. The attorney prepared a will which Mullins signed. After Mullins's death, disappointed heirs might dispute the validity of the will on the grounds that the testator did not know what he was doing when he dictated the terms of the will.

Freedom from Undue Influence Wills are sometimes questioned on the grounds of undue influence. Here, again, it is important to have witnesses who are able to testify that the will was made free from all constraint and by the testator's own free will. When persons come under the influence of others to the degree that they are unable to express their real intentions in a will, such a will may be declared invalid. The court must distinguish between undue influence and the kindness, attention, advice, guidance, and friendliness shown toward the testator by the one named in the will.

EXAMPLE 3 Muriel Jergen suffered a heart attack that confined her to the hospital for several weeks before her death. Muriel's brother, who had greatly influenced her life since childhood, persuaded her to draw up a new will making him the only heir to her estate. The will was declared void by the probate court on the grounds that the brother had exerted undue influence on Muriel in view of her physical condition and her relationship to him.

A **probate court,** also known as a surrogate's court or an orphan's court, is one in which wills are probated, or proved, after the death of the testator.

Form of Will

A will can be very simple. It needs only (1) to identify the testator specifically, (2) to identify clearly the testator's property and the **beneficiaries** (the persons to whom the property is to go), and (3) to be properly signed and witnessed. It must conform exactly to statutory requirements, however, and it should at least be checked by a lawyer before it is signed.

*In this chapter there are a number of terms which have male forms (ending in -*or*) and female forms (ending in -*trix*). When these terms appear for the first time, both forms are listed. Thereafter, only the male form is used. In such cases, the male form refers equally to males as well as to females.

The law of wills varies a little from state to state, but the following general requirements are found in all states.

Must Be in Writing With very minor exceptions, a will must be in writing. A will is an important document transferring title to valuable property. It must be in writing to be properly proved in court and to be recorded in the public record. It may be either handwritten or typewritten.

The will offered for probate must be the original copy, not a carbon. It must not be torn, mutilated, or show any signs of burning; such conditions may be accepted as evidence of the testator's intent to revoke the will. A will should contain no alterations of any kind.

EXAMPLE 4 A will was offered for probate soon after Ellen Cook died. On close examination, it was found that the will had been torn in half and later mended with cellulose tape. The court refused to accept the will for probate, questioning its validity and suggesting the possibility that the testator had deliberately attempted to destroy the will.

■ Some states have statutes that provide for the distribution of only a limited amount of personal property by a **nuncupative,** or oral, **will.** The circumstances under which such a will may be used, however, are very limited. The circumstances are usually confined to emergency situations, such as those involving soldiers and sailors in battle and commercial mariners in disasters at sea.

Must Be Properly Signed Every will must be signed in such a way as to identify the will as that of the testator. In some states a will must be signed at the end, but in other states it is held to be valid if a signature is found anywhere in the will. The signing must take place in the presence of witnesses. Some states allow wills to be signed by someone other than the testator at the testator's request and in his or her presence. This would be done, for example, when a testator is paralyzed and cannot write. The law also allows testators to sign with a mark, such as an *X*. This is so because a signature, in the eyes of the law, is any mark placed on the paper which is intended by the person making it to be his or her signature.

Must Be Witnessed ■ The law specifies the number of witnesses who must be present at the signing. Usually, the number is two, although in some states it is three. Following the testator's signing, the witnesses must then sign in the presence of the testator and, in some states, in the presence of each other.

EXAMPLE 5 In a state requiring three witnesses on a will, Oliver Sullivan made a will and had two persons sign it as witnesses. The will was refused for

---

■ This symbol indicates that there may be a state statute that varies from the law discussed here. Whenever you see this symbol, find out, if possible, what the statute in your state says about this point or principle of law.

```
                    WILL OF SANDRA RIVERA

        I, Sandra Rivera, being of sound and disposing mind and memory, and con-
    sidering the uncertainty of this life, do make, publish, and declare this to
    be my last WILL and TESTAMENT as follows, hereby revoking all other former
    Wills by me at any time made.

        FIRST:  After my lawful debts are paid, I give to The Boys' Camping Asso-
    ciation of Chicago, Illinois, $7,500 in cash.  And to my mother, Mrs. Eileen
    Rivera, the balance of my estate remaining after the above bequest has been
    distributed.

        SECOND:  I hereby appoint Mr. Henry Rappaport, 2910 North Tenth Street,
    Port Deposit, Maryland, to be executor of this my last Will and Testament.

        IN WITNESS WHEREOF, I have hereunto subscribed my name, and affixed my
    seal, this 17th day of November        , 19--, in Chicago, Illinois.

                                        Sandra Rivera
                                        Sandra Rivera

        Subscribed by Sandra Rivera, the Testatrix named in the foregoing Will
    in the presence of each of us, and at the time of making such subscription,
    the above Instrument was declared by the said Testatrix to be her last Will
    and Testament, and each of us, at the request of said Testatrix and in her
    presence and in the presence of each other, signed our names as witnesses
    thereto.
                                            420 Chester Drive
    Pauline Sanchez       residing at   Chicago, Illinois
                                            325 Grand Avenue
    Joseph Carter         residing at   Chicago, Illinois
```

A valid will must be signed by testator and witnesses. What else is required of a valid will?

probate because it had not been prepared in conformity with the state law. Sullivan was considered to have died intestate—that is, without leaving a will.

In most states, minors may witness a will as long as they have a sufficient understanding of what is taking place. Persons named as beneficiaries in a will should *not* be witnesses. If they or their spouses are witnesses to the will, they will not receive their inheritance unless there is a sufficient number of other witnesses to meet the statutory requirement.

Legal Issue No. 5

In a few states, a will written entirely in the handwriting of the testator, called a **holographic will,** is valid without witnesses.

Rights of Surviving Spouse

A surviving spouse is protected by law even when omitted from a deceased spouse's will. A surviving spouse who does not like what he or she is given under a will may waive the will and take an elective share of the estate as determined by state statute.

In some states, the right of dower and curtesy is also an option that is available to a surviving spouse in regard to real estate owned by the decedent. At common law, the **right of dower** was available to a wife upon her husband's death. It was a life interest in one-third of the real property owned by the husband during the marriage. The **right of curtesy** was available to a husband

Legal Issue No. 4

upon his wife's death only if a child was born of the marriage. Curtesy amounted to a life interest in all the real property owned by the wife during the marriage. Many states today either have done away with dower and curtesy rights or have modified them considerably. In states that have retained dower and curtesy, a surviving spouse might elect the right when the decedent's estate is insolvent, that is, owes more money to creditors than it has assets. This is so because the rights of dower and curtesy come first, before the rights of the decedent's creditors.

Omitted Children

Some states have laws protecting children who are unintentionally left out of a will. Forgotten children, under these laws, will receive the share that they would have received had their parent died without a will. Children who are intentionally omitted from a parent's will will receive nothing from the parent's estate.

EXAMPLE 6 Edward Morley's will gave a large sum of money to charity and provided nothing for Edward's son, Dennis. Moreover, it contained a clause stating, "I intentionally omit to provide for my son, Dennis Morley." Because Edward's intent was clear, Dennis will receive nothing from his father's estate. Had the will not contained the clause omitting to provide for Dennis, Dennis might have been able to prove that his father mistakenly omitted him from the will and thereby claim a share of the estate.

Changing or Revoking a Will

If you wish to change a simple will, the best thing to do is to write an entirely new one. If the will is long and involved, however, and only some minor change or addition is needed, it may be added to the original by means of a **codicil,** or supplement, that is either added to the original document or drawn up on a separate piece of paper. In either case, however, it must be prepared with all the formalities of the will itself.

EXAMPLE 7 William Birnbaum prepared a will in which he left his entire estate to his wife, providing that the estate should go to their child if his wife were to die before him. Two years later, another child was born to the Birnbaums. To provide for this second child, Birnbaum drew up a codicil and attached it to the original will. To be valid and enforceable, the codicil had to be properly signed and witnessed, as was done when the will itself was prepared.

Legal Issue No. 3

Under the law of many states, a will may be revoked (withdrawn or canceled) in the following ways: (1) burning, tearing, canceling, or obliterating the will with the intent to revoke it, (2) executing a new will, (3) subsequent marriage of the testator, and (4) the testator's divorce or annulment of marriage as to gifts to the former spouse.

CARRYING OUT THE PROVISIONS OF A WILL

A properly drawn will always names an executor (or executrix). The **executor** (male) or **executrix** (female) is the personal representative of the estate named to carry out the terms of the will. When the testator dies, title to his or her personal property is automatically assigned to the executor. It is then the duty of

The Hendersons named each other as beneficiaries in their wills. May they serve as each other's witnesses as well?

the executor to dispose of the property as provided in the will. Title to real property goes automatically to the testator's heirs. It does not go to the executor first, except if the property must be sold to pay the testator's debts.

As soon as the testator dies, the will is filed for probate. The first job of the probate court is to establish the validity of the will. If no one opposes the probating of the will, this can be a simple matter. Sometimes, however, heirs who are left out of the will may contest it, and long litigation may result.

After the will is properly proved, or probated, the judge authorizes the executor to take charge of the property and distribute it according to the terms of the will. The executor must receive the approval of the court in everything he or she does. After the estate is distributed, the executor is discharged by the court and the estate is declared closed.

If the executor cannot serve because of death, illness, or other reasons, or if the decedent dies without a will, the court will appoint an **administrator** or **administratrix** to perform the duties.

EXAMPLE 8 In her will, Linda Tenser named Ralph Lovett as executor of her estate, to serve without bond. Lovett died a few months before Tenser. Unless Tenser had named another executor in the will, the court, on Tenser's death, would appoint a competent person, acceptable to all parties, to act as the administrator of the estate with the will annexed.

∎ INTESTACY

A person who dies without making a will is said to have died **intestate,** and the property is distributed according to the laws of descent in that particular state. The estate is handled in exactly the same way as in the case of a will, except that the probate court appoints an administrator to look after the estate. The duties of an administrator are comparable to those of an executor, except that the administrator must distribute the estate according to the law of the state.

Distribution of Intestate Property

■ The property of one who dies intestate goes to that person's heirs according to the law of the state where the decedent was domiciled at death. (Table 39-1 exemplifies one state's laws.) In general, the surviving spouse is entitled to one-third or one-half of the estate. The balance is usually divided equally among the children of the decedent. If any children are deceased, grandchildren share equally in their deceased parent's share of their grandparent's estate. If all children are deceased, all grandchildren share equally in their grandparent's estate. If there are no children or grandchildren, the property goes to the decedent's parents, if living, and if not, to brothers and sisters. Similarly, the children of any deceased brothers or sisters (nieces and nephews) take their parent's

TABLE 39-1
DISTRIBUTION OF INTESTATE PROPERTY UNDER A TYPICAL STATE STATUTE*

If The Deceased Is Survived by:	A Surviving Spouse Receives:	Any Remainder Is Distributed:
Issue (lineal descendants such as children, grandchildren, great grandchildren)	One-half (or one-third)† of the estate	Equally to the deceased's children. If any children are also deceased, their children divide their deceased's parent's share equally.
No issue but by kindred (blood relatives)	$50,000 plus one-half of the remainder of the estate (but if the estate is under $50,000, the surviving spouse receives it all)	Equally between the deceased's father and mother or to the survivor of them. *However, if the parents are deceased or have no survivor, then:* Equally among the deceased's brothers and sisters. If any brothers or sisters are also deceased, their children divide their deceased parent's share equally. *However, if there are no living brothers or sisters or nieces or nephews, then:* Equally among the deceased's next of kin (those who are most nearly related by blood including aunts, uncles, and cousins)
No issue and no kindred	The entire estate. *However, if there is no surviving spouse, issue, or kindred, then:* The entire estate escheats to (becomes the property of) the state.	

*Massachusetts   †In some other states

share of the estate. If there are no brothers or sisters or nieces or nephews, uncles and aunts inherit the property. If no uncles or aunts survive the decedent, cousins become the heirs. It is only when a person is survived by no blood relatives that the property **escheats,** that is, becomes the property of the state.

Legal Issue No. 2

Adopted Children

Legal Issue No. 1

Under modern state statutes, adopted children are treated legally as though they were the naturally born children of their adopting parents. They inherit from their adopting parents rather than from their natural parents. Similarly, they are heirs of their adopted brothers and sisters and other adopted relatives.

Suggestions for Reducing Legal Risks

1. An attorney should be consulted when a person draws a will because the will must be clear, definite, and in legal form, including proper signatures of the testator and witnesses.
2. The property in a will must be clearly described or identified.
3. The executed original copy of the will should be placed in the hands of the executor, deposited with the attorney who drew the will, or at the very least, placed in a safe-deposit box or some equally protected place.
4. Several copies of the will should be made and deposited in a safe place or places, and these locations should be made known to some of the principal heirs. Only the original should be signed, however.
5. All subsequent codicils should be accurately dated and should be drawn with all the formality of the original will.
6. In these days of frequent automobile and airplane accidents, many times a husband, a wife, and their children or other relatives lose their lives together in what is known as a common disaster. The exact order in which the deaths occur may affect the distribution of the deceaseds' property. Wills should be drawn to allow for the possibility of a common disaster.
7. If a medium-sized or large estate is involved, an individual should consider the possibility of a trust agreement. A trust is preferred over a formal will if an individual is seeking to protect his or her estate from the loose spending habits of survivors. A trust generally assures the survivors of a continuing, regular income, and if properly drawn, it may provide certain tax advantages that are unobtainable in the case of a formal will. A competent attorney should be consulted before a trust agreement is drafted.

Language of the Law

Define or explain each of the following words or phrases:

decedent	testatrix	right of dower	administrator
probated	probate court	right of curtesy	administratrix
will	beneficiaries	codicil	intestate
heirs	nuncupative will	executor	escheats
testator	holographic will	executrix	

Questions for Review

1. Who may make a will?
2. What factors are considered in determining whether a testator has the capacity to make a valid will?
3. Describe and explain the required form of a will.
4. How is a surviving spouse protected by law even when omitted from the deceased spouse's will?
5. What is the difference between the right of dower and the right of curtesy under the common law?
6. When might a surviving spouse elect the right of dower or curtesy today?
7. How does the law protect children who are omitted from their parent's will?
8. From whom do adopted children inherit under modern statutes?
9. How should a person proceed to change a will?
10. How may a person revoke a previous will?
11. How is a will probated? What is the name of the special court used for this purpose in your state?
12. What happens when a person dies without leaving a will?
13. How is property distributed under the laws of descent in your state?

Cases in Point

In each of the following cases, give your decision and state a legal principle that applies to the case:

1. After Peter Ramirez's death, two wills that he had made were found. One was dated May 20, 1986, and the other was dated June 17, 1987. Which of the wills should be accepted by the court in settling the estate?
2. When Leo Abbey died, he left his wife and three children as survivors. Was his wife entitled to the entire estate if he did not leave a will?
3. Betsy Addis signed her typewritten will and had Paula Cantini, a friend, sign it as a witness. Was this a valid will?
4. Bertha Bogart made out her will according to the laws of her state. Six months later she decided to leave a favorite uncle $2,000 from her estate. She orally notified the executor named in her will to see that her Uncle Henry got $2,000 on her death, but she did not change her will. Is the executor allowed to give Bogart's uncle the $2,000?
5. Ben Blumberg was an elderly man of considerable means. He became seriously ill and decided to make his will. He called for his attorney, but he was very indefinite about the extent of his property and the correct names of the relatives he wanted to benefit under the will. Do you think that Blumberg was competent to make a valid will?
6. Jean Bailey became enraged at her son and tore up the original copy of her will which had included a generous bequest to the son. She subsequently made a new will, leaving her son only $1. Following Bailey's death, the son tried to have the will set aside in favor of the previous will, a copy of which was found among Bailey's papers. Do you think the son will succeed in having the new will set aside?
7. George Chaplin died without leaving a will. Surviving were his wife and two children. His estate amounted to $20,000. Under the laws of descent in your state, how would the property be distributed?
8. Joseph Clancy, whose wife was deceased, died without leaving a will. His only known relatives were his aged mother and one sister. Under the laws of descent in your state, how would Clancy's property be divided?
9. Doris Goff asked her cousin Ed Blair to witness the signing of her will. Blair had been

named a beneficiary in the will. Will Blair receive his legacy under the will when Goff dies?

10. Judith Avery drew up her own will and had it typed with lines indicated for signatures of witnesses. Avery visited her neighbor, Aaron Bacon, and asked him to sign the will as a witness. She then visited her neighbor, Bob Cahill, and asked him to sign as a witness. Following Cahill's signature, Avery then signed the will. Has Avery executed a valid will?

Cases to Judge

1. Joseph Katz signed his will in the presence of two witnesses. Instead of signing their names, however, the witnesses printed their names in the place provided for witnesses' signatures. After the death of Katz, the will was presented for probate, and the witnesses signed an affidavit stating that they were witnesses to the will. The question arose as to whether the printing of the witnesses' names at the end of the will constituted their signatures. How would you decide. Why? *Will of Katz,* 494 N.Y.S.2d 629 (New York)

2. After signing a promissory note at his bank late one Friday afternoon, Howard Gillespie asked the assistant vice president of the bank to take some dictation. He then dictated a codicil to his will, leaving $70,000 to Joan Brammer. The codicil was typed, signed by Gillespie, and left with the bank officer. The following Monday, the bank officer had two bank employees sign the codicil as the only witnesses. Gillespie was not present at the time. He died 5 days later. Was the codicil valid? Why or why not? *Brammer v. Taylor,* 338 S.E.2d 207 (West Virginia)

3. Janet and Fred Del Guercio took title to their house as tenants by the entirety. A year later, Janet conveyed her interest in the property to Fred so that Fred owned it alone. Thirteen years after that, marital difficulties arose, and Janet left the marital residence and brought a divorce action against Fred. Fred died, however, before being served a summons in that action. His will left the house to someone else. Not satisfied with the provisions of Fred's will, Janet sought her elective share of his estate. She did not qualify for this, however, under New Jersey law. What other legal right would you suggest that might be available to Janet to obtain title to the house? Explain. *In Re Del Guercio Estate,* 501 A.2d 1072 (New Jersey)

4. After Mildred Savage died, her niece, Gertrude Seals, offered Mrs. Savage's will to the court for probate. The will, which was handwritten with no witnesses, gave parts of Savage's 40 acres of land to various people. The will was allowed by the lower court after a witness, Mittie Kennedy, testified that she witnessed the signing of the will even though she did not sign as a witness. Nine years later suit was brought by a nephew, John Savage, arguing that the will should not have been allowed because it was executed improperly. How should the appellate court decide? Explain. *Black v. Seals,* 474 So. 2d 696 (Alabama)

5. Julia Dejmal executed her will while a patient in St. Joseph's Hospital. The will was witnessed by Lucille and Catherine Pechacek. Catherine was 19 years old and was employed as an assistant x-ray technician at the hospital. The age of majority at the time in that state was 21. It was contended that the will was not valid because one of the witnesses to it was a minor. Do you agree with the contention? Why or why not? *Matter of Estate of Dejmal,* 289 N.W.2d 813 (Wisconsin)

CASE TO DISCUSS

Matter of Will of Womack
280 S.E.2d 494 (North Carolina)

When Claudia Hester Womack (Miss Hester) died, she was survived by 5 first cousins, 20 second cousins, and 1 third cousin. She was the last survivor of a brother and three sisters, none of whom ever married. Her will left all of her estate to Willie and Frank Boswell on the condition that they lived with her and cared for her for the remainder of her life. The Boswells had known the Womack sisters most of their lives. Floyd Strader, one of the first cousins, contested the will on the grounds that the testatrix lacked testamentary capacity. He also claimed that the will was procured by undue influence.

THE TRIAL

The evidence indicated that Miss Hester was 89 years old, physically disabled, and dependent upon others to bring her food and take care of her daily hygiene. She was described as strong-willed and proud and knowledgeable of the family history. Following her last surviving sister's death, she was grief-stricken and felt very strongly about staying in her own home. One of the relatives mentioned a nursing home to her shortly after her sister's death and several relatives were generally known to have discussed a nursing home. The record reflects that she enjoyed a good relationship with most of her relatives and that although they knew someone had to stay with her and take care of her, they were not able to do it because of other obligations.

The . . . evidence as to Miss Hester's lack of understanding of the kind and extent of her property consisted of testimony that a year or two prior to her death she and Miss Willie, the sister who managed their affairs, were very concerned over the expense of keeping another sister in a nursing home. Miss Hester seldom discussed business affairs. [S]he had been confined to her home for several years. [In] the opinion of Edith Chandler, a second cousin, . . . Miss Hester did not know the nature and extent of her property. . . .

Edith Chandler testified that she believed that Miss Hester knew there was property, but she did not think that Miss Hester had any business dealings about it. She further testified that Miss Hester "knew where the farm stretched out to" but "didn't understand the full value of the land." On cross-examination, however, she admitted that she had never discussed Miss Hester's business affairs with her and had no way of knowing what she knew about her property.

The evidence shows that just prior to Miss Willie's death Frank Boswell helped her with her bank accounts and other business affairs, and after her death he served as Miss Hester's personal representative at the inventory of Miss Willie's safe deposit box. In addition, the evidence shows that four days after Miss Hester's will was written she [declined to be the administratrix] of Miss Willie's estate in favor of Frank Boswell.

The jury found that Miss Hester lacked the necessary mental capacity to make a will and also that the will was procured by undue influence.

THE ARGUMENTS ON APPEAL

Willie and Frank Boswell argued that there was not enough evidence of undue influence or incapacity to disallow the will. The cousin who contested the will argued that Miss Hester lacked an understanding of the nature and extent of her property, thus lacking the capacity to make a will.

QUESTIONS FOR DISCUSSION

1. What is required for a testator to be of sound enough mind to make a will?
2. In your opinion, was Miss Hester of sound mind? Explain.
3. When may a will be declared invalid because of undue influence?
4. In your opinion, did the evidence indicate that the will was procured by undue influence? Explain.
5. If you were an appellate court judge hearing the case, for whom would you decide? Why?

CASE TO BRIEF

After reading *How to Write a Case Brief* on page 78, and examining the sample brief on page 80, write a brief of the following case:

Matter of Estate of Feir
701 P.2d 3 (Arizona)

The principal question raised in this appeal is whether [Harry Feir's] last will and testament was cancelled by his typewritten letter to appellant. We find that it was not and reverse.

The decedent [Feir] died on April 30, 1983, and application was made to the Pima County Superior Court for commencement of intestacy proceedings by his sister, appellee. Her application was opposed by appellant, Sidney S. Kanter, who, as executor of the will of decedent, filed an application for . . . probate of the will. . . .

Prior to 1979, the decedent was a resident of New Jersey. On November 20, 1979, appellant, a New Jersey attorney, at decedent's request prepared the will in question.

On December 8, 1980, decedent sent a typed letter to appellant which [Kanter] provided:

"Dear Sir:
  Please be advised that I am VOIDING my will which you had prepared for me on November 10, 1979. Thank you.
                    Cordially yours,
                    Harry Feir
                    /s/HARRY FEIR

Notary Public of New Jersey
My commission expires May 21, 1985
/s/Gail Ann Calderio"

In September 1981, the decedent moved to Arizona. He died in Tucson on April 30, 1983.

The original of the will in question and a copy of the typewritten letter of December 8, 1980, were among the items found in the decedent's safe-deposit box. . . . The trial court in effect found that the letter to appellant revoked decedent's Last Will and Testament.

Appellant [Kanter] contends that the letter did not operate to revoke the will. He argues that the court's ruling overlooks the similar [New Jersey and Arizona statutes.] [The Arizona statute] provides [that a will is revoked *only* by either:]

  "(1) A subsequent will which revokes the prior will or part expressly or by inconsistency.

  (2) Being burned, torn, cancelled, obliterated or destroyed, with the intent and for the purpose of revoking it by the testator or by another person in his presence and by his direction."
This section is similar to [a section] of the Uniform Probate Code. . . . The official comment to the section in the Uniform Probate Code explains that "revocation of a will may be by either a subsequent will or *an act done to the document.*" (Emphasis added) It is uncontested that the letter was not a subsequent will. It obviously does not comply with the statutory requirements for a will, . . . and thus would not qualify as an instrument of equal formality for purposes of revoking the will. [According to Arizona law:]

  "Except as provided for holographic wills, . . . every will shall be in writing signed by the testator or in the testator's name by some other person in the testator's presence and by his direction, and shall be signed by at least two persons each of whom witnessed either the signing or the testator's acknowledgment of the signature or of the will."
[The Arizona statute] provides for revocation by writing which the letter did not accomplish for the reasons already discussed "or by act" which must be done to the document as expressed in the comment to the Uniform Probate Laws section. The letter did not call for nor accomplish any act to be performed to the document. Although the letter may have expressed the testator's intent to revoke the will, the omission of effecting a cancellation of the document is crucial and will not be overlooked. . . . A will must be revoked in a manner prescribed by statute. . . . The intent to revoke must be accompanied by an act which appears on the purported will. . . .

We find appellee's authority [improper, considering] the situation before us. [In a Colorado case,] the decedent wrote on a duplicate carbon copy of the will, "This Last Will & Testament is now null, & void." The court found that the will had been cancelled as a result of the act of the decedent with respect to the duplicate copy in his possession. In [a Louisiana case,] the decedent revoked his will by a holograph. The act of physically destroying a duplicate original of the will was found sufficient in [an Indiana case]. . . .

The judgment of the trial court is reversed and the cause is remanded with instructions that summary judgment be entered in favor of appellant.

TRIAL PROCEDURES

THE VERDICT, JUDGEMENT, AND EXECUTION

The decision of a jury is called a *verdict*. In a civil case, usually five sixths of the jury must reach agreement in order to arrive at a verdict. The plaintiff and the defendant may agree, however, that a different majority of the jurors be taken as the verdict. To reach a verdict in a criminal case, the jury must agree unanimously. If it cannot do so, a mistrial is called and a new trial may be held at the option of the prosecution.

Following the jury's verdict, the court issues a judgment. A *judgment* (called a *decree* in a court of equity) is the act of the trial court finally determining the rights of the parties. This is the court's decision in the case. A *summary judgment* (called a *judgment on the pleadings* in some states) may be made without hearing evidence if the court finds that it is clear from the pleadings that one party is entitled to win the case as a matter of law. Similarly, if the judge believes that the jury's verdict is incorrect as a matter of law, he or she may issue a *judgment notwithstanding the verdict*. This is a judgment in favor of one party even though the jury found in favor of the other party. Summary judgments and judgments notwithstanding the verdict are initiated by motions made by either party.

If the losing party is ordered to pay money to the winning party and does not do so, the winning party must ask the court for a *writ of execution*. A writ of execution orders the sheriff to enforce a money judgment.

Garnishment may sometimes be used to satisfy a judgment. A court orders a third person who owes money or property to the losing party to turn it over to the court or sheriff. Wages (often limited to 25% of the debtor's take-home pay) and bank accounts are the most common types of property garnished.

THE CASE OF GRAZIO v. WILLIAMSON (continued from page 533)

The jury has made its decision and has filed into the courtroom. The bailiff calls out, "Court! Please rise!" Everyone stands, and the judge enters the courtroom.

When the judge sits down, the bailiff says, "Please be seated!"

"Mr. Foreman," the judge asks, "has the jury reached a verdict?"

Standing, the foreman replies, "Yes, Your Honor, we have."

"What is your verdict?"

"We find in favor of the plaintiff in the amount of $2,500."

The judge, finding the verdict to be consistent with the facts and the law, issues a judgment for the plaintiff for $2,500. The judge then thanks the jury and adjourns the court session.

QUESTIONS AND PROBLEMS

Answer the following questions. Refer to the pages in parentheses to review the *Trial Procedure* sections presented earlier in the text.

1. How does a verdict differ from a judgment?
2. Suppose Williamson failed to pay Grazio the $2,500. What could Grazio do?
3. How could garnishment be used against Williamson?
4. Explain the way a lawyer representing a plaintiff begins a lawsuit. (page 181)
5. Describe two ways a defendant's lawyer may respond to a complaint. (page 181)
6. List five methods of discovery. (page 269)
7. Differentiate between a deposition and interrogatories. (page 269)
8. What is a motion for summary judgment and when may it be made?
9. Describe jury selection. (page 328)
10. Distinguish between a challenge for cause and a peremptory challenge. (page 328)
11. List the elements of opening statements. (page 405)
12. List the elements of closing statements. (page 469)
13. What are jury instructions? (page 533)
14. As lawyer for Williamson, review the case and recommend possible grounds for appeal.

Appendix

A DAY IN COURT— CONDUCTING A MOCK TRIAL

A *mock trial* is a simulation designed to give participants a taste of what it is like to be a part of an actual trial. Participating in a mock trial helps to develop the ability to analyze difficult problems, to organize and prepare materials carefully and logically, to ask questions effectively, to think and speak quickly and clearly, and to listen to other people attentively. Students in law school often participate in mock trials, which they refer to as *moot court* or *appellate court* proceedings.

In real life, people should always ask themselves, ''Is a lawsuit really necessary?'' before they start a court action. *Litigation* (the process of pursuing a lawsuit) may be a costly, highly emotional, and time-consuming process. If it is possible to settle a dispute out of court or to arbitrate a dispute, this should be tried. To *arbitrate* means to call in a third party, an arbitrator, to settle a dispute. If court action can be prevented by some sort of compromise agreement, much time and money may be saved. Such an out-of-court settlement is known as a *compromise of disputed claim*.

If a dispute does come to trial, the courts do two things: First, they determine the rights of the parties; second, they provide a way to enforce these rights or restore people to their rights. The law relating to the determination of rights is called *substantive law*. The law relating to the process of bringing a case to court and enforcing or restoring rights is called *adjective*, or *procedural*, law.

A *trial* is a judicial examination of the issues between the parties before a court, which is an impartial body with a judge and sometimes a jury. It is called an *adversary proceeding* because the parties are opposed to each other, each taking different positions. The actual process of taking a case through court is a complicated one, requiring the services of experienced and skilled attorneys.

DUTIES OF PARTICI-PANTS

As you recall, the participants in a trial are listed on page 82. Most mock trials do without a process server and a sheriff. We will discuss the essential characters in a mock trial here: the judge, the bailiff, the clerk of court, the court reporter, the attorneys for the plaintiff (prosecution in a criminal case), the attorneys for the defendant, the witnesses, and the jurors. In civil cases the plaintiff and defendant may be called as witnesses. Each participant plays a vital role in the trial, with a high degree of responsibility. Some of the roles, such as the judge, the witnesses, and the attorneys, require a considerable amount of preparation outside of the classroom in order to perform adequately.

The Judge

The judge's primary role is to preside over the courtroom. He or she must keep order and see that the trial moves along smoothly. The judge must be thoroughly familiar with the steps in the trial and the rules of evidence (see pages 572 and 573). When an attorney objects to a line of questioning, the judge must be prepared to make an immediate decision on whether to sustain (allow) or overrule (not allow) the objection. In addition, the judge must explain to the jury the law that applies to the case and, in general, supervise the jury's conduct.

SUMMARY OF STEPS IN A CIVIL TRIAL

1. Service of process and other pleadings
2. Methods of discovery
3. Jury selection (in a jury trial)
4. Opening statement by plaintiff's attorney
5. Opening statement by defendant's attorney
6. Direct and cross-examination of plaintiff's witnesses
7. Direct and cross-examination of defendant's witnesses
8. Closing argument by plaintiff's attorney
9. Closing argument by defendant's attorney
10. Judge's instructions to the jury
11. Jury deliberation
12. Jury's verdict
13. Court's judgment
14. Execution of judgment

The Bailiff

After calling the court to order and introducing the judge, the bailiff's principal role is to maintain order in the courtroom. In a mock trial, the bailiff may perform other functions assigned by the teacher, such as overseeing the jury's actions and taking attendance.

The Clerk of the Court

The clerk of the court is responsible for maintaining court records. The clerk keeps a file for each case, accepts all pleadings filed by the attorneys, and issues judgments and orders made by the judge. During a trial, the clerk calls the cases, swears in the witnesses, and assists the judge when called upon to do so.

The Court Reporter

The court reporter takes down the words that are spoken by the participants during the trial. In addition, the reporter marks the physical evidence that is introduced at the trial. This is done under the direction of the judge and consists of marking items "Exhibit A," "Exhibit B," and so on. In a mock trial, two or more people may be assigned this task.

In a real trial, the court reporter's notes are transcribed only at the request of one of the attorneys. Usually, this is done when one of the parties decides to appeal the case to a higher court.

Attorneys for Plaintiff and Defendant

In a mock trial, as many as four people may be assigned as attorneys for each side. One attorney may give the opening statement to the judge and jury, a second attorney may conduct the direct examination of witnesses, a third attorney may conduct the cross-examination of witnesses, and a fourth attorney may give the closing arguments. The attorneys for each side should meet together with their witnesses, discuss the case thoroughly, and plan their roles carefully.

Attorneys assigned to give the opening and closing statements write a rough draft of the statement and review it with the other attorneys for their suggestions before making a final draft. Although prepared in writing beforehand, opening and closing statements are not read to the judge and jury. Instead, they are given extemporaneously, with the speaker keeping as much eye contact with the judge and members of the jury as possible. Closing statements might well be modified as the trial unfolds.

Attorneys assigned to conduct the direct examination also prepare questions in writing which they intend to ask each witness. The attorneys review these questions with their witnesses before the trial. Attorneys assigned to conduct cross-examination should anticipate the testimony from witnesses for the other side, and think about ways to *impeach* (call into question) that testimony. Students playing the roles of attorneys conducting direct and cross-examination need to have a working knowledge of the rules of evidence.

The Witnesses

In a mock trial, witnesses must learn their parts well. This is because they are expected to answer correctly the questions asked by the examining attorneys. If they are not well prepared during cross-examination, it will appear to the jury that they are not telling the truth or that they are mistaken in their testimony. Meeting with the attorneys, discussing the facts of the case, and writing out answers to expected questions are good ways to prepare for the trial. In addition, witnesses should be prepared to answer questions pertaining to the character they are playing, even if it is not indicated in the script. They also should try to adopt the character's personality as closely as possible. A person playing the role of a priest, for example, would probably not use gruff, street language.

The Jurors

Jurors have the responsibility of determining the final outcome of the case. They must listen carefully to the evidence that is presented at the trial. They must decide whether or not the testimony of each witness is believable. They must pay careful attention to the judge's explanation of the law as it applies to the case. They must keep an open mind about the case until all the evidence has been presented. In some states, jurors are allowed to take notes during the trial; in others, they are not allowed to do so. You may wish to follow the rules of your own state with regard to notetaking by members of the jury. Jurors may not discuss the case, even among themselves, until the end of the trial when they deliberate in private. During the deliberation, jurors must speak and vote according to their individual consciences. They must use their talents and abilities to help the group reach a decision that is fair and just.

COURTROOM DECORUM

Strict rules of conduct must be followed during a mock trial. A courtroom is a formal setting. Attorneys always stand when they speak in open court. When examining or cross-examining witnesses, attorneys speak clearly so that they can be heard easily by the witness, the judge, and members of the jury. An attorney stands, rather than raising a hand, when making objections.

Participants in a mock trial should be courteous to each other at all times. No one should speak in a rude manner to anyone else. The judge is addressed respectfully as ''Your Honor,'' and opposing attorneys treat each other with grace and courtesy. Other than attorneys making objections, people do not interrupt others who are speaking. The audience is required to be quiet and attentive. The judge is responsible for seeing that proper rules of conduct are followed during the trial.

TRIAL PROCEDURE

The following is a step-by-step procedure for conducting a mock trial. Read the entire process thoroughly so that you will know what to expect. Then, find your particular role in the procedure and prepare carefully to play that part.

The Opening of Court and Jury Selection

1. In a jury trial, the entire body of jurors (usually 30 or more), called the *venire*, is ushered into the courtroom and sits opposite the jury box in seats usually used by the audience.
2. The bailiff enters the courtroom and calls out: ''All rise! The Court of _____ is now in session! The Honorable Judge _____ presiding!''
3. The judge enters and takes a seat at the bench. Everyone sits down.
4. The clerk calls the first case: ''Case No. 87-236 Andrews v. Larson!''
5. The attorneys for each side rise, and the judge asks if the attorneys are ready.
6. If the attorneys are ready, the judge welcomes the jurors, tells them the general nature of the case and the names of the parties and their attorneys. The clerk of the court picks, without looking, slips containing numbers from a box or barrel at the bench. Jurors assigned those numbers are told to take seats in the jury box. When twelve jurors are selected in this manner, they are examined by the judge and attorneys to see if they are biased or prejudiced. This process is discussed in more detail in the Trial Procedure section on page 328. Jurors who are challenged are replaced by other jurors from the venire in the same way that the original jurors were selected. The process continues until a full jury is selected. Remaining members of the venire, who were not chosen, are ushered back to the jury room (or into the audience).

The Opening Statements

Opening statements are important because they are the first opportunities that the attorneys have to tell the judge and jury about their case. The attorneys

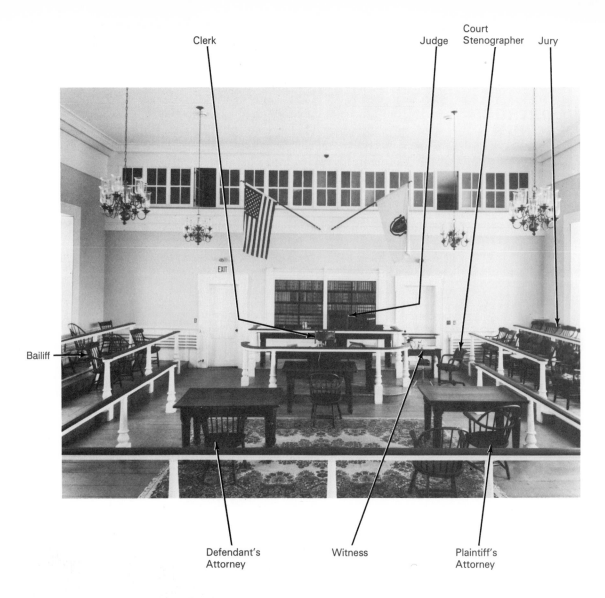

Clerk · Judge · Court Stenographer · Jury · Bailiff · Defendant's Attorney · Witness · Plaintiff's Attorney · EXIT

outline their arguments logically and prepare the jury for the evidence that they will hear. It is a time for storytelling—a time for recreating the facts in the minds of the jurors. A good impression at this time can remain with the jurors throughout the trial.

Opening statements should be clear, concise, and well organized. The elements that should be included in the statement are listed in the Trial Procedure section at the end of Unit 5 (page 405) and model opening statements are presented there and in Figures A-1 and A-2 (pages 567 and 568). Mock trial attorneys should adapt the format to match their facts and arguments.

7. The plaintiff's attorney (or the prosecutor in a criminal case) makes an opening statement.

FIGURE A-1
PLAINTIFF'S MODEL OPENING STATEMENT

May it please the court, ladies and gentlemen of the jury: My name is _____. Here, to help me with this case, are [introduce your colleagues]. We represent the plaintiff, _____. The purpose of this opening statement is to outline in an orderly manner the evidence that we will present. We do this to make it easier for you to see the whole picture of this tragic accident in proper perspective. We want you to see how each bit of evidence fits into the whole picture and thus make it easier for you to perform your duties as members of the group that will see that justice is done.

The evidence will show that on . . . . [Describe, in a logical sequence, the events that occurred.]

Witnesses will testify that . . . . [Summarize your witnesses' testimony.]

One of our witnesses will tell you that . . . . [Emphasize an important point.]

Later, the judge will tell you about the law. I am sure the judge will explain to you that under the law of this state, . . . [Tell briefly about the law favorable to your client and explain the way in which the burden of proof will be met.]

The evidence will show that . . . . [Point to the jury's logical conclusion.]

On the basis of this evidence, we will ask for a verdict in an amount sufficient to compensate [name of plaintiff] for her injuries. Thank you.

8. The defense attorney makes an opening statement.

FIGURE A-2
DEFENDANT'S MODEL OPENING STATEMENT

May it please the court, ladies and gentlemen of the jury: My name is _____. These are my colleagues who will help me today: [Introduce your colleagues.] We represent _____, who is the defendant in this unfortunate case. As you have been told, these opening statements are for the purpose of assisting you in understanding the evidence, and not for arguing the case. My opponent, [name of plaintiff's attorney], has quite effectively told you about some of the evidence that will be presented to you. Unfortunately, you have not yet been given the complete and true picture.

[Name of plaintiff] is suing my client, [name of defendant], because of injuries she received in an accident on _____. We do not deny that [name of plaintiff] was injured, and we do not minimize the seriousness of those injuries. We will show you, however, that . . . . [Tell about something that the jury has not heard that is favorable to your case.]

Plaintiff claims that the injuries were caused by the negligence of [name of defendant]. This we deny. You may have noticed that when [plaintiff's attorney] told about the evidence that [he or she] will produce on this point, [he or she] was very brief. We, however, will produce extensive evidence on this point. The evidence will show that . . . . [Tell about your evidence.]

Our witnesses will testify that . . . . [Tell what the witnesses will say.]

Let me point out once again that the injuries sustained by the plaintiff were most unfortunate, but the true fact is that they were caused by the plaintiff's own carelessness. In this state, ladies and gentlemen, contributory negligence is what is known as an absolute defense. By that, I mean that if you believe that the plaintiff was even slightly contributorily negligent, then she cannot recover any damages.

Given the facts, the plaintiff cannot prove its case as the law requires. All of this evidence will indicate that . . . . [Give a conclusion that you want the jury to reach.]

We submit that plaintiff's accident was a tragic occurrence that took place through no fault of [name of defendant], and, at the close of the case, we will ask you to so find and to return a verdict in favor of the defendant. Thank you.

The Plaintiff's Case in Chief

9. The plaintiff's attorney calls the first witness.
10. When a witness is first called in the trial, the clerk swears that witness in. The witness raises his or her right hand. The clerk asks, ''Do you swear to testify to the truth, the whole truth, and nothing but the truth?'' After replying in the affirmative, the witness is told to be seated at the witness stand.
11. The plaintiff's attorney begins the direct examination by asking the witness to state his or her name and address. The attorney then proceeds with a series of well prepared questions designed to bring out exactly what information each witness can contribute to proving the particular case. Again, the rules of evidence, discussed on page 572, must be followed closely.
12. When objecting to a question, the opposing attorney must stand and say, ''I object!'' The judge will ask the reason for the objection. The attorney may respond, ''Counsel is leading the witness,'' or ''The question is irrelevant and immaterial,'' or ''That is hearsay, Your Honor,'' or ''Counsel is harassing the witness.'' The attorney who asked the question should be given a chance to explain why the question should be allowed. If the judge decides that the question violates a rule of evidence, the judge says, ''Objection sustained!'' If the judge decides that the question does not violate a rule of evidence, he or she says, ''Objection overruled!''
13. At the conclusion of the examination, the attorney says to the opposing attorney, ''Your witness.''

14. The defendant's attorney cross-examines the plaintiff's witness according to rules of evidence.

15. The plaintiff's attorney may re-examine the same witness on any matter brought up on cross-examination.

16. Any new matter may be the subject of cross-examination by the defense attorney.

17. The plaintiff's attorney calls and examines any additional witnesses. These witnesses may be cross-examined by the defendant's attorney. Finally, when finished, the plaintiff's attorney says, "The plaintiff rests, Your Honor."

The Defendant's Case in Chief

18. The defendant's attorneys call and examine their witnesses. The defense attorneys conduct direct examination, and the plaintiff's attorneys may cross-examine these witnesses. In all other respects, the defendant's case in chief is conducted in the same pattern as the plaintiff's. When all the defendant's witnesses have been examined and cross-examined, the defendant's attorney says, "The defendant rests, Your Honor."

Closing Arguments

After the defendant rests, the attorneys for each side make their summations, or closing arguments, to the jury. The closing argument should contain a clear and persuasive summary of the evidence that was presented. In addition, it should emphasize the weaknesses of the other party's case. The elements found in a well prepared closing argument are listed in the Trial Procedure section at the end of Unit 6 (page 469), and model closing statements are presented there and in Figures A-3 (below) and A-4 (page 570).

19. The plaintiff's attorney makes a closing argument first. See the guide for preparing the closing argument below.

FIGURE A-3
PLAINTIFF'S MODEL CLOSING ARGUMENT

May it please the court, ladies and gentlemen of the jury. Soon it will be your obligation to consider the evidence you have heard in this case, both from the defendant's point of view and from the plaintiff's point of view. You must also weigh the instructions that the judge will give to you regarding the law in this case. Right now, it is my privilege to talk to you about the testimony that you have heard and what it has proved.

On the day of the accident . . . . [Summarize the evidence that was favorable to your side.]

The uncontradicted evidence is that . . . . [Point out evidence that was not contradicted.]

The basic issue, then, is really quite simple . . . . [Try to isolate the issue, as you see it, for the jury.]

You have heard the testimony of the plaintiff that she . . . . [Emphasize the strong points of the plaintiff's testimony.]

You have heard the testimony of Mr. _____, who saw the accident and said that . . . . [Highlight this testimony.]

So, then, we have testimony to the effect that . . . . [Summarize the testimony in the plaintiff's favor.]

Now the defendant in this case has constantly stressed the fact that the plaintiff was contributorily negligent. Is this really so? Let's examine the evidence on this point in more detail. Ms. _____ testified that . . . . Similarly, Mr. _____ testified that . . . . The testimony of these witnesses indicates clearly that the plaintiff was not negligent.

We have heard the testimony of Dr. ___[name]___ regarding the plaintiff's injuries. We have also heard the doctor's testimony that the plaintiff's pain will persist for an indefinite period of time.

The law requires us to prove our case by the greater weight of evidence. We have shown that my client was injured by the negligent actions of the defendant, and we have proven the cost of those injuries.

As you consider the evidence, I ask that you find in favor of the plaintiff in the amount of $_____.

20. The defendant's attorney makes a closing argument.

FIGURE A-4
DEFENDANT'S MODEL CLOSING ARGUMENT

Ladies and gentlemen of the jury, if it please the court: You have just heard my colleague, Attorney _____, give you the summation for the plaintiff in this case. It is now my privilege and opportunity to speak to you on behalf of my client and to show you why a verdict should be returned for the defendant.

You will be instructed by the judge that if the plaintiff was in any way negligent, and if this negligence was a contributing factor in the slightest degree to the injury, then you must find for the defendant.

Now, you have heard the testimony of the plaintiff that she . . . .

However, there is the testimony of Mr. _____, which indicates that the plaintiff was, indeed, negligent.

I am sure that all of us regard the injuries that have been sustained by the plaintiff as unfortunate. But your decision in this case must not be rendered out of sympathy for the plaintiff. The decision you arrive at must come exclusively as a result of your weighing the evidence and the testimony that you heard. That evidence does not support the plaintiff's claim. I am confident that you will not allow your sympathies to come in the way of rendering a just and fair verdict. Thank you very much for your consideration.

The Judge's Instructions to the Jury

21. The judge "charges" the jury, that is, explains the law which it must apply to the case. See the Trial Procedure section at the end of Unit 7 (page 533) for more information about the judge's instructions to the jury. A guide for preparing jury instructions is found in Figure A-5 (below).

FIGURE A-5
MODEL INSTRUCTIONS TO THE JURY

Ladies and gentlemen of the jury: You have heard the evidence presented in this case, and now it is time for you to make your decision. The court instructs the jury that "negligence" is the failure to exercise reasonable and ordinary care. This means the degree of care which an ordinarily careful and prudent person would exercise under the same circumstances or conditions. If you believe from the preponderance of the evidence that the defendant failed to meet this test, you may conclude that he was negligent. [The instructions to the jury will vary, of course, according to the law that pertains to each case. See the jury instructions on page 533 for a more complete instruction on negligence.]

The Verdict and Judgment

The verdict and judgement are discussed in detail in the Trial Procedures section at the end of Unit 8 (page 561). In a mock trial the steps are as follows.

22. The jury is ushered by the bailiff to a room where it deliberates in private.
23. Members of the jury select one man or woman to be the foreman. The foreman presides over the jury's deliberations. Secret or open ballots may be taken, from time to time, as the discussion progresses. The foreman encourages the group to make every effort to reach a decision.
24. When ready with a decision, the jury is ushered into the courtroom. The judge asks, "Miss (or Mr.) Foreman, have you reached a verdict?" In a civil case, the foreman announces, "We, the members of the jury, find in favor of [the plaintiff or the defendant]" In a criminal case, the foreman says, "We, the members of the jury, find the defendant (guilty or not guilty)."
25. The judge thanks and dismisses the jury.
26. A written judgment is issued by the court at a later date.

BURDEN OF PROOF

In a criminal case, the prosecution must prove *beyond a reasonable doubt* that the defendant is guilty. The jury must agree unanimously to reach a verdict. If it cannot reach a verdict, a mistrial is called. The prosecution may ask for a new trial with a completely new jury.

In a civil case, the burden is on the plaintiff to prove his or her allegations by a *preponderance of evidence,* that is, evidence of the greatest weight. Five-sixths (10 out of 12) of the jurors must reach agreement to arrive at a verdict. If the plaintiff and the defendant agree, however, a different majority of the jurors can be taken as the verdict.

RULES OF EVIDENCE

Rules of evidence have been developed to ensure that trials are run fairly, in an orderly manner, and in such a way that the truth will come forward and justice will result. Some, but not all, of the rules of evidence are discussed here.

Examination of Witnesses

When attorneys question their own witnesses, it is known as *direct examination*. Attorneys must elicit the testimony without asking questions that suggest the answer that should be given. For example, an attorney might say to a witness, "Miss Young, will you tell the court and jury where you were on the evening of April 30." The attorney could not say, "Miss Young, were you at the high school dance on the evening of April 30?" This would be a *leading question* because it contains the desired answer and could be objected to by the opposing attorney. The jury is expected to judge the whole truth as freely given by the witness. Leading questions tend to select facts the lawyer chooses.

When attorneys question a witness who was called to testify by the opposing party, it is known as *cross-examination*. Attorneys are encouraged to use leading questions when cross-examining a witness in order to focus attention on details of the facts, or to expand the testimony. For example, in cross-examining the witness mentioned above, the opposing attorney might ask, "Isn't it true, Miss Young, that on the evening of April 30, you went to the home of Jane Maxwell?" Leading questions often call for a "yes" or "no" answer.

The scope of cross-examination is limited to matters that were brought up on direct examination. The cross-examiner cannot bring up anything new that was not mentioned in direct examination. An exception to this is anything that relates to the *credibility* (believability) of the witness. The cross-examiner can ask questions about the witness's prior conduct which impeaches his or her truth-telling ability. For example, the cross-examiner might ask, "Isn't it true that you lied about your age when you bought your last car?" The cross-examiner must have evidence of such an occurrence before asking this question, however.

Witnesses' testimony may also be impeached by asking questions about prior criminal convictions. It may also be done by showing that the witness made contradictory statements on an earlier court document.

Witnesses' testimony should be limited to matters that are important and useful in determining the facts in the case. For this reason, attorneys ask questions that call for specific answers. Witnesses sometimes attempt to give more information than the question calls for. This is called a *narrative answer*, or *narration,* and can be objected to by the opposing attorney. Similarly, questions asked by either attorney must be relevant; that is, they must relate to the subject matter of the case. Attorneys may object to irrelevant or immaterial questions.

Hearsay Evidence

Witnesses may only testify about what they heard, saw, or experienced themselves. They cannot tell what they heard someone else say. This is known as *hearsay* and can be objected to. Harry Ames, for example, could not testify that Jane Barret said to him, "I saw a person with blond hair run from the store." Jane Barret would have to testify herself about this. An important exception involves testimony about the parties in the case. A witness is allowed to repeat a statement made by the plaintiff or the defendant. Thus, if Barret were a defendant, Ames could testify as to what she said to him.

| **Expert Witnesses** | Unless a witness is an expert, he or she may not give opinions or conclusions. An *expert witness* is a witness who is asked to give expert opinion on facts or principles that apply to the case. Expert witnesses are allowed to give their opinions based on knowledge gained from study and experience in the field rather than from their personal observation of the facts in a case. Before giving expert testimony, witnesses must first be *qualified* by the attorney calling them. This is done by questioning them about their experience and education in their field of expertise. For instance, a physician might be called as an expert witness in a personal injury case. To qualify this witness, the attorney might ask, ''Where did you study medicine?'', or ''How many cases like this one have you seen?'' |

Documentary, Real, and Parol Evidence

Documentary evidence consists of written instruments such as written contracts, sales slips, letters, and business papers. *Real evidence* consists of actual objects, such as a weapon, an article of clothing, a photograph, or a consumer item.

A special procedure is followed to introduce documentary or real evidence. First, the attorney wishing to introduce the evidence says to the judge, ''Your Honor, I wish to have this item marked for identification as Plaintiff's Exhibit C.'' The clerk marks the item. Then, after showing the item to the opposing attorney, the examining attorney presents the item to a witness already on the stand and asks, ''Do you recognize this item marked Exhibit C?'' After a response, the attorney says, ''Please tell the judge and jury what it is.'' Further questions about the item usually follow. Finally, the attorney says, ''Your Honor, I offer this item into evidence as Plaintiff's Exhibit C and ask that it be admitted.'' The opposing attorney may object at this time if there are grounds for doing so. The judge either admits or refuses to admit the item into evidence. If admitted, it is handed to the judge and jury for their close examination.

Whenever a written contract is introduced into evidence, the *parol evidence* rule must be kept in mind. Under this rule, evidence of oral statements made before the contract was signed cannot be introduced. This is because it is presumed that the parties put in the writing everything they agreed to. Some exceptions to this rule are explained on pages 148 and 149.

Suggestions for Mock Trial Participants

1. Be polite and courteous throughout the trial, even during adverse and difficult conditions.
2. Learn your part thoroughly.
3. Study the facts in the case carefully, paying particular attention to details.
4. Be aware of the law that should be applied to the facts.
5. Except when introducing documentary evidence, never read from prepared statements. Instead, learn your part so that you can speak extemporaneously.
6. Special Advice:
   a. To judges: Politely make it clear that you are in charge and that you take a neutral position in the dispute. Know the rules of evidence.
   b. To witnesses: Tell the truth as you understand it to be.
   c. To attorneys: Don't promise to prove something you cannot prove.
   d. To jurors: Be attentive to every detail.

Questions for Review

1. Why, in real life, should people ask themselves, "Is a lawsuit really necessary?"
2. What is the purpose of arbitration?
3. How does substantive law differ from procedural law?
4. Why is a trial known as an adversary proceeding?
5. List the participants in a mock trial.
6. Describe the principal role of the judge in a trial.
7. What does it mean when the judge sustains an objection? overrules an objection?
8. List, in chronological order, the steps in a trial.
9. Why is it important for witnesses in a mock trial to learn their parts well?
10. Briefly describe the way in which 12 jurors are selected to hear a case.
11. Why are opening statements important?
12. What elements should be included in the opening statement?
13. What elements are found in a well prepared closing argument?
14. What is the difference between direct examination and cross-examination?
15. Explain when leading questions may and may not be used.
16. Describe three ways in which a witness's testimony may be impeached.
17. What kind of testimony may be given by an expert witness that may not be given by an ordinary witness?
18. Give an example of documentary evidence and an example of real evidence.
19. How does the burden of proof in a civil case differ from the burden of proof in a criminal case?

LEGAL PRACTICUM

Henry Perkins is being sued in a civil suit for failing to pay for a car that he bought from George Atkins, who was just released from jail. Perkins counterclaims, alleging he was injured in an accident on his way home from buying the car. Perkins claims that the accident was due to the car's being in a defective condition. Refer to the rules of evidence beginning on page 572 and write your opinions as to whether you would sustain or overrule objections to the following questions if you were the judge. Give reasons for each opinion:

Example: Under direct examination Perkins is asked if he drove within the speed limit on his way home in the newly purchased car. *Answer:* Objection sustained. The attorney is leading the witness in direct examination.

1. Under cross-examination, Perkins is asked if he is divorced from his wife.
2. Under cross-examination, Atkins is asked if he has a criminal record.
3. Atkins is asked what it was like serving time in jail.
4. A witness who saw the accident is asked if Perkins suffered a fractured wrist in the accident.
5. The same witness who saw the accident testifies that another witness, who cannot be found, told him that Perkins caused the accident and that the car was not defective.
6. The same witness who saw the accident is asked if he thought the car was defective.
7. A fellow jail inmate of Atkins testifies that Atkins told him that the car was defective.
8. A medical doctor, after stating her credentials, is asked if Perkins suffered a fractured wrist in the accident.

■ LAW DICTIONARY

This law dictionary contains brief definitions of more than nine hundred legal terms. Some are concise restatements of more detailed definitions given elsewhere in the text. Some are new terms that are not defined in the text but that may be encountered in your future business and legal relationships. For a thorough review of the vocabulary of business law, review the boldfaced terms in each of the 39 separate chapters as well as the entries in this dictionary. Pronunciation: bāke, chăotic, câre, căt, cärt, ăcross, ēat, ĕvade, ĕbb, runnēr, īce, hĭt, ōak, ŏbey, ôrder, cŏt, lōōt, fŏŏt, ūnit, ŭnite, ûrge, ŭp, ′ primary accent, ″ secondary accent.

ABANDONMENT The giving up or surrender of a right or of property with the intent not to reclaim.

ABSOLUTE DEFENSE (also called *real defense*) A defense that is good against everyone, even a holder in due course of a negotiable instrument.

ABSOLUTE DIVORCE Final divorce.

ABSTRACT OF TITLE A summary of the history of the title to land, including all conveyances, mortgages, liens, and other changes affecting a parcel of land.

ACCEPTANCE The act by the drawee of a draft of writing the word *accepted* across the front of the instrument and signing below the word; this act signifies that the drawee agrees to pay the draft. Also, the unqualified assent by an offeree to an offer.

ACCEPTOR The drawee of a draft after he or she has agreed to pay it.

ACCESSORY AFTER THE FACT A person who gives aid and assistance to another with the knowledge that the other person has committed a felony.

ACCESSORY BEFORE THE FACT A person who gets someone else to commit a felony but is not present when the felony is committed.

ACCOMMODATION INDORSEMENT An indorsement, usually in blank, that is made by one party to accommodate another party by adding the security of his or her credit to the instrument.

ACCORD An agreement between a debtor and a creditor as to the allowance or disallowance of their respective claims.

ACCORD AND SATISFACTION The substitution of another agreement for an existing claim and the full execution of the new agreement.

ACQUITTAL A verdict of not guilty; the discharge by a court of a party charged with a crime.

ACT OF BANKRUPTCY Any act, as defined by the laws of bankruptcy, that will cause a person to be adjudged a bankrupt.

ACT OF GOD An accident due to a force beyond human control, such as a flood, an earthquake, or a tornado.

ACTION A lawsuit; a proceeding in a court for the enforcement of a right.

ACTUAL AUTHORITY The authority given to an agent by a principal. It may be expressed in words or it may be implied from the acts of the parties or the nature of the agreement.

ACTUAL DAMAGES Damages that an injured party to a contract can prove to be the result of another party's failure to perform. Also, damages that can be factually proved, as contrasted with speculative damages.

ADDICTION Physical and mental dependence on a substance.

ADHESION CONTRACT A written agreement prepared by the seller that a buyer may not change if the buyer wishes to make a purchase. The seller will only sell under those particular terms and no others.

ADJUDICATORY HEARING A trial of a juvenile case, conducted informally and without a jury.

ADMINISTRATIVE AGENCY (also called a *regulatory agency*) A department of government that is formed for the purpose of administering particular legislation.

ADMINISTRATIVE LAW Rules and regulations made by an administrative agency.

ADMINISTRATOR / ADMINISTRATRIX A person appointed by the court to settle the estate of someone who died intestate, that is, without making a will. An administrator is a man; an administratrix is a woman.

ADULTERATED FOOD OR DRUG Food or drug that contains any substance mixed or packed with it to reduce its quality or strength below the prescribed minimum standards.

ADULTERY A voluntary sexual relationship involving a married person and someone other than his or her spouse.

ADVERSE POSSESSION The open taking possession of real property for a continuous length of time, leading eventually to the acquisition of title to the property.

AFFIDAVIT A signed, written statement sworn before someone who is authorized to take oaths.

AFFINITY Related by marriage.

AFFIRMATIVE ACTION Positive steps to end discrimination which must be taken by companies that participate in government contracts and employ over fifty employees.

AGE OF CONSENT The age at which one acquires the legal ability to marry.

AGE DISCRIMINATION IN EMPLOYMENT ACT A law that prohibits employment agencies, employers of twenty or more employees, and labor unions of more than twenty-five members from discriminating on the basis of age.

AGE OF MAJORITY The age at which a person becomes an adult, which is 18 in most states.

AGENCY The relationship that exists between an agent and a principal.

AGENCY BY ESTOPPEL (e′ stăp ŭl) (also called *apparent agency*) The creation of an agency by acts of the parties, leading third parties to believe that an agency agreement exists to their subsequent injury.

AGENT A person who acts for another in dealings with third parties.

AGENT'S AGENT An agent appointed by another agent who may bind the agent but not the original principal.

AGGRAVATED ASSAULT A felony attempt to commit battery.

AIRBILL A bill of lading issued by an airline.

ALIMONY An allowance made to a divorced person by a former spouse for support and maintenance.

ALIMONY PENDENTE LITE (also called *temporary alimony*) Alimony granted to one of the spouses while he or she is waiting for a divorce or separate support action to be completed.

ALTERATION A change in the terms of a written contract or instrument.

ANNUAL PERCENTAGE RATE The true rate of interest computed according to a special formula.

ANNUITY A guaranteed retirement income which a person secures either by paying a lump-sum premium or by periodically paying a set amount to an insurer.

ANNULMENT A declaration by the court that a marriage was never effective, that it was void from the beginning.

ANSWER A formal written statement containing the defense to an action; a reply to a charge.

ANTICIPATORY BREACH (ăn tĭs′ ĭ pà tō″ ri) The right under the law of contracts to sue on a contract before the time of performance if the promisor has already repudiated the contract.

APPARENT AUTHORITY The rights and powers that a third party may reasonably suppose the agent possesses, which bind the principal as to third parties.

APPEAL The referral, or attempt to refer, a case to a higher court for reexamination and review.

APPELLATE COURT (ă pěl′ ăt) (also called *court of appellate jurisdicton*) A higher court with the right to review cases on appeal from a lower court.

ARBITRATION A method of settling disputes between parties by referring to third parties for settlement.

ARRAIGNMENT (àh răn′ mĕnt) The act of calling a prisoner to the bar of a court to answer an indictment.

ARREST A situation in which a person is deprived of freedom, usually on suspicion of having committed a crime.

ARREST WARRANT An order issued by a court saying that a person has committed a crime and is to be arrested.

ARSON The willful and malicious burning of the dwelling house of another.

ARTICLES OF COPARTNERSHIP The formal name given to a written partnership agreement.

ARTICLES OF INCORPORATION An application for incorporation of a business. The application usually contains the name, object, duration, capital structure, place of business, and proposed directors of the corporation to be formed.

ASSAULT An attempt to commit battery.

ASSET ACQUISITION The purchase by one corporation of all or most of the assets of another corporation.

ASSIGNEE (ăs″ ĭ nē′) The person to whom property or other rights have been transferred or assigned.

ASSIGNMENT The transfer of any property right from one person to another; usually used in connection with the transfer of intangible rights, such as the right to collect money.

ASSIGNOR (ăs″ ĭ nôr′) The person who transfers or assigns property or rights to another.

ASSUMPTION OF THE RISK The defense, in negligence suits, that the plaintiff knew of the risk involved and took the chance of being injured.

ATTACHMENT The act of taking a person's property and bringing it into the custody of the law.

ATTEMPT TO COMMIT A CRIME An act done with the intent to commit a crime that falls short of its commission.

ATTORNEY IN FACT A person appointed by another to act for him or her.

ATTRACTIVE NUISANCE DOCTRINE The rule of law under which property owners must use reasonable care toward children who are attracted to their property by something that is dangerous.

AUCTION A public sale of land or goods, by public outcry, to the highest bidder.

AUCTION WITH RESERVE An auction at which the auctioneer has the right to withdraw goods and not sell them if reasonable bids are not made.

AUCTION WITHOUT RESERVE An auction at which the auctioneer must sell the goods to the highest bidder.

AVOID To make void; to not be bound by (a contract).

BAD CHECK A check issued against a bank balance that is insufficient to cover it, or against a bank in which the drawer has no funds.

BAGGAGE Articles that passengers bring for their own personal use.

BAIL Money or other property that is left with the court to assure the court that the person will return to stand trial.

BAILEE (bāl ē′) The person to whom personal property is delivered under a contract of bailment.

BAILIFF The sheriff's deputy; a minor court officer who assists the sheriff.

BAILMENT The delivery of goods to another for a certain purpose, the goods to be returned later.

BAILMENT LEASE A security device under which the buyer rents goods from the seller. When the amount of the rental paid equals the purchase price, the buyer can take title to the property by paying a token amount, usually $1. (The bailment lease is a type of security interest.)

BAILMENT BY NECESSITY A bailment in which a customer gives up possession of property for the benefit of both parties.

BAILOR (bāl ôr′) The owner of personal property which has been temporarily transferred to another person in a bailment.

BAIT AND SWITCH ADVERTISING An alluring but insincere offer to sell a product or service that the advertiser does not really want to sell.

BALLOON-PAYMENT MORTGAGE A mortgage calling for relatively low fixed payments during the life of the mortgage followed by one large final (balloon) payment.

BANK DRAFT An order for payment of money drawn by an officer of a bank upon either the officer's own bank or some other bank in which funds of the officer's bank are deposited.

BANKRUPT One who has done some act or suffered some act to be done in consequence of which, under the laws of that person's country, he or she is liable to have property seized and distributed to creditors.

BARGAINED FOR In reference to agreements, when a promise is made in exchange for another promise, in exchange for an act, or in exchange for a forbearance to act.

BATTERY The unlawful touching of another person.

BEARER INSTRUMENT A negotiable instrument that may be negotiated by delivery only.

BENEFICIARY (bĕn i fĭsh′ ē ĕr″ ē) The party who is entitled to the proceeds of a life insurance policy; the party who is entitled to the benefit of property held by another as trustee; the party who receives a gift under a will.

BENEFIT Something that a party was not previously entitled to receive.

BID An offer to buy something at a particular price made by a person in the audience at an auction sale.

BIGAMY The act of having two spouses at once.

BILATERAL (bī lăt′ ĕ rĕl) A term used to indicate two simultaneous promises or two obligations.

BILATERAL CONTRACT A contract containing two promises—one by each person.

BILL OF EXCHANGE (also called *draft*) A negotiable instrument by one party ordering another to pay a certain sum of money to a third party named in the instrument.

BILL OF LADING A combination contract and receipt given by the common carrier to the person shipping certain goods.

BILL OF RIGHTS The first ten Amendments to the U.S. Constitution.

BILL OF SALE A written statement evidencing the transfer of personal property from one person to another.

BINDER An oral or written statement putting insurance into force until the regular insurance policy can be issued.

BLANK INDORSEMENT An indorsement in which the holder or payee does no more than sign his or her name on the instrument.

BLOOD TEST The requirement that before a marriage license be issued, the blood of the potential partners be tested for the presence of syphilis.

BODILY INJURY LIABILITY INSURANCE Motor vehicle insurance which protects the policyholder from claims or lawsuits for injuries or death caused by his or her negligent operation of a motor vehicle.

BREACH OF CONTRACT The failure of one of the parties to a contract to do what he or she has previously agreed to do.

BRIBERY The giving or receiving of a reward to influence any official act.

BROKER An agent who carries on negotiations for a principal, acting as an intermediary between the principal and third parties in making contracts involving rights or property.

BULK SALE The sale of the entire stock of merchandise and supplies of a business in one transaction.

BULK TRANSFER A single transaction to transfer the entire stock of merchandise and supplies.

BURGLARY The act of breaking into and entering the dwelling house of another at night with the intent to commit a felony (common-law definition).

BUSINESS JUDGMENT RULE The rule that a corporate manager's decision will stand if the manager has acted in good faith and has done nothing illegal.

BUYER'S GUIDE The large sticker required to be placed in the window of each used vehicle offered for sale, listing warranty and other required information.

BYLAWS The rules which a private corporation adopts for its international regulation.

CAPACITY The legal ability to consent.

CAPITAL The money and property that a business needs to operate.

CAPITAL STOCK The total designated value of shares issued by a corporation.

CARRIER A person or a company that undertakes to transport either persons or goods or both for consideration.

CASH SURRENDER VALUE The amount that a policyholder will receive if he or she decides to cancel an insurance policy.

CASHIER'S CHECK A check issued by the cashier of a bank and drawn against bank funds.

CASUALTY INSURANCE Insurance protecting a person from losses due to accident or disaster.

CAUSE OF ACTION The grounds for a lawsuit.

CEASE AND DESIST ORDERS Orders to stop an activity.

CERTIFICATE OF DEPOSIT A bank certificate stating that the person named has deposited a stated amount of money payable to his or her order.

CERTIFIED CHECK A check that has been accepted by the bank on which it was drawn and has been marked or certified to indicate such acceptance.

CHALLENGE FOR CAUSE To request that a member of a jury be removed because of possible bias.

CHARTER (also called *certificate*) A grant by a state permitting a corporation to exist.

CHATTEL (shă′ tĕl) A piece of personal property.

CHATTEL MORTGAGE A mortgage on personal property.

CHECK A draft drawn on a bank and payable on demand.

CHILD-LABOR LAWS Laws that control the work that children are permitted to do.

CIRCUMSTANTIAL EVIDENCE Evidence that is indirect.

CITATION The identification of a court case, consisting of the names of the parties, the volume number, the name of the reporter, and the beginning page number of the case.

CIVIL ACTION An action at law in which a party seeks to recover damages resulting from the invasion of legal rights of a private nature.

CIVIL DEATH The loss by people in prison of the right to vote, to contract, and to bring and defend against civil lawsuits.

CIVIL LAW A system of codified law based on Roman law, common on the continent of Europe. Or, used in a different context, that division of laws that deals with the rights and duties of private parties, as contrasted with criminal law.

CIVIL RIGHTS ACT OF 1964 A federal law which makes it illegal to discriminate in employment or other areas because of race, creed, color, or sex.

CLAYTON ACT An act passed by Congress in 1914 which strengthened the Sherman Antitrust Act by making specific practices illegal.

CLERK OF COURT The person who receives and files all papers relating to the trial, sets up the trial calendar, and tends to all other clerical matters for the court.

CLOSED-END CREDIT An extension of credit for a fixed amount of money which may not be increased by the debtor without taking out a new loan.

CLOSED SHOP A business in which a person must be a union member in order to be employed. The Taft-Hartley Act made the closed shop illegal.

CLOSING DATE The date on which the purchase price of real property will be paid and the title will be transferred to the buyer.

COAGENTS Two or more agents hired by a principal.

CODE An organized collection of laws.

CODICIL (kŏd′ ĭ sĭl″) A formal supplement to a will.

COINSURANCE-CLAUSE POLICY
A kind of fire insurance in which the insured must keep his or her coverage at an agreed percentage of the value of the property. If the insured does not do so and suffers a loss, the company will pay less than the actual loss.

COLLATERAL SECURITY Additional obligations, usually stocks or bonds, pledged as security for a personal performance of an agreement.

COLLECTIVE BARGAINING AGREEMENT An employment contract negotiated between an employer and a group of employees represented by a union.

COLLISION INSURANCE Motor vehicle insurance which pays for damage to the insured's own car.

COMAKER A person who with another signs a negotiable instrument on its face and becomes primarily liable with the other person for its payment.

COMMERCE CLAUSE The clause in the U.S. Constitution that states that Congress shall have the power to regulate commerce ''among the several states.''

COMMERCIAL PAPER Negotiable instruments, such as notes or drafts, which obligate a maker or drawer for the payment of money.

COMMON CARRIER A carrier of freight or passengers operating under a franchise granted by state authority.

COMMON LAW The part of our law that comes from custom or precedent, usually the long-established law of England that was based on the recorded decisions of the early law courts.

COMMON-LAW MARRIAGE A marriage not solemnized in the ordinary way, but created by an agreement to marry followed by cohabitation.

COMMON STOCK The most usual form of stock issued by a corporation, which represents the interest of the stockholders in the new worth of the corporation. It does not guarantee to its holders the right to profits.

COMMUNITY PROPERTY JURISDICTIONS Nine states whose laws provide that the wealth accumulated during marriage generally belongs equally to both spouses regardless of which spouse received it.

COMPARABLE WORK Work that requires skill, training, and effort of a level similar to that required by another job.

COMPARATIVE NEGLIGENCE The doctrine under which the negligence of

each party is compared and the amount of the plaintiff's recovery is reduced by the percent of the plaintiff's negligence.

COMPENSATION Salary or wages.

COMPLAINT A written statement of the plaintiff's cause of action against the defendant.

COMPREHENSIVE COVERAGE INSURANCE Motor vehicle insurance which protects the insured when his or her car is lost or damaged because of fire, lightning, flood, hail, windstorm, riot, vandalism, and theft.

CONCLUSIVE PRESUMPTION An assumption that cannot be overruled by any other evidence.

CONDITION PRECEDENT (prĕs′ ĕd ĕnt) In sales, a condition that must be fulfilled before title to goods passes to a buyer.

CONDITION SUBSEQUENT (sŭb′ sĕ kwĕnt″) In sales, a condition to be met after title has passed, such as a money-back guarantee.

CONDITIONAL ACCEPTANCE (also called *qualified acceptance*) An acceptance of an offer that occurs only as a result of the addition of another term or condition.

CONDITIONAL SALE A contract in which it is agreed that title to goods shall not pass from the seller to the buyer until the fulfillment of a certain condition, usually the payment of the purchase price.

CONDOMINIUM (kän′ dŭ mĭn′ ē ŭm) Absolute ownership of an apartment unit together with an undivided interest in the structural parts of a building and grounds not under the supervision and care of one individual.

CONSANGUINITY (kŏn″ săn″ gwĭn′ ĭ tē) Blood relationship.

CONSIDERATION In contracts, the impelling influence that causes a contracting party to enter the contract; a benefit received by the promiser or a detriment suffered by the promisee.

CONSIGNMENT Goods directed by one person to another to be sold for the first person and credited to him or her by the second person.

CONSIGNOR A person who directs goods to a consignee for sale.

CONSOLIDATION The combining of two corporations into a new corporation.

CONSPIRACY The crime that occurs when people get together with others to talk about or to plan the commission of a crime.

CONSTITUTIONAL Allowed by the Constitution of the United States and (in some cases) by a particular state's constitution.

CONSTRUCTIVE EVICTION An eviction that occurs when the landlord breaches his or her duties under the lease.

CONSUMER CREDIT PROTECTION ACT Federal legislation protecting consumers from obligation on contracts wherein all credit terms are not clearly disclosed.

CONSUMER PRODUCT SAFETY ACT OF 1972 A federal law which places certain responsibilities on manufacturers and sellers of products to be sure that they are safe and will not injure consumers.

CONSUMER PROTECTION AGENCIES Government agencies set up to investigate consumer complaints and to create programs to help consumers.

CONTEMPT OF COURT A deliberate violation of the order of a judge or court.

CONTRABAND Illegal goods or substances.

CONTRACT Any agreement enforceable at law.

CONTRACT IMPLIED IN FACT A contract that comes about from the actions of the parties rather than from the words that the parties use.

CONTRACT FOR SALE A contract entered into by a buyer and seller to buy and sell goods either at the present time or in the future.

CONTRACT UNDER SEAL A contract whose seal (impression made on a document) is regarded as proof that the parties have exchanged something of value.

CONTRACT TO SELL Under the Uniform Commercial Code, a contract to sell goods at a later date.

CONTRARY TO PUBLIC POLICY Harmful to the public welfare.

CONTRIBUTORY NEGLIGENCE Negligence on the part of the plaintiff who assisted in causing the injuries.

CONTRIBUTORY PENSION PLAN A pension plan that requires the employee to pay part of the cost of the plan.

CONTROLLED SUBSTANCES ACT A federal act which prohibits the unauthorized possession of controlled substances for an individual's own use.

CONVENTIONAL LOAN Mortgage loan made strictly between the lender and the borrower, with no government agency involved.

CONVERSION The unauthorized taking of the personal property of someone else for the use of the person taking it.

COOPERATION The duty of the principal not to interfere with the performance of tasks that the principal assigned the agent.

COPYRIGHT A right granted to an author, photographer, artist, or the agent of any one of these by the government to publish and sell exclusively an artistic or literary work for the life of the author plus 50 years.

CORPORATION An artificial legal entity created by statute that has the right to conduct affairs in its own name and as specified by the charter granted to it.

CORPORATION BY ESTOPPEL The doctrine by which parties who have benefitted by dealing with a business as if it were a corporation are prevented from denying its existence as a corporation.

COUNTERCLAIM A claim which is intended to offset another claim.

COUNTEROFFER An offer in return, which ends the first offer.

COURT OF CLAIMS Special court that judges individual claims against the federal government or a state government.

COURT OF EQUITY A court in which rules of equity rather than rules of law are supplied, giving relief where money damages will not be adequate.

COURT OF GENERAL JURISDICTION County-level court with original jurisdiction for cases involving major crimes and large amounts of money, and with appellate jurisdiction for small claims and local cases.

COURT REPORTER The person who keeps a written record of the trial.

CONVENANT (kŭv′ ĕ nŭnt) A promise contained within a sealed contract.

COVER After a breach of contract by a seller, a purchase of goods in good faith by the buyer substituting for those goods not delivered by the seller.

COVERED WORKERS Workers covered by private pension plans.

CREDIT Time given for the payment for goods or services sold on trust.

CREDITOR A person who sells goods to another on credit or lends money to another.

CRIME A wrong which the government recognizes as injurious to the public; a violation of a public law.

CUMULATIVE PREFERRED STOCK Stock which contains a provision that if the guaranteed dividends are not paid on the stock in any one year, they will be paid in the following years before any dividends are paid to common stock holders.

CURRENCY TRANSACTION REPORT A report by financial institutions to the Internal Revenue Service client deposits, withdrawals, transfers, and other handling of amounts of $10,000 or more.

CURTESY, RIGHT OF (kûr′ tĕ sĭ) Under common law, the estate to which a man is entitled on the death of his wife, provided they have had children born alive who might have been capable of inheriting the estate.

CUSTODIAL PARENT The parent who has custody of a minor.

DAMAGES The money recovered by court action for injury or loss caused by another.

DAYS OF GRACE The period allowed after an insurance premium is due and before the policy will lapse for nonpayment.

DE FACTO CORPORATION A corporation that exists in fact although not under the law.

DE JURE CORPORATION A legally formed corporation that has complied with all the incorporation formalities.

DEBTOR A person who buys goods from another on credit or borrows money from another.

DECEDENT (dĭ sē′ dĕnt) A deceased person.

DECEIT Another name for fraud.

DECREASING TERM INSURANCE A type of term life insurance whose premium stays the same from year to year but whose amount of protection decreases over the years.

DECREE An order made by a court of equity. (Compare *injunction*.)

DECRIMINALIZATION The reclassification of a criminal act to be a lesser violation, usually punishable by a fine.

DEDUCTIBLE CLAUSE A clause in health insurance policies requiring the insured to pay an initial amount before the insurance company will pay anything.

DEED A formal written instrument which transfers ownership of real property.

DEFAMATION The wrongful act of injuring another's reputation by the use of false statements. Defamation is divided into two classes: libel and slander.

DEFAULT A neglect or failure to act.

DEFENDANT The person sued in a civil action: the person charged with a crime in a criminal action.

DEFENSE The answer to a cause of action or indictment.

DEFERRED PAYMENT PRICE The total cost to a buyer who purchases goods on credit.

DELANEY AMENDMENT An amendment to the Food, Drug, and Cosmetic Act that gives the federal government the right to remove from the market any food or food additive shown or believed to cause cancer in humans or animals.

DELEGATION The transfer of a duty or obligation from one person to another.

DEMAND NOTE A note that is payable whenever the payee demands payment.

DEMURRAGE (dě mûr′ ĭj) **CHARGE** Compensation for delay of a vessel or railroad car beyond the time allowed for loading, unloading, or departing.

DEMURRER (dě mûr′ ēr) A formal procedure for disputing the legal basis of the other side's pleading.

DENIED BOARDING COMPENSATION A payment by airlines to passengers who have been denied boarding against their will, or ''bumped''.

DEPOSITION The testimony of a witness given under oath for use in the trial of a case.

DERIVATIVE SUIT A suit filed against corporate management by shareholders on behalf of the corporation.

DESERTION The unjustified, voluntary separation of one spouse from the other, with the intent of not returning, for a period of time set by law.

DESTINATION CONTRACT A contract requiring the seller to deliver the goods to the destination and to transfer title on delivery.

DETENTION HEARING In juvenile cases, a hearing to determine whether there are good reasons for keeping the accused in custody and whether or not there are special circumstances affecting the case.

DETRIMENT In contracts, giving up something (or promising to give up something) that one has a legal right to keep, doing something (or promising to do something) that one has a legal right not to do, or refraining from doing something (or promising not to do something) that one has a legal right to do.

DIRECT SUIT A suit brought against a corporation by one or more shareholders who claim to have been deprived of a shareholder right.

DIRECTORS A group of people who are elected by the stockholders of a corporation to manage the corporation.

DISABILITY INCOME INSURANCE A kind of insurance which pays benefits to the insured when he or she is either totally or partially disabled.

DISAFFIRM To show by a statement or by some act an intent not to live up to a voidable contract.

DISCHARGE The act by which a person is freed from performing a legal obligation.

DISCLOSED PRINCIPAL A principal whose existence is known to a third party.

DISCOUNT The act of subtracting the amount of interest from the amount of a loan when the loan is approved and giving only the difference to the borrower.

DISHONOR To refuse to pay a negotiable instrument when it is due.

DISPARATE IMPACT In reference to employment discrimination, the situation in which an employer's policy seems neutral on the surface but has an unequal impact on members of one or more protected groups.

DISPARATE TREATMENT Intentional discrimination by an employer against an individual or a group belonging to one of the protected categories.

DISPOSITIONAL HEARING In juvenile cases, a court hearing to decide how to dispose of the case.

DISPOSSESS PROCEEDING An action by a landlord to evict a tenant.

DISSIDENT OR INSURGENT SHAREHOLDERS Shareholders who challenge management.

DISSOLUTION In a partnership, a change in the relation of the partners which occurs when any partner ceases to be associated with the carrying on of the business.

DIVIDENDS Profits distributed to the stockholders of a corporation.

DIVORCE A declaration by a court that a valid marriage has come to an end.

DOCUMENT OF TITLE A paper which serves as evidence that the person holding the paper has title to the goods mentioned in the document.

DOMESTIC CORPORATION A corporation which operates in the state in which it is incorporated.

DOMICILE A person's principal place of abode. It is the place to which, whenever a person is absent, he or she has the present intent of returning.

DORMANT PARTNER A partner who takes no active part in the management of the firm and whose connection with the firm is kept a secret from the public, but who has unlimited liability for the firm's debts.

DOUBLE INDEMNITY A clause found in some insurance policies which provides that in the event of the accidental death of the insured, the beneficiary receives double the amount of the face value of the policy.

DOUBLE JEOPARDY A subsequent trial of a person for a crime of which he or she has already been found not guilty in a previous trial.

DOWER (dŏw′ ēr), **RIGHT OF** The provision made by law for a widow out of her late husband's real property.

DRAFT (also known as *bill of exchange*) A request for the payment of money drawn by one person on another.

DRAWEE The party named in a draft who is ordered to pay money to the payee.

DRAWER The party who draws a draft—that is, the party who orders that the money be paid.

DRUG A chemical substance that has an effect on the body or mind.

DRUG ABUSE The use of drugs in a way that can harm the body or mind.

DRUG ADDICTION Occurs when people become physically and mentally dependent on drugs.

DRUG TRAFFICKING The unauthorized manufacture or distribution of any controlled substance or the possession of such a substance with the intention of manufacturing or distributing it illegally.

DUE PROCESS OF LAW Those fundamental rights and principles of justice that limit the government's power to deprive people of their lives, liberty, or property.

DURESS (dŏŏ rĕs′) Overcoming the will of a person by a threat of physical force or bodily detention.

DUTY TO ACCOUNT The duty of

agents to present a record to the principal of all money collected and paid out.

DUTY OF DUE CARE The duty of agents and corporate managers to exercise proper skill and good judgment in conducting the business of the principal or corporation.

DUTY OF LOYALTY The duty of agents and corporate managers to put the interests of the principal or corporation above their own interests.

EASEMENT The right to make use of land belonging to another.

ECCLESIASTICAL LAW The law of the church.

ECONOMIC DURESS Threats of a business nature that cause another, without real consent, to enter into a contract.

ELECTRONIC FUND TRANSFERS The use of computers and electronic technology as a substitute for checks and other paper forms of banking.

EMBEZZLEMENT The wrongful taking away of another's property by a person who has been entrusted with or given rightful control over that property by the owner.

EMINENT DOMAIN (dō mān′) The right of the government to appropriate property for some public use.

EMOTIONAL SUFFERING A wrongful act (tort) involving extreme and outrageous behavior which causes severe emotional distress, but not necessarily bodily injury.

EMPLOYMENT-AT-WILL The doctrine that an employer could fire an employee at any time for any reason—or even without a reason.

ENCUMBRANCE (ĭn cŭm′ brŭn[t]s) A lien or claim attached to property.

ENDOWMENT INSURANCE A kind of insurance which provides protection for a stated time, generally twenty to thirty years. The face value of the policy is paid to the insured at the end of the agreed period, or if the insured dies during that period, the face value is paid to the beneficiary.

ENTRAPMENT A police officer's inducement of someone who is not a law violator to commit a crime.

ENVIRONMENTAL IMPACT STATEMENT A detailed statement discussing the probable environmental impact of a proposed action which is often required before taking such action that might substantially or adversely affect the environment.

EQUAL EMPLOYMENT OPPOR-TUNITY COMMISSION The federal agency that investigates employee claims of discrimination.

EQUAL-PAY RULE A federal law requiring employers engaged in interstate commerce, or receiving federal funds, to pay women equally as men holding the same job.

EQUITABLE ACTION An action seeking an injunction or decree.

EQUITABLE DISTRIBUTION LAWS In divorces, laws allowing judges to distribute property equitably between the husband and wife regardless who has title to the property.

EQUITABLE ESTOPPEL (also called *part performance*) In contracts for the sale of real property, the enforceability of an oral contract when one party, in reliance on the oral promise of the other to sell the property, either makes improvements on the property or changes his or her position in an important way.

EQUITY A branch of law granting relief when there is no adequate relief otherwise available.

ESCHEAT (ĭs[h] chēt′) The reversion of property to the state if the property holder dies without legal heirs.

ESCROW (ĕs′ krō) A written document held by a third person until a prescribed condition comes about.

ESPIONAGE The gathering, transmitting, or losing of information related to the national defense with reason to believe that it will be used to injure this country or to aid a foreign government.

ESTOPPEL (ĕ stȧp′ ŭl) A rule of law that bars a person from denying the truth of his or her deeds, claims, or admissions.

EVICTION The act of depriving a person of the possession of real property, usually through court action.

EVIDENCE Proof, either written or unwritten, of the allegations at issue between parties; that which is used to induce belief in the minds of the jury or of the court.

EXCUSABLE HOMICIDE The killing of a human being by another human being in self-defense.

EXECUTION The performance of an act, or the completion of an instrument; a writ directing an officer to enforce a judgment.

EXECUTOR/EXECUTRIX The party named in a will to carry out the terms of the will. An executor is a man; an executrix is a woman.

EXECUTORY The state of a contract having come into existence through a valid offer and acceptance but with its terms not yet carried out.

EXEMPLARY DAMAGES Damages that act as a punishment to deter other wrongdoers.

EXPERT WITNESS A witness who is asked to give expert opinion on facts or principles that apply to the case.

EXPRESS AGENCY AGREEMENT An agreement to create an agency relationship that involves clearly stated terms.

EXPRESS AUTHORITY Agency authority that involves all the directions or commands that are detailed by the principal when the agency relationship is created.

EXPRESS CONTRACT A contract in which the terms are stated or expressed.

EXPRESS WARRANTY Occurs whenever anyone sells goods and makes a statement of fact or promise about them to the buyer. The statement or promise must relate to the goods and be part of the basis of the bargain.

EXTENDED COVERAGE ENDORSEMENTS (also called *special-extended coverage endorsements*) Insurance policy provisions for protection against losses resulting from windstorm, hail, explosion, riots and other civil commotions, aircraft, vehicles, smoke, and often water.

EXTORTION The taking of money or a thing of value unjustly by a public official or someone else in a situation where the victim consents to the surrender of the item because of the use of force or because the victim has been put in fear.

FACE VALUE In life insurance policies, the stated amount that is to be paid the beneficiary in case of the death of the insured.

FAIRNESS RULE The requirement that corporate managers be fair to the corporation when they are self-dealing.

FALSE ARREST (also called *false imprisonment*) An unlawful physical restraint by a person of another's liberty, whether in prison or otherwise.

FAMILY COURT (also called *probate court* or *surrogate court*) County-level court that supervises the estates of deceased persons.

FEDERAL DISTRICT COURTS The courts of original jurisdiction in the federal system.

FEDERAL FAIR LABOR STANDARDS ACT (also called *Wage and Hour Law*) Federal legislation regulating hours worked, wages, and child labor.

FEDERAL TRADE COMMISSION ACT An act passed by Congress in 1914 and amended in 1938 and again in 1975 which says: ''Unfair methods of competition in or affecting commerce, and unfair or deceptive acts or practices in or affecting commerce are hereby declared unlawful.''

FELLOW GUESTS Guests who are at the same hotel. If a fellow guest causes a fire or other injury, no negligence can be attributed to the hotelkeeper.

FELONY A crime punishable by death or imprisonment in a state or federal prison.

FEUDAL SYSTEM The governing system in which the feudal lord had supreme power within his domain.

FIDUCIARY (fĭ dōō′ shē ēr″ ē) A person who possesses rights and powers to be exercised for the benefit of another person; a trustee.

FINANCE CHARGE The actual cost of a loan in dollars and cents.

FINANCIAL RESPONSIBILITY LAWS Laws which require car owners who are not insured to show proof that they can pay for the damages when they are at fault in an automobile accident.

FINANCING STATEMENT A written notice that a security interest exists.

FIRE INSURANCE A contract in which the insurer promises, for a stated premium, to pay the insured a sum not exceeding the face amount of the policy if a particular piece of real or personal property is damaged or destroyed by fire.

FIRM OFFER Under the Uniform Commercial Code, a merchant's written promise to hold open an offer for the sale of goods. No consideration is necessary for the promise to be binding.

FIRST-DEGREE MURDER Generally, murder committed in any one of the following three circumstances: (1) after premeditation, (2) in a cruel way, or (3) while committing a major crime.

FIXTURE An article of personal property physically attached to real property.

FLEXIBLE-RATE MORTGAGE A mortgage with a rate of interest that changes according to fluctuations in a reference index.

FLOATER POLICY An insurance policy that insures property that cannot be covered by specific insurance because the property is constantly changing in either value or location.

F.O.B. Free on board.

F.O.B. DESTINATION Shipping terms under which the seller must pay the freight charges to the destination.

F.O.B. SHIPPING POINT Shipping terms under which the buyer must pay the freight charges from the shipping point to the destination.

FOOD, DRUG, AND COSMETIC ACT A federal law which prohibits the manufacture and shipment in interstate commerce of any food, drug, cosmetic, or device for health purposes that is injurious, adulterated, or misbranded.

FORBEARANCE The act of refraining to do something (or promising not to do something) which a person has a legal right to do.

FORCED SALE The sale of property, such as a sheriff's sale, against the will of the owner.

FORECLOSURE The legal proceeding which brings about the application of mortgaged property to the payment of a mortgage.

FOREIGN CORPORATION A corporation which operates in a state other than the one in which it is incorporated.

FORGED CHECK A check signed by someone other than the drawer and without authority.

FORGERY The act of falsely making or materially altering a document with intent to defraud.

FRANCHISE A special privilege conferred by a government or a private party to an individual or a corporation.

FRAUD The misrepresentation of a material, existing fact which was known to be false by the party making it, was made with the intention that it be relied upon, was relied upon, and caused the party who was wronged to suffer damages.

FRAUDULENT MISREPRESENTATION Any statement that has the effect of deceiving the buyer. It usually occurs when a seller misstates the facts about something that is important to a consumer.

FRIENDLY FIRE A fire that burns only within its intended boundaries.

FRIENDLY SUITOR (also called *white knight*) An individual or a corporation invited by another corporation's management to take over that corporation in order to prevent a takeover by a hostile bidder; the friendly suitor pledges to keep the same management team.

FRISK A limited search that is done by patting the outer clothing of a person.

FULL INDORSEMENT (also called *special indorsement*) An indorsement made by first writing on the back of a negotiable instrument an order to pay to a specified person and then signing the instrument.

FULL WARRANTY Under the Magnuson-Moss Warranty Act, a warranty in which a defective product will be fixed or replaced free within a reasonable time after a complaint has been made about the product.

FUNGIBLE GOODS (fŭn′ jĭ bl) Movable goods composed of like units which can be estimated and replaced by like units according to weight, measure, and number.

FUTURE GOODS In sales law, goods not yet in existence or manufactured or not yet identified to a contract—that is, set aside to be the subject matter of a contract.

GARNISHMENT A court order authorizing the attachment (taking) of property, usually wages, in order to satisfy an unpaid claim.

GENERAL AGENT An agent who has been given the authority to transact all of his or her principal's business.

GENERAL CONSENT The permission by patients entering a hospital that the hospital do whatever routine procedures are needed to make a diagnosis or administer treatment.

GENERAL PARTNER A partner who takes an active part in the management of a business, is publicly known as a partner, and has unlimited liability for the firm's debts.

GENERAL PARTNERSHIP As defined by the Uniform Partnership Act, an association of two or more persons to carry on a business for profit.

GENERAL RELEASE A statement in writing and under seal terminating an existing obligation between two parties.

GIFT A voluntary transfer of property without consideration.

GOOD FAITH An honest intention not to take advantage of another.

GOODS All things (including those that have been specially manufac-tured) which are movable at the time they are made part of a contract for sale.

GOODWILL The advantage or benefit that is acquired by a business, beyond the capital or stock used therein, resulting from having a body of regular customers and a good reputation.

GRADUATED-PAYMENT MORTGAGE A mortgage whose interest rate is fixed but whose monthly payments increase over the term of the loan.

GRAND JURY A jury that hears evidence prior to an actual trial to determine whether a criminal charge should be brought against an individual.

GRAND LARCENY Stealing something of great value—a felony.

GRANT The transfer of title to real property by means of a deed.

GRATUITOUS (grŭ t[y]ū′ ŭt ŭs) Without value or legal consideration.

GRATUITOUS AGENT An agent who is not legally obligated to fulfill a promise.

GRATUITOUS BAILMENT A bailment in which the bailor lends the goods to the bailee for use without charge or a bailment in which the bailee takes possession of the goods for the bailor and keeps them safely without charge.

GRIEVANCE PROCEDURE A procedure detailed in collective bargaining agreements that gives employees the right to appeal any employer's decision they feel violates just cause.

GROUNDS FOR RELIEF In bankruptcy law, the requirements that creditors must meet to force a debtor into involuntary bankruptcy—the major requirement being that the debtor not pay bills as they come due.

GUARANTEE (găr″ ăn te′) A contract whereby one party agrees to answer for the debt or default of another. Also, a promise or assurance of the quality or life of a product. (See *express warranty*)

GUARANTOR A party who makes a guarantee.

GUARDIAN The party having legal custody of the property or the person of a minor or incompetent.

HEIR A person who inherits by right of relationship.

HOLDER A person who is in possession of a negotiable instrument that is payable either to the person holding it or to the bearer.

HOLDER IN DUE COURSE A party

who has taken a negotiable instrument in good faith and for value without any knowledge that there is anything irregular about the instrument.

HOLDOVER TENANT (also called *tenant by sufferance*) A tenant who remains in possession of real property after his or her interest in the property expires.

HOLOGRAPHIC WILL (häl″ ŭ grăf′ ĭk) A will written in the testator's handwriting.

HOMEOWNER'S INSURANCE A kind of insurance which provides protection for all types of losses and liabilities related to home ownership, including losses from fire, windstorm, burglary, and negligence of the homeowner.

HOMICIDE The killing of a human being by another human being.

HORIZONTAL PRICE FIXING Competitor agreements to sell a product or service at an agreed price.

HOSPITALIZATION INSURANCE Insurance that covers the cost of staying in a hospital.

HOSTILE FIRE (also called *unfriendly fire*) A fire that becomes uncontrollable or escapes from the place where it is supposed to be.

HOTELKEEPER An individual, partnership, or corporation that offers rooms to transients for a price.

IDENTIFIED GOODS Under the Uniform Commercial Code, goods that presently exist and that have been selected or set aside to be the subject matter of a particular contract.

ILLUSORY In relation to contracts, appearing at first to bind both parties but in actuality not doing so.

IMPLIED AUTHORITY The unexpressed authority of an agent to perform acts incidental to the duties of the agency.

IMPLIED CONTRACT A contract created by the acts of the parties rather than by their oral or written agreements.

IMPLIED COVENANT Implied promise.

IMPLIED WARRANTY A warranty that is proved by the acts of the seller or by surrounding circumstances rather than by words spoken or written.

IMPLIED WARRANTY OF HABITABILITY The obligation of the landlord to make those repairs necessary to keep the premises fit to live in.

IMPOUND Take possession of (by police).

INCAPACITY A legal disability, such as infancy, lack of authority, or other personal disability, to make binding agreements.

INCIDENTAL DAMAGES Reasonable expenses resulting from breach of contract that have been incurred by the party who did not breach the contract.

INCOMPATIBILITY A ground for divorce in a few states. The evidence must show that the couple have a personality conflict so deep that there is no chance for a reconciliation.

INDEMNITY An agreement that one party will secure another party against loss or damage due to the happening of a specified event.

INDEPENDENT CONTRACTOR A person who contracts to do a piece of work according to his or her own methods and without being subject to the control of his or her employer except as to the result of the work.

INDICTMENT (ĭn dīt′ mĕnt) A formal charge of a crime made by a grand jury.

INDORSEMENT A name, with or without other words, written on the back of a negotiable paper.

INFANT (also called *minor*) Person under 18.

INFORMED CONSENT Consent given by patients for diagnostic tests or treatments that will involve any danger after being told about the risks involved in the tests or treatments.

INHERITANCE Passage of title to property to a deceased person's heirs.

INJUNCTION A court order issued by a judge ordering a person to do or not to do a certain act.

INJURIOUS Harmful.

INLAND MARINE INSURANCE Insurance that covers (a) goods moved by carriers such as rail, truck, and airplane; (b) such goods as jewelry, fine arts, musical instruments, and wedding presents; or (c) customers' goods in the possession of bailees.

INNOCENT MISREPRESENTATION A statement of fact made by a person who honestly believes it to be true but which, in fact, is false.

INSIDER TRADING Trading in stocks by corporate insiders— managers, officers, majority shareholders, and so on—on the basis of inside information and for the purpose of profiting personally; under securities law, insiders who have important knowledge about some material aspect

of a stock sale must either make that knowledge public or refrain from trading in the stock themselves.

INSOLVENCY The condition of having insufficient property for the full payment of one's debts or of being unable to pay debts as they become due.

INSTALLMENT NOTE A note that is paid in a series of payments.

INSURABLE INTEREST The financial interest that an insurance policyholder has in the person or property that is insured.

INSURANCE A contract whereby one party agrees to reimburse another party if the latter suffers a specified monetary loss.

INSURANCE POLICY The written statement containing the insurance contract that is entered into between the insurer and the insured.

INSURED The person whose life or property is insured.

INSURER A bailee who is absolutely liable for any loss; in insurance, the party that issues the policy, collects the premium, and assumes the risk.

INTANGIBLE PROPERTY Property not perceptible to the senses; generally, rights rather than goods.

INTERFERENCE WITH CONTRACTUAL RELATIONS The tort of intentionally causing a person not to contract with another or intentionally causing a person to breach a contract with another.

INTERLOCKING DIRECTORATE The control of two or more competing companies by the same board of directors.

INTERMEDIATE COURTS Local courts whose function is to hear appeals from courts of general jurisdiction.

INTERNATIONAL LAW The mutual agreements that nations enter into among themselves.

INTERNATIONAL TERRORISM As defined by the U.S. Code (50 USCS 1801), activities that involve violent acts dangerous to human life that are a violation of the criminal laws of the United States or of any state or that would be a criminal violation if committed within the jurisdiction of the United States or any state; that appear to be intended to intimidate or coerce a civilian population, to influence the policy of a government by intimidation or coercion, or to affect the conduct of a government by assassination or kidnapping; and that occur totally outside the United States or transcend national boundaries in terms of the means by which they are accomplished, the persons they appear intended to coerce or intimidate, or the locale in which their perpetrators operate or seek asylum.

INTERSTATE COMMERCE COMMISSION An agency of the federal government which regulates commerce between the states.

INTESTATE A person who dies without leaving a will.

INTRASTATE CARRIERS Carriers that operate within the boundaries of a single state.

INVALID Of no legal force; void.

INVASION OF PRIVACY An act that deprives citizens of their right to privacy and of their freedom from interference with their personal life.

INVOLUNTARY BAILEE A bailee who has made no agreement of any kind.

INVOLUNTARY BANKRUPTCY Bankruptcy in which creditors petition the court in an effort to have a debtor declared bankrupt.

INVOLUNTARY MANSLAUGHTER The act of unintentionally killing someone while committing an unlawful or reckless act.

IRRECONCILABLE DIFFERENCES The breakdown of the marriage relationship. Also referred to in some states as *irremediable breakdown* or *irretrievable breakdown*.

IRREVOCABLE (ĭr rĕv′ ăh kă bl) Not able to be revoked or rescinded legally.

IRREVOCABLE AGENCY An agency that cannot be discharged by the principal because the agent has an interest in the subject matter.

ISSUED In regard to notes or drafts, executed by the maker and handed to the payee.

JOINT CONTRACTS Contracts in which two or more persons hold themselves liable for performance.

JOINT CUSTODY In divorce, the awarding of custody of children to both parents jointly.

JOINT ESTATE An estate owned by two or more persons whose interest will go to the surviving owners at the death of anyone named in the deed.

JOINT LIABILITY A type of liability held by a group of persons which requires that they all must be sued together in the event of a lawsuit.

JOINT AND SEVERAL LIABILITY A type of liability that is held by a group of persons and which allows an injured party the choice, in the event of a lawsuit, of suing all of the parties together or one or more of them separately.

JOINT TENANTS Two or more tenants holding land under conditions whereby the survivor takes the whole interest.

JUDGE The person who presides over all actions in open court.

JUDGMENT The official decision of the court.

JUDGMENT BY DEFAULT A judgment in favor of a plaintiff because of the failure of the defendant to answer the summons or appear.

JUDICIAL DECISION A court's interpretation of the common law, statutes, and constitutions accepted as the law.

JUDICIAL SEPARATION (also called *limited divorce*) A court order which allows a married couple to live separate and apart.

JURISDICTION (jōor ĭs dĭk′ shŭn) The authority given to a court or a judge to try an individual or a disagreement and to make a judgment.

JURY Body of persons selected to determine the truth in questions of fact in either civil or criminal cases.

JUST CAUSE Legitimate reason.

JUSTICE OF THE PEACE COURTS (also called *magistrate's courts*) Local courts established to furnish a way to try small claims cases and to punish petty crimes in communities.

JUSTIFIABLE HOMICIDE The killing of a human being by another human being through the legal execution of a convicted criminal or the killing of a soldier in battle.

JUVENILE COURT A court that has special jurisdiction over delinquents and neglected children up to an age set by state statute.

JUVENILE DELINQUENT A minor, under a certain age, who has committed an act that would be a crime if done by an adult.

LABOR UNION An organization of employees who join together for the purpose of bargaining collectively with their employer concerning their conditions of employment.

LANDLORD A person who owns real property and who rents or leases it to someone else.

LAPSE The termination of a right or

privilege through neglect to exercise it within some limit of time, or through failure of some contingency.

LAPSED POLICY An insurance policy whose premium has not been paid.

LARCENY The wrongful taking and carrying away of the personal property of another with the intent to steal.

LARCENY BY FALSE PRETENSES The taking of someone else's money or property by the intentional use of false statements calculated to mislead the victim and induce the victim's reliance on them.

LAW The rules of conduct that govern people in their dealings with one another.

LAW OF COMMERCIAL PAPER (also called *law of negotiable instruments*) Law developed in recognition of the need to transact business without carrying around large sums of money and to borrow money in order to buy things now and pay for them later—part of the Uniform Commercial Code.

LAW MERCHANT The use by judges of the customs of merchants and traders in settling disputes between businesspeople; the name given to the customs and practices of businesspeople, merchants, and mariners in early English times.

LAW OF SALES Law that governs contracts for the sale of goods.

LAWSUIT A legal action brought by one person against another.

LAY WITNESS A witness who is asked to testify to facts that are within his or her personal knowledge.

LEASE A contract granting the use of certain real property to another for a specified period in return for the payment of rent.

LEGACY A gift of personal property as designated by will.

LEGAL TENDER Money, according to law, that must be accepted in payment of a debt. It consists of the exact amount due in United States currency.

LESSEE A tenant under a lease of real property.

LESSOR A landlord who leases real property to a tenant.

LIBEL An untruthful written or printed statement that injures another person's reputation or reflects upon that person's character.

LICENSE Permission to do or to refrain from doing some act.

LIEN (lēn) A right to retain certain property as security for a claim or debt.

LIFE ESTATE The right of a person to use or receive the income from property for life.

LIMITED DIVORCE (also called *judicial separation*) A court order which allows a married couple to live separate and apart.

LIMITED PARTNER A partner whose liability does not extend beyond the partner's investment.

LIMITED PARTNERSHIP As defined by the Revised Uniform Limited Partnership Act, a partnership formed by two or more persons and having one or more general partners and one or more limited partners.

LIMITED-PAYMENT LIFE INSURANCE A kind of insurance which provides that the payment of premiums will stop after a stated length of time—usually ten, twenty, or thirty years. The amount of the policy will be paid to the beneficiary upon the death of the insured, whether the death occurs during the payment period or after.

LIMITED WARRANTY Under the Magnuson-Moss Warranty Act, a warranty that is not a full warranty.

LIQUIDATED Turned into cash to pay creditors.

LIQUIDATED DAMAGES An amount agreed upon that is to be paid in case of a breach of contract.

LITIGATION (lĭt ŭ gā′ shŭn) A contest in a court of justice for the purpose of enforcing a right; a lawsuit.

LIVING WILL A document that makes an advance statement directing the withholding of life-sustaining measures in the event of terminal illness or injury.

LOAN VALUE The amount that a life insurance policyholder may borrow from the insurance company.

LOCAL COURTS Courts of limited jurisdiction—having jurisdiction only in minor matters, petty crimes, and civil actions involving small amounts of money.

LOCUS SIGILLI (lō′ kŭs sĭ jĭl′ ī) Latin phrase meaning *the place of the seal*. (Also indicated by the abbreviation *L.S.*) Required in the execution of contracts for the sale of interest in real property and in other contracts. Not required in all states.

LODGER (or *roomer*) Any person staying at a hotel, motel, or rooming house for a definite period of time.

LOWER COURTS (also called *trial courts* or *courts of original juris-diction*) Courts that hear cases initially.

LOYALTY In agency law the requirement that agents (including employees, partners, and corporate directors and managers) act in their principals' best interests at all times.

MAGISTRATES Civil officers having judicial powers.

MAJOR MEDICAL INSURANCE A kind of insurance which pays for large hospital and medical bills resulting from serious and prolonged illness.

MAJORITY The age at which minors reach legal maturity, usually 18 years.

MAKER A person obligated as the payor on a promissory note; the person promising to pay.

MALICE AFORETHOUGHT Having an evil intent before a killing takes place.

MALFEASANCE (măl fēz′ ĕn[t]s) The commission of an unlawful act.

MALICIOUS PROSECUTION The bringing of a legal action with malice and without probable cause.

MALPRACTICE Improper professional practice.

MANSLAUGHTER The unlawful killing of one human being by another without malice aforethought.

MARRIAGE BANNS Public notice of a forthcoming marriage.

MARTIAL LAW A system of law which governs the military. In time of war or serious emergency, it may be declared to govern the civilian population.

MASTER In two-party relationships, the person who has the right to control the physical conduct of another.

MATERIAL ALTERATION A change in an instrument that affects the rights of the parties.

MATERIAL FACT A fact that is important, that matters to one of the parties to a contract or transaction.

MECHANIC'S LIEN Claim created by law to ensure that the cost of labor and materials used in repairing or erecting a building shall be paid before the owner of the property is released from liability.

MEDIATION (mēd″ ē ā′ shŭn) The intervention of a third party in a dispute between two or more contending parties.

MEDICAL AND SURGICAL INSURANCE A kind of insurance which pays for doctors' and surgeons'
bills when the insured becomes ill or has to have an operation.

MEDICAL PAYMENTS INSURANCE Motor vehicle insurance which pays for medical (and sometimes funeral) expenses resulting from bodily injuries to anyone occupying the policyholder's car at the time of an accident.

MEDICARE Health insurance protection, consisting of both medical and hospital benefits, available to all Americans 65 years of age and older under social security.

MEMORANDUM A note or instrument stating something that the parties desire to fix in memory by the aid of written evidence.

MERCHANT A person who deals in goods sold in the ordinary course of business, or one who otherwise holds himself or herself out as having knowledge or skill peculiar to those goods.

MERCHANTABLE In reference to goods, passing without objection in the trade under the contract description; fit for the ordinary purposes for which they are used; adequately contained, packaged, and labeled; and conforming to the promises or statements of fact made on the container.

MERGER The acquisition of one corporation by another.

MINOR (also called *infant*) A person under the age of legal maturity, which is usually 18 years.

MISBRANDED In regard to a food or drug, having false or misleading labeling or packaging.

MISDEMEANOR (mĭs″ dĕ mēn′ ĕr) A minor criminal offense of less serious nature than a felony.

MISREPRESENTATION A false statement of fact.

MISTRIAL A trial which has been declared void because of errors in law or fact arising during the prosecution of the case. A mistrial creates the necessity for a new trial before a different jury.

MITIGATION OF DAMAGES The principle that the injured party is obliged to protect the other party from any unnecessary losses.

MONEY ORDER A draft issued by a post office, bank, or telegraph company to transfer money.

MONOPOLIES Business agreements which, because of their exclusive control of an operation, result in the restraint of competition and free trade.

MORATORIUM (màwr″ ŭ tōr′ ē ŭm)

A period of time during which a debtor has the legal right to delay the payment of an overdue account.

MORTGAGE (mȧwr′ gĭj) A lien given on property as security for a loan.

MORTGAGEE A party to whom a mortgage is given (very often a bank) as security for a loan. The mortgagee lends the money and takes a mortgage back as security for the loan.

MORTGAGOR A party who borrows money and gives a mortgage to the lender as security for the loan.

MULTIEMPLOYER PLAN A pension plan under which many different employers give money to a central fund for the benefit of their employees when they retire.

MUNICIPAL COURTS Local courts that serve the same function as justice of the peace courts—trying small claims cases and punishing petty crimes.

MURDER The unlawful killing of a human being by another with malice aforethought.

MUTUAL-BENEFIT BAILMENT A bailment in which both the bailor and the bailee receive some benefit.

MUTUAL MISTAKE (also called *bilateral mistake*) A misunderstanding by both parties to a contract about some important fact.

MUTUAL RELEASE Contract discharge by mutual agreement, with each party releasing the other from the obligation.

NATIONAL LABOR RELATIONS BOARD A board established for the purpose of enforcing the National Labor Relations Act.

NATURAL LAW Rules of conduct that it is believed people would follow if there were no formal laws.

NECESSITIES Things that are needed for the sustenance of human life. They include food, clothing, shelter, and medical care.

NEGLIGENCE The failure to exercise the degree of care which a reasonably prudent person would have exercised under the same circumstances.

NEGOTIABILITY (nē̇ gō″ shĭ ȧ bĭl′ ĭ tĭ) The characteristic of commercial paper (a note, draft, check, etc.) whereby it may be transferred to another person who then becomes the legal holder.

NEGOTIABLE INSTRUMENT A written promise or request for the payment of a certain sum of money to order or to the bearer.

NEGOTIABLE WAREHOUSE RECEIPT A receipt given by a warehouse to a customer whose goods the warehouse is storing. The receipt may be transferred to other people, and the warehouse will release the goods only to the holder of the receipt.

NEGOTIATION The transfer of an instrument in such a way that the transferee becomes a holder.

NEW STOCK ISSUES Stocks offered for sale for the first time.

NO-FAULT DIVORCE LAW Law that eliminates the need to prove that one party is at fault when seeking a divorce.

NO-FAULT INSURANCE Motor vehicle insurance in which the insured's own insurance company pays the insured's own bills when he or she is in an automobile accident, regardless of who is at fault.

NO PAR VALUE STOCK Stock that does not have any stated value.

NOMINAL DAMAGES A small award given to a person whose legal right has been violated but who sustained no actual loss.

NONCONFORMING USES Existing uses of property that do not comply with new zoning laws but that are allowed to continue.

NONCONTRIBUTORY PENSION PLAN Pension plan financed entirely by the employer.

NONNEGOTIABLE WAREHOUSE RECEIPT A receipt, which is not transferable, given by a warehouse to a customer whose goods the warehouse is storing.

NONPROFIT CORPORATION A corporation that is formed for educational, religious, charitable, or social purposes.

NONSTOCK CORPORATION A nonprofit corporation in which membership is acquired by agreement rather than by acquisition of stock.

NOTARY PUBLIC A public official who certifies under seal various documents such as deeds and affidavits. He or she has the power to present and formally protest notes and drafts.

NOTICE OF PROTEST A formal notice that a bill of exchange or note has been dishonored.

NOTIFY EMPLOYER PROCEDURE The procedure whereby newly hired employees without social security numbers are allowed to begin work if they get a receipt from the social security office to show they have applied for the numbers; the employer is notified directly by the Social Security Administration of the employee numbers as soon as they are issued.

NOVATION An agreement whereby an original party to a contract is replaced by a new party. To be effective, the substitution of parties must be agreed to by all three parties involved in the transaction.

NUISANCE (nū′ sȧns) Anything that endangers life or health, gives offense to the senses, violates the laws of decency, or obstructs the reasonable and comfortable use of property.

NUNCUPATIVE WILL (nŭn′ kyoo pāt″ ĭv) An oral will made and declared in the presence of witnesses by the testator.

OCCUPATIONAL SAFETY AND HEALTH ADMINISTRATION The federal regulatory agency established to ensure safe and healthy working conditions for workers throughout the country.

OCEAN MARINE INSURANCE Insurance that covers ships at sea.

OFFER A proposal by one person to another, intended to create a legal duty if it is accepted by the person to whom it is made.

OFFEREE (ôf′ ĕr ē) The person who receives an offer.

OFFEROR (ôf′ ĕr ôr) The person who makes an offer.

OFFICERS A group of people chosen by the board of directors to run the everyday operation of a corporation.

OPEN-END CREDIT An extension of credit which may be increased by the debtor at any time simply by purchasing more goods.

OPEN POLICY An insurance policy in which the amount to be paid by the insurance company is to be determined when the loss occurs.

OPERATION OF LAW In the best interest of society. (See also *quasi-contract* and *public policy*.)

OPTION A binding promise to hold an offer open for a specified period.

OPTIONEE The holder of an option.

ORDER BILL OF LADING A receipt for goods shipped, issued by a carrier and containing a promise by the carrier not to redeliver the goods to anyone until the original order bill, properly endorsed, is presented to the carrier.

ORDER INSTRUMENT A negotiable instrument that may be negotiated by indorsement followed by delivery.

ORDER FOR RELIEF The legal name for a bankruptcy judgment.

ORDER TO STOP PAYMENT An order to a bank by the drawee of a check not to pay the check when it is presented.

ORDINANCE The legislative act of a municipal corporation; a law, statute, or decree.

ORDINARY LIFE INSURANCE (also called *straight life insurance* and *whole life insurance*) A kind of insurance which requires the payment of premiums throughout the life of the insured and which pays the beneficiary the face value of the policy upon the insured's death.

OUTPUT CONTRACT A contract to buy the entire production of a particular product from a producer of goods.

OUTSTANDING CHECKS Checks that have been written but not yet returned to the bank.

PAR VALUE STOCK Stock whose value is stated in the articles of incorporation.

PARENT CORPORATION A corporation that owns and operates another corporation.

PARENTAL LIABILITY LAWS Laws which require the parents of vandals to pay for the damage done by their children.

PAROL (pŭ ràwl′) By word of mouth; oral, verbal.

PAROL EVIDENCE RULE A rule which says that evidence of oral statements made before signing a written agreement is usually not admissible in court to change or contradict the terms of a written agreement.

PAROLE (pŭ rōl′) The conditional release of a prisoner before the expiration of his or her sentence.

PARTIAL DISABILITY The condition in which a person is disabled to the extent that he or she is unable to perform one or more of the basic duties of a job, but is able to do some of the duties.

PARTICIPATING PREFERRED STOCK Stock which gives the holder the right to share in extra earnings along with the common stock holder after he or she has received a fixed rate (percent) or dividend.

PARTNERSHIP An association of two or more persons to carry on as co-owners of a business for profit.

PARTNERSHIP BY ESTOPPEL A partnership that occurs because someone says or does something that leads a third party to believe that a partnership exists.

PARTNERSHIP BY PROOF OF EXISTENCE A partnership that is created simply because of the way that two or more people conduct business with one another.

PATENT A right granted by the government to an inventor or the inventor's agent to manufacture and sell a patented article for a period of seventeen years.

PAWNBROKER A person licensed to lend money on pledged goods.

PAYEE The party named in commercial paper, to whom payment is to be made.

PENSION PLAN Any plan, fund, or program that provides income to employees after they retire.

PEREMPTORY CHALLENGE A request that a member of a jury be removed without cause (for no reason).

PERFECTED A security interest is said to be *perfected* when the secured party has done everything that the law requires to give the secured party greater rights to the goods than others have.

PERIODIC TENANCY (also called *tenancy from year to year*) An interest in real property that continues for successive periods of time until one of the parties ends it by giving proper notice to the other.

PERJURY A false statement made while testifying under oath in court, made willfully concerning some material point.

PERSONAL DEFENSE A defense that can be used against a holder but not a holder in due course of a negotiable instrument.

PERSONAL PROPERTY Things other than real estate.

PERSONAL PROPERTY FLOATER A floater insurance policy that covers personal property in general, wherever located.

PETIT JURY (pĕt′ ē) The trial jury that has the duty of determining the facts at issue after hearing the evidence presented in open court by each party; called a petit jury because the number of jurors is usually smaller than in a grand jury.

PETTY LARCENY The stealing of something of small value—a misdemeanor.

PIERCING THE CORPORATE VEIL The doctrine of holding the shareholders of a corporation personally liable when they have used the corporation as a facade to defraud or commit some other misdeed.

PLAIN-VIEW EXCEPTION The legal ability of police to seize suspicious items that are in plain view without obtaining a warrant.

PLAINTIFF The party who brings an action in court against another party.

PLEA A person's answer to a complaint or charge against that person.

PLEADINGS The written statement of claims and defenses of the parties involved in a court action.

PLEDGE (also called *pawn*) A bailment of goods as security for a debt or other obligation.

PLEDGEE A person to whom property is given as security for a loan.

PLEDGOR A person who pledges (gives) property to another as security for a loan.

POLICE POWER The power to govern; the power to enact laws for the protection of the public health, welfare, morals, and safety.

POLICYHOLDER The owner of an insurance policy.

POLYGAMY The act of having more than two spouses at the same time.

POOLING AGREEMENTS (also called *shareholder agreements* or *voting agreements*) Agreements by a group of shareholders who join together to vote the same way on a particular issue.

PORTABILITY The ability to transfer pension benefits from one job to another.

POSTDATE To date an instrument as of a later date than the one on which it was made.

POUR-OVER PROVISION In bankruptcy law, the protection from creditors of up to $3,750 of any unused portion of the real estate exemption plus $400 of any other unused exemption.

POWER OF ATTORNEY A written instrument which empowers one person to act for or represent another in specified matters.

PRECEDENT (prē sēd′ ent) adj., (prĕs′ė dĕnt) n. A legal decision cited as having an effect upon an action being presented in a court of law or equity.

PREFERRED STOCK Stock which gives owners the right to have their investment returned first in case of dissolution, and the right to receive dividends first before dividends are distributed to holders of common stock.

PREMARITAL AGREEMENT (also called *antenuptial agreement* or *prenuptial agreement*) An agreement between prospective spouses made in contemplation of marriage and to be effective upon marriage.

PREMEDITATION Thinking about an act and planning it in advance.

PREMIUM The amount paid periodically by the insured to the insurer for insurance.

PRESENTENCE HEARING The second phase of a trial, in which the judge or jury listens to lawyers' arguments and examines other evidence to help determine the punishment to be given to a person who was found guilty of a crime during the first phase.

PRESENTMENT The exhibition of a note and demand for payment.

PRESENTMENT FOR ACCEPTANCE The presentation of a draft or a bill of exchange to a drawee with a request for acceptance.

PRESENTMENT FOR PAYMENT The presentation of a draft or a bill of exchange to a drawee with a request for payment.

PRIMA FACIE EVIDENCE (prī′ má fā′ shĭ ē) Evidence that is legally sufficient for proof unless rebutted or contradicted.

PRIMARY LIABILITY Absolute liability to pay a negotiable instrument.

PRINCIPAL A person who appoints and directs the activities of an agent.

PRINCIPAL IN THE FIRST DEGREE A person who actually commits a felony.

PRINCIPAL IN THE SECOND DEGREE A person who does not actually commit the act but who is present, assisting another who is committing a felony.

PRIVATE CARRIERS (also called *contract carriers*) Carriers that haul goods for others under special arrangements.

PRIVATE CORPORATIONS Corporations formed by private citizens for either profit or non-profit purposes.

PRIVATE NUISANCE Something that interferes with one person's enjoyment of life or property—a tort.

PRIVILEGED Statements that are not subject to defamation lawsuits.

PRIVILEGED SPEECH Statements that are not subject to defamation lawsuits.

PRIVITY OF CONTRACT The relationship that exists between two or more contracting parties.

PRO RATA AMOUNT The proportion of an insurance premium that has not been used and that is returned to the insured if the policy is cancelled.

PROBATE (prō′ bāt) The legal procedure of proving or establishing a will.

PROBATE COURT (sometimes called *surrogate court* or *widow's and orphans' court*) A court which supervises the administration of the estates of deceased persons.

PROCEEDS The amount that a beneficiary of a life insurance policy receives upon the death of the insured.

PROCESS SERVER A sheriff, marshal, or other court official who gives notice to the various parties in a lawsuit by handing them official documents.

PRODUCT LIABILITY The responsibility of manufacturers and sellers for products they sell that cause injuries to consumers because the products are defective, unhealthy, or unsafe.

PROFIT CORPORATIONS Private corporations organized for the purpose of making money.

PROMISSORY ESTOPPEL The doctrine that a promise may be enforceable without consideration if that promise reasonably induced another's action, and the breaking of that promise would result in injustice.

PROMISSORY NOTE A written promise by one person to pay money to another at a particular time or on demand.

PROMOTERS (also called *incorporators*) Persons who organize a corporation.

PROPERTY Things we own, including movable items such as automobiles, pencils, and books and nonmovable items such as land and buildings.

PROPERTY DAMAGE LIABILITY INSURANCE Automobile insurance that provides protection when other people bring claims or lawsuits against the insured for damaging their property.

PROPRIETARY LEASE A long-term lease issued to prospective tenants of cooperative apartments by the corporation that owns the building, giving the tenants all the usual rights of ownership.

PROPRIETOR The person who hires an independent contractor. Also, an owner of a business.

PROSECUTE To proceed against a person by legal means.

PROSECUTION The state, as the party bringing legal action against a person accused of a crime.

PROSPECTUS A document published by a corporation setting forth the nature and objects of an issue of stock, and inviting the public to subscribe to it.

PROTEST A statement by a notary public (or other authorized person) that an instrument has been refused payment at maturity.

PROXIMATE RESULTS The reasonably foreseeable results of an action. In fire insurance, damages related to the fire, e.g. smoke and water damage and damage to insured goods moved to a safer location.

PROXY (prŏks′ ē) A document by which one person authorizes another to act for him or her.

PROXY CONTEST A battle between insurgent shareholders and the majority shareholders representing management for the right to vote other shareholders' stock.

PROXY MARRIAGE A marriage solemnized in the ordinary way except that one or both of the parties to the marriage are absent and are represented by an agent who acts in their behalf.

PROXY SOLICITATION PROCESS The process by which shareholders ask other shareholders to transfer their voting rights.

PRUDENT PERSON A wise and careful person.

PUBLIC CARRIER A common carrier that engages in transporting passengers.

PUBLIC CORPORATION An incorporated political unit such as a town, village, city, or school district.

PUBLIC ENEMY A person or group that attempts through violence to overthrow the government.

PUBLIC NUISANCE Anything that interferes with the enjoyment of life or property by a large group of people—a tort.

PUBLIC OFFER An offer made publicly in situations in which the offeree's identity or location is unknown to the offeror.

PUBLIC POLICY The principle of law which holds that no person may lawfully perform an act that has a tendency to be injurious to the public.

PUBLIC UTILITY A private corporation having certain powers of a public nature to enable it to discharge its duties for the public benefit.

PUFFING Expressions of opinion of a

seller regarded by the courts as merely persuasive and not as actionable statements of fact.

PUNITIVE DAMAGES (pū′ nĭ tĭv) Damages, in excess of actual damages incurred by the plaintiff, awarded as a measure of punishment for the defendant's wrongful and malicious acts.

PURCHASE AND SALE AGREEMENT A written statement of the rights and duties of both parties to a contract for the sale, especially, of real property.

QUALIFIED INDORSEMENT An indorsement in which words have been added to the signature that limit or qualify the liability of the indorser.

QUASI CONTRACT A contract implied by law, not by fact; not a contract in the true sense because it lacks the element of mutual assent.

QUIET ENJOYMENT The right of a tenant to the undisturbed possession of the property that he or she is renting.

QUIET POSSESSION Undisturbed possession; as used in the law of sales, the right to hold goods free and clear of the claims of all other persons.

QUITCLAIM DEED A deed which transfers whatever interest the grantor has in real property to the grantee, without warranties.

QUORUM (kwôr′ ŭm) The minimum number of persons who must be present to transact business.

RAISED CHECK A check that has been illegally altered to raise the amount of money written on it.

RATIFICATION The subsequent approval of an act that previously had not been binding.

RATIFY To approve or show an intent to live up to a contract.

REAL DEFENSE (also called *absolute defense)* A defense that is good against everyone, even a holder in due course of a negotiable instrument.

REAL PROPERTY The ground and anything permanently attached to it including land, buildings, growing trees and shrubs. It also includes the airspace above the land.

REASONABLE CARE The degree of care that a reasonable person would exercise in a given situation.

REASONABLE-PERSON TEST A court's test of satisfactory performance based on the judgement of a ''reasonable person.''

REASONABLE TIME The time which is suitable to the end in view. It will vary with the circumstances of each individual situation.

REBUTTABLE PRESUMPTION An assumption that can be overruled by other evidence.

RECEIVER A person legally appointed to receive and hold in trust property that is or may be subject to litigation.

RECONCILIATION A return of friendship.

RECONCILIATION OF A BANK STATEMENT The adjustment of a check register and a bank statement accounting for bank charges, checks in transit, and unrecorded deposits, bringing these records into balance.

REDEMPTION (rḗ dĕm′ shŭn) The act of buying back one's own property after it has been sold.

REFERRAL SCHEME A scheme in which a seller promises to give a buyer a cash rebate or something for free if a certain number of the buyer's referrals also purchase the item.

REGISTRATION STATEMENT A statement required by the Securities and Exchange Commission to indicate the details about securities for sale and about the business making the offer of the securities.

REGULATION B A regulation authorized by the federal Equal Credit Opportunity Act which sets forth rules that must be followed to prevent discrimination against any person on the basis of sex or marital status in any aspect of a credit transaction.

REGULATION Z A regulation authorized by the federal Truth in Lending Act which sets forth specific rules that must be followed by people who extend credit to others.

REGULATORY AGENCY (also called *administrative agency)* A department of government that is formed for the purpose of administering particular legislation.

REHABILITATION The goal of the courts to steer individual offenders in the right direction rather than to impose harsh penalties.

REHABILITATION ACT OF 1973 The act under which employers that participate in government contracts must take affirmative action to employ and promote qualified handicapped people.

REIMBURSEMENT Repayment for money spent on someone else's behalf.

REJECTION The refusal by an offeree of an offer made by an offeror.

RELEASE The giving up, or surrender, of a claim or right of action; an instrument evidencing such a surrender.

REMEDY The legal means to recover a right or to redress a wrong.

RENT CONTROL LAWS Laws that limit the amount of rent that may be charged by a landlord.

RENT DAY The day on which rent is due.

REPLEVY (rĭ plĕv′ ē) A court action for the purpose of recovering possession of personal property wrongfully taken or held.

REPORTERS Books in which court cases are published.

REPOSSESS Take back.

REPRIEVE (rĭ prēv′) To suspend the execution of a sentence for a time.

REQUIREMENT CONTRACT A contract for all the goods a company needs for a particular purpose.

RESCIND (rē sĭnd′) To cancel; to annul; to avoid or void.

RESCISSION (rē sĭ′ shŭn) The annulling of a contract by mutual consent of the parties involved or by court decision as a result of a breach by one of the parties.

RESIDENCE A place where a person actually lives or resides. It may or may not be that person's domicile.

RESPONDEAT SUPERIOR In a master-servant relationship, the principle that the master can be held liable if the servant commits a tort while working for the master.

RESTRAINING INJUNCTION A decree of a court of equity ordering a party to cease and desist from certain acts.

RESTRAINT OF TRADE Contracts or combinations designed to eliminate or stifle competition, effect a monopoly, or artificially maintain prices.

RESTRICTIVE COVENANT A promise by an employee, in an employment contract, not to work for anyone else in the same field of employment; a promise not to start a competing business, for a specified time period within a particular geographical area.

RESTRICTIVE INDORSEMENT An indorsement in which words have been added, in addition to the signature of the transferor, that restrict the further indorsement of the instrument.

REVOCATION (rĕv″ ŭ kā′ shŭn) A taking back, or withdrawal, of an offer by an offeror before it has been accepted by an offeree.

RIDER (also called *endorsement)* In insurance, an attached writing which modifies or supplements the printed policy.

RIGHT OF PRIVACY The right of a

person to be protected from intrusion and invasion of his or her personal life by unauthorized agencies. In hotels, the right of privacy means a guest's right to use his or her room without fear of intrusion by others.

RIGHT-TO-WORK LAWS Laws which prohibit a union shop. The Taft-Hartley Act allows the individual states to pass right-to-work laws if they wish.

RIPARIAN RIGHTS (rī pâr' ĭ ăn) The rights of an owner of land abutting a stream or other body of water to the use of the water, and to the use of water and ice the owner may wish to remove from the body of water.

RISK An event insured against.

RISK OF LOSS Responsibility for loss or damage to goods.

ROBBERY The wrongful taking and carrying away of the personal property of another from the other's person. It is a crime committed against the victim's will by the use of force, violence, or the threat of bodily harm.

ROBINSON-PATMAN ACT An act passed by Congress in 1936 making it illegal for companies to sell goods at lower prices to high-volume purchasers.

ROMAN CODE (also called *Roman law* and *Civil Code*) A comprehensive system of laws established by Emperor Justinian and the emperors who followed him for the better administration of the vast Roman Empire.

ROOMER (or lodger) A person staying at a hotel, motel, or rooming house for a definite period of time.

SALE A contract whereby property is transferred from one person (called the *seller*) to another person (called the *buyer*) for a consideration (called the *price*).

SEAL A particular sign adopted and used by an individual to attest in the most formal manner the execution of an instrument.

SEARCH WARRANT A court order allowing an officer to conduct a search.

SECOND-DEGREE MURDER The unlawful killing of a human being with malice aforethought but without premeditation, not in a cruel way, and not while committing a major crime.

SECONDARY LIABILITY Liability to pay a negotiable instrument by a secondary party (a drawer or indorser) when that instrument has been dishon-

ored and the secondary party has been legally notified.

SECONDARY PARTY A drawer or indorser of an instrument.

SECRET PARTNER A partner who is active in the management of a business but whose connection with the firm is kept secret from the public.

SECURED LOAN A loan in which the creditor has something of value from which he or she can be paid if the debtor does not pay.

SECURED PARTY A lender or seller who holds a security interest on goods belonging to a debtor.

SECURITIES AND EXCHANGE COMMISSION The federal regulatory commission whose purpose is to protect investors.

SECURITY Protection or assurance (usually given in the form of a pledge, mortgage, deposit, or lien) given by a debtor to a creditor to make sure the debt is paid.

SECURITY AGREEMENT A written agreement that creates a security interest. It must identify the goods and be signed by the debtor.

SECURITY DEPOSIT A money deposit given by a tenant to a landlord at the beginning of a tenancy as security for the payment of the rent, or for repairs for damages done by the tenant.

SECURITY INTEREST An interest in personal property which secures payment or performance of an obligation.

SELF-DEFENSE An excusable use of force in resisting attack.

SELF-INCRIMINATION Being a witness against oneself.

SERVANT A person whose physical conduct in the performance of a task is controlled by another.

SHAREHOLDER PROPOSAL A proposal by certain shareholders that management of a publicly held corporation must put on the agenda at a shareholders' meeting.

SHARES Units of ownership of corporations (stock).

SHEPARDIZING Using a set of books called *Shepard's Citations* to determine the subsequent use of a case by the courts.

SHERMAN ANTITRUST ACT A congressional act passed in 1890 seeking to promote free trade without suppression of competition.

SHIPMENT CONTRACT A contract requiring the seller to send the goods to the buyer but not requiring that they be delivered directly to the place of

destination; title is transferred at the time and place that the shipment begins.

SHOPLIFTING The act of stealing goods from a store.

SIGHT DRAFT A written order on the drawee to pay on demand the amount named in the instrument.

SILENT PARTNER A partner who takes no active part in the management of the firm, is known publicly as a partner, and has unlimited liability for the firm's debts.

SINGLE-EMPLOYER PLAN A pension plan in which money is set aside and held by a single employer for the benefit of its employees when they retire.

SLANDER An untruthful oral statement that injures another person's reputation or reflects upon that person's character.

SMALL CLAIMS COURTS Local courts that hear civil, but not criminal, cases involving claims up to amounts ranging from $500 to $5,000, depending on the state law.

SOBRIETY TEST (sō brī' ĕ tē) A test devised to permit police to check a motorist's condition by analyzing the alcohol content of the motorist's blood and by other means.

SOCIAL SECURITY The basic method used in the United States to provide income to people when their regular income stops because of retirement, disability, or the death of someone who had provided them with income.

SOLE PROPRIETORSHIP A form of business that is owned and operated by one person.

SOLEMNIZED Performed by ceremony.

SPECIAL AGENT An agent who has been given the authority to conduct a particular transaction or to perform a specified act for his or her principal.

SPECIAL INDORSEMENT (also called *full indorsement*) An indorsement made by first writing on the back of a negotiable instrument an order to pay to a specified person and then signing the instrument.

SPECIFIC PERFORMANCE A remedy available to a person whose contract has been breached if money damages are not sufficient to give relief. Under this doctrine, the court can order the person who breached a contract to perform the agreement according to the exact terms originally agreed upon.

SPECULATIVE DAMAGES Damages which have not actually been inflicted and cannot be proved.

STALE CHECK A check that is more than six months old.

STARE DECISIS (ster-ē-di-ˈsī-səs) (also called the *law of precedent*) The doctrine "to stand by the decision"—that is, decisions made by the highest appellate court of any state become the law of that state and are followed by other courts in that state thereafter.

STATE SUPREME COURT (also called the *court of appeals* or the *court of errors*) The highest court in any state.

STATUTE A law enacted by a legislature.

STATUTE OF FRAUDS A law requiring written evidence to support certain contracts if they are to be enforced in court.

STATUTE OF LIMITATIONS A law that prevents bringing an action if that action is not begun within a specified time.

STATUTORY AGENT The person appointed by the incorporators of a corporation to receive complaints and summonses if the corporation is involved in litigation.

STATUTORY LAW The body of law passed by governing bodies created for the purpose of passing laws—including the U.S. Congress, the state legislatures, local city councils, or town meetings.

STOCK The transferable representation of ownership of a corporation.

STOCK CERTIFICATE A written instrument stating that a person is the owner of a designated number of shares of stock in a corporation.

STOCK CORPORATIONS Profit corporations that sell shares of ownership in themselves in order to raise capital.

STOCK SUBSCRIPTIONS Contracts to take stock when the corporation completes its organization and is authorized by the state to sell stock to the public.

STOCKBROKER One who buys and sells stock as the agent of others.

STOCKHOLDER OF RECORD An owner of stock whose name is recorded as the registered owner of a designated number of shares of stock in the corporation.

STOP PAYMENT ORDER An order by the drawer of a check to the drawee bank not to pay the check when it is presented.

STOPPAGE IN TRANSIT The right of an unpaid seller to stop goods in transit and order the carrier to hold the goods for the benefit of the unpaid seller, in cases in which the buyer becomes insolvent after the goods have been shipped.

STRAIGHT BILL OF LADING A receipt for goods shipped, issued by a carrier to a shipper and containing the contractual terms under which the goods are received for shipment.

STRAIGHT LIFE INSURANCE (also called *ordinary life insurance*) A kind of insurance which requires the payment of premiums throughout the life of the insured and which pays the beneficiary the face value of the policy upon the insured's death.

STRICT LIABILITY (also called *absolute liability*) The doctrine under which people may be liable for injuries to others whether or not they have done something wrong.

SUBAGENT An agent lawfully appointed by another agent.

SUB-CHAPTER S CORPORATION A corporation in which the stockholders have agreed to have the profits (or losses) of the corporation taxed directly to them rather than to the corporation.

SUBCONTRACTOR One who takes a portion of a contract from the principal contractor or from another subcontractor.

SUBLEASE A lease given by a lessee to a third person conveying the same interest for a shorter term than the period for which the lessee holds it.

SUBPOENA (sŭb pē′ nà) An order or writ commanding a person to appear and testify in a legal action or proceeding.

SUBSIDIARY A corporation owned and operated by another corporation.

SUBSTANTIAL PERFORMANCE A principle of law that allows the collection of the full contract price, less damages for any breach, when a contract has essentially been fully performed and performed in good faith, even though there has been some slight defect in the performance.

SUBSTANTIVE LAW (sŭb′ stăn tĭve) That part of our laws that deals with the determination of rights and duties.

SUBTERRANEAN RIGHTS Rights that an owner of real property has to the ground below the earth's surface.

SUITOR An individual or a corporation that attempts to buy another corporation in a takeover bid.

SUMMONS A notice issued from a court requiring a person to appear therein to answer the complaint of a plaintiff within a specified time.

SUPPLEMENTAL SECURITY INCOME (SSI) A federal program, in addition to social security, which provides additional cash benefits each month for needy people who are either aged, blind, or disabled.

SURROGATE The name given in some states to the judge who has the administration of probate matters.

TAFT-HARTLEY ACT The Labor-Management Relations Act of 1947, providing for the mediation of labor-management disputes.

TAKEOVER BID An attempt to buy enough shares of stock in a corporation to control it.

TANGIBLE Occupying space; able to be touched.

TARGET The corporation sought in a takeover bid.

TEMPORARY ALIMONY (also called *alimony pendente lite*) Alimony granted to one of the spouses while he or she is waiting for a divorce or separate support action to be completed.

TENANCY The interest owned by renters in the real estate they possess.

TENANCY BY THE ENTIRETY Co-ownership of real property by husband and wife.

TENANCY IN PARTNERSHIP Co-ownership of partnership property by all the partners.

TENANCY AT WILL An interest in real property that continues for an indefinite period of time.

TENANCY FOR YEARS An interest in real property which gives the tenant the right to use and occupy the property for a stated period of time.

TENANCY FROM YEAR TO YEAR (also called *periodic tenancy*) An interest in real property that continues for successive periods of time until one of the parties ends it by giving proper notice to the other.

TENANT A person who has temporary possession of and interest in the land of another.

TENANT IN COMMON A co-owner of real property whose heirs inherit that person's share of the property upon the person's death.

TENANT AT SUFFERANCE (also called *holdover tenant*) A tenant who remains in possession of real property after his or her interest in the property expires.

TENDER OF DELIVERY An offer by the seller of goods to turn the goods over to the buyer.

TENDER OFFER An offer to buy the stock of a target corporation in exchange for cash or stock in the suitor corporation.

TENDER OF PAYMENT An offer to pay money due under a contract.

TENDER OF PERFORMANCE An offer to do what a person has agreed to do under a contract.

TERM INSURANCE Insurance which is issued for a particular time period, usually five or ten years.

TESTATOR (tĕs′ tāt″ ŭr) A man who makes a will.

TESTATRIX (tĕs′ tā″ trĭks) A woman who makes a will.

TESTIMONY The spoken or written declaration of a witness given under oath.

THIRD PARTY BENEFICIARY One who receives a benefit as the result of a valid agreement between two other parties made expressly to benefit the third party.

TIME DRAFT A draft that is not payable until the lapse of a particular time period stated on the draft.

"TIME IS OF THE ESSENCE" An expression applicable to those agreements in which time of performance is critical in the carrying out of the agreement.

TIME NOTE A note that is payable at a future date written on the face of the note.

TITLE The right of ownership often evidenced by a certificate of title, bill of sale, or similar document.

TITLE INSURANCE Insurance that pays the value of real property to the insured in the event a prior claim is uncovered.

TITLE SEARCH A search through title records to satisfy the buyer of real property that the seller has good title to the property.

TITLE VII The part of the Civil Rights Act of 1964 that prohibits employment discrimination based on sex, race, color, religion, and national origin.

TORT A person's interference with another's rights, either by an intentional act or through negligence.

TORTFEASOR The person who commits a tort.

TORTIOUS BAILEE (tôr′ shŭs) One who wrongfully retains possession of the lost property of another or is knowingly in possession of stolen property, or who uses a bailed article for a purpose other than that which was agreed upon.

TOTAL DISABILITY The condition in which a person is so disabled that he or she is unable to perform normal job duties for a year or longer.

TRADE ACCEPTANCE A draft used by a seller of goods to receive payment and also to extend credit.

TRADE FIXTURES Those items of personal property brought upon the land by the tenant which are necessary to carry on the trade or business to which the land will be devoted.

TRADE SECRET Inside information about a firm's new products, processes, or inventions.

TRANSFER The taking of a case from juvenile court to criminal court.

TRANSIENT A guest in a hotel or motel whose stay is variable in length. He or she may leave at any time.

TRAVELER'S CHECK A draft purchased from a bank or express company and signed by the purchaser at the time of the purchase and again at the time of cashing as a precaution against forgery.

TREASON A crime involving the levying of war against the United States or the giving of aid and comfort to its enemies.

TREASURY STOCK Stock of a corporation issued by it and later reacquired.

TRESPASS A wrongful injury to or interference with the property of another.

TRUST A property interest held by one person for the benefit of another.

TRUSTEE A person who holds property in trust for another, called the beneficiary. The trustee has legal title to the property and the beneficiary has equitable or beneficial title to the property.

TRUTH IN LENDING ACT Federal legislation regulating consumer purchases on credit and consumer loans.

UNCONSCIONABLE AGREEMENTS (ŭn känch′ ŭ nŭ bl) Contracts which the courts refuse to enforce due to obvious unfair practices wrought upon victimized buyers.

UNDERCAPITALIZED The situation in which shareholders do not keep enough money and property in a corporation for the corporation to establish its own identity.

UNDISCLOSED PRINCIPAL A principal whose identity is not revealed to a third party who is dealing with that principal's agent.

UNDUE INFLUENCE Personal pressure, usually exerted by one in a position of trust, on another person who normally could be expected to trust the person who exerts the pressure.

UNEMPLOYMENT COMPENSATION A system of government payments to people who are out of work to provide them with support until they find another job.

UNENFORCEABLE In regard to contracts, unable to be enforced in court because of some rule of law.

UNFAIR AND DECEPTIVE ACT OR PRACTICE An act or practice that misleads (or has the potential to mislead) consumers.

UNFRIENDLY FIRE (also called *hostile fire*) A fire that becomes uncontrollable or escapes from the place where it is supposed to be.

UNFRIENDLY TAKEOVER BID An attempt by an individual or a corporation to buy a majority of the shares of another corporation with the intention of reorganizing the corporation by ousting the present management.

UNIFORM COMMERCIAL CODE A uniform law relating to certain commercial transactions involving personal property including sales, commercial paper, bank deposits and collections, letters of credit, bulk transfers, warehouse receipts, bills of lading, and other matters.

UNIFORM PARTNERSHIP ACT An act adopted by many states for the purpose of giving uniformity to the regulation of partnership business.

UNIFORM RECIPROCAL ENFORCEMENT OF SUPPORT ACT A uniform law (in a divorce or judicial separation matter) under which a support order of one state will be enforced in every state.

UNILATERAL CONTRACT A contract that contains a promise or promises made only by the offeror and contingent on the fulfillment of specified conditions.

UNILATERAL MISTAKE A mistake made by one of the parties to a contract.

UNINSURED MOTORIST INSURANCE Motor vehicle insurance which provides protection when the insured is injured in an automobile accident caused by another driver who is at fault and who has no bodily injury liability insurance to cover the loss to the injured party.

UNION SHOP   A business in which a worker must join the union within thirty days after being employed. Union shops are illegal in some states.

UNLIMITED LIABILITY   The status of being personally liable for all debts of a business and for the negligent acts of the employees of the business.

U.S. COURT OF APPEALS   The federal court in each judicial circuit that hears appeals from the federal district courts.

U.S. SUPREME COURT   The highest court in the United States.

USED CAR RULE   The rule by the Federal Trade Commission that requires used car dealers to place a large sticker, called a Buyer's Guide, in the window of each used vehicle they offer for sale.

USED VEHICLE   A vehicle that has been driven more than the distance necessary to deliver a new car to the dealership or to test-drive it.

USURY (ūzh' ĕrē)   A charge for the use of money beyond the rate of interest set by law.

UTTERING   Offering a forged instrument to another person, knowing it is forged and intending to defraud.

VA–GUARANTEED LOANS   Mortgage loans made to eligible veterans by private lenders such as banks and other lending institutions and guaranteed by the Veterans Administration to the level of 60 percent of the outstanding balance.

VALID   Legally good.

VALUED POLICY   An insurance policy in which the amount to be paid by the insurance company is definitely stated.

VANDALISM (also called *malicious mischief*)   The willful or malicious causing of damage to property.

VERDICT   The official finding of fact by the jury; the jury's decision.

VERTICAL PRICE FIXING   Price fixing that occurs when manufacturers dictate the price at which a product must be sold by retailers.

VESTING OF RETIREMENT BENEFITS   The act of giving a worker a guaranteed right to receive a future pension.

VOID   Of no legal force or effect.

VOIDABLE   Capable of being voided or nullified, usually at the election of a party to a contract.

VOIDABLE TITLE   The legal right to return goods and get back the money paid for them.

VOLUNTARY BANKRUPT   A person or corporation that asks to be adjudged a bankrupt.

VOLUNTARY MANSLAUGHTER   The act of intentionally killing someone without planning to do so in advance and as the result of great personal distress.

VOTING TRUST   A voting pool under the terms of which shareholders transfer their voting rights to a trustee.

WAIVER   The surrender of some right, claim, or privilege granted by law.

WAIVER OF PREMIUM   A life insurance provision that an insured person who becomes disabled does not have to pay the insurance premium for as long as the disability continues.

WARD   A minor in the custody of a guardian.

WAREHOUSE RECEIPT   A receipt given by a warehouse to a customer whose goods the warehouse is storing.

WARRANT (wŏr' ănt)   To guarantee; an order of a court authorizing an arrest.

WARRANTY   An agreement to be responsible if a good or service is not as represented; also, the covenant of the grantor of real property and of his or her heirs that the grantee will have title to the property.

WARRANTY DEED   A deed that transfers ownership of real property from one person to another and which guarantees that the transferor's title is good.

WARRANTY OF FITNESS FOR A PARTICULAR PURPOSE   An implied warranty that goods will be fit for a particular purpose. This warranty is given by the seller to the buyer of goods whenever the seller has reason to know of any particular purpose for which the goods are needed and the buyer relies on the seller's skill and judgment to select the goods.

WARRANTY OF HABITABILITY   The obligation of a landlord to maintain the premises rented to a tenant in a livable condition.

WARRANTY OF MERCHANTABILITY   An implied warranty that goods are fit for the ordinary purpose for which such goods are used. Unless excluded, this warranty is always given by a merchant who sells goods in the ordinary course of business.

WARRANTY OF TITLE   An implied warranty given by a seller to a buyer of goods that the title being conveyed is good and that the transfer is rightful.

WASTE   A destructive use of property by one in rightful possession.

WATERED STOCK (also called *discounted stock*)   Stock issued for insufficient values, or for no value at all.

WHEELER-LEA AMENDMENT   An act passed by Congress in 1938 which amended the Federal Trade Commission Act to provide protection to the consumer as well as to the business person.

WHITE-COLLAR CRIMES   Crimes that are fraud-related and are carried out in a nonviolent way.

WILL   A document drawn in conformity with the laws of a state indicating how property is to be disposed of after the death of the testator or testatrix.

WILLFUL, WANTON, AND RECKLESS CONDUCT   The intentional commission of an act which a reasonable person knows would cause injury to another.

WORDS OF NEGOTIABILITY   Words (*to the order of* or *to bearer*) required to give an instrument the quality of negotiability.

WORK PERMIT   A document that allows a minor of a certain age to work.

WORKERS' COMPENSATION   A state insurance system that makes payments to workers who are injured on the job.

WRAPAROUND MORTGAGE   An all-inclusive mortgage that includes existing mortgages by ''wrapping around'' old loans.

WRIT   Anything written; a judicial process by which a person is summoned to appear; a legal instrument to enforce obedience to the orders and sentences of the court.

WRONGFUL DISCHARGE   A discharge of an employee that violates public policy, an implied contract, or an implied covenant.

ZONING LAW   An ordinance restricting or permitting certain uses of land in specified areas.

∎ INDEX